Software Requirements
Analysis and Specification

ALAN M. DAVIS
BTG, Inc.

Prentice Hall, Englewood Cliffs, New Jersey 07632

Library of Congress Cataloging-in-Publication Data

Davis, Alan M. (Alan Mark)
Software requirements : analysis and specification / Alan M. Davis.
p. cm.
Includes bibliographical references.
ISBN 0-13-824673-4
1. Computer software—Development. I. Title.
QA76.76D47D38 1990
005.1'2—dc20   89-16392
                                        CIP

Editorial/production supervision: *bookworks*
Cover design: *Victoria A. Heim*
Manufacturing buyer: *Robert Anderson*

About the cover: The selection of Victoria Heim's "Hands on Hands" was inspired by the *What* vs. *How Dilemma* described in section 1. 2. 1.

The publisher offers discounts on this book when ordered in bulk quantities. For more information write:

  Special Sales/College Marketing
  Prentice-Hall, Inc.
  College Technical and Reference Division
  Englewood Cliffs, New Jersey 07632

Printed in the United States of America

10 9 8 7 6 5

ISBN 0-13-824673-4

Prentice-Hall International (UK) Limited, *London*
Prentice-Hall of Australia Pty. Limited, *Sydney*
Prentice-Hall Canada Inc., *Toronto*
Prentice-Hall Hispanoamericana, S.A., *Mexico*
Prentice-Hall of India Private Limited, *New Delhi*
Prentice-Hall of Japan, Inc., *Tokyo*
Editora Prentice-Hall do Brasil, Ltda., *Rio de Janeiro*

TO

Ginny
Marsha
Michael
and my parents,
Barney and Hannah Davis

Contents

v

List of Figures

Foreword

Over the past fifteen years, there has been a great deal of concern about the high cost of software. On one hand projections show that demand for applications outstrips our society's ability to produce them at this time. The software tools applied to assist users, including programmers, in developing solutions are improving only incrementally. On the other hand, the U.S. software industry is saddled with more than $300 billion worth of ill-structured and difficult-to-maintain software inventory. As a consequence the cost of maintenance in large data processing centers has exceeded 60% of their budgets. These problems call for improving and automating the software development process, and while much has been done, analysis and specification of requirements remain a relatively untouched area. Yet it is perhaps the most important aspect of any large software development project.

Beginning in the mid 1970s, there have been a number of techniques and systems developed for the purpose of analyzing and defining requirements. The leading methods include SADT, PSL/PSA, SREM, E-R Data Model, and Data Flow Diagram à la Yourdon. Numerous studies have been conducted to analyze and compare these methods, while others have concentrated on using the techniques/methods. Although proponents of each methodology suggest that their method can suitably carry out the entire analysis process, we have learned that each problem requires a different set of techniques and tools. Therefore it is very refreshing to read this book by Alan M. Davis. I was pleasantly surprised by his heavy emphasis on the fundamental issue of problem solving rather than on techniques or tools. The implicit process model of interactive analysis and specification is very effective and realistic. I particularly appreciate the notion that a requirement specification binds only the solution space and sometimes it is necessary to do some design or even implementation (via prototyping) to determine where the solution boundary lies. This contrasts drastically to some of the pure requirements methodology of stating only *what* and not *how*. For as Davis clearly points out, the *how* of one level is the *what* of another level.

In addition to presenting software requirements analysis as a problem-solving activity, this book has three outstanding features. First of all this is one of the most readable technical books I have encountered. Secondly this book provides a broad coverage of various methodologies, languages, and tools. It also contains a thorough reference list that will benefit anyone interested in this topic. Finally the book presents numerous examples throughout to illustrate both problem-solving principles and techniques applied to requirements analysis.

I consider *Software Requirements: Analysis and Specification* to be a significant contribution to the software engineering field and would recommend its use in a university-level software engineering curriculum.

Raymond T. Yeh
Austin, Texas

Preface

This book focuses on the early phases of the software development life cycle. These early activities are commonly called *software requirements analysis* or *software requirements specification*. I have written this book for two audiences—(1) the practicing systems engineer, software analyst, and requirements writer; and (2) the advanced student of software engineering who wishes to receive specialized education in the early phases of the software development life cycle.

This book is unique because it discusses the latest research results from the requirements arena but at the same time is highly practical. Some authors on the subjects of requirements, specifications, or analysis stress a particular technique and then try to convince you to embrace that technique as *the* technique to apply to your requirements problem. Some authors present compilations of other authors' primary works, which in turn advocate particular techniques. I, however, will not try to convince you that any particular technique will always be right. Instead this book will arm you with a thorough understanding of (1) what you need to accomplish during the requirements phase, (2) how each of a wide variety of techniques can help you accomplish some part of that task, (3) how different aspects of your particular application will strongly suggest using one technique or another, (4) how to compare and contrast all techniques using some common terminology, and (5) how to find a technique that will assist you in analyzing your problem and specifying your product's requirements instead of one that provides you with yet another problem (that is, figuring out how to use the technique itself). I believe that a good technique should lend itself to your problem—not insist that you mold your problem to fit the technique, and this philosophy permeates this book. A good friend of mine, the late Professor Donald B. Gillies, once said, "If you program in Algol long enough, you start to see the entire universe as an Algol program" [GIL72]. Of course this is true not only of Algol and many other programming languages but many engineering techniques, including those used during requirements.

I often hear analysts asking such questions as, "Should I use Structured Analysis or SREM?", or "Should I use USE.IT or SADT?" It is true that all four of these are termed "requirements" techniques by their respective inventors (and all are discussed in this book). However the posers of these questions demonstrate an inherent lack of understanding of the requirements domain and the same naivete as someone who asks, "Should I wear my black shoes or my leather gloves today?" There is no trade-off involved; Structured Analysis and SREM serve two completely different purposes, and USE.IT and SADT serve two completely different purposes. This book provides a new taxonomy of requirements-related activities to enable you to ask the right questions and provide sensible answers to them as well.

After reading this book, you may expect to be able to do the following:

• Given any real-world problem, to organize your ideas to quickly find loose ends that require further analysis and areas that have been overanalyzed.

• Given any real-world problem, to select a set of requirements techniques, tools, and/or languages that will aid in analyzing that problem.

• Once you thoroughly understand your problem, to formulate and organize a specification of the solution system's required external behavior completely, consistently, and unambiguously.

• To select a set of requirements techniques, tools, and/or languages that could be used to augment your specification of external behavior to help alleviate inconsistencies, incompletenesses, and ambiguities.

• Given a document defining software requirements for a system, to determine where it is overspecified, underspecified, inconsistent, ambiguous, or incomplete.[1]

• When presented with "yet another (new) requirements technique," to determine (1) how it relates to other techniques and (2) whether it is applicable to your individual problem.

[1]It is interesting to note that there are no hard and fast rules for this determination. As you will see in reading this book, the correct level of these attributes varies dramatically with the stage of development. For example, a document whose purpose is to define needs and invite potential developers to bid competitively to satisfy those needs must be much more open ended than one whose purpose is to define the to- be-built system's external behavior just prior to software design.

Techniques that are presented in this book are followed by case studies showing how the technique can be applied to aspects of three real problems. The same three problems are used as case studies throughout the book to help you compare and contrast the techniques. The three problems were deliberately selected to represent three very different application domains:

Problem	Application Attributes
1. Automation of a book distribution company	Data intensive; some aspects highly human interactive; other aspects highly batch; multiple simultaneous actions
2. Automation of helicopter landing	Hardware control intensive; synchrony intensive; time sensitive; nondeterministic
3. Transportation of people from New York to Tokyo in 30 minutes	A *very* difficult problem[2]

Clearly no problem is entirely batch, entirely difficult, or entirely data intensive. Every problem has a bit of each of these attributes. The important thing to remember is to employ a technique that makes the difficult parts easier. Therefore when faced with a particular problem, first determine what the most difficult parts are, then find the problem in the preceding list that is most similar to yours, and employ techniques most suitable to that problem.

This book is organized into seven chapters plus an extensive annotated bibliography.

Chapter 1, the Introduction, sets the stage by (1) describing where the software industry is today, (2) motivating the tremendous need for improved software engineering techniques, (3) showing where requirements analysis and specification fit into the total software development life cycle, (4) defining precisely what requirements are (and are not), (5) explaining fundamental differences between problem analysis, and product description, and (6) providing conclusive evidence that failure to detect requirements defects is a major cause of skyrocketing software costs. The chapter concludes with a thorough discussion of software applications in general and the three case studies used throughout the book.

In Chapter 1 we learned that there are two fundamentally different things being done during the requirements phase—problem analysis and product description. Chapter 2 explores the former topic in depth, and Chapters 3–5 explore the latter. The bulk of the second chapter describes, compares, contrasts, and

---

[2]Selecting a very difficult problem as an example in this book has its advantages and its disadvantages. The primary advantage is to help the reader understand how to approach such a problem. The greatest disadvantage is that if this is truly a difficult problem, we will not solve it and in fact should make little headway in solving it (or it would have already been partially solved). Unfortunately this lack of progress may lead some readers to believe that the techniques employed are not useful. The correct conclusion is that solving a really difficult problem is not easy: You simply chip away at small pieces, brainstorm a lot, and hopefully solve it. As Turski [TUR80] said, "To every hard problem, there is a simple solution, and it's wrong."

applies a variety of problem analysis techniques. However prior to that discussion, fundamental principles underlying problem analysis techniques are described. The chapter concludes with examples of applying each of the techniques from the chapter to the three case studies described at the end of Chapter 1.

Chapter 3 introduces the subject of how to write or evaluate a document (that is, the software requirements specifications—SRS) that specifies the external behavior of a software product. A list is provided of all attributes that a "perfect" SRS should exhibit (realizing of course that no SRS can ever be perfect!). Each of these attributes is defined, and many examples from actual SRSs are given to demonstrate each attribute. The chapter concludes with sample outlines for SRSs that can be used as checklists for the novice SRS writer.

In Chapter 3 we learned that there are two types of requirements that belong in an SRS—behavioral and nonbehavioral. Chapter 4 explores the former category of requirements (Chapter 5 explores the latter). The bulk of this chapter describes, compares, contrasts, and applies a variety of techniques that can be used to describe the external behavior of software. Like Chapter 2, Chapter 4 concludes with examples of applying each of the SRS techniques described in this chapter to the same three case studies.

In addition to describing external functional behavior, a properly written SRS also describes the "ilities" of the software. Namely, it describes how adaptable, how maintainable, how reliable, etc. the software should be. Chapter 5 defines many of the attributes of a software product that must be addressed in the SRS to ensure that the as-built product satisfies real needs. Guidance and examples are provided to help you (1) decide which "ilities" should be emphasized in your particular application and (2) see how to specify the product traits in as unambiguous a manner as possible.

Prototyping has been used in engineering disciplines for years but only recently received attention in software engineering. There are two schools of prototyping during the requirements phase—throwaway and evolutionary. Proponents of both schools call what they do simply "prototyping;" rarely is a distinction made in practice. Unfortunately, if you build either type of prototype expecting to achieve results available from the other, you will be grossly disappointed. Chapter 6 thoroughly describes the preceding two types of requirements and explains their respective impact on the requirements process, the software development life cycle, productivity, and product success.

Chapter 7 summarizes key ideas presented in Chapters 1–6, explains where the requirements field is going, and where it is likely to be in the next fifteen to twenty years.

The Glossary defines terms used with special meanings in the requirements domain.

The annotated Bibliography offers a compilation of approximately 600 published articles, books, and reports on the subject of requirements. Many of them are described in a short synopsis.

Depending on how you wish to use the book, you may want to read it in a number of different ways:

If you are a software practitioner who wants to learn about requirements and the types of techniques, tools, and languages available, I suggest you read the entire book. If you have a particular problem and do not know where to turn for advice on how to analyze it, I suggest you read Chapters 1, 2, and 6 only. If you have been asked to write an SRS for a product to be built by your own organization, you should read Chapters 1, 3–6.

If you have been asked to review an existing or proposed SRS, Chapters 1, 3, 4, and 5 can help you.

If you are using this book as a reference to help you find an applicable technique, tool, or language, read Sections 1.1 and 1.2 to gain an appreciation for the difference between problem analysis and writing an SRS—then browse through Chapters 2 and 4 to find appropriate approaches.

Notes to the Teacher

If you are using this book as a text for a graduate or an advanced undergraduate-level course, let me indicate how I organize the course when I teach it:

Topic	Textbook References	Activity	Hours[a]
Administrative introduction	N/A	Lecture/discussion	1.2
Introduction			
Software life cycle	1.1	Lecture/discussion	0.7
What are requirements?	1.2	Lecture/discussion	3.3
Exercise 1 (SRS evaluation)	4	Student team exercise	2.8
Introduction (continued)			
Why are requirements so important?	1.3	Lecture/discussion	0.8
Taxonomy of applications	1.4 & 1.5	Lecture/discussion	0.5
Problem analysis	2	Lecture/discussion	8.0
Exercise 2 (problem analysis)	2	Group participation	4.0
The SRS	3	Lecture/discussion	2.3
Specifying behavioral requirements	4	Lecture/discussion	4.0
Exercise 3 (SRS evaluation)	4	Student team exercise	4.0
Specifying nonbehavioral requirements	5	Lecture/discussion	4.0
Requirements prototyping	6	Lecture/discussion	1.2
Summary	7	Lecture/discussion	1.0
Exam review	N/A	Discussion	2.5
Exam	N/A	Exam	2.7
		Total hours	43.0

[a]Actual class contact time.

Exercises 1 and 3 represent before-the-course and after-the-course exercises on how to recognize inadequacies in an SRS. In both cases, I distribute copies of actual SRSs, then divide the class into teams of three to five each to assess independently the quality of the SRS. Usually I also give each team a unique role to play:

1. Design team
   Wants to be able to build software based on SRS
   Disdains overspecification

2. System testing team
   Wants to be able to test that the software product meets its
      requirements
   Can not tolerate ambiguity

3. System user/customer team
   Wants to be sure product is worth paying for
   Wants an understandable document
   Can not tolerate underspecification

4. Requirements Consultants, Inc., team
   Wants to see formality
   Intolerant of ambiguity

During Exercise 3, I usually walk from team to team to assist each in playing its role realistically. This is followed by formal 15-minute presentations by each team to the entire class. Because each team has a unique position, much controversy is generated concerning the appropriateness of the SRS. In both exercises, students learn how to recognize inadequacies in an SRS. In Exercise 3, they also learn that there are no clear-cut answers to the question, "What is a perfect SRS?"

In Exercise 2, the assembled class simulates the brainstorming that goes on during a typical problem analysis session. I serve as moderator and provide little added value other than as a poser of key questions when the students lose momentum. In this way students learn how to use problem analysis techniques to organize ideas.

REFERENCES

[GIL72] Gillies, D.B. Private communication. Lawrence, Kans., January 1972.

[TUR80] Turski, V. Stated orally at IFIPS Congress 1980, Tokyo. October 1980.

ACKNOWLEDGMENTS

Only one author's name appears on the cover of this book, but I did not write it alone. Dozens of collegues, friends, and relatives provided assistance of all kinds, and without that assistance, this book would never have existed.

Dr. Edward Bersoff, president of BTG, Inc., deserves the most thanks. His moral and financial support, technical ideas, friendship, and high standards of integrity have been inspirational to me and crucial to the creation of this book.

During the ten-year period when the ideas expressed in this book were developed, I had the opportunity of discussing requirements-related issues with many people. Among them are a few individuals who stand out for having provided me with considerable insight into the vast challenges associated with analyzing problems and writing software requirements specifications: Dr. Ed Bersoff of BTG, Inc.; Peter Coad of Object International, Inc.; Ed Comer of Software Productivity Solutions, Inc.; Dr. B. Dasarathy of Concurrent Computers; Bruce Gregor of RS Data Systems Inc.; Tom Miller, formerly with GTE Laboratories; Dr. Tom Rauscher of Xerox Corporation; and Dr. Ray Yeh of International Systems Corporation. Dr. Jim Sherrill and the U.S. Army systems automation officers in the "Defining Software Requirements" course at the Computer Science School in Ft. Benjamin Harrison, Indiana, from March 1986 to December 1987 also deserve special recognition for having unknowingly served as a test bed for many of the ideas in this book. The feedback that they supplied about my successes and failures with teaching this material was used to fine tune the instructional methods used in that course as well as in this book. Early reviewers of this book, namely, Dr. Bob Glass of the *Journal of Systems and Software* and Bill Cureton of Sun Microsystems, Inc., provided much help with the rough spots in early manuscripts. Bruce Gregor was invaluable in developing the Pfleeger Pfliers case study.

A number of people played a key role in creating this book, although they did not realize it at the time. Three individuals in my early professional life gave me inspiration, taught me the meaning of self-confidence, and shaped the very nature of how I think today. These people, Dick Dworak, the late Dr. Don Gillies, and Dr. Tom Wilcox, probably have more to do with who I am today professionally than any others.

The Prentice Hall editor Paul Becker was helpful in providing sound advice about writing this book. He gave me just the right number of reminders to make sure I was always progressing and on the right track. In addition to being a trusted friend, Ms. Marilynn Bersoff deserves my praise and thanks for maintaining her incredible level of quality standards in the physical production of the text and figures that comprise this work. Ms. Eileen Bates and Interactive Development Environments, Inc., provided access to Software

Through Pictures and computing resources to produce all the data flow diagrams contained in this work.

The most special people in my life are my family—my wife, Ginny; my children, Marsha and Michael; and my parents, Hannah and Barney. It is only with you that life has meaning. It is your support, trust, and love that have enabled me to achieve successes such as this book.

To everyone who helped me with this book, thanks for unselfishly sharing your ideas, wisdom, time, support, confidence, and energy. Although you all deserve credit for this book, I take full responsibility for any errors or omissions that may exist herein.

Alan M. Davis
Vienna, Virginia

In memory of
Corey Lantz
1984-1989

1

Introduction

This book provides a thorough discussion of the early phases of the software engineering development life cycle, commonly referred to as *software requirements analysis* or *software requirements specification*. Chapter 1 sets the stage in order to maximize the transfer of knowledge from the rest of the book to you. It begins with some background information about what software engineering is and how the software industry is faring today. Next Chapter 1 defines the subject of the book, software requirements, and provides general information about the documents usually produced during the software requirements process: Who writes these documents and why requirements documents are sometimes acceptably quite vague and other times acceptably quite specific. The chapter also presents empirical evidence to support the need for software developers to do a substantially better job of performing software requirements analysis and specification than they have been doing.

Throughout this book numerous techniques are demonstrated using the same three case studies. In order to understand these case studies and how your particular problem(s) may be related, the chapter concludes with a discussion of a taxonomy of application areas (which emphasizes differences in requirements approaches) and of the three specific case studies to be used later.

1.1 SOFTWARE ENGINEERING

1.1.1 The Software Industry

The computer industry is only about thirty years old. During those thirty years, however, the industry has undergone a degree of change that few others have. The industry has experienced at least three completely different generations of hardware technologies based on inventions that resulted in tumbling prices over a period of time when the average cost of other goods has tripled. One aspect of computer hardware cost is particularly easy to track because of the availability of data and existence of standard measures. Figure 1–1a shows the trend of computer memory costs. The cost per bit of computer memory decreased fiftyfold between 1973 and 1985 and by an additional fiftyfold between 1985 and 1988! Since this is primarily due to dramatically improved integrated circuit fabrication techniques, we can easily extrapolate this data to most integrated circuits and thus most computer hardware. Figure 1–1b (adapted from [MUS83]) shows even more startling data. It plots computer power (i.e., instructions per second) divided by the cost per million bits of memory as a function of time. It shows a thousandfold increase in power per dollar every ten years!

   With this dramatic decrease in cost have also come faster, less power-consuming, smaller-sized, and more reliable computer. These changes have led to computer applications which only a decade ago would not have been possible. Figure 1–2 shows these new marketplaces [MIZ83].

   With new application areas and the increasing complexity of problems that we are trying to solve with computers, there is a corresponding decrease in the probability of designing a correct solution. Also with such rapidly growing marketplaces, there is a need to constantly adapt existing systems. This results in an increasing reliance on software that is *theoretically* easier to modify than hardware (of course with this theoretical ease of change comes a vast amount of additional work in order to manage the change [BER80]). The increasingly important role that software plays is seen most dramatically in the Electronic Industries Associations' regular surveys of the computer industry. For example Figure 1–3, which comes from one of their analyses [EIA85], shows the incredible growth of software costs (250% from 1980 to 1985 and 680% projected between 1980 and 1990) compared to that of hardware costs (110% from 1980 to 1985 and 340% projected between 1980 and 1990) for embedded system development in the U.S. Department of Defense (DoD). The growth in software demand is also quite apparent at NASA (see Figure 1–4 [BOE81]). It is interesting to note that since 1983, the growth of software has been more dramatic in the United States than in the rest of the world (see Figure 1–5 [DOC84]).

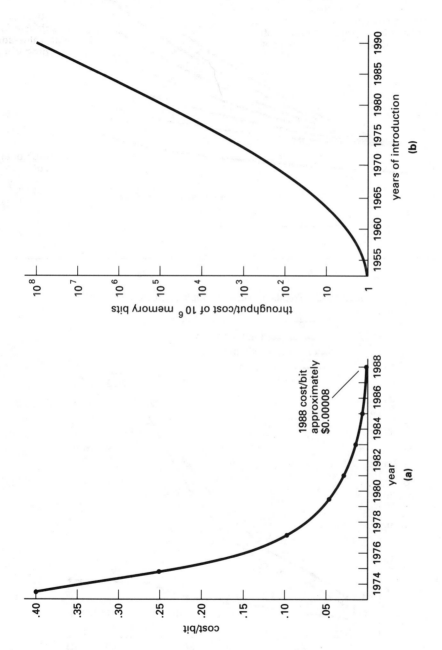

Figure 1-1. Hardware Cost Trends. (a) Rapid Decrease in Memory Costs. (b) Computer Hardware Technology Relative Cost Effectiveness.

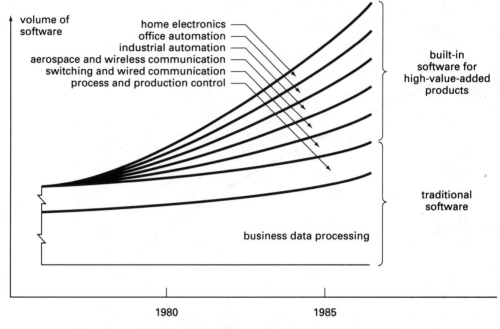

Figure 1-2. Trends in Software Applications. © 1983 IEEE.

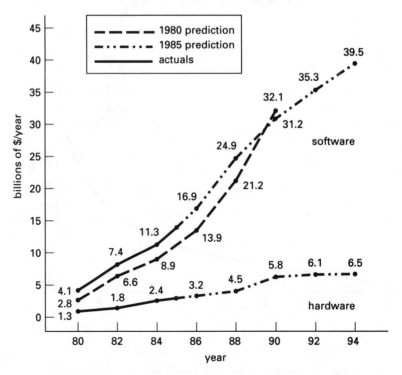

Figure 1-3. DoD Embedded Computer Software/Hardware.

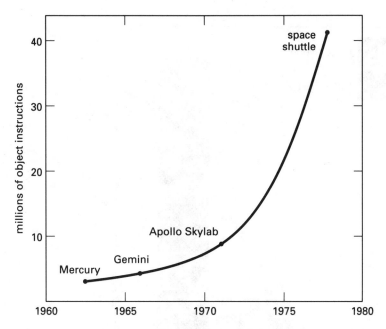

Figure 1–4. Growth in NASA Software Demand. Barry W. Boehm, *Software Engineering Economics,* © 1981, p. 643. Adapted by permission of Prentice-Hall, Inc., Englewood Cliffs, New Jersey.

The preceding data makes it quite apparent that an incredible sum is being spent to develop software. How well is this money being spent? In 1979 the Government Accounting Office (GAO) published a report indicating that many, if not most, of these dollars are being wasted [GAO79]. The GAO selected nine software development projects that were recently completed for the U.S. Federal Government. Although the size of the projects was quite small (the sum of the nine contracts was less than $7M), the findings were depressing (see Figure 1–6): Forty-seven percent of the dollars were spent for software that was *never* used! To make matters even worse, an additional 29% of the dollars were spent for software that was never even delivered,[1] and another 19% resulted in software that was either extensively reworked after delivery or abandoned after delivery but before the GAO study was conducted. All in all, that leaves very little for the successful projects. Of the $317K spent on these so-called successful projects, some additional modifications were required to about $198K of it, and only $119K worth of the software could be used as delivered. That means that less than 2% of the dollars spent resulted in software that met its requirements! The $119K happens to represent a project

---

[1]This phenomenon occurs when software development is paid for in increments, but the developers or customer cannot proceed with the full development. To make matters even worse, this often occurs *after* major overruns have occurred.

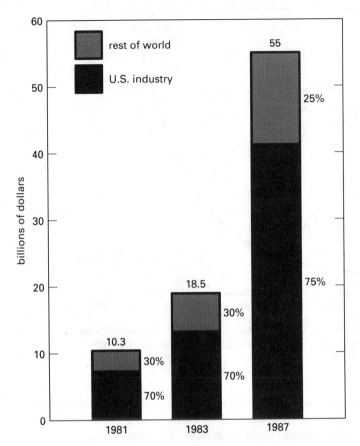

Figure 1-5. U.S. Industry Share of World Software Market 1981–1987.

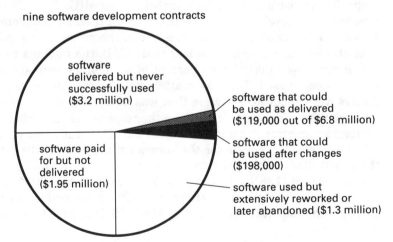

Figure 1-6. How Well Are We Doing?

that was a preprocessor to a COBOL compiler. What made the project unique was that it was relatively simple, the requirements were well understood by all parties up front, and the requirements did not change during the course of the project. Obviously the GAO study occurred many years ago. However if it is representative of today's software industry as well (and I do believe that it is.), then this industry needs to improve how it develops software.

1.1.2 The Software Engineering Discipline

Software engineering is the application of scientific principles to (1) the orderly transformation of a problem into a working software solution and (2) the subsequent maintenance of that software until the end of its useful life. Software engineering is more than just programming; the software engineering process generally starts long before a line of code is written and continues long after the initial version of the program has been completed. People and projects following an engineered approach to software development generally pass through a series of phases, or stages. Royce [ROY70] was the first to coin the phrase "the waterfall model" to characterize the series of software engineering stages. Figure 1–7 shows the original model that Royce presented.

The U.S. Department of Defense [DOD85] prefers to document the software development process as a series of bands along a horizontal belt, as shown in Figure 1–8. Both of these views fail to show the symmetry that exists between the earlier and later stages of the development life cycle. For that reason we will use the symmetrical view of the development process, as shown in Figure 1–9. Let us go through the stages one at a time so we all have a common understanding of how this model works. We will first go through the primary path (indicated by a series of bold arrows on the figure) and then through the remaining three boxes:

1. Software requirements: includes analyzing the software problem at hand and concludes with a complete specification of the desired external behavior of the software system to be built; also called functional description, functional requirements, and specifications by others. This phase is the subject of the current book.

2. Preliminary design: decomposes the software system into its actual constituent (architectural) components and then iteratively decomposes those components into smaller and smaller subcomponents until the subcomponents located at the leaves of the resulting design tree are small enough so that we would expect a person to be able to "get his or her arms around it" easily. In practice that generally means something that will eventually map into, say, fifty to two hundred lines of code. Each of these

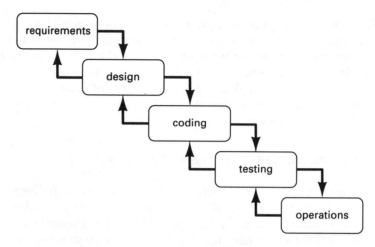

Figure 1–7. Standard Waterfall Life Cycle Model.

modules is documented in terms of its inputs, outputs, and functions; also called specifications, high-level design, architectural design, and functional design by others.

3. Detailed design: defines and documents algorithms for each module in the design tree that will be realized as code; also called program design by others.

4. Coding: transforms algorithms defined during the detailed design stage into a computer-understandable language. This is usually performed in two steps: converting the algorithm into a high-level language (usually performed by people) and converting the high-level language into a machine language (usually performed automatically by a compiler); also called programming.

If humans were perfect, the process would be complete at this point. Unfortunately this is not the case. Therefore we need a testing process to uncover and remove the "bugs."[2]

5. Unit testing: checks each coded module for the presence of bugs. Unit testing's purpose is to ensure that each as-built module behaves according to its specification defined during detailed design; also called module testing and functional testing.

6. Integration testing: interconnects sets of previously tested modules to ensure that the sets behave as well as they did as independently tested

[2]The word *bug* was coined on September 9, 1947, by Admiral Grace Hopper, Ret., when she detected a moth stuck in a relay in the Mark II computer.

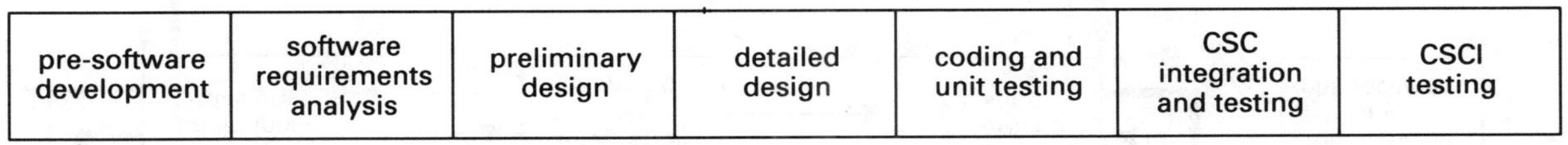

pre-software development	software requirements analysis	preliminary design	detailed design	coding and unit testing	CSC integration and testing	CSCI testing

Figure 1–8. Department of Defense Development Model.

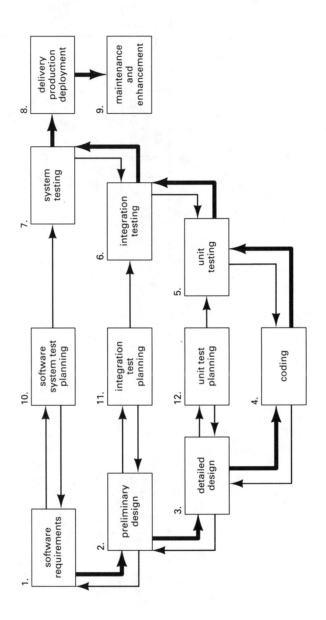

Figure 1-9. Software Engineering Life Cycle.

modules. Ideally each integrated set of modules should correspond to a component in the design tree defined during preliminary design. Thus integration testing's purpose is to ensure that each as-built component behaves according to its specification defined during preliminary design; also called string testing and computer software component (CSC) testing.

7. System testing: checks that the entire (i.e., fully integrated) software system embedded in its actual hardware environment behaves according to the Software Requirements Specification (SRS). Very large systems might include multiple SRSs and be a multistep process consisting of independent functional testing (also called computer software configuration item testing) of each major software component against its SRS followed by an integration of these major software components with each other and checking their combined behavior against system-level requirements.

8. Delivery, production, and deployment: After final system testing, the software and its surrounding hardware become operational.

9. Maintenance and enhancement: The maintenance (continued detection and repair of bugs after deployment) and enhancement (addition of new capabilities) processes are actually a full development life cycle, like the left side of Figure 1–9, but have been drawn as one box to simplify the figure. The reason why it is a full life cycle is simple: If a coding change is made, then the coding and three subsequent testing stages must be performed. If a design change is made, then the design, coding, and three testing stages must be performed. If a requirement change has occurred, then all the stages must be performed.

You will note that arrows between adjacent stages are bidirectional. The reason for this bidirectionality is that during any stage you may learn something causing you to return to the previous stage. For example, during the preliminary design stage, you may discover that some requirement cannot be met or some required performance level can be exceeded, or you may learn about a new requirement that must be met.[3] In any of these cases, it is necessary to return to the requirements stage to update the SRS.

[3]Discovering after the requirements stage that a new requirement must be met could simply result from some new environmental factor that had not been previously considered (for example, a new type of terminal interface might cause you to redefine the requirements for a new network under development). Or the new requirement could be a *derived requirement* which is a requirement that cannot be determined until after some design has been performed (for example, in domestic home construction, you would not know to specify carpeting on the stairs during the requirements stage until the house had been designed with more than one floor).

The remaining three boxes in Figure 1–9 point to the fact that it is inappropriate to wait until the testing stage to determine how you are going to test. Starting from the top and working down,

10. Software system test planning: assesses how the software system will be tested for conformity to the software requirements. It includes the development and documentation of test plans and procedures and might include the full-scale development of a test environment to test the actual system under test. Another purpose of software system test planning is to thoroughly examine the SRS to determine whether it is verifiable, that is, whether or not it has been written in a manner that makes it possible to verify that the software meets its contents. (This property of an SRS is discussed in Section 3.4.4). The arrow in Figure 1–9 pointing from this stage back to the requirements stage represents the path taken in the event that a lack of verifiability is detected.

11. Integration test planning: generates and documents plans and procedures to effect an orderly system integration. This might include developing specifications concerning the order of integration, test data to be used to test sets of components, and feedback to project management concerning relative priorities to apply during detailed design, coding, and unit testing in order to optimize the integration testing activity. This activity might also spawn a software development effort of its own to create *scaffolding software,* that is, software used to temporarily join two components during integration testing that would be removed before final system test.

12. Unit test planning: generates and documents plans and procedures to test each module independently and thoroughly.

Estimates of relative percentages of time and dollars spent on each of these stages vary considerably from researcher to researcher. However, Boehm [BOE81] has collected perhaps the most complete set of data from sixty-three projects performed at TRW. The data, shown in Figures 1–10a (relative cost efforts) and 1–10b (relative duration effort), indicate clearly how time and dollars spent on integration testing and system testing grow disproportionately as the size of the project increases, and time spent on requirements analysis grows disproportionately as the size of the project increases (adapted from [BOE81]).

1.2 REQUIREMENTS

Suppose we were invited to a meeting to discuss telephone service in a new soon-to-be-built hotel. We arrive a little late, the meeting has already started,

	Size of Program under Development			
	2,000 loc [a]	80,000 loc	32,000 loc	128,000 loc
Requirements	6	6	6	6
Preliminary design	15	15	15	15
Detailed design, coding and unit testing	64	61	58	56
Integration and system testing	15	18	21	23
Total (%)	100	100	100	100

[a] loc = lines of code.

(a)

	Size of Program under Development			
	2,000 loc	80,000 loc	32,000 loc	128,000 loc
Requirements	9	10	11	12
Preliminary design	17	17	17	17
Detailed design, coding and unit testing	57	53	49	45
Integration and system testing	16	20	23	26
Total (%)	100	100	100	100

(b)

Figure 1–10. Relative Efforts by Development Stage. (a) By cost. (b) By Duration. Barry W. Boehm, *Software Engineering Economics,* © 1981, p. 90. Adapted by permission of Prentice-Hall, Inc., Englewood Cliffs, N. J.

and as we walk in, we notice that everyone is speaking at the same time. As we listen to each person's words (shown in Figure 1–11), we are surprised to discover that all the participants appear to be talking on different wavelengths:

Person 1 is making a general statement of need. She recognizes that the hotel does indeed need voice communications.

Person 2 says that person 1 is being too general and suggests we interview a large number of regular hotel guests and a variety of hotel employees in order to generate a list of all the telephone features that are needed; for example, local calls, call forwarding, call waiting.

In preparation for this meeting, person 3 signed up for, and just returned from, a five-day course on Structured Analysis and Design Technique (SADT™).[4] He believes that if all eight meeting participants took such a course,

---

[4]™SADT is a registered trademark of SofTech, Inc., Waltham, Mass.

Figure 1-11. Who Is Doing Requirements Analysis?

14

they would all be on a similar wavelength and thus waste less time arguing and spend more time solving the hotel's problem.

Person 4 has procured telephone systems for dozens of hotels. She knows that there are many vendors of private automatic branch exchanges (PABXs) with hotel and motel features. She recommends that we invite sales representatives from five of the major manufacturers, listen to their presentations, then select the one that optimizes price and performance.

Person 5 says, "Look, this hotel is supposed to be the pièce de resistance of the hotel chain. We can't afford to buy just any PABX. Let's decide exactly how we want each feature to operate (for example, we may want a separate button on the phone labeled *long distance* rather than requiring all users to remember that *9* means long distance), allow all telephone equipment vendors to bid competitively on satisfying our precise telephone needs, then select the lowest bidder."

Like the third person, person 6 just returned from a course. He believes that if we buy the Problem Statement Language/Problem Statement Analyzer (PSL/PSA™)[5] system, we could start storing and analyzing all our requirements in a requirements data base.

Person 7 has most recently worked for a large manufacturer of telephone equipment. She has been chief designer on three different telephone switching systems. She says, "Why are we wasting our time on such high levels of abstraction? We all know that every telephone switch is composed of the same five major pieces. Why not start with that assumption and define the necessary inputs, outputs, and interfaces to each of these major components?"

Person 8 believes that using Structured Analysis (SA) will be superior to either SADT or PSL/PSA.

Which person is right? What role should you play? The answers to these questions appear later in this section.

1.2.1 What Are Requirements?

Webster's Ninth New Collegiate Dictionary [WEB84] defines a requirement as "something required; something wanted or needed." The IEEE Standard 729 [IEE83] defines it as "(1) a condition or capability needed by a user to solve a problem or achieve an objective; (2) a condition or capability that must be met or possessed by a system...to satisfy a contract, standard, specification, or other formally imposed document." Neither of these definitions is specific enough to encompass what must be included in requirements while omitting what should be excluded.

---

[5]™PSL/PSA is a registered trademark of Meta Systems, Inc., Ann Arbor, Mich.

Before we attempt to provide a formal definition, let us come to a common understanding about when the requirements phase begins and when it ends. To do so we must first recognize that when you have a problem to solve, you do not necessarily know if the solution will be realized in software, hardware, or a combination of the two. When the solutions are composed of software only (for example, an inventory control system),[6] a development life cycle similar to that shown in Figure 1–12a is followed. When the solutions are composed of both hardware and software (for example, a space shuttle life support system), we would follow a systems development life cycle similar to that shown in Figure 1–12b. Although the ends of the two software requirements phases are the same, their beginnings are quite different. Therefore let us discuss each scenario separately.

In the pure software case, the requirements phase begins when (1) there is recognition that a problem exists and requires a solution or (2) a new software idea arises (the equivalent of an invention in hardware). The recognized problem might be purely application oriented (for example, we need a new inventory control system); business oriented (for example, we must develop a new product

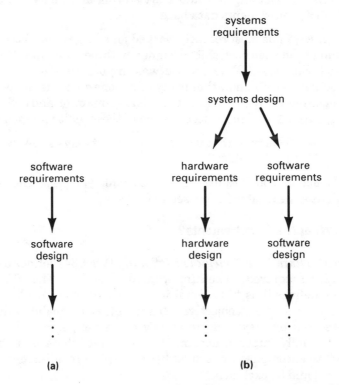

Figure 1-12. Development Life Cycles. **(a)** Software. **(b)** Systems (Software and Hardware).

[6]Of course software is useless unless it is running on hardware. This class of solutions is distinct because its members run on off-the-shelf rather than custom hardware.

to challenge a competitor's, or we must develop a new product to meet our five-year revenue goals); or product improvement oriented (for example, we must rebuild a product to reduce its failure rate or poor maintenance record).

In the systems (that is, software *and* hardware) case, systems design usually precedes the software requirements phase. During systems design, we generally reach agreement on the major system components and their purposes. Software and hardware requirements are then elaborated on for each of these components separately. In such cases the software requirements phase of a major system component begins when the systems design is complete. This corresponds to the time when all major external interfaces to that component have at least been defined.

In any case the end of the software requirements phase is the same; it occurs when we have a *complete* description of the external behavior of the software to be built. As shown in Figure 1–13, this complete description includes documenting all interfaces between the software and its environment (that is, host hardware, other software, humans). This complete description is recorded in a software requirements specification.

A *Software Requirements Specification* (SRS) is a document containing a complete description of what the software will do without describing how it will do it. This definition is fairly universally accepted, so that if we asked some of the people who work in the software requirements arena (for example, Mack Alford, Margaret Hamilton, Ken Orr, Douglas Ross, Dan Teichroew) to define an SRS I suspect that all would give this definition. If we read any of their work (for example, [ALF77, HAM83, ORR81, ROS80, and TEI77]), this definition would either be given or at least implied. However as we further read their work, we would discover that although each offers a unique solution to the problem of requirements, they are each solving a *different* requirements problem. At first this appears to be a paradox, since all seemed to agree initially that the purpose of the requirements phase is to [write an SRS whose purpose is to] define what the software is to do without defining how it is to do it. The resolution of the apparent paradox lies in the recognition of what I call the "what versus how" dilemma.

The "what versus how" dilemma can be briefly defined as "One person's *how* is another person's *what*" and is roughly equivalent to "One person's *floor* is another person's *ceiling*." To help understand this dilemma, let us look at the earlier example of the telephone system for the new hotel (see Figure 1–11):

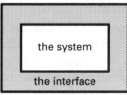

the environment

Figure 1–13. End of the Requirements Phase.

1. Initially we can follow the advice of person 2 to arrive at a common understanding of the real user needs. We would thus learn such things as the need for long-distance calls and the call-waiting feature. This level is clearly a definition of *what* the system will do (that is, it shall satisfy these user needs) without any indication of *how* it will be accomplished. Looked at in this way, this is clearly the "requirements" level. The next step might be to define all possible systems (i.e., the product space) that could satisfy these needs. This step clearly defines *how* these needs might be satisfied and is thus beyond the scope of the requirements phase.

2. On the other hand, we can define the set of all systems that could possibly satisfy user needs as a statement of *what* we want our system to do without describing *how* the particular system we will eventually build or buy will behave. Looked at in this way, this is clearly the "requirements" level. The next step might be to define the exact behavior of the actual software system to be built or bought. This step clearly defines *how* the system behaves and is thus beyond the scope of the requirements phase.

3. On the other hand, we can define the external behavior of the actual product to be built or bought as a statement of *what* the system will do without defining *how* it works internally. Looked at in this way, this is clearly the "requirements" level. The next step might be to define the constituent architectural components of the software system. This step clearly defines *how* the system works internally and is thus beyond the scope of the requirements phase.

4. On the other hand, we can say that the definition of the constituent architectural components of the software system defines *what* makes up the software without defining *how* each component works internally. Looked at in this way, this is clearly the "requirements" level. The next step might be to break large architectural components into smaller and smaller software modules. This step clearly defines the inner workings of the main architectural components, that is, the *how* of the components, and is thus beyond the scope of the requirements phase.

5. On the other hand, we can say that module specifications define *what* the module is to do without defining *how* the module is to satisfy that specification. Looked at in this way, this is clearly the "requirements" level. The next step might be to define algorithms to be used by each module. This step clearly defines *how* the modules work and is thus beyond the scope of the requirements phase.

6. On the other hand, we can say that the module algorithms define *what* process each module should perform without defining *how* the code works. Looked at in this way, this is clearly the "requirements" level. The next step might be to code each of the modules (for example, in Ada, FORTRAN, COBOL). This clearly defines *how* the module is to be implemented and is thus beyond the scope of the requirements phase.

We could probably continue for even three more levels (machine code, micro-code, electron movement), but the preceding six levels are sufficient to demon-strate the heart of the dilemma (see Figure 1–14).

If we reconsider the works of the aforementioned requirements authors, we can easily see that simply stating "requirements are a statement of *what*, not *how*" is insufficient. In particular it is my opinion that Alford's Require-ments Engineering Validation System (REVS) addresses *what* not *how*, where *what* is defined at level 3; Hamilton's USE.IT applies to levels 5 and 6; Orr's Structured Requirements Definition spans levels 1, 4, and 5 (it appears to bypass levels 2 and 3); and Ross's SADT and Teichroew's PSL/PSA can be applied at either levels 1 or 4. Thus we can easily see that although they all offer so-called requirements tools and techniques to address *what*, not *how*, problems in software development, each one is really addressing a different problem!

For the purposes of this book, the requirements phase of the software development life cycle will encompass only levels 1–3.

1.2.2 What Is a Software Requirements Specification?

As mentioned in the preceding section, an SRS is a document containing a complete description of a product's external behavior and thus corresponds to level 3 in the "what versus how" dilemma just described. However, depending on how the software is being developed and who is writing the SRS, it may be detailed or general. To make this clearer, let us look at a number of possible scenarios:

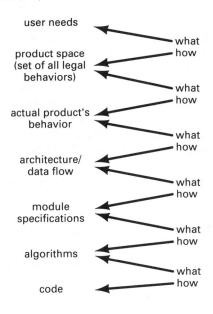

Figure 1-14. "What Versus How" Dilemma.

1. A government agency wishes to procure a custom piece of equipment (with embedded software) via an open competition and must write an SRS to specify its needs.

2. A government contractor has won this competition and must write an SRS to specify the system it will build for the government.

3. A company wants to build a system for its own use and must write an SRS as part of the development process.

4. A company wants to build a product to be sold commercially and must write an SRS to specify the system it will build and sell.

In the first scenario, it is necessary for the SRS to be general enough to facilitate competition but specific enough to ensure that any system that meets the specification truly satisfies the real need. For example,

> The system shall provide helicopter pilots with the ability to determine the current altitude, air speed and vertical velocity without removing their eyes from the windscreen.

can be satisfied with a wide variety of systems and thus facilitates competition. For example, one contractor may bid a thin-screen television screen shaped in the form of a helmet's visor. Another might propose a projector that reflects the requisite data on the windscreen. A third might propose a holographic display projected 50 feet beyond the windscreen. However, a system that supplies the requisite data on the standard instrument panel (requiring the pilot's gaze to be redirected) or supplies different data would not meet the specification.

In the second scenario, the contractor has to be considerably more specific in order to communicate to the government what the system will be, since it is only with such detail that the government can plan the rest of the cockpit and interfaces between the head-up display and its related systems. Specificity also assures the government that the contractor understands the problem, is building the correct system, and the system can be tested. However, this specificity cannot be at the expense of understandability by personnel un-trained in computer science. In this scenario, customers, technical writers [CAS81], designers, analysts, and testers should have input into the SRS writing process.

In the third scenario, the SRS must also be extremely specific in order to serve two functions: (1) the primary source of requirements for the designers to build to and (2) the primary source for system test planners who will generate a thorough set of tests to be used to verify that the as-built system meets the requirements.

In the fourth scenario, the SRS would likely serve both the functions indicated in scenario 3 and two additional functions: (1) as input to the marketing organization to develop sales promotion material, and (2) as an

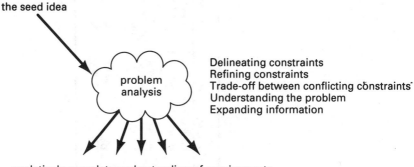

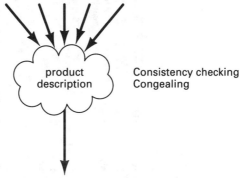

a consistent and complete SRS

Figure 1–15. Kinds of Activities during the Requirements Phase

example of "we know how to build software" to be shown to prospective customers. This implies that in addition to being specific, the SRS must also be easy to understand by personnel untrained in computer science.

1.2.3 Problem Analysis versus Product Description

There are two different types of activities that occur during the requirements phase (see Figure 1–15): problem analysis and product description. The kinds of things done during each is quite distinct.

During problem analysis, analysts spend their time brainstorming, interviewing people who have the most knowledge about the problem at hand, and identifying all possible constraints on the problem's solution. At this time there is a considerable expansion of information and knowledge about the problem. The greatest problems that occur during this time are finding ways of trading off constraints and organizing the plethora of information. Problem analysis must be performed until a complete understanding of the problem is reached.

During product description it is time to take pen in hand, to make some difficult decisions and prepare a document that describes the expected external behavior of the product to be built to solve the now-understood problem. This is a time to organize ideas, resolve conflicting views, and eliminate inconsistencies and ambiguities.

It must be pointed out, however, that the two clouds in Figure 1–15 do not represent two temporally sequential, mutually exclusive phases. There are two reasons for this. First, some product developments require little or no

Activity	This Book	Berzins [BER85]	Boehm [BOE76]	Charette [CHA86]	DoD [DOD85]	Freeman [FRE83]	IEEE [IEE84]	Kerola [KER81]	Roman [ROM84]	Ross [ROS77]	Wasserman [WAS86]	Yourdon [YOU89]
Problem analysis	Problem analysis	Requirements definition	↑ Requirements	Requirements analysis	System requirements	Analysis	N/A	Pragmatic phase	Problem definition	Context analysis	Requirements analysis	Essential modeling
External behavior definition	Writing an SRS	Functional specification	Requirements ↓	Specification	Software requirements analysis	↑ Functional Specification	Requirements	I/O perspective phase	System design	Functional specification	External design	User implementation modeling
Definition of product's constituent components	Preliminary design	Design	Design	Design	Preliminary design	Functional Specification ↓	Design	Constructive phase	Software design	Design	Internal design	Design

Figure 1–16. Inconsistent Requirements Terminology.

problem analysis. In particular, problem analysis is applicable to only new, difficult, or yet-unsolved problems. Why waste time analyzing a problem that is already well understood? Second, given a new, difficult, or yet-unsolved problem, we do not perform problem analysis and then when complete begin writing an SRS. In reality what is done is something like this: Problem analysis is initiated; as parts of the problem become well understood, corresponding sections of the SRS are written; finally the last aspect of the problem is analyzed, and the SRS is finished.

It is remarkable how inconsistent the terminology used in the software industry is. As shown in Figure 1–16, there is no consistent use of the terms *requirements, analysis, specification,* and *design.*

1.3 WHY ARE REQUIREMENTS IMPORTANT?

Previous sections of this chapter have defined the software requirements phase and established its context in relation to the rest of the system development life cycle. We could argue, "Why waste time worrying about requirements? Why not save money by eliminating this unnecessary step?" The purpose of this section is to explain why doing a better job of defining and specifying software requirements is not only worthwhile but also possible and cost effective. The section is structured as a series of hypotheses each followed by empirical evidence in support of the hypothesis.

Hypothesis 1. The later in the development life cycle that a software error is detected, the more expensive it will be to repair.

Supporting Empirical Evidence. In the early 1970s, three companies, GTE [DAL77], TRW [BOE76], and IBM [FAG74] performed independent studies of this phenomenon. Although each of the three companies was apparently unaware of the other two, they all reached roughly the same result. Figure 1–17 gives a compilation of the results. In particular if we arbitrarily assign unit cost to the effort required to detect and repair an error during the coding stage, it was found that the cost to detect and repair an error during the requirements stage was between a fifth and tenth as much and the cost to detect and repair an error during maintenance was twenty times as much. All

Stage	Relative Cost of Repair
Requirements	0.1 – 0.2
Design	0.5
Coding	1
Unit test	2
Acceptance test	5
Maintenance	20

Figure 1–17. Cost (Effort) to Repair Software in Relationship to Life Cycle Stage

together that implies as much as a two hundred to one ratio between the requirements and maintenance stages.

There are two possible explanations for this apparently dramatic increase in the cost of detecting and repairing errors as we progress through the life cycle:

a. If we assume that most errors are detected soon after they have been made, then the only conclusion we can reach is that coding bugs are inherently more expensive to detect and repair than design bugs, which are inherently more expensive to detect and repair than requirements errors, and so forth, or

b. If we assume that most errors are not detected until well after they have been made, then the additional cost may be due to the need not only to correct the original offending error but subsequent investments in the error that have been made during later stages. This is precisely what Mizuno [MIZ83] was showing in one diagram of his COMPSAC '82 keynote address, which is reproduced in Figure 1–18. Assuming that we begin with a real problem, we then write a requirements specification. Some part of that specification will be correct and the remainder erroneous. Then we move on to design. During the design stage, design based on erroneous requirements specification will certainly be incorrect; meanwhile design based on correct requirements specification will result in part in correct design and in part in erroneous design. Then we move on to implementation. During implementation, programs based on design originating from erroneous requirements specification will certainly be incorrect; programs based on erroneous design will certainly be incorrect; meanwhile programming based on correct design will result in part in correct programs and in part in erroneous programs. Then we move on to testing. During testing, the part of the program that is correct will hopefully be demonstrated to work correctly. Some errors will be detected and corrected, some will be detected and left uncorrected, and some will not be detected at all.

Explanation **a** is counterintuitive; let us pursue explanation **b**.

Hypothesis 2. Many errors remain latent and are not detected until well after the stage at which they are made.

Supporting Empirical Evidence. Boehm [BOE75] concluded that 54% of all errors ever detected in software projects studied at TRW were in fact detected *after* the coding and unit testing stages. To make matters even worse, most of these (45%) were attributable to the requirements and design stages rather than the coding stage (9%). This provides possible empirical evidence to support Mizuno's concern (that is, explanation **b**) and hypothesis 2.

Hypothesis 3. There are many requirements errors being made.

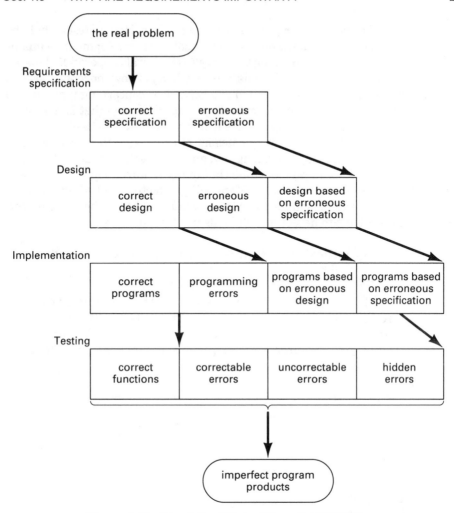

Figure 1–18. Cumulative Effects of Error. © 1983 IEEE.

Supporting Empirical Evidence. DeMarco, as quoted by Tavolato and Vincena [TAV84], reports that 56% of all bugs detected can be traced to errors made during the requirements stage. An experiment by AIRMICS [CEL83] showed that careful analysis (in particular through the use of automated requirements tools) of a previously approved SRS for a large U.S. Army management information system uncovered over five hundred errors in the document. Of course this is only one experiment on only one software project.

Hypothesis 4. Errors made in requirements specifications are typically incorrect facts, omissions, inconsistencies, and ambiguities.

Supporting Empirical Evidence. The Naval Research Laboratory has been performing ongoing research in software development techniques since the mid-1970s. They are using the Navy A-7E aircraft's operational flight program as a realistic test case to demonstrate feasibility of new concepts. Part of this ongoing study [BAS81] has generated extensive data concerning types of errors that are made during the requirements stage. The data shows that 77% of all requirements errors on the A-7E project were nonclerical. Figure 1–19 gives the distribution of these nonclerical errors by category of error: 49% incorrect fact, 31% omission, 13% inconsistency, 5% ambiguity, and 2% misplacement.

Now we might conclude that many requirements errors are being made, these are around awhile before being detected, and we know what kind they are, but the reason for their latency may be due to the fact that the errors are too difficult to detect, which leads us to hypothesis 5.

Hypothesis 5.   Requirements errors can be detected.

Supporting Empirical Evidence.   Let us look at three independent studies:

Bruggere's [BRU79] data shows that the most effective way of finding an error in software is to inspect it (see Figure 1–20). This puts to rest the myth that we should not spend time analyzing nonexecutable forms of the software (for example, requirements and designs) because the computer can more easily find errors when it executes the program.

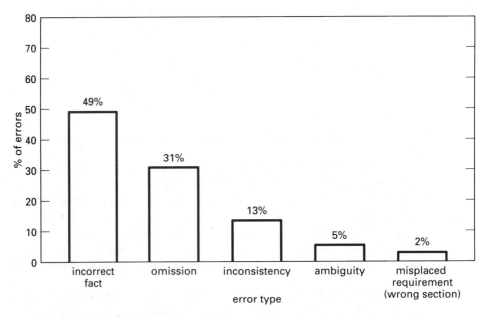

Figure 1-19. Types of Non-Clerical Requirements Errors. © 1981 IEEE Computer Society, Inc.

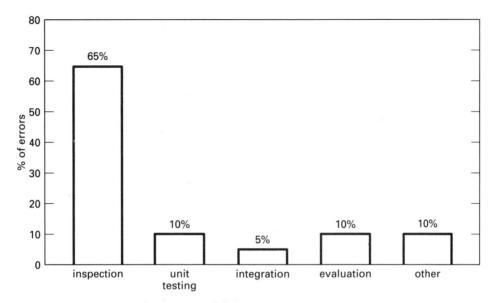

Figure 1–20. Can We Find the Errors?

Basili and Weiss's [BAS81] data shows that 33% of requirements errors in the A-7E specification were detected by manual review (see Figure 1–21).

Data from Celko, et al. [CEL83] shows that the use of automated tools (in this case, REVS [ALF77], IORL [EVE80], and CADSAT [TER80], an adaptation of PSL/PSA [TEI77]) can detect a significant number of errors (302, 542, and 250, respectively) in a previously approved software requirements specification (see Figure 1–22).

If we believe the empirical evidence, we can conclude that

1. Many requirements errors are being made (Hypotheses 3 and 4).
2. Many of these errors are not being detected early (Hypothesis 2).
3. Many of these errors can be detected early (Hypothesis 5).
4. Not detecting these errors may contribute to skyrocketing software costs (Hypothesis 1).

The potential impact of errors in requirements is substantial:

1. The resulting software may not satisfy users' real needs.
2. Multiple interpretations of requirements may cause disagreements between customers and developers, wasting time and dollars and perhaps resulting in lawsuits.

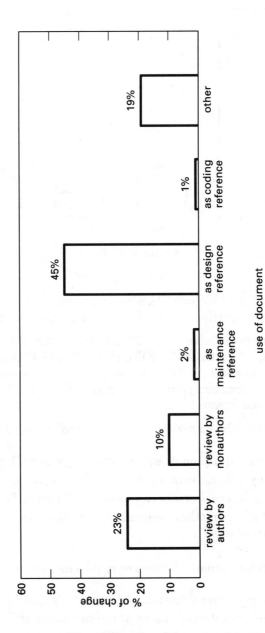

Figure 1-21. Discovering a Need for Change. © 1981 IEEE Computer Society, Inc.

	REVS	IORL	CADSAT
Inconsistent	101	143	115
Ambiguous	70	126	0
Missing	53	0	0
Illogical	38	0	0
Incomplete	26	0	52
Questions	0	0	79
Typos	0	0	4
Others	14	273	0
Total	302	542	250

Figure 1-22. Errors Found by Automated Tools.

3. It may be impossible to thoroughly test that the software meets its intended requirements.
4. Both time and money may be wasted building the wrong system.

1.4 A TAXONOMY OF APPLICATIONS

This book contains descriptions of numerous requirements tools and techniques, many of which have been developed or are specifically suitable for particular subsets of the universe of applications. In order to demonstrate the effectiveness of any tool or technique, it is important to demonstrate its usefulness on an appropriate problem. On the other hand, to compare sets of tools or techniques, it is important to provide consistent problems across tools and techniques. This will not only show the effectiveness or ineffectiveness of a tool or technique in selected application domains but also how tools or techniques mold thought processes differently.

Section 1.5 defines in detail the particular problems used as case studies throughout this book. To explain how these are representative and see relevant similarities in any particular problem that you happen to be solving personally, the current section offers a taxonomy of applications.

The sole purpose of this taxonomy is to partition the world of software applications into classes exhibiting common properties that make one or more requirements tools or techniques uniformly applicable to its members.[7] The taxonomy is created by dividing the entire domain of software applications along five orthogonal axes:

1. Difficulty of problem
2. Relationship in time between data and processing

[7]For this reason more traditional taxonomies, such as scientific versus commercial, are not used here.

3. Number of simultaneous tasks to be performed
4. Relative difficulty of data, control, and algorithmic aspects of problem
5. Deterministic versus nondeterministic.

Each of these is described in the following paragraphs.

For the current purpose, it is sufficient to divide the difficulty of software problems into two basic categories: hard (HA)[8] and not hard (NH). The HA problems are those that have never before been solved or are brand new or have an unknown or inapplicable solution. The NH problems are the others, that is, old problems that have previously been solved and whose solutions are known to be applicable. Some examples are:

HA	NH
Landing a person on Pluto	Telephone communication for a
Transporting people from New	new hotel
York to Tokyo in 30 min	Translating FORTRAN into VAX
Destroying all enemy missiles	machine language
within 10 sec of launch	Interactive text editing
Completely replacing humans in	Patient monitoring
the software development process	Inventory control

Another way of dividing the universe of software applications into subsets is by the temporal relationship that exists between the availability of the input data and the processing [JOR86]: *static* (ST) and *dynamic* (DY).[9] In ST applications all input data is available to the program before it starts processing. In DY applications, input data continues to arrive during processing to effect the program's outcome. Certainly, all interactive systems are DY. Some examples are:

ST	DY
Translating FORTRAN into VAX	Editing
machine language	Inventory control
Payroll	Patient monitoring
Graphics display	Nuclear reactor control
	Telephone communication
	for a new hotel

A third way of dividing the universe of software applications into subsets is by the number of things the software is expected to do simultaneously

---

[8]This does not imply that a relationship exists between these so-called *hard* problems and mathematically *hard* problems, as defined in computational complexity theory.

[9]Harel [HAR85] calls these *transformational* and *reactive,* respectively. ST applications are also called *batch* applications. DY applications are occasionally termed *real time.*

[JOR86]: *sequential* (SE) and *parallel* (PA). In SE applications the software solution is expected to perform only one thing at a time. In PA applications the software solution is expected to perform multiple tasks simultaneously (from the user's perspective). The SE versus PA attribute applies to the solution software itself, not to the environment in which it is contained. Thus an editor is a sequential application (most editors care about only one user), even though it is usually run in an environment (an operating system) that supplies parallel operation. Some examples are given in the table that follows:

SE	PA
Compiling	Telephone switching
Payroll	Process control
Editing	Robotics control
Games	Inventory control (probably)
	Patient monitoring
	Graphics display

A fourth way of dividing software applications into subsets is with respect to that aspect of the software's external behavior most difficult to specify: *data* (DA), *control* (CO), or *algorithm* (AL). In DA applications the most difficult aspect of the software requirements specification process is the definition, description, organization, and format of the data that moves across the interface between the system and its environment. In CO applications the most difficult aspect is the definition and description of how the environment is going to control the system or how the system is going to control its environment. These applications also tend to have strict timing requirements. In AL applications the most difficult aspect is the specification of the transform function that describes interrelationships and interplay between the system's inputs and outputs. Many general application domains exhibit more than one of these attributes (see Figure 1–23). Interesting enough when you ask individuals about their own problems, they usually maintain that all three are extremely difficult. Some examples are:

Payroll	DA	
Inventory control	DA	CO
Editing	DA	AL
Compiling	DA	AL
Graphics display	DA	AL
Patient monitoring	CO	
Telephone switching	CO	AL
Nuclear reactor control	DA	CO

	Data (DA)	Control (CO)	Algorithm (AL)
Real-time systems		X	X
Business data processing	X	X	
Process control systems	X	X	
Support software (e.g. compilers)	X		X
Communications		X	
Information storage and retrieval	X		X
Any individual's problem	X	X	X

Figure 1–23. General Characteristics of Application Domains.

A fifth way of dividing software applications into subsets is by the predictability of system outcome based on a given set of inputs: *deterministic* (DE) and *nondeterministic* (ND) problems.[10] In DE applications the system is expected to provide the same answer all the time, given the same inputs. Its "stimuli and expected responses are well understood and definable" [BER84]. In ND applications the system's responses are not well understood. The systems are less predictable; they are expected to make decisions and draw "conclusions based on the conjoined meaning of the data...from a variety of sources" [BER84]. There may be more than one right answer. Such systems often try to mimic human behavior. Some examples are:

DE	ND
Payroll	Command, control, communications,
Inventory control	and intelligence (C^3I)
Editing	Chess playing
Compiling	Disease diagnosis
Graphics display	Automatic program synthesis

In this book the applicability of all the techniques will be described in terms of these five orthogonal sets of attributes of applications.

---

[10]Jorgensen [JOR86] and Bersoff et al. [BER87] call these *computational* and *decisional*, respectively. Bersoff [BER84] calls these *algorithmic* (or *sequential*) and *inferential*, respectively.

1.5 THREE APPLICATIONS

Figures 1–24 through 1–26 present three different real-world problems as problem scenarios in need of solution. The details given are typical of a problem statement prior to the requirements phase. The three applications and their attributes are:

1. Automating a book distribution company
   NH DY PA DA DE
2. Automating a helicopter landing
   NH DY SE CO AL ND
3. Transporting people from New York to Tokyo in 30 min[11]
   HA DY SE CO DE

The Library of Computer Sciences (LOCS) Corporation specializes in selling computer-related books at low prices to computer specialists. It does this by mailing every month to every one of the current subscribers the following:

A brief synopsis of the latest selection-of-the-month book

A catalog of other available books

A postcard on which subscribers indicate whether or not they want the latest selection-of-the-month and/or other selections from the catalog

When the company started its business three years ago, it did so with a small office and three employees, and all work was performed manually. The company now sells thirty thousand books per month and employs a full-time staff of twenty. Unfortunately all work is still performed manually. The company recently purchased a VAX 11/780 computer system, thinking it would solve the problems. The company has contacted us to evaluate its operations and develop an automated system using the VAX. It is not at all clear at this point whether or not the solution will include automating any or all of the following: payroll and human resources; inventory, conveyor belts, and robots to move books; accounts payable and receivable; and so forth.

Figure 1-24. Automating a Book Distribution Company.

[11]There is an irony in selecting a representative hard problem. If I select one and then demonstrate problem analysis techniques (and thus analyze the problem), either the problem was not so hard, or I solved the problem and it is no longer hard. On the other hand, if I select a really hard, not yet solved problem, then I cannot demonstrate the successful application of any problem analysis techniques.

Pfleeger Pfliers operates a parcel delivery service in a metropolitan area. The president and pfounder, Pfilip Pfleeger, established the company's reputation of extremely rapid delivery (15 to 20 minutes) of any parcel between two locations within the greater Pfiladelphia metropolitan area. He is able to accomplish this with a pfleet of helicopters and a collection of helipads he built on 250 recently purchased abandoned building lots (each with a bicycle garage and bicycle used by the helicopter pilot to transport parcels from the heliport to the destination). For this extremely pfast service, Pfleeger's prices are quite high, but his business base is rapidly expanding in this business community. Last week unfortunately his company encountered two major problems. First on Tuesday the entire city was locked in with heavy pfog, and zero visibility grounded all his helicopters. Needless to say his clients were quite upset; some are actually considering suing him because he had claimed that weather would not prevent his promised 20-min maximum delivery time. Second on Thursday one of his pilots suffered a heart attack on final approach. The helicopter crashed and was totally destroyed (including the parcel). The good news is that the pilot was rescued and is now recuperating in a local hospital. That incident could have been a lot worse, but once again clients are paying a lot of money for this elite service and do not appreciate their important packages being destroyed.

Mr. Pfleeger has decided that the best way for his company to supply the level of service he has promised is to install systems at each of the 250 helipads to control the landing safely. The system must be smart enough to operate effectively in cases of both zero visibility and unconscious pilots. He has given us the contract to develop that automated system.

Figure 1–25. Automating a Helicopter Landing

EXERCISES

1. Which of the following are valid requirements? In each case explain why or why not.
   a. The software shall be written in FORTRAN.
   b. The software shall respond to all requests within 5 seconds.
   c. The software shall be composed of the following twenty-three modules.
   d. The software shall use the following fifteen menu screens whenever it is communicating with the user.
2. Categorize the following software applications by selecting the appropriate attributes from the list
      HA or NH
      ST or DY
      SE or PA
      DA and/or CO and/or AL
      DE or ND

A consortium of companies from Japan and the United States has been created to investigate the feasibility of transporting people between New York and Tokyo in less than 30 minutes. The consortium has in turn hired a team of consultants from many different disciplines (including software) to solve the problem. We are the software delegates on the team. At this early point in time, very few decisions have been made other than that the transportation system should be in operation no later than 15 years from now. Although they are certainly open to additional suggestions, the consortium members have thus far defined four possible general approaches

1. Space shuttle approach: A space shuttle type aircraft is launched from a reusable rocket, enters space, and lands like a glider at its destination.

2. Tunnel approach: A tunnel is dug through the earth connecting New York and Tokyo and air is removed to a level as close as possible to a complete vacuum. An elevatorlike vehicle is dropped down on rails. No outside source of energy is needed for most of the trip, since gravity will take care of the first half of the trip and built-up kinetic energy will suffice for most of the second half. The only necessary external energy source will be the power required to raise the elevator the remaining distance to the surface.

3. Bullet train approach: Tracks are installed across the planet on a great circle route and covered by a glass tube, and the area under the tube is evacuated (as in approach 2). The tube and tracks are of course floated on pontoons when crossing any body of water. The train transports people through the tube.

4. "Beam me up, Scottie" approach: Individuals enter an encoding station at the departure city. All their atoms are analyzed and digitized. The digital data is transmitted via satellite to the destination city where the decoding station captures the data and recreates the traveler out of the digitized atom descriptions.

Figure 1-26. Transporting People from New York to Tokyo in 30 Minutes.

a. A patient-monitoring system that sounds alarms whenever a patient's vital signs exceed acceptable ranges.
b. An elevator control system that controls the movement of elevators and dispatches them to appropriate floors.
c. A robot lawn mower that can be placed on any lawn and will cut all contiguous areas of grass without hitting such items as shrubs, sidewalks, and trees.
d. An automatic hair cutter that you sit under after telling it what style haircut you want and which will cut your hair accordingly.
e. A payroll program that accepts time cards and generates correct paychecks.
f. A private automatic branch exchange (PABX) that provides telephone services.
g. A fully automated automobile production line.

h. An elevator control system that operates multiple elevator cars within a single shaft; spurs at each floor enable the system to move elevators to awaiting passengers outside the primary shaft, as shown in Figure 1–27.

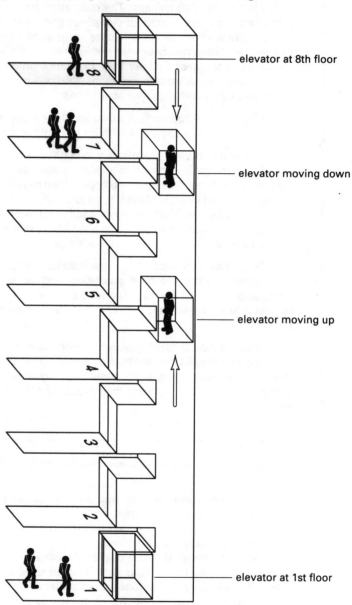

Figure 1–27. Multiple-Car Elevator System.

REFERENCES

[ALF77]   Alford, M. W. "A Requirements Engineering Methodology for Real-Time Processing Requirements." *IEEE Transactions on Software Engineering* **3,** 1 (January 1977): 60–69.

[BAS81]   Basili, V., and D. Weiss. "Evaluation of a Software Requirements Document by Analysis of Change Data." In *Fifth IEEE International Conference on Software Engineering,* Washington D.C.: Computer Society Press of the Institute of Electrical and Electronics Engineers, 1981. pp. 314–23.

[BER80]   Bersoff, E., et al. *Software Configuration Management: An Investment in Product Integrity.* Englewood Cliffs, N.J.: Prentice-Hall, 1980.

[BER84]   Bersoff, E. "Intelligence System Development Methodologies: Slaying the Dinosaur." In *AFCEA Intelligence Symposium,* Fairfax, Virginia: AFCEA International Press, March 1984.

[BER87]   Bersoff, E., et al. "A New Look at the C^3I Software Life Cycle." *SIGNAL Magazine* **41,** 8 (April 1987): 85–93.

[BER85]   Berzins, V., and M. Gray. "Analysis and Design in MSG.84: Formalizing Functional Specifications." *IEEE Transactions on Software Engineering* **11,** 8 (August 1985): 657–70.

[BOE75]   Boehm, B. W., et al. "Some Experience with Automated Aids to the Design of Large-Scale Reliable Software." *IEEE Transactions on Software Engineering* **1,** 1 (March 1975): 125–33.

[BOE76]   Boehm, B. W. "Software Engineering." *IEEE Transactions on Computers* **25,** 12 (December 1976): 1226–1241.

[BOE81]   Boehm, B. W. *Software Engineering Economics.* Englewood Cliffs, N.J.: Prentice-Hall, 1981.

[BRU79]   Bruggere, T. "Software Engineering Management, Personnel, and Methodology." In *Fourth IEEE International Conference on Software Engineering,* Washington D.C.: Computer Society Press of the Institute of Electrical and Electronics Engineers, 1979. p. 367.

[CAS81]   Casey, B. "The Impact of the Technical Communicator on Software Requirements." *Journal of Technical Writing and Communication* **11,** 4 (April 1981): 361–72.

[CEL83]   Celko, J., et al. "A Demonstration of Three Requirements Language Systems." *ACM SIGPLAN Notices* **18,** 1 (January 1983): 9–14.

[CHA86]   Charette, R. *Software Engineering Environments.* New York: McGraw-Hill, 1986.

[DAL77]   Daly, E. Management of Software Development." *IEEE Transactions on Software Engineering* **3,** 3 (May 1977): 229–42.

[DOC84]   U.S. Department of Commerce. *A Competitive Assessment of the U.S. Software Industry.* Washington, D.C.: International Trade Administration, December 1984.

[DOD85]   U.S. Department of Defense. *Military Standard: Defense System Software Development.* DOD-STD-2167. Washington, D.C., June 1985.

[EIA80] Electronics Industries Association. *The DoD Electronics Market: Forecast for the 80s.* Washington, D.C., 1980.

[EIA85] Electronics Industries Association. *DoD Computing Activities and Programs: 1985 Specific Market Survey.* Washington, D.C., 1985.

[EVE80] Everhart, C., et al. *SAMS IORL Demonstration Final Report.* Teledyne Brown Engineering Report SD80-AIRMICS-2428. September 1980.

[FAG74] Fagan, M. *Design and Code Inspections and Process Control in the Development of Programs.* IBM Report IBM-SDD-TR-21-572. December 1974.

[FRE83] Freeman, P. "Fundamentals of Design." In *IEEE Tutorial on Software Design Techniques.* 4th ed. Washington D.C.: Computer Society Press of the Institute of Electrical and Electronics Engineers, 1983. pp. 2–22.

[GAO79] U.S. Government Accounting Office. *Contracting for Computer Software Development—Serious Problems Require Management Attention to Avoid Wasting Additional Millions.* Report FGMSD-80-4. November 1979.

[HAM83] Hamilton, M., and S. Zeldin. "The Functional Life Cycle Model and Its Automation: USE.IT." *Journal of Systems and Software* **3,** 1 (March 1983): 25–62.

[HAR85] Harel, D., and A. Pnueli. *On the Development of Reactive Systems.* Weizmann Institute of Science Report C585-02. Rehovot, Israel, 1985.

[IEE83] Institute of Electrical and Electronics Engineers. *IEEE Standard Glossary of Software Engineering Terminology.* ANSI/IEEE Standard 729-1983. New York, 1983.

[IEE84] Institute of Electrical and Electronics Engineers. *IEEE Guide to Software Requirements Specifications.* ANSI/IEEE Standard 830-1984. New York, 1984.

[JOR86] Jorgensen, P. "Minireview—Software Requirements Specification." In *IEEE COMPSAC 86,* Washington D.C.: Computer Society Press of the Institute of Electrical and Electronics Engineers, 1986. p. 182.

[KER81] Kerola, P., and P. Freeman. "A Comparison of Life Cycle Models." In *Fifth IEEE International Conference on Software Engineering,* Washington D.C.: Computer Society Press of the Institute of Electrical and Electronics Engineers, 1981. pp. 90–99.

[MIZ83] Mizuno, Y. "Software Quality Improvement." *IEEE Computer* **15,** 3 (March 1983): 66–72.

[MUS83] Musa, J., et al. "Stimulating Software Engineering Progress—a Report of the Software Engineering Planning Group." *ACM Software Engineering Notes* **8,** 2 (April 1983): 29–54.

[ORR81] Orr, K. *Structured Requirements Definition.* Topeka, Kans.: Orr and Assoc., 1981.

[ROM84] Roman, G.-C., et al. "A Total System Design Framework." *IEEE Computer* **17,** 5 (May 1984): 15–26.

[ROS77] Ross, D., and K. Schoman. "Structured Analysis for Requirements Definition." *IEEE Transactions on Software Engineering* **3,** 1 (January 1977): 6–15.

[ROS80] Ross, D. T. "Removing the Limitations of Natural Language." In *Software Engineering*, H. Freeman and P. Lewis, eds. New York: Academic Press, 1980. pp. 149–79.

[ROY70] Royce, W. "Managing the Development of Large Software Systems." In *IEEE WESCON*, August 1970. pp. 1–9. Reprinted in *Ninth IEEE International Conference on Software Engineering*, Washington D.C.: Computer Society Press of the Institute of Electrical and Electronics Engineers, 1987. pp. 328–38.

[TAV84] Tavolato, P., and K. Vincena. "A Prototyping Methodology and Its Tool." In *Approaches to Prototyping*, R. Budde et al., eds., Berlin: Springer-Verlag, 1984. pp. 434–46.

[TEI77] Teichroew, D., and E. A. Hershey III. "PSL/PSA: A Computer-Aided Technique for Structured Documentation and Analysis of Information Processing Systems." *IEEE Transactions on Software Engineering* **3**, 1 (January 1977): 41–48.

[TER80] Terrell, K., and L. Johnson. *AIRMICS LARE / CADSAT Analysis Final Report*, Logicon report R-81003A. April 1980.

[TUR74] Turn, R. *Computers in the 1980s.* New York: Columbia University Press, 1974. As reported in M. Shooman, *Software Engineering*, New York: McGraw-Hill, 1983.

[WAS86] Wasserman, A., et al. "Developing Interactive Information Systems with the User Software Engineering Methodology." *IEEE Transactions on Software Engineering* **12**, 2 (February 1986): 326–45.

[WEB84] *Webster's Ninth New Collegiate Dictionary.* Springfield, Mass.: G. and C. Merriam, 1984.

[YOU89] Yourdon, E. *Modern Structured Analysis.* Englewood Cliffs, N.J.: Yourdon Press, 1989.

2

Problem Analysis

In Section 1.2.3, two distinct activities were defined as part of the software requirements stage: problem analysis and product description. The former activity is the subject of this chapter; the latter is the subject of Chapters 3, 4, and 5. Chapter 2 begins with an introduction to the subject of problem analysis, followed by a discussion of the principles that underlie any problem analysis technique, and concludes with an explanation, discussion, and comparison of a number of techniques, tools, and languages that can aid in problem analysis.

2.1 INTRODUCTION TO PROBLEM ANALYSIS

Problem analysis is the activity that encompasses learning about the problem to be solved (often through brainstorming and/or questioning), understanding the needs of potential users, trying to find out who the user really is, and understanding all the constraints on the solution. Assuming that the requirements stage ends with creating a document called the software requirements specification (SRS), which contains a complete description of the external behavior of the product to be built or purchased, problem analysis can be thought of as defining the product space, i.e., the range of all possible software solutions.

The *product space* is that range of problem solutions that meets all known constraints. The sources of constraints may include users, customers, developers, technology, laws, and standards [CRO82]. Let us look at how these interact

41

to create a product space. Potential users may be able to express their particular problem quite well. In such cases, they may know what they want, but that may or may not correspond to what they really need. Potential users may *want* a computer system that will not affect their current nonautomated activities at all, whereas what they *need* is a system that will drastically affect their way of doing business if the system is to pay for itself in a short period of time. For example, a word processing organization may be so comfortable with retyping almost identical copies of figures (because of an inadequate file manager and associated commands) that when they upgrade to a new word processing system (to provide, say, better graphics), they do not want a feature to store and retrieve similar versions of the same figure efficiently. It is the job of the analyst to uncover not only what users say they want but what they really need based on the analyst's assessment of the users' problems. Once discovered, the analyst should be able to divide the universe of software systems into two mutually exclusive sets that correspond to those that would satisfy the users' real needs and those that would not (see Figure 2–1a). The primary factors of user interest tend to be the functions performed, response time, user interface, and reliability.

Customers are differentiated from users in this context as the people who actually possess the money to buy the product. Customers, too, may be able to express their wants quickly but, once again, it is the analyst's task to discover the real needs of the customers. Once uncovered by the analyst, these customer needs divide the universe of software solutions into two mutually exclusive sets corresponding to those that would satisfy the customers' real needs and those that would not (see Figure 2–1b). The primary factors of customer interest include functions performed, development time, cost, maintainability, modifiability, and reliability.

The development organization has yet a different perspective. In addition to wanting to satisfy the customers' and users' desires, the organization is interested in revenue and profits, market share, a product's relationship to existing products, and the ability of its staff to do the required job. Depending on the relationship between the customer and the developer, other factors may become important. For example, if the development organization will be selling copies of the product to many customers in a competitive marketplace, the development organization wants to keep costs as low as possible. In an environment where competition between suppliers occurs only during pre-development, so there is no competition after development commences, there may be less motivation to control costs. On the other hand, if the development organization will be responsible for repairing all defects in the product at no additional cost to the customer, there is strong motivation to build in quality, maintainability, and modifiability from the onset. In cases where the customer bears such cost, the opposite may be true. In environments where development costs are directly reimbursed by a (captive) customer, there may be little

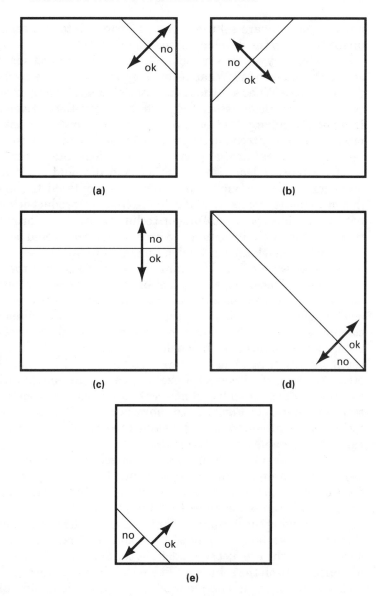

Figure 2–1. Carving the Product Space. **(a)** Users' Needs. **(b)** Customers' Needs. **(c)** Developers' Perspective. **(d)** Technology Risks. **(e)** Input of Laws and Standards.

motivation to reuse parts of existing products. In cases where there is motivation to reduce development costs, software reuse is a lot more common. The bottom line is that however the development organization is motivated, the universe of software solutions can be divided into two sets: acceptable and unacceptable to the developers (see Figure 2–1c).

Technology also has a major impact on the product space. What technology is available now? What technology is likely to be available at product delivery time? What are the risks associated with using existing technology? What are the risks associated with using yet-to-be-developed technology? Imagine a company that believed it was not worth the risk of developing a product using any technology unless a competitor had already sold a competing product incorporating that particular technology. Such a company could never occupy a market leadership position, and it would repeatedly release new products that were out of date before they entered the marketplace. Now imagine another company that believed that any product development that did not plan to incorporate all major technological breakthroughs expected between development inception and product delivery would be out of date before reaching the marketplace. Such a company would probably find that many of its products were delayed indefinitely or aborted due to the unavailability of some piece of technology. The fact of the matter is that neither philosophy works. The only sensible business approach is to assess every piece of technology independently and to take calculated risks on those items that have some combination of high likelihood and high payoff. In the area of hardware, there are many examples of technological breakthroughs that one might decide to count on: new components, materials, integrated circuit fabrication processes, etc. In the area of software, the examples are somewhat more limited and tend to focus on the availability of new software tools: new compilers, new editors, test generators, etc. Figure 2–1d shows how acceptability risks with respect to technology availability may carve the universe of software solutions into two ranges: acceptable and unacceptable.

Laws and standards also have an effect on the product space (see Figure 2–1e). For example, solutions that violate laws and standards (e.g., a garage door opener that interferes with television reception) would fall into the unacceptable range, and those that did not would fall into the acceptable range.

Overlaying the five parts of Figure 2–1 results in a composite Figure 2–2a that clearly shows the goal of problem analysis, namely, to define the product space, where the product space defines the domain of products that will satisfy all constraints on the solution. Within this domain, any product P_i (see Figure 2–2b) would be an acceptable product. Each would exhibit different external behavior but would satisfy all constraints.

Figures 2–1 and 2–2 show the differences between acceptable and non-acceptable solutions with a discrete well-defined line. In reality, the differences are more continuous. Perhaps a better way of showing each of the constraints in Figure 2–1 is through the use of varying degrees of shading, where solid black represents totally unacceptable solutions and solid white represents totally acceptable solutions, and the intermediate shades represent the corre-

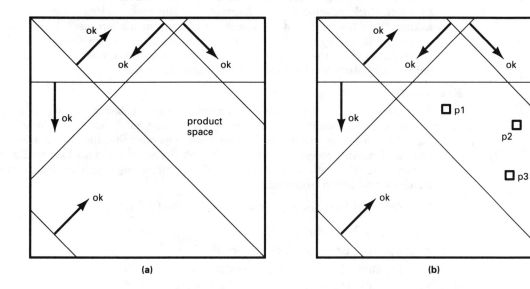

Figure 2–2. Product Space. **(a)** Composite of the Constraints. **(b)** Possible Products.

sponding degrees of acceptability. Then Figure 2–2 would show the composite with lighter areas representing better solutions than darker areas.

It should be pointed out that for most problem analyses, the initial attempt to delineate all constraints results in a product space of negative area, i.e., two or more constraints contradict each other. This is why a major activity during problem analysis is performing trade-offs between constraints, i.e., relaxing one constraint to accommodate another. Classic examples of this are the trade-offs between functionality and cost (e.g., decrease cost by decreasing functionality) and between development time and functionality (e.g., increase functionality by increasing development time).

When the SRS is finally written, it describes the external behavior of the actual product to be built. As such, it limits behavior to some particular P_i in Figure 2–2b.

Uncovering needs and understanding the potential users' problems is not an easy task. It takes a lot of questions and usually a lot of legwork. The most effective technique is speaking to real potential users, watching real potential users doing their current job, and allowing users to play with experimental early versions of the product, commonly called prototypes (prototyping is the subject of Chapter 7). Formulate questions to potential users carefully, for if you are not careful, you may unduly bias the answer by your question. The classic case of this is the so-called Railroad Paradox [WEI82]. Two examples from Weinberg [WEI82] will suffice to illustrate it:

Example 1

A systems analyst in a brokerage firm received a request to change the algorithm by which stock movements were forecast. She surveyed the individual brokers, asking: "How frequently do you use the stock movements forecast?" When they all replied that they never used the forecast, she turned down the request. Of course, the reason the forecast wasn't used was that there was an error in the current algorithm, rendering the output worse than useless.

Example 2

Engineers at a computer manufacturing company were asked to improve the new version of the company's CPU by adding an efficient mechanism for subroutine calls. After a two-month delay, the engineers responded that they had studied a sample of existing programs and found that hardly any of them used subroutines in situations where efficiency was required. Therefore, they said, the request was frivolous, and would be denied.

The Railroad Paradox can be summarized as [WEI82]:

1. Service is substandard
2. Because of **1**, users do not use service
3. Also because of **1**, users request better service
4. Because of **2**, the analyst denies the request, **3**.

2.2 THE PRIMITIVES OF PROBLEM ANALYSIS

There are at least two contrasting schools of thought on how to approach problem analysis, the functional and the object oriented. In the functional world, the problem domain is analyzed from the perspective of functions that must be provided to solve those problems. Most of the analysis deals with functions (or processes) and data or control flows between and among those functions. In the object-oriented world, the problem domain is analyzed from the perspective of objects in the application domain. Most of the analysis deals with objects; classes of objects; attributes of objects; information passed between objects; relationships between objects; and services provided by, or for, objects. In either world, any of the subjects of analysis can be described at many levels of detail. For example, functions can be described at any level from the very abstract (e.g., provide voice communications) to the very specific (e.g., the local call shall be operated by pressing the "X" button). Data items can be described at any level from the very abstract (e.g., payroll data) to the very specific (e.g., John Doe's annual salary for 1989). Objects can be described at any level from the very abstract (e.g., vehicles) to the very specific (e.g., 1989 BMW 750iL).

Because there are so many relationships that can exist between items under analysis and so many levels of possible detail, analysts need techniques to organize the plethora of information that surfaces. In particular, what is needed is a *knowledge structure,* which is just a structured collection of concepts and their interrelationships.

46

To provide a better understanding of this knowledge structure, let us look at an example: an elevator control system for a twenty-story building. During early discussions, someone may comment, "The ergonomics of the control system are important." Later someone else may say, "It is important for the control panel to be reachable by passengers restricted to wheel chairs," and, "The buttons should be labeled with the floor numbers." The latter two comments are subordinate to the former or are at a lower level of abstraction. Thus what we have is an information tree (which is one special case of a knowledge structure), such as that shown in Figure 2–3a. At some later time, two additional comments may be made: "We must address how to handle emergencies," and "The software shall control the temperature." These are then added to the tree, as shown in Figure 2–3b. By using such a tree, we can easily locate underspecified areas of the software requirements (in this case, details of emergency handling), potentially overspecified areas (subtrees with many more small branches than other subtrees), and failures to raise sufficiently abstract concepts (in this case, environmental control is a missing main branch between the trunk and the temperature control). As particular sections of the problem become well understood, it is time to define the specific behavior of that aspect of the software solution in the SRS, as described in Chapter 3.

Yeh and Zave [YEH80] were the first to isolate partitioning, abstraction, and projection as three underlying principles of structuring used during problem analysis. Usually analysts are no more aware of their use than speakers are consciously aware that they are using a noun or a verb. Just as speakers simply speak, analysts simply analyze.

Partitioning captures the "aggregation/part of" structural relation among entities or problems in the real world. It is used when it is difficult or impossible to describe a problem or its solution any way except in terms of its parts. For example, let us say we want to understand the problem of defending a nation against ballistic missiles. It is quite difficult to get our arms around that entire problem, so instead we describe it in terms of its parts. These parts may be target detection, communication, intelligence gathering and resolution, defen-

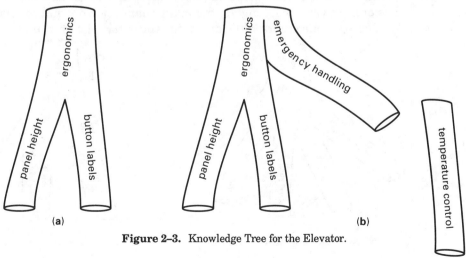

Figure 2–3. Knowledge Tree for the Elevator.

sive weapon launch, and defensive weapon guidance. Note that this is not a
design; we have simply decomposed the problem (function) into five subproblems (subfunctions) to aid in its analysis. When the real system is finally
built, it may be composed of any number of subcomponents with little or no
relationship to these subproblems. If we had analyzed each of the parts
separately, we could then extrapolate and conclude that the entire problem is
the union of the five subproblems, as shown in Figure 2–4.

Abstraction captures the "general/specific" structural relation among entities or problems in the real world. When using abstraction, we define some aspect
of the problem in abstract terms, and provide more details in association with
particular instances of that abstract concept. For example, we may define the
function of identifying threats and recognize that there are three kinds: identifying
submarine threats, identifying surface threats, and identifying air threats, as
shown in Figure 2–5. Let us look at another example where abstraction could be
used during analysis. In specifying the external behavior of an airline reservation
system, we may want to resolve all issues dealing with general dialog patterns
between the system and the user before delving into details of menu screen
formats and error message formats. The former, shown in Figure 2–6a and the
latter, shown in Figure 2–6b, represent two different levels of abstraction of the
same problem. Once these two networks are defined, whenever someone wants
to discuss the order of dialog or the behavior of particular features, the first
network can be shown; and whenever someone wants to discuss the formats of
input or output requirements, the second network can be shown. What we have
performed here is the two-step process represented in Figure 2–7.

Projection is yet another way of structuring aspects of some problems; it
is defined as describing the system from multiple viewpoints. It is analogous
to using two-dimensional diagrams to specify an object, as in Figure 2–8. One
example of using projection during analysis occurs when the analyst for an
elevator control system steps back and says, "Let's look at the elevator from
the perspectives of passengers, the maintenance person, and the fireperson."
Another example occurs while analyzing the external behavior of a telephone

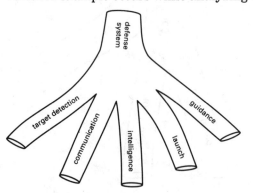

Figure 2–4. Partitioning Example.

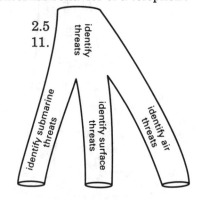

Figure 2–5. Abstraction Example 1.

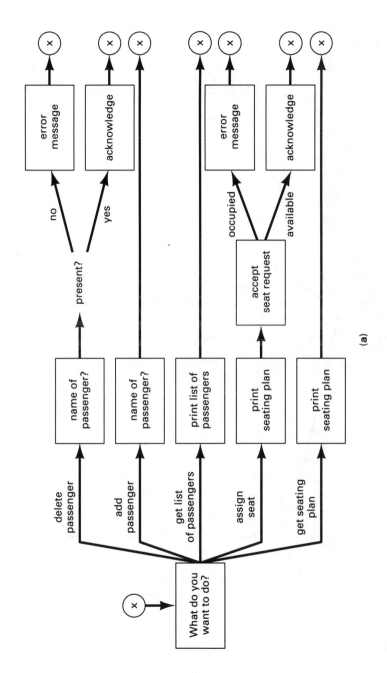

Figure 2-6. Abstraction Example 2: Airline Reservation System. (a) Level 1. (b) Level 2.

(a)

49

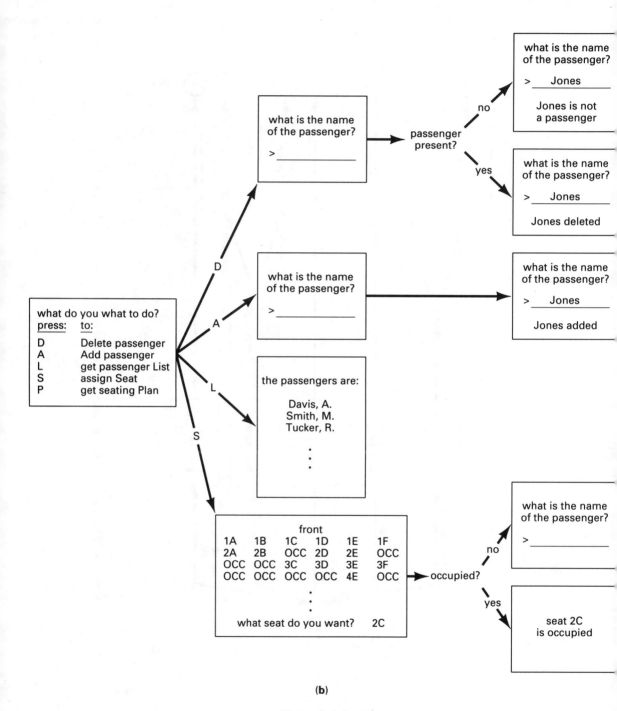

(b)

Figure 2-6. *(cont.)*

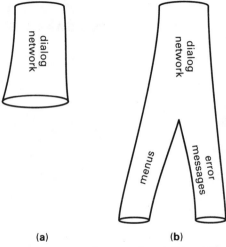

Figure 2-7. Knowledge Structure for Abstraction Example 2. **(a)** Step 1. **(b)** Step 2.

(a)   (b)

switching system during the call-waiting feature. This feature notifies subscribing parties by a clicking sound in their receiver during a phone call whenever another party is trying to call them. Trying to describe the system's complete external behavior from a global viewpoint is quite tedious and error prone. On the other hand, describing desired behavior from the perspectives of each of the three parties involved is much more straightforward, as shown in Figure 2–9. This figure assumes that parties *A* and *B* are having a conversation when party *A* receives an incoming call from party *C*. The behavior of call waiting in Figure 2–9 is shown in the style of the Specification and Description Language (SDL) [ROC82].

In summary, partitioning, abstraction, and projection can each be used in a top-down or a bottom-up manner. All define structural relationships between objects, tasks, functions, or data. Recording the fact that *A* is subordinate to *B* means different things when using the three techniques. In partitioning, it means *A* is a part of *B;* in abstraction, it means that *A* is an example of *B* and thus inherits all of *B*'s attributes; in projection, it means that *A* is one view of *B*.

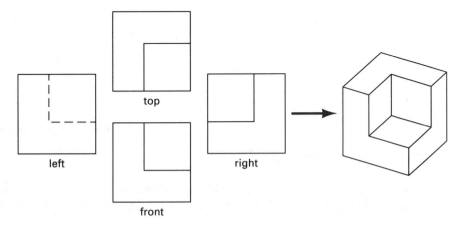

Figure 2–8. Analogy for Projection.

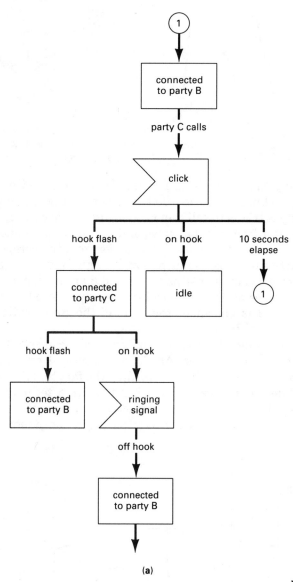

(a)

Figure 2–9. Projection Example.

2.3 SURVEY OF TECHNIQUES

In this section, a variety of problem analysis techniques are compared and contrasted. The section begins with an introduction that includes the definition

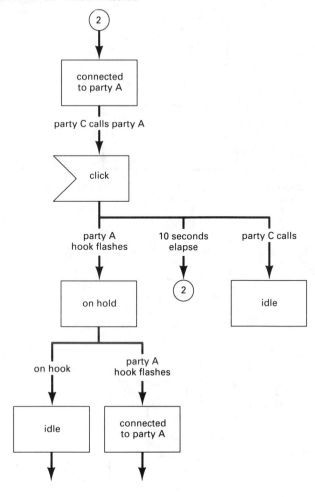

(b)

Figure 2–9. *(cont.)*

of criteria useful for evaluating a problem analysis technique. Following this is a discussion of some of the notations and some of the techniques used during problem analysis. The section concludes with examples of applying the techniques to the three case studies defined in Chapter 1 and a complete comparative analysis of the techniques based on the previously defined evaluation criteria.

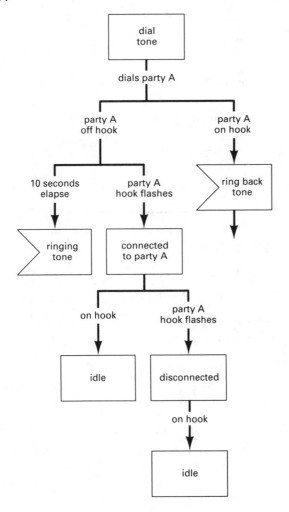

Figure 2–9 *(cont.)*

(c)

2.3.1 Introduction

Many analysts analyze a problem randomly by asking key questions, writing down the answers, asking other questions, etc. The primary advantage of applying a more formal approach to problem analysis is that it simplifies the task. But analysts do not need simplification of the easy parts of their job; they need simplification of the difficult parts. What is difficult about the job? The answer is <u>organizing all the information,</u> relating different people's perspectives, surfacing and resolving conflicts, and avoiding the internal design of the software.

Organizational aids are important because during the analysis of a nontrivial problem, reams of information about the problem are generated. During problem analysis, different people may have very different views of the problem. It is important to be able to track these different perspectives and relate them to each other. When these perspectives are in conflict, a good problem analysis technique will surface the conflict to aid in its resolution rather than burying it. There are some people who function as "professional ambiguators." They walk into meetings between developers and customers who are in disagreement over some system trait and find a way supposedly of resolving the conflict through wordsmanship. For example, the customer may want 5-second response time; the developer wants 15-second response time; the professional ambiguator recommends that the SRS read, "The response time shall be from 5 to 15 seconds." This type of resolution is *not* a resolution at all and has simply aided in obscuring the issue and burying the conflict. In such scenarios, by the way, the customer always loses; developers will do it their way, and the customer will have no recourse because the system meets the stated requirement.

Perhaps the most difficult aspect of problem analysis is avoiding software design. If we examine the requirements and design stages of the software development life cycle, shown in Figure 2–10a, we see that the requirements stage consists of two parts—problem analysis and writing the SRS—and the design stage consists of two parts—preliminary design and detailed design. Problem analysis is primarily a decomposition process: decomposing problems into subproblems with the goal of understanding the entire problem at hand. Preliminary design is also primarily a decomposition process: decomposing software components into smaller software components with the goal of generating an optimal design that meets all requirements. From a technique or tool point of view, decomposition is decomposition regardless of the "stuff" being decomposed. As a result, most techniques and tools applicable to problem analysis are equally effective during preliminary design, and vice versa. There is, however, very good reason for doing them both and not mixing the two. Remember that the goal of problem analysis is understanding, and the goal of preliminary design is optimization, e.g., of performance or maintainability. For critical applications, preliminary design might consume 25 to 30 percent of total project resources. A project team certainly cannot afford to spend that kind of money during the requirements stage—especially not before project members even know what system they are going to build (i.e., there is no SRS yet). Since an analyst will obviously not be permitted to spend sufficient dollars during the requirements stage to do a thorough software design, including trade-off studies between competing design alternatives, such an analyst is forced to use criteria for creating the software design other than those that are

Stage	Aspect	Primary Activity	Primary Goal
Requirements	Problem analysis Writing the SRS	Decomposition Behavior description	Understanding
Design	Preliminary design Detailed design	Decomposition Behavior description	Optimization

(a)

Stage	Aspect	Primary Activity	Primary Goal
System requirements	Problem analysis Writing the system requirements specification	Decomposition Behavior description	Understanding
System design	System design	Decomposition ———	Optimization
Software requirements	Problem analysis* Writing the SRS	Decomposition Behavior description	Understanding
Software design	Preliminary design Detailed design	Decomposition Behavior description	Optimization

* relatively small effort   (b)

Figure 2–10. Similarities Between Requirements and Design. **(a)** Software Only. **(b)** Systems (Software and Hardware).

appropriate. Too often analysts use the simple criteria, "that's how I've always designed such systems." And all this activity is taking place before we even write the SRS! It should be clear at this point why it is so crucial not to perform real design during the problem analysis stage and why it is so difficult to avoid.

The relationship between requirements and design becomes even more complex in problems whose solution lies in a combination of software and hardware. In these cases, a majority of the problem analysis is performed at the systems level. Relatively little problem analysis is required at the software level because (1) the system-level problem analysis (part of the system requirements stage) has uncovered most of the overall environmental, application–domain issues and (2) the subsequent system design stage has clearly specified all external constraints on all software subsystems. Figure 2–10b captures this scenario.

The following subsections discuss a variety of problem analysis techniques. Here are the traits that we would like to see such a technique exhibit

1. Facilitate communication (probably via an easy-to-understand language)
2. Provide a means of defining the system boundary
3. Provide a means of defining partitions, abstractions, and projections
4. Encourage the analyst to think and document in terms of the problem (i.e., the application) as opposed to the solution (i.e., the software)
5. Allow for opposing alternatives but alert the analyst to their presence
6. Make it easy for analysts to modify the knowledge structure

As you read the following sections of this book, keep in mind that different kinds of problems require different kinds of techniques; different aspects of any particular problem may require different kinds of techniques; and there are no panaceas. This means that to be a really effective analyst, you must keep a rich bag of tricks and know when and how to apply the right one at the right time. A famous but anonymous saying is, "If I gave a person nothing but a hammer to work with, he or she would start treating everything like a nail." It is unfortunate that when a software tool is used for the wrong purpose, users usually blame the tool. It is also unfortunate that many tool suppliers sell their tools as useful for any application. They get away with this because their tools *can* be used for many applications; they just are not optimal. For example, you *can* use a hand plane to smooth the hardwood floor of a ballroom, and you *can* use a jointer planer to sharpen toothpicks.

2.3.2 Notations for Problem Analysis

Most of the techniques discussed in Section 2.3.3 use a combination of notations, including data flow diagrams, data dictionaries, entity-relation (ER) diagrams, and Coad object diagrams. The following subsections describe these notations.

2.3.2.1 Data flow diagrams

Data flow diagrams (DFDs) have been used for many years prior to the advent of computers. DFDs show the flow of data through a system. The system may be a company, an organization, a set of procedures, a computer hardware system, a software system, or any combination of the preceding. DFDs are composed of data on the move, shown as a named arrow; transformations of data into other data, shown as named bubbles; sources and destinations of data, shown as named rectangles called *terminators*; and data in static storage (i.e., data bases), shown as two parallel lines, once again named. Figure 2–11 (adapted from [GAN79]) is an example of a DFD. The following observations about DFDs are important:

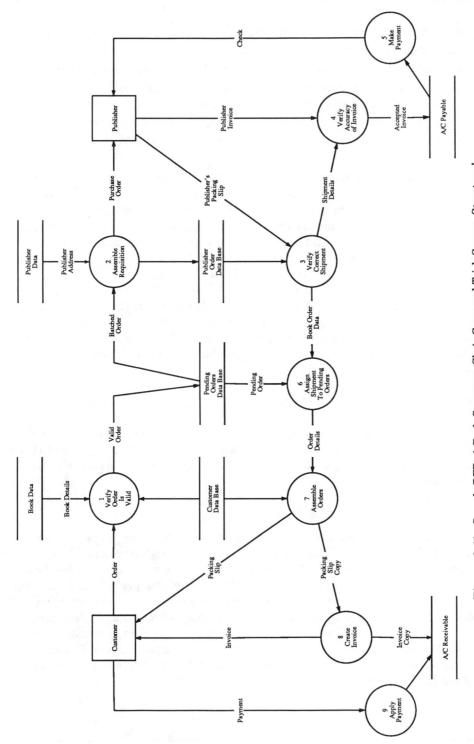

Figure 2-11. Sample DFD: A Book Company. Chris Gane and Trish Sarson, *Structured Systems Analysis: Tools and Techniques*, ©1979, p. 12; Adapted by permission of Prentice-Hall, Inc., Englewood Cliffs, N. J.

1. *All names should be unique.* This makes it easier to refer to items in the DFD. Without unique names, you might be forced to say such things as, "The big circle just to the right of the smallish circle just above the double parallel arrows coming out of the data base."

2. *Remember that a DFD is not a flow chart.* Arrows in a flow chart represent the order of events; arrows in a DFD represent flowing data. A DFD does not imply any order of events. Thus Figure 2–12 does not imply anything about the relative order of the arrival of *X* at *A* or the departure of *Y* from *A:* They may occur simultaneously, independently, *Y* may be generated each time an *X* arrives, or *X* may arrive as soon as *Y* departs. Yourdon's Modern Structured Analysis [WOO88, YOU89] defines the semantics of DFDs such that there *is* a well-defined order.

3. *Suppress logical decisions.* If you ever have the urge to draw a diamond-shaped box in a DFD, suppress the urge! A diamond-shaped box is used in flow charts to represent decision points with multiple exit paths of which only one is taken. That implies an ordering of events, which makes no sense in a DFD.

4. *Do not become bogged down in details.* Defer error conditions and error handling until the end of the analysis. Of course if the purpose of the system is to find errors, for example, hardware diagnostics or patient monitoring, do not defer error conditions and handling.

Nontrivial applications will be simple enough to represent as a single DFD. In cases where you need more detail to analyze the problem at hand sufficiently, the system is documented at the highest, most abstract level (called the context diagram) with just one bubble, showing all system terminators and external inputs and outputs. Then the system is decomposed and represented as a DFD with multiple bubbles. Parts of the system represented by each of these bubbles are then decomposed and documented as more and more detailed DFDs. This process may be repeated at as many levels as necessary until the problem at hand is well understood. It is important to preserve the number of inputs and outputs between levels; this concept is called *leveling* by DeMarco. Thus if bubble *A* has two inputs, *I1* and *I2,* and one output, *O3*, then the expanded DFD that represents *A* should have exactly two external inputs and one external output, as shown in Figure 2–13a (adapted from [DEM79]). As bubbles are decomposed into less and less abstract bubbles, the corresponding data flows may also need to be decomposed. For example, it may be sufficient to label the data flow between the Employee

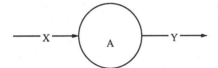

Figure 2–12. Trivial DFD.

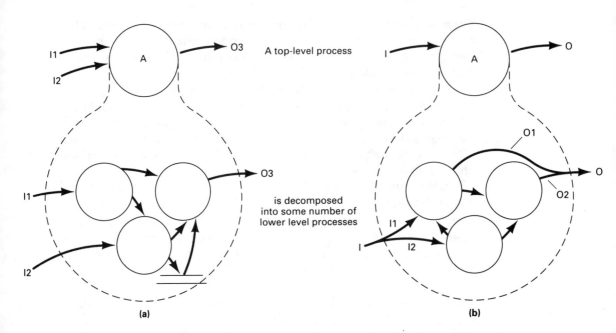

Figure 2–13. Concept of Leveling. **(a)** Rules of Decomposition. **(b)** Data Decomposition.

Record System and Payroll with the name Employee Data. However, when Payroll is further decomposed into Obtain Salary and Dependents, Compute Deductions, and Print Check, we find that we must also decompose the data flow called Employee Data into its constituent components, namely, Employee Name, Pay Rate, Address, Deductions To Date, and Number Of Dependents, each flowing into a unique (or possible multiplicity of) sub-bubble(s). This parallel refinement of data is shown graphically in Figure 2–13b and is recorded in the data dictionary (see Section 2.3.2.2) in the data definition/form field.

Incidentally there is little uniformity in the industry concerning DFD notation. Gane and Sarson [GAN79] use rounded rectangles for bubbles, shadowed rectangles for sources and destinations, and squared off *C*s for data bases; Orr [ORR81] uses rectangles for bubbles, ellipses for sources and destinations, and ellipses for data bases.

Hatley, Pirbhai, Ward, and Mellor [HAT84, WAR86, HAT87] have extended DFD notations to make it easier to analyze and specify real-time systems. These extensions are usually called *structured analysis/real time* (SA/RT). Hatley adds a variety of control extensions. For example, in addition to the standard data flow diagram (DFD), there is a *control flow diagram* (CFD). In addition to the process spec, there is a *control spec* consisting of a Mealy or Moore state transition diagram (see Section 4.2.2.1) and a *process activation table.* A *requirements dictionary* is used as the repository for all processes, data, and control present in the set of diagrams. The DFDs and CFDs are at the same level of abstraction. The processes and stores in a CFD are laid out in exactly the same positions as the ones in the corresponding DFD. As a process completes execution, it (1) generates data flows indicated in the DFD and (2) generates control flows, drawn as dotted arrows emanating from the process in the CFD. Some control flows in the CFD may terminate at other processes, in which case those processes become active. Control flows may also terminate at bars. Such control flows reflect stimuli to the finite state machine in the control spec. The finite state machine then changes state in response to that stimulus and generates a response. The process activation table then shows what other processes become active as a result of the finite state machine's response. Hatley applied his extensions to a commercial flight management computer system.

Ward's notational extensions are similar to Hatley's. Rather than two types of diagrams, the DFD and the CFD, Ward allows the introduction of control information in the standard DFD. Thus in addition to the usual data transformations, data flows, and data stores in a DFD, he allows control transformations (modeled as FSMs—see Section 4.2.2.1), event flows, and buffers (see Figure 2–14 [WAR86] for his notations). Whereas Hatley's FSMs specify the overall behavior of the processes in the DFD/CFD, Ward's FSMs specify the behavior of primitive transforms. Ward also differentiates between two types of data flows and three types of event flows:

Discrete data	A single item of data (e.g., current floor in an elevator control example)
Continuous data	A source of constantly available and perhaps continuously changing data (e.g., current position of doors where 0 is open and 1 is closed and all values in between are possible)

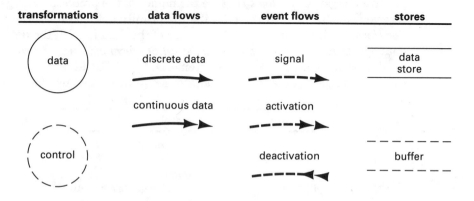

Figure 2–14. Ward Notations for DFD Extensions. © 1986 IEEE.

Signal	Reporting an event (e.g., doors have reached their full open position)
Activation	A direct overt action to initiate another process (e.g., the elevator control system activating the elevator door control process on arrival at a floor)
Deactivation	A direct overt action to stop another process (e.g., the elevator control system deactivating the usual elevator dispatching process on detecting a fire in the building)

2.3.2.2 Data dictionaries

Families of DFDs can become quite complex. One way of helping manage this complexity is to augment DFDs with data dictionaries (DD). Data dictionaries are simply repositories in which to store information about all data items defined in DFDs. Typical information stored includes:

- Name of the data item
- Aliases (other names for item)
- Description/Purpose
- Related data items
- Range of values
- Data flows
- Data structure definition/form

The *name of the data item* is self-explanatory. *Aliases* include other names by which this data item is called, e.g., AR for Accounts Receivable. *Description/Purpose* is a textual description of what the data item is used for or why it exists. *Related data items* capture relationships between data items, e.g., invoice-amount must always be equal to unit-price times number-of-units-sold. *Range of values* records all possible values, e.g., number-of-customers must always be a positive integer. *Data flows* capture the names of the processes that generate or receive the data item. If the data item is primitive, then *data structure definition/form* captures the physical structure of the data item. If the data is itself a data aggregate, then *data structure definition/form* captures the composition of the data item in terms of other data items. DeMarco [DEM79] suggests that this composition be represented in a notation similar to Backus-Naur form:

Meta Symbol	Meaning
+	and (concatenation)
( )	optional
{ }	iteration
[...|...|...]	selection of one alternative
" "	a literal string

For example, the DFD shown in Figure 2–11 might have the data dictionary shown in Figure 2-15. This particular DD shows only four of the fields.

The data dictionary can be used to

- Create an ordered listing of all data items.
- Create an ordered listing of a subset of data items (e.g., all data items generated by *A*, all data items derived through some set of processes from data item *X*, or all data items with "emergency" in its description).
- Find a data item name from a description.
- Perform the completeness and consistency checking described in Section 2.3.3.5.3.
- Generate data definitions automatically (e.g., declarations in Ada[TM1], VAR in Pascal, INTEGER and REAL in FORTRAN, the DATA Division in COBOL). Of course, this is much more helpful when using DDs as an adjunct to software design rather than analysis.

2.3.2.3 Entity–relation diagrams

As the name implies, *entity–relation* (ER) *diagrams* are used to define the existence of entities in the real world and their interrelationships. They are sometimes extended to include attributes of the objects and are then called ERA diagrams. Entities are represented as rectangles, and relationships between entities are represented as diamonds. Attributes, when included, are represented by circles hanging off lines attached to entities. Figure 2–16 is an example of an ER diagram for an elevator control system problem.

2.3.2.4 Coad object diagrams

As part of his Object-Oriented Analysis (OOA), Peter Coad [COA89] developed a notation that combines the essences of ER diagrams and DFDs with a number of additional features. He represents objects as rounded-corner rectangles. Attributes associated with that object are indicated within the object representation itself, as shown in Figure 2–17. Two types of structural relationships may exist between objects: classification and assembly. Classification relationships, shown in Figure 2–18, represent abstraction as defined in Section 2.2 and thus imply that subordinate objects (i.e., in-patient, out-patient) are members of the class of objects (i.e., patient). Assembly relationships, shown in Figure 2–19, represent partitioning as defined in Section 2.2 and thus imply that subordinate objects (i.e., heart, kidney, eye) are parts of the patient object. Note that the lines between the parent and subordinate objects in assembly structures can terminate with either a bar or a crow's foot. These

---

[1]Ada is a registered trademark of the U.S. Department of Defense.

	Data Flows			
Name	**Generated By**	**Used By**	**Description/Purpose**	**Form**
Accepted Invoice	Verify Accuracy of Invoice	Accounts Payable	The subset of publisher invoices which are correct.	publisher + price
Address	Customer Data Base	Assemble Orders	Customers' addresses.	
Batched Order	Pending Orders Data Base	Assemble Requisition	An aggregate of valid orders organized by book title rather than by customer.	{ bookid + no }
Book #				{ numeric digit }
Book Author				{ alphanumeric char }
Book Details	Book Data	Verify Order is Valid	A list of all currently sold books.	{ bookid }
Bookid			Unique book identifier.	publisher + book name + book author + book # + price
Book name				{ alphanumeric char }
Book Order Data	Verify Correct Shipment	Assign Shipment to Pending Orders	A list of books received.	{ bookid + no }
Check	Publisher	Accounts Payable	A negotiable check for payment of books received.	publisher + price
Credit Level				["credit-worthy" | "not credit-worthy"]
Credit Status	Customer Data Base	Verify Order is Valid	An "okay" or "not okay" that defines the credit worthiness of each customer.	customer id + credit level
Customer id			Unique customer identifier.	{ alphabetic char }
Invoice	Create Invoice	Customer	A bill indicating how much the customer owes.	customer id + price
Invoice Copy	Create Invoice	Accounts Receivable	A copy of the invoice used to verify correct payment by customer.	customer id + price
No			Number of items shipped.	{ numeric digit }
Order	Customer	Verify Order is Valid	The actual form used by customers to order books.	customer id + { bookid + no }
Order Details	Publisher Order Data Base	Verify Correct Shipment	Given any purchase order, list of books ordered.	{ bookid + no }
Packing Slip	Assemble Orders	Customer	A list of books included in actual book packaging.	customer id + { bookid + no }
Packing Slip Copy	Assemble Orders	Create Invoice	A copy of the packing slip used to generate the invoice.	customer id + { bookid + no }
Payment	Customer	Apply Payment	A negotiable check for payment of books received.	customer id + price

Figure 2–15. Corresponding Data Dictionary.

	Data Flows			
Name	Generated By	Used By	Description/Purpose	Form
Pending Order	Pending Orders Data Base	Assign Shipment	Copies of valid orders for customers whose books have just arrived from publisher.	{ customer id + bookid + no }
P.O. Details	Assemble Requisition	Publisher Order Data Base	A copy of all the info on the Purchase Order used to verify correct shipments from publishers.	{ bookid + no }
Price				$ + { numeric digit } + . + numeric digit + numeric digit
Publisher				{ alphanumeric char }
Publisher Address	Publisher Data	Assemble Requisition	The address for a publisher.	
Publisher Invoice	Publisher	Verify Accuracy of Invoice	A bill indicating how much is owed to publisher.	publisher + price
Publishers Packing Slip	Publisher	Verify Correct Shipment	A list of books sent by the publisher included in actual book packaging.	{ bookid + no }
Purchase Order	Assemble Requisition	Publisher	The form used to buy books from the publisher.	{ bookid + no }
Shipment Details	Verify Correct Shipment	Verify Accuracy of Invoice	The subset of packing slip for correctly shipped goods.	{ bookid + no }
Valid Order	Verify Order is Valid	Pending Orders Data Base	The subset of the orders that are going to be processed.	customer id + { bookid + no }

Figure 2–15. *(cont.)*

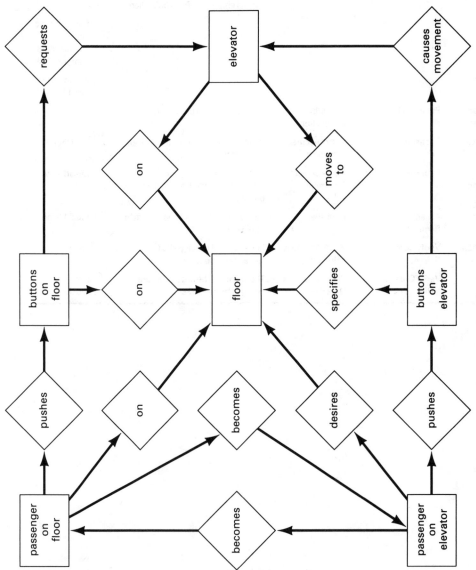

Figure 2–16. Example of an Entity Relationship Diagram for an Elevator Control System.

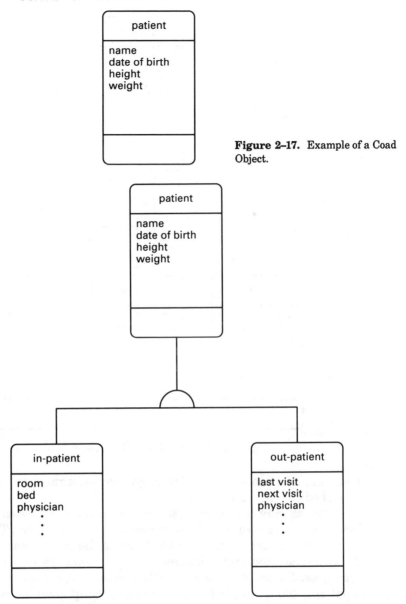

Figure 2–17. Example of a Coad Object.

Figure 2–18. Example of a Coad Classification Structure.

indicate one-to-one, one-to-many, or many-to-many occurrence relationships. In particular for Figure 2–19, a patient has only one heart but more than one kidney or eye. Also note that all the lines in the assembly structure have either an O for optional or a bar for mandatory. In Figure 2–19, these are used to show how every patient *must* have a heart and a kidney, but may not have

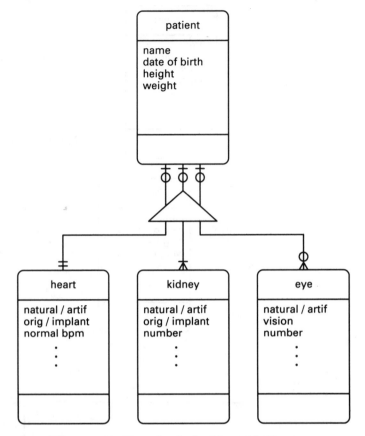

Figure 2–19. Example of a Coad Assembly Structure.

eyes; and that a heart, a kidney, or an eye may exist alone, i.e., their association with a body is optional.

Objects may also have instance connections with each other, but not necessarily have a superordinate/subordinate relationship. These are shown with lines interconnecting two objects using the same notations for numbers of occurrences and optional/mandatory relationships as used for assembly structures. Figure 2–20 shows such a relationship between physician and in-patient, and it records the facts that every in-patient has one primary-care physician and any physician may have multiple (including zero) in-patients.

Objects provide services to their environments. These services are indicated in the lower part of an object representation, as shown in Figure 2–21. In this figure, we capture the services provided by physicians: they can examine patients and can report their observations. Because *all* objects with attributes can occur, i.e., they exist, can be created, deleted, etc., Coad omits "occur" services from the model to reduce clutter. Specifications for services

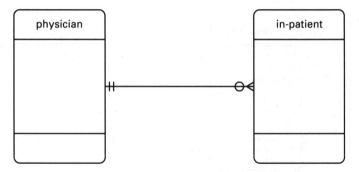

Figure 2–20. Example of an Instance Connection in Coad Diagrams.

Figure 2–21. Example of Services in Coad Diagrams.

are associated with the object that performs the service and are documented as bulleted lists, block diagrams, data flow diagrams, or state transition diagrams. In order for objects to perform services for other objects, messages must be sent. These are represented as dotted arrows on Coad diagrams, with the tail at the object desiring the service, and the head at the supplier. Figure 2–22 provides an example. For every message, the message itself is documented in the specification of the sender's services, and actions taken in response to that message are documented in the specification of the receiver's services.

2.3.3 Approaches to Problem Analysis

By the time you complete problem analysis, it is necessary to have isolated and understood all aspects of the problem and probably have defined the system boundary. There are a number of general ways of approaching this task; for example,

1. One could simply list the inputs to the system, then list all the outputs, and then list all the functions.
2. One could list all the functions of the system first, then list all the inputs and outputs associated with each function.

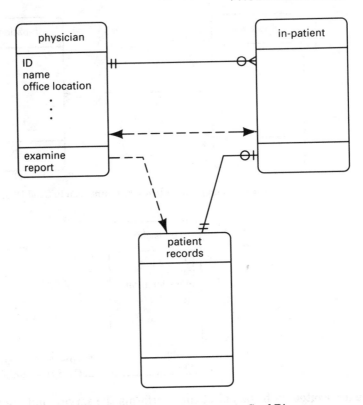

Figure 2-22. Example of Messages in Coad Diagrams.

3. One could define the system as one main function with gross system inputs and outputs and then repeatedly refine that function into more detailed descriptions.

4. One could list all the events that invoke some system response; for each event, define the system response and any other inputs needed to generate the response; then merge together all these small transforms into more and more abstract views of the system.

5. One could define all the objects in the application domain; then for each object, define its attributes, relationships to other objects, and services provided.

The following subsections provide more detail on some general and some specific approaches to performing problem analysis:

1. Listing all inputs and outputs
2. Listing major functions

3. Structured Requirements Definition (SRD)
4. Structured Analysis by Ross
5. Structured Analysis by DeMarco
6. Extensions to Structured Analysis
7. PSL/PSA
8. Object-Oriented Problem Analysis

2.3.3.1 Listing all inputs and outputs

This technique is almost too straightforward to include here; all you do is list the inputs, then list the outputs. It will work for only relatively simple problems. For example, if we want to analyze the problem of software for an elevator control system, we could list the inputs:

- Floor-based "up" and "down" button presses
- Elevator-based button presses
    Floor numbers
    Open door
    Close door
    Emergency
- Elevator-based key switches
    Fireperson mode
    Maintenance mode
    Light switch
    Fan switch
- Door obstruction sensors
    Bumpers
    Electric eye
- Weight limit exceeded

And the outputs:

- Signals to hoist motor
    Up
    Down
- Signals to door controller
    Open
    Close
- Signals to alarms
    Weight limit exceeded
    Emergency alarm

2.3.3.2 Listing major functions

For some analyses, it is difficult to simply enumerate inputs and outputs. For some of these applications, it is easier to first list all the major (categories of) functions of the system and then for each function, analyze and enumerate all related inputs and outputs. For example, if a particular supply depot were to be analyzed, not all inputs and outputs might be apparent. In this case, it might be helpful to first list the main functions of the depot:

* Receive, inspect, and store supplies
* Ship supplies
* Respond to external inventory status requests.

Now for each one, we can list the corresponding inputs and outputs

* Receive, inspect, and store supplies.
  Inputs: Incoming supplies
               Invoices from suppliers
  Outputs: Requisitions for supplies to suppliers
               Payments to suppliers
* Ship supplies.
  Inputs: Requisition for supplies from customers
               Payments from customers
  Outputs: Outgoing supplies
               Invoices to customers
* Respond to external inventory status requests.
  Inputs: Inventory status requests
  Outputs: Inventory status reports

2.3.3.3 Structured requirements definition (SRD)

In his book on requirements definition, Orr [ORR81] describes an alternative method to learning the complete set of inputs and outputs. He calls the method "defining the application context." It is a multistep process as follows:

Step 1. *Define a user-level data flow diagram.* This step requires the analyst to interview each individual who is currently performing some unique task within an organization in order to learn what that individual receives as inputs and generates as outputs. Record the inputs and outputs for each individual in a data flow diagram (Orr calls these *entity diagrams*) as shown in Figure 2–23.

Step 2. *Define a combined user-level data flow diagram.* Merge all like bubbles in the individual data flow diagrams to create one integrated diagram.

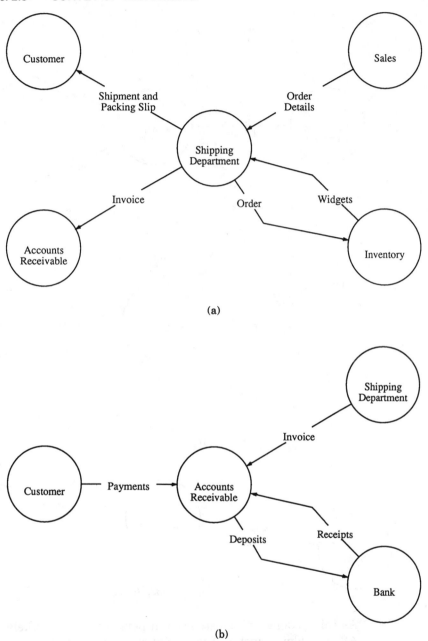

(a)

(b)

Figure 2-23. Sample SRD Data Flow Diagrams. **(a)** Shipping Department Perspective. **(b)** Accounts Receivable Perspective. **(c)** Accounts Payable Perspective. **(d)** Sales Perspective. **(e)** Purchasing Perspective. **(f)** Receiving Department Perspective. **(g)** Inventory Perspective.

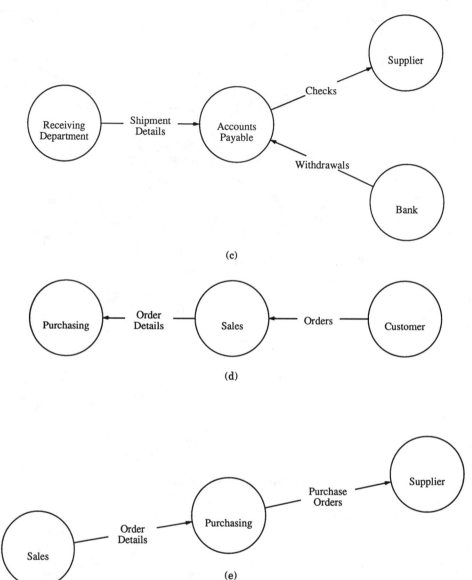

(c)

(d)

(e)

Figure 2–23. *(cont.)*

As this is done, inconsistencies in perspectives will likely be detected. After resolving such differences of opinion, create the single integrated data flow diagram, as shown in Figure 2–24.

Step 3. *Define the application-level data flow diagram.* Draw a dotted line around that part of the diagram that corresponds to the organization or system under analysis, as shown in Figure 2–25a. Then collapse the area sur-

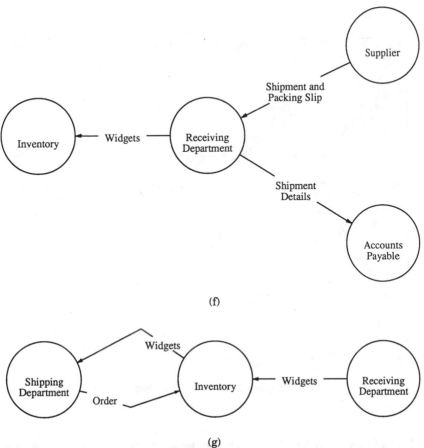

(f)

(g)

Figure 2–23. *(cont.)*

rounded by the dotted line into a single bubble, as shown in Figure 2–25b. This results in a definition of all external system inputs and outputs.

Step 4. *Define the application-level functions.* For each function X performed by the organization for its environment, number the system-level inputs and outputs X_1, X_2, X_3, $\cdots$ to show the order of events that comprise the function. Figure 2–25c shows this step for two functions: Filling Orders (A) and Buying Books (B).

2.3.3.4 Structured analysis and design technique

The Structured Analysis and Design Technique (SADT)™[2] was developed in the early 1970s by Doug Ross at SofTech, Inc. [ROS77]. The most popular aspects of SADT have been thoroughly described by Marca and McGowan

[2]SADT is a registered trademark of SofTech, Inc.

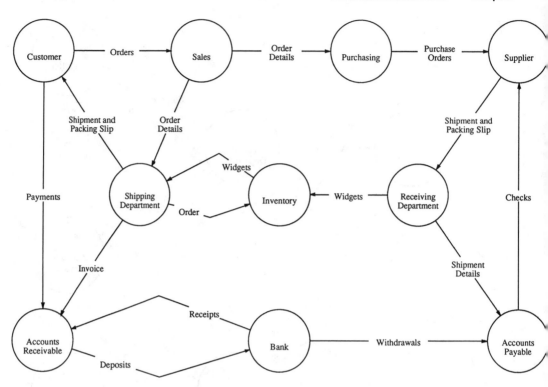

Figure 2–24. Integrated Data Flow Diagram.

[MAR88]. It is Ross's view that nature by itself has no problems; a problem is only what a human being perceives is a problem. The only way of expressing a problem (and of course any solution to that problem) is in terms of natural language, for by definition natural language *is* the language that is natural for humans (who *are* the only parties who perceive the problem). However, since natural language is inherently ambiguous, it might be necessary but certainly not sufficient. Therefore SADT uses a nonambiguous graphical notation in which natural language is embedded. The graphical notation provides for projection, abstraction, and partitioning.

Using SADT, a model of the problem is constructed. The model is composed of a hierarchy of diagrams. Each diagram is composed of boxes and arrows. The uppermost diagram, called the *context diagram* defines the problem most abstractly. See Figure 2–26 for an example of a context diagram for an Army supply depot [MCG82]. The problem is then refined into its sub-problems, and that refinement is documented in another diagram, as shown in Figure 2–27, where each box represents one well-defined piece of the whole problem. Each box can now be detailed into its own SADT diagram to document

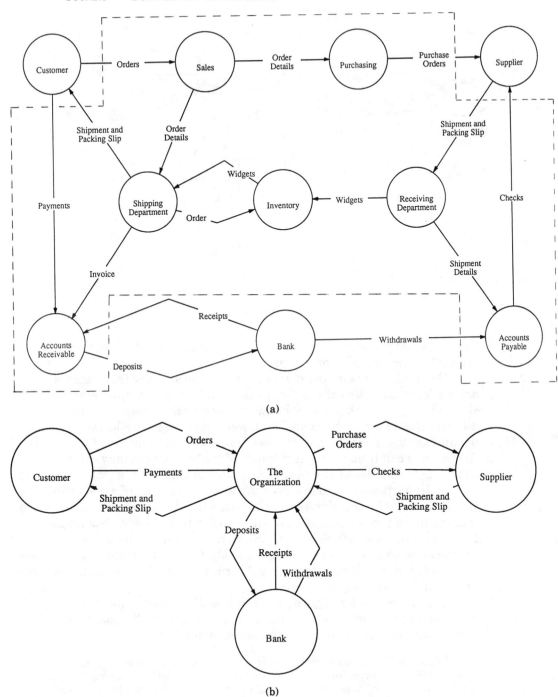

Figure 2–25.   Defining the Application Using SRD. **(a)** Draw a Dotted Line around the Organization. **(b)** Collapse the Dotted Area Into One Bubble. **(c)** Define the Application-Level Functions.

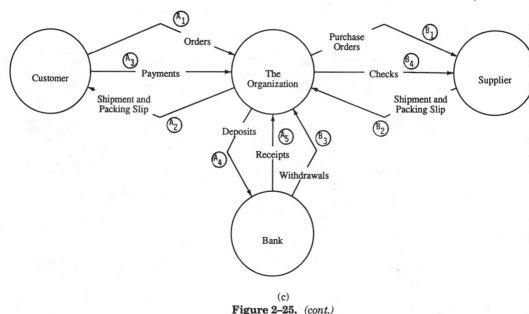

(c)

Figure 2–25. *(cont.)*

the continued refinement of an ongoing understanding of the problem. What results is a hierarchy[3] of diagrams.

Generally boxes in any diagram are arranged along the diagonal, with arrows interconnecting the boxes. Boxes should be given unique names that should always be verb phrases, because they represent functions. In addition all boxes should be numbered in their lower right corner to reflect their relative dominance; use 1 for the box representing the most dominant function, etc. Arrows may exit from the right side only of the box. Arrows may enter the top, left, or bottom sides of the box. Strict rules govern interpretation of those arrows. In particular an arrow pointing into the left side of a box represents things that will be transformed by the box, whereas an arrow pointing down into the top of the box represents *control* that affects how the box transforms things entering the left side [MAR88]. Arrows entering the bottom of a box represent *mechanism* and provide the analyst with the ability to document how the function will operate, who will perform it, or what physical resources are needed to perform the function.

Let us reconsider Figures 2–26 and 2–27 and examine their roles in defining the problem of an Army supply depot. Figure 2–26 captures the main inputs, outputs, and functions of the depot as follows:

[3]Note that Ross contends this is really a network, not a hierarchy, because there could conceivably be two different boxes in two different places in the model representing the same thing and they would "fan in" to one diagram. I prefer to call it a hierarchy to emphasize the fact that items closer to the root node (i.e., the context diagram) are inherently more abstract than those farther away.

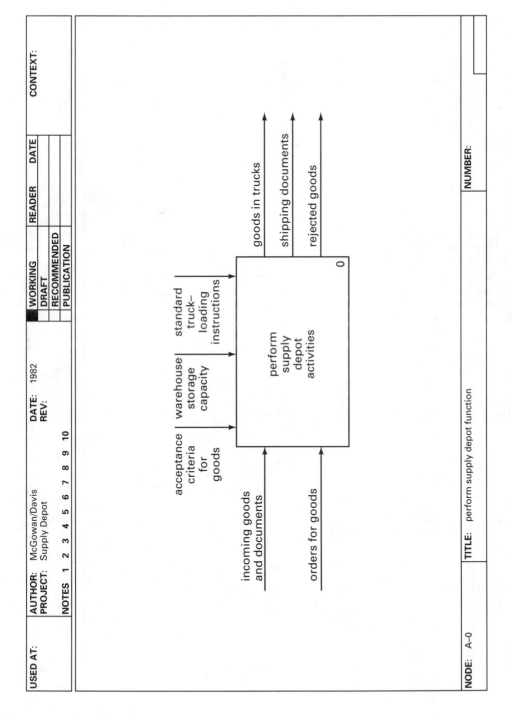

Figure 2-26. SADT Context Diagram: Army Supply Depot.

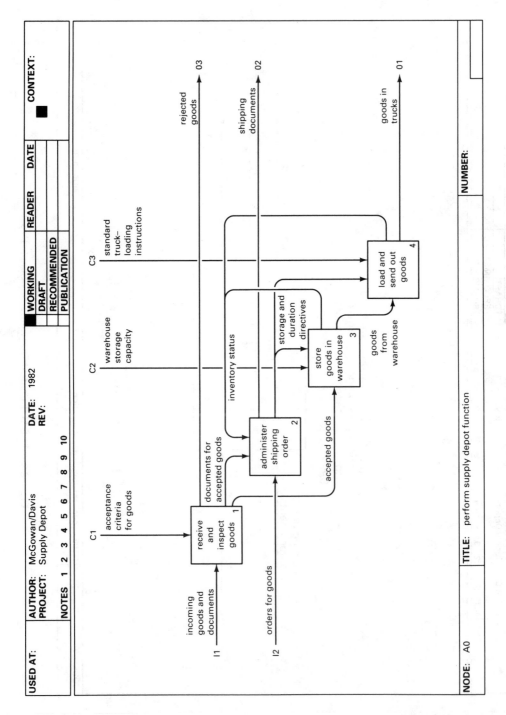

Figure 2-27. SADT Example: Refinement of Army Supply Depot Problem.

- "Incoming goods and documents" enter from supply lines. Based on the "acceptance criteria for goods" and the "warehouse storage capacity," the goods are either stored for future use or returned as "rejected goods."
- Meanwhile as truck convoys arrive with supply needs, they have "orders for goods." Based on the "standard truck-loading instructions" (which state maximum allowable weights per truck type and per truck axle), the "goods in trucks" are generated along with appropriate "shipping documents" to record the delivery of goods.

The next step in the analysis is to provide more detail. More detailed analysis of the supply depot problem results in determining that there are really four different activities that comprise the supply function. Figure 2–27 shows the documentation using SADT of the supply depot problem as four subproblems: receive and inspect the goods, administer the shipping order, store the goods in the warehouse, and load and send out the goods on trucks. Notice that the number and types of arrows in Figures 2–26 and 2–27 have been preserved; in particular there were two inputs into the left on Figure 2–26, and there are two inputs into the left on Figure 2–27; there were three inputs into the top on Figure 2–26, and there are three inputs into the top on Figure 2–27; and there were three outputs out the right-hand side in Figure 2–26, and there are three outputs from the right-hand side in Figure 2–27. This situation will *usually* be the case, although there are exceptions (see Chapter 3 of Marca and McGowan [MAR88]). To assist the analyst and reviewer in verifying that all arrows match, SADT includes the ICOM code notation. Whenever any box in any SADT diagram (let us call it the parent diagram) is detailed into an SADT diagram (let us call it the child diagram), the arrows that flow into or out of that child diagram externally (not the internal arrows) are labeled with a letter and a number. The letter (I, C, O, or M) indicates the role that the arrow played (input, control, output, or mechanism) relative to the box being detailed in the parent diagram. The number indicates the absolute position where that arrow touches the box in the parent diagram. Notice for example the numbering of arrows in Figure 2–27.

    The next step in the analysis is to define any and all information flows between the four subproblems of the supply depot problem, as shown in Figure 2–27. Now each of the subproblems at this level is further decomposed into its subproblems and documented as a diagram in the same manner until the resulting hierarchy of diagrams provides a level of detail sufficient to define the entire problem for the analyst.

    It is important to note that this decomposition is not a software design; all that we are doing here is analyzing the problem using repetitive decomposition. Each box corresponds to a component of the problem, not a component of the solution. Once the analysis is completed but prior to writing the SRS, it is necessary to make the decision of what will be automated. When looking at

Figure 2–27, you might decide to solve the problem by automating all the boxes, but not the arrows; or to automate all the arrows, but not the boxes; or to automate just one of the boxes; or to automate the entire system. Even if the latter strategy were selected, the diagram in Figure 2–27 is still not a design. Designers would eventually (i.e., after the requirements were defined in the SRS) need to perform the appropriate trade-off analyses to determine the ultimate design.[4] That design may coincidentally be the same as the analyst's decomposition, but it would be just that, a coincidence; it could just as likely have been an entirely different design. It is important to remember that the optimal decomposition during analysis is one that helps you understand the problem; the optimal decomposition during design is one that exhibits the appropriate combination of performance, efficiency, reliability, maintainability, modifiability, etc. There is at least one major school of design, headed by Michael Jackson [JAC75], that contends that the only correct design is one that mimics the problem domain. The Jackson approach is discussed in Section 7.1.3.

SADT's first use was in analyzing the design, finance, QA/QC, marketing, manufacturing, inventory control, and product support functions of the aerospace industry in support of the U.S. Air Force Computer Aided Manufacturing (AFCAM) Program. It was used to define both how the aerospace industry is today as well as how it should be [AIR74]. SADT has also been used by ITT Europe since 1974 for training personnel on telephone switches [ROS77a]. The status of SADT as of 1985 was reported by Ross [ROS85].

SADT has been automated by three tools: A.S.A., Design/IDEF, and SPECIF-X. These provide the SADT methodology, notation, and language features; maintain project data bases; maintain and enforce project member roles (SADT methodology defines about a dozen specific roles that individual members of the analysis team play); provide camera-quality documentation; and perform rudimentary consistency checking [VER87, IGL85, MAR88]. A.S.A. operates on SUN, Apollo, and VAX computers; more information about it is available from Verilog, U.S.A., Inc., of Alexandria, Virginia. Design/IDEF runs on Apple MacIntosh computers; more information about it is available from META Software, Inc., of Cambridge, Massachusetts. SPECIF-X operates on Apollo computers; more information about it is available from IGL of Paris, France.

2.3.3.5 Structured analysis and system specification

Structured Analysis and System Specification (SASS) was developed by Tom DeMarco [DEM79] and is a spin-off of the early requirements work of Ross [ROS77] and closely related to the design work of Constantine and Yourdon [YOU79]. In the foreword to DeMarco's book [DEM79], P. J. Plauger states, "It

---

[4]Of course, SADT (or any of the other analysis techniques described in this chapter) can be used effectively to define some aspects of the design as well.

is a pure pleasure to watch the emergence of a new discipline. 'Structured Analysis' has progressed from being a concatenation of buzzwords, to a collection of homilies, to an orderly approach that commands the respect of the most battle-scarred senior analysts." Unfortunately the word *structured* has been so overused that it now means little more than *good*. Alas we have come full circle: The term *structured analysis* is now used by everybody to mean any technique that they perceive is good and that they apply during the requirements or design phases. Structured analysis has thus returned to being little more than a concatenation of buzzwords. Be that as it may, we will use the terms SASS and structured analysis specifically to refer to DeMarco's flavor of the technique.

2.3.3.5.1 *Methodology*

Like SADT, the SASS approach is a pure top-down technique in which the analyst starts by representing the system in a context diagram showing all system inputs and outputs and repeatedly refines the system, representing each refinement as a more detailed diagram. Figure 2–28 [DEM79] shows the overall system development life cycle as defined by DeMarco; it is roughly equivalent in level of detail and purpose to Figure 1–9. According to this approach, the first activity of a system development effort is the survey, followed by structured analysis and the hardware study. Following these are structured design and implementation of the system.

The structured analysis stage in Figure 2–28 is the one that most closely approximates the requirements phase of the life cycle. Therefore let us expand that bubble and see what DeMarco believes should transpire. Figure 2–29 [DEM79] shows an expansion of the structured analysis stage in Figure 2–28. According to SASS, the first activity of structured analysis is to study the current environment (Step 2.1). During this activity, a DFD is drawn showing how data flows through the current nonautomated organization. The bubbles should be labeled with names of organizational units or individuals within those units. This DFD is called the current physical DFD.

The second activity (Step 2.2) of structured analysis is called deriving logical equivalents. During this activity, people's and organizational units' names are replaced with action verbs that define the activity they perform. If two parties both performed the same logical functions, those functions are married into one bubble. Also bubbles that have no value added to a piece of information but simply serve as a checkpoint and pass information through are deleted. Thus if activity A in Figure 2–30a uses data X in order to transform Y into Z but does not modify X before passing it onto B, the current physical DFD shown in Figure 2–30a would be transformed into its logical equivalent as shown in Figure 2–30b.

Once the customer reviews and verifies this current logical DFD, it is time to start defining the effect of automation on the organization. Step 2.3 creates

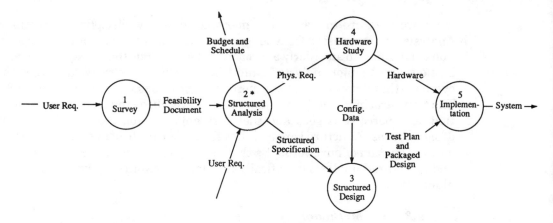

Figure 2–28. Structured Analysis and System Specification. Tom DeMarco, *Structured Analysis and System Specification,* © 1979, P. 26. Adapted by permission of Prentice-Hall, Englewood Cliffs, N. J.

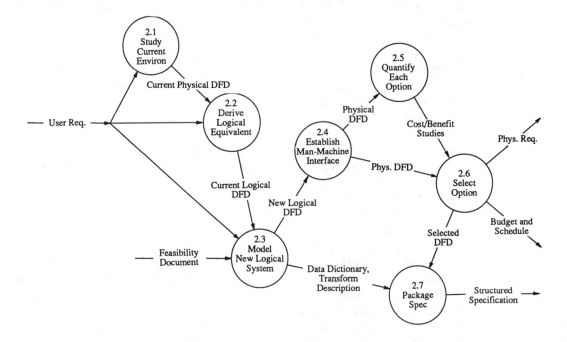

Figure 2–29. Structured Analysis. Tom DeMarco, *Structured Analysis and Systems Specification,* © 1979, P. 26. Adapted by permission of Prentice-Hall, Englewood Cliffs, N. J.

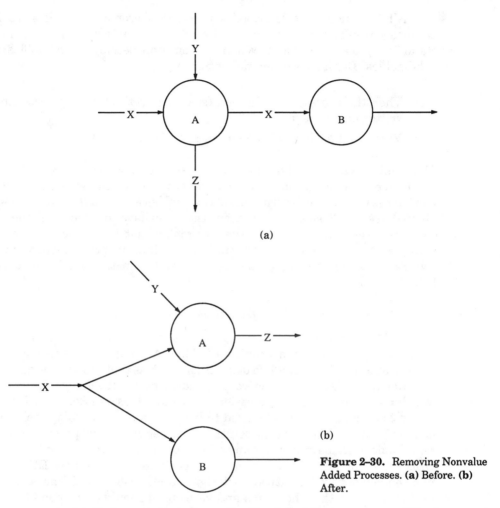

(a)

(b)

Figure 2–30. Removing Nonvalue Added Processes. **(a)** Before. **(b)** After.

a model of the new logical system. During this stage, we modify the current logical DFD to reflect how information will move through the organization *after* the automated system is in place. However, no attempt is made to differentiate between those activities that will eventually be automated and those that will remain manual. The result of this step is the new logical DFD.

The next step (Step 2.4) is to define a number of different automation alternatives and to document each of these as a new physical DFD. Each of these alternatives should show clearly what will and what will not be automated. Step 2.5 analyzes each of these alternatives with the customers through a series of cost/benefit analyses. Finally at Step 2.6, one of the new physical DFDs is selected for implementation; that DFD is passed on to Step 2.7 for final packaging and cleanup.

All four DFDs just described will actually become hierarchies of DFDs because you will need to decompose the bubbles repeatedly in order to understand the problem at hand. When do you stop decomposing bubbles into sub-bubbles? DeMarco's recommendation is:

- When the process specification (see next section) for a process can be written on one page
- When a bubble has only one input and one output

The problem with this advice is that you can *always* write a process specification for a process on one page. Much better advice is, when the nouns and verbs used in the names and descriptions of the bubbles and data flows are no longer able to be seen, felt, smelled, heard, or tasted, you have gone too far. Remember, the purpose of analysis is to analyze the problem, not design the software. One of the best treatises written on the subject of maintaining the analysis perspective rather than the design perspective while creating DFDs appears in [WOO88].

2.3.3.5.2 Process Specifications

DeMarco also advocates using process specifications to describe procedures to be followed by a primitive bubble. A process specification can be written as a structured English description, such as that shown in Figure 2–31 (adapted from [GAN79]), which corresponds to part of the bubble Verify Order is Valid in Figure 2–11 or as decision trees and tables (see Section 4.2.2.2). In either case, caution should be used to keep the discussion completely in the domain of the problem, not the solution. In other words, the process specification should describe either how an action is performed currently at the current DFD stages or how an action must be performed at the new DFD stages independent of how the software is designed and implemented. The best advice in this regard is that the nouns and verbs used should correspond to things that the customer or user can see, touch, smell, hear, or feel.

2.3.3.5.3 "Automated" Tools

With the introduction of low-priced graphics terminals and workstations, structured analysis has become an extremely popular technique to "automate." I put the word automate in quotations because the tools simply liberate the analyst's librarian from the manual chore of maintaining all the DFDs. The tools in no way automate the analysis process. The tools (1) permit the analyst to draw data flow diagrams easily on a graphics terminal, (2) manage the large collection of DFDs and their interrelationships, and (3) create a skeleton of a data dictionary. In particular, they enable users to

Process name: VERIFY CREDIT IS OK

For each <u>order,</u>
    Retrieve   <u>payment-history</u>
    IF   <u>payment-history</u> is not found (i.e., new customer)
    THEN   generate <u>prepayment-request</u>
    ELSE   (existing-customer)
       SO   compute <u>average-order-frequency</u>
                         (i.e., average number of orders per month
                         over last 3 months)
             compute total of balance overdue
             IF   <u>average-order-frequency</u> is GT 2.0
                      (i.e., customer is regular)
             THEN   IF   age of oldest balance overdue is LT 60 days
                     THEN   mark order as OK for credit
                     ELSE   (balance overdue GE 60 days)
                         SO generate <u>prepayment-request</u> plus
                             <u>reminder-of-overdue-balance</u>
             ELSE   (customer is not regular)
                 SO-IF   balance overdue is GT zero
                    THEN   generate <u>prepayment-request</u>
                    ELSE   (no balance owed)
                       SO mark order as OK for credit

Figure 2–31. Structured English Process Specification. Chris Gane and Trish Sarson, *Structured System Analysis: Tools and Techniques,* ©1979, p. 106. Adapted by permission of Prentice-Hall, Englewood Cliffs, N. J.

- Request that a bubble be drawn at any particular place on the screen (usually with a mouse, rollerball, or joy stick).
- Request that a data base be drawn at any particular place on the screen.
- Request that arrows be drawn interconnecting bubbles and/or data bases.
- Name all items.
- Retrieve and edit previously created DFDs.

- While pointing to any particular bubble, request that the bubble be expanded on the screen revealing the next level of underlying detail, i.e., the DFD that represents the indicated bubble.

- While looking at any DFD, request that the entire DFD be contracted down to just one bubble revealing all the aunt and uncle bubbles.

- Examine an automatically generated data dictionary.

- Request a check by the tool for completeness. In this case, completeness means that all bubbles, arrows, and data bases are labeled and all arrows have sources and destinations.

- Request a check by the tool for consistency. In this case, consistency means that all bubbles, arrows, and data bases have unique names and every DFD which is the expansion of a parent bubble exhibits the same number of inputs and outputs as its parent.

- Do analysis or design (but unfortunately few make the distinction).

A partial list of tools that perform these operations, along with their vendors, host hardware, and other features is shown in Figure 2–32.

A description of PRISM is provided by Iconix's president, Rosenberg [ROS85a], and a description of Teamwork/SA is provided by Hecht [HEC86]. A description of a 50-month military project using ProMod was given by Peterson [PET87]. Excelerator and CASE 2000 were compared by Edwards [EDW87]. Design Aid and Teamwork were compared by SPS [SPS88] from a total systems requirements and system design perspective rather than from a software requirements perspective. Many of the tools listed in Figure 2–32 have implemented SA/RT notational extensions (as described at the end of Section 2.3.2.1) as well as the basic structured analysis notations.

2.3.3.6 Modern structured analysis

By the late 1980s, structured analysis had been applied to a wide variety of problems with mixed success. Based on pioneering work by McMenamin and Palmer [MCM84] on essential modeling, Paul Ward and Stephen Mellor [WAR85] proposed a set of modifications to the development methodology originally proposed by DeMarco. Ed Yourdon [YOU89] later expanded on these changes to what some have called the Yourdon's Structured Methodology (YSM) [WOO88]. These changes recognized that

- Full-scale development of both a current physical and a current logical model could easily induce "paralysis through analysis."

- Pure top-down approaches to analysis do not necessarily make sense for very complex systems and may tempt the analyst to perform a real design prematurely.

Tool	Vendor*	Host**	Other Features***
Anatool	Advanced Logical Software 9903 Santa Monica Blvd., #108 Beverly Hills, CA 90212	Macintosh	B, C, D, E, G, H, I
Teamwork/SA and Teamwork/RT	Cadre Technologies, Inc. 222 Richmond Street Providence, RI 02903	APOLLO, VAXstation, IBM PC, Sun, HP	C, D, E
POSE	Computer Systems Advisors 50 Tice Boulevard Woodcliff Lake, NJ 07675	IBM PC	C, D
Envision	Enriched Data Systems P.O. Box 7449 Laguna Niguel, CA 92677	IBM PC	C, D, G, I
PRISM	ICONIX Software Engineering, Inc. 1037 Third Street Santa Monica, CA 90403	Macintosh, IBM PC	C, E, I
STATEMATE	i-Logix 22 Third Avenue Burlington, MA 01803	VAXstation, Sun	A, B, C, E, I
Excelerator and Excelerator/RTS	Index Technology Corp. 101 Main Street Cambridge, MA 02142	IBM PC, VAX, Sun	C, D, E, F, H
Software Through Pictures	Interactive Development Environments, Inc. 150 Fouth Street San Francisco, CA 94103	Sun, APOLLO, VAXstation, HP	B, C, D, E, F, H, I, J
Information Engineering Workbench/ Analysis Workstation	KnowledgeWare 3340 Peachtree Rd., NE, Suite 2900 Atlanta, GA 30026	IBM PC	C, D, F, G, H, I
Automate Plus	Learmonth & Burchett 2900 N. Loop West, Suite 800 Houston, TX 77092	IBM PC	B, C, D, F, H
Prokit WORKBENCH	McDonnell Douglas Information Systems Group P.O. Box 516 St. Louis, MO 63166	IBM PC	C, E
FOUNDATION	Menlo Business Systems, Inc. 201 Main Sst. Los Altos, CA 94022	Tandem	B, C, D, I
Design/2.0/OA	Meta Software 150 Cambridge Park Drive Cambridge, MA 02140	IBM PC, Macintosh	C, G

* All of the vendors listed are actively expanding the capabilities of their tools. This list of features shows the author's understanding of the current status of each of the tools at a particular point in time. Contact the vendors directly for more up-to-date information.

** With the rapid increase in capability of workstations, many of the tool vendors listed here are actively porting their tools to workstations.

*** Legend for other features:

A	=	Simulation capability	F =	Integrated with project management
B	=	Prototyping capability	G =	Customizable graphic symbols
C	=	Design as well as analysis	H =	Multiple workstations can share data bases
D	=	ER modeling capability	I =	Source code frame generation
E	=	Real-time extensions	J =	Open system architecture

Tool	Vendor	Host**	Other Features***
Structured Architect	Meta Systems, Inc. 315 E. Eisenhower Pkwy. Ann Arbor, MI 48108	IBM PC	C, E, H
DesignAid (Part of CASE 2000)	Nastec Corporation 24681 Northwestern Highway Southfield, MI 48075	VAX, IBM PC	C, E, F, G, H
ProMod	ProMod, Inc. 23685 Birtcher Drive Lake Forest, CA 92630	VAX, IBM PC	C, E, I
CARDtools	Ready Systems Corp. 449 Serman Ave. P.O. Box 61029 Palo Alto, CA 94306	VAXstation, VAX, IBM PC	A, B, C, E, I
EPOS-R	Software Products & Services 19 E. 38 Street New York, NY 10016	VAX, IBM 4300, VAXstation, IBM PC, others	C, F, I
MacBubbles	StarSys, Inc. 11113 Norlee Drive Silver Spring, MD 20902	Macintosh	C, E
Microstep	Syscorp International 9420 Research Blvd. Austin, TX 78759	IBM PC	A, B, C, I
TEK/SA	Tektronix, Inc. P.O. Box 500 Beaverton, OR 97077	VAX, Tektronix, VAXstation	C, E
Information Engineering Facility	Texas Instruments P.O. Box 225474 Dallas, TX 75265	IBM PC, TI Business Pro	B, C, I
Kangatool	U.S. Sertek, Inc. 926 Thompson Pl. Sunnyvale, CA 94086		C
Systems Analyst Workbench	Visible Systems Corp. 48 Lexington St. Newton, MA 02165	IBM PC	C, G, H
VS Designer	Visual Software 3945 Freedom Circle Santa Clara, CA 95054	IBM PC	C, D, F, G, H
Analyst/Designer Toolkit	Yourdon, Inc. 1501 Broadway New York, NY 10036	IBM PC, Sun	C, E, G, I

Note: Anatool is a trademark of Advanced Logical Software. VAX and VAXstation are trademarks of Digital Equipment Corporation. Teamwork/SA and Teamwork/RT are trademarks of Cadre Technologies, Inc. APOLLO is a registered trademark of Apollo Computer, Inc. IBM PC is a trademark of International Business Machines, Inc. Sun is a trademark of Sun Microsystems, Inc. POSE is a trademark of CSA, Inc. Envision is a trademark of Enriched Data Systems, Inc. PRISM is a trademark of ICONIX Software Engineering, Inc. Macintosh is a trademark of Apple Computer, Inc. STATEMATE is a trademark of i-Logix, Inc. Excelerator and Excelerator/RTS are trademarks of Index Technology Corporation. Software Through Pictures is a trademark of Interactive Development Environments, Inc. Information Engineering Workbench is a registered trademark of KnowledgeWare, Inc. FOUNDATION is a trademark of Menlo Business Systems, Inc. Prokit WORK-BENCH is a trademark of McDonnell Douglas, Inc. Design/2.0 and Design/OA are trademarks of META Software Corporation. CASE 2000 and DesignAid are trademarks of Nastec Corporation. EPOS is a trademark of SPS, Inc. ProMod is a registered trademark of PROMOD, Inc. TEK/SA is a trademark and Tektronix is a registered trademark of Tektronix, Inc. MacBubbles is a trademark of Star/Sys, Inc. Visible Analyst is a registered trademark of Visible Systems Corporation.

Figure 2-32

- Entity-relationship diagrams are extremely valuable in capturing the complexities of objects and their relationships.

Ward and Mellor's extensions eliminate the current physical model and include a specific methodology for defining either a current or a new logical model. Their methodology can be summarized as follows:

1. Define the system context. This means define all terminators (i.e., objects external to the system under specification that communicate or otherwise interface with the system) and all information flows between those terminators and the system.

2. Define all external events (i.e., stimuli) to the system in a narrative *event list*.

3. For each event, define the system's behavior. This should be captured as a single-bubble DFD with the event as one input and the system's response to that event as one (or more) outputs. In addition any other data required by the system to respond to the event should appear as additional inputs, and any data generated by the system in response to the event but that will be used by other parts of the system should appear as outputs to data stores.

4. Perform upward leveling to create what Yourdon calls the *behavioral model*. Because the result of step 3 is potentially a large quantity of disjoint diagrams, group these together into successively more abstract models. This should be performed in such a way as to preserve the spirit of the environment's structure in the model's structure. Ward presents a number of useful guidelines for selecting this grouping: (a) minimize interfaces, (b) identify hierarchies of control, (c) group common responses, (d) group processes that share common data stores, (e) group common terminators, and (f) group to ensure that names can be given to the abstract groups (i.e., avoid the requirements equivalent of design's coincidental cohesion [YOU79]). Yourdon's advice is simpler: Group diagrams that share common data and group diagrams that can hide information from the rest of the system.

Note that the result of the preceding process is a hierarchy of DFDs that capture the structure of the environment and whose lowest most detailed level is still a pure external view of the system under specification. This solves one of structured analysis's biggest problems, namely, that the model constructed in a top-down manner often implied a design to the reader.

Yourdon's *Modern Structured Analysis* [YOU89] is an excellent compilation of all the wisdom and experience collected during two decades of structured analysis in practice. Yourdon defines systems analysis to include the development of two models: the environmental model and the behavioral model, which together are called the *essential model*. All of the models are composed of data flow diagrams, data dictionaries, entity relationship diagrams, and process specifications that should be thoroughly analyzed for consistency. Using Ward's real-time notational extensions (see Section 2.3.2.1), the data flow diagrams may include control flows and data flows, and control processes can be further defined in terms of finite-state machines. Primitive bubbles in a data flow diagram can be defined using any expressive and user-understandable technique that is appropriate to the particular process or application (Note: Chapter 4 of this book describes most of these techniques). The environmental model consists of (1) a statement of purpose for the system being defined, (2) a context diagram that shows the objects external to the system with which it interacts and their interfaces to the system, and (3) a list of all the events that precipitate a system response. The behavioral model consists of (1) a complete set of leveled DFDs constructed according to Ward's aforementioned methodology; (2) entity relationship diagrams to capture all the objects manipulated by the system, their attributes and interrelationships; (3) state-transition diagrams for all the control processes; (4) a data dictionary; and (5) process specifications for each lowest level process.

2.3.3.7 PSL/PSA

The Problem Statement Language/Problem Statement Analyzer (PSL/PSA)™[5] was originally developed during the early 1970s by Dan Teichroew and the ISDOS Project at the University of Michigan [TEI77]. Its further development is now undertaken by Meta Systems, also in Ann Arbor, Michigan. One of the earliest of the requirements analysis tools, PSA predates the availability of widely available inexpensive graphics terminals. Since Teichroew knew that analysis was primarily an iterative decomposition process but that graphics terminals were not practical, he did the only thing possible: He developed PSL, a completely text (nongraphical) language to describe processes, information flow between processes, and hierarchical decomposition of process and data. Using PSL/PSA is similar to using any of the SASS-type automated tools except that the input is entirely text. For example, the data flow diagram shown in Figure 2–33 can be described in PSL by using the text shown in Figure 2–34 (adapted from [TEI77]). The decomposition of Hourly-Employee-Processing into its subproblems Hourly-Paycheck-Validation, Hourly-Emp-Update, H-Report-Entry-Generation and Hourly-Paycheck-Production is shown graphically in Figure 2–35; In the spirit of top-down development, PSA would expect you first to define the subordinate elements in the parent node (Figure 2–34) and then to define each subordinate node as shown in Figure 2–36.

As shown in Figure 2–37 [TEI77], PSL statements are input into PSA, which in turn stores all the statements in an internal form in a data base. Once

---

[5]PSL/PSA is a registered trademark of Meta Systems, Inc., Ann Arbor, Michigan.

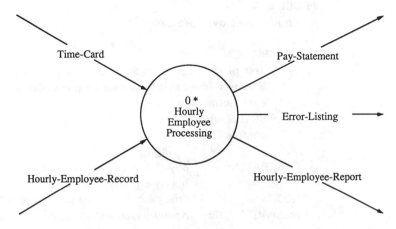

Figure 2-33. Hourly Employee Processing DFD.

stored, the requirements can be updated, deleted, supplemented, etc. What the Problem Statement Analyzer suffers from in regards to an out-of-date input style, it makes up for in its extensive error analysis and reporting capabilities. Commands can be given to PSA to generate a wide variety of reports, including

- Data dictionaries
- Data flow diagrams (printed on a line printer, not a graphics terminal)
- Data flow inconsistency reports, e.g., information generated but not used or information used but not generated
- Data base modification reports, e.g., who modified the requirements data base when
- Reference reports, e.g., summaries of all processes referencing an item of information
- Hierarchical summary reports showing the superordinate/subordinate relationships between information items or processes
- Analysis reports, e.g., process chain or data/process interaction.

PSL/PSA has been augmented with additional abilities over time. In particular PSL/PSA can be used to show system-level input/output (i.e., interaction between the system being analyzed and its environment); decomposition of the problem into subproblems; the actual system's design (not appropriate for the problem analysis phase); the structure of data; data sizing and program sizing; system behavioral dynamics; attributes of the system; and project management functions, such as personnel, schedules, and resources. More recently Meta Systems has produced an interactive front end called the

PROCESS:
- hourly-employee-processing:

DESCRIPTION:
This process performs those actions needed to interpret time cards to produce a pay statement for each hourly employee.;

ATTRIBUTES ARE:
complexity-level
high;

GENERATES:	pay-statement, error-listing, hourly-employee-report;
RECEIVES:	time-card, hourly-employee-record;
SUBPARTS ARE:	hourly-paycheck-validation, hourly -emp-update, h-report-entry-generation; hourly-paycheck-production;
PART OF:	payroll-processing;
DERIVES:	pay statement
USING:	time-card, hourly-employee-record;
DERIVES:	hourly-employee-report
USING:	time-card, hourly-employee-record;
DERIVES:	error listing
USING:	time-card, hourly-employee-record;

PROCEDURE:
1. compute gross pay from time card data.
2. compute tax from gross pay.
3. subtract tax from gross pay to obtain net pay.
4. update hourly employee record accordingly.
5. update department record accordingly
6. generate paycheck.

Note: if status code specifies that the employee did not work this week, no processing will be done for this employee.;

HAPPENS:
number-of-payments TIMES-PER pay-period;

TRIGGERED BY:
hourly-emp-processing-event;

TERMINATION-CAUSES:
new-employee-processing-event;

SECURITY IS:
company-only;

Figure 2–34. Example of Problem Statement Language: Hourly Employee Processing. © 1977 IEEE.

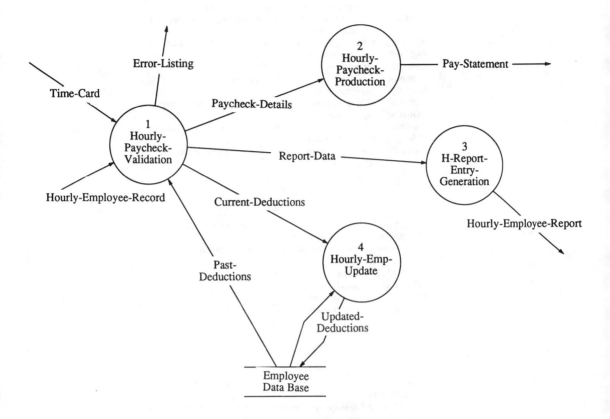

Figure 2–35. The Expanded Hourly Employee Processing DFD.

Structured Architect™[6], which enables DFDs to be entered and updated graphically.

To date, PSL/PSA has been used on more than 140 projects, including numerous large systems for the DoD. Although it *can* be used for problem analysis effectively, it has often been used for only *design,* i.e., the decomposition of the software into its actual subcomponents. Written in FORTRAN, PSA has been hosted on dozens of computers. AT&T Long Lines uses PSL/PSA as a design tool on major information system development efforts [WIN79], and it serves as the underlying data base system for REVS, discussed later in Section 4.2.2.6.

2.3.3.8 Object-oriented problem analysis

The concept of object orientation in software development has its roots in the language Smalltalk. Rentsch [REN82] provides an excellent historic per-

[6]Structured Architect is a trademark of Meta Systems, Inc.

```
PROCESS                          hourly-paycheck-validation
DESCRIPTION:
        This process checks the time card for validity and computes the
        gross and net pay amounts for each employee;
GENERATES:    error-listing, paycheck-details, report-data, current-
                 deductions;
RECEIVES:   time-card, hourly-employee-record, past-deduction;
PART OF:    hourly-employee-processing;
DERIVES:    error-listing
  USING:    time-card, hourly-employee-record;
DERIVES:    paycheck-details
  USING:    time-card, hourly-employee-record, past-deductions;
DERIVES:    report-data
  USING:    time-card, hourly-employee-record, past-deductions;
DERIVES:    current-deductions
  USING:    time-card, hourly-employee-record, past-deductions;
                        .
                        .
                        .
                            (a)


PROCESS                          hourly-paycheck-production
DESCRIPTION:
        Given all the relevant data, this process generates the actual
        paycheck and stub;
GENERATES:    pay-statement;
RECEIVES:    paycheck-details;
DERIVES:     pay-statement
  USING:     pay-check-details;
                        .
                        .
                        .
                            (b)


PROCESS                          h-report-entry-generation
DESCRIPTION:
        Given individual employee pay data, this process collects that
        data and generates a summary report;
GENERATES:    hourly-employee-report;
RECEIVES:    report-data;
DERIVES:     hourly-employee-report
  USING:     report-data;
                        .
                        .
                        .
                            (c)


PROCESS                          hourly-emp-update
DESCRIPTION:
        Updates the employee data base to reflect latest deductions;
GENERATES:    updated-deductions;
RECEIVES:    current-deductions, past-deductions;
DERIVES:     updated-deductions
  USING:     current-deductions, past-deductions;
                        .
                        .
                            (d)
```

Figure 2–36. PSL Examples for Each Subordinate Node of Hourly Employee Processing. (**a**) Hourly-Paycheck-Validation. (**b**) Hourly-Paycheck-Production. (**c**) H-Report-Entry-Generation. (**d**) Hourly-Emp-Update.

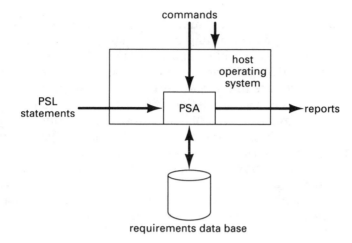

Figure 2–37. PSL/PSA System Architecture. © 1977 IEEE.

spective of object-oriented *programming*. Booch [BOO86] discusses the effect
of object-orientation on *design*. Finally, Borgida [BOR85] and Coad [COA89]
discuss the effect of object orientation on problem analysis.

All object-oriented approaches stress the definition and refinement of
objects in the real world and classes of objects in the real world. A *class* of
objects can be thought of as an abstraction that represents one or more
objects or other classes of objects. Thus if we have objects called manufacturers, wholesalers, and retailers, they might all be members of the class of
objects called companies. Also in any object-oriented approach, objects (and
classes of objects) possess *attributes,* and all objects *inherit* the attributes
of the classes of which they are members. Since problem analysis is the
analysis and description of the real world, its entities, their attributes, and
their relationships, it makes sense to use object-oriented concepts in problem analysis. The primary motivation for object orientation is that as a
system evolves, its functions tend to change, but its objects remain un-
changed. Thus a system built using object-oriented techniques may be
inherently more maintainable than one built using more conventional
functional approaches.

By far the most thorough methodology for using an object orientation
during problem analysis has been put forth by Peter Coad [COA89, COA89a]
under the name Object-Oriented Analysis (OOA). OOA is a five-step methodology using the notations described in Section 2.3.2.4. The five steps correspond
to specifying objects, structures, subjects, attributes, and services. At the time
this book was being written, OOA was still under rapid evolution. This section
provides only a summary of OOA at a particular point during its infancy. A
more up-to-date and detailed description can be found in [COA89a].

Objects are "an encapsulation of attributes and exclusive services; an abstraction of the something in the problem space, with some number of occurrences in the problem space" [COA89a]. Unlike other authors, Coad provides explicit guidance on how to identify objects. His advice is to examine structure in the real world (e.g., nurses and physicians are members of the medical profession), identify other systems with which the current or proposed system will interact (e.g., Blue Cross/Blue Shield); identify those things in the real world that need to be remembered for later retrieval (e.g., patient's blood pressure); identify specific roles played by individuals (e.g., physician, patient); identify physical locations that need to be known (e.g., physician's office address); identify organizations that humans belong to (e.g., AMA, HMOs); identify catalogs that have to record quantities of repetitive, static information about things (e.g., patient medical history).

The identification of *structure* is one of the most important steps in OOA. It is fundamental in defining objects and minimizing the complexity of the analysis. There are two types of structure: *classification* and *assembly*. They enable you to use abstraction and partitioning, respectively, in describing objects. Classification enables you to define one class of objects that captures common attributes and services and enables all objects that are members to inherit those attributes and services. The example given in Section 2.3.2.4 showed how in-patients and out-patients were both members of the class patients. I have personally found in practice that this structure can be realized both top down and bottom up. For instance, in the medical example, we may be analyzing in-patients separately from out-patients and then realize they have much in common and that it would be useful to define the more abstract concept of patient. On the other hand, we might be analyzing in-patients when we realize that the attributes and services associated with cardiac-care patients are different than those associated with psych patients, so that it would be useful to define two less abstract objects, cardiac-care and psych, which would be subordinate to the class of in-patients. The other type of structure is assembly. It captures the concept of "what is a part (or component) of what." For example, patients and physicians may be parts of an HMO plan. As in the case of classification, you create these in practice in both a top-down and bottom-up fashion.

At this point in the process, the model starts to become somewhat complex. To simplify the understanding of the model, the next step is to examine the objects and their underlying structures to arrive at a less complex, more abstract view. This view is called the *subject* view and entails the definition of subjects. Each classification structure and assembly structure becomes one subject. According to Coad, each remaining object also becomes a subject, although if there are a considerable number of these, I would recommend that you search the problem space for additional candidate structures among the remaining objects, in order to reduce the number of subjects. Once the subjects are defined, a subject diagram is constructed. It looks just like an object diagram except that its contents are limited to the names of the subjects. When the next two steps are completed, you will augment the subject diagram to reflect any instance connections or message connections that result from defining attributes and services, respectively.

The next step is defining *attributes* associated with objects. From the real-world perspective, these express some important aspect of the object. From the computer perspective, these represent some value or aspect that must be stored for all instances of the object. Thus for example, if the object is a patient, then some of the attributes may be height, weight, name, social security number, date of birth, etc. The definition of attributes must be made hand-in-hand with the definition of structures. As sets of objects evolve to have attributes in common (for good reason, not coincidental), you may consider defining a class of objects to "hold" the common attributes. Every object that is a member of a class of objects possesses all attributes unique to that object as well as those of its class. This is called *inheritance*. During the process of defining attributes, a situation often occurs where the attribute of one object *is* another object. For example, in an elevator control system, one possible attribute of an elevator is the current floor, or one possible attribute of a floor is the number of elevators currently present on that floor. When this occurs, it is far easier not to include these attributes, but instead to add instance connections between these related objects. *Instance connections* define one-to-one, one-to-many, and many-to-many relations that exist in the real world between instances of objects.

The last step is specifying the services performed by each object. According to Coad, there are three types of services: occur, calculate, and monitor. *Occurrence services* are related to the creation, deletion, and modification of instances of the object. Rather than specifying add, delete, change, test, and select services for every object, Coad suggests using a single abstract service type called "occur," which is omitted from the model due to its omnipresence. *Calculate services* are used when one object needs the calculated result from another object. Each "calculate" service is explicitly placed in the model. *Monitor services* are those where instances of an object monitor some other process for a condition, an event, etc. For every service, you must specify its external behavior in a *service specification*. These should be as short and focused as possible and most importantly, should use terminology from the problem domain. *Message connections* are precisely data flows and control flows in the data flow world. The primary difference is that in the Coad world, you think of them in association with services, i.e., you are motivated by the need for message flow rather than simply its existence. In particular if instances of object A provide some service for instances of object B, then there may be a need for B to pass a message to A to represent either data being passed for processing or the control signal to initiate the service. Similarly there may be a need for A to pass a message to B to represent either data resulting from the service or the control signal representing completion of the service.

Finally the entire problem analysis is documented in three packages: the OOA model itself (which includes diagrams), a dictionary (with definitions of all attributes), and service specifications (one for each object). Coad's 1989 paper [COA89] is an excellent source for step-by-step instructions and helpful advice about OOA. The methodology and notation are further expanded in [COA89a].

2.3.4 Applying Problem Analysis Techniques: Example 1

As defined in Section 1.5, the first example is the automation of a book distribution company. As we learned in Section 2.3.3, there are at least eight approaches to performing problem analysis. Let us examine each of these approaches. In this particular case, it would be nontrivial to list all inputs and outputs unless we were extremely familiar with such types of companies from previous experience. Similarly the primary functions of the company may not be apparent. Orr's Structured Requirements Definition appears to be a sound approach in this case because we wish to analyze a currently manual process with the intent of automating it and there are a variety of disparate viewpoints on the process.

2.3.4.1 Structured requirements definition

To employ the SRD approach, we interview personnel from each of the major divisions of the company and ask them to tell us what their job involves. As each person describes his or her role, we record on a DFD all the interfaces between that individual and others. Let us assume that we have been given the organization chart shown in Figure 2–38. We decide to speak to representatives from the eight organizational units that show no subordinates, i.e., sales distribution, order filling, buying, inventory, membership, personnel, accounting, and printing.

Figure 2–39 records the results of initial interviews. The next step in SRD is to merge the DFDs into one large DFD. When that is attempted, there arise three obvious inconsistencies in perspectives:

* Order Filling claims (see Figure 2–39b) to send book requisitions to Inventory and to receive books in return, while Inventory claims (see Figure 2–39d) that it receives book requisitions from Sales that it responds to with books. This is only a minor discrepancy; Sales is really

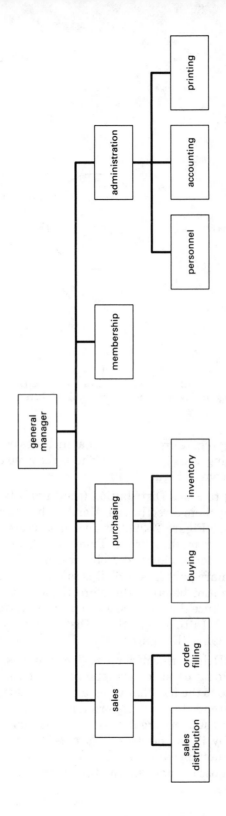

Figure 2-38. LOCS Corporation Organization Chart.

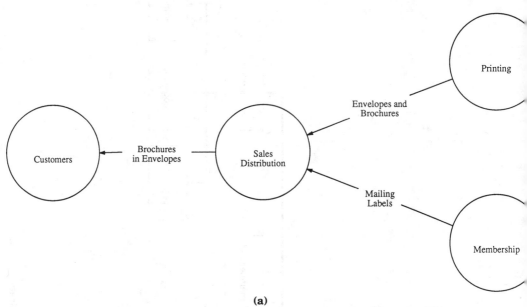

(a)

Figure 2–39. SRD DFDs for LOCS. **(a)** Sales Distribution. **(b)** Order Filling.
(c) Buying. **(d)** Inventory. **(e)** Membership. **(f)** Personnel. **(g)** Accounting. **(h)**
Printing.

only an aggregate organization that includes both Sales Distribution and
Order Filling (see Figure 2–38). This is resolved by updating Figure 2–39d
to that shown in Figure 2–40.

- According to Sales Distribution (see Figure 2–39a), mailing labels are
  received by them directly from Membership. However according to Membership (see Figure 2–39e), it does not create mailing labels at all but
  instead sends mailing lists to Printing, which in turn generates mailing
  labels. This latter view is corroborated by Printing in Figure 2–39h. One
  of the primary purposes of SRD is to uncover misunderstandings in how
  an organization behaves; therefore, these types of discrepancies are to be
  expected. Since there can be only one reality, we know that the issue can
  be resolved. In this case, Sales Distribution was mistaken. We correct
  Figure 2–39a with Figure 2–41.

- When SRD is performed on real companies, functional and support
  organizational perspectives tend not to be complementary. This is primarily due to the fact that when a functional organization is asked what
  it does, it tends to stress its primary functional purpose rather than its
  interface to support organizations. Thus many of the information flows
  reported by Personnel (see Figure 2–39f) and Accounting (see Figure
  2–39g) do not appear on other DFDs. These should be resolved by either
  deleting those support information flows (if there is no plan to automate

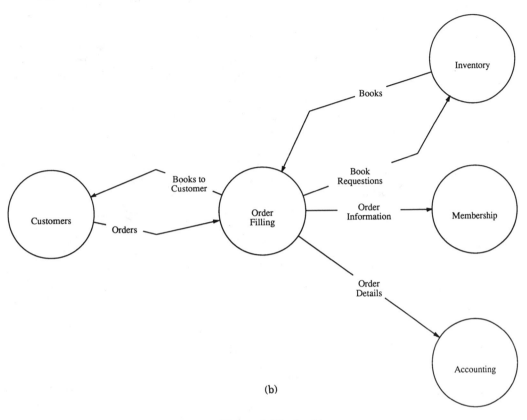

(b)

Figure 2–39   *(cont.)*

them) or adding them to all functional organizations' DFDs (to achieve consistency). In this case, we have chosen to delete them.

Once the preceding issues are resolved, we can easily merge the individual DFDs into one consistent DFD, as shown in Figure 2–42. It now becomes quite evident how the company works. As shown clearly in Figure 2–42,

1. Printing prints advertisements to join the book club. Membership sends this enrollment information to Potential Customers. Some of those people respond with applications to join the book club.
2. On a regular (e.g., monthly) basis, Membership sends mailing lists to Printing, which in turn runs off envelopes and mailing labels for all current members. It also prints a brochure to be mailed to all current members (Customers) advertising all available books.
3. Sales Distribution packs the brochures in the envelopes and mails them to all current Customers.

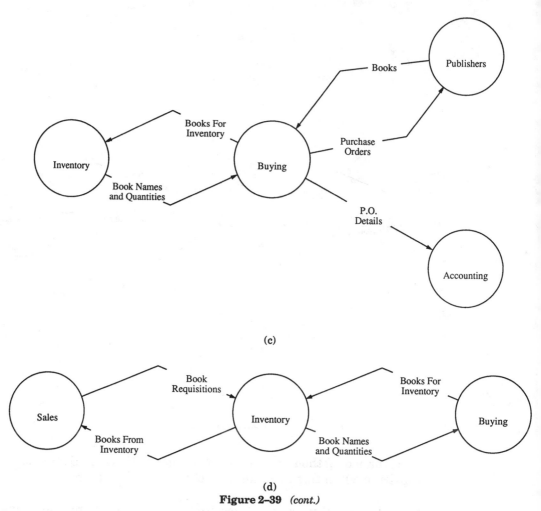

(c)

(d)

Figure 2–39 *(cont.)*

4. Customers who desire to order books, place orders and send them to Order Filling. Order Filling sends corresponding book requisitions to Inventory.

5. If Inventory does not have a book in stock, it sends the required book names and quantities needed to Buying, which assembles and sends a purchase order to Publishers, who send back the books to Buying, which replenishes Inventory. Buying also sends copies of purchase order details to Accounting, which makes withdrawals from the Bank (via check) and mails checks to the Publishers.

6. Meanwhile if Inventory has the books in stock (or has received them from Buying), it sends the books to Order Filling, which (a) tells Membership so it can update its records for the number of books each Customer has

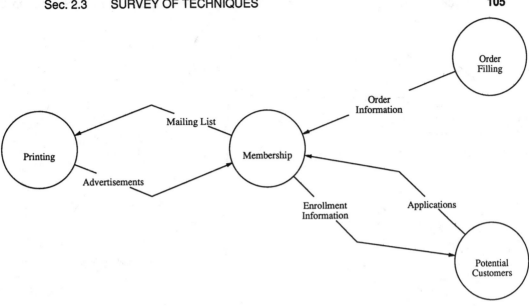

(e)

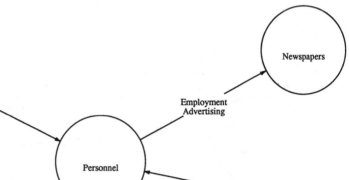

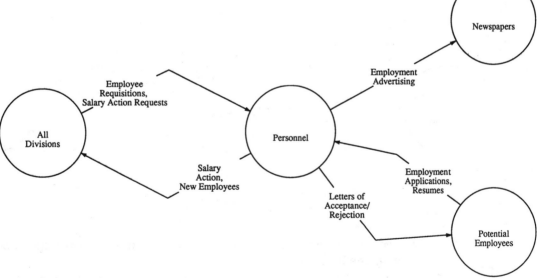

(f)

Figure 2–39 *(cont.)*

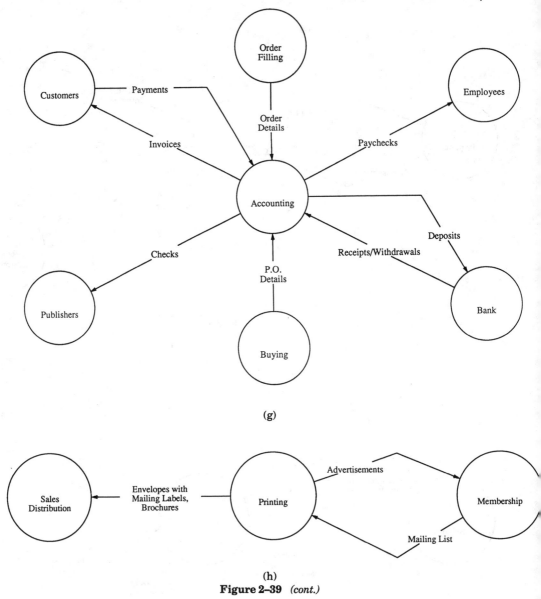

(g)

(h)
Figure 2–39 *(cont.)*

ordered, (b) tells Accounting so it can send invoices to the Customer, and
(c) sends the books to the Customer.

7. On receipt of the books and the invoice, the Customer sends payments to
Accounting, which makes deposits into the Bank and receives receipts in
return.

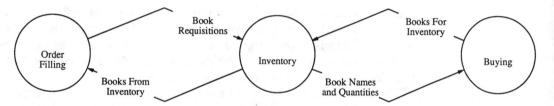

Figure 2–40. Updated Figure 2–39d.

Figure 2–41. Updated Figure 2–39a.

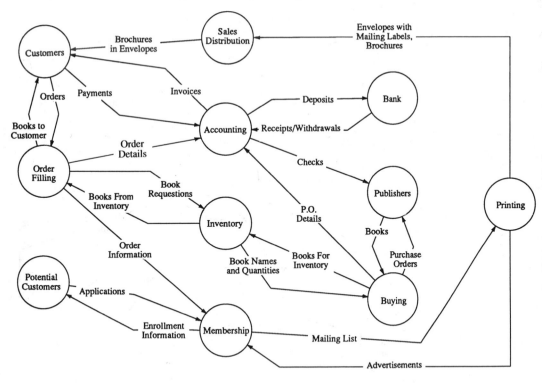

Figure 2–42. DFD for LOCS.

At this point in time, we have a much better understanding of how the company operates (i.e., the problem) but no idea of how automation will solve the problem. That is a good sign that we are correctly performing problem analysis—we are neither defining the external behavior (i.e., writing the SRS) or designing the internals of the software system.

The next step in SRD is to collapse that part of the DFD corresponding to the company into just one bubble. In this case, all bubbles except Customers, Potential Customers, Bank, and Publishers comprise the company. When we collapse these into one bubble, preserving all its external interfaces, we arrive at Figure 2–43. Furthermore at our current level of heightened understanding of the company, we can now isolate three major functions of LOCS: A—soliciting new customers, B—selling books, and C—buying books. The next step in using SRD is to define these functions in terms of the information flows defined in Figure 2–43. Using the notation A_i, B_i, and C_i to denote the ith step in function A, B, and C, respectively, to label the arcs, we arrive at Figure 2–44.

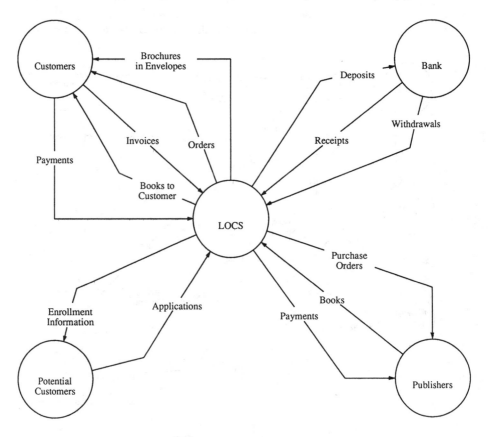

Figure 2–43. Collapsed DFD for LOCS.

2.3.4.2 SADT

For a problem as simple and straightforward as the book club, there is probably little need to analyze the problem at hand beyond the level of specifying all inputs, outputs, and major functions of the company. The next logical step for *this* problem would probably be to make the difficult decisions concerning what you want to automate and then begin defining the automated system's intended external behavior and characteristics, which would all be documented in the SRS.

However, let us assume that for some reason we choose to analyze the book club further using SADT. Prior to beginning, we would have already defined all the inputs and outputs of the company, using any technique (e.g., using SRD). The next step is to record this in a context diagram using SADT as shown in Figure 2–45. Next it is time to decompose the problem into subproblems. This can be done in many ways; for example, we could refine our understanding of the company by examining each of the company's organiza-

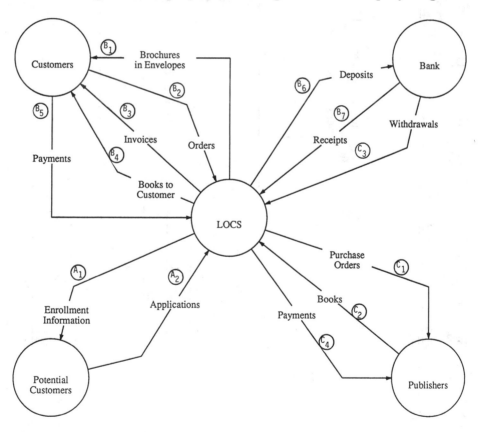

Figure 2–44. Primary LOCS Functions.

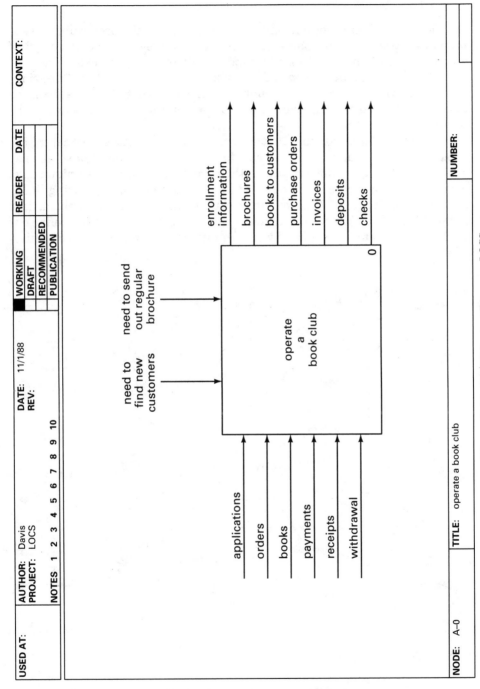

Figure 2-45. SADT Context Diagram: LOCS.

tional components, or we could refine our understanding of the company by examining each of the company's main functions. The right way is the one that provides you, the analyst, with the most insight into the problem at hand. It is also quite acceptable, and often recommended, to decompose from multiple perspectives, since multiple perspectives often provide far more insight than any one perspective alone. Let us do just that. First we will examine the company from the perspective of its organizational components. This detailing of Figure 2–45 is shown in Figure 2–46. To create this diagram, the following steps were taken:

- Define first-level company organization (i.e., the four boxes).
- Allocate each company level input and output to an organizational element.
- Define all information flows between the organizational elements.

The next step is the production of a diagram for each of the four elements by refining them further. These are shown in Figure 2–47.

We can also detail Figure 2–45 in terms of the company's major functions; for example, Figure 2–48 provides such a detailing. As before, we want to decompose each of these major functions into its major subfunctions to gain a clearer understanding, as shown in Figure 2–49. Figures 2–48 and 2–49 provide a very different perspective than Figures 2–46 and 2–47.

The reader should be cautioned when examining any of these diagrams that in the real world (as opposed to reading this book), one would spend many hours interviewing, discussing, brainstorming, and analyzing (as I did when I wrote this book) in order to arrive at the diagrams. SADT (and most of the problem analysis techniques discussed here) provides an aid to documenting the results of the analysis—it does not do the analysis itself. However, do not underestimate the power of such a documentation aid. Documentation is as important to analysis as language is to thought. There is no way of expressing, conceiving, or organizing thought without language; there is no way of expressing, conceiving, or organizing analysis without documentation aids.

2.3.4.3 SASS

The primary differences between SASS and SADT are that SASS introduces data bases into the DFDs and demands current and new perspectives. For this application, we have chosen to use Structured Analysis/RT.[7] Figures 2–50 through 2–52 represent the current physical DFD. Figures 2–50, 2–53, and 2–54 represent the current logical DFDs. In this case, the decision was made not to change the data flows as a result of automation; thus the new

---

[7]This application is obviously not real time. It should be clear to the reader that this author believes there is value in modeling control aspects of a problem whether or not it is real time.

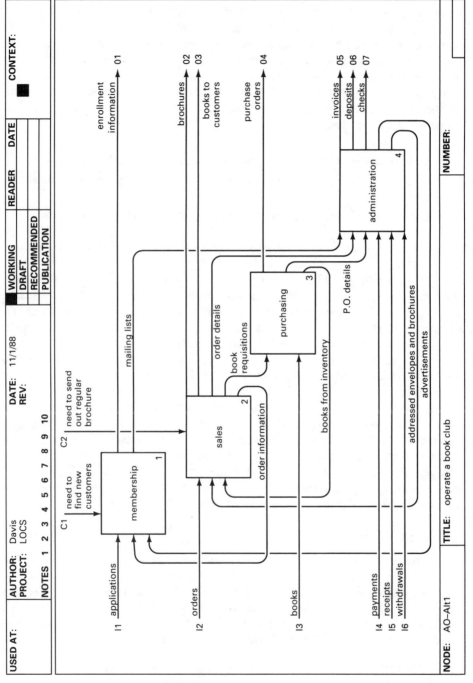

Figure 2-46. SADT First-Level Decomposition: LOCS by Organization.

112

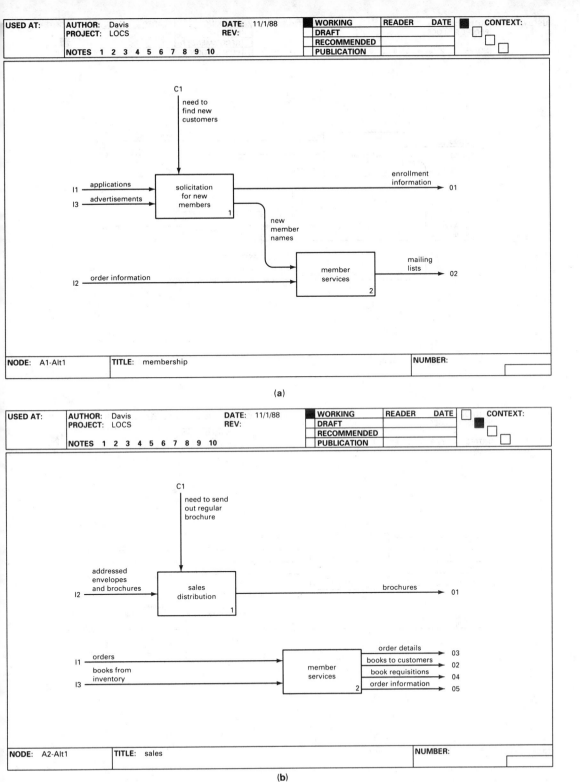

C1
need to
find new
customers

I1 applications

I3 advertisements

solicitation
for new
members
1

enrollment
information O1

new
member
names

I2 order information

member
services
2

mailing
lists O2

NODE: A1-Alt1 | **TITLE:** membership | **NUMBER:**

(a)

C1
need to send
out regular
brochure

addressed
envelopes
and brochures

I2

sales
distribution
1

brochures O1

I1 orders

books from
inventory

I3

member
services
2

order details O3
books to customers O2
book requisitions O4
order information O5

NODE: A2-Alt1 | **TITLE:** sales | **NUMBER:**

(b)

Figure 2–47. SADT Second-Level Decomposition: LOCS by Organization. (a) Membership. (b) Sales. (c) Purchasing. (d) Administration.

113

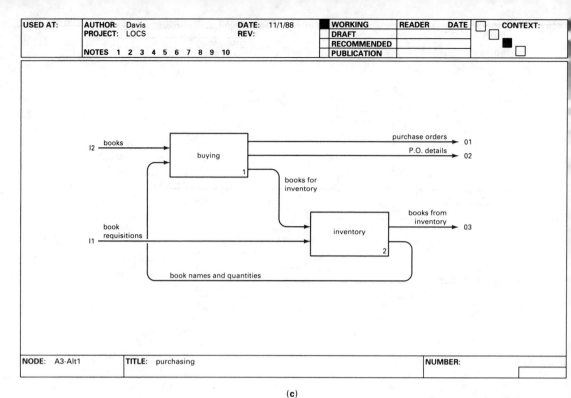

I2 → books → buying 1

purchase orders → O1
P.O. details → O2

books for inventory

I1 → book requisitions

inventory 2 → books from inventory → O3

book names and quantities

NODE: A3-Alt1	TITLE: purchasing	NUMBER:

(c)

USED AT:	AUTHOR: Davis PROJECT: LOCS	DATE: 11/1/88 REV:	■ WORKING DRAFT RECOMMENDED PUBLICATION	READER DATE	□	CONTEXT:
	NOTES 1 2 3 4 5 6 7 8 9 10					

I2 → order details
I3 → P.O. details
I4 → payments
I5 → receipts
I6 → withdrawals

accounting 1

invoices → O1
deposits → O2
checks → O3

I1 → mailing lists

printing 2

addressed envelopes and brochures → O5
advertisements → O4

NODE: A4-Alt1	TITLE: administration	NUMBER:

(d)

Figure 2–47. (cont.)

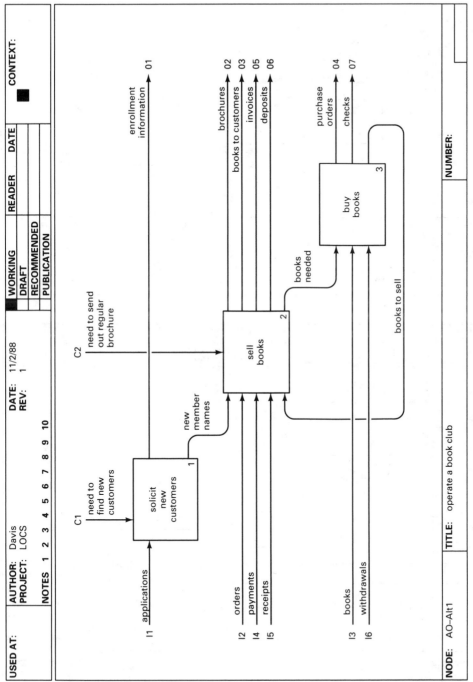

Figure 2-48. SADT First-Level Decomposition: LOCS by Function.

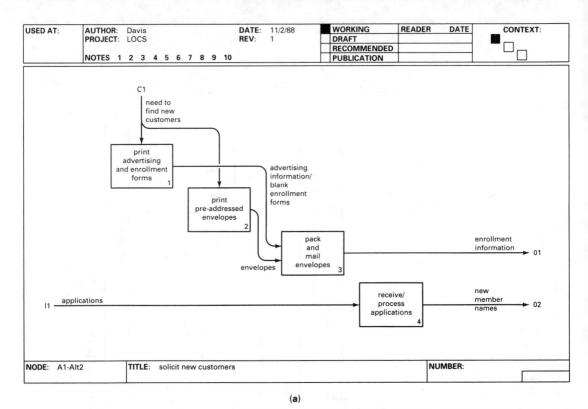

NODE: A1-Alt2   TITLE: solicit new customers   NUMBER:

(a)

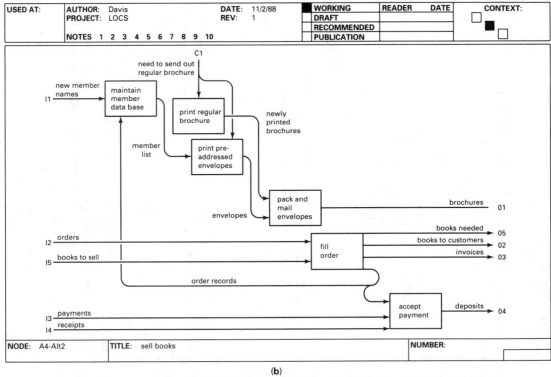

NODE: A4-Alt2   TITLE: sell books   NUMBER:

(b)

Figure 2–49. SADT Second-Level Decomposition: LOCS by Function. **(a)** Solicit New Customers. **(b)** Sell Books. **(c)** Buy Books.

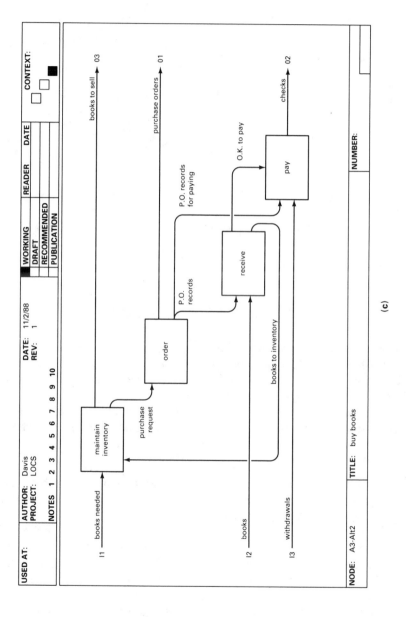

Figure 2-49. *(cont.)*

(c)

117

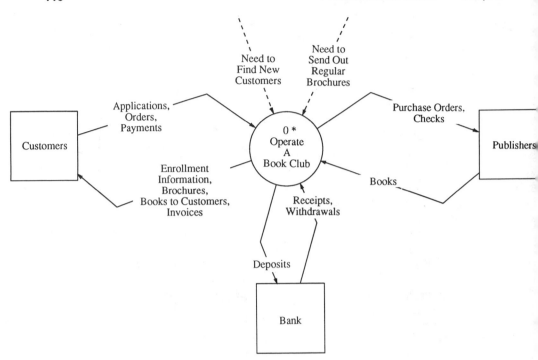

Figure 2–50. SASS Context Diagram: LOCS.

DFDs are the same as the current DFDs. Remember when creating new DFDs, it is not the time to design the target software. Note the similarity of Figures 2–50 through 2–54 to Figures 2–45 through 2–49, respectively. The primary differences are change in notation, physical layout on the page, and the addition of data bases. Figures 2–55 and 2–56 show data dictionaries that correspond to the two decompositions (physical and logical), respectively.

2.3.4.4 Object-oriented problem analysis

Let us assume that we are starting from scratch on this problem analysis, that the analyses described in Sections 2.3.4.1–2.3.4.3 have not occurred. Let us follow Coad's five-step method [COA89].

The first step is to identify the objects of LOCS. To uncover these objects, we look at other systems we may want to interact with. In this case, two possibilities are the publisher and the bank. We look at those things that have to be remembered. In this case, they might include customers' orders for books and purchase orders to order books from publishers. We look at specific roles played by individuals. As far as individuals about whom information *must* be maintained, there is an obvious one: the customer. As far as individuals who play other types of roles in the LOCS world, there are many possible candi-

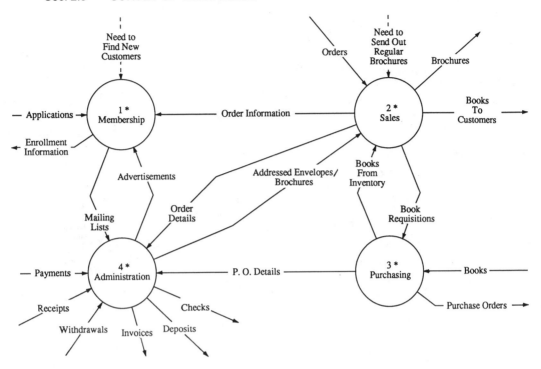

Figure 2–51. First-Level Physical DFD: LOCS.

dates: salespeople, buyers, clerks, customer representatives, truck drivers, forklift operators, accounts receivable personnel, accounts payable personnel, inventory experts, etc. At one extreme, we could try to identify all these as separate roles, or at the other extreme, we could group them all together in one object called LOCS employee. I suspect *at this point* that many will have no role to play in the final definition of the problem *if* we arbitrarily decide to automate the LOCS primary functions (i.e., selling books) rather than support functions, such as payroll. Rather than forgetting this group entirely, let us tentatively include three objects: customer interface personnel (including salespeople, customer representatives, and accounts receivable personnel, for example), publisher interface personnel (including buyers, truck drivers, and accounts payable personnel, for example), and internal LOCS personnel (including clerks, forklift operators, and inventory experts, for example). Since all of these employees will involve some common attributes (e.g., start date, social security number, salary), it may also make sense to define a class called LOCS employee with the three objects as members of it. We should also look at physical locations; at this point, the obvious ones are the physical location(s) of LOCS, locations of customers, and locations of publishers. The latter two

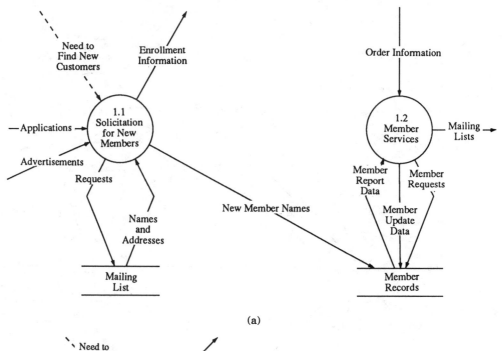

(a)

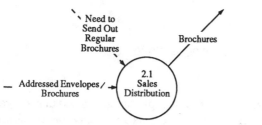

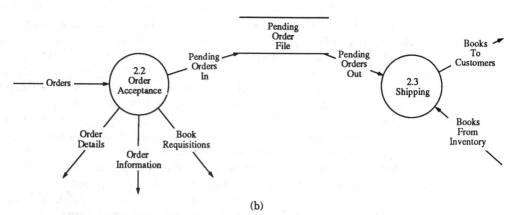

(b)

Figure 2–52. Second-Level Physical DFD: LOCS. **(a)** Membership. **(b)** Sales.
(c) Purchasing. **(d)** Administration.

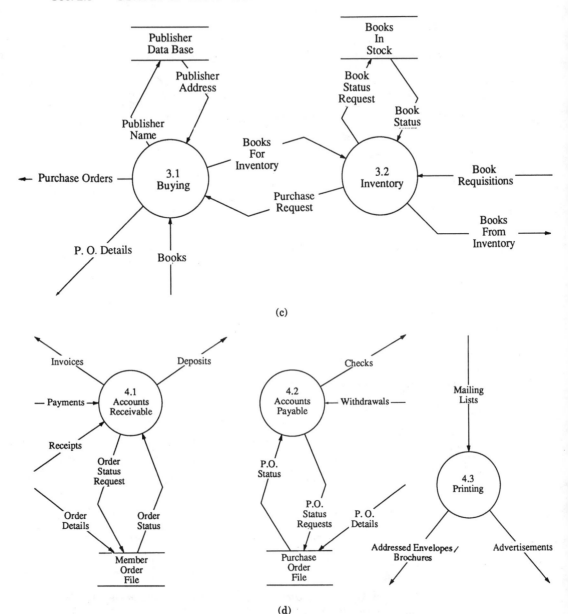

(c)

(d)

Figure 2–52 *(cont.)*

seem more logical to include as attributes of customer and publisher objects rather than as objects themselves. The physical location(s) of LOCS is meaningful to capture as an object if LOCS was physically distributed, e.g., multiple warehouses or sales offices, but let us assume that this is not the case.

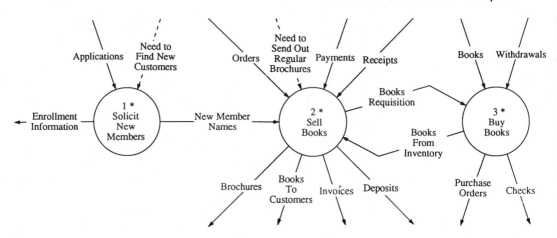

Figure 2–53. First-Level Logical DFD: LOCS.

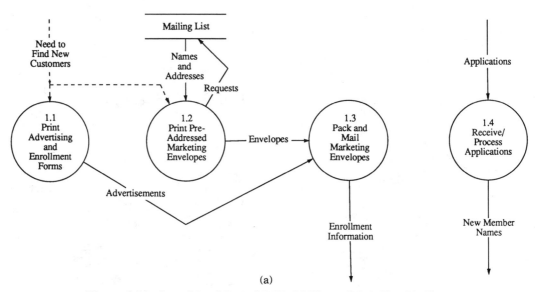

(a)

Figure 2–54. Second-Level Logical DFD: LOCS. **(a)** Solicit New Members. **(b)** Sell Books. **(c)** Buy Books.

Organizations to which people belong may be meaningful if LOCS acquired mailing lists related to customers' memberships in various societies and then tracked their progress as a function of these societies. Also if LOCS had multiple sub-book clubs, one for theory, one for the PC market, one for software engineering, then the membership of the customer would be helpful as well.

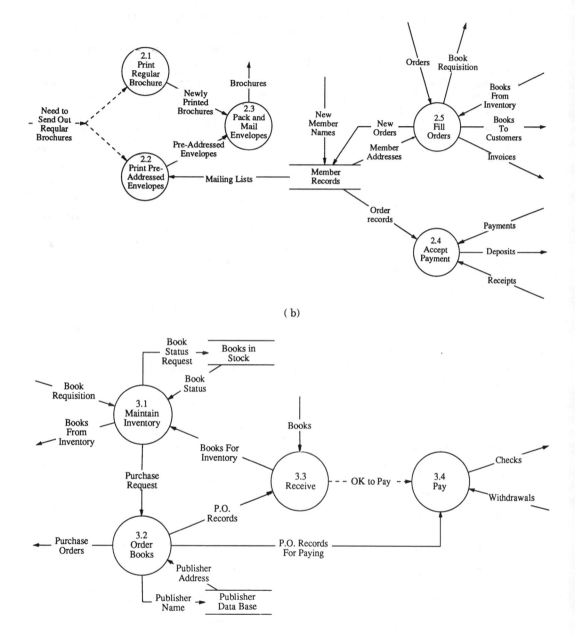

(b)

(c)

Figure 2–54 *(cont.)*

	Data Flows			
Name	**Generated By**	**Used By**	**Description/Purpose**	**Form**
Address				{ alphanumeric char }
Advertisements	Printing	Solicitation for New Members	Brochures used to advertise the book.	
Applications	Customers	Solicitation for New Members	Completed forms used to join book club.	customer name + address
Addressed Envelopes/ Brochures	Printing	Sales Distribution	Monthly newsletter packaged and mailed to advertise books.	customer name + address + brochures
Book #				{ numeric digit }
Book Author				{ alphabetic char }
Bookid			Unique book identifier.	publisher + book name + book author + book # + price
Book Requisition	Order Acceptance	Inventory	A request by Sales to Inventory to receive X copies of a book to satisfy a customer order.	{ bookid + no }
Book Status	Books in Stock	Inventory	The number of copies of a book in inventory.	{ bookid + no }
Book Status Request	Inventory	Books in Stock	A request to find out how many books are in stock.	{ bookid }
Bookname				{ alphanumeric char }
Books	Publishers	Buying	The wholesale supply of products.	
Books to Customers	Shipping	Customers	Boxed books en route to customers.	
Books for Inventory	Buying	Shipping	After books are received from the publisher, they are shipped to inventory for storage.	
Books from Inventory	Inventory	Shipping	Books about to be boxed and mailed to customers.	
Brochures	Sales Distribution	Customers	Monthly newsletters mailed to members to advertise books.	
Checks	Accounts Payable	Publishers	Payments to publishers (suppliers) for purchased books.	{ publisher + price }
Customer id			Unique customer identifier.	{ alphanumeric char }
Customer name				{ alphabetic char }
Deposit				price
Deposits	Accounts Receivable	Bank	Deposits into bank of check paid LOCS by customers.	{ deposit }
Enrollment Information	Solicitation for New Members	Customers	Advertisements in envelopes.	

Figure 2–55. Data Dictionary for Physical Decomposition: LOCS.

| Name | Data Flows | | Description/Purpose | Form |
	Generated By	Used By		
Invoice				customer id + { book + no } + price
Invoices	Accounts Receivable	Customers	Bills sent to customers mailed under separate cover from books.	{ invoice }
Mailing Lists	Member Services	Printing	A formatted list of the names and addresses of all current members.	{ customer name + address }
Member Report Data	Member Records	Member Services	Retrieved information (e.g., address or name) about a member.	[customer name | address]
Member Requests	Member Services	Member Records	A request for storage or retrieval of information about a current member (e.g., a request for the name and address).	["store" | "retrieve"] + [customer name | customer id]
Member Update Data	Member Services	Member Records	New information about existing members to be stored, (e.g., name or book ordered by member).	[customer name | customer id] + [address | (bookid + no)]
Names and Addresses	Mailing List	Solicitation for New Members	A list of names and addresses of potential new members.	{ customer name + address }
Need to Find New Customers	Book Club Corporate Executives	Solicitation for New Members	Based on revenue/profit projections, a signal to indicate the need to advertise for new club members.	
Need to Send Out Regular Brochures	Calendar	Sales Distribution	A signal (probably once/month) that it is time to mail out brochures advertising book selections.	
New Member Names	Solicitation for New Members	Member Records	Names and addresses from enrollment forms for new members.	{ customer name + address }
No			A count of books	{ numeric digit }
Order				customer id + { book + no }
Order Details	Order Acceptance	Member Order File	Financial date concerning books purchased by members.	customer id + { bookid + no } + price
Order Information	Order Acceptance	Member Services	Details of book orders by members.	customer id + { bookid + no }
Order Status	Member Order File	Accounts Receivable	Current balance due on account.	customer id + price
Order Status Request	Accounts Receivable	Member Order File	Member number used to retrieve current balance due.	customer id
Orders	Customers	Order Acceptance	Book orders from customers.	{ order }
Payment			Cash, credit card # or personal check.	
Payments	Customers	Accounts Receivable	Cash, credit card # or check for customer to purchase book.	{ payment }

Figure 2–55. *(cont.)*

	Data Flows			
Name	**Generated By**	**Used By**	**Description/Purpose**	**Form**
Pending Orders In	Order Acceptance	Pending Order File	An order that has not yet been filled or stored.	customer id + { bookid + no }
Pending Orders Out	Pending Order File	Order Acceptance	A retrieved order that has not yet been filled.	customer id + { bookid + no }
P.O. Details	Buying	Purchase Order File	The key information about a purchase from a publisher.	publisher + { bookid + no } + price
P.O. Status	Purchase Order File	Accounts Payable	A record by publisher of dollars owed.	publisher + { bookid + no } + price
P.O. Status Requests	Accounts Payable	Purchase Order File	A request for the outstanding balance by publisher.	publisher
Price				$+{ numeric digit } + · + numeric digit + numeric digit
Publisher				{ alphanumeric char }
Publisher Address	Publisher Data Base	Buying	Mailing addresses for publishers.	{ publisher + address }
Publisher Name	Buying	Publisher Data Base	Name of publisher whose address we desire.	publisher
Purchase Order			An order to buy books.	publisher + { bookid + no } + price
Purchase Orders	Buying	Publishers	Orders to buy books.	{ purchase order }
Purchase Request	Inventory	Buying	When inventory has insufficient copies of a book, it uses this to request the purchase of restocking copies.	{ bookid + no }
Receipt			Receipt for bank deposit.	price
Receipts	Bank	Accounts Receivable		{ receipt }
Requests	Solicitation for New Members	Mailing Lists	A request to obtain names and addresses of potential new members.	
Withdrawals	Bank	Accounts Payable	Cash from bank to pay bills.	

Figure 2–55. *(cont.)*

126

Name	Data Flows Generated By	Data Flows Used By	Description/Purpose	Form
Address				{ alphanumeric char }
Advertise-ments	Print Advertising and Enrollment Forms	Pack and Mail Envelopes	Brochures used to advertise the books.	
Applications	Customers	Receive/Process Applications	Completed forms used to join book club.	customer name + address
Book #				{ numeric digit }
Book Author				{ alphabetic char }
Bookid			Unique book identifier.	publisher + book name + book author + book # + price
Book Requisition	Fill Orders	Maintain Inventory	A request by Sales to Inventory to receive X copies of a book to satisfy a customer order.	{ bookid + no }
Book Status	Books in Stock	Maintain Inventory	The number of copies of a book in inventory.	{ bookid + no }
Book Status Request	Maintain Inventory	Books in Stock	Asks for the availability of a book.	{ bookid }
Bookname				{ alphanumeric char }
Books	Publishers	Receive	The wholesale supplier of products.	
Books to Customers	Fill Orders	Customers	Boxed books en route to customers.	
Books for Inventory	Receive	Maintain Inventory	After books are received from the publisher, they are shipped to inventory for storage.	
Books from Inventory	Maintain Inventory	Fill Orders	Books about to be boxed and mailed to customers.	
Brochures	Pack and Mail Envelopes	Customers	Monthly newsletters mailed to members to advertise books.	
Checks	Pay	Publishers	Payments to publishers (suppliers) for purchased books.	{ publisher + price }
Customer id			Unique customer identifier.	{ alphanumeric char }
Customer name				{ alphabetic char }
Deposit				price
Deposits	Accept Payment	Bank	Deposits into bank of check paid LOCS by customers.	{ deposit }
Enrollment Information	Pack and Mail Marketing Envelopes	Customers	Advertisements in envelopes.	
Envelopes	Print Pre-Addressed Marketing Envelopes	Pack and Mail Marketing Envelopes	Pre-addressed envelopes for prospective member.	
Invoice				customer id + {book + no}+ price

Figure 2–56. Data Dictionary for Logical Decomposition: LOCS.

	Data Flows			
Name	**Generated By**	**Used By**	**Description/Purpose**	**Form**
Invoices	Fill Orders	Customers	Bills sent to customers mailed under separate cover from books.	{ invoice }
Mailing Lists	Member Records	Print Pre-Addressed Envelopes	A formatted list of the names and addresses of all current members.	{ customer name + address }
Member Addresses	Member Records	Fill Orders	Addresses for current members.	{ customer name + address }
Names and Addresses	Mailing List	Print Pre-Addressed Marketing Envelopes	A list of names and addresses of potential new members.	{ customer name + address }
Need to Find New Customers	Book Club Corporate Executives	Solicit New Members	Based on revenue/profit projections, a signal to indicate the need to advertise for new club members.	
Need to Send Out Regular Brochures	Calendar	Sell Books	A signal (probably once/month) that it is time to mail out brochures advertising book selections.	
New Member Names	Receive/Process Applications	Member Records	Names and addresses from enrollment forms for new members.	{ customer name + address }
New Order			Info about who bought which books.	customer id + { bookid + no }
New Orders	Fill Orders	Member Records		{ new order }
Newly Printed Brochures	Print Regular Brochure	Pack and Mail Envelopes	Brochures before placing in envelope.	
OK to Pay	Receive	Pay	A signal saying that we should pay for book received.	
Order				customer id + { bookid + no }
Order Records	Member Records	Accept Payment	Records of who owes what money.	{ customer id + price }
Orders	Customers	Fill Orders	Book orders from customers.	{ order }
Payment			Cash or credit card # or personal check.	
Payments	Customers	Accept Payment	Cash, credit card, or check for customer to purchase book.	{ payment }
P.O. Records	Order Books	Receive	The key information about a purchase from a publisher.	{ purchase order }
P.O. Records for Paying	Order Books	Pay	Publisher name and amount of money owed to them.	{ publisher + price }
Pre-Addressed Envelopes	Print Pre-Addressed Envelopes	Pack and Mail Envelopes	Pre-addressed envelopes for current members.	

Figure 2–56. *(cont.)*

Name	Data Flows		Description/Purpose	Form
	Generated By	**Used By**		
Price				$ + { numeric digit + } · + numeric digit + numeric digit
Publisher				{ alphanumeric char }
Publisher Address	Publisher Data Base	Order Books	Mailing addresses for publishers.	{ publisher + address }
Publisher Name	Order Books	Publisher Data Base	Name of publisher whose address we desire.	publisher
Purchase Order			An order to buy books.	publisher + { bookid + no } + price
Purchase Orders	Order Books	Publishers	Orders to buy books.	{ purchase order }
Purchase Request	Maintain Inventory	Order Books	A request to buy X copies of book Y.	{ bookid + no }
Receipt			Receipt for bank deposit.	price
Receipts	Bank	Accept Payment		{ receipt }
Requests	Print Pre-Addressed Marketing Envelopes	Mailing List	A request to obtain names and addresses of potential new members.	
Withdrawals	Bank	Pay	Cash from bank to pay bills.	

Figure 2–56. *(cont.)*

Let us assume that this is also not the case. In the category of catalogs, there are at least three that might make sense: a catalog of all books in print, a catalog of all books sold by LOCS, and a catalog of all customers—if they were relatively stable. Let us assume that we do not need the first, that the second would be helpful, and that the third would be helpful but has already been captured in "customer" as a role. Figure 2–57 captures our first pass at object definition.

We have already defined one structure in our model. Are there others that could prove helpful? In the direction of more abstract objects, the answer is probably no. It *is* true that we could define a class called company that has both banks and publishers as members, but I do not believe that this adds any more understanding. We could also define an object called order that has both customer orders and purchase orders as members, but it also would aid us little in providing additional insight or simplification. In the other direction, toward less abstract objects, the answer is also probably no. Any refinement of any of the objects in Figure 2–57 could be more simply represented as attributes of those objects. The only exception might be if there were subcategories of customers (e.g., frequent buyers, bonus program members, red-binder club members) or multiple types of banks.

The subject layer in this particular application reduces its complexity only slightly. The LOCS employee structure can easily collapse into one structure. There remain six other objects, an indication that we should revisit the aggregation of these objects into more abstract structures. The option of combining customer order and purchase order was dismissed in the previous paragraph. How about combining the customer and the customer order or the publisher and the purchase order? In both these cases, the resulting subject becomes (1) difficult to name and (2) a source of hiding important information rather than a source of hiding details. Therefore, we will not create any other subjects, and the resulting subject diagram is shown in Figure 2–58.

Turning our attention now to attributes, Figure 2–59 shows a rich set of attributes for each of the objects in Figure 2–57. There are quite a few meaningful instance connections to be specified in this model and these help considerably in understanding the LOCS problem domain. Figure 2–59 captures the following instance connections:

- Every customer is assigned a single customer interface person, but customer interface people may be assigned more than one customer.
- Every customer order must be associated with a unique customer, but any particular customer may have zero, one, or more outstanding customer orders.
- Every customer order must order at least one book and *may* order multiple books. In addition any particular book may appear on zero, one, or more outstanding customer orders.

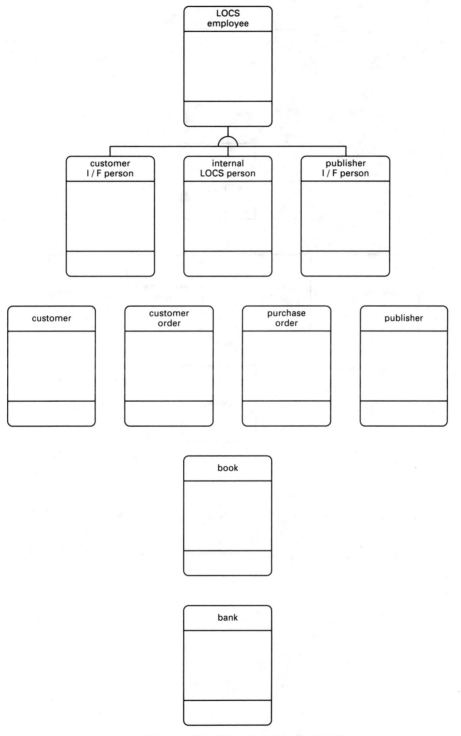

Figure 2–57. Object Definition for LOCS.

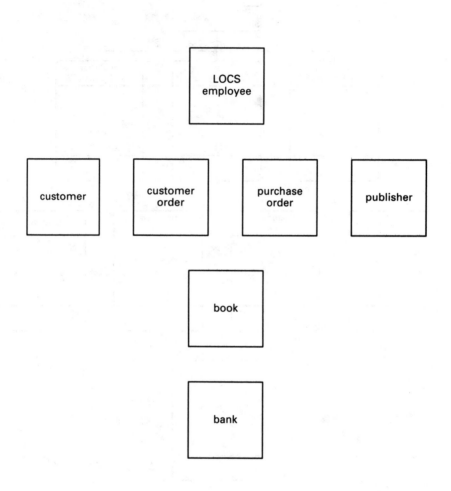

Figure 2–58. OOA Subject Layer for LOCS.

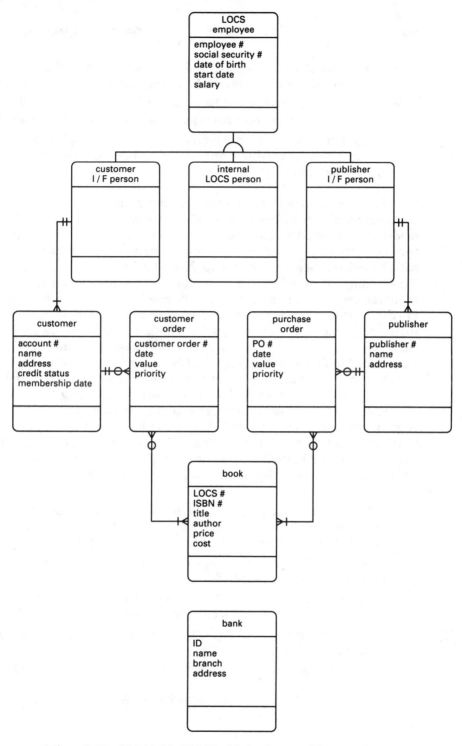

Figure 2–59. OOA Model of LOCS with Attributes and Instance Connections.

- Every publisher is assigned a single publisher interface person, but publisher interface people may be assigned more than one publisher.
- Every purchase order must be associated with a unique publisher, but there may be zero, one, or more purchase orders for any one publisher.
- Every purchase order must order at least one book and may order multiple books. In addition any particular book may appear on zero, one, or more outstanding purchase orders.

The next step is to define the services and their associated message connections. Figure 2–60a itemizes the necessary services. All objects in the model are assumed to have "occur" services to indicate that instances of those objects may be added (e.g., we may write up a new customer order), may be deleted (e.g., we may stop doing business with a particular publisher), may be modified (e.g., we may issue a customer address change request), may be tested (e.g., we may check the number of outstanding purchase orders for a publisher), or may be selected (e.g., a customer interface person may select a particular customer's records for examination). There are no specific "calculate" services. "Monitor" services have been added to four of the objects: LOCS employees have the responsibility of monitoring the status of all orders, customers, publishers, and banks; customers have the responsibility of monitoring LOCS (e.g., invoices, books received); publishers have the responsibility of monitoring LOCS as well (e.g., payments made by LOCS); and banks have the responsibility of monitoring LOCS (e.g., their credit status). Message connections, shown as dotted arrows in Figure 2–60a, show most of the information flows required between objects to enable the services to be performed:

- Customer interface people may request that a customer or a customer order be added, deleted, selected, or modified. A customer may also request that a customer order be added, deleted, selected, or modified.
- Internal LOCS people may request that a customer order or a purchase order be selected or modified.
- Publisher interface people may request that a publisher or a purchase order be added, deleted, selected, or modified.
- A customer order or a purchase order may make queries of the book objects concerning price, author, etc.
- LOCS employees may make queries of the bank and vice versa.

Figure 2–60b shows the final subject diagram with the message connections.

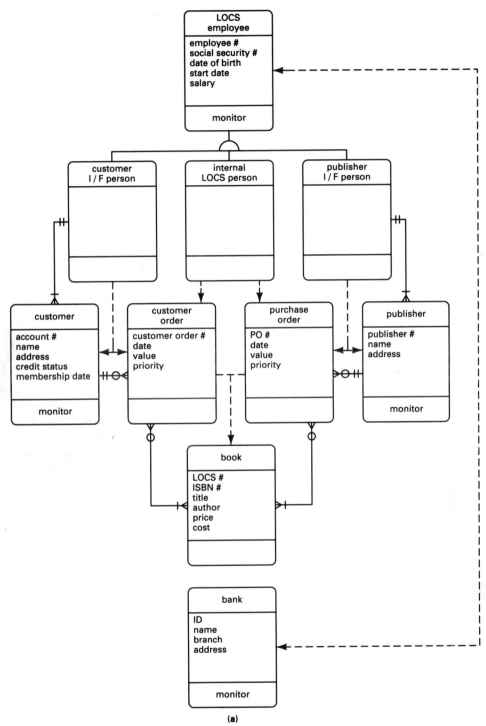

(a)

Figure 2–60. Final OOA Model of LOCS. **(a)** with Services and Message Connections. **(b)** Subject Layer.

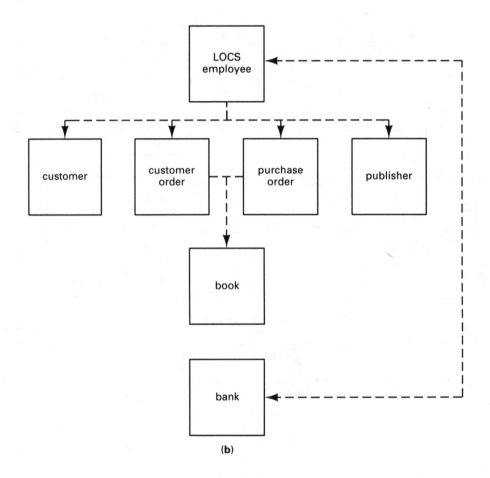

Figure 2–60. *(cont.)*

2.3.5 Applying Problem Analysis Techniques: Example 2

As defined in Section 1.5, the second example is automating the landing of courier helicopters. This problem is quite a bit more complex than the previous example, automating the book company. In fact this is a *systems* problem more than a *software* problem. As shown in Figures 1–12b and 2–10b, systems problems require system-level requirements specification and system design prior to addressing software requirements per se. When we take on the challenge of solving a brand new software problem, we cannot simply put pen to paper and write an SRS. Instead we must first understand the context, the environment, and constraints on that software. In the case of writing an SRS for software that is a component of a larger system under development, most of the software's context, environment, and constraints are explored and in fact documented during system requirements analysis, system requirements specification, and system design activities. These three activities are outside the scope of this book. On the other hand, it is impossible to proceed with the software requirements phase for the development of this helicopter landing system without knowing the results of these system-level activities. For that reason, the remainder of this section will provide a sample of system-level analysis, specification, and design results. Incidentally methodologies (and their associated tools) such as TRW's Distributed Computing Design System (DCDS) [ALF85] and Teledyne Brown's Technology for Automated Generation of Systems (TAGS) [TEL87] have been specifically built to address these system-level problems.

During the extensive system-level problem analysis, many constraints would be delineated, and many questions would be raised and resolved. Here are some

1. Will the system be based totally on the ground? Totally on the helicopter? Distributed on both platforms?
2. Where will weather information come from? Standard aviation weather reports (e.g., ATIS) are airport-, not lot-based.
3. What will activate the automated landing system? A button pressed by the pilot? Detection of an unstable attitude and configuration (indicating, for example, an unconscious pilot)? Detection of extreme weather conditions?
4. How will a pilot inform the system of which vacant building lot is the desired landing point?
5. What are the reliability requirements? Will the software need to detect hardware faults? What will the software do then? Reconfigure the hardware? Notify the (unconscious?) pilot?
6. What happens if two helicopters want to land at the same vacant lot?

7. Heavy fog is one situation in which the automated system would land the helicopter because zero visibility would exceed the human pilot's ability to land. What weather conditions make the automated system unable to land the helicopter (e.g., gale-force winds)? Who or what detects these excessive conditions and turns off the automated system? Then what happens to the helicopter?

8. What are the acceptable horizontal distance tolerances for landing?

9. What are the acceptable vertical and horizontal velocity tolerances for landing?

Here are some of the assumptions that we will make that are typical of those made during system design and are necessary to know prior to performing the software requirements activity:

1. Due to the fact that there are 250 vacant lots on which helicopters may land, we will want to minimize the cost of lot-based equipment.

2. The problem of dispatching, routing, and landing multiple helicopters will require a centralized controller of some kind to provide coordination and global optimization.

3. In non-VFR weather, the helicopter will need to locate itself precisely at the lot site. A transmitter at the site will be inadequate for this purpose because tall buildings will obscure line-of-sight transmissions. Therefore unique transmitters will be placed atop key tall buildings in the city to enable helicopter sensors to detect exact directional information relative to these sources. Then the helicopter (or the central controller) can perform triangulation to determine each helicopter's exact location.

4. Once the helicopter is directly above the landing pad, the helicopter will need to approach and land accurately. This will be accomplished by a downward-pointing point source transmitter aboard the helicopter, a low-cost point source reflector on the pad, and an array of sensors arranged in three concentric rings on the belly of the helicopter capable of detecting deviations from precisely above the pad.

5. Safe approach and landing and the ability to set barometric pressure-sensitive instruments will require accurate weather data from the landing site. Therefore a barometric pressure gauge and wind speed and direction detectors will be situated at every lot. Since tall buildings will obscure transmissions of weather data from the lot to an en route helicopter, an inexpensive modem will be installed at every lot. When the centralized controller learns that a helicopter is needed at a particular lot, it will call the lot via the modem, establishing a phone connection that will remain open until the landing is complete. The centralized controller will learn about the weather conditions and relay them to the helicopter. Meanwhile

during final approach, the helicopter can receive local weather directly from the landing pad via a small inexpensive ground-based transmitter that turns itself on only after the central controller makes telephone contact with it.

The preceding assumptions were made only after much analysis. The following subsections, which demonstrate the use of SRD, SADT, and SASS, respectively, provide some insight into the early problem analyses that were performed and led to the preceding assumptions. By the way, for the purposes of this exercise, we will ignore two significant problems: (1) today's helicopter technology makes it difficult to execute a pure vertical approach and landing, and (2) it is unlikely that the FAA would approve this entire scheme because of the dangers associated with flying helicopters at low altitude in densely populated areas.

2.3.5.1 Structured requirements definition

To apply SRD, we interview each of the people who currently performs manually some aspect of what will be automated. Unfortunately in this case, the only person who fits the bill is a pilot. We could interview a pflock of Pfleeger pilots, but all would provide the same perspective. An alternative is to interview pilots, ground guides, air traffic controllers, and weatherpeople. Each of these people would certainly contribute to our overall understanding of automated helicopter landing, but these people provide perspectives from a vantage point external to the system. Thus we would not even be performing SRD. To show why this approach fails, examine Figure 2–61, which shows the perspectives from the four aforementioned vantage points.

The next steps according to SRD are to merge the perspectives and draw a dotted line around the system, resulting in Figure 2–62. When we collapse the system, we arrive right back at Figure 2–61a as a result of deleting those parts that have only second-order effects on the system (e.g., the weatherperson, radar, and visual sighting of the aircraft by the ground guide). Therefore to no surprise, SRD really did not work. We could have predicted that SRD was going to be less than effective because the essence of the helicopter landing system is not the automation of a task currently performed by a group of people manually. It is instead *performed* manually by a person serving just one role, the pilot, even though the pilot is supported by many other roles. It is the pilot's job that is to be automated, not the others' jobs.

2.3.5.2 SADT

In this subsection, I will share with you my first three attempts at analyzing this particular problem. In each case, I started with the context diagram shown in Figure 2–63.

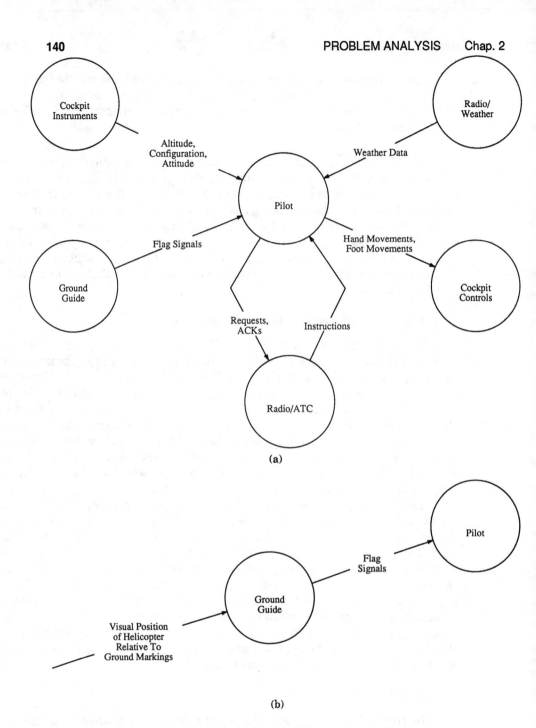

(a)

(b)

Figure 2–61. Four "Perspectives" of the Helicopter Landing Problem.
(a) Pilot Perspective. **(b)** Ground Guide Perspective. **(c)** ATC Perspective.
(d) Weatherperson Perspective.

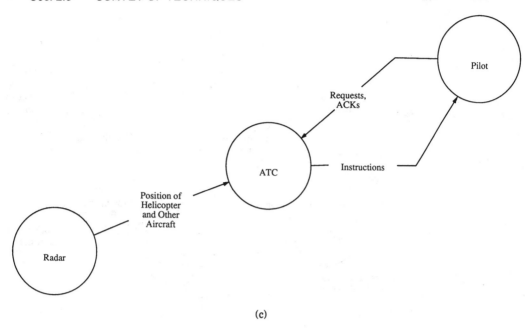

(c)

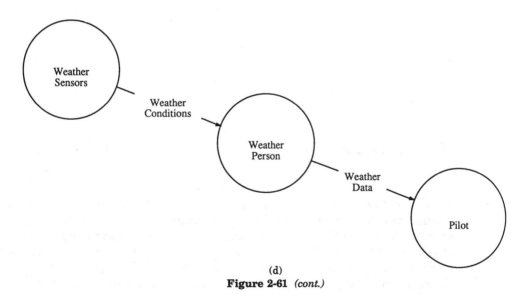

(d)

Figure 2-61 *(cont.)*

My first attempt at the analysis was based on my miniscule 10 hours of fixed-wing aircraft flight instruction. I vividly recalled how landing safely did not seem to me to be algorithmic; instead it seemed that the experienced pilot

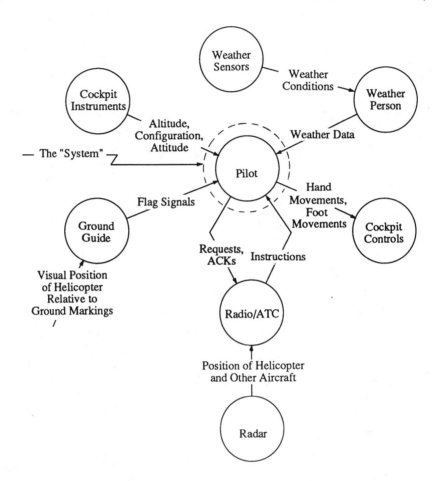

Figure 2–62. Combined Perspectives for the Helicopter Landing Problem.

simply, instinctively, automatically, quite naturally, put the aircraft on the ground, as easily as an automobile driver turns a corner. Thus thinking back to those days, I could only see the landing process as taking in all the dozens of stimuli (weather data, location of aircraft, configuration and attitude of aircraft, etc.) and quite magically converting it all into the right outputs. Therefore my first pass at the analysis resulted in just three boxes: Take in all signals, determine next move, make the move. As shown in Figure 2–64, I never progressed far enough to allocate system-level inputs and outputs; I could see right away that I had created the standard "input, process, output" triad and that all inputs would go into the first box, all outputs would come out of the

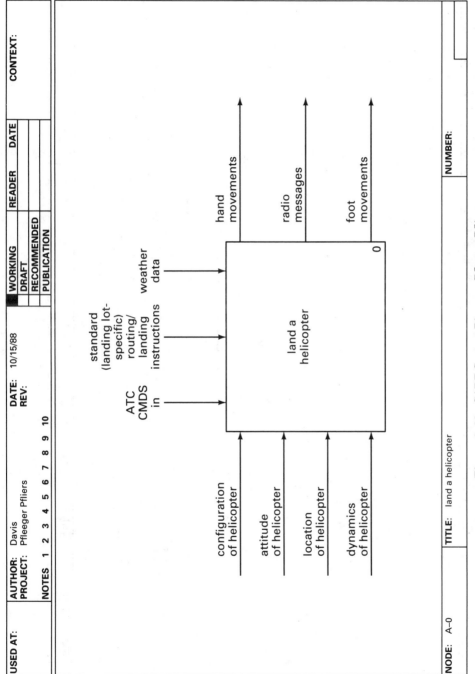

Figure 2-63. SADT Context Diagram: Pfleeger Pfliers.

143

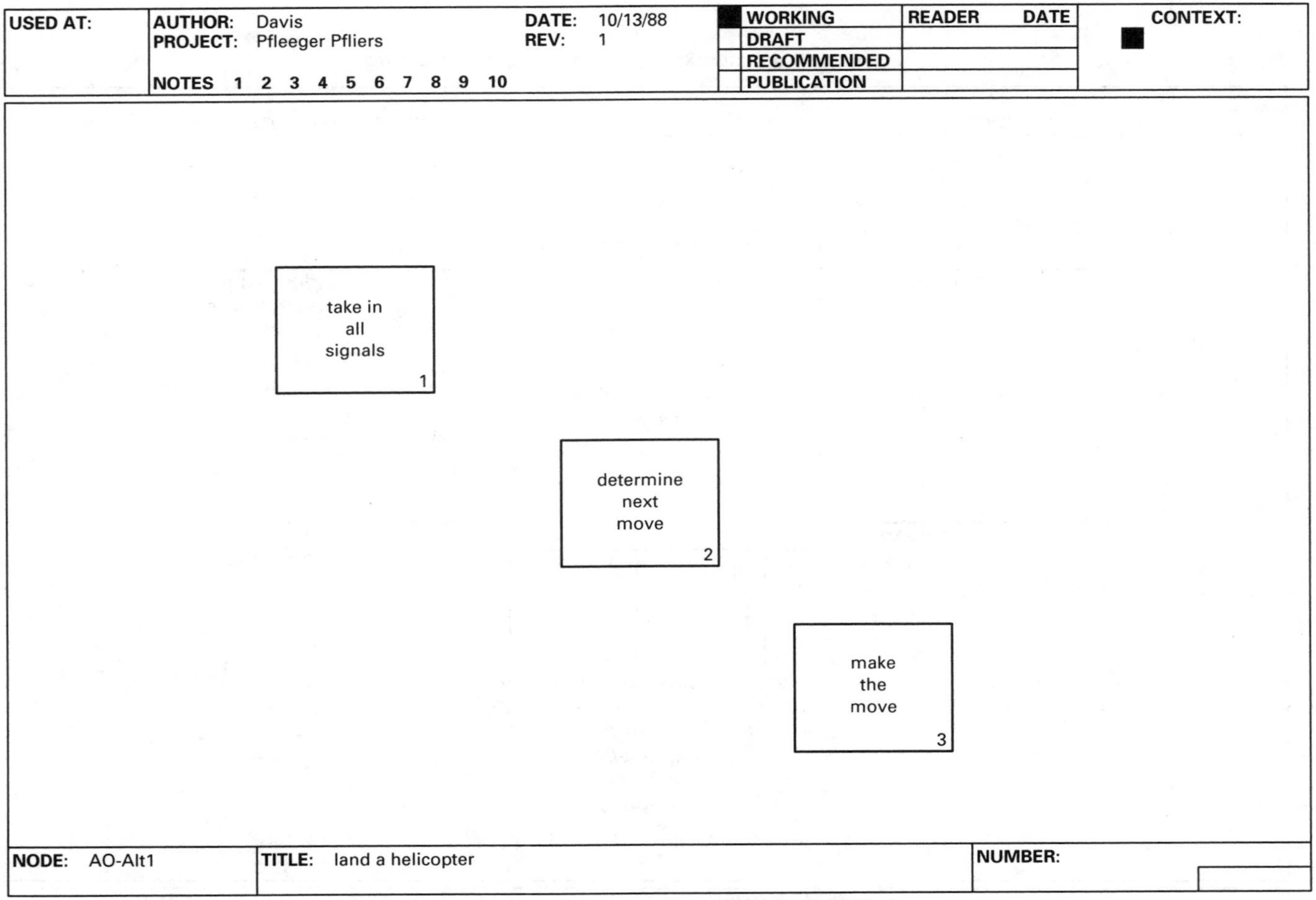

Figure 2–64. First Pfleeger Pfliers Analysis Dead End.

last box, and I would have two cascading arrows linking the three boxes like three cars on a train. I have been on this route before, so I knew that a decomposition that could be applied to *any* problem (any problem can be decomposed into input, process, output), would be ineffective at providing me with specific insight into the particular problem at hand. Thus I dropped this route with little further thought.

The next pass at analysis was somewhat more insightful. For this one, I did some serious thinking about the key goals that the pilot must keep in mind: (1) Make sure gauges are reporting data accurately, (2) make sure you are on the correct approach, and (3) keep your aircraft under control. Thus my second pass had three boxes: Adjust instruments for barometric pressure, determine and follow the optimal approach path, and maintain flight stability, as shown in Figure 2–65.[8] I next allocated each of the overall system inputs and outputs to the subproblems. Notice in this case that some inputs (e.g., dynamics of helicopter) and outputs (e.g., foot movements) are allocated to more than one box. Notice also that I needed to refine some aggregate data items (e.g., weather data) into their constituent, more primitive, data items (e.g., barometric pressure, temperature, wind speed, wind direction). After fully documenting this as Figure 2–65, I recognized that *determining* and *following* the optimal approach path are really two independent activities occurring at different times, using different inputs, and generating different outputs. I also considered these two activities at the same level of abstraction as "maintain flight stability." (I was nagged then and am still nagged now by the idea that "adjust instruments for barometric pressure" is really at a lower level of abstraction, but I have not found a convenient way of aggregating it into other functions or providing it with different descriptive words to make it sound like it is at the right level of abstraction.) I was also bothered by the generic "radio messages" output, which seemed too vague; by the loss of key air traffic controller communications, such as "requesting clearance to occupy airspace or land" and receiving such clearances or other ATC instructions. Most of these problems were solved in my third attempt, as shown in Figure 2–66, which shows the decomposition of the overall problem into five subproblems: (1) Communicate with ATC, (2) adjust instruments for barometric pressure, (3) determine optimal approach path, (4) maintain flight stability, and (5) follow approach path to target.

---

[8]The terms *stick* and *collective* are used in this and later figures for the primary controls for the helicopter pilot. In particular the stick enables the pilot to make the helicopter move forward, backward, and to the side. The collective control effects the speed of the main rotor and the pitch (or angle) of the rotor blades. These two factors (i.e., speed and pitch) *collectively* determine the amount of lift achieved by the helicopter.

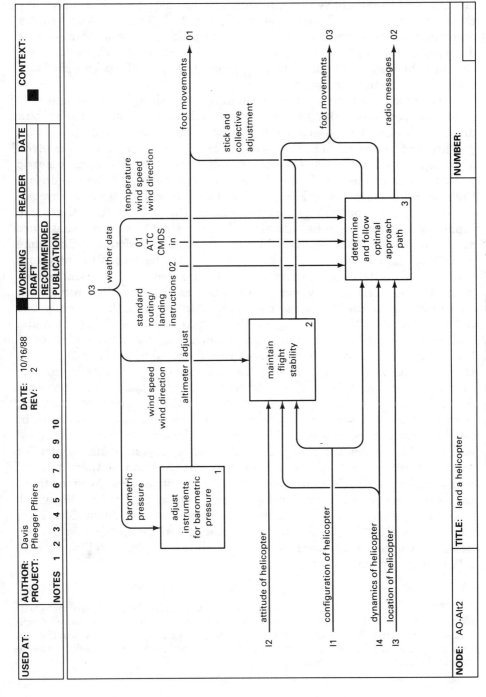

Figure 2–65. Second Pfleeger Pfliers Analysis.

146

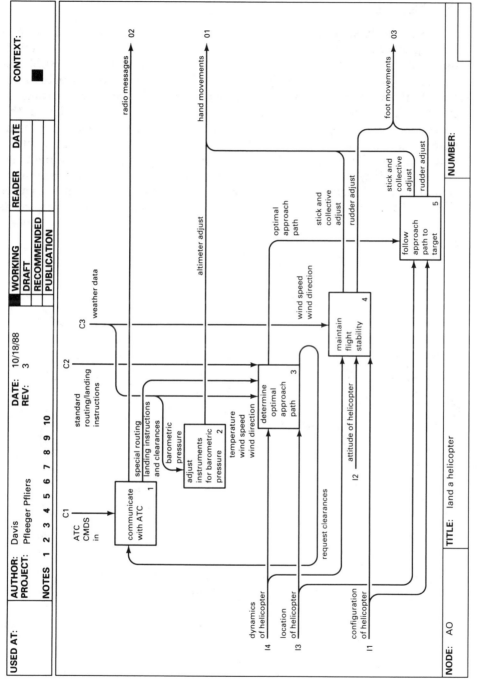

Figure 2-66. Third Pfleeger Pfliers Analysis.

147

2.3.5.3 SASS

SADT helped us understand some of the aspects of the manual helicopter landing process. SASS will help us understand some other aspects and force us to look at how the process changes with automation. According to SASS, the logical DFDs express the way things currently work from the viewpoint of the data. In the current physical DFD, bubbles represent unique organizations, or individuals. In the current logical DFD, bubbles represent activities. In this particular application, there is only one player whose activities are being automated. Therefore the current physical DFD will not be particularly helpful and is omitted. The current logical DFDs are shown in Figures 2–67 and 2–68. Notice that since we are modeling the functions of the system prior to automation and those functions are currently performed by a human pilot, Figures 2–67 and 2–68 model the pilot as part of the system and the helicopter as

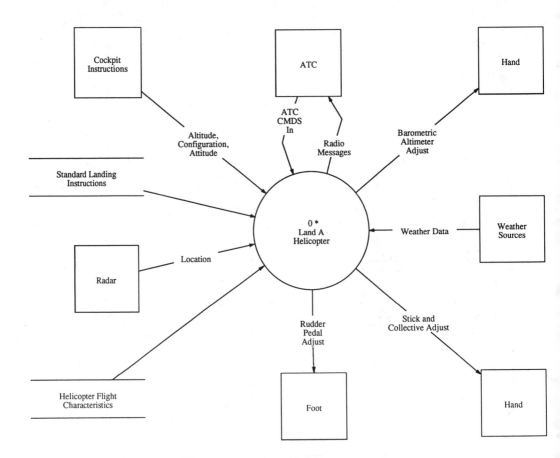

Figure 2–67. SASS Context Diagram (Current): Pfleeger Pfliers.

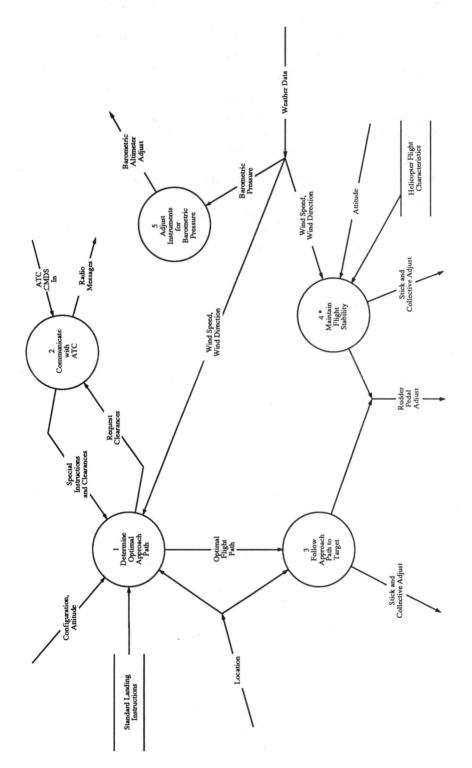

Figure 2–68. First-Level Current DFD: Pfleeger Pfliers.

149

external to the system. This might at first be a bit confusing to you if you are more accustomed to seeing DFDs used during *design,* where the DFD almost always models the machine (i.e., the helicopter) and the human is external to the DFD.

In the LOCS example, the automated system would not significantly alter the process of running the company, and we thus bypassed the new DFDs. In the case of Pfleeger Pfliers, the new system will undoubtedly make significant changes in the external interfaces and the process. Therefore it behooves us to attempt to synthesize new DFDs. Our new context diagram, shown in Figure 2–69, captures the overall system boundary and its interfaces. As mentioned earlier, this is a system problem and as such, most *software* problem analysis is performed in the context of *system* design (see Figure 2–10b). Thus our next level of decomposition should capture the results of our system design, which implies four major subsystems, as shown in Figure 2–70.

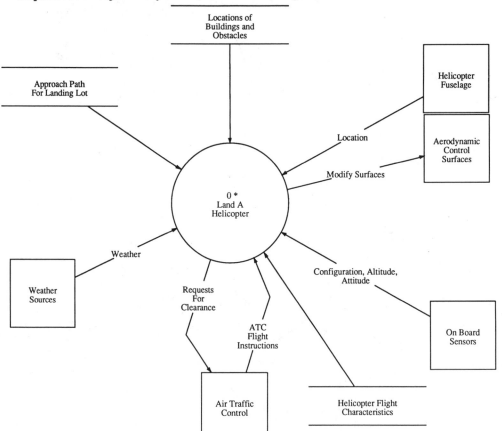

Figure 2–69. SASS Context Diagram (New): Pfleeger Pfliers.

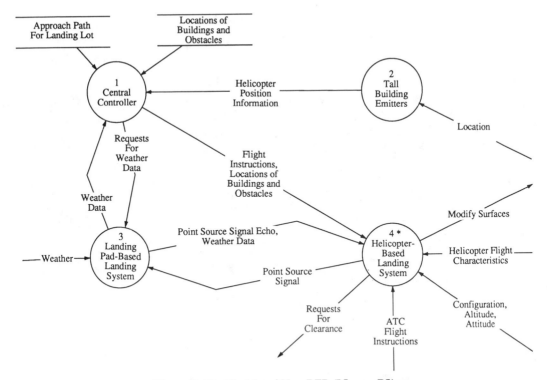

Figure 2-70. First-Level New DFD: Pfleeger Pfliers.

The Helicopter-Based Landing System, represented by the lower right bubble in Figure 2–70 contains most of the functionality associated with the automated landing system per se. Therefore let us refine it one more time to be sure we fully understand the problem. This time we can preserve the purpose of the analysis-time decomposition by optimizing it based solely on "which decomposition most helps us understand" instead of trying to worry about cost, performance, maintainability, or reliability. At this point in the analysis, I visualize four main subfunctions: Mission Acquisition, Determine Exact Current Location, Sense Current Helicopter Status, and Modify Helicopter Status, shown in Figure 2–71. The purpose of Mission Acquisition is to find out what we are trying to accomplish for this helicopter; Determine Exact Current Location uses the downward-pointing point source on the helicopter, the reflector on the ground, and the three-ring array of sensors on the helicopter's belly to determine its exact position relative to the lot; Sense Current Helicopter Status ascertains the helicopter's situation relative to achieving its mission and its degree of stability; Modify Helicopter Status manipulates the aerodynamic surfaces of the helicopter (i.e., engine power,

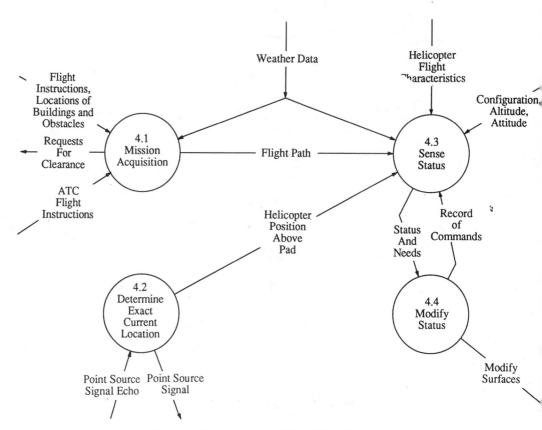

Figure 2–71. Second-Level New DFD: Pfleeger Pfliers.

main rotor blade pitch, tail rotor power, and tail rotor pitch) in order to make the helicopter achieve its mission.

Determining whether or not we have been successful in performing this problem analysis should be based on whether or not we now understand and appreciate the expected functions and behavior of an automated helicopter landing system. If we do, then we have succeeded. Otherwise we should continue the decomposition process in order to generate additional levels of detail. The data dictionaries for the current (i.e., Figures 2–67 and 2–68) and new DFDs (i.e., Figures 2–69 through 2–71) are shown in Figures 2–72 and 2–73, respectively.

2.3.5.4 Object-oriented problem analysis

To apply Coad's Object-Oriented Analysis (OOA) technique, we start by defining the objects present in the problem domain. The first place to look for candidates is in other systems. Some candidates are the helicopter itself and

	Data Flows			
Name	**Generated By**	**Used By**	**Description/Purpose**	**Form**
Altitude	Cockpit Instruments	Determine Optimal Approach Path	Helicopter's height in feet above sea level.	height
ATC CMDS In	ATC	Communicate with ATC	Radio Messages from ATC.	
Attitude	Cockpit instruments	Maintain Flight Stability	The degrees of roll and pitch of the helicopter.	roll + pitch
Barometric Altimeter Adjust	Adjust Instruments for Barometric Pressure	Hand	Physical hand adjustment of instrument.	
Barometric Pressure	Weather Sources	Adjust Instruments for Barometric Pressure	Current barometric pressure at landing site.	{ numeric digit }
Commands			A message to turn left or right or increase or decrease altitude at a location or at a time.	["left" | "right" | "up" | "down"] + [direction | height] + [location | time]
Configuration	Cockpit Instruments	Determine Optimal Approach Path	Positions of major aerodynamic surfaces and landing gear of helicopter.	
Direction			N = 0°, E = 90°, S = 180°, W = 270°.	{ numeric digit }
Direction from Benchmark			The direction (N = 0°, E = 90°, S = 180°, W = 270°) from a fixed location in the city.	direction
Distance			In feet.	{ numeric digit }
Distance from Benchmark			Helicopter's distance in feet from a fixed location in the city.	distance
Height			In feet above sea level	{ numeric digit }
Location			Number of feet latitudinally and longitudinally relative to a fixed benchmark location in the city.	{ numeric digit } + { numeric digit }
Location	Radar	Determine Optimal Approach Path and Follow Approach Path to Target	Helicopter's current position relative to a fixed location in the city.	Distance from benchmark + direction from benchmark
Optimal Flight Path	Determine Optional Approach Path	Follow Approach Path to Target	A trajectory from here to landing site	{ command }
Pitch			The degree of tilt forward/backward (between −90° and +90°)	signed numeric digit + (numeric digit)
Radio Messages	Communicate with ATC	ATC	Radio messages to ATC.	

Figure 2–72. Data Dictionary for Current DFD: Pfleeger Pfliers.

	Data Flows			
Name	Generated By	Used By	Description/Purpose	Form
Relative Humidity			At landing site.	{ numeric digit }
Request Clearances	Determine Optimal Approach Path	Communicate with ATC	Once we determine best path, this is a request of ATC to follow each step	command
Roll			The degree of tilt to the left or right (between −90° and + 90°)	signed numeric digit + (numeric digit)
Rudder Pedal Adjust	Follow Approach Path to Target and Maintain Flight Stability	Foot	A physical adjustment of foot pedal to change the tail rotor speed or pitch.	
Special Instructions and Clearances	Communicate with ATC	Determine Optimal Approach Path	Confirmations and denials for requested clearances and other flight commands.	{ command }
Stick and Collective Adjust	Follow Approach Path to Target and Maintain Flight Stability	Hand	A physical adjustment to two hand controls to modify roll, pitch, or vertical velocity.	
Temperature			In farenheit at landing site.	{ numeric digit }
Time			Using 24 hour notation.	numeric digit + numeric digit + numeric digit + numeric digit
Visibility			In feet at landing site.	distance
Weather Data	Weather Sources	Land a Helicopter	The weather at the landing site.	temperature + relative humidity + barometric pressure + wind speed + wind direction + visibility
Wind Direction	Weather Sources	Determine Optimal Approach Path and Maintain Flight Stability	Direction of wind at the landing site.	direction
Wind Speed	Weather Sources	Determine Optimal Approach Path and Maintain Flight Stability	Speed of wind at the landing site.	{ numeric digit }

Figure 2–72. *(cont.)*

154

	Data Flows			
Name	**Generated By**	**Used By**	**Description/Purpose**	**Form**
Altitude	On Board Sensors	Sense Status	Helicopter's height in feet above sea level.	height
ATC Flight Instructions	ATC	Mission Acquisition	Digitized radio messages from ATC to turn left or right or increase or decrease altitude.	{ command }
Attitude	On Board Sensors	Sense Status	The degrees of roll and pitch of the helicopter.	roll + pitch
Command			A message to turn left or right or increase or decrease altitude at a location or at a time.	["left" | "right" | "up" |"down"] + [direction | height] + [location | time]
Configuration	On Board Sensors	Sense Status	Positions of major aerodynamic surfaces and landing gear of helicopter.	
Control Surface Modification			A command to modify the state of some helicopter control surface.	surface + ["increase" | "decrease"] + { numeric digit }
Direction			N = 0°, E = 90°, S = 180°, W = 270°.	{ numeric digit }
Direction Data	Helicopter Fuselage	Tall Building Emitters	Signals bounced back from the fuselage to emitter/sensors on the tall buildings tell the system what direction the helicopter is relative to that building. (N = 0°, E = 90°, S = 180°, W = 270°)	direction
Distance			In feet.	{ numeric digit }
Flight Instructions	Central Controller	Mission Acquisition	Digitized radio messages from the landing system's central controller and scheduler to turn left or right or increase or decrease altitude.	{ command }
Flight Path	Mission Acquisition	Sense Status	A series of commands that define the desired path for the helicopter.	{ command }
Height			In feet above sea level.	{ numeric digit }
Helicopter Position Above Pad	Determine Exact Current Location	Sense Status	The exact distance and direction of the helicopter relative to the center of the landing pad.	distance + relative direction
Helicopter Position Information	Tall Building Emitters	Central Controller	Exact location of each helicopter	location
Location			Number of feet latitudinally and longitudinally relative to a fixed benchmark location in the city.	{ numeric digit } + { numeric digit }
Locations of Buildings and Obstacles	Central Controller	Mission Acquisition	Digitized information concerning exact locations and heights of all nearby buildings or other impediments to flight.	
Modify Surfaces	Modify Status	Aerodynamic Control Surfaces	Commands to servomotors to move the actual control surfaces of the helicopter.	

Figure 2–73. Data Dictionary for New DFD: Pfleeger Pfliers.

	Data Flows			
Name	**Generated By**	**Used By**	**Description/Purpose**	**Form**
Pitch			The degree of tilt forward or backward (between −90° and +90°).	signed numeric digit + (numeric digit)
Point Source Signal	Determine Exact Current Location	Landing-Pad Based Landing System	Signal from the belly of the helicopter to be reflected off the point source reflector located on landing pad.	
Point Source Signal Echo	Landing-Pad Based Landing System	Determine Exact Current Location	The point source signal bounced back to the 3-ring array of sensors on the helicopter's belly.	
Record of Commands	Modify Status	Sense Status	A handshake acknowledging the movement of a control surface.	{ control surface modification } + "completed"
Relative Direction			Forward = 0°; Right = 90°, Back = 180°, Left = 270°.	{ numeric digit }
Relative Humidity			At the landing site.	{ numeric digit }
Requests for Clearance	Mission Acquisition	ATC	Digitized radio messages from the landing system to ATC to turn left or right or increase or decrease altitude.	"request permission to" + command
Requests for Weather Data	Central Controller	Landing-Pad Based Landing System	A phone call over modems to the landing site (computer to computer).	
Roll			The degree of tilt to the left or right (between −90° and +90°).	signed numeric digit + (numeric digit)
Sensor Signals	Tall Building Emitters	Helicopter Fuselage	Signals from the tall building to be reflected off the helicopter to determine its location.	
Status and Needs	Sense Status	Modify Status	Requests to move aerodynamic control surfaces of helicopter.	{ control surface modification }
Surface			Any of the aerodynamic control surfaces of the helicopter.	["main rotor speed" | "tail rotor speed" | "main rotor blade pitch angle (forward)" | "main rotor blade pitch angle (rear)" | "main motor blade pitch angle (right)" | "main motor blade pitch angle (left)"]
Temperature			In farenheit at the landing site.	{ numeric digit }
Time			Using 24-hour notation.	numeric digit + numeric digit + numeric digit + numeric digit
Visibility			In feet at the landing site.	distance

Figure 2–73. *(cont.)*

| Name | Data Flows | | Description/Purpose | Form |
	Generated By	Used By		
Weather	Weather Sources	Landing-Pad Based Landing System	The weather at the landing site.	temperature + relative humidity + barometric pressure + wind speed + wind direction + visibility
Weather Data	Landing-Pad Based Landing System	Central Controller and Mission Acquisition and Sense Status	Current weather conditions at landing site.	weather
Wind Direction			At the landing site.	direction
Wind Speed			In knots at the landing site.	{ numeric digit }

Figure 2–73. *(cont.)*

its control surfaces, air traffic control and weather sources. The next set of candidates for objects includes things that must be remembered by the system. Some candidates are weather conditions at the landing site, sequences of flight commands, and current configuration, altitude, attitude, and position of the helicopter. In the category of roles played, the pilot is the obvious candidate. Air traffic controllers could also have been considered had their essence not already been captured in "air traffic control" as an external system. Location objects include the exact location of the landing site. In itemizing descriptive catalogs, obvious candidates for objects are the exact locations of *all* landing sites (which subsume the previously defined object of the exact location of the *current* landing site), locations of all buildings and obstacles, and flight characteristics of the current helicopter. Thus our first pass at object definition is shown in Figure 2–74.

As we examine Figure 2–74, a number of anomalies quickly surface:

- Configuration, altitude, attitude, and position of the helicopter *are* things to be remembered but seem to be more like attributes of the helicopter than objects themselves. Let us make them attributes.

- Flight characteristics of a helicopter also seem to be more like attributes of the helicopter and less like objects themselves.

- Weather sources and weather conditions arose from two different types of questions in the object definition process. However, an object called weather with some well-defined attributes could be more meaningful.

- Although the *location* of sites and buildings and obstacles appears to be the only things we need to know at this point, it may be helpful to call the objects simply site and obstacle (including building) and give them suitable attributes.

The resulting refined list of objects is shown in Figure 2–75.

The next step is to add two types of structure to the model: classification and assembly. We should first check the model for any structures that may exist between existing objects. No obvious classification structures exist. Concerning assembly structures, however, a control surface is clearly part of a helicopter. This should cause us to think about other parts of a helicopter that should be included in the model. How about flight controls? Radio? Cockpit instruments? On-board sensors? These may all be useful, so let us add them to our model. Are there sets of other existing objects that can be grouped together into a more abstract object? It does not seem so. Are there objects present that need to be refined into less abstract, more primitive objects? Once again the answer is probably no. The result is Figure 2–76.

Like the previous example, the complexity of this model also is not greatly reduced by defining a subject layer. The only obvious new subject is the helicopter, whose inclusion allows us to eliminate the five parts of the helicop-

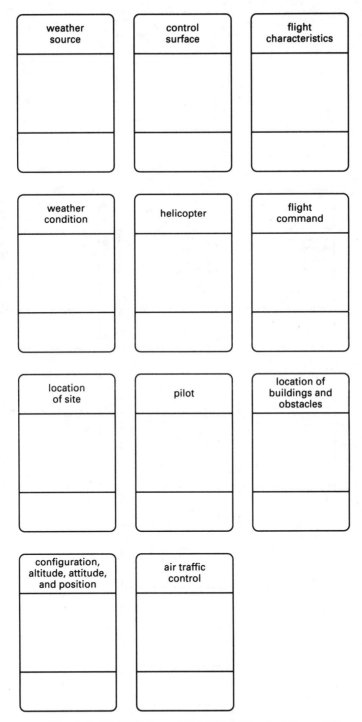

Figure 2–74. First Pass at Object Definition for Pfleeger Pfliers

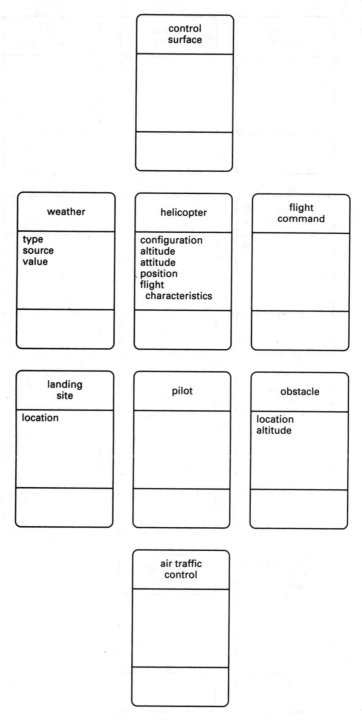

Figure 2-75. Refined Object Definition for Pfleeger Pfliers.

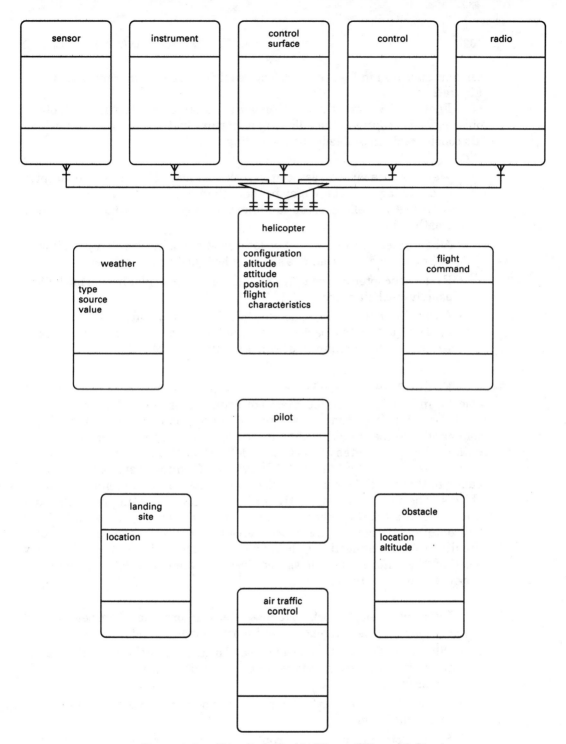

Figure 2–76. Object Definition for Pfleeger Pfliers with Structure.

ter that appeared in Figure 2–76. The resulting subject diagram is shown in Figure 2–77.

Figure 2–78 shows the remaining attributes associated with each of the objects. It also captures the following important instance connections, which aid considerably in problem understanding:

- Weather data must be associated with (i.e., sensed by) either a helicopter or a landing site. There may be more than one item of weather data per source. Any helicopter or landing site may exist without associated weather data.

- A helicopter may or may not be located at a landing site, but if so, it may be at only one, and that one site may hold just one helicopter.

- Every helicopter has exactly one pilot, and every pilot in this model has exactly one helicopter.

- Air traffic control may issue multiple flight commands, each one associated uniquely with a particular helicopter. However helicopters can exist without flight commands, as can air traffic control.

Figure 2–79a summarizes all necessary services performed by the objects and their associated message connections. First "occur" services exist for all objects that may have instances added (e.g., a new flight command may be issued, a new instrument added to the cockpit, a new building built as a potential obstacle), deleted, modified, tested, or selected. There are no specific "calculate" services. "Monitor" services were next added to three of the objects to reflect their active role in monitoring other objects: The pilot "listens" to the radio, "observes" the instruments, and "monitors" the weather, obstacles, etc.; air traffic control "monitors" all the helicopters, weather, etc.; and the sensors "monitor" their environment. Finally message connections, shown as dotted arrows in Figure 2–79a show most of the information flows required between objects to enable the services to be performed:

- Instruments in the cockpit request status information from sensors and control surfaces and report that information to the pilot.

- Pilots use their hands and feet to "send messages" to the aircraft controls, which in turn send messages to the aircraft control surfaces to modify themselves.

- The weather is regularly reported to the helicopter weather sensors and to air traffic control.

- Both pilots and air traffic controllers may make queries concerning information about landing sites and obstacles.

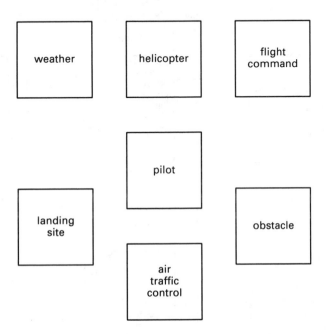

Figure 2–77. OOA Subject Layer for Pfleeger Pfliers.

- Both pilots and air traffic controllers may make requests of the radio to transmit messages and the radio may alert both pilots and air traffic controllers of available messages.

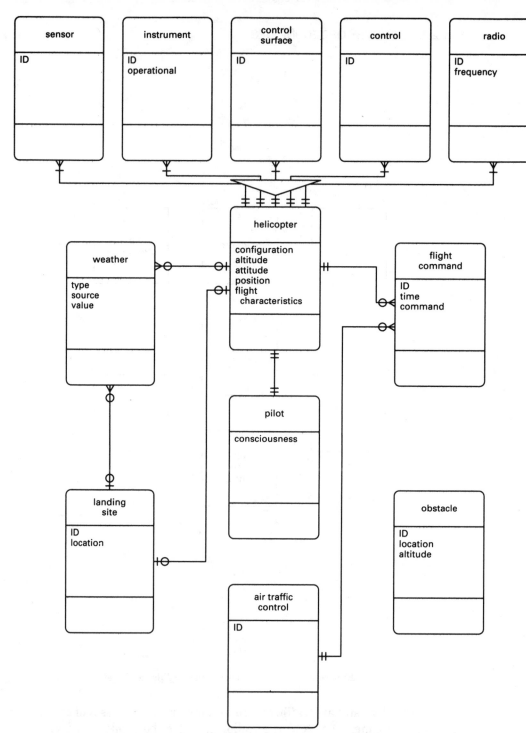

Figure 2-78. OOA Model for Pfleeger Pfliers with Attributes and Instance Connections.

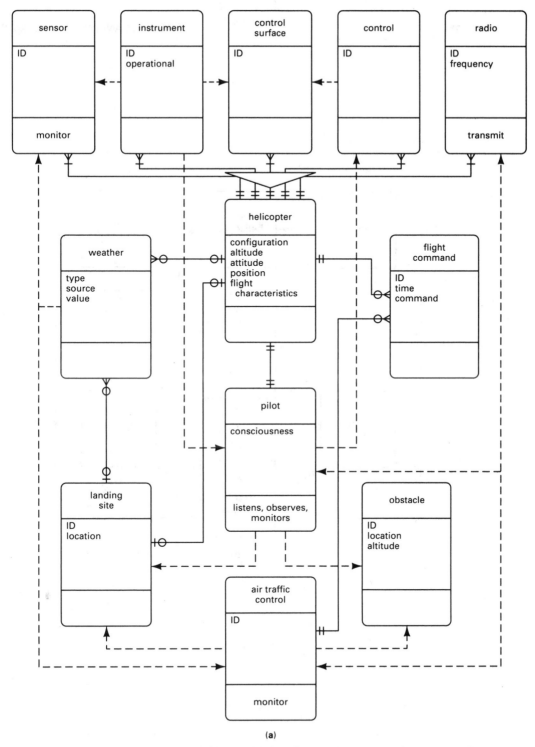

Figure 2–79. Final OOA Model for Pfleeger Pfliers. **(a)** with Services and Message Connections. **(b)** Subject Layer.

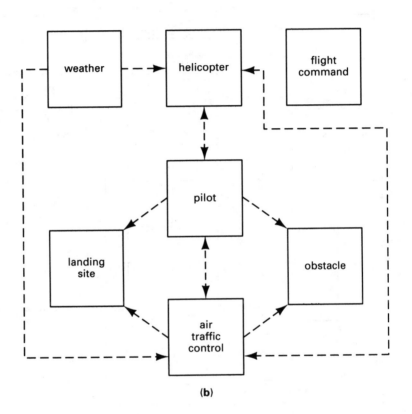

(b)

Figure 2–79. *(cont.)*

Figure 2–79b shows the final subject diagram with the message connections.

2.3.6 Applying Problem Analysis Techniques: Example 3

As defined in Section 1.5, the third example is the problem of transporting people from New York to Tokyo in 30 minutes. This problem is orders of magnitude more complex than either of the two preceding problems. Using *any* technique, it will be almost impossible to ascertain even the overall system inputs and outputs. Certainly SRD will be ineffective because we cannot interview people who currently transport people between New York and Tokyo manually. Similarly using SADT or SASS to model how people are currently transported from New York to Tokyo will at best be only marginally helpful. It is true that understanding current transportation methods (i.e., ship and aircraft) may shed some light on the problem, but I suspect that a system to transport people in 30 minutes will have little in common with existing methods. Modeling existing transportation methods would at best lead us to two dead ends; namely, a super-fast airplane and a super-fast ship. So, what do we do?

The right approach is to begin maintaining a knowledge structure, as described in Section 2.2. At the root of the structure is the general statement of the problem, i.e., transporting people from New York to Tokyo in 30 minutes. Now we start an extensive exploratory process including feasibility analyses and demonstrations; prototype construction and experimentation; and interviewing experts in transportation, materials, geology, space travel, atomic physics, time travel, quantum mechanics, bridge construction, earth plate dynamics, etc. Each time we learn something new, we place it somewhere in the knowledge tree. A good start in the tree construction may be to define four primary trunks growing out of the root, corresponding to the four general approaches defined in Figure 1–26: (1) space shuttle approach, (2) tunnel approach, (3) bullet train approach, and (4) "beam me up, Scottie" approach.

The next step may be to establish four independent analysis teams to explore the four alternatives. This would make sense only if we expected little overlap between the knowledge needed to demonstrate understanding and feasibility of the approaches. Let us follow the escapades now of each of these four teams. Remember that the real goal of each team is to prove or disprove the feasibility of the approach.

2.3.6.1 The space shuttle approach

Some of the questions to which I want to have answers are:

1. What are the population and environmental impacts of a space shuttle launch from near New York City? What must be done to reduce those impacts?

2. Assuming the presence of a space shuttle launch pad near New York City, a suitable landing facility in Tokyo, and existing space shuttle technology, how long would a trip from New York to Tokyo take?

3. If longer than 30 minutes, what must be done to reduce that time? At launch? During suborbit? During landing?

4. What are the safety considerations? What must be done to improve safety?

5. What is the demand for the service? How many space shuttle crafts would be needed to provide enough seats (include maintenance time)? How many passengers can be transported on existing shuttle craft? If insufficient, then we may need to redesign an entirely new vehicle. If so, (a) What are passenger capacity requirements? (b) What price are passengers willing to pay? (c) What will the life span of a vehicle be? How long is an acceptable amortization schedule? (d) How will the new vehicle be launched? How will it land? (e) At what speed must the craft travel? Is this feasible? (f) What new technologies must be developed? Materials? Fuels? Engines? Reliability? Wings?

And there are hundreds or even thousands of other equally basic questions.

In short I could imagine 18 to 24 months of asking basic questions in an attempt to bound the alternatives. The problem analysis would end when the domain was well understood. As shown in Figure 2–80, I suspect that some of the primary determinants are going to be development cost, safety, passenger throughput, acceptable speed, and laws of physics. Feasibility is determined by whether or not the shaded area is finitely positive.

2.3.6.2 The tunnel approach

For this approach, there is an entirely different set of questions to ask:

1. Do we have the digging apparatus to build such a tunnel?

2. What temperatures would be encountered?

3. What pressures will exist on the walls of the tunnel?

4. How long would it take to dig? At what cost?

5. What types of life support and safety are required for the digging staff?

6. Assuming the shaft could be dug, what type of vehicle (elevator cab) is required?

7. What speed would it reach using only gravity as the power source? How much of a vacuum would be necessary? Will this be sufficient to achieve the 30-minute transit time?

8. How much further than the center of the tunnel would the vehicle continue to travel before all its kinetic energy dissipates? What power

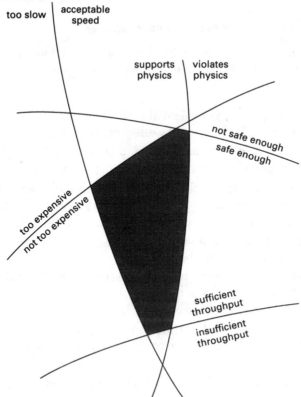

Figure 2–80. Space Shuttle Problem Analysis.

sources will be needed to continue the vehicle's movement beyond that point?

9. What types of life support and safety are required for the passengers?

10. As the vehicle falls, how will we prevent it from hitting the walls? Frictionless rails? Air cushion? Initially correct trajectory plus immobile passengers?

11. How can we allow two-way traffic? (Oh-oh, there's a tough one!)

12. Over what period of time can the tunnel cost be amortized? What will maintenance costs be? Will cost per passenger be practical?

13. Where do we put the tunnel effluent as we dig? Can we do something useful with it?

As in the space shuttle approach, I could once again imagine spending 18 to 24 months asking basic questions.

2.3.6.3 The bullet train approach

For this approach, a different set of questions must be asked; however, there is considerable overlap between these questions and the tunnel approach's questions:

1. Do we have the physical ability to float stable platforms on the ocean for the tracks? What are the effects of weather?
2. What are effects on marine and land fauna by the tracks?
3. How long would it take to construct the tracks? At what cost?
4. Assuming the tracks could be constructed, what type of "train" is required? How do we achieve necessary speeds? Fuel? Engines?
5. Will this be sufficient to achieve the 30-minute transit time?
6. What types of life support and safety are required for the passengers? What G forces will be present?
7. As the train moves, how will we reduce friction with its rail(s)? Frictionless rails? Air cushion?
8. How can we allow two-way traffic?
9. Over what period of time can the track construction cost be amortized? What will maintenance costs be? Will cost per passenger be practical?

Once again, it looks like 18 to 24 months of heavy questioning.

2.3.6.4 The "beam me up, Scottie" approach

This approach has an entirely different set of questions to ask and answer:

1. Can we decompose a person into a set of bits?
2. How many bits are required to store all the information sufficient to define all a human's atoms and their configuration? How long will the encoding process take?
3. To achieve 30-minute transit time, what is the required bandwidth?
4. Can we achieve the necessary bandwidth? At what frequency? Via satellite?
5. Given that we can achieve the bandwidth, do we have the ability to decode the digital data stream and reconstruct the human? What pool of raw materials is necessary? Atoms? Molecules? How long will the decoding process take?
6. What are the implications of the process for other purposes beside transportation? Surgery? Limb replacement? Creating "perfect" humans? Space travel?

7. What are the safety considerations? What happens to the atoms in the passenger's immediate environment during encoding?

8. What can go wrong and what are the implications? Power loss? Noisy transmission? A fly on the passenger's nose?

9. Where is the essence (soul? consciousness?) of the person during transport? Are thoughts themselves captured, frozen, transmitted, and thawed, so that passengers perceive nothing other than a blink of an eye and "poof!" they are in Tokyo?

2.3.6.5 Summary

The problem analysis techniques described in this chapter aid in organizing and documenting the analysis process. They may also provide some general insights into how to approach a problem. However, they do not perform the analysis itself. Thus for really difficult problems, such as this one, the techniques can successfully be used to document the analysis results but cannot compensate for the fact that a successful analysis has not been done at this time. Because of the complexity of this particular problem, and the fact that it has yet to be solved, it will be mentioned again only briefly in Chapter 4.

2.3.7 Comparison of Techniques

In Section 2.3.1, six ideal traits of a problem analysis technique were given:

1. Facilitate communication (probably via an easy-to-understand language)
2. Provide a means of defining the system boundary
3. Provide a means of defining partitions, abstractions, and projections
4. Encourage the analyst to think and document in terms of the problem (i.e., the application) as opposed to the solution (i.e., the software)
5. Allow for opposing alternatives but alert the analyst to their presence
6. Make it easy for analysts to modify the knowledge tree

The following paragraphs discuss to what extent SRD, SADT, SASS, PSL/PSA, and OOA exhibit these traits.

In 1984, I would have claimed that SRD, SADT, and SASS were non-friendly; the data flow diagrams that they employed were difficult for non-computer-oriented personnel to understand. However, I have now worked with hundreds of specialists in medicine, weapons, telephony, manufacturing, logistics, aviation, construction, and management, who have little understanding or appreciation for computers, and I have found that with very few exceptions, they can understand a set of well-written (i.e., using the customers' terminology) problem analysis data flow diagrams. The same is probably true for OOA, but there exists much less experience to verify it. Incidentally the AIRMICS branch of the U.S. Army [CEL83] found PSL/PSA easier to understand than REVS (see Section 4.2.2.5) but harder to understand than IORL [EVE80].

For a tool or technique to enable the analyst to define the system boundary means that there should be an explicit way of saying that *this* entity belongs to the system or to its environment and *that* attribute describes the system or describes its environment. Although none of the techniques provide that specific function overtly, SADT, SASS, and PSL/PSA all permit the analyst either to model the system separately from its environment or to start the analysis with two bubbles: the system and its environment. From that point on, it becomes quite clear what is in the system and what is not. Of course be aware that during much of the problem analysis activities, we may not know or care what the system boundary is. However by the time the entire requirements phase is complete, we must know. Yourdon [YOU89] specifically recommends deferring this decision until construction of the user implementation model, part of the SRS. OOA also appears to discourage this early definition of the system boundary, although the software solution's structure so well parallels the real world that it may not matter.

Concerning the techniques' abilities to define partitions, abstractions, and projections, SRD appears to provide no real means of defining partitions or abstractions. At first glance, it appears to be perfect for defining projections; after all, SRD is little more than the process of asking people for their perspectives of a system. However, I do not believe that SRD has much in common with projection, because a projection is a set of contrasting views of the system from external viewpoints, just like Figures 2–8 and 2–9; people interviewed during SRD all offer internal viewpoints—in effect they are part of the system (see Figure 2–81). This is not meant to be a criticism of SRD; SRD works very well when automating tasks currently performed manually, but it does not offer the projection trait. SASS, SADT, PSL/PSA and OOA all provide abstraction and partitioning as basic aspects of their methodologies; however only OOA provides unique notation to differentiate them. Only SADT specifically recognizes and encourages multiple external viewpoints [ROS77a], i.e., projection.

The next trait is probably the most important trait of any problem analysis technique: It should encourage the analyst to think and document in terms of the problem not the solution; i.e., it should help the analyst avoid falling into design (see Section 2.3.1 for a thorough discussion of why this is so bad). Unfortunately most of the techniques fare poorly in this category. DeMarco's structured analysis (without Ward's or Yourdon's methodological extensions), SADT, and PSL/PSA are all notoriously poor in this regard. The

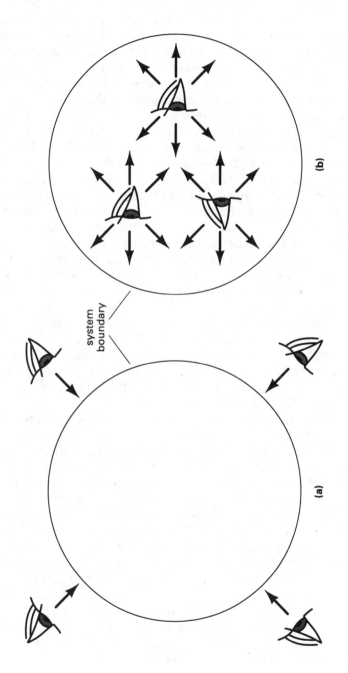

Figure 2–81. Projection versus SRD. **(a)** Projection Viewpoints. **(b)** SRD Viewpoints.

explanation for this is that these techniques have been developed as both problem analysis *and* design techniques. After all, decomposing stuff into sub-stuff is independent of the stuff. All three of these techniques are used often by people for design who claim to be doing requirements and either declare the techniques to be ineffective or valuable far beyond an intended level. Two particular experimenters published papers describing their frustrations. In both cases, the authors were attempting to compare the relative effectiveness of two requirements tools. In the case of Furia [FUR79], Grumman was comparing PSL/PSA to REVS (which is like comparing apples and oranges—their purposes are almost entirely disjoint). In the case of Dooley [DOO80], Babcock and Wilcox was comparing SADT to REVS (also apples and oranges). Dooley was even so bold as to declare that design and code were trivial after using SADT. Of course design was trivial; they had already performed design during the requirements phase. The Ward [WAR85] and Yourdon [YOU89] extensions to DeMarco's structured analysis, which emphasize creating an essential model using context diagrams, event lists, and upward leveling, do assist tremendously in keeping you at the correct level. In contrast, users of SRD and OOA rarely fall into design. In the case of SRD as described herein, the methodology is limited to interviewing working personnel and recording their observations on paper in their terminology, thus keeping the initial problem analysis in the problem domain. However, subsequent stages of SRD not explained in this book strongly discourage the analyst from remaining in the problem domain. In the case of OOA, it appears relatively straightforward to ensure that your objects, attributes, connections, and structures remain in the problem domain. However, regardless of which technique you use, human discipline is the best way of guaranteeing that you stay out of the design domain.

Opposing alternatives should be recordable during a problem analysis session; a user-oriented technique would permit this conflict but alert you to its presence. This trait is more a function of the particular tool implementation than the raw technique itself. All of the automated tools for SASS, SADT or PSL/PSA have consistency-checking capabilities. It is obviously impossible for a tool to differentiate between an intentional inconsistency (used to record a tentative disagreement between individuals) and an unintentional inconsistency (caused by error). PSL/PSA does deserve special points here for its extensive reporting capabilities and flexibility. In the AIRMICS experiment [CEL83], PSL/PSA reported 115 inconsistencies in the data it processed.

Finally the ease of modifying problem analysis information is directly related to the user orientation of the automated tools. As mentioned earlier, SADT, SASS, and PSL/PSA have all been automated.

In conclusion, different techniques are applicable to different types of applications. Figure 2–82 shows, in general, this relationship (see Section 1.4 for definitions of the applications types).

Techniques	Application Attributes				
	EA/HA	ST/DY	SE/PA	DA/CO/AL	DE/ND
SRD	EA	—	—	DA	DE
SADT	—	—	—	DA/CO	—
SASS					
DeMarco (original)	—	ST	SE	DA	DE
w/Ward & Yourdon					
extensions	—	—	—	DA/CO	DE
PSL/PSA	—	ST	—	DA	DE
OORA	—	—	—	DA/CO	—

Note: "—" indicates that the technique is equally suitable to all values of the application attribute.

Figure 2–82. Applications versus Techniques.

2.4 SUMMARY

This chapter has presented a variety of representative problem analysis techniques, most of which have been automated. Each fills a particular niche in the world of problem analysis; none is a panacea. The most important item to remember is to use the right tool for the right job. While using any technique or tool, be constantly aware and driven by your goal: understanding a real problem. Do not become so involved with the intricacies of a technique or tool that you lose sight of that goal. If you are spending more time figuring out how to understand the technique than figuring out how to solve your problem, you may be using the wrong technique. When you have completed your goal and understand the problem, stop! Just because the technique says "follow these twenty-six steps" do not be lured into displacing your goal (i.e., understanding the problem) with another (i.e., following the tool).[9]

As a beginning analyst, you will need to decide consciously which tools you need and how to use them. As you gain experience this will become more and more subconscious. An analogy to carpentry is appropriate here. As an inexperienced carpenter desiring to build some furniture, you must read books about what tools you need, books about how to operate various tools, and books telling you when to use various tools. You discover that you cannot buy a solid piece of 8′ × 4′ maple and must consciously decide to construct it from pieces

---

[9]A few years ago, I was in the process of leaving a major aerospace corporation's facilities. In my attaché case were a half-dozen or so documents clearly stamped in red "COMPANY PRIVATE" (I also had authorization to be in possession of the documents). As I exited, the security guard stopped me to inspect my attaché case. He thumbed through its contents and said, "Okay. Have a nice day." Out of curiosity, I asked him what he was looking for. He responded with "cameras or tape recorders." When I finally got to my car, I burst into laughter at the situation. The guard (and perhaps the company) had completely displaced their real goal (i.e., protecting the company's secrets) with another (i.e., preventing the movement of devices that can steal the company's secrets).

of $8' \times 1'$ lumber. You try to align the four strips of wood only to discover that they are not smooth and even, and you must read about what tool is needed and how to use it. After reading about how to use a jointer/planer, you must then buy one and try it out on test specimens before subjecting your precious maple wood to its blades. Then you read about types of glues, etc., etc., etc. Everything you do must be done consciously. As an experienced carpenter desiring to build such a table, you simply do it. You buy the proper wood, smooth the surfaces, glue, and clamp it. You do not have to think about it any more than an automobile driver has to think about how to make the vehicle turn left.

When an experienced analyst is faced with a new problem, the right tools and techniques are simply selected and used, often completely subconsciously. Just as the carpenter maintains a rich set of tools, the analyst must do so, too.

EXERCISE

Gather in a group of five to fifteen people and brainstorm the issues surrounding some difficult new problem. Spend 3 to 5 hours. Rotate the responsibility of discussion leader/recorder. Record all your ideas on a flip chart, a white board, or 5×7 index cards tacked to a soft wall or large bulletin board. Emphasize the use of partitioning, abstraction, and projection. Attempt to construct a knowledge structure. You may also wish to experiment with various techniques defined in this chapter. At the end, ask yourselves if you understand the problem better. Some suggested topics are:

1. An automated barber
2. An automated home builder
3. An automated systems analyst
4. The elevator of Figure 1–27
5. The "New York to Tokyo in 30 minutes" problem.

REFERENCES

[AIR74]   Air Force Materials Laboratory. *Air Force Computer-Aided Manufacturing Master Plan,* Vol. II, Appendix A, and Vol. III. Wright Patterson Air Force Base Report AFML-TR-74-104.

[ALF85]   Alford, M. "SREM at the Age of Eight, the Distributed Design System." *IEEE Computer* **18,** 4 (April 1985): 36–46.

[BOO86] Booch, G. "Object-Oriented Development." *IEEE Transactions on Software Engineering* **12,** 2 (February 1986): 211–21.

[BOR85] Borgida, A., et al. "Knowledge Representation as the Basis for Requirements Specifications." *IEEE Computer* **18,** 4 (April 1985): 82–91.

[CEL83] Celko, J., et al. "A Demonstration of Three Requirements Language Systems." *SIGPLAN Notices* **18,** 1 (January 1983): 9–14.

[COA89] Coad, P. "OOA—Object-Oriented Analysis." In *COMPSAC '89,* Washington D.C.: Computer Society Press of the Institute of Electrical and Electronics Engineers, 1989.

[COA89a] Coad, P., and E. Yourdon. *OOA—Object-Oriented Analysis.* Englewood Cliffs, N.J.: Prentice Hall, 1989.

[CRO82] Cronhjort, B., and B. Gallmo. *A Model of the Industrial Product Development Process.* L. M. Ericsson Information System Report 1982-09-01-C-TB-BG-82010. Bromma, Sweden, 1982.

[DEM79] DeMarco, T. *Structured Analysis and System Specification.* Englewood Cliffs, N.J.: Prentice Hall, 1979.

[DOD83] U.S. Department of Defense, *Military Standard Ada Programming Language.* ANSI/MIL-STD-1815A-1983. Washington, D.C., 1983.

[DOO80] Dooley, B., et al. "Experience with Software Tools for Nuclear Process System Applications." In *IEEE COMPSAC 80,* Washington D.C.: Computer Society Press of the Institute of Electrical and Electronics Engineers, 1980. pp. 646–54.

[EDW87] Edwards, W. "Excelerator and CASE 2000 Design Aid: Management Considerations and Systems Analysis Support Tools." In *Conference on Methodologies and Tools for Real-Time Systems.* Washington, D.C.: National Institute for Software Quality and Productivity, 1987. pp. N-1–N-20.

[EVE80] Everhart, C. "A Unified Approach to Software (System) Engineering." *IEEE COMPSAC 80,* Washington, D.C.: Institute of Electrical and Electronics Engineers, 1980. pp. 49–55.

[FUR79] Furia, N. "A Comparative Evaluation of RSL/REVS and PSL/PSA Applied to a Digital Flight Control System." In *AIAA Second Computers in Aerospace Conference,* Washington D.C.: American Institute of Aeronautics and Astronautics, 1979. pp. 330–37.

[GAN79] Gane, C., and T. Sarson. *Structured Systems Analysis.* Englewood Cliffs, N.J.: Prentice-Hall, 1979.

[HAT84] Hatley, D. "The Use of Structured Methods in the Development of Large Software Based Avionics Systems." In *AIAA/IEEE Sixth Digital Avionics Systems Conference,* Washington D.C.: American Institute of Aeronautics and Astronautics, 1984. pp. 6–15.

[HAT87] Hatley, D., and I. Pirbhai. *Strategies for Real-Time System Specification.* New York: Dorset House, 1987.

[HEC86] Hecht, A., et al. "Automating Structured Analysis." *IEEE COMPSAC 86,* Washington, D.C.: Institute of Electrical and Electronics Engineers, October 1986. pp. 100–104.

[IGL85] *SPECIF-Simulation Integration Project.* Institut De Genie Logiciel Technical Publication T/0053/DT, Paris, October 1985.

[JAC75] Jackson, M. *Principles of Program Design.* Orlando, Florida: Academic Press, 1975.

[MAR88] Marca, D., and C. McGowan. *Structured Analysis and Design Technique.* New York: McGraw-Hill, 1988.

[MCG82] McGowan, C. Private correspondence. Waltham, Massachusetts, 1982.

[ORR81] Orr, K. *Structured Requirements Definition.* Ken Orr and Associates, Topeka, Kansas, 1981.

[PET87] Peterson, V. "A Case Study in the Application of the ProMod Software Development System." *Conference on Methodologies and Tools for Real-Time Systems,* Washington, D.C.: National Institute for Software Quality and Productivity, 1987. pp. P-1–P-8.

[REN82] Rentsch, T. "Object-Oriented Programming." *ACM SIGPLAN Notices* **17,** 9 (September 1982): 51–57.

[ROC82] Rockstrom, A., and R. Saracco. "SDL—CCITT Specification and Description Language." *IEEE Transactions on Communications* **30,** 6 (June 1982): 1310–1317.

[ROS85] Rosenberg, D. "PRISM—Productivity Improvement for Software Engineers and Managers." In *Eighth International Conference on Software Engineering,* Washington D.C.: Computer Society Press of the Institute of Electrical and Electronics Engineers, 1985. pp. 2–6.

[ROS77] Ross, D. "Structured Analysis (SA): A Language for Communicating Ideas." *IEEE Transactions on Software Engineering* **3,** 1 (January 1977): 16–34.

[ROS77a] Ross, D. T., and K. E. Schoman, Jr. "Structured Analysis for Requirements Definition." *IEEE Transactions on Software Engineering* **3,** 1 (January 1977): 6–15.

[ROS85] Ross, D. "Applications and Extensions of SADT." *IEEE Computer* **18,** 4 (April 1985): 25–34.

[SPS88] Software Productivity Solutions. *Computer-Aided Systems and Software Engineering Products for Time-Critical Applications Development.* Naval Air Development Center, Warminster, Pennsylvania, April 1988.

[TEI77] Teichroew, D., and E. A. Hershey III. "PSL/PSA: A Computer-Aided Technique for Structured Documentation and Analysis of Information Processing Systems." *IEEE Transactions on Software Engineering* **3,** 1 (January 1977): 41–48.

[TEL87] Teledyne Brown Engineering. *Technology for the Automated Generation of Systems (TAGS) Overview,* April 1987, Huntsville, Alabama.

[VER87] Verilog, USA, Inc. *A.S.A. Technical Presentation,* Alexandria, Virginia, October 1987.

[WAR85] Ward, P., and S. Mellor. *Structured Development for Real-Time Systems.* Englewood Cliffs, N.J.: Prentice-Hall, 1985.

[WAR86] Ward, P. "The Transformation Schema: An Extension of the Data Flow Diagram to Represent Control and Timing." *IEEE Transactions on Software Engineering* **12,** 2 (February 1986): 198–210.

[WEI82] Weinberg, G. *Rethinking Systems Analysis and Design.* Waltham, Mass.: Little and Brown, 1982; republished by New York: Dorset House, 1988.

[WIN79] Winters, E. E. "An Analysis of the Capabilities of Problem Statement Language: A Language for System Requirements and Specifications." In *IEEE COMPSAC 79,* IEEE Catalog 79-90968. Washington D.C.: Computer Society Press of the Institute of Electrical and Electronics Engineers, 1979. pp. 283–88.

[WOO88] Woodman, M. "Yourdon Data Flow Diagrams: A Tool for Disciplined Requirements Analysis." *Information and Software Technology* **30,** 9 (November 1988): 515–33.

[YEH80] Yeh, R., and P. Zave. "Specifying Software Requirements." *Proceedings of the IEEE* **68,** 9 (September 1980): 1077–1085.

[YOU79] Yourdon, E., and L. Constantine. *Structured Design.* Englewood Cliffs, N.J.: Prentice-Hall, 1979.

[YOU89] Yourdon, E. *Modern Structured Analysis.* Englewood Cliffs, N.J.: Yourdon Press, 1989.

[ZAV81] Zave, P., and R. Yeh. "Executable Requirements for Embedded Systems." In *Fifth IEEE International Conference on Software Engineering,* Washington D.C.: Computer Society Press of the Institute of Electrical and Electronics Engineers, March 1981. pp. 295–304.

3

The Software Requirements Specification

In Chapter 2 the subject of problem analysis was discussed. During problem analysis the problem is repeatedly decomposed until it is finally understood thoroughly. However, the software requirements phase is not complete until the Software Requirements Specification (SRS) has been written. Chapter 3 introduces the subject of the SRS, describes its appropriate content, explores the attributes of a well-written SRS, and offers advice on how to organize an SRS. Chapters 4 and 5 continue the discussion of the SRS, providing more details about two types of requirements that appear in an SRS: behavioral and nonbehavioral requirements.

3.1 INTRODUCTION

Before the software requirements stage is complete, an SRS must be written. The SRS contains a complete description of the external behavior of the software system. It is possible to complete the entire problem analysis before starting to write the SRS. However, it is more likely that as the problem analysis decomposition process yields aspects of the problem that are well understood, the corresponding section of the SRS is written.

As mentioned in Chapter 1, the SRS serves a number of purposes depending on who is writing it. First the SRS could be written by a potential user (or customer) of a system. Second the SRS could be written by a developer of the system. The two scenarios create entirely different situations and establish entirely different purposes for the document. In the former case, the primary purpose of the SRS is to define the need. This document sometimes serves as a basis for a competitive bidding process among companies who desire to satisfy that need. In order to encourage competition (which potentially helps the customer receive the best product at the least cost), the SRS should be as general as possible. Let us say for example that a building owner wishes to buy an elevator control system. The SRS should be general enough to enable a number of elevator companies (each with a different dispatch algorithm and a different elevator flight path) to respond, but it should also be specific enough to eliminate clearly from the competition a company offering a series of ramps connecting the floors and a parade of elephants walking up and down the ramps transporting people on their backs. Ideally the SRS should carve the universe of systems into two independent sets: a set containing all systems satisfying the users' real needs and one containing all those that would not.

On the other hand, an SRS written by a development organization as the first step of the software development process must be far more specific. This type of SRS is the subject of our discussion in this chapter, and it performs an entirely different set of functions from the so-called SRS described in the preceding paragraph. Its purpose is to provide a means of

- Communication among customers, users, analysts, and designers
- Supporting system-testing activities
- Controlling the evolution of the system

Let us now discuss these three in more detail.

The first purpose of the SRS is to provide a means of communication among all parties. A well-written SRS reduces the probability of the customer being disappointed with the final product. Assuming the SRS is not ambiguous, it defines the external behavior of the system to be built, and there can be no misinterpretation. If there is a disagreement between customer and developer concerning external behavior, it is worked out during the requirements stage, not during acceptance testing, when it is much more costly to correct. Unfortunately many developers prefer to keep the SRS fairly ambiguous in order to provide themselves with more flexibility during design. However, this flexibility significantly increases the customer's risk. The SRS should be very specific about how the system will look externally to the system's environment (or the user). This does have a second-order effect on limiting possible designs, but it is not part of the design; in fact some designers claim such a specification is too constraining. If the SRS writer finds it impossible to specify external behavior without supplying a design, then the SRS should contain a note to the effect that:

> WARNING: THE "DESIGN" CONTAINED HEREIN IS SUPPLIED AS AN AID IN UNDERSTANDING THE PRODUCT'S EXTERNAL BEHAVIOR ONLY. THE DESIGNERS MAY SELECT ANY DESIGN THEY WISH PROVIDED IT BEHAVES EXTERNALLY IN A MANNER IDENTICAL TO THE EXTERNAL BEHAVIOR OF THE ABOVE SYSTEM.

Why should the "design" used in the SRS not be used as *the* design? The answer is simple: The "design" in the SRS was chosen because it helped make requirements more understandable; the real design is chosen to optimize such qualities as maintainability, performance, space, and modifiability.

The second purpose of the SRS is to serve as the basis for system testing and verification activities. The purpose of system testing is to stimulate the system with representative test scenarios in order to show that the as-built system meets requirements. If the SRS is ambiguous or inconsistent or some requirement stated therein is untestable, then such testing is impossible. The SRS is the primary input to the system test planning and generation process.

The third purpose of the SRS is to help control the evolution of the software system. Let us assume that a software product is either under development or has been deployed, and a customer says, "I want the software to do X." How does anyone know if that is a new requirement or an old one? The answer is to read the SRS and find out. If it is determined to be a new requirement, then the appropriate process to incorporate the customer's request is to (1) update the SRS, (2) update the design, (3) update the code, and so forth. The SRS serves as the definition and the only definition of what the software is supposed to do. Thus formal control of the contents of the SRS is precisely formal control of the evolution of the software system. This control process is part of the discipline of software configuration management (SCM) [BER80], which is outside the scope of this book. SCM works effectively during the maintenance and enhancement stages as well as during initial development stages.

3.2 WHAT SHOULD BE INCLUDED IN AN SRS?

Simply stated an SRS must include a complete yet concise description of the entire external interface of the system with its environment, including other software, communication ports, hardware, and human users.[1] This includes two types of requirements: behavioral and nonbehavioral.

---

[1]Yourdon's User Implementation Model [YOU89] captures that part of the SRS corresponding to the system's interface with the human user only.

Behavioral requirements define what the system does. These describe all the inputs and outputs to and from the system as well as information concerning how the inputs and outputs interrelate. In other words we must completely define the transform function of the system software being specified. This description of how inputs map into outputs are typically called behavioral descriptions or operational specifications and are quite nontrivial, as will be seen in Chapter 4.

The nonbehavioral requirements define the attributes of the system as it performs its job. They include a complete description of the system's required levels of efficiency, reliability, security, maintainability, portability, visibility, capacity, and standards compliance, to name but a few. These subjects are covered in depth in Chapter 5.

3.3 WHAT SHOULD *NOT* BE INCLUDED IN AN SRS?

Given the purpose of the SRS just defined, it becomes clear that the following do not belong in an SRS:

- Project requirements (for example, staffing, schedules, costs, milestones, activities, phases, reporting procedures)
- Designs
- Product assurance plans (for example, configuration management plans, verification and validation (V&V) plans, test plans, quality assurance plans)

There are some very good reasons why each of these should be explicitly excluded from an SRS, as described in the following paragraphs.

Why exclude project requirements from an SRS? The SRS and the project requirements have entirely different lifespans. Although some believe that the software product is just the code, the software product must be considered to be the SRS, design documentation, the code, test plans, user's manuals, and so forth. Given that fact, the lifespan of the SRS is the same as the lifespan of the product, for example, 5 years, 10 years, 15 years, or so. On the other hand, items like milestones, development costs, and staffing are of concern only during development (or for historical value later). Thus their lifespan is only as long as the development project. Clearly it makes no sense to include these two types of information in the same document.

Why exclude design from the SRS? There are a number of reasons for doing this: to help partition the documentation, different audiences, and potential lack of sound design principles. Let us discuss each of these reasons separately. First, if we really wanted to, we *could* package all requirements, all designs, all code, all test plans, and all user documentation in one binder.

It *could* be done, but why do it? The greatest advantage of packaging them separately is the ability to define plateaus (usually called baselines) in the development process that (1) signal completion of a major project milestone and thus denote progress and (2) can be used to control change to the system. Second, requirements and design specifications have different intended audiences. The SRS's audience includes system users, system testers, customers, designers, and requirements writers themselves. The audience for the design documentation includes unit and integration testers, coders, and designers themselves. Third, requirements writers are chosen for their ability to analyze and specify, not for the ability to synthesize efficient designs. The correct design process requires a precarious trade-off between many factors and may consume 15 to 25% of total development costs. Few projects can afford to spend this kind of money during the requirements stage of the software development life cycle.

Why exclude product assurance plans from the SRS? The two primary reasons are the same as the first two for excluding design from the SRS. In particular there is no reason to combine relatively unrelated subjects in the same document, and the audience for product assurance plans is altogether different than the one for the SRS. Product assurance plans should be documented in the software quality evaluation plan (SQEP), the software configuration management plan (SCMP), and the software test plan (STP).

3.4 ATTRIBUTES OF A WELL-WRITTEN SRS

If a perfect SRS could exist it would be

- correct
- nonambiguous
- complete
- verifiable
- consistent
- understandable by non-computer specialists
- modifiable
- traceable
- annotated.

Each of these qualities is explained in the following sections:

3.4.1 Correct

An SRS is *correct* if and only if every requirement stated therein represents something required of the system to be built. There is no real way of teaching this quality, since it depends totally on the application at hand. If the software must respond to all button presses within 5 seconds and the SRS states that "the software shall respond to all button presses within 10 seconds," that requirement is incorrect.

3.4.2 Nonambiguous

An SRS is *nonambiguous* if and only if every requirement stated therein has only one interpretation [IEE84]. Imagine that a sentence is extracted from an SRS, given to ten people who are asked for their interpretation. If there is more than one such interpretation, then that sentence is probably ambiguous.

At a minimum all terms with multiple meanings must appear in a glossary. However there is much more of a problem with ambiguity than can be solved with just a glossary. In particular using natural language invites ambiguity because natural language is inherently ambiguous. A few examples will clearly demonstrate this:

Example 1. Air traffic controller problem

> For up to twelve aircraft, the small display format shall be used. Otherwise the large display format shall be used.

This requirement could have been extracted from an SRS for an air traffic controller (ATC) system. The two display formats were defined somewhere else in the SRS as follows. In the *small display format,* ATCs see the status of all aircraft in their sector in the format, shown in Figure 3–1a. That is, under each aircraft position on the screen, there appear the flight carrier and number, altitude, heading, and destination. However when a large number of aircraft are present, the screen switches to the *large display format,* shown in Figure 3–1b. In this format clutter is reduced by eliminating all flight data from the screen except for flight carrier and number. Presumably there would be another terminal nearby where the ATC could make queries in order to determine other data concerning flights of interest.

The ambiguity lies in the phrase "for up to twelve." Does it mean "for up to and including twelve" or "for up to and excluding twelve"? Does it matter? Analysts writing the SRS might argue that it really does not matter, since it is difficult to believe that twelve aircraft on the screen would be cluttered but eleven would not or that thirteen would be too cluttered but not twelve. However, such ambiguities (even as in this case where either of the two possible interpretations could be valid) can lead to devastating results in the final product.

Imagine that two software engineers have responsibility for writing the software to display flight data on the screen. As shown in Figure 3–2, one engineer has responsibility for generating the little windows packed with appropriate data, and the second has responsibility for displaying the little windows of data. Furthermore let us assume that the first engineer assumes that the crossover from small- to large-screen formats occurs between eleven and twelve aircraft and

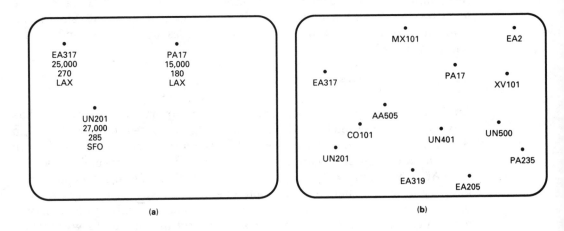

Figure 3-1. Example 1: Air Traffic Control Display Formats. **(a)** Small Display Format. **(b)** Large Display Format.

Figure 3-2. Example 1: The Two Modules Being Written.

the second engineer assumes that it occurs between twelve and thirteen. Everything is fine as long as the number of aircraft remains below twelve. While that is the case, the generator packs little windows full of four lines of data, and the displayer displays the little windows appropriately. When twelve aircraft appear, the generator packs the little window with only one line of flight data, but the displayer expects and thus picks up four lines of flight data, as shown in Figure 3-3. If we are lucky, the other three lines contain garbage; if this occurred, the ATC would occasionally witness garbage on the screen and report it in the daily log. However, the other three lines might contain leftover flight data from another flight. If that were the case, when there are exactly twelve aircraft on the screen, the ATC would see all twelve positions along with normal-looking but totally incorrect flight data concerning all the aircraft. The consequences of this scenario are potentially disastrous! And this all occurred because analysts writing the SRS believed it was acceptable to keep the document ambiguous, since either interpretation of the ambiguous requirement was acceptable. The correct solution is to add the phrase "and including" or "and excluding" to the original statement.

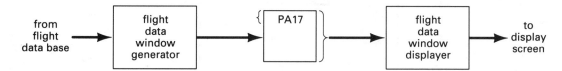

Figure 3–3. Example 1: The Erroneous Window Transfer.

Here is another example:

Example 2. Nonfriendly aircraft problem

> Aircraft that are nonfriendly and have an unknown
> mission or the potential to enter restricted airspace
> within 5 minutes shall raise an alert.

This requirement could have been extracted from an SRS for some type of military system designed to raise alerts in the event that a restricted airspace is violated improperly. The main question is what the relative priorities are of the "and" and "or." In other words does the requirement mean that

> Aircraft that are *either* nonfriendly and have an
> unknown mission *or* have the potential to enter restricted
> airspace within 5 minutes shall raise an alert.

Or does the requirement mean that

> Aircraft that are nonfriendly *and either* have an
> unknown mission *or* the potential to enter restricted
> airspace within 5 minutes shall raise an alert.

Either one could be correct, but these statements have two entirely different meanings. Let us look at two applications where each of the preceding interpretations is correct. In the first application, the intent is to have the system monitor air traffic near a bomb-testing area. An alert should sound if *any* aircraft is about to enter the test area (see positions of friendly aircraft F_1 and nonfriendly aircraft N_1 in Figure 3–4). Also if a nonfriendly aircraft is just passing by (see position N_2 in Figure 3–4) and has not communicated its mission (it might be a surveillance mission), an alert should sound. This corresponds to the first interpretation. In the second application, the intention is to have the system monitor air traffic near an aircraft carrier. An alert should never be sounded for any friendly aircraft. However, the presence of nonfriendly aircraft should raise an alert in either of two cases: (1) If the aircraft is about to enter the restricted airspace surrounding the aircraft carrier (see position N_1 in Figure 3–5), or (2) if the aircraft is just passing by (see position N_2 in Figure 3–5) and has not communicated its mission. This corresponds to the second interpretation. Interestingly enough if this ambi-

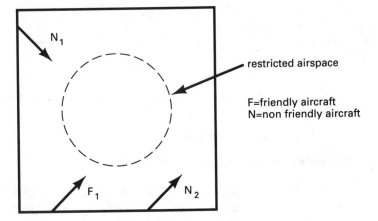

Figure 3–4. Example 2. "Bombing Test-Area" Restricted Airspace.

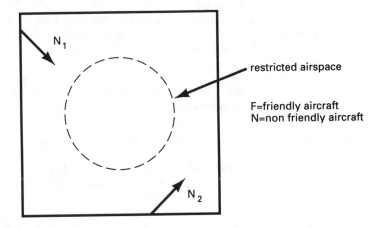

Figure 3–5. Example 2. "Aircraft Carrier" Restricted Airspace.

guity actually were to appear in a real SRS for either of these two applications and the incorrect interpretation were made by the designer, quite unexpected behavior would occur. In the first application, friendly aircraft would be allowed to stray over the bombing test area. In the second application, friendly aircraft would never be allowed to approach, let alone land on, the aircraft carrier.

3.4.3 Complete

A SRS is *complete* if it possesses the following four qualities:

1. Everything that the software is supposed to do is included in the SRS. This is the most difficult of the attributes to define or detect violations of. A violation is difficult to detect because it implies that something is not in the SRS; it is not simple to find something that is not present by examining what is present. The only ones able to detect such an oversight or omission are those who own the problem to be solved by the software. One effective technique for locating a violation uses a prototype, which is the subject of Chapter 6.

It is tempting to include the following sentence in the definition of completeness: The SRS must specifically state those things that the software is not supposed to do. However, this becomes impossible to achieve considering the size of the universe with which the software is not supposed to interact. A simple example suffices. Suppose in a telephone system we state the requirement that

> if party A calls party B and party B is idle,
> then party B's phone shall ring.

This seems perfectly reasonable. Later during testing testers verify that the requirement has been satisfied by the system. However, what is to prevent the developer from satisfying the requirement by building a system that rings all phones in the telephone system whenever party A calls an idle party B? To prevent this the requirements writer would be forced to write

> if party A calls party B and party B is idle,
> then party B's phone shall ring
> and no other phone shall ring.

The problem here is that there may be a valid reason for party C's phone to ring at the same time! An alternative is to write at the beginning of the SRS that

> the system shall do the things stated in this SRS,
> and nothing else.

This is also a dead end because software *does* do things not stated in its requirements, for example, induce the hardware to emit patterns of electromagnetic interference.

2. Definitions of the responses of the software to all realizable classes of input data in all realizable classes of situations is included. Note that it is important to specify the responses to both valid and invalid inputs [IEE84]. This implies that for every system input mentioned in the SRS, the SRS specifies what the appropriate output will be. However, the appropriate output may not be just a function of the input; it may also be a function of the current state of the system. For example, in a telephone switching system, the software's response to detection of the user dialing 9 is a function of the state of the system, which in turn is a function of what the user did previously. Thus if the user's phone handset is in its cradle, no system output is generated (that is, the input is ignored); if the user is listening to a dial tone, the system output might be a distinctive dial tone; and if the user has already started dialing a phone number, the 9 is collected as one more digit of the phone number. In other words the SRS must establish a complete mapping from the cross product of the input domain (I) and state domain (S) into the cross product of the output domain (O) and the state domain (S), that is,

$$\text{SRS}: I \times S \rightarrow O \times S$$

3. All pages are numbered; all figures and tables are numbered, named, and referenced; all terms and units of measure are provided; and all referenced material and sections are present [IEE84]. This is completeness from a word processing perspective.

4. No sections are marked "To Be Determined (TBD)." Inserting the three letters "TBD" in a section of an SRS should be avoided whenever possible. When included, the TBD should be appended with a notation of *who* has responsibility for determining the contents and *when* the section will be completed. This approach ensures that the TBD is not interpreted carte blanche as an excuse to delay completion of the SRS indefinitely as if the TBD meant "To Be Done Tomorrow," and of course tomorrow never occurs. By including the name of the responsible party and a date, we ensure that the TBD expires at some point.

3.4.4 Verifiable

An SRS is *verifiable* if and only if every requirement stated therein is verifiable. A requirement is *verifiable* if and only if there exists some finite cost effective process with which a person or machine can check that the actual as-built software product meets the requirement [IEE84].

It is important to realize that verifiability is a function of the way the SRS is written. (Many people think it is purely a function of the product as-built.) There are a number of reasons why a requirement may be nonverifiable. First, any ambiguity would certainly lead to nonverifiability; obviously there is no way to verify that the software exhibits a trait if that trait is defined ambiguously. For example, the statement "The product shall have an easy-to-use human interface" is ambiguous, that is, has multiple interpretations because opinions of what is easy to use varies greatly from individual to individual and thus cannot be verified to be an attribute of the final product. Second, using nonmeasurable quantities such as "usually" or "often," implies the absence of a finite test process and thus implies nonverifiability. For example, the statement that "The product shall usually ignite the red light when the button is pushed" is nonverifiable because if you try to verify compliance with the requirement by pushing the button a thousand times you may be tempted to declare the test successful if the red light ignited six hundred times. However it may be that if you pushed the button a thousand more times, the red light would never ignite again. In other other words the only way to test that "usually" is the case would be to push the button an infinite number of times. Third, any requirement that is equivalent to a statement of the halting problem ([TUR36] or read any textbook on computability or automata theory) cannot be verified. For example, it can be demonstrated that verification of the statement "the program shall not enter an infinite loop" is equivalent to the halting problem and thus is nonverifiable.

3.4.5 Consistent

An SRS is *consistent* if and only if no subset of individual requirements stated therein conflict. This may be manifested in a number of ways [IEE84]. For example,

1. Conflicting terms: Two terms are used in different contexts to mean the same thing. For example, one place in the SRS uses the term "prompt" to denote a message displayed by the software to ask the user to enter some information, whereas another place in the SRS uses the term "cue" to denote the identical situation.

2. Conflicting characteristics: Two parts of the SRS demand the product to exhibit contradictory traits. For example, in one place, the SRS states that "All inputs to the software shall be via selection of an option in a displayed menu," and in another place, it states that "The user command language shall consist of the following typed commands...."

3. Temporal inconsistency: Two parts of the SRS demand the product to obey contradictory timing characteristics. For example, one place in the SRS states that "System input A will occur only while system input B is occurring," and another place in the SRS states that "System input B may start 15 seconds after an occurrence of system input A."

3.4.6 Understandable by Non-Computer Specialists

In an attempt to make an SRS less ambiguous, more verifiable, complete, and consistent, we might be tempted to resort to extremely formal notations. Unfortunately such notations often make it impossible for non-computer specialists to understand the SRS. Primary readers of the SRS in many cases are customers or users, who tend to be experts in an application area but are not necessarily trained in computer science. Perhaps one way of achieving the goal is to use formal notations but develop a tool to translate the resulting formal SRS into an equivalent easy-to-understand prose automatically. This is the approach taken by Balzer et al. on the GIST project [BAL82]. However, I question why the formal version is needed at all. If there exists a complete nonambiguous mapping between the formal and informal representations, then the informal representation will satisfy all the required attributes, including understandability by the non-computer specialist.

3.4.7 Modifiable

While the six preceding sections discussed attributes of the *content* of the SRS, this section and the two subsequent ones discuss attributes of SRS *format* and *style*.

An SRS is *modifiable* if its structure and style are such that any necessary changes to the requirements can be made easily, completely, and consistently [IEE84].

Modifiability implies that there exists a table of contents, an index, and cross-references where necessary. Thus if a requirement must be modified later, we can check and easily locate the section of the SRS that has to be modified. For example, if we want to change the required maximum response time of a dial tone in a telephone switching system from 5 seconds to 3 seconds, we would look in the index under "dial tone" to locate all the references to dial tone in the document in order to make the necessary changes.

One technique that can be used to improve the readability of a SRS is to repeat selected requirements in different locations in the document. This attribute of a SRS is called *redundancy*. For example, in describing the external interface of a PABX, we must define interactions between the user and the telephone switch. Thus when describing the external view of a local call, the SRS may state that

> Starting with an idle telephone, the user should lift the handset,
> the system shall respond with a dial tone, then the user should
> dial the seven-digit phone number of the party the user is
> trying to reach....

When describing the external view of a long-distance call, the SRS may state that

> Starting with an idle telephone, the user should lift the handset,
> the system shall respond with a dial tone, then the user should
> dial a 1 followed by the ten-digit phone number of the party
> the user is trying to reach....

Note that the restatement of the first three steps makes the document considerably more readable. However, with the additional readability comes the potential for decreased modifiability because a later modification to only one occurrence would render the SRS inconsistent. To make redundancy acceptable, an index or cross-reference table is essential for locating multiple occurrences of requirements. Another option would be to use the automatic consistency checking capability of any of the many automated requirements tools available (see Chapter 4).

3.4.8 Traceable

An SRS is *traceable* if the origin of each of its requirements is clear and if it facilitates the referencing of each requirement in future development or enhancement documentation [IEE84].

There are four types of traceability (see Figure 3–6):

1. Backward-from-requirements traceability implies that we know why every requirement in the SRS exists. It implies that each requirement explicitly references its source in previous documents.

2. Forward-from-requirements traceability implies that we understand which components of the software satisfy each requirement. It demands that each requirement in the SRS explicitly references a design component.

3. Backward-to-requirements traceability implies that every software component explicitly references those requirements that it helps to satisfy. It implies that each requirement in the SRS has a unique name or reference number.

4. Forward-to-requirements traceability implies that all documents that preceded the SRS can reference the SRS. Like backward-to-requirements traceability, this implies that each requirement in the SRS has a unique name or reference number.

Let us assume that an SRS contains the requirement

> The system shall respond to any occurrence of request X
> within 20 seconds.

Now the software has actually been built and when it undergoes its final test, response time is measured consistently at 60 seconds. There are two ways of correcting this problem: (1) Redesign or recode the software to make it more efficient, or (2) change the requirement from 20 to 60 seconds. If no reference is present in the SRS at this location to indicate that 20 seconds was anything but a randomly selected timing constraint, we may be tempted to use solution 2 (and this *may* be perfectly satisfactory). However if the application was a patient-monitoring system and the reason for the 20-second response time was that an earlier white paper demonstrated conclusively that in the particular hospital environment in which this patient-monitoring system was to be

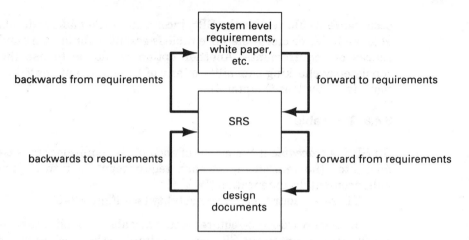

Figure 3–6. Traceability Expectations of an SRS.

installed and with the existing nurse to patient ratio, a nurse needed to make at least three queries of the system per minute in order to ensure the absence of emergency conditions with any patients. In such a case, backward-from-requirements traceability would insist on a reference being entered in the SRS at the site of the timing requirement back to the white paper. Then when solution 2 is considered, it is quickly dismissed after checking the white paper.

Of even more importance is traceability between the SRS and the design, that is, forward-from- and backward-to-requirements traceability. The most common way of implementing this is with a *requirements traceability matrix* (RTM). Although the RTM is not created during the requirements stage, the work done during the requirements stage to organize the requirements hierarchically (or at a minimum to number each requirement uniquely) has a major effect on the ease of later implementing the RTM. In its simplest form, an RTM is a two-dimensional table with one row for every requirement in the SRS and one column for each design component. An X is placed in each entry where the indicated design component helps satisfy the indicated requirement. When completed, a row with no Xs indicates that there exists a requirement that will not be met, that is, no part of the design contributes to its satisfaction. A column with no Xs indicates an extraneous design component. The advantage of the RTM is evident during maintenance: It greatly reduces the effort to locate the causes of product failures (by examining entries in the row corresponding to the unsatisfied requirement) and to analyze all possible adverse effects of a planned software change (by examining entries in the column corresponding to the component being changed).

3.4.9 Annotated

The purpose of annotating requirements contained in an SRS is to provide guidance to the development organization. Two types of annotations are of most help—relative necessity and relative stability.

Occasionally a development organization may spend an inordinate amount of time trying to satisfy a particular requirement, then discover afterward that the customer would have preferred the product on time without that particular requirement satisfied rather than have the product six months late with the requirement satisfied. This scenario would have been avoided if the relative necessities of individual requirements had been stated initially. One way of doing this is to append to every individual requirement in the SRS, an E, D, or O in parentheses to indicate essential, desirable, or optional. Of course the concept of an "optional requirement" is oxymoronic, but the fact is there *are* relative importances among requirements. For example, the life support system on board the space shuttle is essential, and instant orange juice is only optional, but both may actually appear in the overall system-level requirements specification. Thus annotating each of the requirements with an E, D, or O would tell the developers in what order to implement requirements and which requirements were worthy of delaying the schedule.

In addition, annotating each requirement with an indication of how volatile the requirement is provides the development organization with guidance on where to build flexibility into its design. Thus on the space shuttle, for example, annotating the requirement "for a life support system" as stable and the requirement "to support n crew members" as volatile provides designers with knowledge sufficient to integrate fully the life support system with the rest of the space shuttle and have a variable that would be referenced whenever the SRS referred to the number of crew members.

3.4.10 Summary

Achieving all of the preceding attributes in an SRS is impossible. For example, as we attempt to eliminate inconsistency and ambiguity (usually by reducing the natural language in the SRS language), the SRS becomes less understandable to the non-computer specialist (one attempt to combine readability, nonambiguity, and consistency is reported in [DAV82]). As we attempt to be absolutely complete, cost of the SRS skyrockets and the document becomes extremely large and difficult to read. If we try to increase modifiability by eliminating all redundancy, the SRS becomes quite choppy, difficult to follow, and ambiguous. Figure 3–7 shows some of these effects. The only conclusion we can reach is that

> THERE IS NO SUCH THING AS A PERFECT SRS!

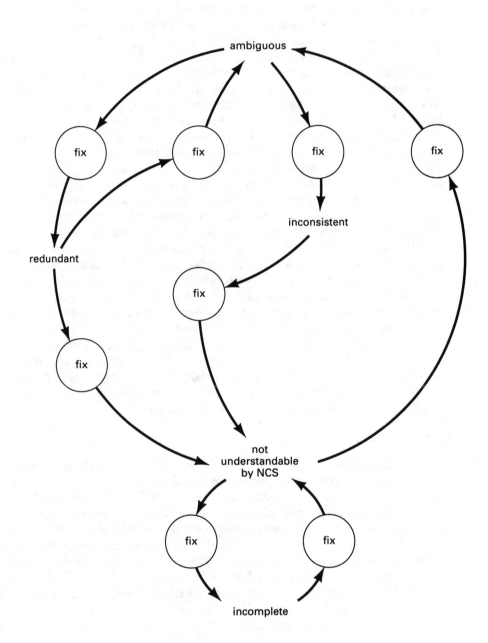

Figure 3–7. A Perfect SRS Is Impossible.

3.5 HOW TO ORGANIZE AN SRS

This section discusses three different ways of organizing the contents of an SRS:

- Department of Defense (DoD) DI-MCCR-80025A
- NASA's SFW-DID-08
- IEEE/ANSI 830-1984
- Naval Research Laboratory's A-7E Operation Flight Program SRS

The first two are examples of typical U.S. Government documentation standards that provide a single standard outline to be used for writing SRSs. The third is a commercial documentation standard that provides a good deal of guidance and flexibility concerning the choice of outline to be used when writing an SRS. The fourth is presented as a case study of a particular SRS written for a specific application.

3.5.1 Department of Defense DI-MCCR-80025A

Until 1984 the DoD had a variety of software development standards. Finally in that year after six years of hard work and compromise, the Joint Logistics Commanders (JLC) approved a new single standard for developing software throughout the Army, Navy, and Air Force. That standard was once called SDS (Software Development Standard), then DOD-STD-2167; it is now called DOD-STD-2167A (pronounced D-O-D Standard 2167A) [DOD88]. Associated with most military development standards, including DOD-STD-2167A, is a volume of Data Item Descriptions (DIDs, for short and pronounced like the word "did"). Each DID contains a standard outline and a set of instructions for creating a different piece of deliverable documentation. One such DID is numbered DI-MCCR-80025A[2] and corresponds to the Software Requirements Specification. Figure 3–8 shows the standard outline contained in that DID. According to DOD-STD-2167A, system-level requirements are documented in a *system/segment specification* (SSS). If the system is extremely complex, a subsequent system design may reveal the existence of a multitude of major subsystems. This system design is documented in a *system/segment design document* (SSDD). The requirements for each of these individual subsystems is further elaborated on in other SSSs. This results in a hierarchy similar to that shown in Figure 3–9. Those subsystems to be implemented in software are termed *computer software configuration items* (CSCIs). Requirements for each CSCI are documented in an SRS. Thus a system composed of seven CSCIs

---

[2]The DI stands for data item; MCCR stands for mission critical computer resources.

1. Scope
    1.1 Identification
    1.2 CSCI overview
    1.3 Document overview

2. Applicable documents
    2.1 Government documents
    2.2 Non-Government documents

inputs and outputs →
3. Engineering requirements (for a CSCI)
    3.1 CSCI external interface requirements
    3.2 CSCI capability requirements
        3.2.X   Capability X
    3.3 CSCI internal interfaces
    3.4 CSCI data element requirements
    3.5 Adaptation requirements   *Anotation*
        3.5.1   Installation-dependent data
        3.5.2   Operational parameters
    3.6 Sizing and timing requirements
    3.7 Safety requirements
    3.8 Security requirements
    3.9 Design constraints
    3.10 Software quality factors
    3.11 Human performance/human engineering requirements
        3.11.1   Human information processing
        3.11.2   Foreseeable human errors
        3.11.3   Total system implications (e.g., training, support, operational environment)
    3.12 Requirements traceability

4. Qualification requirements
    4.1 Methods (demonstrations vs. test vs. analysis vs. inspection)
    4.2 Special (e.g., facilities, formulae, tools)

5. Preparation for delivery

6. Notes (e.g., glossary, formula derivations, abbreviations, background information)

Appendices

Figure 3–8. DI-MCCR-80025A (SRS) Outline.

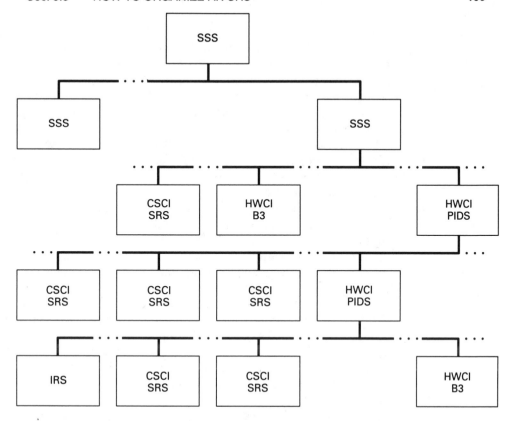

Figure 3–9. A System Decomposition Hierarchy.

would include seven SRSs, one for each CSCI. Those subsystems to be implemented in hardware are termed *hardware configuration items* (HWCIs), and their requirements are recorded in a *prime item development specification* (PIDS) or a *B3 specification,* depending on whether or not they contain their own software subsystems, respectively.

Each SRS is written to stand alone; however if complex interfaces between sibling CSCIs exist, a separate *interface requirements specification* (IRS) may be written for each system that possesses such multiple CSCIs. It is important to recognize that an IRS documents external interfaces between CSCIs; the IRS does not contain descriptions of interfaces between subcomponents of a CSCI (which would make it part of the design stage).

Looking at Figure 3–8 we see that Sections 1 and 2 of the SRS contain general background information and Section 3 contains detailed requirements for this CSCI. Section 3.1 of the SRS sets the stage by delineating all the CSCI's inputs and outputs (and may be replaced by an IRS). The majority of the behavioral requirements are contained in Section 3.2 of the SRS. These are discussed fully in Chapter 4 of this book. Section 3.3 describes interfaces and information flows among functional capabilities (for example, receiving, inventory control, and shipping functions), not among design components of the CSCI. Section 3.4 contains information about the static data requirements of the CSCI that are implied by external requirements. Section 3.5 captures the same idea as the aforementioned annotation with respect to volatility. This is presented in Section 3.4.9 of this book. Sections 3.6–3.11 of the SRS contain most of the nonbehavioral requirements for the software. These are fully discussed in Chapter 5 of this book. Section 3.11 describes attributes of the interface between the software and its users. Section 3.12 aggregates all references from the SRS backward to earlier documents; see Section 3.4.8 of this book for a discussion. Section 4 of the SRS describes how the software is to be approved by the Government; Section 4 is clearly not software requirements because it defines what people will do to inspect the software instead of what the software will do. However, Section 4 must be included for a project that has to obey DI-MCCR-80025A.

In summary, DI-MCCR-80025A provides excellent guidance on organizing an SRS. It has one section, Section 4, that does not really contain software requirements, but the DID's strengths far outweigh this minor oversight. This DID's greatest advantage over earlier DIDs for the DoD and its commercial contractors is the fact that it has eliminated SRS sections for documenting the software design. Earlier DoD standards also used different names for the SRS: MIL-STD-490 calls it a *B5 specification;* MIL-STD-483 calls it a *part I specification;* MIL-STD-1679A called it a *program performance specification* (PPS); and DOD-STD-7935 calls it a *functional description* (FD).

3.5.2 NASA's SFW-DID-08

The National Aeronautics and Space Administration's (NASA's) data item description for the software requirements specification is called SFW-DID-08. Figure 3–10 shows NASA's recommended organization. Sections 1 and 2 are similar to the DoD's SRS. Section 3 describes all possible features of the system from a pure user view. In particular it shows how the user accesses the system and controls its execution. Section 4 contains all requirements for the CSCI; Section 4.1 lists all behavioral and performance requirements. If the system has multiple modes,[3] a table may be included that cross-references modes and functions. Subsections of Section 4.1 delineate each function's inputs, processing requirements, and outputs. Section 4.2 contains the amount of internal memory and timing required by the CSCI. Sections 4.3 and 4.4 correspond to Sections 3.9 and 3.1 of the DoD standard, respectively. Like Section 3.1 of the

---

[3]The term *modes* is used here with the connotation used by Parnas et al. on the A-7E project (see Section 3.5.4); NASA uses the term *states.*

1. Introduction
   1.1 Identification
   1.2 Scope
   1.3 Purpose
   1.4 Organization
   1.5 Objectives
2. Applicable documents
   2.1 Reference
   2.2 Information
   2.3 Parents
→ 3. User scenario descriptions
4. Requirements
   4.1 Functional and performance requirements
      4.1.X Function X   *no internal interface*
3.6 4.2 Timing and sizing requirements
3.9 4.3 Design standards and constraints
3.1 4.4 Interface requirements   *external interface requirements*
→ 4.5 Programming requirements
3.5 4.6 Adaptation requirements   *Annotation*
      4.6.1 System environment
      4.6.2 System parameters
      4.6.3 System capacities
3.4 4.7 Data base requirements
→ 4.8 Quality factors
non-behavioral 4.8.1 Correctness
under one section 4.8.2 Reliability
      4.8.3 Efficiency
      4.8.4 Integrity
      4.8.5 Usability
      4.8.6 Maintainability
      4.8.7 Testability
      4.8.8 Flexibility
      4.8.9 Portability
      4.8.10 Reusability
      4.8.11 Interoperability
      4.8.12 Additional factors
5. Qualification requirements
   5.1 Qualification methods
   5.2 Qualification levels
   5.3 Acceptance tolerance
   5.4 Tools/facilities
   5.5 Special qualification requirements
6. Preparation for delivery
7. Notes
8. Appendices
9. Glossary

Figure 3-10. SFW-DID-08 (SRS).

DoD standard, the interfaces section may be replaced with a complete independent document in the event that interfaces are extremely complex—DoD calls this the interface requirements specification (IRS), while NASA calls it the *interface requirements document* (IRD). Section 4.5 defines the programming language and compiler. Sections 4.6 and 4.7 correspond to Sections 3.5 and 3.4 of the DoD standard, respectively. Section 4.8 is one of the highlights of this standard; it colocates all nonbehavioral requirements for the system in one main section. Sections 5–7 and the appendices correspond precisely to Sections 4–6 and the appendices of the DoD standard.

3.5.3 IEEE/ANSI 830-1984

The Institute of Electrical and Electronics Engineers (IEEE) has a major standardization program under way for electrical engineering and software engineering activities. In 1984 it approved the *Guide for Software Requirements* (IEEE 830-1984), and one year later it was approved by the American National Standards Institute (ANSI) [IEE84]. Unlike the DoD and NASA standards, the IEEE standard does not attempt to provide just one standard outline for all software projects. Instead it offers a variety of outlines for specific software requirements, each one tailored for a particular class of problem. Figure 3–11 shows the basic overall outline that all SRSs should follow. The specific tailoring occurs in Section 3, entitled "Specific Requirements." In looking through Figure 3–11, Section 1 is self-explanatory. Section 2.1 describes the relationship of software to its environment (a picture helps). Section 2.2 provides a general overview of all the functions of the software. Section 2.3 provides general characteristics of eventual users (for example, educational background, amount of product training). Section 2.4 expresses such things as

1. Introduction
    1.1 Purpose of SRS
    1.2 Scope of product
    1.3 Definitions, acronyms, and abbreviations
    1.4 References
    1.5 Overview of rest of SRS
2. General description
    2.1 Product perspective   } ←software overview
    2.2 Product functions
  + 2.3 User characteristics
    2.4 General constraints
    2.5 Assumptions and dependencies
3. Specific requirements
    Appendices
    Index

Figure 3–11. ANSI/IEEE STD-830-1984. © 1984 IEEE.

host hardware limitations, interfaces, and implementation language requirements. Section 3 is discussed in the following paragraph. Following Section 3 are the appendices, including history, cross-references, and sample formats for inputs or outputs.

In recognition of the fact that different types of systems need different emphases in their requirements, IEEE/ANSI 830-1984 offers four different alternatives for organizing specific requirements. Alternative I (see Figure 3–12) organizes specific requirements as follows: First in Section 3.1, each of the main categories of functional (behavioral) requirements are defined. For each an introduction to the function is provided followed by a definition of inputs, processing, and outputs associated with that function. After delineating all functions in this manner, all external interface requirements (Section 3.2) are defined for users, hardware, other software, and communications. Section 3.3 includes all performance requirements (called capacity and performance in this book), such as number of terminals, users, and transactions. Section 3.4 gives design constraints, including all standards that software development must comply with and all limitations of the support hardware, such as memory, speed, and number of ports. Section 3.5 covers all other system software nonbehavioral attributes, such as availability, security, and maintainability. Section 3.6 specifies other requirements, such as data base or operational requirements.

Alternative II (see Figure 3–13) recognizes the fact that requirements for a system may be more easily specified by describing all external user, hardware, software, and communication interfaces in terms of particular functional requirements using these interfaces. Thus for alternative II, Section 3.1 describes each category of functional (behavioral) requirements in terms of an introduction, inputs, processing, outputs, and external interfaces. Sections 3.2–3.5 contain the remainder of the requirements.

Alternative III (see Figure 3–14) is for software systems where performance and design constraints and nonbehavioral attributes of performance are not global for the entire system and can be more easily defined in association with particular functional requirements and external interfaces. Thus in Section 3.1, each of the categories of functional requirements is given in terms of an introduction, inputs, processing, outputs, performance and design constraints, and nonbehavioral attributes. Following this the external user (Section 3.2.1), hardware (Section 3.2.2), software (Section 3.2.3), and communications (Section 3.2.4) interfaces are defined in the same way, that is, in terms of performance and design constraints and nonbehavioral attributes.

In alternative IV (see Figure 3–15), the software being specified is so complex that there are no globally true requirements. Every type of requirement for the software is described in terms of its functional requirements. The primary contribution of IEEE 830-1984 is its host of advice on how to write an SRS, and what to avoid when writing one.

3. Specific requirements
→ 3.1 Functional requirements
   3.1.1   Functional requirement 1
      3.1.1.1   Introduction
      3.1.1.2   Inputs
      3.1.1.3   Processing
      3.1.1.4   Outputs
   3.1.2   Functional requirement 2
      .
      .
      .

   3.1.n Functional requirement n
      .
      .
      .

→ 3.2   External interface requirements
   3.2.1   User interfaces
   3.2.2   Hardware interfaces
   3.2.3   Software interfaces
   3.2.4   Communications interfaces
→ 3.3   Performance requirements
  3.4   Design constraints
   3.4.1   Standards compliance
   3.4.2   Hardware limitations
      .
      .
      .

  3.5   Attributes
   3.5.1   Availability
   3.5.2   Security
   3.5.3   Maintainability
   3.5.4   Transferability/conversion
      .
      .
      .

  3.6   Other requirements
   3.6.1   Data base
   3.6.2   Operations
   3.6.3   Site adaptation
      .
      .
      .

Figure 3–12. ANSI/IEEE STD-830-1984 Alternative I. © 1984 IEEE.

non behavioral (handwritten annotation pointing to 3.4 Attributes)

Figure 3–13. ANSI/IEEE STD-830-1984 Alternative II. © 1984 IEEE.

3.5.4 NRL A-7E OFP SRS

Since 1978 the Naval Research Laboratory (NRL) has undertaken the task of entirely re-engineering the software for the on-board Operational Flight Program (OFP) for the A-7E aircraft [BAS81, HEN80]. The subject software has been around for twenty years and undergone so many changes that it has become almost entirely unmaintainable. Working closely with David Parnas, NRL's goal was to demonstrate the feasibility of applying information hiding, abstract interfaces, formal specifications, cooperating sequential processes, process synchronization routines, and resource monitors to a complex real-time system [BAS81]. The first step in the re-engineering effort was to write a new SRS [HEN78,

3. Specific requirements
  3.1 Functional requirements
    3.1.1 Functional requirement 1
      3.1.1.1 Introduction
      3.1.1.2 Inputs
      3.1.1.3 Processing
      3.1.1.4 Outputs
      3.1.1.5 Performance requirements
      3.1.1.6 Design constraints
        3.1.1.6.1 Standards compliance
        3.1.1.6.2 Hardware limitations
        .
        .
        .
      3.1.1.7 Attributes
        3.1.1.7.1 Availability
        3.1.1.7.2 Security
        3.1.1.7.3 Maintainability
        3.1.1.7.4 Transferability/conversion
        .
        .
        .
      3.1.1.8 Other requirements
        3.1.1.8.1 Data base
        3.1.1.8.2 Operations
        3.1.1.8.3 Site adaptation
        .
        .
        .
    3.1.2 Functional requirement 2
      .
      .
      .
    3.1.n Functional requirement n
      .
      .
      .

  3.2 External interface requirements
    3.2.1 User interfaces
      3.2.1.1 Performance requirements
      3.2.1.2 Design constraints
        3.2.1.2.1 Standards compliance
        3.2.1.2.2 Hardware limitations
        .
        .
        .
      3.2.1.3 Attributes
        3.2.1.3.1 Availability
        3.2.1.3.2 Security
        3.2.1.3.3 Maintainability
        3.2.1.3.4 Transferability/conversion
        .
        .
        .
      3.2.1.4 Other requirements
        3.2.1.4.1 Data base
        3.2.1.4.2 Operations
        3.2.1.4.3 Site adaptation
        .
        .
        .
    3.2.2 Hardware interfaces
      .
      .
      .
    3.2.3 Software interfaces
      .
      .
    3.2.4 Communications interfaces
      .
      .
      .

Figure 3–14. ANSI/IEEE STD-830-1984 Alternative III. © 1984 IEEE.

3. Specific requirements
  3.1 Functional requirement 1
    3.1.1 Introduction
    3.1.2 Inputs
    3.1.3 Processing
    3.1.4 Outputs
    3.1.5 External interfaces
      3.1.5.1 User interfaces
      3.1.5.2 Hardware interfaces
      3.1.5.3 Software interfaces
      3.1.5.4 Communication interfaces
    3.1.6 Performance requirements
    3.1.7 Design constraints
      3.1.7.1 Standards compliance
      3.1.7.2 Hardware limitations

    3.1.8 Attributes
      3.1.8.1 Availability
      3.1.8.2 Security
      3.1.8.3 Maintainability
      3.1.8.4 Transferability/conversion

    3.1.9 Other requirements
      3.1.9.1 Data base
      3.1.9.2 Operations
      3.1.9.3 Site adaptation

  3.2 Functional requirement 2

  3.*n* Functional requirement *n*

Figure 3–15. ANSI/IEEE STD-830-1984 Alternative IV. © 1984 IEEE.

HEN80]. It is important to recognize the uniqueness of this particular task: creating a new SRS for operational software that was already in use. The outline of the resulting SRS shown in Figure 3–16 supports this unique situation. Because the new re-engineered software absolutely had to operate in the exact environment as the old software, certain factors were definite driving forces.

0. Introduction
   0.1 Overview
   0.2 Notation
   0.3 Table formats
1. The TC-2 computer
   1.1 Purpose
   1.2 Data manipulation
   1.3 Control transfer
   1.4 Interrupt system
   1.5 Input/output
2. Inputs and outputs (between OFP and its environment)
   - Acronym
   - Description
   - Range, accuracy
   - Format
   - Instructions to read or transmit it
   - Comments
3. Modes of OFP operation
   3.0 Introduction
   3.1 Legal mode combinations
   3.2 Alignment modes
   3.3 Navigation modes
   3.4 Transitions between modes
   3.5 Navigation update modes
   3.6 Weapon delivery modes
   3.7 Test mode
4. Functions
   - Which inputs and outputs
   - Relationship of output to input
   - Listed in relation to modes when appropriate
   - Demand or periodic (i.e., what triggers it)
5. Timing requirements
   - For each function
   - Minimum and maximum limits
6. Accuracy constraints on software functions
7. Undesired events
   - All desired behaviors in response to all undesired events
   - Ordered by who/what detects the event
8. Subsets
   - Logical subsets of product to assist in implementation
9. Possible changes and enhancements
10. Glossary of terms, abbreviations, and acronyms in A-7 community
11. References (documents and people)
12. Indices to data items, modes, and functions
13. Dictionary of terms used in specification

Figure 3–16. A-7E SRS Outline.

Section 0 of the new SRS supplies general background information about the purposes, philosophy, and physical organization of the SRS itself. Generally Sections 1–6 define software requirements, and Sections 7–13 provide auxiliary information to help locate or interpret requirements and guidance for designers about likely future directions of the software requirements. In particular Section 1 provides an overview of the hardware environment of the software. If following strict DoD documentation standards, this would have been documented in a B3 specification. On the other hand, it makes sense in this case to place this information in the SRS because this software is not being developed in parallel with the hardware but re-engineered to operate on the identical, preexisting hardware. Section 2 defines all external data items that the software must deal with, without regard to what the software does with them. A useful shorthand notation was developed by the NRL team to make it easier to recognize the role of a data item with respect to the software. Specifically single slashes surround inputs (for example, /MARKSW/), double slashes surround outputs (for example, //GNDTRK//), and dollar signs surround mnemonic constants (for example, YES). Section 3 defines all modes of operation of the operational flight program; mode names are always surrounded by stars (for example, *SHRIKE*). Section 4 defines actual behavioral requirements for the program, that is, it defines all functions performed by the program in generating outputs from inputs. Each function is defined in terms of inputs, modes, and conditions. Conditions are prefaced by "@T" or "@F" to indicate the truth or falsity of a condition, for example, @T(/ACAIRB/=NO). Complex conditional expressions can also be shortened by defining them as mnemonics surrounded by exclamation points (for example, !ground track angle!) so that condition checks can become more readable, for example, @T(!ground track angle! gt 45). Section 5 provides all the stimulus–response and response–response timing constraints for the system. Note that the response–stimulus and stimulus–stimulus timing constraints previously appeared in the section on inputs and their characteristics. Section 6 specifies how accurate outputs must be. Making Section 7 a separate section underlines the importance of specifying in an SRS not only what you want the software to do when it is given valid, expected inputs, but also what it is expected to do when invalid or unexpected inputs arrive [PAR76]. Sections 8 and 9 are demonstrations of Parnas's subsetting and software family building philosophy [PAR76a, PAR78] in action. Sections 10 and 13 are in essence both glossaries. However, Section 10 provides a glossary of A-7 terminology for the reader unfamiliar with the aircraft, while Section 13 provides a glossary of terms unique to this SRS for the reader unfamiliar with its terminology. Section 11 lists documents and people that can be contacted for more information about the actual A-7E aircraft or the requirements document itself. Finally, Section 12 is an index to help quickly locate specifications associated with every data item, mode, or function.

Although the exact outline selected for the A-7E is probably not applicable to many other projects, its readability demonstrates the powerful effect of tailoring SRS outlines to specific project and product needs. Similarly notational conventions used in this SRS provide the community with a new idea of how to more easily convey understanding and meaning to a reader of an SRS.

EXERCISES

1. Which of the following statements are ambiguous? Explain why.
   a. The system shall exhibit good response time.
   b. All customers [shall] have the same control field.[4]
   c. The system shall be menu-driven.
   d. There shall exist twenty-five buttons on the control panel, numbered PF1 to PF25.
   e. The software size shall not exceed 128K of RAM.
   f. The elevator shall move smoothly and without jerking.
   g. The system shall be fail-safe.
2. Which of the following pairs of requirements are inconsistent? Of those that are consistent, is there anything else wrong with them?
   a. The response time for all commands shall be less than 0.1 second.
      The response time for the BUILD command shall be less than 5 seconds.
   b. The response time for all commands shall be less than 5 seconds.
      The response time for the BUILD command shall be less than 1 second.
   c. The response time for the BUILD command shall be less than 5 seconds.
      The response time for the BUILD command shall be less than 1 second.
   d. The response time for all commands shall be exactly 2 seconds.
      The response time for the BUILD command shall be exactly 3 seconds.
3. Are there other attributes of an SRS (besides those listed in Section 3.4) that are desirable? List a few and describe why.
4. The 1985 version of DOD-STD-2167 allowed software developers to write an IRS for each CSCI. The 1988 version demands one IRS for each set of cooperating CSCIs. Explain what you believe are the pros and cons surrounding this decision.

REFERENCES

[BAL82] Balzer, R., et al. "Operational Specifications as the Basis for Rapid Prototyping." *ACM Software Engineering Notes* **7,** 5 (December 1982): 3–16.

[BAS81] Basili, V. R., and D. Weiss. "Evaluation of a Software Requirements Document by Analysis of Change Data." In *Fifth International Conference on*

[4]Reprinted from [FRE82].

Software Engineering, Washington D.C.: Computer Society Press of the Institute of Electrical and Electronics Engineers, March 1981. pp. 314–23.

[BER80]   Bersoff, E., et al. *Software Configuration Management*. Englewood Cliffs, N.J.: Prentice-Hall, 1980.

[DAV82]   Davis, A., "The Design of a Family of Applications-Oriented Requirements Languages," *IEEE Computer,* **15,** 5 (May 1982): 21–28.

[DOD88]   U.S. Department of Defense. *Military Standard: Defense System Software Development*. DOD-STD-2167A. Washington, D.C., February 1988.

[FRE82]   Freedman, D., and G. Weinberg. *Handbook of Walk-throughs, Inspections, and Technical Reviews*. Waltham, Mass.: Little and Brown, 1982.

[HEN78]   Heninger, K., et al. *Software Requirements for the A-7E Aircraft*. Naval Research Laboratory Memo 3876. Washington, D.C., November 1978.

[HEN80]   Heninger, K. "Specifying Software Requirements for Complex Systems: New Techniques and Their Application." *IEEE Transactions on Software Engineering* **6,** 1 (January 1980): 2–13.

[IEE84]   Institute of Electrical and Electronics Engineers. *IEEE Guide to Software Requirements Specifications*. ANSI/IEEE Standard 830-1984. New York, 1984.

[PAR76a]   Parnas, D. "On the Design and Development of Program Families." *IEEE Transactions on Software Engineering* **2,** 1 (March 1976): 1–9.

[PAR78]   Parnas, D. "Designing Software for Ease of Extension and Contraction." In *Third International Conference on Software Engineering,* Washington D.C.: Computer Society Press of the Institute of Electrical and Electronics Engineers, 1978. pp. 264–77.

[PAR76]   Parnas, D., and H. Wurges. "Response to Undesired Events in Software Systems." In *Second International Conference on Software Engineering,* Washington D.C.: Computer Society Press of the Institute of Electrical and Electronics Engineers, 1976. pp. 437–46.

[TUR36]   Turing, A. "On Computable Numbers, with an Application to the Entscheidungsproblem." *Proceedings of the London Mathematical Society* **2,** 42 (1936): 230–65.

[YOU89]   Yourdon, E. *Modern Structured Analysis*. Englewood Cliffs, N.J.: Prentice-Hall, 1989.

4

Specifying Behavioral Requirements

In Chapter 3 we learned that a properly written SRS specifies both behavioral and nonbehavioral requirements. Chapter 4 elaborates on the need for, and the techniques available to aid in, specifying the behavioral requirements. Chapter 5 treats the same topics for nonbehavioral requirements.

4.1 INTRODUCTION TO BEHAVIORAL REQUIREMENTS

Behavioral requirements define precisely what inputs are expected by the software, what outputs will be generated by the software, and the details of relationships that exist between those inputs and outputs. In short, behavioral requirements describe all aspects of interfaces between the software and its environment (that is, hardware, humans, and other software). Thus for example, if we wished to build a box with four buttons and two lights and wanted it to behave in a particular way, our behavioral requirements might state

1. There shall be four inputs. They shall be buttons.
   They shall be named *B1, B2, B3,* and *B4.*
2. There shall be two outputs. They shall both be lights. They shall be
   named *L1* and *L2.*
3. *B1* shall be the "power on" button.
4. *B4* shall be the "power off" button.
5. *B2* and *B3* shall be the "action" buttons.
6. After *B1* has been pushed but before *B4* is pushed,
   the system shall be termed "powered on."

7. After *B4* has been pushed but before *B1* is pushed, the system shall be termed "powered off."

8. While powered off, *B2* and *B3* shall have no effect on the system's behavior.

9. When powered off, no lights shall be lit.

10. Since the latest powering on, if *B2* has been pushed more often than *B3*, then *L1* shall be lit.

11. Since the latest powering on, if *B2* has not been pushed more often than *B3*, then *L2* shall be lit.

12. At no time shall more than one light be lit.

13. If either light bulb malfunctions (that is, burns out), the other bulb shall flash on and off in 2-second increments regardless of the number of *B2* and *B3* presses. This flashing shall cease when *B4* is pressed and restart when *B1* is pressed. When the malfunctioning bulb is replaced, the bulb shall cease to flash, and the system shall return to its normal operation.

This is an example of an English language description of the behavior of an extremely trivial system. As systems become more complex however, it becomes increasingly difficult to explain behavior in an unambiguous manner. Even in the preceding trivial system, there may be some doubt about whether or not the system keeps records of *B2* and *B3* presses that occur during periods of malfunctioning bulbs. The answer is critical to understanding the behavior of the system after the malfunctioning bulb has been replaced.

One of the reasons for this ambiguity is the inherent ambiguity in any natural language. In spoken language, intonation, hand movements, and body language provide some clarification, but in our example, not even the spoken word would help alleviate ambiguity. We can think of natural language as a set of atomic elements assembled by SRS writers into documents. Due to the relatively low level of the atoms and the lack of well-defined semantics for each atom, resulting sentences, paragraphs, and requirements become ambiguous.

One solution to this problem is to visualize a shell[1] around the natural language with well-defined semantics. For example, we did just that (albeit matter of factly) with the terms "inputs" and "outputs" in the preceding specification. Although the dictionary gives numerous meanings, the terms were used here in a very specific manner. There was no need to clarify them because it was assumed that all readers of this book have been indoctrinated into computers sufficiently to assign unique semantics to these two terms immediately. We could construct another shell around English that would provide a richer set of semantically clear constructs. When used in this context,

---

[1]*Shell* is being used here in the UNIX[R] sense as a layer of additional capabilities constructed from capabilities at the lower level but not hiding the lower level. UNIX is a registered trademark of AT&T.

this type of shell is often called a model. A model simply provides us with a richer, higher level, and more semantically precise set of constructs than the underlying natural language. Using such a model reduces ambiguity, makes it easier to check for incompleteness, and may at times improve understandability. The reason for the qualifier "at times" in the previous sentence is that as a model becomes increasingly complex, the model itself becomes increasingly more difficult to understand, independent of understanding what is being specified by that model.

The bulk of this chapter is contained in the next section, which surveys techniques for specifying behavioral requirements. With only a few exceptions, each of the surveyed techniques is based on some relatively formal underlying model.

4.2 SURVEY OF TECHNIQUES

The primary purpose for using a requirements specification technique is to reduce the inherent ambiguity of natural language and to let the computer do the difficult work of detecting inconsistencies, redundancies, incompletenesses, and ambiguities. In this section many techniques will be described, compared, and contrasted. The section begins with an introduction that includes the definition of criteria to be used to evaluate techniques. Following this are actual descriptions of formal underlying models, and the techniques and tools that use them. Examples of how the techniques compare and contrast when applied to the three case studies defined at the end of Chapter 1 and analyzed at the end of Chapter 2 are given next. The section concludes with an analysis of the degree to which each of the techniques meet the criteria defined earlier in order to see how well the techniques satisfy the needs of requirements writers.

4.2.1 Introduction

Most requirements specifications today are written in natural language and vary in length from a few pages to five thousand.[2] The size of the document rarely has a relationship to the complexity of the problem. Larger documents are usually created by organizations who aim for more completeness, but in their attempt to create the complete document, they create monsters. The larger the natural language document becomes, the more impossible to keep

---

[2]Incidentally the only SRS I have ever seen as large as five thousand pages was for a central office switching system. That document was used primarily to bring to meetings to say "Look what a great job we are doing writing requirements specifications. Aren't you impressed?" As far as I know, the document was too large to be useful for anything else, let alone as an input to design or a basis for test generation!

it consistent and to maintain it. Fear of ruining such a document becomes a major deterrent to the product's evolution! Let me make my position clear: I am *not* opposed to large SRSs; I *am* opposed to large SRSs written in natural language. My position on SRSs is similar to my position on office buildings; I am *not* opposed to one hundred-story office buildings; I *am* opposed to one hundred-story office buildings constructed entirely of wood.

The solution to the skyscraper problem is simple: Use steel; the solution to the SRS problem is also simple: Use a formal technique. However be aware that wood has its proper place even in a one hundred-story building, and natural language has its proper place in a SRS. When do we use a formal technique and when do we use something else? The answer is:

Use a formal technique when we cannot afford to have the requirement misunderstood.

Chapter 3 stated that one of the primary members of an SRS's reading audience is the customer. The customer is usually an individual expert in some application domain (that is, the one at which the system under specification is aimed) but not necessarily in computer science. Therefore for an SRS written in a formal language to be readable by the customer, it cannot rely on knowledge of computer science. Formality does not necessarily imply difficulty in being read or understood by customers untrained in computer science. We *can* have formality and readability simultaneously [DAV82a]; there are however a number of specification schools that advocate extreme levels of formality in requirements specification (for example, [BER82], [BJO87], [JON80], [LIN79], and [MIL87]). For the most part, these authors are trying to create the ultimately nonambiguous and correct specification: One that can be used as the basis for proving the correctness of programs. Such a level of specification is worthwhile, but beyond the scope of this book.

Just as the most difficult aspect of problem analysis is avoiding the tendency to design (see Section 2.3.1), this is also the most difficult aspect of requirements specification. Figure 2-10a is reproduced here as Figure 4-1 to remind you why the tendency to design is both natural and dangerous. It is natural because in preparing an SRS, we are specifying the external behavior of the software system and this is very similar to specifying the external behavior of software modules. It is also natural because for anything but the most trivial systems, it is necessary to organize the SRS into sections corresponding to major (system) functions. This organization could very well serve as a design; in fact some design approaches (for example, [BER80] and [JAC75]) advocate this as the best design method to employ to optimize

Stage	Aspect	Primary Activity	Primary Goal
Requirements	{ Problem analysis Writing the SRS	Decomposition Behavior description }	Understanding
Design	{ Preliminary design Detailed design	Decomposition Behavior description }	Optimization

Figure 4–1. Similarities Between Requirements and Design.

maintenance costs. As fully explained in Section 2.3.1, (1) the cost of doing a thorough trade-off analysis to determine the optimal design is too great to incur during the requirements phase, and (2) it is dangerous to design a system before having even determined what it should do externally.

The following subsections discuss a variety of behavioral requirements specification techniques and their underlying models. In order to judge these fairly, we should initially define what traits we would like to see such a technique exhibit; for example,

1. Proper use of the technique should reduce ambiguity in the SRS.
2. Proper use of the technique should result in an SRS that is helpful to and understandable by customers and users who are not computer specialists.
3. Proper use of the technique should result in an SRS that can serve effectively as the basis for design and test.
4. The technique should provide automated checking for ambiguity, incompleteness, and inconsistency.
5. The technique should encourage the requirements writer to think and write in terms of external product behavior, not the product's internal components.
6. The technique should help organize information in the SRS.
7. The technique should provide a basis for automated prototype generation and automated system test generation.
8. The technique should facilitate SRS modification.
9. The technique should permit annotation and traceability.
10. The technique should employ underlying models that facilitate the description of a system's external behavior within the intended application environment.

Keep in mind that the ability of a requirements writer to specify a system correctly is primarily a function of the number of techniques that writer knows how and when to apply. Remember the following guidelines:

1. *Given any specific problem, the skills of developers and users must be considered before selecting a technique.*

2. *Given any specific problem and the skills of developers and users, there still may be more than one ideal approach.*

3. *No single approach will suffice in a complex world.* Knowing one technique well will help in some aspects of some problems, but we need a richly packed toolbox to be really effective.

4. *Do not fall in love with the latest fad.* Many requirements writers follow a particular technique taught by some self-proclaimed guru.

5. *"Know-when" is as important as "know-how".* Even if the requirements writer knows all existing techniques, he or she would be ineffective if the wrong tool were used at the wrong time.

Techniques needed to specify the external behavior of real-time systems are quite different than those required for non–real-time systems. Therefore the following two sections discuss techniques suited for real-time and non–real-time applications, respectively.

4.2.2 Techniques for Real-Time Systems

This section explores SRS techniques ideally suited for real-time applications (these are DY applications, as defined in Section 1.4):

> Finite state machines
> Decision tables and decision trees
> Program Design Language (PDL)
> Statecharts
> Requirements Engineering Validation System (REVS)
> Requirements Language Processor (RLP)
> Specification and Description Language (SDL)
> PAISLey
> Petri nets

4.2.2.1 Finite state machines

A *finite state machine* is a hypothetical machine that can be in only one of a given number of states at any specific time. In response to an input, the machine generates an output and changes state. Both the output (O) and the next state (S_N) are purely functions of the current state (S_C) and the input (I). Thus

$$S_N = F(S_C, I)$$

$$O = G(S_C, I)$$

To show how such a model enriches our ability to describe external behavior, let us try to describe your behavior as you read these words. If all we have is the English language, we are saddled with inherent ambiguity. On the other hand, we can model you (that is, the system under specification) as a finite state machine and this book and these words you are now reading as your environment (see Figure 4-2). Now we can use the words "state," "stimulus," "action," and "response" unambiguously. For example,

1. You are in a certain state (of mind) now. It is a function of all your life's experiences, all the things that may have happened to you during the past twenty-four hours, all the things you ever learned, etc.

2. These words are coming at you one at a time, and as they do, they serve as stimuli to you.

3. As each word is received by you, you change your state and you respond. Single words coming at you one at a time have little effect on your state; all they do is trigger you to store the words or concepts in your short-term memory and make a temporary change in your state.

4. When you get near the end of a sentence however, you begin to glean the overall concept being conveyed and only then do you respond with a discernible output (for example, a sigh, raise eyebrows, say "hmmmm") and only then do you make a (hopefully) permanent change in your state

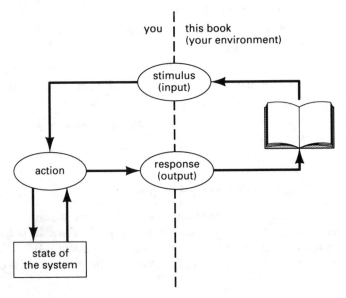

Figure 4–2. A Simple Application of FSMs.

(i.e., you have learned something). Usually such permanent state changes occur only at the ends of sentences.

5. It is possible for your environment to force you to convert the usually temporary state change of the words in the middle of a sentence into a more permanent one. The easiest way of doing this is simply to stop in the middle of. See what I mean?

6. What you learn (i.e., the permanent changes in your state) is purely a function of the stimuli (i.e., these words) and your current state. The former is obviously true; the latter must also be true, for if it were not, then all readers regardless of background would learn the same things from reading these words (which is obviously not true).

7. Your responses are also purely a function of the stimuli and your current state. Obviously when I have written something boring, you respond differently than when I write something insightful. Obviously your current state also affects your response. For example, some of you (based on your background) are responding right now in a certain way because you are fascinated by either the high degree of self-referential statements in this section [HOF86] or because I appear to be speaking to you even though you are reading this "right now" years after I am writing this "right now!"

All of the preceding would have been a lot more difficult to understand had we not previously established the notion of the finite state machine as the underlying model. In general it is possible to model both the system and its environment as finite state machines (see Figure 4-3).

There are two notations commonly used to define finite state machines: *state transition diagrams* (STDs, for short) and *state transition matrices* (STMs, for short). In STDs a circle denotes a state; a directed arc connecting two states denotes the potential to transition between the two indicated states; and the label on the arc, which has two parts separated by a slash, means the input that triggers the transition and the output with which the system responds. For example, Figure 4-4 shows a small part of the specification of the external behavior of a telephone switching system. Starting with the *idle* state on the left side, there is exactly one arc emanating from it. It is labeled *off hook / dial tone* and terminates at the *dial tone* state. That means that when the system is in the *idle* state and receives the stimulus *off hook,* it will generate a *dial tone* and enter the *dial tone* state. There are four arcs emanating from the *dial tone* state, and the path taken will be a function of whether the system receives an *on hook* (the system will generate *quiet* and return to the *idle* state), a *9* (the system will generate a *distinctive dial tone* and enter the *distin. dial tone* state), a *dial idle number* (the system will generate a *ring back tone* and enter the *ringing* state), or a *dial busy number* (the system will generate a *busy tone* and enter the *busy* state).

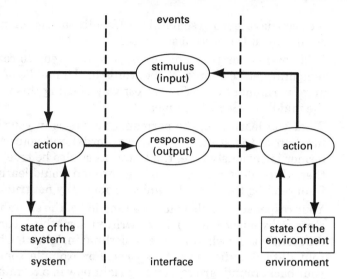

Note: actors may be computers, people, software, or general hardware.

Figure 4–3. The Environment and the System Modeled as FSMs.

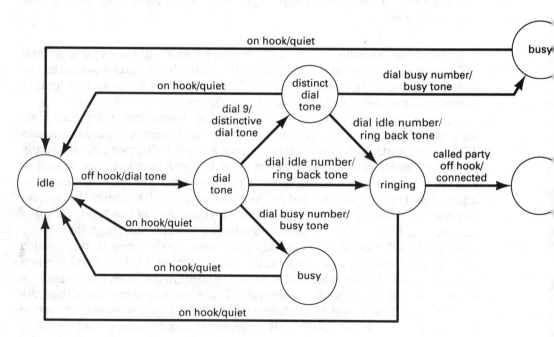

Figure 4–4. State Transition Diagram Example.

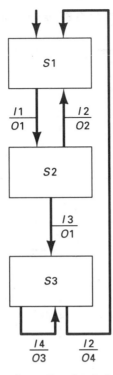

Figure 4-5. SA/RT Tool State Transition Diagram Notation.

It *is* possible to describe the behavior shown in Figure 4-4 in natural language; in fact most of the previous paragraph is just that. However as soon as we stop speaking of states, inputs, and outputs, the behavioral description becomes extremely difficult to create or understand. Many of the structured analysis/RT tools described in Section 2.3.3.2 permit the modeling of control processes using finite state machines within DFDs. Since DFDs and state transition diagrams both use bubbles and arrows as their standard notation, someone reading a new diagram may become confused before determining which one it is. To alleviate this potential problem, most structured analysis/RT tools have adopted a rectangle as the notation of choice for a state in a state transition diagram, as shown in Figure 4-5.

Remember that Figure 4-4 is part of an SRS; it is not a design. The implication to the designer reading Figure 4-4 in the SRS is

> Dear designer: I don't care how you design the system, but when it is all done and I observe it as a black box, I want it to behave externally as if it were designed as the finite state machine shown. Signed, the Requirements Writer.

The second way of describing the behavior of a finite state machine is the STM. In an STM a table is drawn with all the possible states labeling the rows and all possible stimuli labeling the columns. The next state and the required system response appear at each intersection (see Figure 4-6).

Until this point, we have assumed that the system response is a function of the transition (that is, on the STD the response was on an arc, and on the

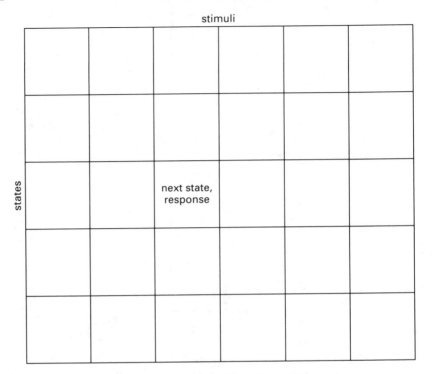

Figure 4–6. STM for Finite State (Mealy) Machines.

STM the response was in an intersection). This is the *Mealy model* of a finite state machine. An alternative is the *Moore model* in which system responses are associated with the state rather than the transition between states. On Moore STDs, arcs are labeled with only the stimulus name, and circles are labeled with the state name and the system response. On Moore STMs, intersections of columns and rows contain only the name of the next state, and a separate column is drawn to indicate the system response associated with each state (see Figure 4-7). Moore and Mealy machines are identical with respect to their power; trivial algorithms exist to transform either one into the other (see any introductory textbook on automata theory for the algorithm— e.g., [KAI72]). The choice between Mealy and Moore is yours and should basically be guided by which one is most expressive and understandable for the particular application. Figure 4-8 shows a small subset of a telephone switching system's external behavior using a Moore STM.

Finite state machines have been used effectively for requirements specifications for telephony applications (e.g., [WHI81] and [KAW71]). They also serve as the underlying model of many of the techniques to follow, including statecharts, REVS, RLP, and SDL.

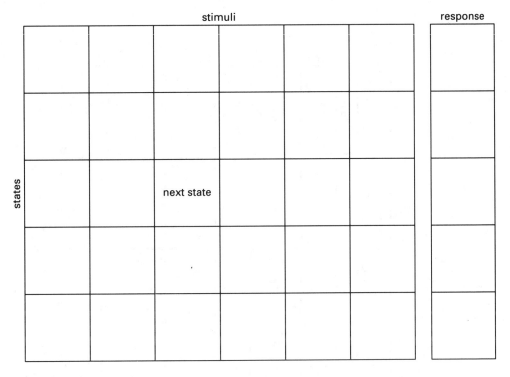

Figure 4–7. STM for Finite State (Moore) Machines.

4.2.2.2 Decision tables and decision trees

It is sometimes necessary to describe the required external behavior of some aspect of a system, but the finite state machine approach makes no sense. For example, if we want to specify the external behavior of a software-controlled elevator door on an elevator control system, we would easily agree that

- If the elevator stops at a floor and the *open door* button is pushed, the elevator doors shall open.
- If the *close door* button is pressed, the elevator doors shall close.
- If the time limit is exceeded, the elevator doors shall close.

We would also readily agree that the SRS should include the preceding three statements, but what if a combination of these conditions is true. For example, what do we do when the time limit is exceeded and the open door button is pressed. In general, required system responses to all combinations of these stimuli is difficult to describe using a finite state machine and even

Stimulus \ State	Lift Phone	Dial 9	Dial 1-8	Dial 0	Hang up Phone	Seventh Digit Collected	Outputs
Idle	Dial tone	—	—	—	—	—	Quiet
Dial tone state	—	Distinctive dial tone	Collecting 7 digits	Operator	Idle	—	Dial tone to calling party
Distinctive dial tone state	—	Collecting 7 digits	Collecting 7 digits	Operator	Idle	—	Distinctive dial tone to calling party
Operator state	—	—	—	—	Idle	—	Connect calling party to operator
Collecting 7 digits state	—	Collecting 7 digits	Collecting 7 digits	Collecting 7 digits	Idle	If called party busy, busy otherwise, ringing	No tone to calling party
Ringing state	…	…	…	…	…	…	Ringing signal to called party; ringback tone to calling party
Busy state	…	…	…	…	…	…	Busy tone to calling party

Figure 4–8. Finite State Machine Telephony Example.

more difficult to describe in English. One simple solution involves a decision table. Decision tables and decision trees have been known for decades; their uses and capabilities were recently explored thoroughly by Moret [MOR82] and Chvalovsky [CHV83].

Decision tables and *decision trees* relate sets of conditions to prescribed actions. To construct a decision table, first draw a row for each condition (or stimulus) that will be used in the process of making a decision, as shown in Figure 4-9. Next draw a column for every possible combination of outcomes from those conditions (if there are n conditions and each has a binary result, there will be 2^n columns). Then add rows at the bottom of the table for each action (or response) you want the system to perform (or generate) and fill in the boxes to reflect which actions you want performed for each combination of conditions. Figure 4-10 shows a decision table for a software-controlled elevator door problem. Even though it has sixty-four columns, the table is easier to create and understand than an STD or STM and considerably easier to understand than the corresponding description in English.

A decision tree captures the same information as a decision table but is graphic rather than tabular. It is roughly a flow chart without loops and without fan-in. In general a decision tree takes up more room than the corresponding decision table because of the blank space required between nodes. On the other hand, a decision tree captures the order of evaluating conditions, and thus it is often possible to save considerable space due to the all-encompassing effect of some conditions. For example, the decision tree in Figure 4-11 shows the same behavior as the decision table in Figure 4-10.

If there is an aspect of a system whose behavior can easily be modeled using a decision table or tree, how do you decide which to use? A decision table is always good (1) for initial analysis of behavior, (2) when most combinations of conditions are possible, and (3) if you suspect you omitted something from the analysis due to the problem's complexity. The decision tree is good (1) for final packaging (some find a tree easier to understand because it has a start and an end, unlike a table) and (2) when certain key conditions overwhelmingly determine a decision outcome, as when the elevator door is blocked or the open door button is pressed in the example.

Decision tables can easily be "automated" with any standard spreadsheet package, such as Symphony.[3] The external behavior of at least two products were specified using decision tables [BUH79, MAT77].

4.2.2.3 Program Design Language

Program Design Language (PDL) is now the de facto standard for specifying detailed designs for software modules. Also known as structured English and pseudo code, PDL is simply free-form English with certain key words reserved with special meanings. The most commonly used PDL today, pro-

---

[3]Symphony is a trademark of Lotus Development, Inc.

one column for every combination of condition outcomes

all combinations of answers

fill in with the actual required system behavior

list all conditions that influence decisions

list all possible decisions

	rule #1	rule #2	rule #3	rule #4	rule #5	rule #6	rule #7	rule #8
condition #1	Y	Y	Y	Y	N	N	N	N
condition #2	Y	Y	N	N	Y	Y	N	N
condition #3	Y	N	Y	N	Y	N	Y	N
action #1	X	X	X				X	
action #2		X	X	X				
action #3						X		
action #4	X			X	X			

Figure 4–9. Decision Table.

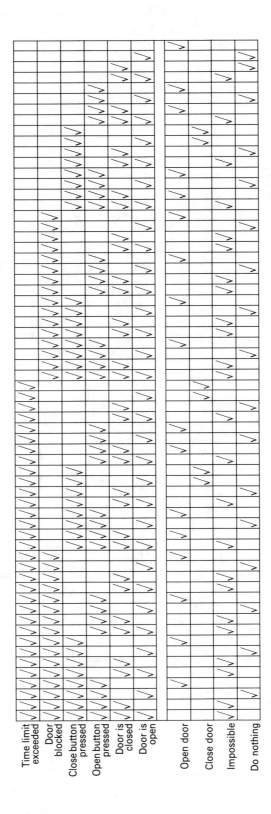

Figure 4–10. A Decision Table for an Elevator Door Control.

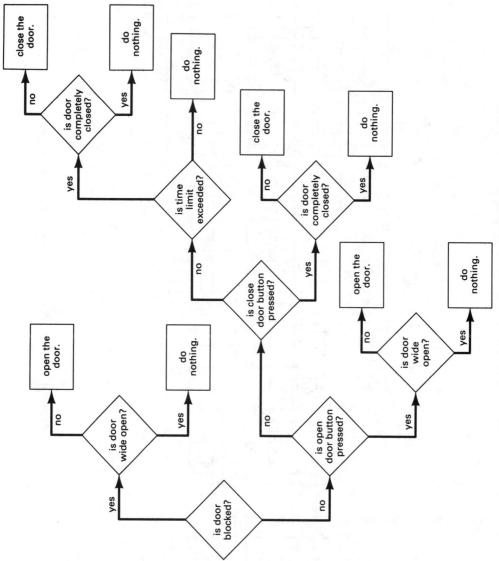

Figure 4-11. A Decision Tree for an Elevator Door Control.

cessed by a tool called PDL [CAI75] produced by Caine, Farber, and Gordon of Pasadena, California, uses the following key word constructs: IF...THEN...ELSE...ENDIF, DO...ENDDO, UNDO, CYCLE, and DO CASE. The tool itself accepts the free-form Englishlike input, reformats it, generates cross-references between selected key words, underlines key words, and reports on poorly nested or unended IFs or DOs. Although primarily developed for specifying design logic, PDL can be used for behavioral requirements as well.

Many people who see PDL in SRSs claim that requirements writers have overstepped their bounds and fallen into design; I disagree. I believe that these objections are being voiced only because people are so accustomed to seeing PDL during design that they refuse even to read the PDL to find out what it says. Format does not make something appropriate for the requirements or the design phase; the content does. For example, let us return to the elevator door control problem. As you recall we agreed that it is important during the requirements phase to completely specify the desired external behavior of the doors resulting from all possible combinations of external stimuli that might be present. Figure 4-12 shows a PDL specification for the same behavior as Figures 4-10 and 4-11.

One of the greatest problems in using PDL during the requirements phase is the natural tendency to design. The best advice to help avoid designing is to insist initially on the nouns, verbs, and adjectives to be used in the SRS. The rule to be used in selecting these terms is simple: They should be things that can be seen, smelled, felt, heard, or tasted by some person or thing that is an external observer of the final system. This approach of preselecting key words

```
IF door blocked
THEN IF door not wide open
        THEN open door
        ENDIF
ELSE IF open-door button pressed
        THEN IF door not wide open
                THEN open door
                ENDIF
        ELSE IF close-door button pressed
                THEN IF door not completely closed
                        THEN close door
                        ENDIF
                ELSE IF time limit exceeded
                        THEN IF door not completely closed
                                THEN close door
                                ENDIF
                        ENDIF
                ENDIF
        ENDIF
ENDIF
```

Figure 4–12. PDL for an Elevator Door Control. © 1986 IEEE Computer Society

was demonstrated for telephony by Davis [DAV79] and Casey [CAS81] and for a flight control application by Heninger [HEN79]. In the first two cases, the observer is the human user of the telephone system. In the last case, the observer is the total hardware/software/pilot environment of the A-7E operational flight program. McMenamin and Palmer [MCM84] make another suggestion for avoiding design. Typically using PDL forces us to state a particular order for a series of activities when one is not really absolutely required. They suggest using a PARALLEL construct to imply that a set of requirements exist but in no particular order.

4.2.2.4 Statecharts

Extensions to finite state machines (FSM) called *statecharts* were proposed by Harel [HAR87, HAR88, HAR88a] that make it even easier to model complex real-time system behavior unambiguously. Ward [WAR85], Hatley [HAT84], and Yourdon [YOU89] had all proposed modeling real-time systems as hierarchies of data flow diagrams in which the behavior of selected processes is defined as a finite state machine. However their leveling conventions relied on hierarchical relationships inherent in DFDs; there was no concept in these extensions to structured analysis that captured hierarchies of finite state machines. The Harel extensions provide a notation and set of conventions that facilitate the hierarchical decomposition of finite state machines and a mechanism for communication between concurrent finite state machines. Salter [SAL76] had originally suggested the hierarchical definition of FSMs but did not present the formal basis or semantics behind them.

The first extension to FSMs suggested by Harel allows a transition to be a function of not only an external stimulus but also the truth of a particular condition. In Figure 4-13, the transition between states S_1 and S_2 would occur when stimulus i is received and condition C is true. Anyone who has ever attempted to use an FSM to describe the behavior of a local call on a telephone switching system will immediately see an obvious use for this simple extension. As shown in Figure 4-14, the condition becomes a convenient notation for specifying that the new state (that is, *busy tone* or *ringback tone*) is a function of whether or not the party being called (the *callee*) is busy.

The next simple extension is the *superstate*. The superstate can be used to aggregate sets of states with common transitions. For example, let us assume that two states S_1 and S_2 both transition to state S_3 on the same stimulus, i. Using regular STDs, Figure 4-15a would result. However, with the superstate concept, we can use the shorthand shown in Figure 4-15b. Telephony once again provides an excellent example. In particular the *caller* going

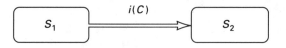

Figure 4–13. Conditional Transition Extension to FSMs.

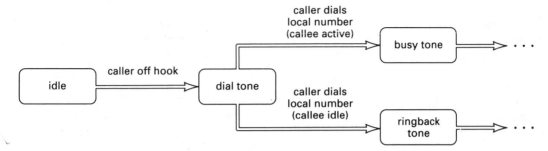

Figure 4–14. Using the Condition Transition Extension for a Local Telephone Call.

on hook causes a transition from most call states back to the *idle* state; Figure 4-16 demonstrates this application of the superstate. It is apparent that superstates can in fact be conceived of and defined before they are decomposed into subordinate states; thus superstates provide a formal basis for iterative refinement and successive decomposition of FSMs. For instance in the telephone example, we could have begun our description of the external behavior of the switch with Figure 4-17. After analyzing the behavior at this level, we could refine the *caller active* state into its subordinate states, as shown in Figure 4-16.

The preceding examples demonstrate how refinement and superstates work with transitions out of superstates and their subordinate states. The same can be said of transitions into superstates except that the resulting refined statechart becomes underspecified with respect to the true destination of an incoming transition. For example, assume we have defined the statechart shown in Figure 4-18a. Next we refine state S_2 into the more detailed decomposition shown in Figure 4-18b. At this point in time, it is not clear what really happens when stimulus i arrives while in state S_1. Do we enter state S_{21} or S_{22}? The solution to this is to extend the incoming arrows to their appropriate next (subordinate) state, as shown in Figure 4-18c.

Harel also introduces the concept of the *default entry state,* which is the subordinate state of a superstate into which the FSM enters if no other subordinate state is specified as the next state. One specifies such a default entry state with a small arrow, as shown in Figure 4-19. Thus, Figure 4-19 implies that there is a transition from state S_1 to state S_{21} in the event of stimulus i and is therefore equivalent to Figure 4-18c. The default entry state is equivalent to the start states of finite state machines.

In the preceding paragraphs, we described the process of decomposing a state (say, S_2) into subordinate states (say, S_{21} and S_{22}). The implied semantics of this refinement are that of an "or" function; namely, that when we are in state S_2 at the higher level of abstraction, we are really in either state S_{21} *or*

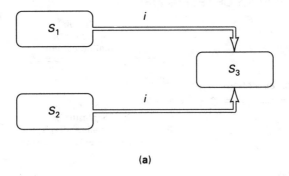

(a)

S₄ superstate

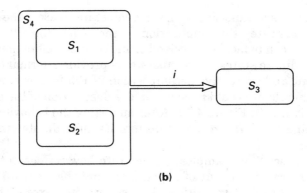

(b)

Figure 4–15. The Superstate Extension to FSMs.

state S_{22} at the lower level of abstraction. Harel also introduces a different kind of state refinement, the "and" function. An "and" decomposition in statecharts is represented by splitting a box with dashed lines. For example, Figure 4-20a shows a simple statechart; Figure 4-20b shows the refinement of state S_2 into its two subordinate states S_{21} and S_{22}. The semantics behind this notation are well defined. In particular, when we are in state S_2, we are states

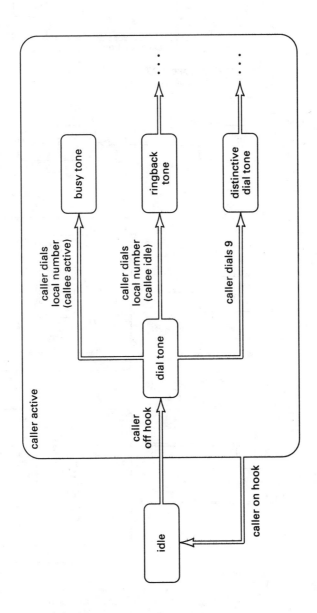

Figure 4-16. Using the Superstate Extension in Telephony.

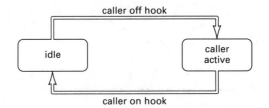

Figure 4–17. The Higher Level Statechart.

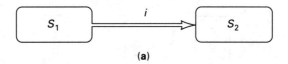

(a)

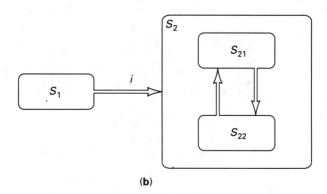

(b)

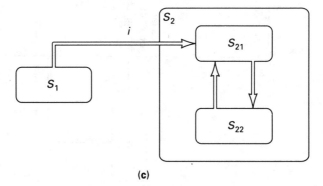

(c)

Figure 4–18. Refining States with Incoming Transitions. **(a)** Highest Level Statecharts. **(b)** Refinement of State S_2. **(c)** Completing the Transition Specifications.

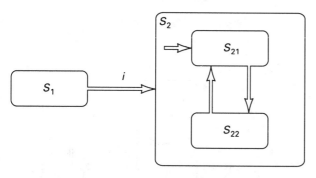

Figure 4-19. Default Entry State Example.

in S_{21} *and* S_{22}. This becomes more meaningful when states S_{21} and S_{22} are further refined, as shown in Figure 4-20c. On receipt of stimulus i_1 in state S_1, we enter both states S_{211} and S_{222} simultaneously. Now if stimulus i_4 arrives, there is a transition from states S_{211} *and* S_{222} simultaneously into states S_{212} and S_{223}. On the other hand, if stimulus i_6 arrives while we are in states S_{211} and S_{222}, only the S_{22} machine changes from state S_{222} to S_{221}, leaving us in both S_{211} and S_{221}. The term used by Harel to describe this type of decomposition is *orthogonal,* to emphasize the independence of state machines S_{21} and S_{22}.

The simplicity, applicability, and elegance of Harel's orthogonal decomposition becomes most apparent when we compare equivalent behavioral descriptions using conventional state transition diagrams. Figure 4-21 shows the equivalent to Figure 4-20c using conventional STDs. Not only has the number of states increased, but the monolithic structure of Figure 4-21 makes it extremely difficult to understand in comparison to the statechart in Figure 4-20c.

Earlier we discussed the ability to specify triggering a transition not only on a stimulus arrival but also on the truth of a condition (for example, see Figures 4-13 and 4-14). In concert with the orthogonality refinement, Harel has also defined the ability to specify a transition based on whether an FSM is in a particular state. For example, Figure 4-22 shows a modification to Figure 4-20c in order to specify that the transition from state S_{213} to state S_{211} will occur only if machine (superstate) S_{22} is in state S_{222}.

In summary Harel's statecharts provide natural extensions to FSMs to make them more suitable for specifying external behavior of real-time (i.e., DY) systems. These extensions provide for the hierarchical decomposition of states and specification of transitions dependent on global conditions and being in particular states. An example of using statecharts to describe external behavior is given in Section 4.2.5.4. An excellent description of how statecharts was applied to one particular application, an automobile cruise control, has been provided by Smith and Gerhart [SMI88]. Smith and Gerhart also have identified one shortcoming of statecharts; although notations provide for the unambiguous and concise specification of processes and objects and their interaction,

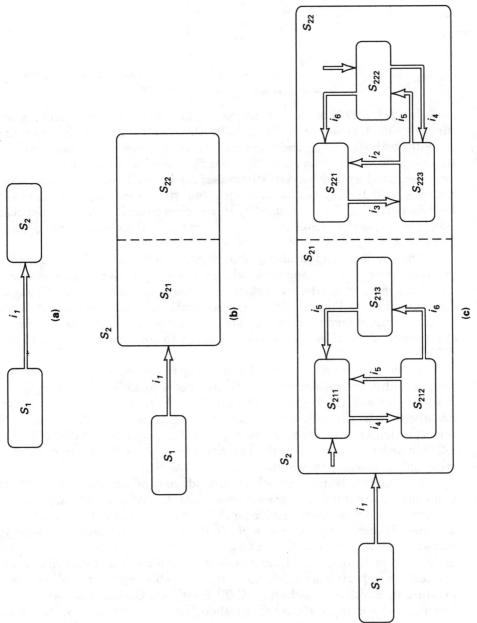

Figure 4-20. Refinement Using the "and" Function. (a) Highest Level Statechart. (b) Refinement of State S_2. (c) Refinement of States S_{21} and S_{22}.

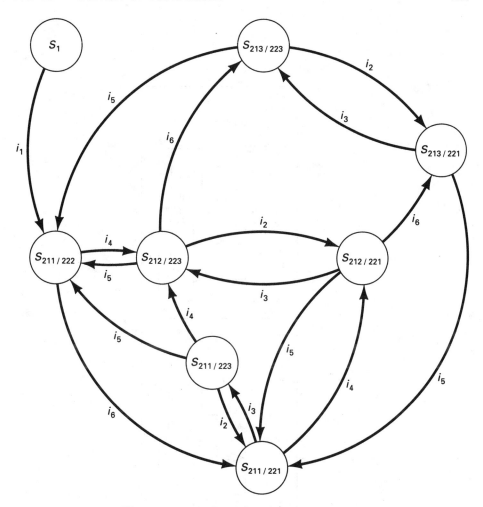

Figure 4–21. An Equivalent Conventional STD.

these fall short of acceptability for specifying multiple instances of a particular process or object. For example, in the electronic funds transfer (EFT) problem analyzed by Smith and Gerhart, they were able to model all of the various objects and their interrelationships. However the authors found it extremely difficult to specify relative priorities or protocols between multiple (but identical) EFT terminals. The reason is that each state name, condition, and object must have a unique name. Thus it is necessary to identify each of the EFT terminals by name, for example, *eft*1, *eft*2, and *eft*3. This may work for a few terminals but obviously not for a large number. We need some way of specifying a class of object and a way of identifying particular instantiations without giving them unique names and redefining their behavior.

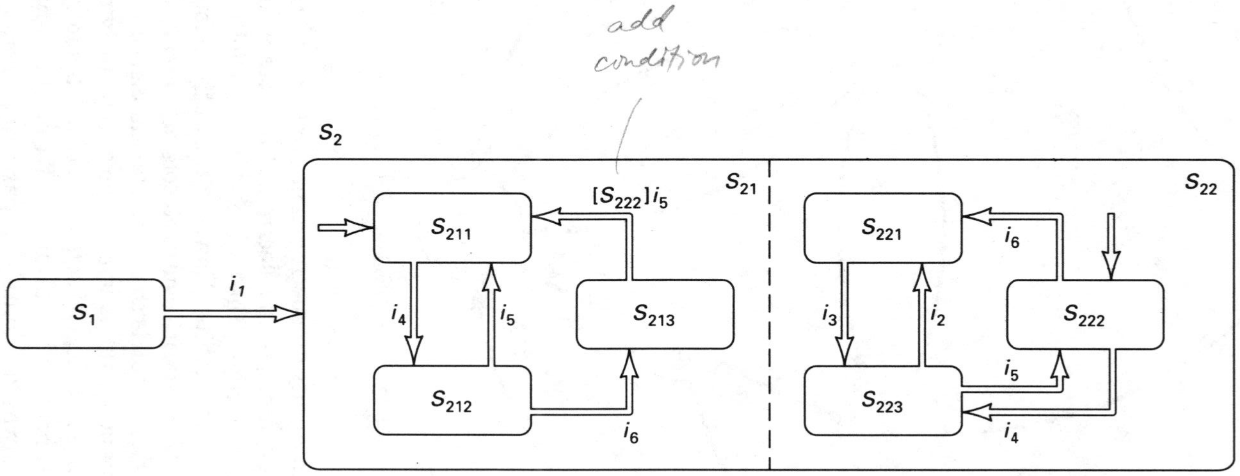

Figure 4-22. Specifying Transitions Dependent on States.

I-Logix, Inc., in Burlington, Massachusetts, has developed a tool called STATEMATE that captures all of Harel's statecharts and then some.[4] Using STATEMATE, requirements writers can describe the system from three perspectives [ILO85, HAR87a].

- The *functional view* allows creation of data flow diagrams.
- The *behavioral view* allows creation of statecharts.
- The *structural view* allows creation of actual designs of system and environmental components.

These views can be created in any order but are considered fully interdependent in that they must all describe the identical system, or said another way, there must exist a system for which the three views are possible. Notations for DFDs are similar to the tools discussed in Section 2.3.3.2; notations used for statecharts are identical to that of Harel.

One of the most powerful features of STATEMATE is its simulation capability. While watching any of the three views on the screen, we may "turn on" the system and see it actually behave in simulated real time. This is most effective when both the system and its environment have been modeled. This way the simulation runs autonomously without interaction between the user and the tool. Watching the behavioral view is extremely helpful for understanding the expected external behavior of the system. Once the simulation is running, active states appear in a different color, so that we can easily see the total state of the system (that is, the cross product of all active states), and as transitions occur, new states flash to alert the user of the impending state change.

4.2.2.5 Requirements Engineering Validation System

The *Requirements Engineering Validation System* (REVS) [DAV77] is a set of tools that analyzes requirements written in the *Requirements Statement Language* (RSL) [BEL76] developed using the *Software Requirements Engineering Methodology* (SREM) (pronounced as if it were spelled "shrem") [ALF77]. The tools, language, and methodology were developed by TRW, Inc., for the U.S. Army Ballistic Missile Defense (now called the Strategic Defense Command) Advanced Technology Center in Huntsville, Alabama. RSL is an extension to conventional FSMs. In particular for some large, complex real-time system, it may not make sense to describe the external behavior of the entire system as one large finite state machine. Harel's extensions (described in previous subsections), which provide the hierarchical decomposition of FSMs, may also not be simple or straightforward to apply. In particular some applications are *stimulus rich,* which means that customers view the system

---

[4]STATEMATE is a trademark of i-Logix, Inc.

they want to buy or build in terms of its rich set of stimuli. For such systems it is simpler for customers to think of their problem (or requirements for the solution system's external behavior) as organized into a set of units, where each unit describes all required system responses to a single stimulus. The best way of recognizing application of this type is to visualize potential customers asking questions about the product. If questions concern stimuli names, for example, in the case of a helicopter landing system,

What happens if a large gust of wind suddenly arrives?
What happens if the pilot accidentally pushes on the throttle too much?
What happens if a landing strut breaks?

then the application is one for which organization by stimuli makes sense and REVS is ideal. If on the other hand, questions concern sequences of stimuli, or user features, for example, in the case of a telephone switching system,

How do I make a long distance call?
How do I forward a call?
How do I respond to a call waiting?

then the application is one for which organization by stimuli probably will not make the SRS more readable and REVS becomes less helpful. By the way I know of no way of categorizing this class of applications other than by using the preceding role playing. Note that you cannot fake the answer very well. Try for example to ask stimulus-oriented questions about the telephony example (and remember you are the customer asking these questions!).

What happens if I dial a 9?
What happens if I hang up?
What happens if I dial an 0?

These are highly unlikely questions. In fact the only valid answer is to ask another question, "What are you trying to do? Make a long distance call? Call the operator? What?" In other words the important issue in telephony is, "What does the user/environment want to do?" rather than "What happens when this stimulus arrives?"

The organizational unit of the SRS corresponding to all expected behaviors of the system in response to a given stimulus is called an *R-net* [ALF76]. We can think of an R-net as a column of the state transition matrix, and thus the R-net is simply an organizational piece of a full FSM. The R-net notation is shown in Figure 4-23. Figure 4-24 shows an example of an R-net for the *dial*

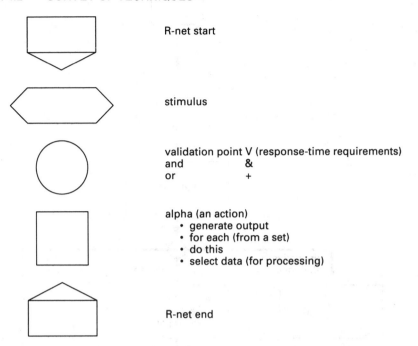

R-net start

stimulus

validation point V (response-time requirements)
and   &
or   +

alpha (an action)
  • generate output
  • for each (from a set)
  • do this
  • select data (for processing)

R-net end

Figure 4–23.   R-net Notation.

9 column in Figure 4-8. Figure 4-25 defines the same behavior in RSL. REVS accepts sets of RSL specifications; checks them for inconsistency, ambiguity, and incompleteness; reports such violations; and creates a requirements data base for later use and analysis.

The SREM methodology is a seven-step process (adapted from [ALF85]).

1. *Define kernal:* Identify all stimuli and all responses; write an R-net for each stimulus; define all the alphas (that is, processing requirements) in the R-nets.

2. *Establish baseline:* Enter all R-nets written in RSL into REVS for translation, consistency checking, and requirements data base creation.

3. *Define data:* For each alpha, define all data inputs and outputs.

4. *Establish traceability:* Trace all detailed requirements back to top-level requirements; ensure that all top-level requirements are satisfied.

5. *Simulate functionality:* Write prototype code for selected sections of the system and simulate the functionality of the specified system.

6. *Identify performance requirements:* Define traceable testable performance requirements.

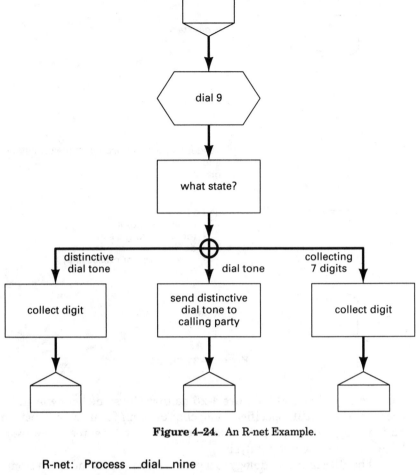

Figure 4–24. An R-net Example.

R-net: Process __dial__nine

Structure:
      Input__interface digit__9__dialed__by__calling__party
      What__state
      Do (state = dial tone)
              Send__distinctive__dial__tone__to__calling__party
     (state = collecting 7 digits)
              Collect__digit
              Terminate
     (distinctive dial tone)
              Collect__digit
              Terminate

     End
   End

Figure 4–25. An RSL Example.

7. Demonstrate feasibility: Write prototype code for selected sections of the system and simulate performance characteristics of the specified system.

Figure 4-26 shows the various tools that comprise REVS (adapted from [DAV77]). REVS has been operational since 1977; originally hosted on a Texas Instruments Advanced Scientific Computer and a CDC 7600, it was later rewritten in PASCAL and rehosted on VAX. The most recent implementation was written in Ada and hosted on VAX and IBM PC-AT computers. TRW has also extended this effort to earlier phases of systems development, particularly systems design [ALF85]. The resulting tool, called the Distributed Computing Design System (DCDS) includes a system-level requirements methodology (SYSREM); a system-level requirement language (SSL); and a system design language, called the Distributed Design Language (DDL). System-level components are defined in terms of functional networks (F-nets). Tools used during software requirements also ensure conformity between R-nets and these F-nets.

4.2.2.6 Requirements Language Processor

The *Requirements Language Processor* (RLP) [DAV78, DAV79a] is part of an overall *Requirements Processing System* (RPS) that was developed by GTE Laboratories in Waltham, Massachusetts. The motivation for developing RLP was similar to that of REVS: Namely, that monolithic FSMs seemed to be too unwieldly for requirements specification of complex real-time systems. Whereas REVS uses the R-net as the organizational unit of the SRS, RLP uses the *stimulus-response sequence,* which is a trace of a two-way dialog between the system under specification and its environment. Selecting which sequences to use is straightforward: Use sequences that define *typical* dialogs. These typical dialogs should correspond to actual user-oriented, user-known, external system features.

The decision of whether or not to use RLP in a particular application should be based on questions a typical customer or user would ask about the product. If the questions are about features (for example, long-distance calls, call forwarding) rather than particular stimuli (for example, dialing 0, dialing 9), then RLP may be the answer. Also RLP is *multilingual* [TAY80, DAV82a], which means that it supports a wide variety of requirements languages, each tailored to a specific application. For example, it might be desirable to use RLP for four different applications: battlefield command and control, patient monitoring, ballistic missile defense, and nuclear reactor control. We would define those four languages in language definition tables, as shown in Figure 4-27 (adapted from [DAV80]). Once these tables exist, requirements writers would select an appropriate language, write requirements using that language, and run RLP. RLP checks requirements for correct syntax and semantics; detects and reports violations; detects and reports inconsistencies, ambiguities and

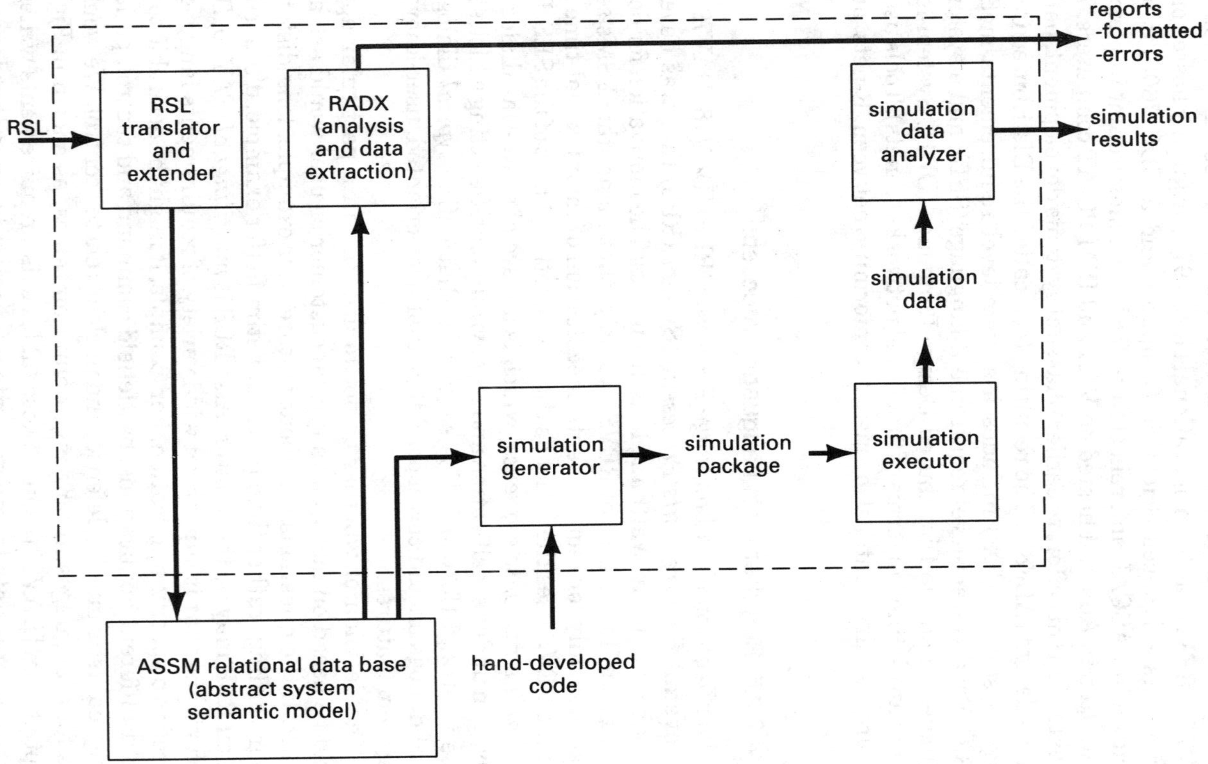

Figure 4-26. REVS Tools.

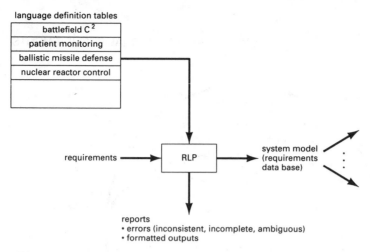

Figure 4-27. The Requirements Language Processor Architecture.

incompletenesses in the requirements; and generates a requirements data base. This data base can later be used to drive automatic system test generation [BAU78, DAV78, DAV80, DAS81, CHA85], automated requirements simulation [DAV82], and automatic program synthesis [DAV82b].

Using a sequence of stimulus-response pairs to define typical dialogs would appear to work in applications that are scenario or feature intensive. We would expect scenarios that look like Figure 4-28; however two problems arise that make scenarios more complex—states and fan-out. First, not all features begin in a single *idle* or *initial* state (for example, the call-waiting feature from the called party's perspective begins when that party is involved in another phone conversation). If all features began in the same state, then the completely integrated set of features would resemble Figure 4-29, where each feature is a sequence of stimuli and responses, as indicated previously. Since this is not the case, it is necessary to specify the beginning and ending states for each sequence. But to show how features interconnect (for example, that the call-waiting feature from the called party's perspective begins in the *connected* state, where the *connected* state is the same one that occurs in the middle of the local call when two parties are connected), it is also necessary to specify names of intermediate states that are passed through during typical scenarios. These state names can then be used by RLP to merge separately

Stimulus 1

Response 1

Stimulus 2

Response 2

Stimulus 3

Response 3

.

.

.

Figure 4-28. Simple Stimulus-Response Sequence.

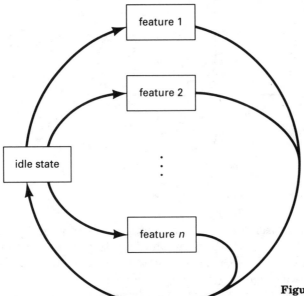

Figure 4-29. Features in Which They All Start at the Same State.

written features into one integrated system-level requirements data base. Thus Figure 4-27 becomes a bit more complex, as shown in Figure 4-30.

The second complicating factor is fan-out. Most interesting scenarios provide choices for the environment and the system. An example of the former occurs during a local call when either of the two parties who are connected may hang up the phone. An example of the latter occurs after dialing a local number, since the system will provide the calling party with either a ringback tone or a busy tone, depending on the state of the called party. To achieve these capabilities, the stimulus-response sequence must check system resources (IF <predicate> THEN...ELSE...) and wait for particular stimuli to arrive (WAIT FOR

```
(Initial)  State     0
Stimulus   1
Response   1
State   1
Stimulus   2
Response   2
State   2
Stimulus   3
Response   3
           .
           .
           .
```

Figure 4-30. A More Complex Stimulus-Response Sequence.

<stimuli set>). Thus the really useful stimulus-response sequence becomes Figure 4-31. Figure 4-32 shows a complete example of the external behavior of a local call [DAV82a]. RLP also has the capability of translating textual requirements languages into SDL, as defined in the following section.

4.2.2.7 Specification and Description Language

The *Specification and Description Language* (SDL) [ROC82] was developed in the late 1970s by CCITT for the external behavioral and internal design of telephone switching systems. SDL is based on FSMs (see Section 4.2.2.1) and can be used to specify R-nets or stimulus–response sequences. The basic building blocks are shown in Figure 4-33. Figure 4-34 shows the SDL for the identical segment of an SRS shown in Figure 4-32.

4.2.2.8 PAISLey

The *Process-oriented, Applicative, and Interpretable Specification Language* (PAISLey) was developed by Pamela Zave while at the University of Maryland and at AT&T Bell Laboratories. As defined in its two definitive works [ZAV81, ZAV82], PAISLey is a language for the requirements specification of embedded systems (type HA, DY, and probably CO, defined in Section 1.4) using an operational approach. *Operational* means that the resulting specification can be executed (or interpreted) and the resulting behavior would mimic the behavior required of the system to be built. From that perspective, statecharts, REVS, and RLP all provide operational approaches to requirements specification. PAISLey's uniqueness is its incredibly simple language, with rigor and formality adopted from the disciplines of asynchronous processes and functional programming. Be forewarned that simplicity in language does not necessarily make "programs" in the language simple to read. In fact the opposite is usually the case; APL and LISP are among the simplest

```
(Initial)   State   0
WAIT  FOR stimulus 1 or stimulus 4
IF stimulus 1 occurred
THEN  response 1
          state 1
          WAIT FOR stimulus 2
          IF <predicate>
          THEN response 2
                 state 2
          ELSE response 3
                 state 3
ELSE    response 4
          state 4
```

Figure 4-31. A Useful Stimulus Response-Sequence.

```
FEATURE:   local to local call
        IN idle state
        WAIT FOR calling party to go off hook
        IN receiving dial tone state
        WAIT FOR calling party to go on hook OR dial local number
        IF calling party is on hook
        THEN IN idle state
        ELSE IF called party is busy
                THEN IN receiving busy tone state
                        WAIT FOR calling party to go on hook
                        IN idle state
                ELSE IN receiving ringback tone state
                        WAIT FOR calling party to go on hook OR
                          called party to go off hook
                        IF calling party is on hook
                        THEN IN idle state
                        ELSE
                                DO WHILE (called party is off hook)
                                    Connect (called party, calling party)
                                    WAIT FOR called party to go on hook OR
                                        calling party to go on hook
                                    IF called party is on hook
                                    THEN WAIT FOR called party to go off hook OR
                                        calling party to go on hook
                                    ELSE IN disconnected calling party state
                                        WAIT FOR called party to go on hook
                                END DO
        END FEATURE
```

Figure 4–32. Stimulus-Response Sequence Example.

languages but far from easy to read. *Asynchronous processes,* exemplified by the cooperating *and*-ed finite state machines of Harel described in Section 4.2.2.4, are independently operating autonomous abstractions of computations that usually communicate with each other via some protocol, such as interrupts, messages, and handshakes. *Functional programming* is a technique used to describe behavior by defining functions that map inputs into outputs rather than by defining procedures that when executed transform inputs into outputs. One advantage of the functional approach is the elimination of side effects and history sensitivity that may be present in other approaches.

When using PAISLey, the requirements writer decomposes both the system under specification and its environment into sets of asynchronous interacting processes. For example, Figure 4-35 shows the decomposition of a

NOTATION	MEANING

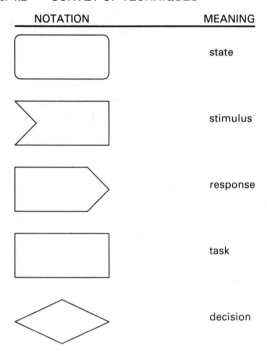

state

stimulus

response

task

decision

Figure 4–33. SDL Notation.

patient-monitoring system into five processes and its environment into four processes (adapted from [ZAV82]).[5] Once this has been accomplished, each process must be defined. This is done by defining the range of possible states that the process may enter (that is, the state space), and by declaring and defining sets of functions to define how processes change state (successor functions) and interact (exchange functions). Processes that are part of the environment are treated no differently than processes that are part of the system. Figure 4-36 shows a small subset of some of these definitions and declarations of processes and functions (adapted from [ZAV82]). In Figure 4-36a we define

- The patient (that is, the patient-cycle) as a process mapping elements in the set patient-state into other elements of the set patient-state. This implies that the patient (1) functions independently of everything else in the system and the environment and (2) is capable of changing his or her state (for example, from a heart rate of 80 bpm to a heart rate of 30 bpm).

---

[5]Note that only the patient and the CRT interact directly with the system. The nurse and doctor have been added to help understand the entire environment and possible interactions (however indirect) between patient and CRT.

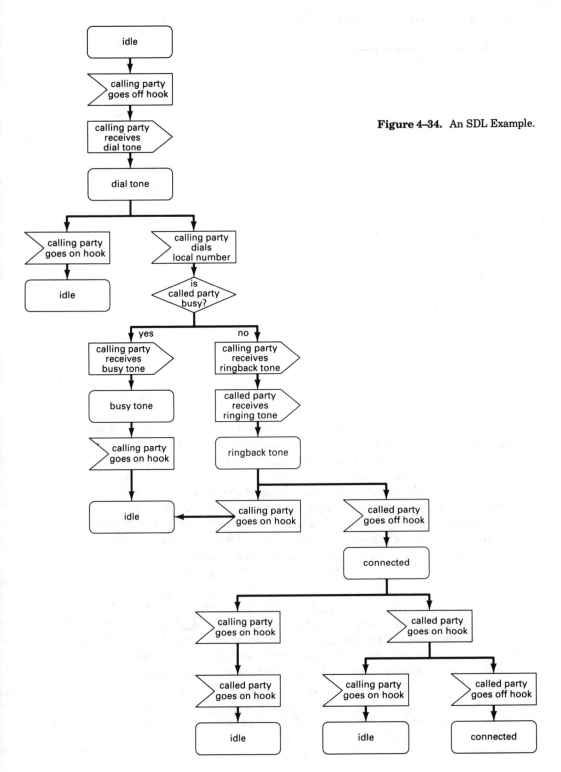

Figure 4–34. An SDL Example.

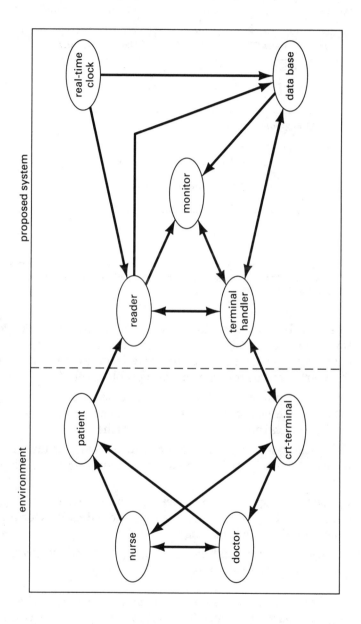

Figure 4-35. Asynchronous Processes for a System and Its Environment. © 1982 IEEE.

```
(patient-cycle:   PATIENT-STATE  → PATIENT-STATE;
patient-check-cycle:   ALERT-STATUS → ALERT-STATUS;
retrieve:   DATABASE * REQUEST  → DATABASE * VITAL-SIGN-TOLERANCE;
sense:   PATIENT-STATE → ACTUAL-VITAL-SIGNS;
check:   VITAL-SIGN-TOLERANCE * ACTUAL-VITAL-SIGNS  → ALERT-STATUS;
update:   DATABASE * ACTUAL-VITAL-SIGNS → DATABASE;
```

(a)

```
patient-check-cycle[n] =

proj[(1, (check[(sense[n],
                 retrieve[(patient-database,n)]
              )],
          update[(patient-database, sense[n])]
          ))];
```

(b)

Figure 4–36. Sample PAISLey Statements. **(a)** Partial Declaration of Processes and Their Successor Functions. **(b)** Definition of the Primary Patient-Monitoring Functions.

- The overall patient-checking process (i.e., patient-check-cycle) as a function mapping alert-status into alert-status; for example, it is capable of changing the current status of alerts from "all patients fine" to "patient 5's heart rate has fallen below acceptable levels."
- Successor mappings of the patient data base retrieval process (i.e., retrieve), which extracts acceptable vital sign tolerances for any patient, while leaving the data base itself unscathed.
- The patient-sensing function (i.e., sense), which reads hardware sensors attached to the patient and converts them into actual digital vital sign data.
- Successor mappings of the checking process (i.e., check), which compares current vital signs to acceptable ranges of vital signs for that patient and raises an alert if out of range.
- The data base update function (i.e., update), which stores newly sensed vital signs in the data base.

In Figure 4-36b we define the primary function of the system, that is checking each patient. It specifies that for any patient it will do two things: Check the patient for acceptable vital sign values and then update the data base with new vital signs. Meanwhile checking the patient requires the system to sense current vital signs and compare them to acceptable values previously stored in the patient data base.

Figure 4-36 is only a partial specification of the behavior of the patient-monitoring system shown in Figure 4-35. Still needed are descriptions of updating acceptable vital sign tolerances for patients, the action of the real-time clock as an initiator of the patient-check-cycle and source of the current time for data base storage, and many other functions.

Some critics of PAISLey claim that the resulting specification is a design specification, not a requirements specification. Two primary reasons for this claim are that the resulting specification is difficult, if not impossible, for the typical customer or user to understand and that writing in PAISLey requires much rigorous, detailed thought. Zave defends PAISLey against this claim [ZAV82] by saying that customers and users need not view the same representation of requirements and that the difference between requirements and design is subtle, the software synthesis process is a series of iterations in which each level implies requirements for the next level. This phenomenon, called the "What versus How" dilemma, was discussed in Section 1.2.1. While this book draws the line between requirements and design at the level where you stop looking at the external and start looking at the internal, Zave draws the line at the point just before computer resources are allocated to processes. Given her definition, PAISLey certainly is applicable during the requirements phase. Given the definition in Section 1.2.1, the answer is somewhat more debatable. I could easily argue here the same position that I argued in Section 4.2.2.1, namely, we are defining *external* behavior by describing the *internal* workings of a hypothetical machine, and the final system must exhibit the same external behavior as the specified machine but need not exhibit the same internal structure. However, Zave offers an alternative software development life cycle. This new life cycle calls for repeated transformations on the specifications so that they eventually become the code itself. Thus Zave is not reluctant to allow the pseudodesign of PAISLey to become the real design of the system.

Zave does state that the primary motivation for decomposition of the system into virtual processes during the requirements phase is to *specify* functionality, concurrency, synchrony, and performance easily and precisely. This differs quite a bit from the motivation for decomposing the system into physical processes during the design phase, which is to *achieve* required levels of functionality, concurrency, synchrony, and performance. Along this line Zave does offer three alternatives to creating a design after writing an SRS using PAISLey [ZAV86]:

1. Use the requirements architecture. Define any undefined sets and mappings in the implementation language; translate the PAISLey specification into the implementation language. Note that this alternative actually bypasses the design phase and goes right to the code, and Zave

recognizes that for most applications, the resulting system would not meet performance requirements.

2. Apply a series of architectural transformations on the specification. Each transformation introduces a modified architecture with improved performance while maintaining the functionality invariant [PAR83].

3. Use the SRS in the traditional life cycle. Do design from scratch using the executable SRS as an oracle against which to check for correct system behavior.

PAISLey is also capable of accepting and analyzing performance requirements, which are discussed in Section 5.3.3.2.5.

A set of PAISLey tools, including a parser, a consistency checker, and an interpreter have been implemented [ZAV86]. The parser finds and reports syntactic or semantic violations; the consistency checker performs static analyses on the specification; and the interpreter supplies interactive execution of PAISLey specifications. One experiment using PAISLey on a real system development effort is reported in [BER87].

4.2.2.9 Petri nets

Petri nets were first introduced in 1962 by C. A. Petri [PET62] and well described by Peterson [PET77]. Like the finite state machines described in Section 4.2.2.1, Petri nets are abstract virtual machines with a very well-defined behavior. They have been used for many years to specify process synchrony during the design phase of time critical applications. However more recently there has begun to be interest in applying them during the requirements phase.

Petri nets are usually represented as graphs composed of two types of nodes—circles (called places) and lines (called transitions). Arrows (directed arcs) interconnect places and transitions, as shown in Figure 4-37. Dots (called tokens) move from place to place according to the rule that tokens may pass through a transition only when (1) a clock pulse has arrived[6] and (2) all the arrows entering that transition are emanating from places that contain tokens. In addition for purposes of this discussion, let us assume that only one token is permitted at any one place.[7] Thus the arrival of a clock pulse at Figure 4-38a will result in Figure 4-38b. Also let us assume that in the case of a fan-out, the token will be replicated, and a copy will follow every path that it can. Thus the arrival of a clock pulse in Figure 4-39a will result in Figure 4-39b. Note that P4 fails to fire because P1 was not previously active (i.e., it had no token), whereas P_5 and P_6 did fire because P_2 and the combination of P_2 and P_3 were active, respectively.

---

[6]Petri nets can also be defined such that clock pulses are not required, but clock-driven nets are somewhat simpler to understand and thus will be assumed here.

[7]In general, places may contain multiple tokens. A Petri net that never allows two tokens to arrive at the same place is termed *safe*. Our assumption in this discussion is that places correspond to conditions and that multiple tokens arriving at a place are *or*-ed together (this is an early interpretation of Petri nets. See p. 80 of [PET81]).

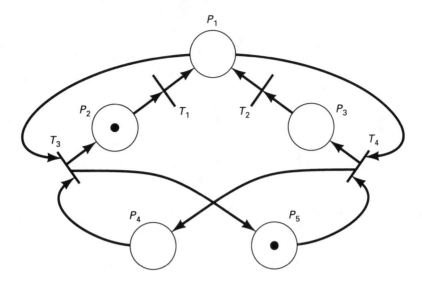

Figure 4–37. A Sample Petri Net. © 1982 IEEE.

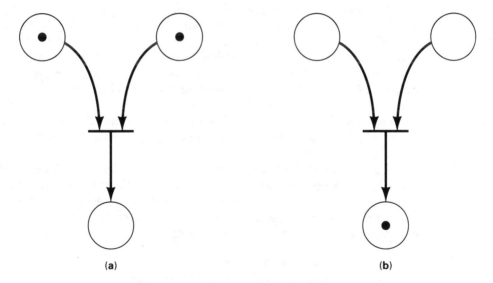

(a)   **(b)**

Figure 4–38. Token Merging in Petri Nets. **(a)** Before. **(b)** After.

Let us return now to the Petri net originally shown in Figure 4-37 and observe its behavior over a period of time through a series of clock pulses. It has been reproduced as Figure 4-40a. When a clock pulse arrives, the token at P_2 easily makes the transition to P_1 because there is only one arc going into transition T_1. On the other hand, the token at P_5, which wants to move through transition T_4 is unable to do so because the other arc coming into T_4 emanates from inactive place P_1. Thus after the first clock pulse, we have Figure 4-40b.

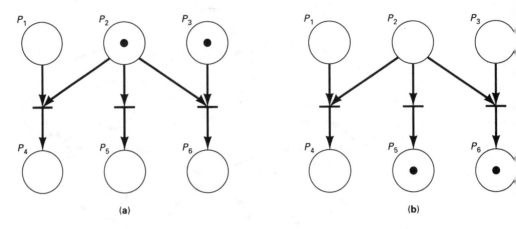

Figure 4–39. Fan-out in Petri nets. **(a)** Before. **(b)** After.

Now another clock pulse arrives. The token at P_1 is ready to fire T_3 or T_4. It is unable to fire T_3 because there is no token at P_4. However T_4 can fire because there are tokens at both P_1 and P_5. Note that there are two arcs emanating from T_4, so when T_4 fires, two tokens are created at P_3 and P_4, resulting in Figure 4-40c. At the next clock pulse, P_3 easily makes the transition to P_1, but P_4 is stalled at T_3 due to the lack of a token at P_1. Thus after the clock pulse, we have Figure 4-40d. At the arrival of the next clock pulse, P_1 and P_4 join forces to fire T_3, which results in tokens arriving at P_2 and P_5, as shown in Figure 4-40e. Note that figures 4-40a and 4-40e are identical; we have just analyzed a Petri net that happens to have a cycle of length four (that is, every four time periods, the cycle repeats).

To show how the Petri net in Figure 4-40 may be useful in writing an SRS, let us associate real-world meanings with some of the places. For example, let us associate two light bulbs with places P_2 and P_3. We could use this Petri net with a 1-second clock to define unambiguously the requirement for a two-light system to do the following:

1. There are two light bulbs.
2. Every other second, there shall be no lights on.
3. Every other second, there shall be exactly one light on.
4. Each time a light comes on, the lights alternate.

Places P_2 and P_3 do just that. Note that the Petri net possesses absolutely no ambiguity, whereas the preceding four English sentences may be misunderstood. However, Figure 4-40 is an overly complex Petri net to describe the preceding requirement. Figure 4-41 shows a much simpler Petri net with

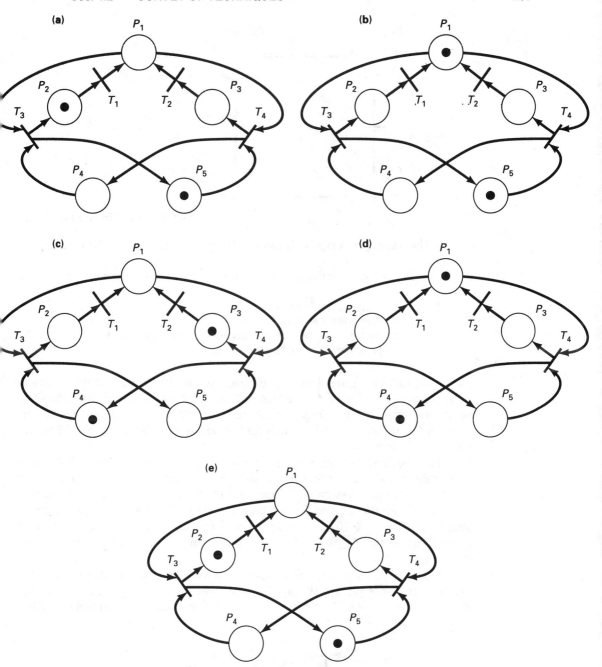

Figure 4–40. A Petri Net Sequence Example.

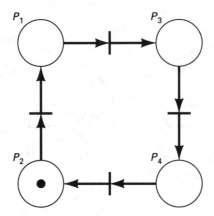

Figure 4-41. A Simple Petri Net.

exactly the same property with respect to light bulbs associated with P_2 and P_3.

Now let us say we want to specify a system with the following properties:

1. There are two light bulbs.
2. For the first 2 seconds, one light is on.
3. For the next 2 seconds, that light goes off and the other goes on.
4. From then on every 2 seconds the lights alternate.

The Petri net in Figure 4-40 can be used to specify these requirements as well. All we do is associate the two light bulbs with places P_4 and P_5. Once again we remove all traces of ambiguity. However once again there also exists a trivial Petri net that will do the same job: Use Figure 4-42 with a 2-second clock pulse.

The real payoff from Petri nets comes with the need to specify complex synchrony requirements unambiguously. For example, if we wanted to specify requirements for a system with four light bulbs, two of which behaved like P_2 and P_3 and two like P_4 and P_5 and together they all behaved in synchrony, as defined by Figure 4-40, we would be hard pressed to describe that behavior unambiguously in English or by using a Petri net much simpler than the one presented.

Let us now look at a specific application where a Petri net is helpful during the requirements phase; the application involves automating a warehouse. Figure 4-43a shows a Petri net that captures the timing requirements of this

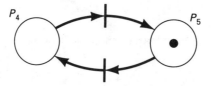

Figure 4-42. Another Simple Petri Net.

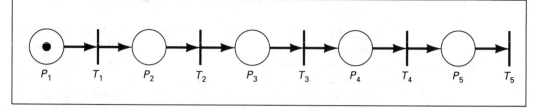

(a)

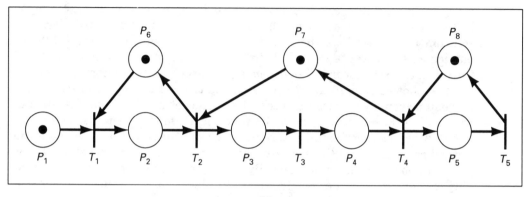

(b)

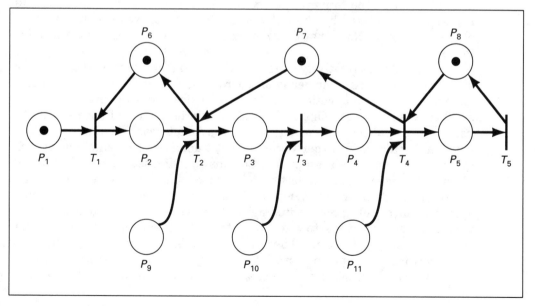

(c)

Figure 4-43. A Petri Net Example for a Warehouse. (a) Version 1. (b) Version 2. (c) Version 3.

application. At place P_1 a truck arrives at the loading dock. At place P_2 paperwork is processed and inventory is checked. At place P_3 all conveyor belts move from the loading dock to the warehouse; the belts are transporting people, robots, and forklifts. At place P_4 conveyor belts move from the warehouse to the loading dock with all the requisite merchandise. At place P_5 goods are loaded onto the truck. This is a fine use of a Petri net and at first glance shows quite well how more than one truck can be handled at a time. However on closer examination, there is a problem: If one truck is being processed at P_4 and the next truck is being processed at P_3, conveyor belts must move in both directions at once—an obvious impossibility. The solution is to introduce three new places, as shown in Figure 4-43b. In particular P_7 prevents P_3 and P_4 from being active simultaneously. I call the token in P_7 the *escort token* because it escorts tokens representing trucks (that is, those on the P_1 and P_5 track) along the critical region of P_3 and P_4. As soon as conveyor belts have completed the return of all merchandise to the loading dock, not only does the token at P_4 move to the next step, P_5, but P_7 becomes reactivated and ready to escort the next token through the critical region. P_6 and P_8 serve similar functions but for single steps; these prevent two tokens from accidentally falling into the same station. Presumably this entire Petri net would also need places corresponding to physical buttons, as shown in Figure 4–43c: the P_9 button would be pressed by the order taker when paperwork was complete; the P_{10} button would be pressed by loaders when the conveyor belt was fully loaded with merchandise, and P_{11} would be pressed by the unloaders when the conveyor belt was completely unloaded. Note that this Petri net no longer requires a clock pulse to work.

Petri nets are relatively simple to understand and best used to describe aspects of intended system behavior where (1) ambiguity cannot be tolerated, for example, the application may be life critical, and (2) precise process synchrony is important. One of the best descriptions of how Petri nets can be used for real applications is given in [AGE79]. An interesting extension to Petri nets making it possible to derive component-timing requirements from overall system requirements is presented by Coolahan and Roussopoulos [COO83] and discussed in more detail in Section 5.3.3.2.6 of this book. Yoeli and Barzilai [YOE77] provide extensive examples of applying Petri nets to the requirements specification of telephone switching systems. Bruno [BRU86] describes a useful set of extensions to Petri nets to make them more expressive for requirements specifications. These extensions include assigning attributes and priorities to tokens and associating predicates with transitions to bar or allow the movement of selected tokens. One final note: Grude [GRU89] reports the existence of a published bibliography of 2634 references to Petri nets [DRE88] and of the *Petri Net Newsletter,* which reports on the status of Petri net tools [PET].

4.2.3 Techniques for Non–Real-Time Systems

As mentioned earlier the purpose of stating behavioral requirements is to define precisely all system inputs, outputs and relationships existing between those inputs and outputs. For real-time systems, a major part of that effort is capturing the timing and causal relationships that exist between inputs and outputs. Most of the techniques discussed in Section 4.2.2 were aids to accomplishing that. Non–real-time systems (that is, the ST class of problems defined in Section 1.4) tend to be data (DA) or algorithm (AL) intensive. For these applications, dynamic relationships between inputs and outputs are not so important as (1) static properties of the inputs and outputs themselves and (2) types of processing needed for inputs in order to create outputs.

Static properties of inputs and outputs include file, record, and field formats; screen formats; error messages; report formats; and media. Most of these topics are covered in Section 5.4 on human factors.

Processing requirements for ST applications tend to fall into two categories (or combinations thereof)—algorithms for translating inputs into outputs and sets of semantics for the input that drives the output generation process.

Algorithms can most easily be defined using PDL (see Section 4.2.2.3). However I have serious doubts about the appropriateness of defining algorithms in an SRS, even for data processing applications. It seems to me that the algorithm is not a requirement; it is an implementation. This may be a subtle difference, but an applicative, functional approach to defining the input to output relationship (for example, as used in PAISLey—Section 4.2.2.8) seems much less restrictive and implementation independent than an algorithm. On the other hand, if we are writing an SRS for a payroll system, an algorithm, such as the following may be appropriate:

```
DO for each employee in company
    accept time card
    check validity of hours worked
    retrieve current personnel record
    compute wages and deductions
    update personnel record
    generate check
ENDDO
```

Perhaps the line between what is and is not an acceptable algorithm should be drawn using the same criteria as mentioned numerous times before in this book: If verbs and nouns correspond to things or actions that the user or the environment knows about or can see, smell, feel, hear, or taste, then it is acceptable to include the algorithm in the SRS.

The mapping between inputs and outputs has been described in terms of formal semantics most often in the case of compilers, one narrow application within the ST domain. The Vienna Development Method (VDM) [BJO78, BJO87, JON80] has been used extensively to define the formal semantics of programming languages and as the basis for automatic synthesis of translators from those languages into machine language. VDM has also been used to define a relational data base system [NEU80]. Although developers of VDM claim wide applicability due to the fact that VDM is based on discrete mathematics, VDM has not been successfully demonstrated in applications outside a very narrow range. Other formal semantic bases of specification (e.g., [NAK80] and [BRO80]) have similar application problems. Chi [CHI85] provides comparisons of algebraic, event algebraic, and set theoretic approaches to specifying requirements. There is no doubt that formal discrete mathematics-based specification methods enable us to define requirements in a rigorous, unambiguous, consistent fashion. These also provide the only possible basis for proving the correctness of the final software solution. For these reasons they will continue to prosper and be the subject of further research; they will be used more and more in cases where the software must be proven absolutely correct. For the most part, a layperson would not be expected to use them. Gehani and McGettrick [GEH86] provide one of the best collections of papers on this subject.

4.2.4 Applying Behavioral Requirements Techniques: Example 1

The SRD analysis of the book distribution company called LOCS in Section 2.3.4.1 resulted in a thorough understanding of the book company's organization and how information flows among organizational entities. Furthermore the SADT and SASS analyses in Sections 2.3.4.2 and 2.3.4.3 helped us understand the primary functions of the organization, which are to

1. solicit new customers
2. sell books
3. buy books

These are performed by four organizations:

1. membership
2. sales

3. purchasing

4. administration

This analysis resulted in a clear understanding of corporate inputs and outputs. In order to write an SRS, a key decision has to be made: What will be automated? Clearly if the decision is to automate the entire company (that is, fire all employees and wheel in a group of robots), we already know the system's inputs and outputs; they are the company's inputs and outputs. Among the more likely alternative decisions concerning what to automate are

1. Any one or two of the three functions listed previously

2. Any subset of the four organizations listed previously

3. Storage, modification, and retrieval of all information currently embodied on forms

4. All of the preceding plus automatically routing information to interested parties

The actual decision about what to automate is probably the result of hours of discussion between key personnel in the book company and the system development organization. The two main forces will be the area of need (that is, what is the problem in the company that caused it to seek an automation solution) and cost per each feature. Of course, the temptation now is to ask the company what their real problem is. Unfortunately, there is no real company; this is just a fictitious example that I have fabricated and implanted in your head while you read this book. Therefore, let us make the assumption that for whatever reason, alternative 4 has been selected.

It would seem relatively straightforward to transform the corporate view of its inputs and outputs as shown in Figure 4-44 (reproduced from Figure 2-46), for example, into an automated system view of its inputs and outputs, but this is not the case. It is not so trivial as turning Figure 4-44 inside out. In fact it is necessary to define the functions to be performed by the system as we define the inputs and outputs. There is one aspect of turning Figure 4-44 inside out that *is* trivial: the definition of the generators of system inputs and receivers of system outputs; they are precisely the four organizations specified in Figure 4-44. To that end we can create an initial picture of an automated system as shown in Figure 4-45. The difficulty arises in our decision about how to label the data or information on the eight arrows currently numbered 1 through 8.

Let us use the goal of filling in system inputs and outputs as a means of selecting system functions. Starting with arrow 1 in Figure 4-45, we ask, "What outputs will the automated system provide the membership organization?" We can get some ideas by looking at Figure 4-44; Note that there are four inputs

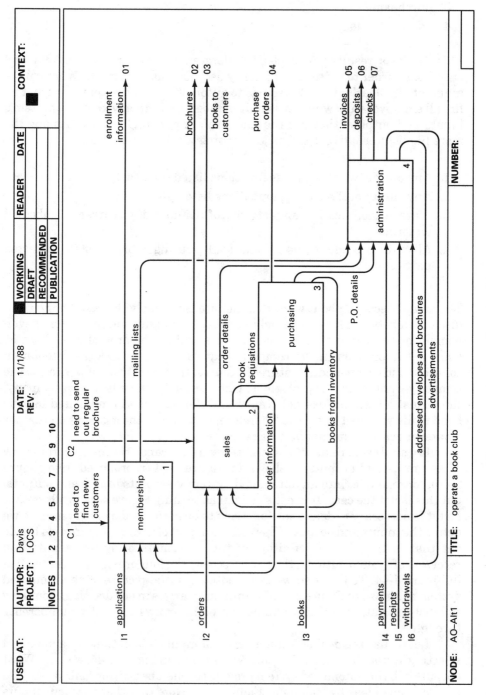

Figure 4-44. Corporate Inputs and Outputs.

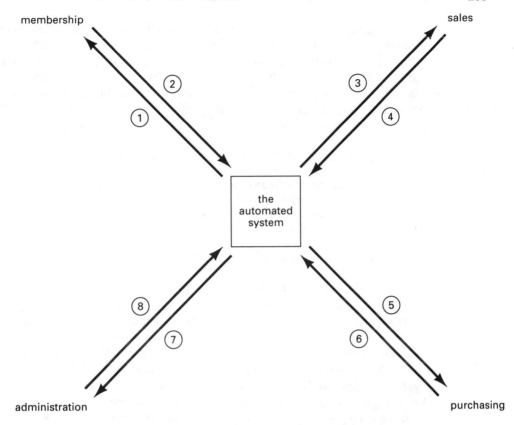

Figure 4–45. The LOCS Automated System (First Pass).

to membership in that figure. Which of these if any will be generated by the system? Let us decide that "need to find new customers" will not be an output of the system (It *could* be if we chose to define one of the system functions as "determine if sufficient revenues are being generated by the company; if not, then initiate a membership drive"). "Applications" are generated by new customers, not by the automated system. "Order information" is a likely candidate to be included on arrow 1; it makes sense if we define two system functions to be:

1. **The system shall maintain a list of all outstanding orders for books from customers.**
2. **The system shall inform membership whenever a book is ordered to ensure that customer queries are dealt with appropriately.**

The last input to membership in Figure 4-44 is "advertisements," whose generation we choose not to automate. Thus arrow 1 in Figure 4-45 is simply "order information."

Turning our attention to arrow 2 in Figure 4-45, the best place to look for ideas is among the outputs of membership in Figure 4-44. There are two—"enrollment information" (physical advertisements to be mailed, and not to be automated) and "mailing lists" from which administration will generate mailing labels for envelopes. Clearly it makes sense for the automated system to retain this list, accept changes from membership, and provide current lists to administration. Thus we add the following functions to the system:

3. **The system shall maintain a list of names and addresses for all current customers.**
4. **The system shall accept these changes to the membership list:**
   - **new members**
   - **cancel membership**
   - **change address**
   - **change name**
   - **record book order**

and arrow 2 becomes "changes to membership list."

For arrow 3 in Figure 4-45, we look at the inputs to sales in Figure 4-44. There are four—"need to send out regular brochures" (this is a monthly alarm clock that triggers the mailing of brochures by sales and can certainly be automated; thus we include "reminder to mail out monthly brochures" on arrow 3); "orders" (which will be generated by customers, not by the automated system); "addressed envelopes and brochures" (which are physical and will not be automated); and "books from inventory" (which we will not automate, although we *could* by including robots and/or conveyor belts as part of the automation). Thus arrow 3 becomes "reminder to mail out monthly brochure," and we must acknowledge a new functional requirement of the system:

5. **The system shall remind the sales organization monthly of the need to mail out brochures.**

For arrow 4 in Figure 4-45, we look at outputs from sales in Figure 4-44. There are five—"brochures" and "books to customers" (both of which are physical and will not be automated), and "order details," "book requisitions" and "order information" (all of which are aspects of orders being sent to the other three organizations). Acknowledging functional requirement 1, we can fulfill the new need for more widely available order data by adding the following functional requirements:

6. **The system shall accept new orders from customers.**
7. **The system shall allow cancellation of old orders.**
8. **The system shall provide the following data about orders on request:**
   - **list of books ordered over any period of time**
   - **list of books on order from any publisher**

- **list of books on order by any customer**
- **for any book, number on order and customers.**

Functional requirement 8 provides for the last three outputs from sales in Figure 4-44. However, functional requirement 6 implies a system input from sales: Arrow 4 becomes "new order information."

For arrow 5 in Figure 4-45, we look at the inputs to purchasing in Figure 4-44; there are just two—"book requisitions" and "books." "Books" are physical and will not be automated. "Book requisitions" were intended to show purchasing how many books have been ordered so purchasing can compare this to current inventory. Functional requirement 8 satisfies the essence of book requisitions, but we have to provide some support to purchasing for current inventory. Thus we need two new functional requirements:

9. **The system shall maintain a current book inventory status.**
10. **The system shall accept the following changes to inventory status:**
    - **removal of *X* books of type *Y* from inventory**
    - **arrival of *X* books of type *Y* to inventory**
    - **back ordering of *X* books of type *Y*.**

Arrow 5 becomes "book requisitions" and "inventory status."

For arrow 6 in Figure 4-45, we look at outputs from purchasing in Figure 4-44; there are three: "books from inventory" (which we will not automate), "purchase orders" and "P.O. details." We should be able to generate "purchase orders" automatically on request of purchasing. So we have three new functional requirements:

11. **On request, the system shall generate a purchase order for any quantity of any particular book.**
12. **The system shall maintain the status of all outstanding purchase orders.**
13. **The system shall generate a list of all outstanding P.O.s.**

Functional requirement 11 implies additional functional requirements:

14. **The system shall maintain a list of all publishers, their addresses and books.**
15. **The system shall accept the following changes to the publisher list:**
    - **add a new publisher and address**
    - **add a new book to a publisher's list**
    - **delete a book from a publisher's list**
    - **delete a publisher.**

The only system inputs (i.e., arrow 6) required are a "request to issue P.O." and "changes to publisher book availability list." Functional requirement 11 also implies a system output, a "purchase order" going to the publishers.

For arrow 7 in Figure 4-45, we look at inputs to administration in Figure 4-44; there are six. "Mailing lists" are available to administration via functional requirement 3. Assuming that administration will manually address and assemble brochures and envelopes, we have one candidate for arrow 7, namely, "mailing lists". "Order details" and "P.O. details" are already available to administration via functional requirements 8 and 13, but these must also be reflected on arrow 7. "Payments" from customers will be received by administration, leading to one more requirement, which will not affect arrow 7:

> 16. **The system shall accept information concerning receipt of payments from customers.**

The last two inputs to administration in Figure 4-44 are "receipts" and "withdrawals," but these have no effect on the automated system unless we also wanted to automate the company's checking account status. Thus arrow 7 now becomes "mailing list," "order details," and "P.O. details."

Finally for arrow 8 in Figure 4-45, we look at outputs from administration in Figure 4-44; there are five. We can handle "invoices" the same way as "purchase orders"; namely, we can add:

> 17. **On request, the system shall generate an invoice to the customer.**

We include "request to issue invoice" as part of arrow 8. "Deposit" and "checks" do not apply for the same reason given for "receipts" and "withdrawals." Finally "addressed envelopes and brochures" and "advertisements" are physical and will not be automated.

The resulting updated version of Figure 4-45 appears in Figure 4-46. We now have a relatively good (albeit general) understanding of what the system is supposed to do (i.e., functional requirements 1–17) and what its inputs and outputs are (i.e., Figure 4-46). Note also that there has been no design decomposition of the system at this time. In fact the decompositions performed during problem analysis all became part of the product's environment, not the system itself.

At this point it is probably useful to select some techniques that could be employed to specify the external functional behavior of the preceding system in an SRS. Which techniques are appropriate? Let us go through them one by one to analyze their suitability.

4.2.4.1 Finite state machines

Rather than using monolithic finite state machines, I would prefer to describe some aspects of the human interface in terms of either an R-net or an RLP-like stimulus-response sequence. In this particular case, either might

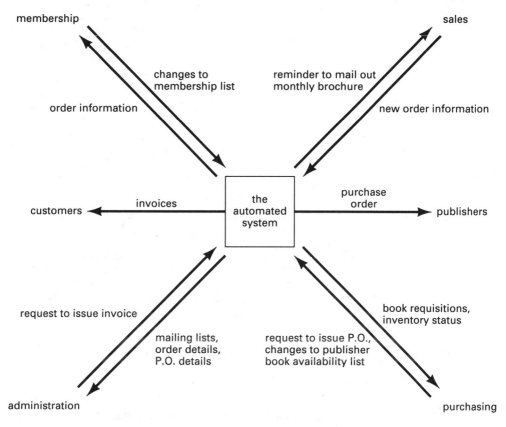

Figure 4–46. The LOCS Automated System (Second Pass).

work. The R-net approach may be used to describe separately the sequence of required activities whenever a new order is placed, and whenever a shipment of books arrives, etc. Similarly the RLP approach may be used to separately describe dialogs necessary for a customer to order a book, and for *purchasing* to issue a purchase order, etc.

4.2.4.2 Decision tables and decision trees

Decision tables and trees are most applicable for describing the intended behavior of the system in particular decision-making roles. Scanning the current list of seventeen functional requirements, none is really decision intensive. However if we had decided to allow the system to determine when inventory was insufficient and automatically issue purchase orders, we would have had an ideal candidate for either decision tables or trees. The decision tree would look something like Figure 4-47.

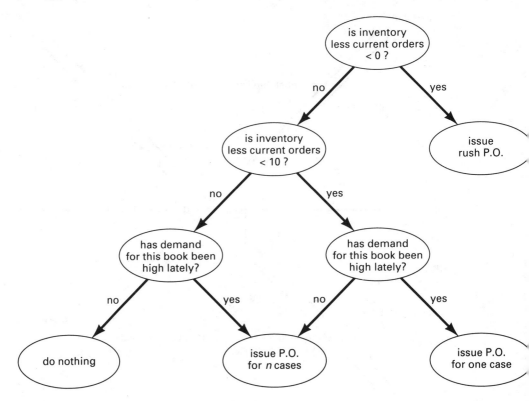

Figure 4–47. A Decision Tree for a Modified LOCS.

4.2.4.3 Program Design Language

PDL is most useful in requirements specifications for describing outputs of a system as a nontrivial combination or sequence of combinations of inputs. In this particular case, the mapping function from inputs to outputs will be relatively straightforward and therefore PDL is probably not helpful.

4.2.4.4 Statecharts

Statecharts are probably overkill for a problem as straightforward as our example. On the other hand, it may be helpful pedagogically to see how much we can accomplish. As I am writing these words I know not how successful we will be. If you are now reading these words, then *you* already know that we are going to be somewhat successful (and you thus have an advantage over me at this moment), because if I go through this exercise and decide that there is nothing to learn from it, I will remove or at least rewrite this paragraph long before this book goes to print.

In examining the seventeen functional requirements given in Section 4.2.4, it becomes evident that the system can be thought of as a set of cooperating asynchronous processes (or state machines):

1. Filling customer orders
2. Maintaining customer status
3. Advertising books
4. Maintaining the inventory
5. Ordering books from publishers
6. Maintaining publishers list.

Using statecharts, I would start with Figure 4-48 which captures the six above processes, each of which may be in its own state. The state machine for filling customer orders is relatively straightforward as shown in Figure 4-49. Problems, however, arise when we try to define a series of states for maintaining customer status. Figure 4-50 shows my failed attempt. What stimulus or condition triggers the state change from *add new member* back to *waiting*? It actually should be the completion by the system of the *add new member* activity. There is no way to represent this...and rightly so. What Figure 4-50 really is is a data flow diagram, as shown in Figure 4-51, which shows movement of data as opposed to changes in state. By the way, the developers

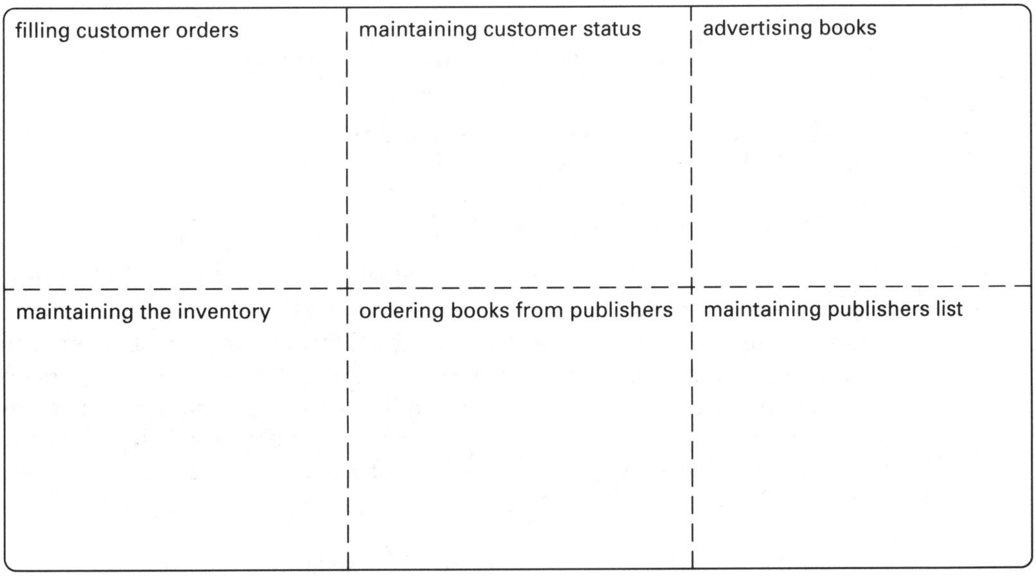

Figure 4–48. Initial Statechart for LOCS.

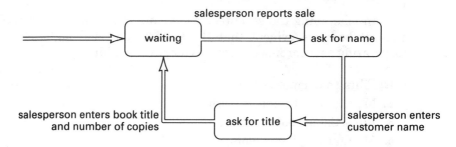

Figure 4–49. Filling Customer Orders Statechart.

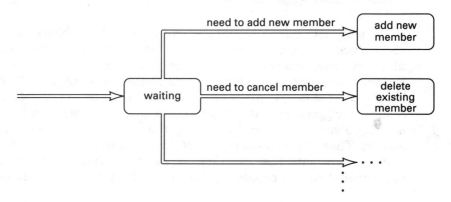

Figure 4–50. Maintaining Customer Status Statechart.

of STATEMATE [HAR87a, HAR88a, ILO85] combine both the finite-state machine-like statecharts with data flow diagrams.

4.2.4.5 Requirements Engineering Validation System

REVS is particularly helpful in describing a set of possibly interrelated system activities that occurs as a result of a particular stimulus. Because this application is more feature-oriented than stimulus-oriented, only one R-net is given here; a more user-oriented specification of external behavior is presented in Section 4.2.4.6. Figure 4-52 shows an R-net that specifies system responses to a request by a salesperson to enter a new customer order. Other R-nets could be created to define system responses to all other stimuli, such as canceling an order and adding a new customer.

4.2.4.6 Requirements Language Processor

The RLP-supported stimulus-response sequences can be used to specify dialogs corresponding to each of the interactive system features; these are a

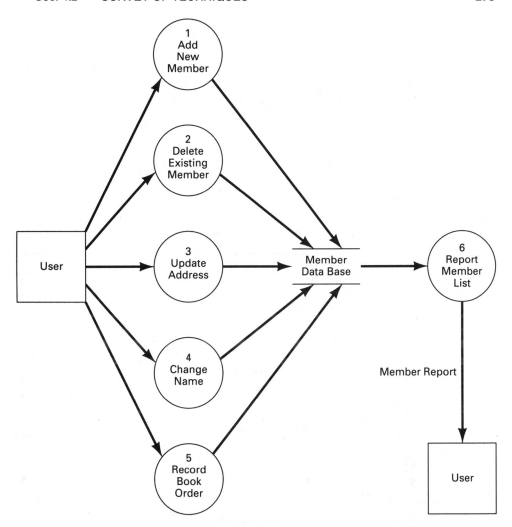

Figure 4–51. Maintaining Customer Status DFD.

subset of the seventeen functional requirements in Section 4.2.4. Each interactive feature is spelled out as a sequence in inputs and outputs. The ideal user interface for this system might include menus, either bezel button or PF-key activated. As such, a user interface/screen interaction specification tool, such as USE [WAS86], is probably more appropriate than RLP; however to demonstrate how stimulus-response sequences can be used to specify the functional behavior, we will provide them here. Figure 4-53 shows stimulus-response sequences for four of the system features.

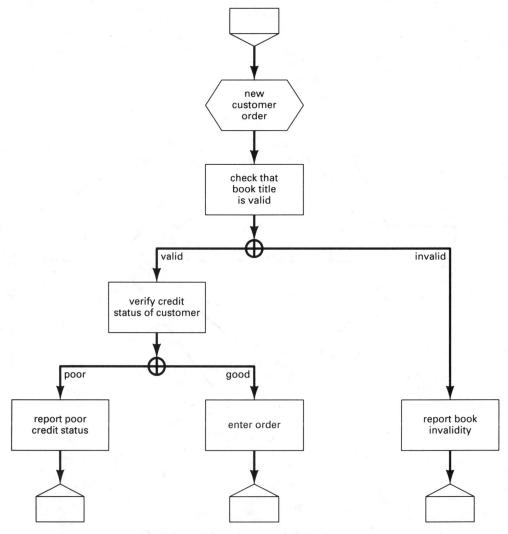

Figure 4–52. R-net for One Aspect of LOCS.

4.2.4.7 Specification and Description Language

SDL was developed primarily for telephony applications but can be applied to any real-time system. Figure 4-54 shows a small part of an SDL specification of the LOCS requirements.

4.2.4.8 PAISLey

PAISLey does not appear to be applicable to this problem because it does not involve an embedded system. Nonetheless it is possible to describe this

MAIN MEMBERSHIP MENU
IF MEMBERSHIP WANTS TO ADD A NEW MEMBER
THEN MEMBERSHIP RECEIVES NEW MEMBER MENU
    MEMBERSHIP ENTERS NEW MEMBER NAME
    MEMBERSHIP ENTERS NEW MEMBER ADDRESS
    SYSTEM ASSIGNS MEMBER ID #
    SYSTEM STORES NEW MEMBER RECORD
MAIN MENU

(a)

MAIN MEMBERSHIP MENU
IF MEMBERSHIP WANTS TO CANCEL A MEMBER
THEN SYSTEM ASKS FOR MEMBER ID #
    MEMBERSHIP ENTERS MEMBER ID #
    SYSTEM DISPLAYS MEMBER RECORD
    SYSTEM ASKS FOR VERIFICATION
    IF MEMBERSHIP ENTERS DELETE AUTHORIZED
    THEN SYSTEM DELETES MEMBER RECORD
MAIN MENU

(b)

MAIN MEMBERSHIP MENU
IF MEMBERSHIP WANTS TO MODIFY A MEMBER
THEN MODIFY MEMBER MENU
    SYSTEM ASKS FOR OLD NAME
    MEMBERSHIP ENTERS OLD NAME
    IF MEMBERSHIP WANTS TO MODIFY NAME
    THEN SYSTEM ASKS FOR NEW NAME
        MEMBERSHIP ENTERS NEW NAME
    ELSE IF MEMBERSHIP WANTS TO MODIFY ADDRESS
        SYSTEM ASKS FOR NEW ADDRESS
        MEMBERSHIP ENTERS NEW ADDRESS
    SYSTEMS UPDATES MEMBER RECORD

(c)

MAIN SALES MENU
IF SALES WANTS TO ENTER ORDER
THEN SYSTEM ASKS FOR MEMBER ID #
    SALES ENTERS MEMBER ID #
    SYSTEM ASKS FOR BOOK ID #
    SALES ENTERS BOOK ID #
    SYSTEM RECORDS ORDER
    SYSTEM ASKS IF MORE BOOKS ORDERED
    SALES ENTERS MORE OR NO MORE
    WHILE (MORE) DO
        SYSTEM ASKS FOR BOOK ID #
        SALES ENTERS BOOK ID #
        SYSTEM UPDATES ORDER
        SYSTEM ASKS IF MORE BOOKS ORDERED
        SALES ENTERS MORE OR NO MORE

(d)

Figure 4–53. Stimulus-response Sequences to Describe the Features of LOCS. **(a)** Adding a New Member. **(b)** Deleting a Member. **(c)** Modifying Member Records. **(d)** Entering a New Order.

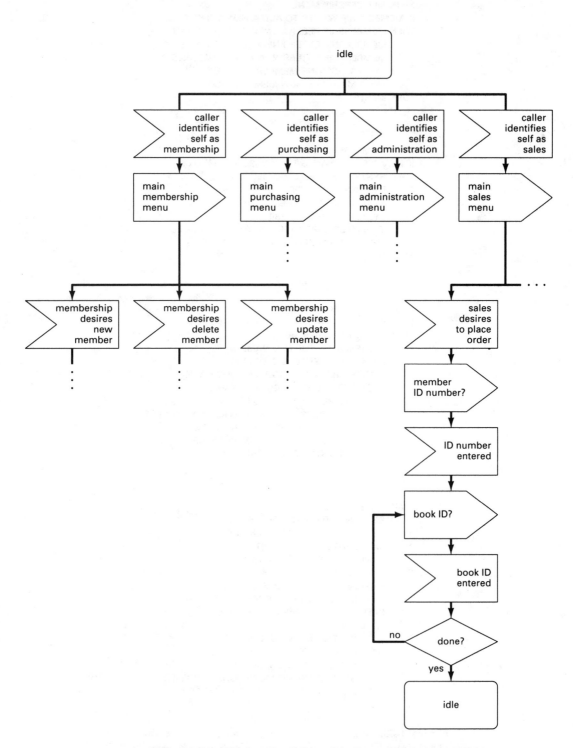

Figure 4–54. SDL for a Small Part of the External Behavior of LOCS.

problem and its environment as a set of asynchronous autonomous processes. In particular the system can be envisioned as three processes—customer order handler, purchase order handler, and membership handler—where all three perform their tasks relatively independently. Figure 4-55 shows these three processes and the six environmental processes. Next we generate PAISLey

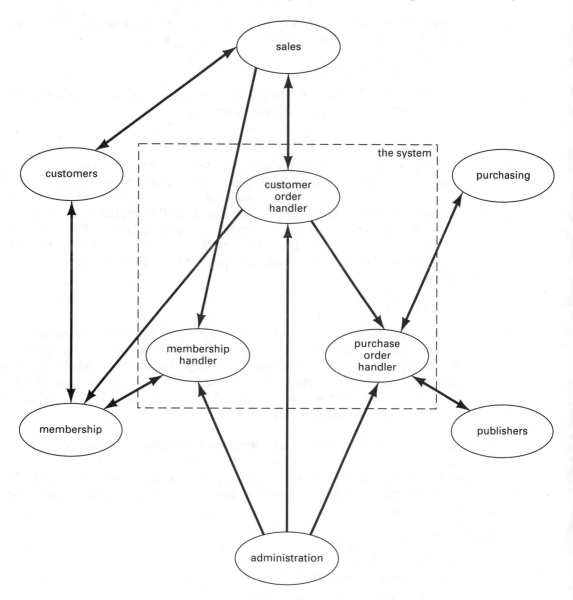

Figure 4–55. The Primary Entities in LOCS.

```
new-order:    ORDER-DATABASE * NEW-ORDER-DATA  →ORDER-DATABASE;
new-po:       PO-DATABASE * NEW-PO-DATA  →PO-DATABASE;
new member:   MEMBER-DATABASE * NEW-MEM-DATA  →MEMBER-DATABASE;
order-retrieve: ORDER-DATABASE * REQUEST  →ORDER-DATABASE * ORDER-DATA;
```

Figure 4–56. PAISLey Statements for a Small Part of LOCS.

statements to declare and define the processes and their successor functions; Figure 4-56 shows a few of these.

4.2.4.9 Petri nets

It is unlikely that there will be synchrony issues in this problem significant enough to warrant using a Petri net.

4.2.4.10 Non–real-time aspects

Although the example under study here is highly interactive, it also has a large number of non–real-time qualities, including the requirement of understanding data base queries and generating numerous reports. It would make sense during the requirements phase to nail down the actual format of these. For example, when doing a retrieval of selected orders from the order data base, it would be helpful to define the exact syntax of the queries in Backus-Naur Form [BAC58] and the exact format of the report in some report generator language.

4.2.4.11 Summary

I hope after you have read as much of this book as you have, that you no longer expect to have a simple answer here. Most of the techniques applied in this example were helpful in some way; no one technique would have facilitated the description of all external requirements. In the spirit of "use a tool to make complex aspects of a problem simpler," I believe that RLP and SDL are probably the ones that will help the most.

4.2.5 Applying Behavioral Requirements Techniques: Example 2

Example 2 is the Pfleeger Pfliers' helicopter landing system. In Section 2.3.5 we described the results of a system design that partitioned the system into four subsystems:

1. A central controller
2. Tall building emitters
3. Landing pad-based landing system
4. Helicopter-based landing system

Each of these corresponds to a computer software configuration item (CSCI) and as such should each be documented in a separate SRS [DOD88]. The remainder of this section will show how each of the SRS techniques described in Section 4.2.2 can be applied to some aspect of at least one of these four SRSs.

4.2.5.1 Finite state machines

There are a number of places where finite state machines may be helpful in the specification of this application. For example, the helicopter is in six general states during a flight—take off, climb, enroute (during which constant air traffic controller (ATC) communication is advised), descent, approach, and landing. Figure 4-57 captures some of that spirit in a state transition diagram; however this application is clearly stimulus-oriented (see Section 4.2.2.5 for an explanation of this concept). Therefore more extensive use of FSMs are discussed in Section 4.2.5.5.

4.2.5.2 Decision tables and decision trees

By its very nature the helicopter landing system must make many decisions, including when to contact ATC, when to lift off, when to descend, when to abandon a trip, which helicopter to route to which lot for which package, when to reroute a bicycle from one site to another, and so forth. To give an idea of a decision table for this application, let us examine the problem of deciding (1) whether or not to land and (2) if landing, the type of landing that should be executed. At least seven factors influence this decision:

1. Is the pilot conscious?
2. Is there fuel?
3. Is the visibility poor (that is, rated at instrument flight rules [IFR]) or good (that is, rated at visual flight rules [VFR])?
4. Are cockpit instruments that report windspeed, vertical velocity, altitude, attitude, configuration, heading, and so forth, to the pilot working properly?
5. Is there wind shear? Is the wind so strong that landing is dangerous?
6. Is the automated landing system operational?
7. Has authorization been received from air traffic control to descend and approach the landing pad?

Given these factors there are five possible decisions:

1. Land using the automatic landing system
2. Allow the pilot to land visually

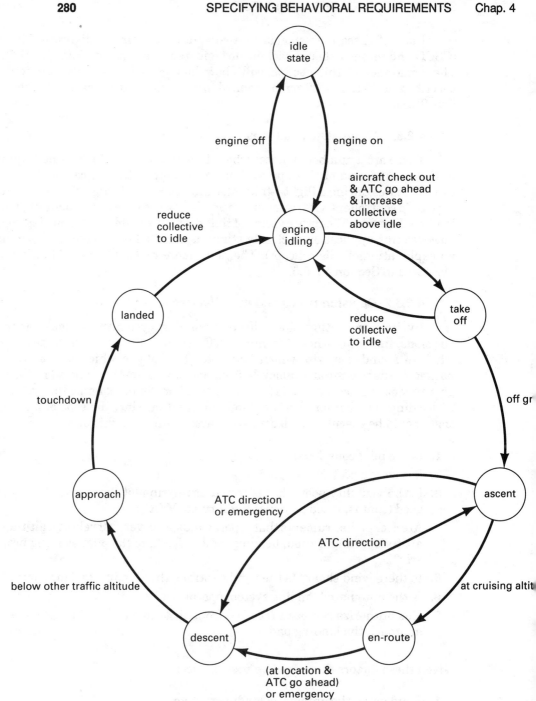

Figure 4–57. An STD Showing Gross States of the Helicopter's Flight.

3. Fly away, i.e., abort the landing attempt
4. Allow the pilot to land with an instrument approach and a visual land
5. Emergency; head ASAP for a designated crash site to minimize injury to passengers and pedestrians

Figure 4-58 captures this decision process. Using a decision table ensures that every combination of factors has been considered in the specification. Figure 4-59 depicts this same decision process as a decision diagram. It is somewhat easier to read because it has a well-defined start and sequence of questions to ask. It is also somewhat less redundant because it recognizes that certain conditions (for example, no fuel present) can have only one outcome regardless of other factors.

4.2.5.3 Program Design Language

Program Design Language is most appropriate in two situations: (1) If we wish to capture a relatively simple relationship between inputs and outputs or (2) if we have no other tool at our disposal. One such scenario in the case of Pfleeger Pfliers is controlling the rate of descent of the helicopter while lowering itself onto the landing pad. Using McMenamin and Palmer's notation [MCM84] for specifying simultaneous requirements, Figure 4-60 specifies this simple requirement. The reason for the third IF statement in the example is that as the helicopter descends and the automated system detects that the helicopter is slightly off its target horizontally (i.e., it is not directly above the landing pad), the system will change the blade pitch (via the stick) to effect a tilting of the fuselage to return the helicopter to its proper position. However, this tilting decreases the net lift of the helicopter, which then begins to descend faster. Rather than waiting for the loss in lift, the third IF statement anticipates the lift loss and compensates for it simultaneously with the stick movement.

4.2.5.4 Statecharts

In order for the automated landing system to behave appropriately, it must at all times have knowledge of the condition of both the helicopter and the vacant lot in which the helicopter is to land. The lot's condition can be characterized by *and*ing the states of four particular aspects of the lot: the presence of a helicopter on the landing pad, the presence of a bicycle at the landing pad, the presence of a customer's package at the landing pad, and the weather at the lot; the statechart shown in Figure 4-61 defines this relationship. Each of the four aspects can now be modeled as their own statecharts, as shown in Figures 4-62 through 4-65. Note that the L-helicopter statechart in Figure 4-62 records the fact that the lot must know if a helicopter is enroute to it or on departure as well as if one is on the ground; this provides data

| Pilot conscious |
| Fuel present |
| Visibility (IFR, VFR) |
| Instruments working |
| Wind okay |
| Auto system working |
| Clearance received |

Decision

| Automatic land |
| VFR land |
| Abort landing |
| Instrument approach/ visual land |
| Ditch/crash |

Figure 4-58. A Decision Table for Pfleeger Pfliers.

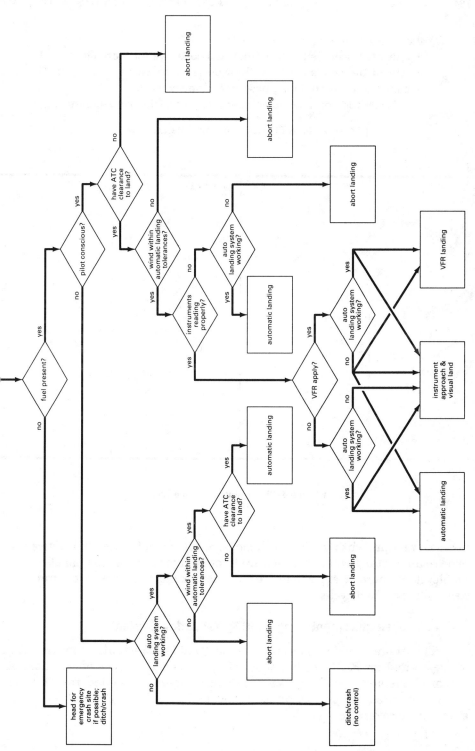

Figure 4-59. A Decision Tree for Pfleger Pfliers.

283

DO the following in no particular order:
    IF rate_of_descent is too fast THEN add collective for more lift
    IF rate_of_descent is too slow THEN decrease collective for less lift
    IF adjusting position during descent by moving stick
        THEN add collective to compensate for anticipated decreased lift

Figure 4–60. A PDL Example from Pfleeger Pfliers.

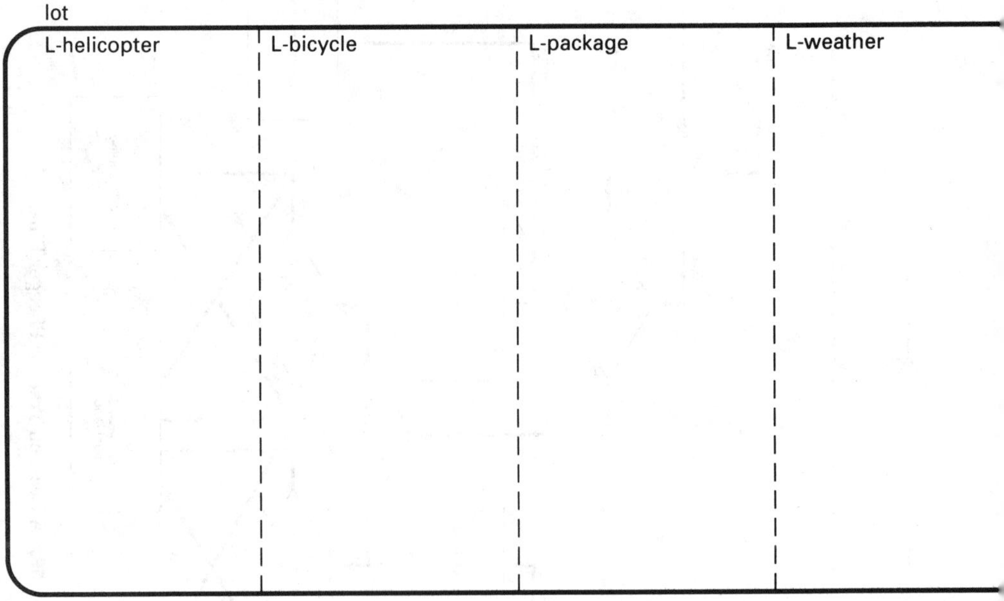

lot

L-helicopter	L-bicycle	L-package	L-weather

Figure 4–61. A Statechart of a Lot.

necessary for preventing midair collisions. Similarly in Figure 4-63, notice the need to understand where bicycles are located. It is pointless to land at a lot if no bicycle is there or expected to arrive soon; it might be better to land at a nearby lot with a bicycle.

4.2.5.5 Requirements Engineering Validation System

This application is certainly real-time (that is, DY); it also appears to be ideally suited for REVS rather than RLP, because the types of questions a potential customer would typically ask are stimulus oriented rather than feature oriented. In particular R-nets would be written for each relevant stimulus, for example

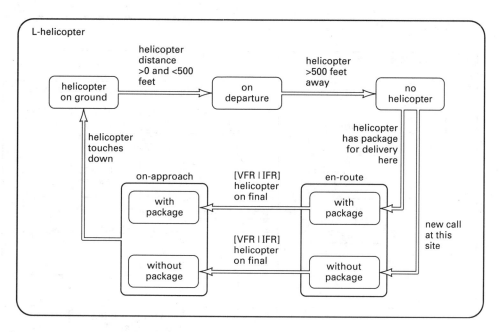

Figure 4–62. A Statechart for Capturing a Lot's View of a Helicopter.

Gust of wind

Pilot becomes unconscious

Pilot becomes conscious

Change in weather to VFR

Change in weather to IFR

Change in weather to "no flight activity allowed"

During final approach

   horizontally off target—first ring

   horizontally off target—second ring

   horizontally off target—third ring

Too slow rate of descent

Too rapid rate of descent

Too slow rate of ascent

Too rapid rate of ascent

Wind direction change

The R-net example given here specifies the automatic landing system's required external behavior when it detects it is slightly off the mark horizon-

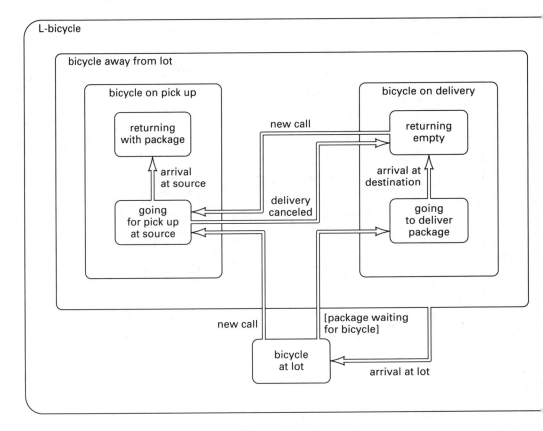

Figure 4–63. A Statechart for Capturing a Lot's View of a Bicycle.

tally during its final approach to a landing pad. In order to fully understand this R-net example as well as the Petri net example given in Section 4.2.5.9, it is necessary to understand how the proposed landing system maintains the helicopter directly above its landing pad during final approach. On the bottom of the helicopter fuselage there is a set of forty-eight sensors arranged in three concentric rings of sixteen sensors each. Within each ring sensors are placed 21.5 degrees apart (see Figure 4-66). In the center of the array is a downward-pointing point source emitter (PSE). Figure 4-67 shows how the landing pad's reflector behaves when (a) the helicopter is directly above its target and (b) slightly forward of its target. Note that if the point source reflection is sensed by any sensor on the rear half of the array (i.e., between 112.5 and 247.5 degrees), the helicopter is too far forward. If the point source reflection is sensed by any sensor on the front half of the array (i.e., between 292.5 and 67.5

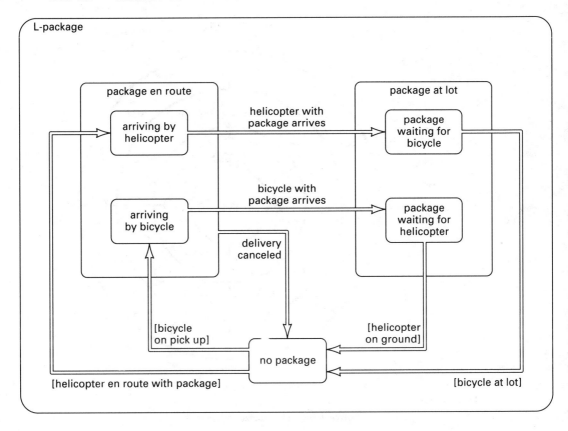

Figure 4–64. A Statechart for Capturing a Lot's View of a Package.

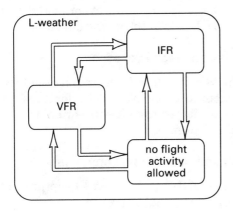

Figure 4–65. A Statechart for a Lot's View of Weather.

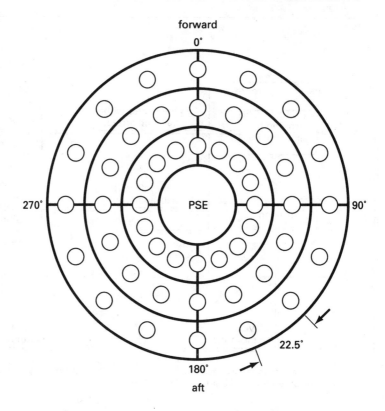

Figure 4–66. The Horizontal Deviation Sensor Array.

degrees), the helicopter is too far to the rear. In a similar fashion, deviations to either side can also be detected. Figure 4-68 is an R-net that captures the external behavior of the automatic landing system when a first-ring sensor is activated in each of the four possible quadrants of horizontal deviance. Similar R-nets could be created for second- and third-ring deviations.

4.2.5.6 Requirements Language Processor

RLP's strength lies in its ability to help the requirements writer organize requirements of a DY system in terms of its user features. This particular application is more stimulus-oriented than feature-oriented. In fact it has just one main feature—to land a helicopter.

4.2.5.7 Specification and Description Language

Figure 4-69 shows how SDL can be used to capture gross helicopter reactions to various stimuli during final approach.

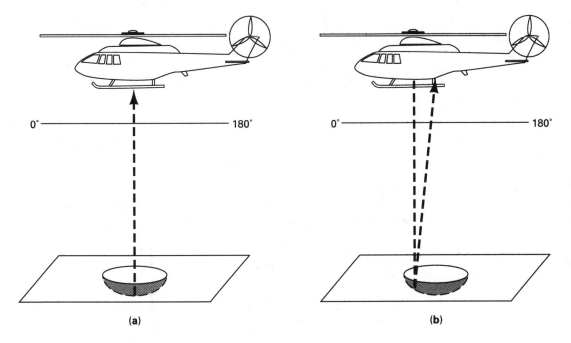

(a)   (b)

Figure 4–67. The Horizontal Deviation Subsystem. (a) Helicopter Directly above Reflector. (b) Helicopter Slightly Forward of Reflector.

4.2.5.8 PAISLey

The proposed system essentially replaces pilots in their current environment. Figure 4-70 shows primary entities in the system and its environment and their potential effects on each other. Figure 4-71 shows some of the PAISLey statements that define processes and their successor functions.

4.2.5.9 Petri nets

There are other characteristics of the three-ring array of sensors on the helicopter's belly that help the automated landing system determine whether or not the helicopter is directly over the landing pad. In particular the wider the ring on which the signal is detected, the farther off course the helicopter is. And the farther off course, the longer the pilot or the automated landing system must hold the stick in a pitch or roll situation to compensate. For example, the helicopter flight characteristics may be such that a first-ring deviation at 90 degrees can be recouped by 2 degrees of right roll for 2 seconds, a second-ring deviation at 90 degrees can be recouped by 2 degrees of right roll for 4 seconds, and a third-ring deviation at 90 degrees can be recouped by 2 degrees of right roll for 6 seconds. In addition as mentioned before, a change

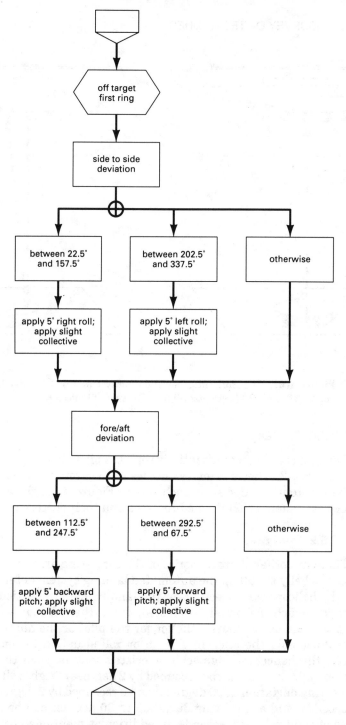

Figure 4–68. An R-net for One Aspect of Pfleeger Pfliers.

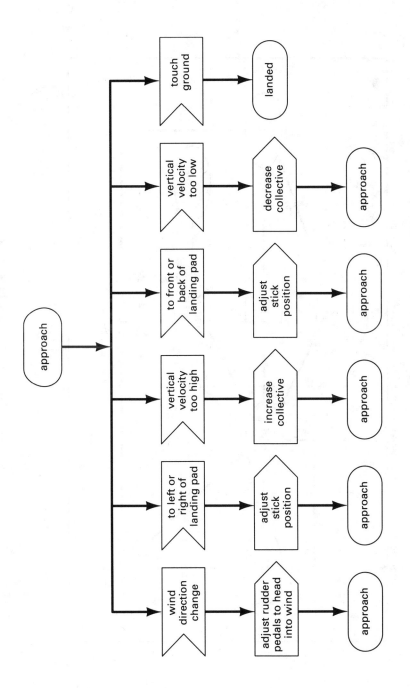

Figure 4-69. SDL Example for One Aspect of Pfleeger Pfliers.

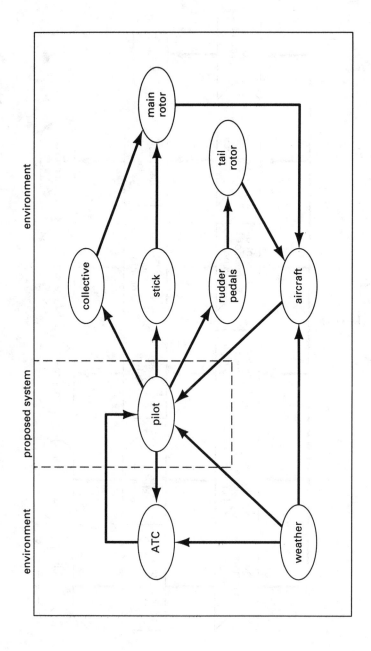

Figure 4-70. Primary Entities in Pfleeger Pfliers.

weather-cycle: WEATHER-STATE ⟶ WEATHER-STATE;
aircraft-cycle: AIRCRAFT-STATE * MAIN-ROTOR-STATE * TAIL-ROTOR-STATE * WEATHER- STATE
⟶ AIRCRAFT-STATE;
main-rotor-update: MAIN-ROTOR-STATE * COLLECTIVE-POSITION * STICK-POSITION
⟶ MAIN-ROTOR-STATE;
tail-rotor-update: TAIL-ROTOR-STATE * RUDDER-PEDAL-POSITION
⟶ TAIL-ROTOR-STATE;
rudder-control: RUDDER-PEDAL-POSITION * PILOT-LEG-MOVEMENTS
⟶ RUDDER-PEDAL-POSITION;
stick-control: STICK-POSITION * PILOT-RIGHT-ARM-MOVEMENTS
⟶ STICK-POSITION;
collective-control: COLLECTIVE-POSITION * PILOT-LEFT-ARM-MOVEMENTS
⟶ COLLECTIVE-POSITION;
modify-cycle: ATC-COMMANDS * WEATHER * AIRCRAFT-STATUS
⟶ PILOT-LEG-MOVEMENTS * PILOT-LEFT-ARM-MOVEMENTS
* PILOT-RIGHT-ARM-MOVEMENTS
* PILOT-TO-ATC-INFORMATION;

Figure 4–71. Some PAISLey Statements for Pfleeger Pfliers.

in the attitude of the helicopter automatically decreases the net angle of attack which in turn reduces lift. To compensate for this loss of lift, the pilot or the automatic landing system must increase the collective. Once again timing is critical. Let us assume that for this particular helicopter, a 2-second roll requires little or no increase in collective but a 4-second roll of 2 degrees requires a 5% increase in collective for 2 seconds, and a 6-second roll of 2 degrees requires a 5% increase in collective for 4 seconds. Figure 4-72 shows only the lower right quadrant of the three-ring array of sensors. Just above the quadrant is a Petri net that captures the roll and collective modifications necessary for maintaining a stable and correct flight path in the case of a 90-degree first-, second-, and third-ring sensor signal detection. To the left of the quadrant is a Petri net that captures similar behavior in the event of a 180-degree first-, second-, and third-ring sensor signal detection; of course these show a change in pitch rather than roll. Similar Petri nets can be constructed for the other three radii of sensors within this same quadrant, but these would require changes to both pitch and roll. And finally Petri nets can be created for the other three quadrants as well.

4.2.5.10 Summary

Each of the examples in this section detailed a particular aspect of the external behavior of the helicopter landing system using a different technique. It is true that some of the techniques could have been used in most of the examples, just like you could use a hammer to drive nails, drive screws, plane wood, and cut wood. However, each example shown was selected specifically to demonstrate the effectiveness of that particular technique to capture an aspect of the helicopter landing system's requirements.

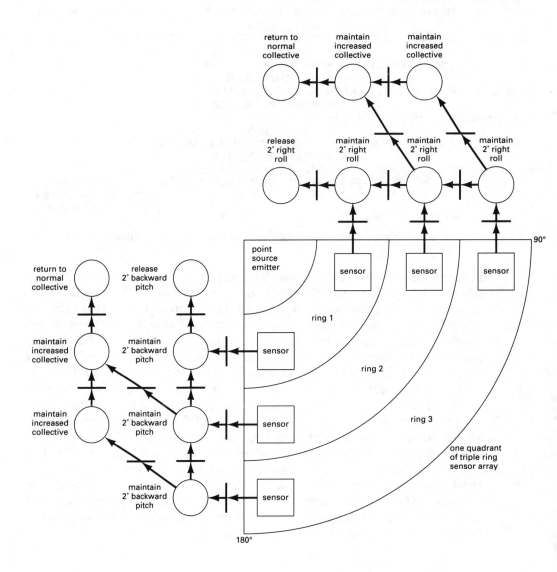

Figure 4–72. Petri Net Applied to Final Approach Control (Alignment Above Landing Pad).

4.2.6 Applying Behavioral Requirements Techniques: Example 3

As discussed previously in Chapters 1 and 2, the problem is to transport people from New York to Tokyo in 30 minutes; it is a very difficult problem. Its solution will be extremely large by any unit of measurement: physical size of resulting system, cost, number of lines of code, difficulty, size of SRS, and so forth. Given any of the four approaches to solving this problem, we can obviously think of many ways of applying behavioral techniques described in this chapter. For example, we could use finite state machines to define the user interface for any of the four approaches. We could use decision tables and trees to specify how the space shuttle determines whether to reenter the atmosphere or complete another orbit, how the tunnel elevator determines when to start providing power to ease its way to the surface after losing a certain amount of kinetic energy, how the bullet train determines when to stop, how the decoder unit in the "beam me up Scottie" approach determines whether to retrieve an oxygen, hydrogen, carbon, or nitrogen atom next. We could use PDL or RLP to define the sequence of steps that operators must go through for the space shuttle's take-off, tunnel elevator's departure, or bullet train's departure and the transmission of the beamed-up passenger, and so forth.

There is thus no difficulty in finding aspects of the application suitable for each technique. Similarly there is little difficulty in actually applying techniques to those aspects. The challenge is that we want to apply techniques to those situations most critical to the specification of the system's external behavior or that aid the most in terms of convincing the reader that the SRS describes a system truly able to solve the problem at hand. Unfortunately this problem is so complex and so poorly understood that we are unable to apply techniques to its really critical aspects because (1) we do not really know what those critical aspects are and (2) if we did, we could not now solve the underlying problems well enough to specify their solution's external behavior. If I did show you an example such as those listed in the previous paragraph, I would be doing you a disservice; I would be showing you the use of techniques just for the sake of showing you the techniques. You would not learn anything about when you should apply them. Therefore rather than showing applications of these techniques while ignoring the real issues, I have chosen not to demonstrate them here.

4.2.7 Comparison of Techniques

In Section 4.2.1, ten criteria were defined for evaluating requirements specification techniques; these were

1. Its use should reduce ambiguity in the SRS.

2. Its use should result in an SRS that is helpful to and understandable by customers and users who are not computer specialists.

3. Its use should result in an SRS that can serve effectively as the basis for design and test.

4. It should provide for automated checking for ambiguity, incompleteness, and inconsistency.

5. It should encourage the requirements writer to think and write in terms of external product behavior, not the product's internal components.

6. It should help organize information in the SRS.

7. It should provide a basis for automated prototype generation and automated system test generation.

8. Its use should facilitate SRS modification.

9. Its use should permit annotation and traceability.

10. It should employ underlying models that facilitate the description of a system's external behavior within the intended application environment.

The following paragraphs analyze, compare, and contrast the techniques in the contexts of each of the preceding criteria. Figure 4-73 summarizes these observations in tabular form and provides each with a score from zero (poor) to ten (excellent).

1. Ambiguity is introduced into a document when words with multiple meanings are used and sentence constructs possess multiple interpretations. Following a set of even the most basic human-enforced rules for constructing sentences and using words can significantly reduce ambiguity in an SRS [CAS81, HUF78, OHN85]. Thus any method is better than natural language. Using PDL will probably have only an insignificant effect on reducing ambiguity because all words except keywords are treated as comments on many PDLs.[8] The use of finite state machines, decision tables, decision trees, SDL, and Petri nets provide an additional (and significant) level of ambiguity prevention. In particular these models provide formal semantic bases, so that once writer and reader are familiar with the underlying concept, meanings for a large number of keywords and sentences used in the SRS can be communicated with little loss in understanding or intended meaning. Statecharts, REVS, RLP, and PAISLey all provide even richer sets of semantics and are thus more expressive and contribute to reducing inherent ambiguity in requirements.

---

[8]Recent work in the "Ada as a PDL" community [BYR86, IEE85] pushes strongly in favor of "when it can be expressed in formal Ada, do so." In my opinion this defeats the purpose of a PDL even as a design tool, but certainly as a requirements tool.

2. It is difficult to be objective in determining whether or not a particular technique aids the understanding of an SRS by a customer untrained in computer technology. On the other hand, such understandability appears to be inversely proportional to the level of complexity and formality present. Obviously PDL, which is primarily natural language, is almost as easy to read as natural language. Decision trees appear in the nontechnical literature regularly with no explanation, so they, too, are extremely understandable. Finite state machines, REVS, RLP, and SDL all require about the same amount of instruction for computer-naive users to *read* and *comprehend* SRS sections using those approaches. Incidentally among these four approaches, there appears to be a significant range of training needed in order to *use* the approach effectively. I *have* successfully taught hundreds of non–computer-oriented personnel at least to *comprehend* the basics of all these approaches in less than an hour per approach. Statecharts, PAISLey, and Petri nets appear to be much more difficult to comprehend than the others, but for three unrelated reasons. In particular, statecharts are probably difficult because of their semantic richness. Concepts added by statecharts to finite state machines offer expressive power, and reduce the size of the resulting specification, but many of the new concepts are not intuitive to the layperson (albeit 100% intuitive to any computer scientist with basic skills in automata theory and asynchronous processes). Conceptually PAISLey suffers from the same problem as statecharts; practically however PAISLey suffers from one additional problem—a language once again difficult to understand. Petri nets appear to be difficult to comprehend by non-computer trained people, perhaps because there is no beginning or end to the notation (as opposed to decision trees or RSL or PAISLey, for example). Or the difficulty may lie in keeping track of the locations of tokens during two successive time periods.

3. For a technique to make an SRS more useful to designers and system testers, it must lower its ambiguity level and increase its understandability to computer-oriented people who design and test. I contend that the very reason why some techniques score low points for ambiguity is the same reason why they score low points for understandability among testers and designers.

4. Miller and Taylor [MIL81] define three distinct levels of errors detectable in an SRS:

a. *Static structural.* for example, signals transmitted through inappropriate ports, signals received by an entity but not sent by an entity

b. *Behavioral.* for example, two requirements conflict; a specification is ambiguous, incomplete, or redundant (see Davis [DAV79] for further discussion of this class of error)

c. *Protocol.* for example, deadlocks between subsystems (see Sunshine [SUN79] for further discussion of this class of error)

Criterion	Natural Language	FSMs	DTs	PDL	Statecharts
1 Reduce ambiguity	0 Natural languages are inherently ambiguos	6 Formal semantic basis reduces ambiguity	6 See FSMs	2 Insufficient formality to reduce ambiguity	9 Rich set of semantics reduce ambiguity
2 Under-standable to computer-naïve personnel	10 Obviously understandable to computer-naive personnel	7 Requires an hour or two of instruc-tion to facilitate understanding by computer-naïve personnel	10 Appear in litera-ture regularly without explan-ation	10 Almost as easy to read as natural language because most of it is natural language	5 Many FSM extensions not intuitive to computer-naïve personnel
3 Basis for design and test	0 With no formality there is no basis	7 The formal model enables one to unambigiously define intended product behavior and thus serve as a basis for both design and test	7 See FSMs	2 Being little more than natural language, the lack of formality provides no basis	9 With the additional expressive power over FSMs, there is less potential for ambiguity and thus a more formal basis for design and test
4 Automated checking	0 No processor is available to perform any checking	7 Static structural and and behavioral errors can be detected	0 See natural language	1 Static structural errors can be detected	9 Static structural, behavioral, and protocol errors can be detected
5 External view not internal view	0 No help provided	3 Needs human disci-pline in defining the external entities up front	3 See FSMs	0 No help provided	5 Structural view pro-vided explicitly and independent of behavioral views
6 SRS organizational assistance	1 Paragraph and chapter	2 Machine	2 Table or tree	2 Module	9 Semantic richness of hierarchical alter-natives; multiple viewpoints
7a Prototype generation	0 None	10 Yes, using IDE tools	0 None	0 None	10 Yes, using i-Logix tools
7b Automatic test generation	0 None	0 None	0 None	0 None	0 None
8 Modifiability	6 With a word proces-sor and text editor	6 See natural language	6 Use spreadsheet	6 See natural language	6 See natural language
9 Annotation and traceability	4 Just write it down as a comment	4 See natural language	4 See natural language	4 See natural language	7 Traceability features available
10 Appropriate applications	Any application where misinter-pretation of requirements is acceptable or at least noncritical	Any DY application that is small enough to not warrant statecharts, REVS or RLP. For example, small process control applications	Those particular parts of any appli-cation which are decision-intensive. Note that decision-intensity is a subset of AL applications	See natural language	Any complex DY application; especially those with sufficient complexity and criti-cality to warrant the multiple view-points and extra expressive power

Figure 4–73. A Comparison of SRS approaches.

REVS	RLP	SDL	PAISLey	Petri nets
9 See statecharts	9 See statecharts	6 See FSMs	9 See statecharts	6 See FSMs
7 See FSMs	7 See FSMs	7 See FSMs	4 Many concepts are not inultive to the non-computer scientist; hard-to-understand language for same audience	4 Synchrony and Petri nets appear to be difficult for noncomputer scientists to grasp
9 See statecharts	9 See statecharts	7 See FSMs	9 See statecharts	See FSMs ⌐
7 See FSMs	7 See FSMs	0 Sec natural language (potential exists for static structural and behavioral error checking)	9 See statecharts	Unknown
7 Same as RLP but slightly lower because R-net is more design oriented than stimulus-response sequence	8 Once external entities are defined, specifier stays naturally in the requirements domain	8 See RLP	3 A common criticism of PAISLey is its design orientation. Zave is not concerned if design is performed during requirements	2 Very difficult to use Petri nets in the applications domain. Many people versed in Petri nets are designers
9 R-net plus hierarchies of alphas	7 Stimulus-response sequence; the feature	7 Stimulus-response sequence; the feature	9 See statecharts	2 net
7 Yes, using TRW tools plus auxiliary coding	2 Feasibility demonstrated, but not implemented	Unknown	10 Yes, using Bell Labs tools	Unknown
0 None	10 Yes, using GTE tools	0 None	0 None	0 None
6 See natural language	6 See natural language	2 Not automated	6 See natural language	6 See natural language
7 See statecharts	4 See natural language	4 See natural language	4 See natural language	4 See natural language
DY applications that are stimulus-oriented; for example: many defense systems	DY applications that are feature-oriented; for example, telephony	SDL was specifically developed for telephone switching systems, but is probably applicable to all RLP applications. See RLP.	PAISLey was developed for complex DY systems	Those particular parts of any application in which synchrony is critical to the specification of external behavior. These are probably a subset of the CO applications

Figure 4–73. *(cont.)*

Clearly natural language does not provide automatic checking for any of these; PDL will be capable of detecting static structural errors. Finite state machines (using an automated tool like the IDE's Transition Diagram Editor [WAS86]), REVS, and RLP all provide automatic checking for behavioral and static structural errors.[9] Statecharts (using an automated tool like i-Logix's STATEMATE described in Section 4.2.2.4) and PAISLey both provide full protocol error checking in addition to behavioral and static structural checking. Pure Petri nets show synchrony very well, but we need the Yoeli and Barzelai extensions [YOE77] to specify fully protocols between asynchronous entities. Unfortunately I have not personally used any of the automated Petri net tools [GRU89] and thus am unable to assess their ability to check automatically for protocol violations. Decision trees and decision tables do not have the ability to specify protocol, and although they are used to specify behavior, I know of no tools to check automatically for consistency. Finally, SDL can be used to specify protocol but to my knowledge has not been automated to any degree.

5. PDL provides no help at all to the requirements writer who must remain at the requirements level and not proceed to design. Finite state machines, decision tables, and decision trees require a considerable amount of human discipline to define first external entities and then use the approach to describe attributes of, and existing relationships between, those entities. Statecharts are slightly better because they provide a structural viewpoint independent from behavioral and data flow viewpoints; however the i-Logix methodology does not specifically encourage the user to define requirements for an entity before defining that entity's internal structures. Finally, REVS, RLP, and SDL provide much better assistance due to their requirement to deal with only previously defined explicit external signals, although all can be easily misused. REVS probably scores slightly lower than RLP and SDL because the view of "what will the system do in response to this input signal" is somewhat more of an inside-out view than the "what do I have to do to make the system perform this function" view exhibited by RLP and SDL.

6. Finite state machines, decision tables, decision trees, PDL, and Petri nets all provide rudimentary SRS organizational assistance. In particular, the FSM and Petri net approaches offer the underlying machine model as the only organizational entity. Decision tables and trees provide the table and tree, respectively. PDL provides a module that can be used for anything desired. REVS enables SRS writers to organize behavioral requirements into R-nets, each corresponding to a system stimulus. Both SDL and RLP enable SRS writers to organize behavioral requirements into user-oriented features. Statecharts and PAISLey provide at least two levels of organization because of their ability to model synchrony, data flow, and external behavior separately.

---

[9]According to one study [CEL83], REVS detected 302 errors in an SRS for a large U.S. Army MIS application.

7. Automatically generating prototypes is possible with FSMs (when using IDE's tools, for example), statecharts (when using i-Logix's tools, for example), and PAISLey with little need to intervene other than by defining requirements in their respective languages. REVS provides prototype generation capability, but it requires considerable auxiliary coding effort on the user's part [FUR79]. The feasibility of automatic prototype generation using RLP has been explored but not implemented [DAV82, LEE85, WAN86]. None of the other approaches support prototype generation except Petri nets [GRU89]. RLP has the capability to generate system-level tests automatically directly from requirements [CHA85].

8. The ability to modify an SRS when using a formal approach is directly related to its ability to paginate, index, and create tables of contents automatically. It is also closely related to the quality of the human interface possessed by the tools. FSMs (with IDE's tools, for example), PDL, statecharts (using i-Logix's STATEMATE), REVS, RLP, Petri nets, and PAISLey all use editors to modify the SRS, and all generate appropriate reports and tables. As mentioned before, decision tables and trees, and SDL, have not been automated. On the other hand, spread sheets can be used for decision tables.

9. None of the approaches explicitly provide annotation, although any of the tools with underlying data bases could probably be modified to add a field to contain annotations. Traceability to design documents is explicitly available from REVS and statecharts but not from the others. Of course any approach associated with an automated tool that provides at least an ability to add comments to requirements permits the requirements writer to record annotations and cross-references manually.

10. The bottom row in Figure 4-73 summarizes appropriate types of applications for each technique, based on classes of applications defined in Section 1.4.

4.3 SUMMARY

In addition to natural language, Chapter 4 surveyed nine different approaches to specifying external behavior. It is important to remember that the same warning applies here as in problem analysis techniques of Chapter 2: There are no panaceas; each approach serves a unique purpose; each offers the ability to specify a particular aspect of a software system's external behavior. It is not wise to try to specify an entire system using any one technique any more than it is wise to construct any piece of furniture using just one tool. However if only one technique is available, I suggest (1) writing most of the SRS in your natural language (using a word processor) and augmenting selected sections with the unambiguous specification that results from using the particular technique and (2) using an automated tool to ensure the absence of errors. Take a minute or two now to reread Section 2.4; all of the advice given there for problem analysis applies equally well here for specification. Of course there is a major difference: (1) During problem analysis, always keep your eye clearly focused on your goal, that is, understanding your problem; stop when you have reached *this* goal; and (2) while writing an SRS always keep your eye clearly focused on your goal, that is, describing the complete external behavior; stop when you have reached *this* goal.

EXERCISES

1. Describe aspects of each of the following applications in which finite state machine-based approaches may be applicable. If not applicable, explain why.
   a. A robot lawn mower (see question 2c in Chapter 1)
   b. An elevator control system
   c. A nuclear reactor control system
   d. An inventory system
   e. A payroll system
   f. A compiler
   g. An "automatic pilot" for an automobile
   h. A sort program
   i. A telephone switching system
   j. An automated barber
   k. A patient-monitoring system
   l. An airline reservation system
2. Describe aspects of each of the applications in question 1 in which decision tables or trees may be applicable. If not applicable, explain why.
3. For the real-time aspects of each of the applications in question 1, describe why you would select statecharts, REVS, RLP, or PAISLey.
4. Describe aspects of each of the applications in question 1 in which Petri nets may be applicable. If not applicable, explain why.

REFERENCES

[AGE79] Agerwala, T. "Putting Petri Nets to Work." *IEEE Computer* **12,** 12 (December 1979): 85–94.

[ALF76] Alford, M. and I. Burns. "R-nets: A Graph Model for Real-Time Software Requirements." *Symposium on Computer Software Engineering.* New York: Polytechnic Press, 1976. pp. 97–108.

[ALF77] Alford, M. W. "A Requirements Engineering Methodology for Real-Time Processing Requirements." *IEEE Transactions on Software Engineering* **3,** 1 (January 1977): 60–69.

[ALF80] Alford, M. W. "Software Requirements Engineering Methodology (SREM) at the Age of Four." In *IEEE COMPSAC '80,* Washington D.C.: Computer Society Press of the Institute of Electrical and Electronics Engineers, 1980. pp. 866–74.

[ALF85] Alford, M. W. "SREM at the Age of Eight, the Distributed Design System." *IEEE Computer* **18,** 4 (April 1985): 36–46.

[BAC58] Backus, J., et al. "Preliminary Report—International Algebraic Language." *Communications of the ACM* **1,** 12 (December 1958): 8–22.

[BAU78] Bauer, J., et al. "The Automatic Generation and Execution of Function Test Plans for Electronic Switching Systems." *ACM Software Engineering Notes* **3,** 5 (November 1978): 92–100.

[BEL76] Bell, T. E., and D. C. Bixler. "A Flow-Oriented Requirements Statement Language." In *Symposium on Computer Software Engineering.* New York: Polytechnic Press, 1976. pp. 109–22.

[BER82] Berg, H., et al. *Formal Methods of Program Verification and Specification.* Englewood Cliffs, N.J.: Prentice-Hall, 1982.

[BER87] Berliner, E., and P. Zave. "An Experiment in Technology Transfer: PAISLey Specification of Requirements for an Undersea Lightware Cable System." In *Ninth IEEE International Conference on Software Engineering,* Washington D.C.: Computer Society Press of the Institute of Electrical and Electronics Engineers, 1987. pp. 42–50.

[BER80] Bersoff, E., et al. *Software Configuration Management: An Investment in Product Integrity.* Englewood Cliffs, N.J.: Prentice-Hall, 1980.

[BJO78] Bjorner, D., and C. Jones. *The Vienna Development Method.* New York: Springer Verlag, 1978.

[BJO87] Bjorner, D. "On the Use of Formal Methods in Software Development." In *Ninth IEEE International Conference on Software Engineering,* Washington D.C.: Computer Society Press of the Institute of Electrical Electronics Engineers, 1987. pp. 17–29.

[BRO80] Broy, M., et al. "Semantic Relations in Programming Languages." In *IFIPS '80,* Amsterdam: North-Holland, 1980. pp. 101–6.

[BRU86] Bruno, G., and C. Manchetto. "Process-Translatable Petri Nets for the Rapid Prototyping of Process Control Systems." *IEEE Transactions on Software Engineering* **12,** 2 (February 1986): 346–57.

[BUH79] Buhrke, R., et al. "Design Choices for a Large PCM Switch with Multiprocessor Control." *GTE World-Wide Communications Journal,* **17,** 4 (July 1979), pp. 114–21.

[BYR86] Byrnes, C., and R. Hilliard II. *The WIS Ada Design Language.* Mitre Corporation Report, contract F19628-86-C-001. Billerica, Mass., 1986.

[CAI75] Caine, S., and E. K. Gordon. "PDL—a Tool for Software Design." In *AFIPS National Computer Conference.* Vol. 44. Montvale, New Jersey: AFIPS Press of the American Federation of Information Processing Societies, 1975. pp. 271–76.

[CAS81] Casey, B. E., and B. J. Taylor. "Writing Requirements in English: A Natural Alternative." In *IEEE Software Engineering Standards Workshop,* Washington D.C.: Computer Society Press of the Institute of Electrical and Electronics Engineers, 1981. pp. 95–101.

[CEL83] Celko, J., et al. "A Demonstration of Three Requirements Language Systems." *ACM SIGPLAN Notices* **18,** 1 (January 1983): 9–14.

[CHA85] Chandrasekharan, M., et al. "Requirements-Based Testing of Real-Time Systems: Modeling for Testability." *IEEE Computer* **18,** 4 (April 1985): 71–80.

[CHI85] Chi, U. H. "Formal Specification of User Interfaces: A Comparison and Evaluation of Four Axiomatic Approaches." *IEEE Transactions on Software Engineering* **11,** 8 (August 1985): 671–85.

[CHV83] Chvalovsky, V. "Decision Tables." *Software Practice and Experience* **13** (1983): 423–29.

[COO83] Coolahan, J. E., and N. Roussopoulos. "Timing Requirements for Time-Driven Systems Using Augmented Petri Nets." *IEEE Transactions on Software Engineering* **9,** 5 (September 1983): 603–16.

[DAS81] Dasarathy, B. "Test Plan Generation for the Requirements Validation of Real-Time Systems." In *IEEE Workshop on Automatic Test Program Generation,* Washington D.C.: Computer Society Press of the Institute of Electrical and Electronics Engineers, 1981.

[DAV77] Davis, C., and C. Vick. "The Software Development System." *IEEE Transactions on Software Engineering* **SE-3,** 1 (January 1977): 69–84.

[DAV78] Davis, A. M., and W. Rataj. "Requirements Language Processing for the Effective Testing of Real-Time Software." *ACM Software Engineering Notes* **3,** 5 (November 1978): 61–66.

[DAV79] Davis, A. M., and T. G. Rauscher. "Formal Techniques and Automatic Processing to Ensure Correctness in Requirements Specifications." In *IEEE Specifications of Reliable Software Conference,* Washington D.C.: Computer Society of the Institute of Electrical and Electronics Engineers, 1979. pp. 15–35.

[DAV79a] Davis, A. M., et al. "RLP: An Automated Tool for the Processing of Requirements." In *IEEE COMPSAC '79,* Washington D.C.: Computer Society of the Institute of Electrical and Electronics Engineers, 1979. pp. 289–99.

[DAV80] Davis, A. M. "Automating the Requirements Phase: Benefits to Later Phases of the Software Life-Cycle." In *IEEE COMPSAC '80,* Washington D.C.: Computer Society of the Institute of Electrical and Electronics Engineers, 1980. pp. 42–48.

[DAV82] Davis, A. M. "Rapid Prototyping Using Executable Requirements Specifications." *ACM Software Engineering Notes* **7,** 5 (December 1982): 39–44.

[DAV82a] Davis, A. M. "The Design of a Family of Applications-Oriented Requirements Languages." *IEEE Computer* **15,** 5 (March 1982): 21–28.

[DAV82b] Davis, A. M. "The Role of Requirements in the Software Synthesis of Real-Time Systems." In *International Symposium on Current Issues in Requirements Engineering Environments,* Y. Ohno, ed. Amsterdam: North-Holland Publ., 1982. pp. 151–58.

[DOD88] U.S. Department of Defense. *Military Standard: Defense System Software Development.* DOD-STD-2167A. Washington, D.C., February 1988.

[DRE88] Drees, S. et al. "Bibliography of Petri Nets 1988." Arbeitspapiere der GMD Nr. 315.

[FUR79] Furia, N. "A Comparative Evaluation of RSL/REVS and PSL/PSA Applied to a Digital Flight Control System." In *AIAA Second Computers in Aerospace Conference,* Washington D.C.: American Institute of Aeronautics and Astronautics, 1979. pp. 330–37.

[GEH86] Gehani, N., and A. McGettrick, eds. *Software Specification Techniques.* Reading, Penn.: Addison Wesley, 1986.

[GRU89] Grude, Y. Letter to ACM Forum. *Communications of the ACM* **32,** 1 (January 1989): 5–6.

[HAR87] Harel, D. "Statecharts: A Visual Formalism for Complex Systems." *Science of Computer Programming* **8** (1987): 231–74.

[HAR87a] Harel, D., et al. "The ADCAD Methodology and STATEMATE1 Working Environment." In *Conference on Methodologies and Tools for Real-Time Systems.* Washington, D.C.: National Institute for Quality and Productivity. 1987. pp. I-1–I-10.

[HAR88] Harel, D. "On Visual Formalisms." *Communications of the ACM* **31,** 5 (May 1988): 514–30.

[HAR88a] Harel, D., et al. "STATEMATE: A Working Environment for the Development of Complex Reactive Systems." In *Tenth IEEE International Conference on Software Engineering,* Washington D.C.: Computer Society Press of the Institute of Electrical and Electronics Engineers, 1988.

[HAT84] Hatley, D. "The Use of Structured Methods in the Development of Large Software Based Avionics Systems, In *AIAA/IEEE Sixth Digital Avionics Systems Conference,* Washington D.C.: American Institute of Aeronautics and Astronautics, 1984, pp. 6–15.

[HEN79] Heninger, K. L. "Specifying Software Requirements for Complex Systems: New Techniques and Their Applications." *IEEE Transactions on Software Engineering* **6,** 1 (January 1980): 2–12.

[HOF86] Hofstadter, D. *Metamagical Themas.* New York: Basic Books, 1985.

[HUF78] Huff, S. L., and S. E. Madnick. *An Approach to Constructing Functional Requirements Statements for System Architectural Design.* Center for Information Systems Research, MIT Sloan School of Management Technical Report 6, Cambridge, Mass., June 1978.

[IEE85] Institute of Electrical and Electronics Engineers. *Ada as a Program Design Language.* ANSI/IEEE Standard 990-1986. New York, 1986.

[ILO85] i-Logix, Inc. *STATEMATE1: The STATEMATE1 Working Environment for System Development.* Burlington, Mass.: i-Logix, 1985.

[JAC75] Jackson, M. *Principles of Program Design.* New York: Academic Press, 1975.

[JON80] Jones, C. *Software Development: A Rigorous Approach.* Englewood Cliffs, N.J.: Prentice-Hall International, 1980.

[KAI72] Kain, R. *Automata Theory: Machines and Languages.* New York: McGraw-Hill, 1972.

[KAW71] Kawashima, H., et al. "Functional Specification of Call Processing by State Transition Diagram." *IEEE Transactions on Communications* **19**, 5 (October 1971): 581–87.

[LEE85] Lee, S., and S. Sluizer. "On Using Executable Specifications for High-Level Prototyping." In *Third IEEE International Workshop on Specification and Design,* Washington D.C.: Computer Society Press of the Institute of Electrical and Electronics Engineers, 1985. pp. 130–34.

[LIN79] Linger, R., et al. *Structured Programming: Theory and Practice.* Reading, Mass.: Addison-Wesley, 1979.

[MAT77] Matsumoto, Y. "A Method of Software Requirements Definitions in Process Control." In *IEEE COMPSAC '77,* Washington D.C.: Computer Society Press of the Institute of Electrical and Electronics Engineers, 1977. pp. 128–32.

[MCM84] McMenamin, S., and J. Palmer. *Essential Systems Analysis.* Englewood Cliffs, N.J.: Prentice-Hall, 1984.

[MIL81] Miller, T., and B. J. Taylor. "A System Requirements Methodology." In *IEEE Electro '81 Conference,* Washington D.C.: Computer Society Press of the Institute of Electrical and Electronics Engineers, 1981. pp. 18.5.1–18.5.5.

[MIL87] Mills, H., et al. *Principles of Computer Programming: A Mathematical Approach.* Newton, Mass.: Allyn and Bacon, 1987.

[MOR82] Moret, B. "Decision Trees and Diagrams." *ACM Computing Surveys* **14**, 4 (December 1982): 593–623.

[NAK80] Nakagawa, M. "Specifying the Underlying Control Structures of Programming Languages in Their Denotational Semantics." In *IFIPS '80,* Amsterdam: North-Holland, 1980. pp. 89–94.

[NEU80] Neuhold, E., and T. Olnhoff. "The Vienna Development Method and Its Use for the Specification of a Relational Data Base System." In *IFIPS '80,* Amsterdam: North-Holland, 1980. pp. 5–16.

[OHN85] Ohnishi, A., et al. "Requirements Model and Method of Requirements Definition." In *IEEE COMPSAC '85,* Washington D.C.: Computer Society Press of the Institute of Electrical and Electronics Engineers, 1985. pp. 26–32.

[PAR83] Partsch, H., and R. Steinbruggen. "Program Transformation Systems." *ACM Computing Surveys* **15**, 3 (September 1983): 199–236.

[PET] *Petri Net Newsletter.* GMD-F1, P.B. 1240, D-5205 St., Augustin, FRG.

[PET77] Peterson, J. "Petri Nets." *ACM Computing Surveys* **9**, 3 (September 1977): 223–52.

[PET81] Peterson, J. *Petri Net Theory and the Modeling of Systems.* Englewood Cliffs, NJ: Prentice Hall, 1981.

[PET62] Petri, C. A. "Kommunikation mit Automaten." Ph.D. Diss. University of Bonn. Bonn, FRG, 1962.

[ROC82] Rockstrom, A., and R. Saracco. "SDL—CCITT Specification and Description Language." *IEEE Transactions on Communications* **30,** 6 (June 1982): 1310–18.

[SAL76] Salter, K. "A Methodology for Decomposing System Requirements into Data-Processing Requirements." In *Second IEEE International Conference on Software Engineering,* Washington D.C.: Computer Society Press of the Institute of Electrical and Electronics Engineers, 1976. pp. 91–101.

[SMI88] Smith, S., and S. Gerhart. "STATEMATE and Cruise Control: A Case Study." In *IEEE COMPSAC '88,* Washington D.C.: Computer Society Press of the Institute of Electrical and Electronics Engineers, 1988. pp. 49–56.

[SUN79] Sunshine, C. *Formal Methods for Communication Protocol Specification and Verification.* ARPA Report 3460/3681. November 1979.

[TAY80] Taylor, B. "A Method for Expressing Functional Requirements of Real-Time Systems." In *IFAC/IFIP Workshop on Real-Time Programming,* Oxford, England: Pergamon Press, 1981. pp. 111–20.

[WAN86] Wang, Y. "A Distributed Specification Model and Its Prototyping." In *IEEE COMPSAC '86,* Washington D.C.: Computer Society Press of the Institute of Electrical and Electronics Engineers, 1986. pp. 130–37.

[WAR85] Ward, P., and S. Mellor. *Structured Development for Real-Time Systems.* Englewood Cliffs, N.J.: Prentice-Hall, 1985.

[WAS81] Wasserman, A. "User Software Engineering and the Design of Interactive Systems." In *Fifth IEEE International Conference on Software Engineering,* Washington D.C.: Computer Society Press of the Institute of Electrical and Electronics Engineers, 1981. pp. 387–93.

[WAS85] Wasserman, A. I. "Extending State Transition Diagrams for the Specification of Human–Computer Interaction." *IEEE Transactions on Software Engineering* **11,** 8 (August 1985): 699–713.

[WAS86] Wasserman, A., et al. "Development Interactive Information Systems with the User Software Engineering Methodology." *IEEE Transactions on Software Engineering* **12,** 2 (February 1986): 326–45.

[WHI81] Whitis, V.S., and W. N. Chiang. "A State Machine Development for Call-Processing Software." In *IEEE Electro '81 Conference,* Washington D.C.: Computer Society Press of the Institute of Electrical and Electronics Engineers, 1981. pp. 7/2-1–7/2-6.

[YOE77] Yoeli, M., and Z. Barzilai. "Behavioral Descriptions of Communication Switching Systems Using Extended Petri Nets." *Digital Processes* **3,** 4 (1977): 307–20.

[YOU79] Yourdon, E., and L. Constantine. *Structured Design.* Englewood Cliffs, N.J.: Prentice-Hall, 1979.

[YOU89] Yourdon, E. *Modern Structured Analysis.* Englewood Cliffs, N.J.: Prentice-Hall, 1989.

[ZAV81] Zave, P., and R. T. Yeh. "Executable Requirements for Embedded Systems." In *Fifth IEEE International Conference on Software Engineering,* Washington D.C.: Computer Society Press of the Institute of Electrical and Electronics Engineers, 1981. pp. 295–304.

[ZAV82] Zave, P. "An Operational Approach to Requirements Specification for Embedded Systems." *IEEE Transactions on Software Engineering* **8,** 3 (May 1982): 250–69.

[ZAV86] Zave, P., and W. Schell. "Salient Features of an Executable Specification Language and Its Environment." *IEEE Transactions on Software Engineering* **12,** 2 (Feburary 1986): 312–25.

5

Specifying Nonbehavioral Requirements

Knowing how to specify behavioral requirements for a software system is only half the battle. All applications, from the most trivial to the most complex, have additional requirements that define the overall qualities or attributes to be exhibited by the resulting software system. In 1976, Barry Boehm [BOE76] generated a hierarchical list of qualities exhibited by software (see Figure 5–1). Although many have attempted similar lists, none have been better than Boehm's. Chapter 5 discusses how to specify the degree of each of these qualities as requirements for the software system being built. In general, an SRS need not specify every one of these; it is necessary to emphasize those factors of particular importance to the particular application. For example, if the application is life critical, reliability becomes paramount. If the product is to be long lived, then portability and modifiability are usually critical. If the system is real-time, then reliability, efficiency, and human engineering are often most important. If the application has all these aspects, then all factors become important. Of course these are broad generalizations that will not apply to all situations; it is important to remember to spend your efforts on those that are critical and not to waste your time on those that are not.

The following five sections cover the seven qualities defined by the third tier of factoring in Figure 5–1.

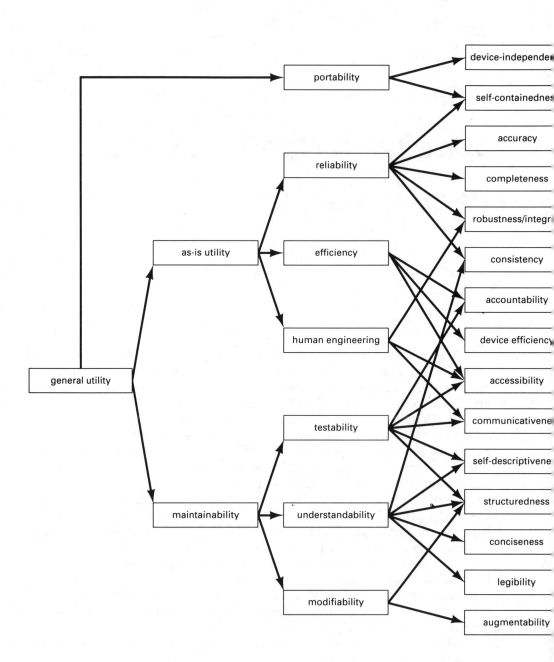

Figure 5–1. The Software Quality Characteristics Tree. © 1976 IEEE Computer Society.

5.1 PORTABILITY

Portability is the degree to which software running on one host computer environment can easily be converted to one running on another host computer environment. If the application will be short lived (for example, a to-be-used-once test environment), impossible to port (for example, satellite based), or expected to live a relatively long time but is not expected to be ever upgraded (for example, an elevator control system may experience little upgrade from installation to building demolition), portability need not be addressed. On the other hand, portability requirements are absolutely essential to include in an SRS for any other type of application.

Portability is almost impossible to quantify. The closest quantification of portability I have seen is "maximum time to port to host system X," but this falls grossly short of anything useful because (1) we rarely know the next generation host and (2) maximum time is relatively meaningless. Would you design your software any differently if it had to be ported in two weeks rather than one day? Skelton [SKE86] presents very sketchy definitions of four levels of portability (which he calls migratability), but these are so casually defined that few conclusions can be reached. A considerably better way of specifying portability is in terms of (1) source language, (2) host operating system, and (3) compiler selection. I have specifically excluded object-oriented design, isolating hardware dependent code, designing with abstractions, and packages, all of which are sensible design approaches that unquestioningly improve portability, maintainability, and modifiability characteristics of software. However, portability rarely appears as the primary motivation for their use.

Programming language selection has a considerable effect on the resulting product's portability level because a program written in language X for which compilers exist for two different machines can be easily ported between those two machines simply by switching compilers. Although language selection should ideally be made during the design stage and not during the requirements stage, its role in portability is so significant that it may be completely appropriate to decree the language in the SRS. It must be realized that language selection is often political and rarely has a technical basis. Removing all political considerations from a project probably points a project with stringent portability requirements in the direction of either C or FORTRAN (for nonbusiness) or COBOL (for business).[1] These three languages are among my last choices for a project from an aesthetic point of view, but their idiosyncrasies have long ago disappeared or become understood, they are well shaken down, they are available on just about any computer system, and in the case of FORTRAN and COBOL were standardized nationally very early. On the other hand, most implementations of FORTRAN extend beyond the standard vanilla, so you must use discipline to remain within the portable

[1] C is a registered trademark of AT&T.

standard. Ada probably has the best chance of being truly standard and thus affords its users the best potential for portability. The DoD insists on only one Ada; no supersets or subsets are permissible. The DoD certifies Ada compilers, and when this certification is present, we can be assured of having the entire standard Ada and only the standard Ada. Compilers for Ada are likely to become widespread on all major host computers. PASCAL must take a distant fifth place in the race for portability; it was standardized too late and hundreds of developers of PASCAL compilers took free reign in modifying Niklaus Wirth's original PASCAL, which was developed primarily for student use. Assembly language will be the least portable alternative for any application.

In some cases selecting a specific operating system can enhance a program's portability; this is particularly true for "portable" operating systems. The operating system to date that has demonstrated its ability most often to be ported is probably UNIX. With such a requirement, applications written to run on UNIX on one machine should be able to be ported fairly easily to other machines that support UNIX.

Selecting a specific compiler, like selecting a language, should ideally occur late in the design stage. However, some compilers greatly enhance portability of the product, and thus it may be beneficial to specify a specific compiler in the portability section of the SRS. In particular some compilers are termed *retargetable,* that is, easily modifiable to generate code for any target computer system. Thus if we specify in the SRS compiler W for language X targeted to computer Y, and compiler W is known to be retargetable, the chances are likely that W can later be modified to generate code for some next-generation computer system Z with a minimum of effort and thus port the application software from host Y to host Z with no changes to the application source itself.

By all means, specify in the SRS the likelihood that the software will have to be ported in the future. If it is not stated, designers and coders will have no way of knowing that they must plan for it.

5.2 RELIABILITY

Reliability of software is defined to be the ability of the software to behave consistently in a user-acceptable manner when subjected to an environment in which it was intended to be used. This section concentrates on practical techniques for specifying software reliability. Requirements specification of reliability is discussed from four perspectives: the meaning of 99.999% reliability, traditional techniques from hardware, techniques to measure numbers of bugs in software, and the relative need for reliability in software. Musa et al. [MUS87] is the best source of information about the theory and meaning of software reliability itself.

5.2.1 What does 99.999% Reliable Mean?

SRSs for systems with high reliability requirements occasionally contain the phrase "the system shall be 99.999% reliable." Be careful in using that type of expression; it means different things to different people. For example, in telephony it means that the telephone system may occasionally lose a phone call here and there, but it may not go down completely more than five minutes every year. On the other hand, patient-monitoring systems may also have the same requirement. Does it mean that it is okay occasionally to lose a patient provided the system does not go down completely? Quite the contrary, it may go down completely provided it alerts the medical staff so that patients can be monitored manually. The 99.999% implies that when it is operating, it may not incorrectly monitor more than one patient out of every hundred thousand.

5.2.2 Traditional Techniques from Hardware

The theory and practice of hardware reliability are well established disciplines. Unfortunately however, the metrics developed for hardware have somehow escaped into the software domain. It is important to understand these metrics in order to see how absurd many of them are when applied to software.

The most popular metric is some variation of mean time to failure (MTTF). In the hardware world, MTTF makes sense. Every physical component, whether a steel beam or an integrated circuit, reacts with its environment and will slowly degrade until it no longer satisfies its intended purpose. The rate of failures of most electronic components exhibits what is called a bathtub curve, such as that shown in Figure 5–2. Given a large population of a particular component, many will fail soon after development; this so-called infant mortality rate is usually the result of inaccuracies in the manufacturing process. Once this early period of failures has been completed, components are expected to last a certain time without failing. For example, one integrated circuit might have a MTTF of one hundred thousand hours, meaning that on the average, it can be expected to fail after about 11.5 years of relatively constant operation. When a system is constructed with many interconnected components, the system's MTTF is some well defined function of the MTTFs of each of its components. A component fails because it has reacted with its environment and has decomposed in some way according to the laws of physics. Because two "identical" components (with the same MTTF of, say, one hundred thousand hours) are unlikely to fail at the same time, the reliability of a hardware system can be increased by incorporating redundancy.

MTTF has also been used to define necessary levels of software reliability [JEL72, LIT73, MUS75, GIL77, SCH78]; however, this is somewhat fallacious. Let us say we have a piece of software and it runs for 11.5 years without failure, then the software suddenly stops working. There are only two possible expla-

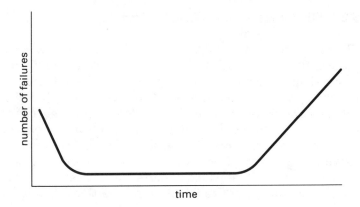

Figure 5–2. A Bathtub Curve.

nations: A software maintenance person has made an error and introduced a new bug, or the software user has employed the software in a way in which it had never before been used and thus uncovered a bug that had always been there. In neither case is there a relationship between the event and the software's reliability at time of deployment. In the first case, the bug was introduced years after and thus certainly had no relationship to the software's initial level of reliability. In the second case, the time until failure was purely a function of the "reliability" (i.e., predictability) of the user, not the software. In support, however, of MTTF for software is the argument put forth by Musa that MTTF is a function of both the predictability of the user and the number of bugs in the software [MUS87]. Thus if two programs solved the same problem and each had the same bugs, the programs would demonstrate different MTTFs when used in different environments, but two programs having a different number of bugs used in identical environments would also demonstrate different MTTFs.

Two other techniques from hardware reliability that have somehow crept into software are mean time to repair (MTTR) and total down time per time period; both have the same problems as MTTF.

5.2.3 Counting Bugs

Most software engineers today believe that quality, in general, and reliability, specifically, must be built in initially (that is, designed and implemented in) rather than tested in after the fact. This is not a new idea and dates back to at least 1969 [SAU69]. If this is the case, then one way of forcing developers to build in quality is to define a maximum testing interval. For example, we could state initially that developers should do whatever is needed so that it takes no more than two months to test the software. The problem with this approach is that the development/test organization could simply stop testing after two months and declare success. Prospective customers would have no way of knowing if the software was really well designed or if the testing process had simply been stopped prematurely. An equally unacceptable approach would be to determine initially the maximum number of bugs that could be found during testing. Once again the development/test organization could simply stop testing after the requisite number of bugs had been found. By the way, even if either of these approaches made sense, statements concerning length of the testing interval or number of bugs found during testing would not be appropriate for an SRS. These are attributes of the software development process rather than the software product itself.

What is really needed is a requirement in the SRS that when the software is delivered, it will "work;" but what does it mean to work? One meaning is to have no bugs, where a bug is defined to be some defect in the software. If no bugs is the ultimate, then five bugs per one thousand lines of code is better than ten bugs per one thousand lines of code, and so forth. Perhaps there is a way of stating in the SRS that

> The software shall have no more than one bug per thousand lines of code.

But how can we know how many bugs are in the software when it is delivered? It will not help to wait until the software is mothballed and then count the bugs that were found during its lifetime, and declare that the software had or had not met the SRS. What good is it to know then? We need to know at delivery time; one way of doing so is to use Monte Carlo techniques.

A *Monte Carlo technique* involves determining some aspect of the real world through statistical analysis of random events. A good example is the application of Monte Carlo techniques to determine the area of a nonstandard shape. For example, there does not exist an obvious equation for calculating the area of the shape in Figure 5–3a. I do not know the equation for the area of an amoeba. An effective way of calculating the area involves circumscribing the shape of a known area, say, a 2 inch by 2 inch square, around the unknown shape, as shown in Figure 5–3b, then dropping a large number of random points in the square. For each point, record whether the point falls inside or outside of the shape. The number of points falling inside the shape divided by the total number of points dropped will be proportional to the area of the shape divided by the known area; that is,

$$\frac{\text{Number of points in shape}}{\text{Total number of points}} = \frac{\text{Area of shape}}{\text{Known area of square}}$$

Solving for the area of the shape,

$$\text{Area of shape} = \frac{\text{Number of points in shape} \times \text{Known area of square}}{\text{Total number of points}}$$

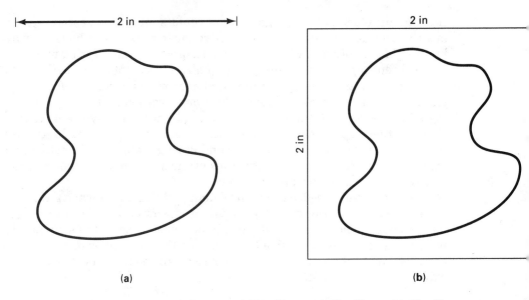

Figure 5–3. Find the Area of This Shape. **(a)** The Shape. **(b)** The Shape Circumscribed.

For example, let us drop one million points in the square of known area. Let us assume that 400,000 of them fall in the shape, then

$$\text{Area of shape} = \frac{400,000 \times 4 \text{ square inches}}{1,000,000} = 1.6 \text{ square inches}$$

The same theory applies in determining the number of bugs in a software product by using what Gilb calls *bebugging* [GIL77] and Mills calls *inspection statistics* [MIL72]. Just before system-level testing, we secretly insert a known number of bugs; these are called *seeded bugs*. The test team is not told where the bugs are or how many there are. As shown in Figure 5–4, the unknown numbers of bugs can be represented as a shape of unknown area (where its area corresponds to the number of bugs) and that subset of seeded bugs as a shape of known area within the unknown shape. Now an independent test team tries to uncover bugs in the software. As these random bugs are located, some will turn out to be previously seeded bugs (i.e., the points will fall within the little square), and some will be previously unknown bugs (i.e., the points will fall within the large shape but outside the little square). Thus the same proportion as before holds

$$\frac{\text{Points in square}}{\text{Total number of points}} = \frac{\text{Area of square}}{\text{Area of shape}}$$

Using the meanings of the points and shapes,

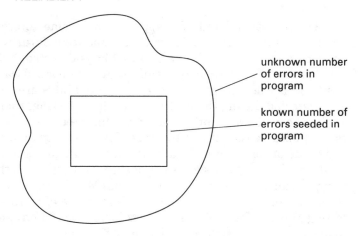

unknown number
of errors in
program

known number of
errors seeded in
program

Figure 5–4. Bebugging Process

$$\frac{\text{Number of detected seeded bugs}}{\text{Number of detected bugs}} = \frac{\text{Number of seeded bugs}}{\text{Number of bugs in system}}$$

Solving for the only unknown, the number of bugs in the system, yields

$$\text{Number of bugs in system} = \frac{\text{Number of seeded bugs} \times \text{Number of detected bugs}}{\text{Number of detected seeded bugs}}$$

For example, let us secretly seed ten bugs in the software. Then we test. The test team detects 120 bugs, of which six had previously been seeded. Then

$$\text{Number of bugs in system} = \frac{10 \times 120}{6} = 200 \text{ bugs}$$

But now we must remove the 120 detected bugs as well as the four previously seeded (i.e., 10 – 6) bugs that had not been detected to find out how many bugs really remain in the system. Thus,

$$\text{Number of bugs in system} = 200 - 120 - 4 = 76$$

Unfortunately there are a number of fallacies in the preceding approach. First, not all bugs are created equal. It is better to have one hundred bugs in a system, each of which causes a minor inconvenience or irritation, than one bug that kills a person. Second, the existence of one bug may hide the presence of another bug. Third, not all bugs can be found equally easily. For example, if we seed the software with ten easy-to-find bugs, results will be biased toward few bugs remaining; if we seed the software with ten hard-to-find bugs, results will be biased toward a large quantity of bugs remaining. And fourth, fixing bugs often creates other bugs (i.e., the domino effect) [LIT73], so that we cannot assume we can subtract 120 from 200 in the preceding example.

On the other hand, the approach has some interesting and positive attributes. First, the way it works is somewhat intuitive. After all, if one hundred bugs are seeded, one hundred bugs detected, but none of them are among those seeded, we may assume that it is poor software (and the formula results in a value of infinity). If one hundred bugs are seeded, one hundred bugs detected during the first two months of testing, then no more detected during the next two months, and all one hundred are those previously seeded, we may assume that the software is of good quality (and the formula results in a value of zero). Second, although the technique is not perfect, it at least yields results that have some relationship to the quality of the software—something we cannot say with assurance about MTTF. And third, in the worst case, we can at least use the technique as a measure of testing effectiveness (i.e., testing is over when all seeded bugs have been found) and as a measure of completeness of testing (i.e., testing is $X\%$ complete when $X\%$ of the seeded bugs have been found).

5.2.4 Reliability in Perspective

If we ask any company that develops software how important reliability is, most will say that reliability is of paramount importance. In many cases the reason is that low product reliability means low customer satisfaction, which means reduced revenues and then major financial loss to the company building the software. It is more relevant to analyze the impact of low reliability on software users rather than on software vendors and developers. Software that could result in death if it malfunctioned (e.g., an intensive-care patient-monitoring system) would seem to require the most reliability and therefore the most attention to reliability in the SRS. However, there are software applications where malfunctioning software can kill hundreds of thousands of people (e.g., nuclear reactor control systems). Surely these applications require more attention to reliability in their implementation and of course in their SRSs. However, there are yet more critical software applications! In such applications a malfunction could destroy all of civilization as we know it today (e.g., a malfunctioning nuclear weapon control system could conceivably start a nuclear war). Thus, there are clearly hierarchies in defining the level of detail appropriate when specifying reliability requirements:

- Destroy all humankind
- Destroy large numbers of human beings
- Kill a few people
- Injure people
- Cause major financial loss
- Cause major embarrassment

- Cause minor financial loss
- Cause mild inconvenience

5.2.5 Summary

Software reliability is probably the most difficult of all nonbehavioral requirements to state in an SRS. Many claim that the term reliability should not even be applied to software. A suggested reliability requirement is that

> No more than five bugs per 10K lines of executable code may be detected during integration and system testing. No more than ten bugs per 10K lines of executable code may remain in the system after delivery, as calculated by the Monte Carlo seeding technique defined in Appendix III. The system must be 100% operational 99.9% of the calendar time during its first year of operation.

Musa et al. [MUS87] contains a wealth of additional ideas on software reliability, mostly statistical based.

5.3 EFFICIENCY

Software *efficiency* refers to the level at which the software uses scarce system resources. Types of scarce resources include machine cycles (timing constraints), memory, disk space, buffers, and communication channels. Remember that we want to specify limitations on these resources at requirements specification time. If the software being specified is a stand-alone system and it only interfaces with the outside world through its host computer and perhaps a user, then usually machine cycles and memory are the only significant efficiency considerations.

When the software being described in the SRS is a subsystem of a much larger system (and there are probably other SRSs being written for other major software subsystems), overall system design has already been performed. This overall system design has defined buffer space, buffer sizes, and other types of communication channels between these software subsystems. In such applications, required buffer use must be specified, including maximum and mean number of requested buffers per time period, maximum and mean number of reserved buffers at any one time, and maximum and mean time that buffers are held.

5.3.1 Capacity

Capacity is easy to quantify: Specify how many users, how many terminals, how many ships? Aircraft? Patients? Nodes in network? Employees? Pay grades? Rooms in hotel? For every possible input, specify in the SRS how many can be expected. Since capacity requirements often increase in the future, it may also be helpful to indicate how volatile the stated capacity is likely to be in the future.

Also important for capacity (especially in DY applications) is the rate at which things arrive. For example, what is the maximum at any one time? Maximum per hour? How will peak versus normal periods compare? How long will peak periods last? A few seconds or a few days? Once again it is helpful to state likely changes to these rates and peak periods projected into the future.

Here is an example:

> The system shall handle up to and including twenty simultaneous terminals and users performing any activities without degradation of service below that defined in Section *I.J.K.* Other systems may make short requests of this system at a maximum rate of 50 per hour and long requests at a maximum rate of 1 per hour, also without degradation.

5.3.2 Degradation of Service

If the SRS states that the software shall be able to handle X widgets at a time, the onus is on the developers to build the software to meet that requirement. But what if $X + 1$ widgets arrive? Unfortunately the SRS does not obligate the real world, the real environment of the system! As an example, an air traffic controller system may require that

1. The system shall track the movements of up to fifty aircraft.
2. New positions of all aircraft shall be displayed no less often than once per 5 seconds.

What will happen if a fifty-first aircraft arrives? Some possibilities are

- The software "bombs," i.e., it enters a fatal, nonrecoverable state.
- The software continues to track the first fifty aircraft but ignores the fifty-first.
- The software prints an error message to the ATC announcing violation of its requirements.
- The software notifies the pilot to exit the sector immediately.
- The software tracks all fifty-one aircraft, but updates all their positions once every 7 seconds rather than once every 5 seconds.

If the SRS does not state which alternative is correct, then designers are free to implement any of the five alternatives. Clearly the best alternative from the users' (or passengers') perspective is the last one, and the worst are the first and second. The third and fourth are not much better than the first and second. From the developers' perspective, the easiest thing to do is to assume the capacity stated in the SRS is the capacity and not worry about the capacity being exceeded. Unfortunately this will probably lead to alternative 1.

The moral is that for many performance requirements, it is necessary not only to state what capacity is to be accommodated, and what performance levels are acceptable within those capacities, but also what the desired system behavior is in the case the environment exceeds capacity. In general, the alternatives are complete system failure, ignoring inputs in excess of capacity, providing degraded service to all inputs, and providing acceptable service to existing inputs and degraded service to inputs exceeding capacity. The correct choice is purely a function of the application. For example, in the ATC example, the best decision is probably to provide slightly degraded service to all aircraft (because we cannot afford to "lose" an aircraft), but in a telephone example, callers in excess of switch capacity should probably be ignored and not even receive a dial tone (because we can afford to "lose" a new caller).

5.3.3 Timing Constraints

Timing constraints define response time requirements for software and/or its environment. In the simplest cases, a few short sentences are all that is required, for example, the editor shall echo all key presses within 10 msec, shall complete tasks demanded by editing commands in category I within 5 seconds, averaging 1 second; and those in category II within 20 seconds, averaging 5 seconds. However, timing constraints for class DY applications are in general a lot more complex and deserve special attention.

5.3.3.1 Theory

In 1985 Dasarathy [DAS85] provided a generalization to the timing constraint problem, which paved the way for the straightforward inclusion of such constraints into any of the models described in Section 4.2.2. In particular Dasarathy [DAS85] stated that four types of timing constraints are sufficient for the requirements specification of real-time systems:

- Stimulus-response
- Response-response
- Stimulus-stimulus
- Response-stimulus.

where stimulus denotes an action performed by the user or environment on the system, and response denotes an action performed by the system on the user or environment.

Stimulus-response is the constraint that the system must produce a *response* in accordance with a specified timing relationship to an earlier user (or environment) *stimulus* to that system. This timing relationship may be either a minimum time, a maximum time, or both; for example,

Minimum stimulus-response constraint example: The system shall generate a dial tone within 15 seconds of a user taking the phone off the hook.

Maximum stimulus-response constraint example: The system shall arm the door alarm no sooner than 1 minute after the "alarm on" button is pressed in order to allow the person to exit the premises without triggering the alarm.

Note also that the stimulus and the response specified in the timing constraint need not be immediately adjacent in time, i.e., other stimuli and responses may occur in between. A key idea of the stimulus-response constraint is to specify the timing constraint that must exist between any stimulus and any subsequent response.

The second type of timing constraint, the *response-response* enables us to specify a temporal relationship that must exist between two arbitrary system responses to the environment. As before, this relationship may be a minimum, maximum, or a combination; for example,

Minimum response-response constraint example: The system shall initiate the door-closing operation within 20 seconds of locking the landing gear in the retracted state.

Maximum response-response constraint example: The system shall generate a "launch missile" command no sooner than 5 seconds after generating a "start battery warm-up" command.

As before, the two responses need not be adjacent in time.

The third type of constraint, *stimulus-stimulus,* enables us to specify expected behavior of a user (or environment) of a system in terms of minimum or maximum timing constraints between two stimuli. Once again these may be a minimum, maximum, or a combination of constraints; for example,

Minimum stimulus-stimulus constraint example: Users must type their password within 15 seconds of typing their identification, or they will be denied access to the data base.

Maximum stimulus-stimulus constraint example: Pilots must not press the "launch weapon" button sooner than 10 seconds after pressing the "fire ready" button.

The fourth type, *response-stimulus,* enables us to specify a temporal relationship that must exist between a system response and a subsequent user stimulus; for example,

Minimum response-stimulus constraint example: The user must dial the complete phone number within 1 minute of hearing the dial tone.

Maximum response-stimulus constraint example: The user may not make a menu selection sooner than 5 seconds after completion of the menu display.

Note that the first two types of timing constraints define timing requirements on the system being specified; that is, they imply that designers of the software may employ any architectural or algorithmic solutions they choose but the function must be implemented in such a way to perform the function rapidly (or slowly) enough to meet the timing requirement. The latter two types of timing constraints imply that the system be able to detect a violation of timing constraints by the users or environment and then perform an alternative action. Thus these latter two types do not imply that software must be rapid (or slow) but that there must be additional software to (1) detect inappropriately timed user stimuli and (2) generate alternative responses to the user, e.g., warnings or error messages. On the other hand, if the PAISLey approach [ZAV81, ZAV86] (see Section 4.2.2.8) is taken in which both the system and its environment are specified as two cooperating processes, then Dasarathy's timing constraints can really be reduced to just two types: stimulus-response and response-response. In other words, Dasarathy's four types of timing constraints are just these two taken from two perspectives: from the system's perspective and from its environment's perspective.

5.3.3.2 Specification of timing constraints using models

The following sections discuss how timing constraints can be expressed in some of the models defined in Section 4.2.2.

5.3.3.2.1 Finite State Machines

Response-stimulus timing constraints where the stimulus immediately follows the response with no intervening stimuli or responses are the easiest to represent. For example, Figure 5–5 uses a state transition diagram to define a maximum 15-second response time for a user to do task *X*. If the user does *X*, the user receives the normal system response. On the other hand, if 15 seconds elapse before the user does *X*, then the user receives the alternative system response. In situations where the response and the stimulus are separated by other responses and stimuli, it is necessary to define timers (called *alarms* by Wasserman [WAS85]). Using timers involves turning them on at specific points in time and transitioning later based on time elapsed in the timer. The example in Figure 5–6 shows a timer being reset to zero sometime in the past. Then when we enter state *S*, we will transition to the

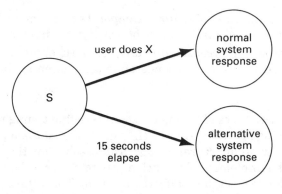

Figure 5–5. Response-Stimulus
Timing Constraint in an FSM

alternative system response immediately if the timer has already clocked 15 seconds. Otherwise the user will receive the normal system response as long as X is completed before the timer reaches 15 seconds. The same strategy works for stimulus-stimulus timing constraints.

Stimulus-response timing constraints where no other intervening stimuli or responses occur are also straightforward, as shown in Figure 5–7. In this case the system must enter state T within 5 seconds of the user completing X. The same type of timer will work for stimulus-response as for response-stimulus timing constraints where there are intervening stimuli and responses (see Figure 5–8). Of course if more than one timer is needed, give them names. Response-response timing constraints work the same way as stimulus-response.

5.3.3.2.2 *Program Design Language and Requirements Language Processor*

In both PDL as well as languages processable by RLP, a simple suffix to requirements statements suffices to define response-stimulus timing constraints [TAY80, WAN86]:

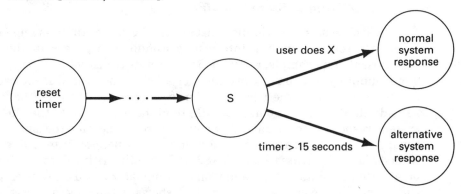

Figure 5–6. Another Response-Stimulus Timing Constraint in an FSM

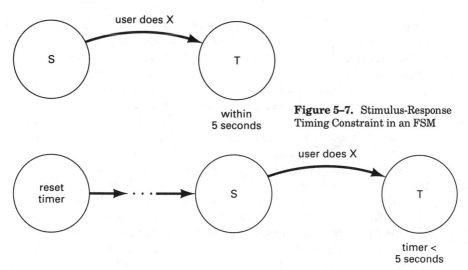

Figure 5–7. Stimulus-Response Timing Constraint in an FSM

Figure 5–8. Another Stimulus-Response Timing Constraint in an FSM

IF USER DOES *X* WITHIN 15 SECONDS

or to define stimulus-response timing constraints

CALLING PARTY RECEIVES DIAL TONE WITHIN 5 SECONDS

When other stimuli or responses intervene, it is necessary to use timers as before. Unfortunately the resulting specifications do not remain so readable:

RESET TIMER

.

.

.

IF USER DOES X WITHIN 15 SECONDS OF TIMER RESET

and

RESET TIMER

.

.

.

CALLING PARTY RECEIVES DIAL TONE WITHIN 5 SECONDS OF TIMER RESET

5.3.3.2.3. *Statecharts*

Harel [HAR87] offers an elegant and straightforward extension to statecharts to model stimulus-stimulus and response-stimulus timing constraints. One of the statechart extensions to finite state machines discussed in Section 4.2.2.4 was the condition or the event that can trigger a transition between states. A special type of event, called the *timeout,* is used to model timing constraints. In particular, *timeout (event, number of time units)* is an event that occurs when the given *number of time units* has transpired since the *event.* Figure 5–9 shows the same requirement as that shown in Figure 5–5. The event *entered S* occurs when we enter state *S.* With the ability to specify any event in the first parameter, it becomes obvious how to specify either stimulus-stimulus or response-stimulus timing constraints even with other intervening stimuli or responses. Statecharts also offer a shorthand notation. Examples in Figure 5–10 demonstrate how to specify minimal and maximal timeouts [HAR87].

The current version of statecharts does not include the ability to specify either stimulus-response or response-response timing constraints explicitly. However if both the environment and the system are modeled as statecharts, response-stimulus and stimulus-stimulus timing constraints on the environment are identical to stimulus-response and response-response timing constraints for the system.

More recently, Jahanian and Mok [JAH88] have extended Harel's work by providing a set of semantics for statecharts (they call them modecharts) in the Real Time Logic (RTL) language. RTL can be used to specify statecharts via the following constructs:

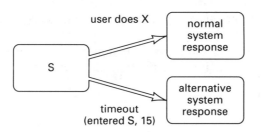

Figure 5–9. Response-Stimulus Timing Constraint in a Statechart.

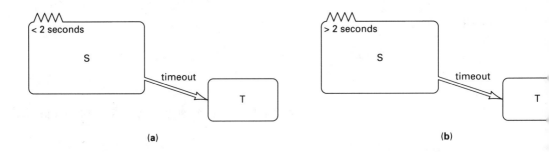

Figure 5–10. Timeout Shorthand in Statecharts. (a) Minimum Timeout. (b) Maximum Timeout.

$\uparrow A$	Event marking the initiation of action A
$\downarrow A$	Event marking the completion of action A
ΩB	External event B
$@(\uparrow A, i)$	Time of the ith occurrence of the start of action A
$+, -, *, /$	Usual arithmetic operators
$=, <, \le, >, \ge$	Usual algebraic operators
$\cup, \exists$	Usual universal and existential qualifiers
$\neg, \wedge, \vee$	Logical operators (not, and, or)
$\rightarrow$	Implies
$(S{:=}T)$	Statechart (or state) S has been entered (T means true)
$(S{:=}F)$	Statechart (or state) S has been exited (F means false)
$(S_i - S_j)$	Transition from statechart (or state) S_i to statechart (or state) S_j
$S[x,y]$	Entered statechart S at time x and exited statechart S at time y
$S[x,y)$	Entered statechart S at time x and exited at or after time y
$S[x,y>$	Entered statechart S at time x and exited after time y
$S(x,y)$	Entered statechart S before or at time x and exited at or after time y
$S(x,y]$	Entered statechart S before or at time x and exited at time y
$S(x,y>$	Entered statechart S before or at time x and exited after time y
$S<x,y>$	Entered statechart S before time x and exited after time y
$S<x,y]$	Entered statechart S before time x and exited at time y
$S<x,y)$	Entered statechart S before time x and exited at or after time y

Thus for example, the statechart shown in Figure 4–16 has the following representation:

1. $\forall t\ idle(t,t\,) \wedge \Omega\ caller\ off\ hook$
   $\rightarrow \exists j\ @((idle - dial\ tone), j\,) = t$
2. $\forall t\ dial\ tone(t,t\,) \wedge \Omega\ caller\ dials\ local\ number \wedge callee\ busy$
   $\rightarrow \exists j\ @(dial\ tone - busy\ tone), j\,) = t$
3. $\forall t\ dial\ tone(t,t\,) \wedge \Omega\ caller\ dials\ local\ number \wedge callee\ idle$
   $\rightarrow \exists j\ @(dial\ tone - ringback\ tone), j\,) = t$
4. $\forall t\ dial\ tone(t,t\,) \wedge \Omega\ caller\ dials\ 9$
   $\rightarrow \exists j\ @(dial\ tone - distinctive\ dial\ tone), j\,) = t$
5. $\forall t\ caller\ active(t,t\,) \wedge \Omega\ caller\ on\ hook$
   $\rightarrow \exists j\ @(caller\ active - idle), j\,) = t$

This means

1. At all times, if we are in the *idle* state and the *caller* goes *off hook*, we will enter the *dial tone* state.
2. At all times, if we are in the *dial tone* state and the *caller dials* a *local number* while the *callee* is *busy*, we will enter the *busy tone* state.
3. At all times, if we are in the *dial tone* state and the *caller dials* a *local number* while the *callee* is *idle*, we will enter the *ringback tone* state.
4. At all times, if we are in the *dial tone* state and the *caller dials 9*, we will enter the *distinctive dial tone* state.
5. At all times, if the *caller* is *active* and the *caller* goes *on hook*, we will enter the *idle* state.

If we wanted to specify that the dial tone must arrive within 20 seconds, we would write

$$\forall t\ idle[t,t) \wedge \Omega\ caller\ off\ hook$$

$$\rightarrow \exists\ t'\ \exists\ j\ @((idle - dial\ tone), j\ ) \wedge t' < t + 20$$

That is, at all times *t*, if we are in the *idle* state and the *caller* goes *off hook*, we will enter the *dial tone* state at some subsequent time *t'*, such that *t'* is less than 20 seconds after time *t*.

5.3.3.2.4 *Requirements Engineering Validation System*

Specifying stimulus-response and response-response timing constraints is relatively straightforward in RSL and R-nets. Validation points (drawn as circles) are inserted in the R-net and labeled; for example, there are three validation points, *V1*, *V2*, and *V3* in the R-net shown in Figure 5–11 [DYE77]. Minimum and maximum time limits may be defined for any validation path in an R-net. A validation path is a series of validation points. If a time limit is not a constant but is instead a function of data, REVS provides the ability to write a PASCAL program to compute the required timing constraint as a function of the data. As in the case of statecharts, no feature is available to provide response-stimulus or stimulus-stimulus timing constraints specifically (see the comment in the second paragraph of Section 5.3.3.2.3).

5.3.3.2.5 *PAISLey*

In PAISLey it is possible to associate a timing requirement with any successor or exchange function definition given in the entire specification [ZAV86]. These timing requirements can be stated as a minimum or maximum time limit (as in REVS), a random variable, or a distribution between two

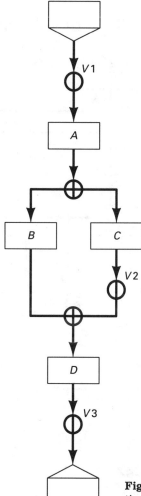

Figure 5–11. Illustration of Validation Paths in REVS.

limits. When the specification is "executed," the simulator prints the timing of each event. Also since timing constraints can be stated at multiple levels in the PAISLey specification, consistency checks can be run, feasibility validated, and new timing constraints derived in a relatively straightforward manner.

5.3.3.2.6 Petri Nets

Response-stimulus timing constraints can be stated in Petri nets but not quite so easily as in finite state machines. Figure 5–12 shows the Petri net equivalent of the Figure 5–5 FSM. A token arrives at place P_0 when a user has

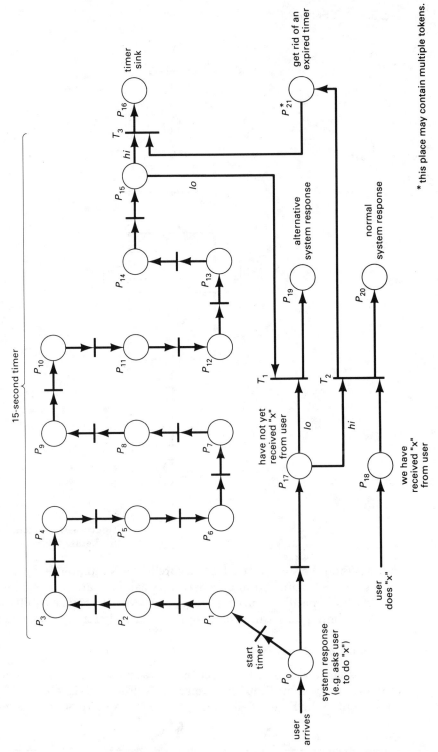

Figure 5-12. Response-Stimulus Timing Constraints in Petri Nets.

* this place may contain multiple tokens.

been asked to do x. Once asked, a timer token proceeds to P_1 through P_{15}, proceeding one place per second, arriving at P_{15} in exactly 15 seconds. Meanwhile a token sits at P_{17} waiting for either the 15 seconds to elapse (at which time the P_{17} token is consumed by firing transition T_1) or for the user to complete x (at which time the P_{17} token is consumed by firing transition T_2). If 15 seconds does elapse, P_{19} is fired, activating the alternative system response (for example, "Sorry. You didn't complete x fast enough."). On the other hand, if the user completes x before 15 seconds, P_{20} is fired, activating the normal system response (for example, "Thank you for doing x."). If the user completes x in precisely 15 seconds, we give the user the benefit of the doubt by giving him or her the normal system response; that is why lo and hi priorities are placed on the two arcs emanating from P_{17} to remove any doubt associated with nondeterminism. However whenever a user receives the normal system response, that user has spawned a timer token in the P_1 to P_{15} track. This renegade timer token may force a premature alternative system response to the next user who comes along. To remove these renegade timer tokens, place P_{21} has been added. Its mission at T_3 is to remove all renegade timer tokens that reach place P_{15}. Note that the arc connecting P_{15} and T_3 has been given a higher priority than the arc connecting P_{15} and T_1. This is to ensure that a timer token is always removed if there is a token at P_{21} and never has a chance to give a subsequent user at P_{17} an alternative system response through T_1 accidentally. Identical structures can be used to specify stimulus-stimulus timing constraints.

Stimulus-response and response-response timing constraints require an extension to standard Petri nets; extensions suggested by Coolahan and Roussopoulos [COO83] are used here. Above each place, the required execution time T_i is recorded. For example, in the Petri net shown in Figure 5–13 (adapted from [COO83]), places P_1, P_2, and P_3 have timing constraints placed on them of 1, 0.5, and 0.25 seconds, respectively, specifying the maximum allowable times for the system to perform the operations at those three places.

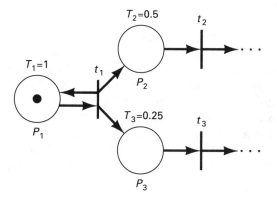

Figure 5–13. A Petri Net Showing Execution Times.

5.3.4 Memory Requirements

For most applications, memory restrictions are best stated as a maximum total amount of memory utilization rather than either a maximum amount of object code or a maximum amount of data storage because any good programmer can easily minimize either program space on data space at the expense of the other. The exception to this recommendation is in those applications where the host computer system architecture defines different types of read only (i.e., ROM) executable (for systems level software), ROM non-executable (for systems data), read/write (i.e., RAM) executable (for applications software), and RAM non-executable (for applications data).

5.4 HUMAN ENGINEERING

It is remarkable how many people think of themselves as experts in creating the ultimate system in terms of user friendliness. It is also remarkable how many systems are discarded by users due to poor user interfaces. Major sections of a number of recent books [BAI82, DUM88, SHN80] have helped by providing sensible guidance, but their impact has been negligible on most major systems being built today. Systems are still being built with input languages composed of literally thousands of different alphanumeric commands. Mantei and Teorey [MAN88] have attempted to analyze cost benefit trade-offs of human factors. This section of the book discusses types of user interfaces and recommends an appropriate level of detail for the requirements specification of such interfaces. Traditionally software designers want to "design" user interfaces. However requirements writers are much closer to users' needs and thus far more capable of defining the details of the user interface. Furthermore the user interface is a description of the interface between the software and one part of its environment (the user) and thus fits nicely into the domain of the requirements writer.

5.4.1 Interactive Styles

The oldest type of user interface is the *command language*. Using a command language, users type any desired command into the system. Most systems permit typing either the full command name (e.g., deletefile) or some abbreviated form (e.g., df). The greatest advantages of this type of input mechanism are that (1) users can do whatever they want whenever they wish without having to move through a long series of screens and (2) the software can be easily ported to different host computers because just about every system and every terminal permits typed command inputs. The greatest disadvantage is that the user may need to memorize a large vocabulary of commands.

Another means of user interface is the traditional *menu-based* system. In this approach, the user is presented with a series of menus from which a single selection is made (see Figure 5–14). Selections are generally made by pressing the one letter key followed by an ENTER or RETURN key. A simple and convenient extension to this basic approach uses *program function keys* (PFKs), which are special purpose, usually application programmable, keys added to the standard keyboard. Menus are displayed with PFK numbers (e.g., PF1, PF2) instead of letters. A single key press of the desired PFK selects an option, instead of the double key press (i.e., the selection key plus the ENTER or RETURN key). Menus of this type resemble Figure 5–15. Special program function keys have been added by some manufacturers (e.g., some of Hewlett Packard's HP 9XXX series computers) on the screen bezel itself. With these buttons moved so close to the screen, it becomes possible to display options on the screen immediately adjacent to the button, as shown in Figure 5–16, thus eliminating the need to display the required key's name. The greatest advantage of this approach over previously discussed approaches is its ability to reserve a majority of the screen for the actual application and use only the bottom portion of the screen for menu options. In turn this makes it possible to display engineering drawings or maps on the screen and use bezel buttons to select zoom and pan types of options simultaneously while watching the

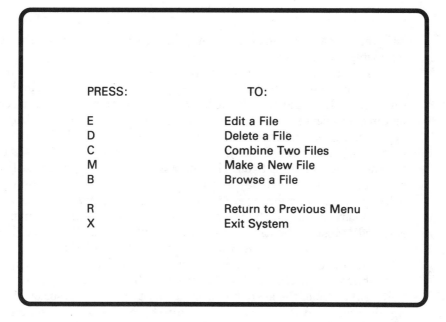

PRESS: TO:

E   Edit a File
D   Delete a File
C   Combine Two Files
M   Make a New File
B   Browse a File

R   Return to Previous Menu
X   Exit System

Figure 5–14. A Traditional Menu.

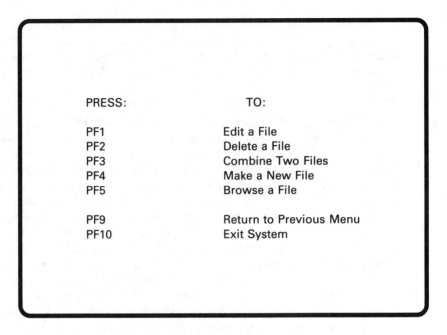

PRESS:	TO:
PF1	Edit a File
PF2	Delete a File
PF3	Combine Two Files
PF4	Make a New File
PF5	Browse a File
PF9	Return to Previous Menu
PF10	Exit System

Figure 5–15. A Traditional Menu with PF Keys.

drawing or map instead of the old-fashioned menu that erases the drawing or map while displaying a menu.

An alternative and less costly menu selection technique that frees a majority of the screen for the application is that selected by IBM for its Personal Computers. In this approach, menu options are displayed (usually horizontally on top of the screen) and a cursor can be moved back and forth from option to option using left and right pointing arrows on the keyboard. When the appropriate option has been highlighted by the cursor, the user presses ENTER to tell the computer what to do. This approach reduces the need for PF keys but requires an additional key press to move back and forth between menu selection and the main area of the screen (unlike bezel buttons, where the cursors can remain in the main area of the screen while the menu option is selected). Most applications using this approach also allow a single key press to select an option by typing the first letter of the option only.

The next major breakthrough in user interface came as a result of the availability of low-cost "picking" devices, such as mouses, joy sticks, and roller balls. All three of these enable users easily to move a cursor on the screen to any location and pick that spot, usually by pressing a button on the device itself. This ability made such old-fashioned menus as those shown in Figures 5–14 and 5–15 obsolete overnight. All you need to do to select any menu option is move the cursor to the desired option and press the button.

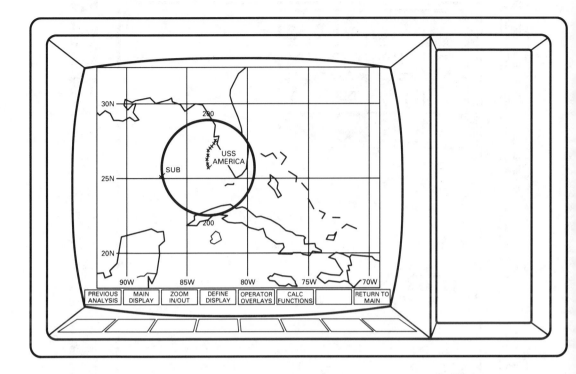

Figure 5–16. A Menu Using Bezel Buttons. © 1989 BTG, Inc. Reprinted with Permission.

Once picking via a mouselike device became popular, it was an extremely short jump to icon-driven options rather than menu-driven ones. An *icon* is a small picture that imparts a certain meaning to its observers. Although icon-driven design has been the rule for at least ten years on large CAD systems, it really did not become widely available until the PC market took off. MacPaint[2] is one of the earliest examples of such a product; it can be used expertly with little or no training or reading of a reference manual (see Figure 5–17, which shows a MacPaint 2.0 screen).

User interfaces took one additional major step forward in the mid-1980s—the window. A *window* is a region on the screen that provides a particular view of a particular process. In the traditional user interface, the full screen was in effect a window and provided the standard user view of the process to which the terminal was attached. In modern workstations, it is possible to specify multiple windows on the screen. The user can in effect treat each window as a separate traditional terminal screen. For example, in one

[2]MacPaint is a registered trademark of Apple, Inc.

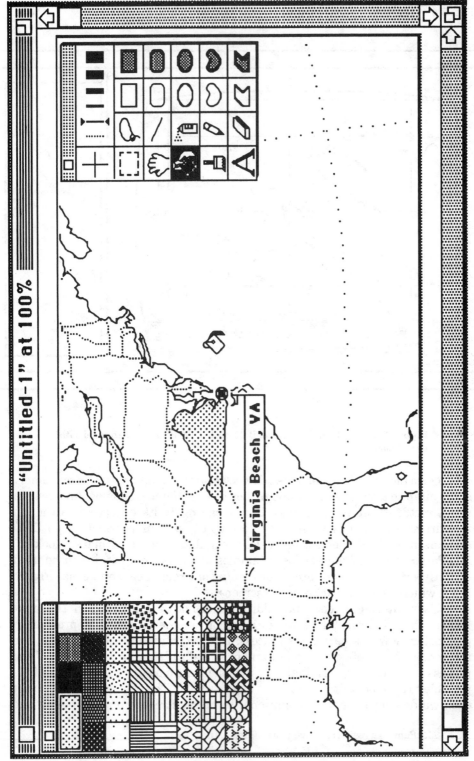

Figure 5-17. MacPaint Screen.

window the user can begin editing file X; in another window the user can start editing file Y. Both windows can be active simultaneously. By moving the cursor to one window, "picking" a piece of text using the editor, then moving the cursor with the text to the other window, it is possible to effect edits easily across two open files. The use of windows becomes even more interesting when the workstation uses a server-based window system [PRO88] and is attached to a local area network (LAN) with multiple workstations and servers. In such an environment, the user can create multiple windows, each logged on to a different computer, each executing independently and simultaneously.

The next major breakthrough in user interface technology was the advent of standard user interface tool kits [PRO88] for workstations. These tool kits contain (1) a collection of user interface primitives accessible by an application, (2) a user interface controller program that enables application developers to relate various user inputs to specific routines to be executed and automatically invokes those routines when applicable, and (3) a variety of menu/screen utilities to manipulate information on the screen. A number of these tool kits with server-based window systems, such as X11 and NeWS, are now available commercially.

The purposes of the preceding discussion is to familiarize you with the types of human interfaces available. When writing the human engineering section of an SRS, we must be extremely careful to specify the user interface to a level of detail that ensures customers receive the best quality easy-to-use interface they are willing to pay for. If the boundary of the system under specification includes the users, then clearly user interface does not belong in the SRS; but if the system boundary excludes the user, then that entire interface should be part of the SRS, and the level of detail is purely a matter of taste. Let us assume that the goal is to have a traditional menu-driven system. There are four levels of detail that can be stated in the SRS

1. The system shall have an easy-to-use human interface.
2. The system shall be menu driven.
3. The system shall be menu driven; Appendix A shows sample menus.
4. The system shall be menu driven; Appendix A shows all menus to be used.

The first level is clearly ambiguous and inadequate; the second level leaves much interpretation to the designer, who could consider the message "Please select A, B, C, or D" as a menu. The third and fourth levels are just right; they leave no doubt in designers' minds about what to build and no doubt in customers' minds what they will receive.

The preceding specification suggestions apply to either a single full-screen display or any one window in a multiple-window environment. Specifying a particular window system (e.g., X11 or NeWS) or a particular user interface tool kit (e.g., View2 from Sun Microsystems or Xt+ from AT&T) in the SRS is helpful (1) in providing a flavor for the user interface and (2) in defining part of the software system's environment with which the software system must interface. But specifying the window system or tool kit is not sufficient to specify an entire user interface in an SRS and lies somewhere between levels 2 and 3 as far as the level of specificity goes.

5.4.2 Error Messages

In general SRS writers tend not to specify error messages by the system to the user. There is a common feeling that the types of error messages are not predictable prior to the detailed design or coding stages. I contend that unless there is a sound understanding of the types of error messages the system can generate, there is insufficient knowledge of the system's expected normal behavior to be able to consider the requirements stage complete. Thus it is appropriate to itemize types of errors that can be detected by the software. In fact in Section 3.4.3 the definition of completeness includes specification of expected system outputs from all acceptable as well as unacceptable inputs. It is also a good idea to define in an appendix to the SRS the exact text of all error messages. This greatly enhances a customer's or user's view of the system's user friendliness. It is common among many software developers not to define error messages until as late as the end of the testing stage. During coding they insert such error messages as "error 42" and do not replace them with real messages until just prior to deployment, if at all. I know not what motivates this behavior. Is it that "Designing a good user interface is too trivial for me to concern myself with"? Or is it that "I'll save time by deferring it to later"?[3] Or is it that "My users are so smart that they'll understand 'error 42' "? Or is it that "Why do today what I can do tomorrow?"[3] Or is it that "Why should I document them now; they'll just change anyway."[3] Whatever the reason, never buy a software product or support software product development without seeing error messages spelled out in the SRS.

5.4.3 Summary

The same advice given for screen interfaces and error messages applies to all other system outputs (e.g., report formats). If the SRS does not clearly define what the output looks like, then (1) the SRS writer has not given enough thought to the product, (2) the product is not ready for the design stage, and (3) if development is allowed to proceed, customers deserve what they get: an unfriendly product. With tools such as RAPID/USE[WAS86] which enable specifiers to easily experiment with various interactive styles and to create operating prototypes rapidly, there is little excuse to produce products with poor user interfaces. If there is strong political pressure on a project to not

---

[3]These arguments can be used just as easily for all requirements!

specify the user interface, at least define the attributes and backgrounds of expected users.

5.5 TESTABILITY, UNDERSTANDABILITY, AND MODIFIABILITY

Testability, understandability, and modifiability are closely related. It is very difficult in an SRS to quantify their required levels in a final product. This is unfortunate because these are among the most important contributors to full life cycle cost of software. Specifying required levels of cohesion and coupling [YOU79] in the design is probably the best the industry has to offer at this point. Cohesion should be expressed as minimally acceptable for any one module and a minimally acceptable average for all modules in the design. Coupling should be expressed as maximally acceptable for any pair of modules and a maximally acceptable average for all pairs of modules in the design.

Certain languages are also inherently more understandable and thus more maintainable and modifiable. There is certainly a great deal of controversy concerning which languages fit into which categories, but most people agree that in general the higher the language, the easier it is to understand, modify, and maintain. "Higher" means that the building blocks, primitive operations, control structures, and data types are closer to the application and further from the underlying machine. In addition some languages enable us easily to construct abstractions from available primitive elements and thus raise the effective level of the language.

Finally one additional suggestion is to specify in the SRS conformity to a previously written and approved set of programming standards. These standards should include, at a minimum:

> Naming conventions
>> components
>> data
> Invocation conventions
>> calling
>> interrupts
>> synchronization
>> message formats
> Component header
>> format
>> content
> In-line documentation style
> Use of control constructs
> Use of global/common variables

Use of named constants

Modularity standards.

EXERCISES

1. In Section 5.2.1 two categories of applications were defined regarding how to interpret 99.999% reliability: (1) the telephone category, which meant that occasional sporadic failures on individual tasks were okay but it had to be globally operational 99.999% of the time and (2) the patient-monitoring category, which meant performing correctly on 99.999% of individual tasks but going down globally more often. In which of these two categories do the following high-reliability systems fall:

   a. Automated teller machine
   b. Air traffic control system
   c. Spacecraft life support system
   d. Automated automobile assembly line

2. In Section 5.2.4 eight levels of applications were defined to help us gain perspective on the reliability issue. Define a similar set of levels that can be used to provide similar perspectives on the relative importance of

   a. Portability
   b. Efficiency
   c. Human engineering
   d. Testability
   e. Understandability
   f. Modifiability

REFERENCES

[BAI82] Bailey, R. *Human Performance Engineering.* Englewood Cliffs, N.J.: Prentice-Hall, 1982.

[BOE76] Boehm, B., et al. "Quantitative Evaluation of Software Quality." In *Second IEEE International Conference on Software Engineering,* Washington D.C.: Computer Society Press of the Institute of Electrical and Electronics Engineers, 1976. pp. 592–605.

[COO83] Coolahan, J. E., and N. Roussopoulos. "Timing Requirements for Time-Driven Systems Using Augmented Petri Nets." *IEEE Transactions on Software Engineering* **9,** 5 (September 1983): 603–16.

[DAS85] Dasarathy, B. "Timing Constraints of Real-Time Systems: Constructs for Expressing Them, Methods of Validating Them." *IEEE Transactions on Software Engineering* **11,** 1 (January 1985): 80–86.

[DUM88] Dumas, J. *Designing User Interfaces for Software.* Englewood Cliffs, N.J.: Prentice-Hall, 1988.

[DYE77] Dyer, M. E., et al. *REVS Users Manual,* SREP Final Report. Vol. 2. TRW Report 27332-6921-026. Huntsville, Ala., August 1977.

[GIL77] Gilb, T. *Software Metrics.* Cambridge, Mass: Winthrop Publ., 1977.

[HAR87] Harel, D. "Statecharts: A Visual Formalism for Complex Systems." *Science of Computer Programming* **8** (1987): 231–74.

[JAH88] Jahanian, F., and A. Mok. "Modechart: A Specification Language for Real-Time Systems." *IEEE Transactions on Software Engineering.* Considered for publication, 1988.

[JEL72] Jelinski, Z., and P. Moranda. "Software Reliability Research." In *Statistical Computer Performance Evaluation,* W. Freiberger, ed., New York: Academic Press, 1972. pp. 465–84.

[LIT73] Littlewood, B., and J. Verrall. "A Bayesian Reliability Growth Model for Computer Software." In *IEEE Symposium on Computer Software Reliability,* Washington, D.C.: Computer Society Press of the Institute of Electrical and Electronics Engineers, 1973. pp. 70–77.

[MAN88] Mantei, M., and T. Teorey. "Cost/Benefit for Incorporating Human Factors in the Software Life Cycle." *Communications of the ACM* **31,** 4 (April 1988): 428–39.

[MIL72] Mills, H. *On the Statistical Validation of Computer Programs.* IBM Federal Systems Division Report FSC-72-6015. Gaithersburg, Md., 1972.

[MUS75] Musa, J. "A Theory of Software Reliability and Its Application." *IEEE Transactions on Software Engineering* **1,** 9 (September 1975): 312–27.

[MUS87] Musa, J., et al. *Software Reliability.* New York: McGraw-Hill, 1987.

[PRO88] Probst, R. "Open-Look Toolkits." *Sun Technology* **1,** 4 (Autumn 1988): 76–86.

[SAU69] Sauter, J. "Reliability in Computer Programs." *Mechanical Engineering* **91** (February 1969): 24–27.

[SCH86] Scheifler, R., and J. Gettys. "The *X* Window System." *ACM Transactions on Graphics* **5,** 2 (April 1986).

[SCH78] Schick, G., and R. Wolverton. "An Analysis of Competing Software Reliability Models." *IEEE Transactions on Software Engineering* **4,** 2 (March 1978): 109–20.

[SHN80] Shneiderman, B. *Software Psychology.* Cambridge, Mass.: Winthrop, 1980.

[SHO72] Shooman, M. "Probabilistic Models for Software Reliability Prediction." In *Statistical Computer Performance Evaluation,* ed. W. Freidberger, New York: Academic Press, 1972. pp. 485–502.

[SKE86] Skelton, S. "Measurements of Migratability and Transportability." *ACM Software Engineering Notes* **11,** 1 (January 1986): 29–34.

[SUN86] Sun Microsystems. *NeWS Technical Overview.* Sunnyvale, Calif., October 1986.

[TAY80] Taylor, B. "Introducing Real-Time Constraints in Requirements and High-level Design of Operating Systems." In *National Telecommunications Con-*

ference, Washington D.C.: Computer Society Press of the Institute of Electrical and Electronics Engineers, 1980. pp. 18.5.1–18.5.5.

[WAN86] Wang, Y. "A Distributed Specification Model and Its Prototyping." In *IEEE COMPSAC 86,* Washington D.C.: Computer Society Press of the Institute of Electrical and Electronics Engineers, 1986. pp. 130–37.

[WAS85] Wasserman, A. I. "Extending State Transition Diagrams for the Specification of Human–Computer Interaction." *IEEE Transactions on Software Engineering* **11,** 8 (August 1985): 699–713.

[WAS86] Wasserman, A. I., et al. "Developing Interactive Information Systems with the User Software Engineering Methodology." *IEEE Transactions on Software Engineering* **12,** 2 (February 1986): 326–45.

[YOU79] Yourdon, E., and L. Constantine. *Structured Design.* Englewood Cliffs, N.J.: Prentice-Hall, 1979.

[ZAV78] Zave, P. "Formal Specification of Complete and Consistent Performance Requirements." *Eighth Texas Conference on Computing Systems,* Dallas, November 1978. pp. 4B-18–4B-25.

[ZAV81] Zave, P., and R. Yeh. "Executable Requirements for Embedded Systems." In *Fifth International IEEE Conference on Software Engineering,* Washington D.C.: Computer Society Press of the Institute of Electrical and Electronics Engineers, 1981. pp. 295–304.

[ZAV82] Zave, P., "An Operational Approach to Requirements Specification for Embedded Systems." *IEEE Transactions on Software Engineering* **8,** 5 (May 1982): 250-69.

[ZAV86] Zave, P., and W. Schell. "Salient Features of an Executable Specification Language and Its Environment." *IEEE Transactions on Software Engineering* **12,** 2 (February 1986): 312–25.

6

Requirements Prototyping

Prototyping is the technique of constructing a partial implementation of a system so that customers, users, or developers can learn more about a problem or a solution to that problem. It is a partial implementation because if it were a full implementation, it would be *the* system, not a prototype of it. The purpose of the partial implementation is a fundamental part of the definition and differentiates a prototype from a subset. A subset is also a partial implementation; however, the purpose of a *subset* is to provide early functionality, whereas the purpose of the prototype is to learn something. Thus a prototype could be a subset, and vice versa, but they are not the same.

There are two schools of prototyping—throwaway and evolutionary. In the *throwaway* approach, the prototype software is constructed in order to learn more about the problem or its solution and is usually discarded after the desired knowledge is gained. In the *evolutionary* approach, the prototype is constructed in order to learn more about the problem or its solution; once the prototype has been used and the requisite knowledge gained, the prototype is then adapted to satisfy the now better understood needs. The prototype is then used again, more is learned, and the prototype is re-adapted. This process repeats indefinitely until the prototype system satisfies all needs and has thus evolved into the real system. Followers of the throwaway prototyping school (e.g., [BOE84, DAV82, GOM81, GOM83]) generally call what they do simply "prototyping." Followers of the evolutionary prototyping school (e.g., [BAL82, BAS75, MCC82, MAS83, ZEL80]) generally call what they do simply "prototyping."

343

The two approaches use the same name but are entirely different approaches to software development. It was not until the mid-1980s that literature appeared which recognized these differences [BER87, DAV88, FLO84, GOM86, HEK87]. Chapter 6 explores the impact of prototyping on requirements, life cycle, and productivity.

6.1 IMPACT OF PROTOTYPING ON REQUIREMENTS AND THE SOFTWARE LIFE CYCLE

For complex systems (i.e., HA and/or DY applications in Section 1.4), (1) requirements are often poorly understood, (2) requirements usually change during the development process, and (3) current requirements remain only partially understood until after users have had an actual opportunity to use a system. At first glance this last item appears to condemn the traditional view of the software development life cycle. How can we follow the traditional life cycle and have a working product prior to writing an SRS? However, with a little more analysis of the situation, it becomes apparent that both throwaway and evolutionary prototyping are completely compatible with the traditional life cycle. For a counterargument, see Firestone [FIR87].

A throwaway prototype can be built during any synthesis phase in the software life cycle, as shown in Figure 6–1. During the requirements phase, a quick-and-dirty throwaway prototype can be constructed and given to a potential user or customer in order to (1) determine the feasibility of a requirement, (2) validate that a particular function is really necessary, (3) uncover missing requirements, or (4) determine the viability of a user interface. Armed with the experience of having used the prototype, the team completes the SRS with increased assurance that the right system is being specified. If all requirements can be uncovered, well understood and agreed on without the prototype, do not build one. Similarly, during the preliminary design phase, a quick-and-dirty prototype can be constructed to validate that a particular architecture actually exhibits the required set of properties, i.e., it has the potential to meet the requirements. Once again if there is general agreement about design alternatives, do not create a prototype. Finally, during detailed design, a quick-and-dirty prototype can be built to validate that a particular algorithm will have sufficient oomph to meet its requirements (this is most effective after attempts to perform algorithm analysis have failed). In all three cases, there are two important goals that should not be forgotten: The prototype should be *quick* and *dirty*. Its development should be quick because its advantage exists only if results from its use are available in a timely fashion. It should be dirty because there is no justification for building quality into a product that will be discarded. Among the dirty characteristics to be considered are no design, no comments, no test plans, implementation in some relatively unmaintainable

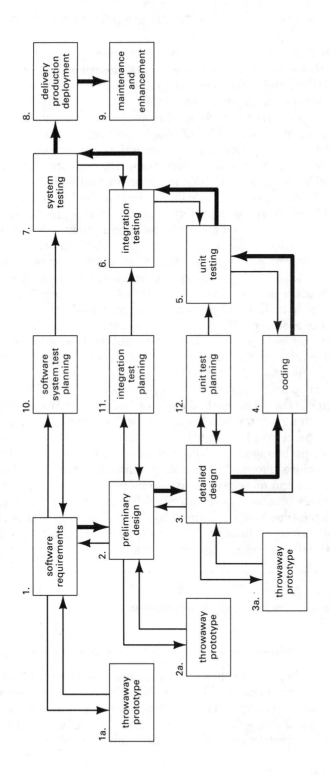

Figure 6-1. The Software Engineering Life Cycle and Throwaway Prototypes.

language that facilitates fast synthesis of programs (e.g., SNOBOL, LISP, APL). Of the three throwaway prototypes just described (i.e., requirements, preliminary design, and detailed design), only the first is relevant to this book; the other two will not be mentioned again.

The most common scenario for a throwaway requirements prototype calls for (1) writing a preliminary SRS, (2) implementing the prototype based on those requirements, (3) achieving user experience with the prototype, (4) writing the real SRS and then, (5) developing the real product. In Gomaa's experiment at General Electric [GOM83], users had difficulty visualizing how a highly interactive integrated circuit fabrication control system would be used. General Electric created a prototype in APL in three months using three people. They expended around 6% of the total real product development cost to develop the prototype. To help reduce costs, they ignored all exception conditions, all recovery software, hardware interfaces, and performance (including response time). After prototype development, Gomaa's group trained actual product users on the use of the prototype during scheduled two-hour courses and demonstrations. Users were given four weeks to experiment with and evaluate the prototype. User evaluations revealed many misunderstandings between users and specifiers, and many ambiguities and inconsistencies in the SRS; showed that a number of necessary functions had been inadvertently omitted from the SRS; surfaced confusing interactions in the user interface; and gave users a much better understanding of their own problem. This implies that if the prototype had not been built, but the production system based on the SRS as written had been, the resulting product would probably not have been perceived by users to be a good product. Incidentally after working out all problems in the SRS, the real product was created in FORTRAN using a more rigorous methodology, and after product release, users were satisfied and had no requirements problems.

Evolutionary prototypes are entirely different entities. In particular, an evolutionary prototype may not be built in a "dirty" fashion. The evolutionary prototype evolves into the final product, and thus it must exhibit all the quality attributes of the final product. Remember that

---

It is impossible to retrofit quality, maintainability, and reliability!

Because we do not know how to retrofit these attributes into a product, they must be built in. Because they must be built in, prototype development will *not* be particularly rapid. The rigorous software development life cycle shown in Figure 1–9 exists for the very purpose of ensuring that the software product exhibits acceptable levels of quality, maintainability, and reliability.

Thus there are few shortcuts to generating an evolutionary prototype. The only sensible way of building an evolutionary prototype then is to follow the traditional life cycle—deploy the product, obtain experience using it, then based on that experience, go back and redo the requirements, redesign, recode, retest, and redeploy. After gaining more experience, it is time to repeat the entire process again, as shown in Figure 6–2. This ensures the creation of all necessary documents and the presence of all necessary reviews. In fact the only shortcuts that should be taken in building evolutionary prototypes are (1) building only those parts of the product that are understood (leaving other parts to later generations of the prototype) and perhaps (2) lowering the importance of performance (to paraphrase Dijkstra [DIJ70]: "It is easier to make a working program faster then to make a fast program work"). Most researchers who advocate quick-and-dirty prototypes that later evolve into working production systems are just that, researchers; they do not appreciate the incredible effort required during the design stage to generate a design that can withstand the punishments of the real world and stay operational and maintainable.

A common scenario these days results when a throwaway prototype is delivered to a customer and the customer responds with, "Oh, I love it! Can you just add a few more lines of code and make it a production quality product?" This is equivalent to a person seeing a cowboy town street facade from a movie set and saying "Oh, what a lovely town. Can you just add a few boards and pipes behind the facades and make it a real town?" Or, the pilot who walks into a hanger (see Figure 6–3), sees a huge piece of equipment, and finds it is an aircraft flight simulator. After flying around for awhile in simulated flight, the pilot emerges to exclaim, "Oh, I love that aircraft! Can we throw some wings on it and let me fly it for real?" In these cases the product being examined is a great simulator of activity; it is not a good performer. In other words, the movie

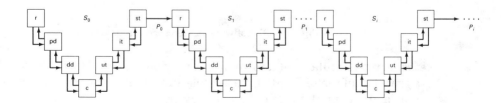

Figure 6–2. The Software Life Cycle and Evolutionary Prototypes.

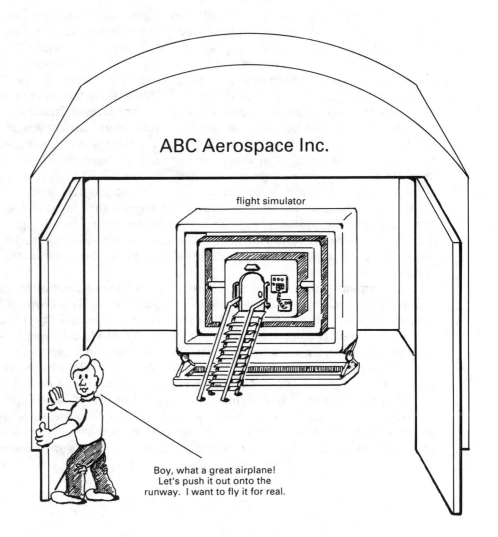

Figure 6–3. Software vs. Aerospace Prototypes.

set is a great simulator of a town; it is a very poor town. The flight simulator
is a great simulator of flight; it is a terrible aircraft. And the software prototype
is only a great simulator of product behavior.

To see why this is so, let us look at a hypothetical prototype of a
hypothetical airline reservation system. The potential customer sees a screen
that provides a variety of options, as shown in Figure 6–4. The customer is
impressed. The customer presses "P" and instantly sees the screen in Figure
6–5 requesting a flight number. The customer responds by typing "134," and

PARS

The Prototype Airline Reservation System

Press	To
A	Add a passenger to a manifest
D	Delete a passenger from a manifest
S	Get a seating plan
R	Reserve a seat
P	Get a list of passengers
X	Exit

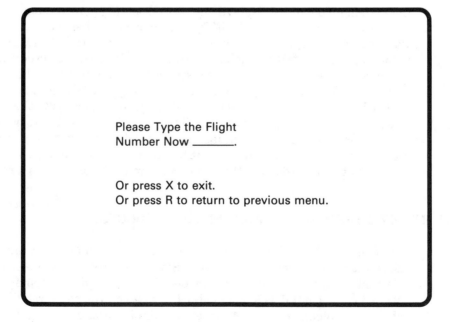

Figure 6–4. Menu 1—Sample Prototype System.

Please Type the Flight
Number Now ______.

Or press X to exit.
Or press R to return to previous menu.

Figure 6–5. Menu 2—Sample Prototype System.

```
┌─────────────────────────────────────────────────────────────┐
│                                                               │
│               Flight 134 Seating Plan                         │
│                                                               │
│      ─────────────────────────────────────────────           │
│                                                               │
│     Row    Seat:      A         B         C        D          │
│                                                               │
│      1            Yourdon    Harel     Boehm     Balzer       │
│      2            Yeh        Gries     DeMarco   Avail        │
│      3            Alford     Aho       Avail     Basili       │
│      4            Zeldin     Hamilton  Avail     Ross         │
│      5            Dijkstra   Hoare     Mills     Parnas       │
│                                                               │
│                                                               │
│     Press M to see more rows                                  │
│     Or press X to exit                                        │
│     Or press R to return to previous menu                     │
│                                                               │
└─────────────────────────────────────────────────────────────┘
```

Figure 6–6. Menu 3—Sample Prototype System.

the system responds by displaying an actual seating plan, as shown in Figure 6–6. Now the customer is hooked! The customer cannot believe that this system was written in just one week! The customer could now press "R" twice to return to Menu 1 to select "D" to delete, say, passenger Dijkstra. If the customer now asked to see the seating plan, Dijkstra would still be there. In fact if the customer asked for the seating plan for *any* flight, the same plan would be shown, because there is no data base and no real functionality in the prototype. The prototype is simply a set of canned screens with the ability to bounce from one to another in an intelligent fashion. There do *not* exist "just a few lines of code" that could be added to make it function any more than there are a few boards that can be added to the movie set to make it function as a real town.

6.2 IMPACT ON PRODUCTIVITY AND PRODUCT SUCCESS

Boehm et al. [BOE84] conducted an experiment to compare prototyping and the traditional development life cycle. Seven teams of students were asked to select either of the two life cycle models; three selected prototyping, and four selected traditional development. Each was given the same relatively small software development task. A large number of statistics were gathered comparing results of the seven teams' efforts. However, as you examine the data be careful not to jump to premature conclusions. The traditional teams were required to produce an SRS, a design specification, a software product, a user's manual, and a maintenance manual. Prototyping teams were required to produce a software product (i.e., the prototype), a user's manual, and a maintenance manual. Notice that the prototyping approach did not call for an SRS or design documentation. Without these, the resulting prototype must surely be considered a throwaway prototype, not a maintainable product. Thus comparisons made here appear to be between a production quality (or as production quality as can be expected from a student environment) product developed by the traditional technique and a throwaway prototype. The data would have been more meaningful if they compared the production quality product developed traditionally and the production quality product developed after experimentation with a throwaway prototype. But nonetheless the experimental results are interesting.

The first result of the experiment was that the prototypes were consistently smaller (i.e., 40% on the average) in size than the traditional products. This should be no surprise considering the aforementioned flaw in the experiment. The second result was that no significant difference was seen in team productivity (as measured by delivered source lines of code/person hours) between the two approaches. This should not be surprising considering the fact that a great majority of Intermediate COCOMO's [BOE80] significant contributors to productivity were invariant between and among these teams. However, it would have been interesting to compare productivities of the two sets of teams had the prototyping teams been required to produce the same levels of documentation as the traditional teams. Obviously if you do less, your productivity appears to increase—the difference becomes evident during maintenance when the absence of key documentation causes productivity to decline.

The third result of the experiment was that the traditionally developed products were more functional and more robust than the throwaway prototypes. The authors rated the prototypes however considerably easier to use and learn to use. One possible explanation is that in this experiment, teams were able to select their approach. Teams who selected prototyping for this highly interactive application may have had a greater affinity for good user interfaces than those who selected the traditional approach. The final result of the experiment was somewhat contradictory: the prototyping approach tended to result in less coherent designs, poor integration characteristics, but better maintainability.

An alternative way of examining the effects of prototyping is from the point of view of user needs satisfaction [DAV88]. For nontrivial applications, user needs and expectations of an automated system are constantly growing, as shown in Figure 6–7 [DAV88]. In traditional development, needs are

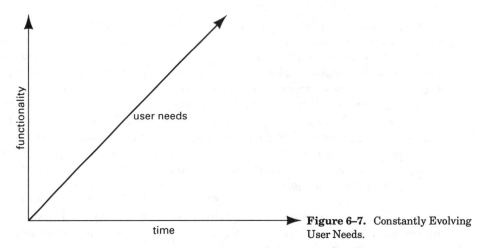

Figure 6–7. Constantly Evolving User Needs.

perceived at some point in time t_0, and software development efforts commence. Finally at some future point in time t_1 (see Figure 6–8 adapted from [DAV88]), a system emerges that probably falls short of satisfying even the original t_0 requirements because these were so poorly understood and/or explored at that time. Now the software begins to undergo enhancements in order to try to catch up to the user's continuously evolving needs. Eventually at time t_2, the product reaches the point where it has been so extensively modified that additional changes would render the system unreliable. At this point the software becomes static, and a new development effort is initiated, resulting finally in a product at time t_3, and the cycle repeats. The shaded area in Figure 6–8 is

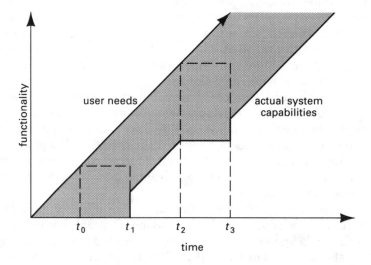

Figure 6–8. Software Products Fall Short of Meeting All Current User Needs.

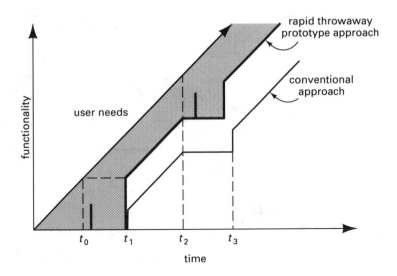

Figure 6–9. Throwaway Prototyping Approach

some measure of the shortfall of the product (or how the product is being created) to satisfy user needs.

Throwaway prototypes solve this problem in part by helping ensure that requirements are well understood before development proceeds. Thus as shown in Figure 6–9 (adapted from [DAV88]), when the product is finally created at time t_1, it is more likely to satisfy a larger percentage of the t_0 user needs due to the creation and use of a prototype early in the development life cycle (shown as a bold vertical band just to the right of t_0 in Figure 6–9). There is no particular reason why the length of development (i.e., $t_1–t_0$) should be either shorter or longer than the conventional approach. However, note that the size of the shaded area in Figure 6–9 is significantly smaller than the corresponding area in Figure 6–8, indicating that in general throwaway prototypes increase the average satisfaction of user needs.

Using evolutionary prototyping has a considerably different effect on needs satisfaction. In particular as shown in Figure 6–10 (adapted from [DAV88]), an evolutionary prototype can generally be created more quickly than a full-scale development because the first version generally implements only a well-understood subset of functions. But in addition the slope of line A-B in Figure 6–10 is greater than the corresponding line in the conventional approach because evolvability usually becomes a major design objective during evolutionary prototype development. Note that once again, the shaded area is considerably smaller than with the conventional approach.

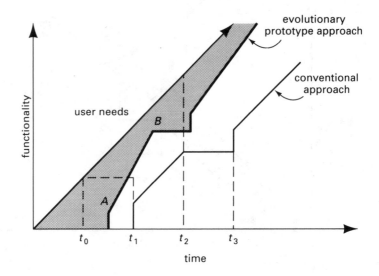

Figure 6–10. Evolutionary Prototyping Approach.

6.3 SUMMARY

The two prototyping schemes discussed here are quite different in both approach and effect. For this reason it is absolutely critical to define initially which approach is being taken. The differences are remarkable:

	Throwaway	*Evolutionary*
Development approach	Quick and dirty No rigor	No sloppiness Rigorous
What to build	Build only difficult parts	Build understood parts first Build on solid foundation
Design drivers	Optimize development time	Optimize modifiability
Ultimate goal	Throw it away	Evolve it

Both approaches result in better satisfaction of user needs; both also reduce total costs but in quite different ways. Throwaway prototypes save dollars by helping ensure that the real system will actually meet real requirements. Evolutionary prototypes save dollars by (1) having to retreat to only the latest increment when a mistake is made and (2) increasing the likelihood that version i+1 will meet users' real needs because users have already used version i and supplied feedback on its performance.

REFERENCES

[BAL82]   Balzer, R., et al. "Operational Specifications as a Basis for Rapid Prototyping." *ACM Software Engineering Notes.* **7,** 5 (December 1982): 3–16.

[BAS75]   Basili, V., and A. Turner. "Iterative Enhancement: A Practical Technique for Software Development." *IEEE Transactions on Software Engineering* **1,** 4 (December 1975): 390–96.

[BER87]   Bersoff, E., et al. "Alternative Life Cycle Models." *SIGNAL* **41,** 8 (April 1987): 85–93.

[BOE80]   Boehm, B. *Software Engineering Economics.* Englewood Cliffs, N.J.: Prentice-Hall, 1980.

[BOE84]   Boehm, B., et al. "Prototyping versus Specifying: A Multiproject Experiment." *IEEE Transactions on Software Engineering* **10,** 3 (May 1984): 290–303.

[DAV82]   Davis, A. M. "Rapid Prototyping Using Executable Requirements Specifications." *ACM Software Engineering Notes* **7,** 5 (December 1982): 39–44.

[DAV88]   Davis, A., et al. "A Strategy for Comparing Alternative Software Development Life Cycle Models." *IEEE Transactions on Software Engineering* **14,** 10 (October 1988): 1453–61.

[DIJ79]   Dijkstra, E. In statement made at *Fourth International Conference on Software Engineering,* Munich, West Germany, 1979.

[FIR87]   Firestone, D. "Ada Community Concerns regarding DOD-STD-2167." *Conference on Methodologies and Tools for Real-Time Systems,* Washington, D.C.: National Institute for Software Quality and Productivity, 1987. pp. AA-1–AA-17.

[FLO84]   Floyd, C. "A Systematic Look at Programming." In *Approaches to Prototyping.* Edited by R. Budde et al. Berlin: Springer Verlag, 1984. pp. 1–18.

[GOM81]   Gomaa, H., and P. Scott. "Prototyping as a Tool in the Specification of User Requirements." In *Fifth International Conference on Software Engineering,* Washington D.C.: Computer Society Press of the Institute of Electrical and Electronics Engineers, 1981. pp. 333–42.

[GOM83]   Gomaa, H. "The Impact of Rapid Prototyping on Specifying User Requirements." *ACM Software Engineering Notes* **8,** 2 (April 1983): 17–28.

[GOM86]   Gomaa, H. "Prototypes—Keep Them or Throw Them Away?" *Infotech State of the Art Report on Prototyping,* edited by M. Lipp, Oxford, England: Pergamon Infotech Ltd., 1986.

[HEK87]   Hekmatpour, S. "Experience with Evolutionary Prototyping in a Large Software Project." *ACM Software Engineering Notes* **12,** 1 (January 1987): 38–41.

[MCC82]   McCracken, D., and M. Jackson. "Life Cycle Concept Considered Harmful." *ACM Software Engineering Notes* **7,** 2 (April 1982): 29–32.

[MAS83] Mason, R., and T. Carey. "Prototyping Interactive Information Systems." *Communications of the ACM* **26,** 5 (May 1983): 347–54.

[ZEL80]   Zelkowitz, M. "A Case Study in Rapid Prototyping." *Software—Practice and Experience* **10,** 12 (December 1980): 1037–42.

7

Some Final Thoughts

Chapter 7 presents a few final thoughts about the requirements domain. In particular it describes some additional techniques that either help peripherally in writing requirements or whose advocates claim are useful during the requirements phase. Chapter 7 also makes some projections about the future of the software industry as a whole and the future role of requirements in software development.

7.1 OTHER TYPES OF "REQUIREMENTS" TECHNIQUES

7.1.1 Word Processors and Data Base Systems

In today's electronic world, conventional typewriters are less and less common-place in the office. Virtually all documents generated by a software development project today are produced at least by a word processor. Once an SRS is in a word processing environment, it is relatively easy to search for key words, search for redundancies, and automatically generate correct tables of contents and indices. Furthermore if the word processor is integrated with a data base system, it becomes possible to store the requirements traceability matrix (see Section 3.4.8), internal SRS cross-references, and annotations about volatility and necessity. These can be stored in separate records along side the actual SRS text. By doing so it is relatively easy to generate both clean SRSs and SRSs containing additional information embedded within it and to ensure that the SRS and RTM are always updated in unison.

7.1.2 USE.IT

This section discusses USE.IT [HAM83], a set of tools developed by Higher Order Software (HOS), Inc., of Cambridge, Massachusetts. Personal experience with USE.IT, based on live demonstrations and reading half a dozen or so papers, has led me to conclude that there is little or no overlap between early phases of software development as defined in this book (i.e., problem analysis and software requirements specification) and USE.IT. However, developers of the techniques and tools occasionally refer to their own work as automation of the translation from requirements to implementation. Therefore I recognize that there probably exist numerous readers of this book who expect to hear about USE.IT.

USE.IT is a set of tools that automate a functional life cycle model as defined by HOS [HAM76], the methodology defined by HOS, Inc. In the HOS methodology, the overall system is defined as a single mathematical function that maps system inputs into outputs. Then, following a set of six formally defined laws, the function is repeatedly decomposed into simpler functions, which are in turn decomposed into yet simpler functions. Finally, the functions at the most primitive level are translated (automatically) into operational code. The relationship between any two successive levels in the hierarchy is one of control (i.e., calling or invocation hierarchy). Thus the result of this process is a *detailed design* of the software solution. In fact, the developers state [HAM76] that HOS provides "a specification language [for] adhering to…the formal set of laws to the *design* of a given problem" and that "the *design* for a particular software system is based on [the application of] six axioms that describe control."[1]

The life cycle with USE.IT consists of four discrete steps all controlled by a management function, as shown in Figure 7–1 (adapted from [HAM83]). The first step is to define "requirements" using the AXES Specification Language to define the functional decomposition process just described. This so-called requirements definition involves defining the software executive, software subsystems, and all the calling (or invocation) hierarchies between all those software components. The second step is to analyze the "requirements." The Analyzer Tool checks the "requirements" for logical completeness and consistency. The third step is to use the Resource Allocation Tool (RAT) to search a library of existing software components to see if any functions defined in AXES have been previously coded. If any are found (i.e., have previously been coded, debugged, and stored in the library), these are retrieved and pieced together to create operational code for the target system. The final step of USE.IT is to compile and execute the generated code.

HOS provides an excellent set of guiding principles for software *design*. The USE.IT approach demonstrates one of the most impressive and successful

---

[1] Italics mine.

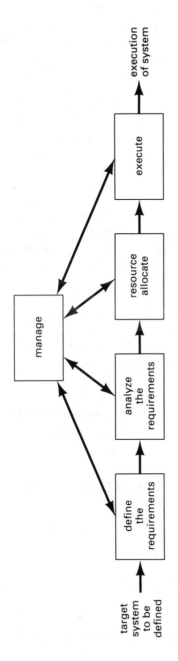

Figure 7-1. The USE.IT Functional Life Cycle Process.

systems for storing and retrieving reusable software components from a library once the design is complete. Using AXES makes the heretofore difficult tasks of cataloging, specifying, storing and relocating such components possible and practical. This is an excellent contribution to software engineering; it is not an aid to requirements specification.

Hamilton and Zeldin criticize developers of compilers and operating systems for "concerning themselves with complex resource allocation algorithms" [HAM83]. They contend that if those developers had used USE.IT, such algorithms would be unnecessary. What Hamilton and Zeldin have failed to recognize is that compilers and operating systems are tools that perform resource allocation as one of their primary functions, just as RAT in USE.IT is a tool that performs the same function. The reason why compilers, operating systems, and RAT do this is identical: so application programmers need not worry about it!

The USE.IT developers also criticize toolsmiths for forcing software developers to use different languages for each stage of software development [HAM83]. However to argue in favor of this in general is to argue that architects should dispense with the use of blueprints and start designing with two by fours, hammers, and nails. There is good reason for different perspectives to require different abstraction mechanisms and different media. Of course, USE.IT solved the problem of multiple languages by discarding requirements and preliminary design stages, retaining the detailed design stage, and automatically synthesizing code from the detailed design through reusable components. Hence it is left with just one language.

In summary, USE.IT provides the software engineering community with

- A formal basis for detailed design specifications
- An impressive tool for the interactive decomposition of functions
- An impressive set of tools for automatically translating detailed designs into code
- An impressive application of libraries of reusable components for the automatic synthesis of software

However, there is little application of the approach to software requirements analysis or specification.

7.1.3 Jackson System Development

The *Jackson System Development* (JSD) methodology [JAC82, CAM83, CAM86] was developed by Michael Jackson and John Cameron of Michael Jackson Systems, Ltd., in the late 1970s. Based on Jackson Structured Programming (JSP), JSD applies basic JSP principles to the entire life cycle. JSD is a three phase process—modeling, networking, and implementation. During the modeling phase, processes are selected, modeled, and defined; during the networking phase, the specification is expanded; and during the implementation phase, processes are constructed, packaged, and resources allocated. The methodology does not subscribe to a traditional life cycle model, as shown earlier in Figure 1–9, and there is no clear cut activity in JSD that corresponds precisely to the requirements phase. For that reason only earlier activities of JSD will be discussed here, that is, those that parallel most closely the requirements phase.

In JSD, like PAISLey, the system is defined as a set of autonomous sequential processes. During the modeling phase, each entity that occurs in the real world is represented as a process whose states correspond precisely to the life states of the real-life entity. Processes may communicate with each other via message passing through infinitely long queues or via sharing internal process state information. Notations used for these two concepts are shown in Figure 7–2. A process may also represent a primitive control function, such as sequence (i.e., do this process, then this process, then this process), iteration (i.e., do these processes n times), or selection (i.e., do this process or that process). It is thus possible to construct hierarchies of processes where the inner processes represent control and the leaf nodes represent actual functioning processes, as shown in Figure 7–3. JSD supports the concept of projection (see Section 2.2) by allowing multiple process hierarchies to represent different views of the same real-world scenario. Each view can even have its own set of states, and thus the real state of the scenario being specified is the cross product of each of the projected states.

Using JSD, an event model is created after process models have been defined. The event model describes the organizational dynamics of the system. The last modeling step is to define the states of each process (that is, data stored by each process). It is this final modeling stage that most closely follows JSP. Note that this entire methodology is not top-down. This is because Jackson believes that it is better to have "a well-defined incomplete system...than an ill-defined complete system." When JSD continues, models built earlier are slowly transformed into executable code. Like other approaches discussed before, JSD seems to lack a distinct design stage during which the architecture

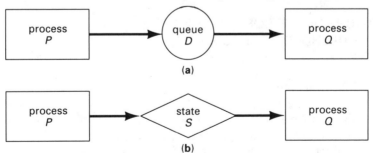

Figure 7–2. JSD Process Communication.

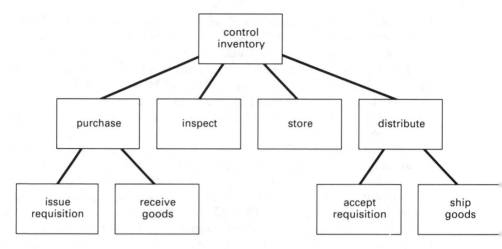

Figure 7–3. JSD Process Hierarchy Example.

is optimized by criteria other than architecture matching the real world's structure. This is clearly in support of Jackson's view of design: A design that does not match the structure of the real world is not just poor, it is wrong! There is no doubt in my mind that writing the SRS using JSD and then allowing the SRS's structure to become the real software architecture has a high probability of optimizing the software's maintainability. However, remember that a product whose architecture is not chosen with regard to performance may fail to meet its requirements.

The Jackson approach has a great deal of appeal. It is discussed here rather than earlier because it is not really clear whether it is problem analysis, requirements specification, or system design methodology. Of course, the answer is that it does not matter; it is a complete life cycle approach to transforming a real problem into a working solution based on very sound and intuitive principles. Numerous published examples of JSD applications have appeared in the literature, all conveniently reprinted by Cameron [CAM83].

7.2 FUTURE OF THE SOFTWARE INDUSTRY
AND THE ROLE OF REQUIREMENTS

7.2.1 Introduction

The software industry is growing at a phenomenal rate. As shown in Figure 7–4 [MUS85], data processing already exceeds 8% of U.S. gross national product and is growing at approximately 12% per year. On the other hand, the number of available software engineers in the industry has increased at only

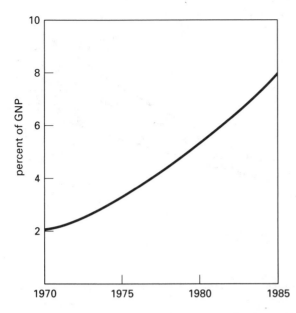

Figure 7–4. Data Processing as a Percentage of U.S. Gross National Product. © 1985 IEEE Computer Society.

approximately 4% annually [CHA86, MUS85, STE80]. Charette [CHA86] and Musa [MUS85] provide sound arguments based on a variety of data, including Dolotta's [DOL76], to support the claim that the software industry as a whole is experiencing a 4% increase in productivity per year. The net effect of this, shown as the shaded area in Figure 7–5 [DOD82], is a significant shortfall in available software engineers. How will this be overcome? Will work that needs to be done not be done? How would we as a society even know that this were the case? What should be gleaned from Figure 7–5 is a significant need in the industry to improve productivity. Ironically enough there is no lack of productivity-enhancing tools and techniques. There is however a significant failure to use available concepts in the industry today [COM84, YEH83, ZEL84]. Acknowledging this poor state of technology transfer, the U.S. DoD has established the Software Engineering Institute [BAR85, LIE86] to assist in that transfer. Numerous other initiatives began in the 1980s to try to develop revolutionary new techniques in software. These include the software technology program of MCC [FIS83, MYE85], the European Common Market's European Strategic Programme on Research in Information Technology (ESPRIT) [NAS83, ELM85], the Software Productivity Consortium (SPC) [YUD86, YUD86a, DEL88], and the software areas of the Fifth-Generation Computer System (FGCS) Project in Japan [MCC83, MOT82, MOT83, MOT84]. All are searching for significant breakthroughs that will result in a major increase in software engineering productivity.

Perhaps the technology with the highest potential payoff to software productivity and the highest risk is expert systems. Expert systems in general and knowledge-based systems specifically are being applied to a wide variety

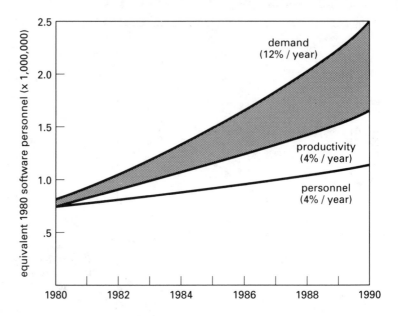

Figure 7–5. Trends in Software Supply and Demand.

of applications that require significant human intelligence and are not easily characterizable algorithmically. Obviously one such application involves translating a problem into a working software solution, that is, software engineering. In my opinion, expert systems today are where the pharmaceutical industry was in the 1860s: ninety-five percent of what was sold as medicine (i.e., "snake oil") in the 1860s was later proven to be totally useless. The remaining 5% formed the basis of a major and successful drug industry. Similarly 95% of what is sold today as expert systems to automate software development is totally useless. However there is the remaining 5%, which will probably revolutionize how we develop software. Unfortunately (1) there are many snake oil salespeople, and (2) it is not easy to differentiate between those who have a useful practical solution and those who do not.

This subsection briefly describes four areas where research in the next ten years may uncover results that could revolutionize how the requirements stage of software development is conducted—the analyst's intelligent assistant, automatic translation of informal requirements into a formal SRS, automated program synthesis from requirements, and automatic system test generation from requirements.

7.2.2 Analyst's Intelligent Assistant

Problem analysis is one of those areas with a few people who are really good at it, but those who are good are really, really good. Those who do analysis well seem to have an uncanny ability for asking exactly the right question at the right time, and probably more important, they are able instantaneously to see relationships that exist between a new piece of information and previously gleaned information. Good analysts tend to have (1) highly developed analytic skills and (2) a great deal of knowledge about the problem's application domain. Perhaps if we could populate a knowledge base with primitive inferences from both of these domains, we could create a knowledge-based system that mimics analysts performing their job.

7.2.3 Automated Translation of Informal Requirements into a Formal SRS

Today, most SRSs are written in natural language. As such these tend to be ambiguous, incomplete, and difficult to maintain. Techniques are necessary to translate such SRSs into those that are more formal, more demonstrably unambiguous and complete and easier to maintain. Balzer et al. [BAL78] were obviously well ahead of their time when suggesting this still unfulfilled approach in 1978. The system they developed, called SAFE, was able to translate such requirements as those shown in Figure 7–6 into formal specifications [BAL78]. One of the common criticisms of this approach is "what if the computers misinterpret the informally written requirements?" The counterargument is that if the translation were not performed, then the informal SRS would serve as *the* SRS and human designers would also misinterpret the requirements. At least the computer knows when it is looking at an ambiguous statement and can announce its presence and any assumptions being made.

1.   ((Messages ((received from (the sensor))) (are
     processed) for (automatic distribution assignments))

2.   ((The message) (is distributed) to (each (assigned)
     combat group))

3.   ((The number of (copies of (a message) ((distributed)
     to (a combat group)))) (is) (a function of (whether ((the
     group) (is assigned) for (action) or (information)))))

4.   ((The rules for ((editing) (messages))) (are) (: ((save)
     (only (alphanumeric characters) and (spaces)))
     ((eliminate) (all redundant spaces)))))

5.   (Then (the message) (is searched) for (all keys))

6.   ((When ((a key) (is located) in (a message)) ((perform)
     (the action ((associated) with (that type of (key)))))))

Figure 7–6. The SAFE System Sample Input. © 1978 IEEE Computer Society.

7.2.4 Automated Program Synthesis from Requirements

Once the SRS is formally written (by either people or a translator like SAFE from informally stated requirements), it may be possible to synthesize the software automatically from requirements. Of course, this operation is now performed by people who do trade-off analyses of various architectures and algorithms before finalizing a design. This translation from a formal SRS to operational software is usually thought of as a two-step process—synthesis of a design and optimization of the design. Initial synthesis of the design may be performed (1) with a canned architecture used for all applications [DAV82], (2) with the requirements-implied architecture for operationally specified requirements [ZAV81], or (3) with a knowledge base containing expert knowledge of optimal designs [BAR79]. There is a vast literature base of techniques for performing transformations on software that optimize performance while holding external behavior invariant [BAR79, DAR81, PAR83].

Many people argue that if we could translate requirements directly into code, then the requirements would have to be so detailed that it would be as difficult to write those requirements as to write code today. Even if this were the case, I claim there is a net savings. The first column in Figure 7–7 shows how software was developed in the late 1950s. Note that in effect we went through all stages of the life cycle but all stages were performed relatively informally except for the formal process of writing machine (or assembler) language code. Each informal stage must be translated by hand into the next stage. Since the 1960s we have in general programmed in high-level languages for implementation, preceding it with more informal stages that are still translated by hand. Of course once we program in a high-level language, we need not perform the manual translation into machine code; instead we allow the compiler (i.e., an "automatic program synthesizer") to translate for us. As we continue in this industry for the next few decades, we will see the level of formality becoming higher and higher. Those who claim that writing a formal requirements specification will take as much time as writing a formal programming language program are in part correct: Writing anything in a formal manner takes much more energy than writing it in an informal way. However "programming" in a requirements language is inherently more productive than programming in a high-level language, because of higher levels of abstraction and proximity to the real problem domain. This of course is the same reason why we are more productive in a higher level language than in machine language. There is however another reason why each column in Figure 7–7 is more efficient and conducive for increased productivity than its previous column. Let us assume the worst case: Formality is formality, and writing something formal is equally difficult regardless of the abstraction level built into the language. Let us call this constant effort F for formal; let us assume the same for informal efforts and call that effort I for informal. Look now at

Stage	1950s	Post 1950s	FUTURE		
Requirements	Informal	Informal	Informal	Informal	Formal
High-level design	Informal	Informal	Informal	Formal	Not performed
Detailed design	Informal	Informal	Formal	Not performed	Not performed
High-level language	Informal	Formal	Not performed	Not performed	Not performed
Machine language	Formal	Not performed	Not performed	Not performed	Not performed

Figure 7-7. Software Synthesis Stages.

each of the columns in the figure. Note how the efforts of each column decrease when moving from left to right: 4I+F, 3I+F, 2I+F, I+F, F.

7.2.5 Automatic System Test Generation from Requirements

In looking at Figure 1–9, it is evident that the SRS serves two primary purposes. First, it is the basis of software design and coding; second, it is the basis for system test planning and generation. As in the case of program synthesis discussed in Section 7.2.4, the automatic synthesis of system test plans must begin with a formal SRS. In operationally specified SRSs, test generation is the process for determining input data (or stimuli) and correct output data (or responses) that force the system through as many meaningful paths in the operational specification as possible. This is a problem similar to generating path predicates in unit test data generation [HUA75]. A number of systems to do this have either been proposed or constructed, but none has ever been applied to real projects [CHA85, CHO78, DAS81, DAS82, DAV80, MIL75, RAM76]. Some problems associated with such test generation were discussed by Ntafos [NTA79].

7.3 CONCLUSIONS

When I set out to create this book, my plan was to provide readers with insights into the early phases of the software life cycle. Only you can judge the success or failure of that endeavor. There are however a number of stones that I have turned which should have made you somewhat uneasy. For example, the book preaches using the right tool for the right job at all times—just like a skilled carpenter. This is good pie-in-the-sky advice, difficult to argue with, but there are at least two problems with its implementation—cost and interface. If you went out today to buy, say, a half-dozen or so of the types of tools described herein, you would probably spend between a quarter and a half million dollars—before you even began to build your product! Let us suppose you had the resources. You buy the tools, you receive the training necessary to know how and when to apply them; now what? In the case of carpentry, it is perfectly fine to first saw a piece of wood, then sand it, then drill it, then tap in a screw with a hammer, than continue driving in the screw with a screw driver. There is no reason to worry about compatibility among tools used. Is this practical today for requirements tools? The answer is largely "no." For example, if you bought TRW's REVS and GTE's RLP and i-Logix's STATEMATE, each would do a fine job on particular aspects of your job, but they would probably not communicate with each other satisfactorily. You would find yourself re-entering the same information multiple times, creating incompatible data bases and incompatible outputs.

An integrated requirements workbench is needed. Central to that workbench is a requirements specific data base, which would allow for multiple perspectives:

Problem analysis versus external description

Opposing points of view

Levels of abstraction

DFD versus behavioral versus ER versus IPO versus simulation

The data base would also allow you easily to attach tools that require a particular subset of the preceding perspectives. Unfortunately we are still a few years away from this.

What should you do today? Learn many of the techniques in depth. This should certainly include Structured Analysis, Structured Analysis/RT, statecharts, finite state machines, decision tables/trees, and any others of particular relevance to your application. Then acquire one to three tools that will help you with the toughest aspects of the problem at hand. You can also optimize the chance of future compatibility among tools by selecting tools that (1) practice the open-system architecture philosophy, (2) publish internal tool data base access methods and (3) encourage incorporation of new tools.

REFERENCES

[BAL78]   Balzer, R., et al. "Informality in Program Specifications." *IEEE Transactions on Software Engineering* **4**, 2 (March 1978): 94–103.

[BAR85] Barbacci, M., et al. "The Software Engineering Institute: Bridging Practice and Potential." *IEEE Software* **2,** 6 (November 1985): 4–21.

[BAR79] Barstow, D. *Knowledge-Based Program Construction.* Amsterdam: North Holland Publ., 1979.

[BOO86] Booch, G. "Object-Oriented Development." *IEEE Transactions on Software Engineering* **12,** 2 (February 1986): 211–21.

[BOR85] Borgida, A., et al. "Knowledge Representation as the Basis for Requirements Specification." *IEEE Computer* **18,** 4 (April 1985): 82–91.

[CAM83] Cameron, J. "JSD Principles and Small Examples." Pt. 4. In *Tutorial: JSP and JSD: The Jackson Approach to Software Development.* IEEE EH0206-3. Washington D.C.: Computer Society Press of the Institute of Electrical and Electronics Engineers, 1983.

[CAM86] Cameron, J. "An Overview of JSD." *IEEE Transactions on Software Engineering* **12,** 2 (February 1986): 222–40.

[CHA85] Chandrasekharan, M., et al. "Requirements-Based Testing of Real-Time Systems: Modeling for Testability." *IEEE Computer* **18,** 4 (April 1985): 71–80.

[CHA86] Charette, R., *Software Engineering Environments.* New York: McGraw-Hill, 1986.

[CHO78] Chow, T. S. "Testing Software Design Modeled by Finite State Machines." *IEEE Transactions on Software Engineering* **4,** 3 (May 1978): 178–87.

[COM84] Computerworld Argentina. "Panorama de la Ingenieria de Soft." *Computerworld Argentina* (in Spanish) **2,** 34 (October 1984): 6.

[DAR81] Darlington, J. "An Experimental Program Transformation and Synthesis System." *Artificial Intelligence* **16** (1981): 1–46.

[DAS82] Dasarathy, B., and M. Chandrasekharan. "Test Generation for Functional Validation of Real-Time Systems." Presented at *Sixth IEEE International Conference on Software Engineering.* Unpublished poster session, September 1982.

[DAS81] Dasarathy, B. "Test Plan Generation for the Requirements Validation of Real-Time Systems." In *IEEE Workshop on Automatic Test Program Generation.* Washington D.C.: Computer Society Press of the Institute of Electrical and Electronics Engineers, 1981.

[DAV80] Davis, A. "Automating the Requirements Phase: Benefits to Later Phases of the Software Life Cycle." In *IEEE COMPSAC '80,* Washington D.C.: Computer Society Press of the Institute of Electrical and Electronics Engineers, 1980. pp. 42–48.

[DAV82] Davis, A. M. "The Role of Requirements in the Automated Synthesis of Real-Time Systems." In *International Symposium on Current Issues of Requirements Environments,* Y. Ohno, ed. Amsterdam: North Holland Publ., 1982. pp. 151–58.

[DEL88] Delfossi, C. "Software Productivity Consortium: Experience and Prospects for a Large American Consortium." *International Workshop: Software Engineering and Its Applications,* Toulouse, France, Nanterre, France: EC2. December 1988.

[DOD82] U.S. Department of Defense. *Strategy for a DoD Software Initiative.* Washington, D.C., October 1, 1982.

[DOL76] Dolotta, T., et al. *Data Processing in 1980–1985: A Study of Potential Limitations to Progress.* New York: Wiley, 1976.

[ELM85] Elmore, J. "Software Development Directions in Europe." Unpublished plenary address, *IEEE COMPSAC '85,* Chicago, October 1985.

[FIS83] Fischetti, M. "MCC: An Industry Response to the Japanese Challenge." *IEEE Spectrum* **20,** 11 (November 1983): 55–56.

[HAM76] Hamilton, M., and S. Zeldin. "Higher Order Software—A Methodology for Defining Software." *IEEE Transactions on Software Engineering* **2,** 1 (March 1976): 9–32.

[HAM83] Hamilton, M., and S. Zeldin. "The Functional Life Cycle Model and Its Automation: USE.IT." *Journal of Systems and Software* **3,** 1 (March 1983): 25–62.

[HUA75] Huang, J. C. "An Approach to Program Testing." *ACM Computing Surveys* **7,** 3 (September 1975): 113–28.

[JAC82] Jackson, M. *Systems Development.* Englewood Cliffs, N.J.: Prentice-Hall, 1982.

[LIE86] Lieblein, E. "The Department of Defense Software Initiative—a Status Report." *Communications of the ACM* **29,** 8 (August 1986): 734–44.

[MCC83] McCorduck, P. "Introduction to the Fifth Generation." *Communications of the ACM* **26,** 9 (September 1983): 629–30.

[MEY87] Meyer, B. "Reusability: The Case for Object-Oriented Design." *IEEE Software* **4,** 2 (March 1987): 50–64.

[MIL75] Miller, E., and R. Melton. "Automatic Generation of Test Case Datasets. *ACM SIGPLAN Notices* **10,** 6 (June 1975): 51–58.

[MOT82] Moto-Oka, T., ed. *Fifth-Generation Computer Systems.* Amsterdam: North Holland Publ., 1982.

[MOT83] Moto-Oka, T. "The Fifth Generation: A Quantum Jump in Friendliness." *IEEE Spectrum* **20,** 11 (November 1983): 46–47.

[MOT84] Moto-Oka, T., and H. Stone. "Fifth-Generation Computer Systems: A Japanese Project." *IEEE Computer* **17,** 3 (March 1984): 6–13.

[MUS85] Musa, J. "Software Engineering: The Future of a Profession." *IEEE Software* **2,** 1 (January 1985): 55–62.

[MYE85] Myers, W. "MCC: Planning the Revolution in Software." *IEEE Software* **2,** 6 (November 1985): 68–73.

[NAS83] Nasko, H. "European Common Market." *IEEE Spectrum* **20,** 11 (November 1983): 71–72.

[NTA79] Ntafos, S., and S. Hakimi. "On Path Cover Problems in Digraphs and Applications to Program Testing." *IEEE Transactions on Software Engineering* **5,** 5 (September 1979): 520–29.

[PAR83] Partsch, H., and R. Steinbruggen. "Program Transformation Systems." *ACM Computing Surveys* **15,** 3 (September 1983): 199–236. This article contains almost two hundred references to other works on program transformations.

[POW88] Power, L. In statements made during "CASE Perspectives," a panel at *IEEE COMPSAC '88*, Chicago, October 6, 1988.

[RAM76] Ramamoorthy, C. V., et al. "On the Automated Generation of Program Test Data." *IEEE Transactions on Software Engineering* **2**, 4 (December 1976): 293–300.

[REN82] Rentsch, T. "Object-Oriented Programming." *ACM SIGPLAN Notices* **17**, 9 (September 1982): 51–57.

[STE80] Stephen, D. "Digital Data Processing—Software and Hardware." *DoD Electronics Market: Forecast for the 80s, the EIA Ten-Year Forecast.* Washington, D.C.: Electronic Industries Association., 1980. p. 88–116.

[YEH83] Yeh, R. T. "Software Engineering." *IEEE Spectrum* **20**, 11 (November 1983): 91–94.

[YUD86] Yudkin, H. "Software Productivity." Unpublished plenary address, IEEE COMPSAC '86, Chicago, October 1986.

[YUD86a] Yudkin, H. "Need for Mission-Critical System Software Productivity Improvement." *Conference on Software Reusability and Maintainability,* Washington, D.C.: National Institute for Software Quality and Productivity, 1986. pp. A-1–A-27.

[ZAV81] Zave, P., and R. Yeh. "Executable Requirements for Embedded Systems." In *Fifth IEEE International Conference on Software Engineering,* Washington D.C.: Computer Society Press of the Institute of Electrical and Electronics Engineers, 1981. pp. 295–304.

[ZEL84] Zelkowitz, M. V., et al. "Software Engineering Practices in the U.S. and Japan." *IEEE Computer* **17,** 6 (June 1984): 57–66.

Glossary [1]

Abstraction A *problem analysis* principle in which a problem is analyzed in general, then refined into subproblems, all of which exhibit the traits of the original problem.

Algorithm Same as a recipe. The sequence of steps the software will take to perform a required task; defined during *design* for every module in the system.

Algorithmic *Deterministic.*

Algorithmic design *Detailed design.*

Analyst A person who performs *problem analysis.*

Annotation A technique to indicate the relative importance and/or volatility of each *requirement* in an *SRS*.

Architecture A set of software modules (usually defined hierarchically) and their interfaces that define the structure of the software; defined during *design.*

B5 specification As defined by *DOD-STD-490,* a *software requirements specification* and an optional *interface requirements specification.*

---

[1]Note: *Italicized* terms are defined elsewhere in this glossary.

Batch *Static.*

Behavioral requirements Those *requirements* that specify the *inputs* (*stimuli*) to the system, the *outputs* (*responses*) from the system, and behavioral relationships between them; also called *functional* or *operational requirements.*

Bug Any error in software.

Capacity The number of real-world objects (or events) and the rate at which those objects (or events) arrive that the software is required to handle.

CFD *Control flow diagram.*

Coding The stage of the *software life cycle* immediately following *design* during which *algorithms* are transformed into some computer programming language; also called *implementation.*

Cohesion A measure of how closely related the tasks performed by a specific module are.

Complete An *SRS* is complete if and only if everything that eventual users or customers need is specified therein.

Computational *Deterministic.*

Consistent An *SRS* is consistent if and only if no subset of individual *requirements* described in it conflict.

Control flow diagram A *data flow diagram* that shows control lines as well as data flow.

Correct An *SRS* is correct if and only if every *requirement* stated therein represents something that is required.

Coupling A measure of the strength of the interrelatedness between two modules.

CSC testing *Integration testing.*

CSCI testing *System testing.*

Data dictionary A data base (i.e., a data repository) for storing all information concerning all data (information) elements defined during a *problem analysis* or *design.*

Data flow diagram (DFD) A graphical *language* for describing flow of data. It is composed of arrows (for data) and circles (for transformations on that data).

Data item description (DID) A U.S. Government-defined standard for the outline and content of a document, including all *specifications.*

Decision table A tabular chart showing the logic relating all combinations of conditions to a set of actions (decisions); see *decision tree.*

Decision tree A branching chart showing the logic relating various combinations of conditions to a set of actions (decisions); see *decision table.*

Decisional *Nondeterministic.*

Design The *architecture* of the software and the *algorithms* used therein. The stage of the *software life cycle* where the architecture and algorithms are selected; immediately follows the *requirements* stage.

Detailed design The second half of *design* where *algorithms* for software modules are defined; also called *lower level design* or *algorithmic design.*

Deterministic An application where the same predictable *output* is produced given the same set of *inputs;* also called *computational* and *algorithmic.*

DFD *Data flow diagram.*

DID *Data item description.*

DI-MCCR-80025A The *DID* for the *SRS* according to *DOD-STD-2167A.*

DOD-STD-2167A The U.S. Department of Defense standard for mission critical software development and its associated *DID*s.

DOD-STD-490 The U.S. Department of Defense standard for *specification* practices associated with system development and its associated *DID*s.

DOD-STD-7935 The U.S. Department of Defense standard for non–mission critical software development and its associated *DID*s.

Dynamic An application where data is made available to the program only after it starts processing; also called *real-time.*

Efficiency The degree to which software utilizes scarce system resources.

Environment That portion of the universe not part of the system but interfacing with the system.

Evolutionary prototype A *prototype* constructed in order to learn more about the problem or its solution and then usually built on or expanded to become the final system eventually.

Evolvable prototype *Evolutionary prototype.*

FD *Functional description.*

Finite state machine (FSM) A virtual machine that can be in any one of a set of finite states and whose next states and outputs are functions of input and current states only. It is often useful to describe the behavior of a complex system as if it were a finite state machine.

FSM *Finite state machine.*

Functional description (FD) As defined by *DOD-STD-7935,* a *software requirements specification.*

Functional requirement *Behavioral requirement.*

High-level design *Preliminary design.*

Human engineering The ease with which software can be requested to do jobs for which it was intended.

IEEE/ANSI 830-1984 An IEEE and ANSI standard for organizing an *SRS.*

Implementation *Coding.*

Inferential *Nondeterministic.*

Input An item that comes into a system.

Integration testing The stage of the *software life cycle* immediately following *unit testing* during which previously unit-tested software modules are integrated together to see if these function correctly as a team; also called *CSC, integration,* and *string testing.*

Interface requirements specification (IRS) As defined by *DOD-STD-2167A,* a *specification* containing a description of interfaces between major software subsystems, each described in its own *SRS.*

IRS *Interface requirements specification.*

Jackson Structured Programming (JSP) A *technique* developed by Michael Jackson Systems, Ltd., where relatively small software systems are designed with the identical structure as the data structure that models the real world.

Jackson System Development (JSD) A *technique* developed by Michael Jackson Systems, Ltd., where systems are *model*ed using sets of autonomous processes, communicating via messages or state sharing.

JSD *Jackson System Development.*

JSP *Jackson Structured Programming.*

Language A vocabulary, a set of rules for composing sentences from that vocabulary, and a set of semantics for each possible meaningful sentence.

Lower level design *Detailed design.*

Methodology A set of *techniques* or methods (a misnomer; it should mean the *study* of techniques or methods).

Model *M* is a model of a system *S* if *M* can be used to answer a well-defined set of questions about *S* to a tolerance adequate for a stated purpose.

Modifiability A measure of how easy it is to modify operational software to meet new *requirements* while maintaining its *reliability*.

Modifiable An *SRS* is modifiable if its structure and style are such that any necessary changes to the *requirements* can be made easily, completely, and consistently.

Nonambiguous An *SRS* is nonambiguous if and only if every *requirement* stated therein has only one interpretation.

Nonbehavioral requirements *Requirements* that describe the required overall attributes of the system, including *portability, reliability, efficiency, human engineering, testability, understandability,* and *modifiability*.

Nondeterministic An application where *outputs* may vary from occurrence to occurrence of identical *inputs;* also called *decisional* and *inferential*.

Object-oriented design Same as *object-oriented development* but applied exclusively to *design*.

Object-oriented development An approach to developing software where every component represents an object in the real world, its attributes, and its possible actions; objects can be grouped together into classes to facilitate attribute and action assignments.

Object-oriented problem analysis An *object-oriented development* technique applied to *problem analysis*.

Object-oriented programming An *object-oriented development* technique applied to *coding*.

Operational requirement *Behavioral requirement*.

Operational specification A *specification* (*requirements* or *design*) that can be executed or simulated in order to ascertain intended behavior.

Output An item that comes out of a system.

PAISLey *Process-Oriented, Applicative, and Interpretable Specification Language*.

PPS *Program performance specification*.

Parallel An application where multiple tasks are performed simultaneously.

Partitioning A *problem analysis* principle in which a problem is analyzed by decomposing it into subproblems, each of which is a part of the entire problem and the entire problem is usually the union of the subproblems.

PDL *Program design language.*

Petri net A virtual machine where tokens move from place to place according to a well-defined set of rules.

Portability The degree to which software running on one computer can be converted to run on another.

Preliminary design The first half of *design* where the software *architecture* is defined; also called *high-level design.*

Problem analysis The process of brainstorming and/or interviewing to help understand a problem in the problem domain or the scope of the *product space;* also called *software requirements analysis.*

Problem Statement Language (PSL) A *language* for *problem analysis* developed by Meta Systems, Inc.

Problem Statement Analyzer (PSA) An automated *tool* developed by Meta Systems, Inc., that processes the *Problem Statement Language.*

Process-Oriented, Applicative, and Interpretable Specification Language (PAISLey) A *language* and associated *tool* developed by AT&T for the *problem analysis* and *requirements specification* of embedded systems.

Product assurance The combination of *software configuration management, V&V, quality assurance,* and *testing.*

Product description The process of writing an *SRS.*

Product space The subset of the universe of products where any member would satisfy the *requirements.*

Program design language (PDL) Free-form English with embedded keywords with specific meanings.

Program performance specification (PPS) *Software requirements specification.*

Projection A *problem analysis* principle of stepping back from a problem or its solution and looking at it from multiple external perspectives.

Prototype A partial implementation of a system constructed primarily to enable customers, users, or developers to learn more about a problem or its solution.

PSL/PSA *Problem Statement Language/Problem Statement Analyzer.*

Quality assurance The discipline that ensures software meets its standards.

Quick and dirty prototype *Throwaway prototype.*

R-net A unit of an *SRS* corresponding to a column of a *finite state machine.* It thus describes all system behaviors required in response to a particular *stimulus;* developed by TRW; see also *REVS, SREM,* and *RSL.*

Rapid prototype *Throwaway prototype.*

Real-time *Dynamic.*

Redundancy The presence of a *requirement* at least twice in an *SRS.*

Reliability The ability of software to behave in a user-acceptable manner when subjected to the *environment* in which it was intended to function.

Requirement Something that is needed. The first stage of the *software life cycle* in which the *software requirements specification* is written.

Requirements Engineering Validation System (REVS) A set of *tools* developed by TRW to ensure the *consistency, nonambiguity,* and *completeness* of *requirements* written in *RSL;* see also *SREM* and *R-net.*

Requirements language Any language used to specify *behavioral* or *nonbehavioral requirements.*

Requirements Language Processor (RLP) An automated *tool* developed by GTE to ensure *consistency, nonambiguity,* and *completeness* of *requirements* written as *stimulus-response sequences.*

Requirements Processing System (RPS) A set of *tools* developed by GTE to automate the *requirements* stage of the *software life cycle.* The chief tool is the *Requirements Language Processor.*

Requirements specification A document describing all of a system's required attributes that can be witnessed externally. It defines what the software will do externally without describing how it will function internally.

Requirements Statement Language (RSL) A *language* developed by TRW for the *specification* of external behavior of *real-time* systems; see also *SREM, REVS,* and *R-nets.*

Requirements traceability matrix (RTM) A table that cross-references individual *requirements* to *design* components.

Response An *output* from a *real-time* system.

Response time The time that elapses between a *stimulus* to a system and the corresponding *response* from that system.

REVS *Requirements Engineering Validation System.*

RLP *Requirements Language Processor.*

RSL *Requirements Statement Language.*

RTM *Requirements traceability matrix.*

RPS *Requirements Processing System.*

SADT *Structured Analysis and Design Technique.*

SA/RT *Structured Analysis / Real Time.*

SASS *Structured Analysis and System Specification.*

SCM *Software configuration management.*

SDL *Specification and Description Language.*

Sequential An application in which one task is performed at a time.

Software configuration management (SCM) The process of establishing software baselines in order to control (not prevent) and monitor changes to those baselines and thus manage the evolution of the software.

Software engineering The disciplined process of transforming recognized needs into an operational software solution.

Software life cycle Series of stages from the beginning of a software project (when one recognizes the existence of an unsatisfied need) through development, deployment, and maintenance and ending when the software is permanently mothballed or destroyed.

Software requirements analysis *Problem analysis.*

Software Requirements Engineering Methodology (SREM) *Methodology* developed by TRW for the U.S. Army Strategic Defense Command (nee Ballistic Missile Defense) Advanced Technology Center for translating user needs into a *software requirements specification* written in *RSL;* see also *REVS* and *R-net.*

Software requirements specification (SRS) A *requirements specification* for a software system or the software part of a software/hardware system; also called *program performance specification* and *functional description.*

SOW Statement of work.

Specification A document; for example, a *requirements specification* is a document containing *requirements;* a design specification is a document containing the *design;* a test specification is a document containing the *testing* process.

Specification and Description Language (SDL) A graphical and text language developed by CCITT to write *requirements* or *design specifications* for telephone systems.

SRD *Structured Requirements Definition.*

SREM *Software Requirements Engineering Methodology.*

SRS *Software requirements specification.*

SSS *System / segment specification.*

Statechart An extension to *finite state machines* developed by D. Harel.

STATEMATE An automated *tool* by i-Logix, Inc., that implements *statecharts.*

Static An application where all input data is available to the program before it starts processing; also called *batch.*

Stimulus An *input* in a *real-time* system.

Stimulus-response sequence A unit of an *SRS* corresponding to a user feature of a *finite state machine.* It thus describes the complete dialog that transpires between a system and its *environment* (for example, the user) in performing some user-relatable function.

String testing *Integration testing.*

Structured analysis A term originally coined by Douglas Ross, now used to refer to any one of a variety of top-down *problem analysis techniques;* see *Structured Analysis and Design Technique* and *Structured Analysis and System Specification.*

Structured Analysis and Design Technique (SADT) A *problem analysis technique* developed by SofTech, Inc.

Structured Analysis and System Specification (SASS) A *problem analysis technique* developed by Tom DeMarco.

Structured analysis/real time An extension to *structured analysis* to include modeling control paths and *behavioral requirements.*

Structured Requirements Definition (SRD) A *problem analysis technique* developed by Ken Orr and Associates that uses *DFD*s and an interviewing process to help understand the *inputs, outputs,* and functions of an organization.

Subset A partial implementation of a system constructed primarily to provide early functionality.

System integration testing For large complex systems composed of multiple software systems where a separate SRS is written for each system; this stage of the *software life cycle* integrates separately *system tested* software systems to see if the entire aggregate meets overall *system requirements specification.*

System requirements specification A *requirements specification* for the overall system without discriminating between the medium (e.g., software or hardware) in which the *requirements* will be satisfied.

System segment specification (SSS) As defined by *DOD-STD-2167A,* a *system requirements specification.*

System testing The stage of the *software life cycle* immediately following *integration testing* during which the fully integrated software is checked to see if it meets all *requirements* stated in the *software requirements specification;* also called *CSCI testing.*

TBD To be determined.

Technique A set of rules to follow to accomplish a task.

Testing A phase of the *software life cycle* that includes three distinct stages— *unit testing, integration testing,* and *system testing;* for complex applications, may also include *system integration testing.*

Testability A measure of the inherent difficulty of detecting and repairing *bugs* in software.

Throwaway prototype A *prototype* software system that is constructed in order to learn more about the problem or its solution and usually discarded after the desired knowledge is gained.

Timing constraint A *requirement* for the software to respond in a minimum or maximum time limit (see *response time*) or for the software to respond differently when the *environment* fails to conform to specific minimum or maximum time limits.

Tool A piece of software that can be used by people to help them perform a task; occasionally enforces or demands a *technique.*

Traceable An *SRS* is traceable is the origin of each of its *requirements* is clear and if it facilitates referencing each *requirement* in future development or enhancement documentation.

Understandability A measure of the inherent difficulty of understanding the purpose and process intended by a piece of software.

Unit testing The stage of the *software life cycle* immediately following *coding* during which software modules are checked by themselves to see if these meet *design specifications.*

VDM *Vienna Development Method.*

Validation The process of checking the results of each stage of the *software life cycle* to see if it has the correct relationship to results from the previous stage.

Verifiable An *SRS* is verifiable if and only if every *requirement* stated therein is verifiable. A *requirement* is verifiable if and only if there exists some finite cost effective process with which a person or machine can check that the software product meets the *requirement*.

Verification The formal process of checking *designs, code, test* plans, and final software products against *requirements*.

Vienna Development Method (VDM) A *technique* and *language* developed in Europe for the formal *specification* of semantics of transformation from *inputs* to *outputs*.

Word processor A software package that facilitates entry, storage, editing, and printing a text.

Annotated Bibliography

This bibliography is a compilation of every requirements-related item I know of in the literature. Most of these items are described in a few sentences to help you determine whether or not you want to read them. The bibliography is useful in two ways: First you can read or browse through it, looking for items of interest; second you can refer to the topic-bibliography cross-reference table that follows on page 481. This table enables you to locate bibliographical entries corresponding to topics of interest easily. The notation used in this bibliography for all items is [**author year-of-publication**].[1]

1. **[Abbott 1986].**
   Abbott, R. *An Integrated Approach to Software Development.* New York: Wiley, 1986.

   A general textbook on software engineering, this book uses the term "requirements" to denote what we have called problem analysis, and the term "behavioral specification" for what we have called requirements specification. Although the logic of the book is sometimes difficult to follow, this is one of the best treatises available on early phases of software development and well worth reading. Chapters 2–5 are on the requirements phase.

2. **[Abbott and Moorhead 1981].**
   Abbott, R., and D. Moorhead. "Software Requirements and Specifications." *Journal of Systems and Software* **2,** (1981): 297–316.

---

[1]References in the body of this book to additional information appear at the end of each chapter and use the notation [AAAYY], where AAA are the first three letters of the first author and YY are the last two digits of the year of publication.

3. **[Adler 1988].**
   Adler, M. "An Algebra for Data Flow Diagram Process Decomposition." *IEEE Transactions on Software Engineering* **14,** 2 (February 1988): 169–83.

4. **[Agusa et al. 1979].**
   Agusa, K., et al. "Verification of Requirements Description." In *Twelfth Hawaii International Conference on System Science,* Washington D.C.: Computer Society Press of the Institute of Electrical and Electronics Engineers, 1979.

5. **[Agusa and Ohnishi 1982].**
   Agusa, K., and A. Ohnishi. "Verification System for Formal Requirements Description". In *Sixth International Conference on Software Engineering,* Washington D.C.: Computer Society Press of the Institute of Electrical and Electronics Engineers, 1982. pp. 120–26.

   Describes the application of assertions and formal verification to the realm of requirements specification. Once requirements are entered into a data base using PSL/PSA, assertions are written, entered, and syntactically analyzed by a tool developed by the authors, named ASL/ASA (Assertion Statement Language/Assertion Statement Analyzer). Finally, a Requirements Descriptions Verifier (RDV) uses the requirements as axioms and the assertions as theorems, and using theorem-proving techniques, it proves the theorems. Although the approach is certainly unique and interesting, there is the possibility that the authors have lost sight of what one is really trying to do during requirements specification. I claim that if a collection of assertions could be written concerning the system and these are more concise than the requirements, then the assertions *are* the requirements. Examples are given of the ASL language. 7 refs.

6. **[Alavi and Wetherbe 1982].**
   Alavi, M., and J. C. Wetherbe. "Reducing Complexity in Information Requirements Planning." *Systems, Objectives, and Solutions* **2,** 3 (August 1982): 143–58.

   Advocates breaking down requirements into logical application groups (LAGs) to reduce the complexity of the system development task. 20 refs.

7. **[Alexander and Potter 1987].**
   Alexander, H., and B. Potter. "Case Study: The Use of Formal Specification and Rapid Prototyping to Establish Product Feasibility." *Information and Software Technology* **29,** 7 (September 1987): 388-94.

   A short article reporting on the successful use of a prototype to demonstrate feasibility of a tool to help configure and interface heterogeneous systems. The methodology used has three steps—model using objects, specify using "me too," and build the prototype. According to the authors, the major advantage is a common understanding of, and nomenclature for, objects being modeled and functions being performed. 20 refs.

8. **[Alford and Burns 1975].**
   Alford, M. W. , and I. F. Burns. "An Approach to Stating Real-Time Processing Requirements." Presented at *Conference on Petri Nets and Related Methods,* MIT, Cambridge, Mass., July 1–3, 1975.

9. **[Alford and Burns 1976].**
   Alford, M. W., and I. F. Burns. "R-Nets: A Graph Model for Real-Time Software Requirements." In *Symposium on Computer Software Engineering.* New York: Polytechnic Press, 1976. pp. 97–108.

Defines a technique useful for specifying overall black-box system requirements for real-time systems with a minimum amount of human interaction. One of the best statements differentiating system requirements from both module specifications and system design. Provides a thorough list of attributes that apply to properly written requirements specifications. Precisely defines the eight types of requirements that comprise the invariants between different designs solving the same problem. 16 refs.

10. **[Alford 1977].**
Alford, M. W. "A Requirements Engineering Methodology for Real-Time Processing Requirements." *IEEE Transactions on Software Engineering* **3,** 1 (January 1977): 60–69.

This classic paper describes the Software Requirements and Engineering Methodology (SREM) developed by TRW for the U.S. Army SDCATC to generate requirements specifications for large complex weapons systems. SREM consists of a language that supports disambiguation, design freedom, testability, modularity, and readability; a set of software tools whose use assures consistency, completeness, and correctness; and an approach for writing and processing requirements. RSL demands a pure black-box view of the system in terms of inputs, outputs, and the names of processing steps. The methodology itself is a four-step process—translation, decomposition, allocation, and feasibility analysis. 18 refs.

11. **[Alford et al. 1977].**
Alford, M., et al. *Management of Requirements Development Using SREM Technology.* TRW Technical Report 237332-6921-028. Huntsville, Ala., 1977.

A set of slides representing a one-day course intended to provide managers with an overview of REVS, SREM, RSL, and R-nets.

12. **[Alford et al. 1977a].**
Alford, M. W., et al. *Software Requirements Engineering Methodology.* SREP Final Report, Vol. 1, TRW. Huntsville, Ala., August 1977. See Benoit and Dyer for Vols. 2 and 3.

Detailed report of technical and management approaches used by TRW in fulfilling its contract with the U.S. Army to develop a requirements engineering methodology suitable to ballistic missile defense. 6 refs.

13. **[Alford 1978].**
Alford, M. W. "Software Requirements Engineering Methodology (SREM) at the Age of Two." In *IEEE COMPSAC '78,* Washington D.C.: Computer Society Press of the Institute of Electrical and Electronics Engineers, 1978, pp. 332–39.

Provides an update on the current status of SREM. Describes how SREM technology has been transferred to eight locations on TI and CDC equipment for a variety of applications. 8 refs.

14. **[Alford 1979].**
Alford, M. "Requirements for Distributed Data Processing Design." In *First International Conference on Distributed Computing Systems,* Washington D.C.: Computer Society Press of the Institute of Electrical and Electronics Engineers, 1979, pp. 1–14.

Three concepts, system requirements, system design, and system development plan, are formally defined and described in terms of the objects described in each, types of decomposition valid within each domain, and types of transformations legal within each. For example, in the domain of system requirements, decomposition is legal only on data using a structured data tree. On the other hand, in the domain of system design, decomposition results only in creating subsystems. A methodology is given to help define the overall distributed system as a set of nodes communicating over a set of channels using a set of protocols, followed by a definition and allocation of system requirements. A short example of the methodology is given using a patient-monitoring system. 14 refs.

15. **[Alford 1979a].**
Alford, M. "SREM." Panelist report in W. Bail, "User Experiences with Specification Tools." *ACM Software Engineering Notes.* **9,** 3 (July 1979): 10–11.

16. **[Alford 1980].**
Alford, M. W. "Software Requirements Engineering Methodology (SREM) at the Age of Four." In *IEEE COMPSAC '80,* Washington D.C.: Computer Society Press of the Institute of Electrical and Electronics Engineers, pp. 886–74.

Updates the current status of SREM. Contrasts SREM with Jackson, PSL/PSA, HOS, SADT, and IORL. Updates potential users about system availability and performance statistics. 18 refs.

17. **[Alford 1980a].**
Alford, M.W. "Software Requirements in the 80s: From Alchemy to Science." In *Proceedings of the ACM '80 Conference,* New York: ACM Press of the Association for Computing Machinery, pp. 342–49.

Provides a methodology to separate design decisions from implementation of that decision and eliminates as much of the handcrafting of software as possible. The paper claims that using automated requirements and design analysis tools can reduce maintenance costs by up to 80%. 10 refs.

18. **[Alford 1984].**
Alford, M. W. "Derivation of Database/Management Design from System Requirements." In *IEEE International Conference on Data Engineering,* Washington D.C.: Computer Society Press of the Institute of Electrical and Electronics Engineers, 1984.

19. **[Alford 1985].**
Alford, M. W. "SREM at the Age of Eight; the Distributed Computing Design System." *IEEE Computer* **18,** 4 (April 1985): 36–46.

Provides a detailed summary of the origins of REVS, SREM, and RSL. Describes extensions to SREM to facilitate system-level requirements engineering (that is, SYSREM) and designing distributed computed systems (DCDS). 7 refs.

20. **[Alford 1987].**
Alford, M. W. "The DCDS Multiple-View Approach to Bridging the Requirements Analysis/Design Gap." In *Conference on Methodologies and Tools for Real-Time Systems: IV,* Washington, D.C.: National Institute for Software Quality and Productivity, 1987.

21. **[Alspaugh 1986].**
Alspaugh, T., et al. *Software Requirements for the A-7E Aircraft,* version 5.10. Naval Research Laboratory. Washington, D.C., August 1986. Updated version of [Heninger et al. 1978].

22. **[American Society for Testing Materials 1977].**
American Society for Testing Materials. *Standard Guidelines for Developing Functional Requirements for Computerized Laboratory Systems.* Document ASTM E 623-77. Philadelphia, 1977.

For the particular application of automated equipment for laboratory use, this document specifically defines the organization and content of a requirements specification. Categories of information discussed include nature of project; specific goals; expected results; financial, operational, and manpower constraints; future requirements; desired control functions; characteristics of input, data reduction, and output; reliability; environment; implementation restrictions; human interfaces; and basis for system evaluation. No refs.

23. **[Andreu and Madnick 1977].**
Andreu, R. C., and S. E. Madnick. *An Exercise in Software Architectural Design: From Requirements to Design Problem Structure.* Center for Information Systems Research, MIT Sloan School of Management, technical report 3. Cambridge, Mass., November 1977.

Describes a methodology that can be used to (1) eliminate requirements specification statements that are irrelevant to the choice of product architecture, (2) define the design interdependencies that exist between requirements specification statements, and (3) interpret the significance of the design subproblem defined by each requirements subset. 4 refs.

24. **[Andreu and Madnick 1977a].**
Andreu, R. C., and S. E. Madnick. *Completing the Requirements Set as a Means towards Better Design Frameworks: A Follow-up Exercise in Software Architectural Design.* Center for Information Systems Research, MIT Sloan School of Management, technical report 4. Cambridge, Mass., December 1977.

25. **[Ardis 1979].**
Ardis, M. "Specification of Reliable Software—What Next?" *ACM Software Engineering Notes* **4,** 3 (July 1979): 19–21.

Panel report from the *Specifications of Reliable Software Conference*; containing a brief summary of the positions of the five panelists—Doug Ross, Peter Neumann, Jim Horning, Ray Yeh, and Marv Zelkowtiz. A good summary of the entire conference, albeit short.

26. **[Averhill and Vestal 1979].**
Averhill, E., and S. C. Vestal. "Requirements Methodology." In *AIAA Second Computers in Aerospace Conference,* Washington D.C.: American Institute of Aeronautics and Astronautics, 1979, pp. 130–34.

Very sketchy description of an experimental, unused requirements methodology. Although the authors define the methodology as a series of eleven steps divided into two stages, definitions of each step are so vague that they are of little use to the reader. In the authors' own words, "It is not possible to define a complex, creative process exactly upon first try." I agree but wish that papers were written only after authors have thought extensively about a problem and are well past their first try. 14 refs.

27. **[Azuma et al. 1984].**
Azuma, M., et al. "Integrating and Standardizing Requirements Engineering for Business Systems—an Experimental Study." In *IEEE COMPSAC '84,* Washington D.C.: Computer Society Press of the Institute of Electrical and Electronics Engineers, 1984.

28. **[Babb 1982].**
Babb, R. G., II. "Coherent Realization of Systems Requirements." In *International Symposium on Current Issues of Requirements Engineering Environments,* edited by Y. Ohno. Amsterdam: North Holland Publ., 1982. pp. 103–5.

Describes a technique called Program/System Design using simulation to verify that every level of successive refinement of a system design still meets customers' needs. Although the paper discusses "executable requirements," it appears to be primarily an executable design specification, which, after repeated refinements, results in an actual implementation of the system originally defined by the requirements. 10 refs.

29. **[Bail 1979].**
Bail, W. "User Experiences with Specification Tools." *ACM Software Engineering Notes* **4,** 3 (July 1979): 7–14.

A report of the panel at the *Specifications of Reliable Software Conference* on April 3–5, 1979. Each of the panelists—Tom Berson, Ray Slegel, Ed Jacks, Larry Johnson, Larry Robinson, Mack Alford, Clarence Feldman, and Al Hershey—discusses his experience either using or developing specification tools (HDM, SREM, SADT, CADSAT).

30. **[Balkovich and Engelberg 1976].**
Balkovich, E. E., and G. P. Engelberg. "Research Towards a Technology to Support the Specification of Data Processing System Performance Requirements." In *Second International Conference on Software Engineering,* Washington D.C.: Computer Society Press of the Institute of Electrical and Electronics Engineers,. 1976. pp. 110–15.

Describes a methodology using Petri nets for specifying requirements of real-time systems. This General Research Corporation research was sponsored by the U.S. Army Ballistic Missile Defense Advanced Technology Center. 19 refs.

31. **[Bally et al. 1977].**
Bally, L., et al. "A Prototype Approach to Information System Design and Development." *Information and Management* **1,** 1 (1977): 21–26.

32. **[Balzer, R. 1975].**
Balzer, R. *Imprecise Program Specifications.* USC Report ISI/RR-75-36. December 1975.

33. **[Balzer et al. 1978].**
Balzer, R., et al. "Informality in Program Specifications." *IEEE Transactions on Software Engineering* **4,** 2 (March 1978): 94–103.

Explores the feasibility of automatically transforming informal, ambiguous requirements into formal unambiguous specifications. The paper describes a prototype tool that accepts informal natural language specifications, interacts with the user concerning assumptions that it is making, and finally transforms the text into a formal specification. A few relatively simple examples are given. 14 refs.

34. [Balzer and Goldman 1979].

Balzer, R., and N. Goldman. "Principles of Good Software Specification and Their Implications for Specification Language." In *IEEE Conference on Specifications of Reliable Software,* Washington D.C.: Computer Society Press of the Institute of Electrical and Electronics Engineers. 1979, pp. 58–67.

Presents and discusses a list of principles affecting the module specification phase. Although primarily aimed at modules, most of the principles apply equally well to system and software requirements. The principles are (1) separate what from how, (2) describe specifications in a process-oriented manner, (3) describe how the component being specified relates and interacts with its environment, (4) describe the component in terms of how it is perceived by its users, (5) describe sample test inputs and outputs as part of the specification, (6) be tolerant of incompleteness and change, and (7) remember that a specification must be localized (i.e., function isolation) and its components loosely coupled. 15 refs.

35. [Balzer et al. 1982].

Balzer, R., et al. "Operational Specifications as the Basis for Rapid Prototyping." *ACM Software Engineering Notes* **7,** 5 (December 1982): 3–16.

Describes the Gist specification language and technique. Requirements written in Gist are organized into three sections: (1) a definition of all possible system states, (2) a mapping from all possible system states and stimuli into system responses, and (3) a list of constraints limiting the first two sections and defining the unique product being specified. All three sections describe system actions in terms of objects in the application domain. Features of the system being specified are written as "demons," which behave as independent processes. The combined set of processes define a nondeterministic machine, which is resolved whenever any nondeterministic path reaches a system response state. An example is given of a package-routing specification. Details of the example are possible to follow, although the notation using five different type fonts is awkward. 11 refs.

36. [Balzer et al. 1988].

Balzer, R., et al. *RADC System / Software Requirements Engineering Testbed Research and Development Program.* Report TR-88-75, Rome Air Development Center. Griffiss Air Force Base, N.Y., June 1988.

Report commissioned by RADC of a blue-ribbon panel of requirements experts (Balzer, Konrad, Ramamoorthy, Royce, Rzepka, Sherman, Stucki, Welch, Yeh) to define a ten-year R&D program to develop a test-bed on which to validate the usefulness of new requirements tools and techniques. This excellent report proposes four thrusts—prototyping, analysis, tool integration and evaluation, and formal specifications. Along the way the panel provides (1) excellent insight into how RADC currently writes requirements; (2) a meaningful discussion of the backgrounds (past and future) of readers of an SRS; (3) panelists' personal views on intermixing requirements and design; (4) a comparison of 2167-implied methodology and the proposed requirements test-bed methodology; and (5) a thorough list of all issues, tools, and projects relating to the proposed test-bed along with cost estimates, schedules, and issues. 54 refs.

37. **[Baroudi et al. 1986].**

Baroudi, J., et al. "An Empirical Study of the Impact of User Involvement on System Usage and Information Satisfaction." *Communications of the ACM* **29,** 3 (March 1986): 232–38.

Presents tentative data to support user involvement in the requirements definition process. 38 refs.

38. **[Basili and Turner 1975].**

Basili, V., and A. Turner. "Iterative Enhancement: A Practical Technique for Software Development." *IEEE Transactions on Software Engineering* **1,** 4 (December 1975): 390–96.

A case study of applying evolutionary prototyping to a compiler development effort. 11 refs.

39. **[Basili and Weiss 1981].**

Basili, V., and D. Weiss. "Evaluation of a Software Requirements Document by Analysis of Change Data." In *Fifth International Conference on Software Engineering,* Washington D.C.: Computer Society Press of the Institute of Electrical and Electronics Engineers. 1981, pp. 314–23.

Describes an experiment to determine the feasibility of using data collection methods to analyze the maintainability of a requirements document. Data collection methods are discussed, as are results of applying the methods to the U.S. Navy's A-7 flight software requirements. The paper reaches general conclusions regarding the usefulness of data collection methods and maintainability of the A-7 specification. 19 refs.

40. **[Bass 1985].**

Bass, L. J. "An Approach to User Specification of Interactive Display Interfaces." *IEEE Transactions on Software Engineering* **11,** 8 (August 1985): 686–98.

Describes Karlsruhe Screen-Based Application Support System (KSBASS), which allows specifiers or users of interactive database systems to specify hierarchical relationships between fields in a form. Once specified, KSBASS automatically generates forms in an aesthetic and correct fashion. 10 refs.

41. **[Batini et al. 1986].**

Batini, C., et al. "A Layout Algorithm for Data Flow Diagrams." *IEEE Transactions on Software Engineering* **12,** 4 (April 1986): 538–46.

A graph–theoretical analysis of the layout of DFDs. Once an optimal placement is made of boxes, and locations on the boxes from which arcs will emanate, it employs algorithms similar to those used by automatic integrated-circuit-routing tools to generate an aesthetic layout of a DFD. 17 refs.

42. **[Bauer et al. 1978].**

Bauer, J., et al. "The Automatic Generation and Execution of Function Test Plans for Electronic Switching Systems." *ACM Software Engineering Notes* **3,** 5 (November 1978): 92–100.

An early report describing two tools, the Test Plan Generator (TPG) and the Automatic Test Executor (ATE) developed at GTE. The TPG generates tests automatically from a requirements specification; the ATE uses those tests to perform requirements testing of a real-time (e.g., switching) system. 9 refs.

43. [Bauer and Finger 1979].
Bauer, J. and A. Finger. "Test Plan Generation Using Formal Grammars." In *Fourth International Conference on Software Engineering,* Washington D.C.: Computer Society Press of the Institute of Electrical and Electronics Engineers, 1979, pp. 425–32.

Describes using sentence generation in formal grammars to generate tests automatically from requirements specifications. 15 refs.

44. [Belford et al. 1976].
Belford, P. C., et al. "Specifications: A Key to Effective Software Development." In *Second International Conference on Software Engineering,* Washington D.C.: Computer Society Press of the Institute of Electrical and Electronics Engineers. 1976, pp. 71–79.

A very early and now outdated paper describing the SDCATC's plans to define a decomposition technique, a specification language, a set of software tools, and a management-enforced methodology. Papers that define results in more detail have since been written by numerous contractors involved in this effort. Interesting reading for historians or those interested in motivating factors behind TRW's RSL, REVS, and SREM. 10 refs.

45. [Belford and Taylor 1976].
Belford, P. C., and D. S. Taylor. "Specification Verification—A Key to Improving Software Reliability." In *Symposium on Computer Software Engineering.* New York: Polytechnic Press, 1976. pp. 83–96.

Proving the correctness of software presupposes the existence of a proper requirements specification. This paper emphasizes the need to verify specifications formally before program design or implementation is attempted. The paper proposes writing specifications in a formal language; writing an analyzer and simulator to confirm that the specifications lack inherent conflicts, discrepancies, omissions, and incompleteness, and embody the customer's actual needs. 22 refs.

46. [Belford 1978].
Belford, P. C. "Experience Utilizing Components of the Software Development System." In *IEEE COMPSAC '78,* Washington D.C.: Computer Society Press of the Institute of Electrical and Electronics Engineers, 1978. pp. 340–45.

Describes components of the Software Development System (SDS) developed for the U.S. Army SDCATC. SDS consists of REVS, a process design language, a standard system verification diagram, and comprehensive verification and validation testing procedures. 14 refs.

47. [Belkhouche 1985].
Belkhouche, B. "Compilation of Specification Languages as a Basis for Rapid and Efficient Prototyping." In *Third IEEE International Workshop on Software Specification and Design,* Washington D.C.: Computer Society Press of the Institute of Electrical and Electronics Engineers. 1985, pp. 16–19.

Brief description of a Tulane University data abstraction to PL/I translator. 11 refs.

48. [Bell and Bixler 1976].
Bell, T. E., and D. C. Bixler. "A Flow-Oriented Requirements Statement Language." In *Symposium on Computer Software Engineering.* New York: Polytechnic Press, 1976, pp. 109–22.

Describes a language called Requirements Statement Language (RSL) developed by TRW for the U.S. Army SDCATC. 15 refs.

49. [Bell and Thayer 1976].

Bell, T. E., and T. A. Thayer. "Software Requirements: Are They Really a Problem?" In *Second International Conference on Software Engineering,* Washington D.C.: Computer Society Press of the Institute of Electrical and Electronics Engineers, 1976. pp. 61–68.

Classic paper describing two controlled experiments (one small student project and one large-scale software problem) that analyze types of problems in requirements specification as perceived by involved parties. Categorizes types of errors found in a requirements document; dismisses the philosophy that anything a customer wants can be a requirement. Also dismisses use of the term requirements to define what is stated in any phase that must be fulfilled in the subsequent phase. 9 refs.

50. [Bell et al. 1977].

Bell, T. E., et al. "An Extendable Approach to Computer-Aided Software Requirements Engineering." *IEEE Transactions on Software Engineering* **3,** 1 (January 1977): 49–60.

The Requirements Engineering and Validation System (REVS) that processes RSL is described in detail. Provides an excellent overview of early research on requirements performed by TRW for the U.S. Army SDCATC. Overviews the history of the requirements methodology SREM and the requirements language RSL. 20 refs.

51. [Ben-Menachem and Marliss 1980].

Ben-Menachem, M., and G. Marliss. "A Review of Requirements Analysis Technologies." Paper presented at *Fifteenth Annual Conference of the IPA,* Jerusalem, November 1980.

A superficial comparison of HIPO, structure charts, Warnier-Orr diagrams, USE.IT, SADT, information analysis, JSD, REVS, and PSL/PSA. 15 refs.

52. [Ben-Menachem et al. 1981].

Ben-Menachem, M., et al. "Rapid Prototyping of EDP Systems." Paper presented at *Sixteenth Annual Conference of the IPA,* Jerusalem, November 1981.

An interesting paper that (1) defines the ideal environment for prototyping and (2) describes one particular prototyping effort. This paper states that the primary purpose of a prototype is to test user requirements in order to decrease user criticism, change orders, and maintenance costs. A brief set of guidelines are provided to define the ideal prototyping environment—a fast-to-generate programming language (e.g., APL, RAMIS II, FOCUS, SETL, SNOBOL); a highly interactive debugging environment; and a reusability library to construct prototypes from previously tested primitives rapidly. 5 refs.

53. [Benoit et al. 1977].

Benoit, W. E., et al. *REVS Maintenance Manual, SREP Final Report.* Vol. 3. TRW Report CDRL C005. Huntsville, Ala., August 1977. See Alford and Dyer for Vols. 1 and 2.

A thorough description of the internal workings of TRW's REVS software. The BNF syntax and semantics are given for all RSL statements. For all modules, flow charts, inputs, outputs, and functional descriptions are given in this two-inch thick report. 19 refs.

54. [Berliner and Zave 1987].

Berliner, E., and P. Zave. "An Experiment in Technology Transfer: PAISLey Specification of Requirements for an Undersea Lightwave Cable System." In *Ninth IEEE International Conference on Software Engineering,* Washington D.C.: Computer Society Press of the Institute of Electrical and Electronics Engineers, 1987, pp. 42–50.

Reports on the partial success of using PAISLey on a real product. 14 refs.

55. [Berzins and Gray 1985].

Berzins, V., and M. Gray. "Analysis and Design in MSG 84: Formalizing Functional Specifications." *IEEE Transactions on Software Engineering* **11,** 8 (August 1985): 657–70.

What a great opening:

> There is a fair amount of agreement that the early stages of the software life cycle consist of requirements definition, functional specification, and design. There is a lack of agreement on the meaning of these terms, and no precise definition of the activities that are performed in each stage. The result is often a chaotic process, where all aspects of design are mixed together, resulting in software products that have cumbersome and complicated user interfaces and that do not satisfy user needs.

Berzins uses the term "requirements definition" where we have used "problem analysis," and the term "functional specification" where we have used "writing the SRS." A language called MSG.84 is presented to define functional specifications formally. MSG.84 is designed for system designers to read easily; it is expected that some tool could be developed in the future to translate MSG.84 automatically into a language for users to comprehend easily. MSG.84 is based on the actor model of computation, messages and events for communication, and abstraction. Using these concepts, the writer of an MSG.84 SRS can create transforms, FSMs, and data abstractions. A specification is provided for a trivial example—a simple editor. 34 refs.

56. [Bethke et al. 1981].

Bethke, F. J., et al. "Improving the Usability of Programming Publications." *IBM Systems Journal* **20,** 3 (1981): 306–20.

Although not written specifically for requirements specifications, this paper defines the attributes of any well-written document that describes software. These attributes are consistency, use of pointers, useful organization, simplicity, concreteness, naturalness, completeness, accuracy, and relevance. The paper describes a useful method of organizing a document around user-perceived tasks and provides a methodology to incorporate this organization and evaluate the degree to which a document processes the preceding attributes. 7 refs.

57. [Bianchi et al. 1980].

Bianchi, G., et al. "Requirements Specification—Today and Tomorrow." Panel discussion at the *IFIP/IFAC Real-Time Programming Workshop,* Oxford, England: Pergamon Press, 1981, 1980, pp. 121—27.

A general discussion by five people concerning the difference between writing a requirement specification for the ultimate system user or the system designer. The discussion lacks direction. No refs.

58. **[Biewald et al. 1980].**

Biewald, J., et al. "Real-Time Features of EPOS: Formulation, Evaluation, and Documentation." In *IFIP/IFAC Real-Time Programming Workshop,* Oxford, England: Pergamon Press, 1980, pp. 95–100.

Used in all phases of software development, the EPOS system enforces a systematic top-down design of a real-time system. EPOS-R, used during requirements writing, is described only briefly as an outline in which free-form English is inserted. 7 refs.

59. **[Birrell and Ould 1985].**

Birrell, N., and M. Ould. *A Practical Handbook for Software Development.* Cambridge, Eng.: Cambridge University Press, 1985.

Chapter 5 provides brief summaries of PSL/PSA, SASS, SADT, SREM, USE.IT, FSMs, Petri nets, Jackson System Development, CORE, and SDS/RSRE. Compares most by using a common example, an image-processing system called VISTA. Contains one of the most extensive bibliographies on software engineering available. 500 refs.

60. **[Blackhurst and Gandee 1976].**

Blackhurst, I., and J. S. Gandee. "Call Description Language." *Electrical Communication* **52** (1976): 202–6.

Describes a language called CDL that can be used to define functional characteristics of telephone systems. Once specified in CDL, the specification is checked for consistency by a CDL compiler. The compiler also automatically generates code to be run (i.e., interpreted) on the actual target machine. No refs.

61. **[Blackledge 1981].**

Blackledge, P. "The Selection of a Specification Language." In *Fourth International Conference on Software Engineering for Telecommunication Switching Systems,* London: Institution of Electrical Engineers, July 1981. pp. 25–30.

Defines a set of criteria for a requirements language suitable for specifying telecommunication systems. A large number of languages and their associated support tools are described and analyzed. The criteria are formality, comprehensibility, conciseness, limiting to *what* and not *how,* complexity handling, modifiability, and tolerance of incompleteness. 72 refs.

62. **[Blank and Krijger 1983].**

Blank, J., and M. Krijger, eds. *Software Engineering: Methods and Techniques.* New York: Wiley, 1983.

63. **[Bleser and Foley 1982].**

Bleser, T., and J. D. Foley. "Towards Specifying and Evaluating the Human Factors of User-Computer Interfaces." In *ACM Human Factors in Computing Systems,* New York: ACM Press of the Association for Computing Machinery, 1982, pp. 309–14.

64. **[Blum 1989].**

Blum, B. "Controversy: Volume, Distance, and Productivity." Unpublished manuscript; may appear in *Journal of Systems and Software.* 1989-1990

65. **[Blumofe and Hecht 1988].**
Blumofe, R., and A. Hecht. "Executing Real-Time Structured Analysis Specifications." *ACM Software Engineering Notes* **13,** 3 (July 1988): 32–40.

Describes an extension to Cadre's Teamwork tool that simulates the movement of data through a data flow diagram. The only simulation performed is in the presence or absence of a data item or control signal; no data paths have values. Two useful errors in DFDs are detected—deadlock detection and unreachable states. 12 refs.

66. **[Boar 1984].**
Boar, B. *Application Prototyping.* New York: Wiley, 1984.

Discusses the feasibility of prototyping business applications in lieu of writing requirements. No refs.

67. **[Boar 1986].**
Boar, B. "Application Prototyping: A Life Cycle Perspective." *Journal of Systems Management* (February 1986): 25–31.

68. **[Boehm 1974].**
Boehm, B. W. "Some Steps toward Formal and Automated Aids to Software Requirements Analysis and Design." In *IFIPS,* Amsterdam: North-Holland, 1974, pp. 192–97.

One of the earliest papers that addresses the need for automated requirements tools. The author stresses that requirements must define the needs of the prospective user in terms of sequences of preferred actions. Some techniques for checking relationships between requirements and design are explored. 16 refs.

69. **[Boehm et al. 1975].**
Boehm, B. W., et al. "Some Experience with Automated Aids to the Design of Large-Scale Reliable Software." *ACM SIGPLAN Notices* **10,** 6 (June 1975): 105–13; also appears in *IEEE Transactions on Software Engineering,* **1,** 1 (March 1975): 125–33.

A good analysis of the types of errors that occur in large and small programming projects. Very little in the paper addresses requirements per se, but the paper discusses the high degree of success achieved when a thorough consistency analysis is performed at one level (in this case, design) before tackling the next level (in this case, implementation). 16 refs.

70. **[Boehm 1976].**
Boehm, B. W. "Software Engineering." *IEEE Transactions on Computers* **25,** 12 (December 1976): 1226–41.

A classic paper defining the term "software engineering" and outlining the phases of the software life cycle. Pages 1227–30 define requirements and briefly describe and contrast available requirements languages and tools. 104 refs.

71. **[Boehm 1979].**
Boehm, B. W. "Guidelines for Verifying and Validating Software Requirements and Design Specifications." In *EuroIFIP Congress,* Amsterdam: North-Holland, 1979, pp. 711–20.

72. **[Boehm 1979a].**
    Boehm, B. W. "Software Requirements Engineering," in "Software Engineering: R&D Trends and Defense Needs." In *Research Directions in Software Technology*, ed. P. Wegner. Cambridge, Mass.: MIT Press, 1979. pp. 44–51.

    A good general description of the 1979 state-of-the-art in requirements. Boehm discusses the use of English, PSL/PSA, and REVS as requirements tools. The implication of automatic programming on requirements is also briefly explored. Although this entire paper (pp. 44–86) is a must for software engineering technologists, the section on requirements itself is by necessity too brief to provide much insight. 17 refs.

73. **[Boehm 1984].**
    Boehm, B. W. "Verifying and Validating Software Requirements and Design Specifications." *IEEE Software* **1,** 1 (January 1984): 75–88.

    Defines manual and automated techniques for uncovering incompleteness, inconsistencies, and infeasibilities in SRSs. 16 refs.

74. **[Boehm et al. 1984].**
    Boehm, B. W., et al. "Prototyping vs. Specifying: a Multiproject Experiment." *IEEE Transactions on Software Engineering* **10,** 3 (May 1984): 290–303.

    Results of a university experiment where seven teams of students were given a choice of using prototyping or traditional approaches to the same problem. The study is somewhat flawed because it compares the traditionally developed system to a throwaway prototype rather than to the system developed based on what was learned from using the throwaway prototype. 13 refs.

75. **[Boehm 1986].**
    Boehm, B. W. "A Spiral Model of Software Development and Enhancement." *ACM Software Engineering Notes* **11,** 4 (August 1986): 16–24. Reprinted in *IEEE Computer* **21,** 5 (May 1988): 61–72.

    Presents an alternative to the waterfall model, called the *spiral model*. Each iteration in the spiral model includes the definition of objectives and constraints, a risk analysis, and implementation of the plan. It may include a prototype, or full-scale product development. 17 refs.

76. **[Booch 1986].**
    Booch, G. "Object-Oriented Development." *IEEE Transactions on Software Engineering* **12,** 2 (February 1986): 211–21.

    Details of designing systems in which each layer of the decomposition is composed solely of objects that mirror the real world's real or abstract entities. Although aimed entirely at the design stage, concepts of object-oriented design apply well to requirements. 33 refs.

77. **[Borgida et al. 1985].**
    Borgida, A., et al. "Knowledge Representation as the Basis for Requirements Specification." *IEEE Computer* **18,** 4 (April 1985): 82–91.

    Recognizing that there is a need to perform a problem analysis of the environment prior to writing an SRS, this paper (1) presents a language called RML that can be used to capture attributes of, and interrelationships between, objects in the real world and (2) advocates that this serve as the SRS. 13 refs.

78. **[Borgida and Greenspan n. d.].**

Borgida, A., and S. Greenspan. "A Requirements Modeling Language and its Semantics." Unknown origin. pp. 111–34.

Uses the term "requirements specification" for the step in which analysts capture all information about the organization that has a problem. Thus Borgida and Greenspan use this term in the same way as I use the term "problem analysis." This paper defines the requirements modeling language (RML) that can be used to capture models of the real world using an object-oriented approach augmented with assertions. Using RML one models the world by defining entities in the world (modeled as objects), events that change those entities (modeled as objects), and assertions about objects. RML also encourages multiple viewpoints of all entities, events, and assertions and of course provides for the definition of object classes and the inheritance of traits among classes. The majority of this paper provides the formal specification of the RML language. 30 refs.

79. **[Bosyj 1976].**

Bosyj, M. *A Program for the Design of Procurement Systems.* M.S. thesis. Massachusetts Institute of Technology, 1976.

Describes a program called PROCTOR that presents multiple-choice questions to a potential computer customer in order to define computer-processing requirements for a company. The program is designed for use by companies whose primary business is wholesale and retail without manufacturing functions. Answers to the questions are stored in a data base called OWL, which was designed to store conceptual knowledge. 31 refs.

80. **[Boute 1981].**

Boute, R. T. "Towards System Specification Languages." *Fourth International Conference on Software Engineering for Telecommunication Switching Systems,* University of Warwick, Coventry, U.K., London: Institution of Electrical Engineers July 1981. pp. 31–37.

A condemnation of using pure finite state machines for specifying complex real-time systems. This criticism is based on (1) insufficient level of abstraction, (2) insufficient power of expression, and (3) lack of "structured" rules. The author proposes using nondeterministic multistring dialogue grammars as an improved alternative. 21 refs.

81. **[Boydstun et al. 1980].**

Boydstun, L. E., et al. "Computer-Aided Modeling of Information Systems." In *IEEE COMPSAC '80,* Washington D.C: Computer Society Press of the Institute of Electrical and Electronics Engineers, 1980, pp. 37–41.

Describes the automatic derivation of dynamic system modeling programs from the PSL/PSA system description data base. The system's performance and design characteristics are written in the System Description Language (SDL), a language based on the entity–relationship–attribute model. Modeling programs are generated using SIMSCRIPT. Because the simulation program is derived automatically from SDL, a change in the system definition automatically makes the corresponding change to the simulation. 15 refs.

82. **[Brackett and McGowan 1977].**
Brackett, J. W., and C. L. McGowan. *Applying SADT to Large System Problems.* SofTech Report TP-059. Waltham, Mass., 1977. Also appears in *Conference on Life Cycle Management* (August 1977): 539–51.

Provides an excellent overview of SADT, stressing its ability to document a wide range of problem analyses in a variety of applications. Some actual case studies using SADT are described. 11 refs.

83. **[Braek 1979].**
Braek, R. *Functional Specification and Description Languages as a Practical Tool for Improved System Quality.* University of Trondheim Electronics Research Laboratory Report no. STF44-A79166. September 1979. Also presented at *Third World Telecommunication Forum,* Geneva, September 1979.

Contains a wide variety of both useful and highly contradictory suggestions. First on the plus side, the paper proposes writing requirements specifications from a situation-orientation perspective rather than activity orientation. This concept might be new to telephony, but it certainly is not new to requirements definition. Also on the plus side, the author claims that situation-oriented requirements provide more design options. On the minus side however, the paper proposes an awkward methodology that even a phase diagram (Figure 2.1) cannot help explain. Also on the minus side, a set of picture drawing rules are given that have little or no intuitive meaning; the conventions are obviously the result of years of inbreeding within one particular company and not particularly useful to anyone else. The author states that "we must therefore consider situation oriented descriptions as having superior quality assurance properties...and should therefore be applied whenever practically possible." It might be true, but this illogical paper did not convince me. 6 refs.

84. **[Brandenstein et al. 1987].**
Brandenstein, A., et al. "Prototyping: A New Role for DARPA." *AFCEA's The Evolving World of C³I Conference,* Washington, D. C.: AFCEA Press, July 1987.

Describes a new charter for DARPA—Prototyping. In particular this role is for product prototypes, not necessarily software prototypes. These types are recognized: Experimental (to demonstrate technological feasibility), developmental (to gain confidence before full-scale development), and preproduction (to validate detail characteristics prior to quantity production). Most of the paper deals with organizational issues within DARPA and prototype acquisition strategies. Software per se is not mentioned. No refs.

85. **[Brathwaite 1988].**
Brathwaite, K. *Analysis, Design, and Implementation of Data Dictionaries.* New York: McGraw-Hill, 1988.

This book uses the term data dictionary (DD) in the broadest possible way—any repository for information in which that information has interrelationships. Chapters are devoted to how to design an in-house DD; how to enter data into a DD; use of DDs in distributed data processing and office automation, and as a tool for data base design, security, standards, and performance. 20 refs.

86. **[Bravaco and Yadav 1985].**
Bravaco, R., and S. Yadav. "Requirement Definition Architecture—an Overview."
Computers in Industry **6**, 4 (August 1985).

87. **[Bruno and Manchetto 1986].**
Bruno, G., and G. Manchetto. "Process-Translatable Petri Nets for the Rapid
Prototyping of Process Control Systems." *IEEE Transactions on Software Engi-
neering* **12**, 2 (February 1986): 346–57.

Describes PROT nets (an extension to Petri nets) that can be used to provide
operational specifications for real-time systems in general, and process control
systems specifically. PROT nets extend Petri nets in a variety of ways: Nets may
have types, tokens may carry attributes and may be assigned priorities, transitions
may be decomposed, and predicates may be placed on transitions to selectively
allow or bar the movement of particular tokens over them. An example is given of
the application of PROT nets to an automated conveyor-based warehouse transportation system. There is a brief summary of how PROT nets can be automatically
translated into Ada to prototype applications rapidly. 39 refs.

88. **[Bruno and Morisio 1987].**
Bruno, G., and M. Morisio. "An Executable Specification Methodology: Its Application to Computer-Integrated Manufacturing Systems." In *IEEE COMPSAC '87,*
Washington D.C.: Computer Society Press of the Institute of Electrical and Electronics Engineers. 1987, pp. 714–20.

Provides a language and describes a tool that supports PROT nets (see other Bruno
paper). A simple example is given. 21 refs.

89. **[Bruno et al. 1988].**
Bruno, G., et al. "A Knowledge-Based System Approach to the Development of a
System Functional Requirement Specification Processor." In *IEEE COMPSAC '88,*
1988, pp. 387–94.

Based on the theory presented in [Davis and Rauscher 1979a], this paper describes
a tool called the System Functional Requirement (SFR) processor that checks SRSs
for incompleteness, inconsistency, ambiguity, and redundancy. This tool is unique
because it is knowledge-based, with the knowledge base containing information
about the application domain for which the SRS is being written. 15 refs.

90. **[Bruyn et al. 1988].**
Bruyn, W., et al. "ESML: An Extended Systems Modeling Language Based on the
Data Flow Diagram." *ACM Software Engineering Notes* **13**, 1 (January 1988):
58–67.

A proposal to combine the best attributes of Ward/Mellor and Hatley/Pirbhai
extensions to structured analysis. Flow (i.e., data) transformations are shown
as solid rectangles with rounded corners. Control transformations are dotted
rectangles with rounded corners. Terminators are rectangles. Value bearing
(i.e., data) flows are solid arrows with two kinds of arrow heads to reflect
continuous versus intermittent data. Non–value-bearing (i.e., event) flows are
dotted arrows. Seven special-purpose messages can be transmitted. The notation for data stores differentiates between depletable and nondepletable stores.
Control transforms can be represented only as finite state machines. A number
of examples are given. 9 refs.

91. **[Bryssine 1988].**

Bryssine, A. "The Real-Life Use of SADT and MACH in Projects Relating to Technical Management at Sodeteg TAI." *International Workshop: Software Engineering and Its Applications,* Toulouse, France, December 1988. Nanterre, France: EC2.

92. **[Budde and Sylla 1984].**

Budde, R., and K.-H. Sylla. "From Application Domain Modelling to Target System." In *Approaches to Prototyping,* R. Budde et al., eds. Berlin: Springer-Verlag, 1984.

Proposes a well-thought-out approach to prototyping using object-oriented development. As in the case of most object-oriented approaches, problem analysis leads quite naturally into an obvious system design. The Budde approach performs problem analysis followed by a prototype construction that serves as a blueprint for full-scale development. As much functionality as possible is incorporated into the prototype, but performance, recovery, and portability are lightly downplayed. One unique idea here is that the prototype's architecture should be identical to the final product. 13 refs.

93. **[Burns et al. 1979]**

Burns, F., et al. *Current Software Requirements Engineering Technology.* TRW Systems Group. Huntsville, Ala., August 1979.

94. **[Cairns 1975].**

Cairns, G. "Meeting Software Requirements." *Computing Weekly* **18,** 449 (June 1975).

95. **[Cameron 1983].**

Cameron, J. *Tutorial: JSP and JSD: The Jackson Approach to Software Development.* In IEEE Catalog EH0206-3. Washington D.C.: Computer Society Press of the Institute of Electrical and Electronics Engineers, 1983.

96. **[Canning 1977].**

Canning, R. "Getting the Requirements Right." *EDP Analyst* **15,** 7 (July 1977): 1–14.

97. **[Carlson 1979].**

Carlson, W. "Business Information and Analysis Technique (BIAIT)—the New Horizon." *Database* (Spring 1979): 3–9.

98. **[Carrio 1987].**

Carrio, M., Jr. "The Technology Life Cycle and Ada." Origin unknown, 1987. Available from Teledyne Brown Engineering, Huntsville, Ala. Provides a short synopsis of problems in the traditional waterfall life cycle and suggests the need for prototyping, reuse, knowledge-based systems, generic instantiations, data base applications, and automated tools. 18 refs.

99. **[Casey 1981].**

Casey, B. "The Impact of the Technical Communicator on Software Requirements." *Journal of Technical Writing and Communication* **11,** 4 (1981): 361–72.

Discusses how a professional communicator can provide valuable input to the requirements development process. Specifically four services are addressed—analyzing the expected specification audience, analyzing the functional needs of the customer, analyzing the human factors, and the actual writing of the requirements specification. 9 refs.

100. **[Casey and Taylor 1981].**

Casey, B. E., and B. J. Taylor. "Writing Requirements in English: A Natural Alternative." In *IEEE Software Engineering Standards Workshop,* Washington D.C.: Computer Society Press of the Institute of Electrical and Electronics Engineers. 1981, pp. 95–101.

Suggests why currently available formal requirements systems are not being widely used. One reason is that formal languages are difficult for the lay-person to understand. This paper proposes using enough key words in an English language specification so that limited consistency checking with an automated tool is feasible, but not so many key words that the resulting document becomes unreadable. The proposed language is called *behavioral English.* Examples are given of how to state various classes of requirements in a specification in behavioral English. 11 refs.

101. **[CCITT 1977].**

CCITT. *Programming Languages for Stored-Program Control Exchanges.* Vol. VI.4. International Telecommuncations Union. Geneva, 1977.

Defines the System Design Language (SDL) that can be used to describe the external behavior, design, and implementation of real-time systems. The CCITT has officially approved the graphic format of this language but not the textual form.

102. **[Celko et al. 1983].**

Celko, J., et al. "A Demonstration of Three Requirements Language Systems." *ACM SIGPLAN Notices* **18,** 1 (January 1983): 9–14.

A comparative analysis of PSL/PSA, IORL, and REVS. Requirements were written using all three requirements systems for the Standard Army Maintenance System (SAMS). A comparison was made of the three tools based on five areas (1) amount of time needed, (2) types and number of reports produced, (3) ability to trace requirements back to the original SAMS specification document, (4) types of errors detected by systems in the SAMS requirements specification, and (5) ease of learning to use the tool. According to the results, IORL was most easily learned, and the REVS least; IORL was the cheapest to use, REVS the most expensive. The REVS analysis and graphics capabilities were the best of all. PSL/PSA offered the most flexibility and had the largest user base. 11 refs.

103. **[Chafin 1980].**

Chafin, R. L. "The System Analyst and Software Requirements Specification." In *IEEE COMPSAC '80,* Washington D.C.: Computer Society Press of the Institute of Electrical and Electronics Engineers. 1980, pp. 254–58.

Describes human interface problems between various players involved in the requirements specification phase in detail. The systems analyst must resolve discrepancies between customer and developer in terms of frame of reference, common terminology, depth of detail, and time span. 19 refs.

104. **[Chandrasekharan et al. 1985].**

Chandrasekharan, M., et al. "Requirements-Based Testing of Real-Time Systems: Modeling for Testability." *IEEE Computer* **18,** 4 (April 1985): 71–80.

Provides an excellent summary of the formal basis for the Requirements Language Processor (RLP). Describes how test coverage criteria and test constraints can be used to drive a tool to generate an effective set of system tests automatically from an SRS. Also provides some useful data on the complexity of (1) writing FSM-based SRSs for large applications and (2) generating tests. In particular a large telephone switching system (of approximately 500K lines of code) could be specified with five hundred states and three thousand transitions between states. The test generation process took only a few seconds of CPU time. 35 refs.

105. **[Chang et al. 1987].**

Chang, C. K., et al. "A New Design Approach of Real-Time Distributed Software Systems." In *IEEE COMPSAC '87,* Washington D.C.: Computer Society Press of the Institute of Electrical and Electronics Engineers, 1987, pp. 474–79.

Although the title of this paper implies that it presents a *design* approach, the term is used generically to refer to the entire development process. The approach was used experimentally on the 5 ESS switching system. In essence this paper says that the design process entails modeling the behavior of the system with respect to its environment, in five steps: (1) user needs, (2) generic services, (3) service views, (4) functional components, and (5) kernel views. The first corresponds to problem analysis, the next two correspond to defining external behavior, and the last two to design. This paper presents an extended modified Petri net (EMPN) language for specifying data flow, timing, and multiple external views of software behavior. 27 refs.

106. **[Chapin 1979].**

Chapin, N. "Some Structured Analysis Techniques." *Data Base* **10,** 3 (March 1979): 16–23.

107. **[Charette 1986].**

Charette, R. *Software Engineering Environments.* New York: McGraw-Hill, 1986. Although a general software engineering textbook, this book contains one of the broadest surveys of requirements tools and techniques in the literature prior to the book you are now reading. Charette uses the terms *requirements analysis* for problem analysis, and *specification* for writing an SRS. Chapters 3 and 4 explore these two topics, respectively.

108. **[Chen and Chou 1988].**

Chen, P., and C. Chou. "The Requirement Model in a Knowledge-Based Rapid Prototyping System." In *IEEE COMPSAC '88,* Washington, D.C.: Computer Society Press of the Institute of Electrical and Electronics Engineers, 1988, pp. 418–26.

109. **[Cheng et al. 1982].**

Cheng, L., et al. "Simulation of an I/O-Driven Requirements Language." In *IEEE COMPSAC '82,* Washington, D.C.: Computer Society Press of the Institute of Electrical and Electronics Engineers, 1982, pp. 433–41.

Describes a tool that accepts as input a specification of a system using IORL and checks it for consistency. The consistency checking emphasizes issues relating to concurrency and timing—message-passing and deadlocking problems. 13 refs.

110. **[Cherry 1987].**
      Cherry, G. "PAMELA II: Full Support for Object-Oriented Design and Behavioral
      Specification." In *Methodologies and Tools for Real-Time Systems: IV.* Washington,
      D.C.: National Institute for Software Quality and Productivity. September 1987.

111. **[Chi 1985].**
      Chi, U. H. "Formal Specification of User Interfaces: A Comparison and Evaluation
      of Four Axiomatic Approaches." *IEEE Transactions on Software Engineering* **11,** 8
      (August 1985): 671–85.

      Specifies a simple commercial line editor using four different approaches—alge-
      braic, Guttag-Horning extended algebraic, event algebra, and set theoretic. 28 refs.

112. **[Childs et al. 1983].**
      Childs, D., et al. "Software Analysis and Management System (USAMS)—Evalu-
      ation of SREM/REVS/RSL and PSL/PSA." In *IEEE Symposium on Application and
      Assessment of Automated Tools for Software Development,* Washington, D.C.:
      Computer Society Press of the Institute of Electrical and Electronics Engineers,
      1983.

113. **[Chmura and Weiss 1982].**
      Chmura, L., and D. Weiss. *The A-7E Software Requirements Document: Three Years
      of Change Data.* Navy Research Laboratory Memorandum Report 4938. Washing-
      ton, D.C., November 1982. 16 refs.

114. **[Chow 1977].**
      Chow, T. S. "Testing Software Design Modeled by Finite State Machines." In *IEEE
      COMPSAC '77,* Washington, D.C.: Computer Society Press of the Institute of
      Electrical and Electronics Engineers, 1977, pp. 58–64.; also in *IEEE Transactions
      on Software Engineering* **4,** 3 (May 1978): 178–87.

      Discusses how testing can be partially automated when requirements for a system
      have been specified purely as sequences of stimuli and corresponding system
      responses. An example shows that tests can be generated and informal statements
      made about the resulting reliability of the tested software. 18 refs.

115. **[Christensen and Kreplin 1984].**
      Christensen, N., and K.-D. Kreplin. "Prototyping of User Interfaces." In *Approaches
      to Prototyping,* R. Budde et al., eds. Berlin: Springer-Verlag, 1984. pp. 58–67.

      Brief summary of the use of prototypes to aid in the requirements specification of
      text-oriented interactive software. 6 refs.

116. **[Churchman 1975].**
      Churchman, W. "Functional Approach to Turnkey System Procurement." In *NCC
      '75,* Montvale, New Jersey: AFIPS Press of the American Federation of Information
      Processing Societies, 1975, pp. 789-92.

      Advocates that computer systems should not be purchased solely by examining
      physical characteristics. The paper describes in very general terms five other
      characteristics (besides physical) that should be defined before purchasing comput-
      ers. No refs.

117. **[Chvalovsky 1983].**
Chvalovsky, V. "Decision Tables." *Software-Practice and Experience* **13** (1983): 423–49.

118. **[Clapp 1987].**
Clapp, J. "Rapid Prototyping for Risk Management." In *IEEE COMPSAC '87*, Washington D.C.: Computer Society Press of the Institute of Electrical and Electronics Engineers, 1987, pp. 17–22.

Brief summary of the key reasons for prototyping. 5 refs.

119. **[Clements 1981].**
Clements, P. C. *Function Specification for the A-7E Function-Driver Module*. Naval Research Laboratory. Washington, D.C., November 1981.

120. **[Coad and Yourdon 1989].**
Coad, P., and E. Yourdon. *OOA—Object-Oriented Analysis*. Englewood Cliffs, N.J.: Prentice Hall, 1989.

121. **[Combelic 1978].**
Combelic, D. "User Experience with New Software Methods." In *National Computer Conference* (AFIPS) **47** (1978): 631–33. Montvale, New Jersey: AFIPS Press of the American Federation of Information Processing Societies.

122. **[Computer Science Corporation 1973].**
Computer Science Corporation. *A User's Guide to the THREADS Management System*. November 1973.

123. **[Conn 1977].**
Conn, A. P. "Specification of Reliable Large-Scale Software Systems." Ph.D. diss. U. of California at Berkeley, 1977.

Using the term *specification* to mean a formal description of a system at any stage of its development (e.g., requirements, design), the author defines a language suitable for specification. This thesis also describes the types of automatic checking that a computer could perform on such specifications. Details of the language syntax and semantics as well as a number of examples are given. 87 refs.

124. **[Conn 1979].**
Conn, A. P. "A Methodology for Broadening the Scope of Computer Requirements Definition." In *AIAA Second Computers in Aerospace Conference*, Washington D.C.: American Institute of Aeronautics and Astronautics, 1979, pp. 135–42.

An excellent addition to the knowledge base of requirements. States that most traditional requirements methodologies are primarily suitable for the specification of classes of systems that are well understood and for which actual systems have previously been built. The methodology described in this paper addresses classes of systems that are poorly understood, for which their requirements, their interfaces, and their environment are still vaguely understood. The methodology stresses the easy writing of free-form English, a framework for iteratively building on vaguely stated requirements and eventually producing a nonambiguous, consistent specification. Once English statements are defined (excellent examples are given), a requirements abstraction is used to cluster requirements and hide the yet-to-be-defined details of a requirement at any particular level. An *alternative* statement is introduced to allow the expression of alternative, and possibly contradictory, requirements. Again an excellent example is given. 23 refs.

125. [Conn 1979a].

Conn, A. P. "Representation of Decisions in a Requirements Specification Language." In *IEEE COMPSAC '79,* Washington D.C.: Computer Society Press of the Institute of Electrical and Electronics Engineers. 1979. pp. 113–16.

Assuming requirements specifications are defined as a tree of abstractions, this paper explores types of control structures needed to define decisions to be made by the system under specification. The author basically concludes that decision tables written as CASE and ELSE statements (for flexibility) are necessary. The author states that he is building a support system that supports these and other constructs. 8 refs.

126. [Conn 1979b].

Conn, A. P. "Towards Computer Assisted Requirements Definitions for Large-Scale Software Systems." Presented at *First International Symposium on Policy Analysis and Information Systems,* 1979, pp. 319–25.

Describes the use of an abstraction-based methodology to refine requirements. Simple but useful examples show how environmental and activity requirements can be stated. An interactive tool is described that stores requirements; prompts for additional information; and enables requirements writers to reorganize, refine, or restructure requirements. Requirements abstractions consist of specifications of interfaces, attributes, and functions. 12 refs.

127. [Conn 1980].

Conn, A. P. "Maintenance: A Key Element in Computer Requirements Definition." In *IEEE COMPSAC '80,* Washington D.C.: Computer Society Press of the Institute of Electrical and Electronics Engineers. 1980. pp. 401–6.

Emphasizes the need to consider maintenance as part of the entire iteratively applied software development process. Three qualities of the requirements phase are emphasized: (1) Requirements must be machine readable, (2) an audit trail of all changes to the requirements must be maintained, and (3) requirements should be hierarchically organized. This hierarchy should not correspond to the system design process but is essential for defining and accessing levels of details of the requirements. 21 refs.

128. [Coolahan and Roussopoulos 1983].

Coolahan, J. E., and N. Roussopoulos. "Timing Requirements for Time-Driven Systems Using Augmented Petri Nets." *IEEE Transactions of Software Engineering* **9,** 5 (September 1983): 603–16.

Well-written paper describing a method of using timing contraints defined in a requirements specification to derive detailed timing requirements that apply to individual modules in a software design. These individual timing requirements for modules are derived as sets of inequalities and thus enable the designer to do intelligent trade-off analyses in the event that particular modules perform more slowly or rapidly than originally expected. The theory described in the paper is developed using extended Petri nets. The Petri nets are augmented with time delays at places, transitions, and arbitrary paths through the Petri net (i.e., valid sequences of places and transitions). 13 refs.

129. **[Cooper and Hsia 1982].**

Cooper, J. W., and P. Hsia. "Scenario-Basd Prototypes for Requirements Identification." In *ACM SIGSOFT Workshop on Rapid Prototyping,* New York: ACM Press of the Association for Computing Machinery, 1982, pp. 17.1–17.11.

The first half of this paper describes inadequacies of most requirements languages and tools for helping the customer and the developer ascertain the product's requirements. Unfortunately most of this paper's survey of languages and tools comes from an AIRMICS study that examined tools used primarily during software design. On the other hand, had actual requirements tools and languages been surveyed, the same conclusion would probably have been reached. The second half of the paper proposes creating a technique of rapid prototyping driven off a set of scenarios that describe samples of the users' view of the system. The goal is to expend considerably less than the 10% of total system development cost as proposed by Gomaa. This paper is a proposal to do research; it is interesting because it asks some probing, though unanswered, questions. 44 refs.

130. **[Cox 1973].**

Cox, H. "The Constitution of an Adequate Software Specification." In *IEEE Organization and Management of Computer-Based Control and Automation Projects,* Washington D.C.: Computer Society Press of the Institute of Electrical and Electronics Engineers. 1973. pp. 35–41.

131. **[Cronhjort and Gallmo 1982].**

Cronhjort, B., and B. Gallmo. *A Model of the Industrial Product Development Process.* Ericsson Information Systems Report 1982-09-01 C TB BG 82010. Bromma, Sweden, 1982.

Uses the term *requirements analysis* to describe the initial planning stage, which starts with an analysis of competition, users' needs, technology, company goals, existing products, environment, laws, and standards and ends with a detailed description of a new product's behavior and characteristics. 3 refs.

132. **[Cunningham and Salih 1981].**

Cunningham, R. J., and A. M. Salih. "The Use of Verficiation-Oriented Software Specification in Telecommunication Engineering." *Fourth International Conference on Software Engineering for Telecommunicaton Switching Systems,* London: Institution of Electrical Engineers, 1981. pp. 38–42.

Describes a technique of using assertions for the formal specification of sequential function, data, and multiprocessing. 13 refs.

133. **[Cunningham et al. 1985].**

Cunningham, R. J., et al. "Formal Requirements Specification—The Forest Project." In *Third IEEE International Workshop on Specification and Design,* Washington D.C.: Computer Society Press of the Institute of Electrical and Electronics Engineers. 1985. pp. 186–91.

Three-fourths of this interesting short paper tears to pieces standard approaches to formal requirements specification (e.g., unnatural, unreadable, idiomatic, contentious semantics, flat). This paper demands that requirements specifications be written formally but not exhibit these traits. The authors are strong believers in proving the correctness of the result. The remaining fourth of this paper says the authors are looking at various existing techniques in order to select the best from each for their creation, called FOREST. 7 refs.

134. [DARPA 1987].

Defense Advanced Research Projects Agency. "Rapid Prototyping: Its Role in the Acquisition Process." *SIGNAL* **42,** 1 (September 1987): 73–76.

Brief summary of a panel session on DARPA's new role to encourage rapid prototyping of all systems, not just software. No refs.

135. [Dasarathy 1983].

Dasarathy, B. "Abstraction Mechanisms for Telecommunications Systems Specification." in *IEEE International Workshop on Software Development Tools for Telecommunications Systems,* Washington D.C.: Computer Society Press of the Institute of Electrical and Electronics Engineers, 1983.

Criticizing finite state machines for their lack of expressive power, this paper offers a number of useful alternatives for specifying real-time systems. The term *specification* is used here because the paper's author views the process of defining requirements through the final system implementation as a continuum in which increasingly more concrete levels of abstraction are incorporated into the model. The alternatives described include hierarchies of finite state machines, processes, Petri nets, set theory abstractions, and data abstractions. Each one is only briefly described in the paper, which is an abstract of a more complete talk. 16 refs.

136. [Dasarathy 1985].

Dasarathy, B. "Timing Constraints of Real-Time Systems: Constructs for Expressing Them, Methods of Validating Them." In *IEEE Real-Time Systems Symposium,* Washington D.C.: Computer Society Press of the Institute of Electrical and Electronics Engineers. 1982. Also appears in *IEEE Transactions on Software Engineering* **11,** 1 (January 1985): 80–86.

An excellent paper defining all classes of timing constraints that may appear in the requirements specification of real-time systems. Timing constraints can be classified using a number of different criteria. For example, they can be categorized as constraints on the system being specified or the environment of the system. Similarly they can be classified as maximal (no more than t time units may elapse), minimal (no less than t time units may elapse), or durational (an event must occur for t time units). In addition the author has isolated four classes of maximal and minimal timing contraints that apply to real-time systems—stimulus-stimulus, stimulus-response, response-stimulus, and response-response. These describe timing contraints between pairs of stimuli, between a stimuli to the system and the system response, between a system response and a subsequent stimulus, and between two responses, respectively. Note that the first and third define timing constraints on the system's environment, and the second and fourth define timing constraints on the system itself. 10 refs.

137. [Davis and Rataj 1978].

Davis, A. M., and W. J. Rataj. "Requirements Language Processing for the Effective Testing of Real-Time Systems." *ACM Software Engineering Notes* **3,** 5 (November 1978): 61–66.

An outdated paper describing the Requirements Language Processor (RLP) and how its use can help in the system testing of the specified system. The RLP generates a finite state machine model of the specified system. This model is then fed into a test plan generator, which produces a test plan capable of verifying whether a system behaves in the same way as the specified system is supposed to behave. 6 refs.

138. **[Davis and Rauscher 1979].**

Davis, A. M., and T. G. Rauscher. "A Survey of Techniques Used for Requirements Definition of Computer-Based Systems." *GTE Automatic Electric World-Wide Communications Journal* **17,** 5 (September 1979): 161–70.

Surveys six models of systems in use by a variety of requirements tools and methodologies. Compares and contrasts these models with regard to their usefulness and applicability to classes of problems. Models analyzed include finite state machines, stimulus-response sequences, input-process-output, R-nets, extended Petri nets, and bi-partite graphs. 20 refs.

139. **[Davis and Rauscher 1979a].**

Davis, A. M., and T. G. Rauscher. "Formal Techniques and Automatic Processing to Ensure Correctness in Requirements Specifications." In *IEEE Specifications of Reliable Software Conference,* Washington D.C.: Computer Society Press of the Institute of Electrical and Electronics Engineers, 1979, pp. 15–35.

Formally defines requirements for real-time systems, formally defines classes of errors that can occur in requirements, and briefly describes a tool called the Requirements Lanaguage Processor (RLP), which can determine the presence of those errors in a requirements specification. 23 refs.

140. **[Davis et al. 1979].**

Davis, A. M., et al. "RLP: An. Automated Tool for the Automatic Processing of Requirements." In *IEEE COMPSAC '79,* Washington D.C.: Computer Society Press of the Institute of Electrical and Electronics Engineers, (November 1979): 188–94. 1979. pp. 289–99. Also appears in *GTE Automatic Electric Worldwide Communications Journal* **17,** 6

Describes services provided to users of the Requirements Language Processor (RLP), which automatically checks consistency of requirements specifications. RLP processes requirements specifications written in any of a variety of applications-oriented requirements languages. From such specifications, RLP produces pretty-printed reports and a requirements data base that contains a finite state machine description whose behavior is identical to the system specified in the requirements. In addition RLP reports the presence of any inconsistency, incompleteness, or ambiguity. 23 refs.

141. **[Davis 1980].**

Davis, A. M. "Automating the Requirements Phase: Benefits to Later Phases of the Software Life Cycle." In *IEEE COMPSAC '80,* Washington D.C.: Computer Society Press of the Institute of Electrical and Electronics Engineers, 1980, pp. 42–48.

Describes how using an automated consistency-checking tool during requirements analysis can trigger cost savings during later stages of software development. A number of automated tools are described that depend on the earlier use of a requirements analyzer. These tools perform automatic test generation, system simulation, design, and prototype synthesis. 13 refs.

142. **[Davis 1982].**

Davis, A. M. "Rapid Prototyping Using Executable Requirements Specifications." *ACM Software Engineering Notes* **7**, 5 (December 1982): 39–44.

Describes a tool called the Feature Simulator that provides a rapid prototype of a real-time system. The tool is driven purely by the system's requirements. A number of techniques are presented that make the rapid prototype useful and easy to use. 15 refs.

143. **[Davis 1982a].**

Davis, A. M. "The Design of a Family of Applications-Oriented Requirements Languages." *IEEE Comptuer* **15**, 5 (May 1982): 21–28. Reprinted in *Selected Reprints in Software*, 2d ed. IEEE Computer Society. 1982. pp. 118–25. An earlier version appears in *GTE Automatic Electric Worldwide Communications Journal* **19**, 5 (September 1981): 169–74.

Describes attributes of well-designed readable machine-processable languages for specifying requirements of real-time systems. The thesis is that using a good language is more likely to result in a requirements specification that is understood by customers, designers, and managers. A variety of existing languages are analyzed and compared. An ideal set of languages is proposed that exhibit common properties. Each is tailored to a particular application area, all assume the identical system model, and all are organized by features and share common constructs for control and timing constraints. 28 refs.

144. **[Davis 1982b].**

Davis, A. M. "The Role of Requirements in the Automated Synthesis for Real-Time Systems." In *International Symposium on Current Issues of Requirements Environments*, edited by Y. Ohno. Amsterdam: North Holland Publ., 1982. pp. 151–58.

Describes a method of automatically generating software for real-time systems from a requirements specification. The scheme relies on a standard system architecture that can be table-driven to perform a variety of application domain functions. The automatic generator transforms requirements into tables that drive the real-time system. The variety of attributes that a requirements specification must possess in order to enable this are described in detail. 27 refs.

145. **[Davis 1988].**

Davis, A. M. "A Comparison of Techniques for the Specification of External Behavior of Systems." *Communications of the ACM* **31**, 9 (September 1988): 1098–1115.

A survey paper comparing and contrasting a dozen different tools/languages/techniques that aid in writing an SRS. 60 refs.

146. **[Davis 1988a].**

Davis, A. M. "A Taxonomy of the Early Stages of the Software Development Life Cycle." *Journal of Systems and Software* **8**, 4 (September 1988): 297–311.

Provides a taxonomy of the requirements phase of the software development life cycle to enable (1) a student of software engineering to compare and contrast different requirements techniques intelligently, (2) a researcher or toolsmith in the requirements domain to relate his/her work to the work of others, and (3) a company in need of a requirements tool to more accurately define what that need is. 38 refs.

147. **[Davis et al. 1988].**

Davis, A. M., et al. "A Strategy for Comparing Alternative Software Development Life Cycle Models." *IEEE Transactions on Software Engineering* **14,** 10 (October 1988): 1453–61.

Based on the assumption that user needs are either not well known at requirements definition time or user needs evolve continually during the development process, this paper provides a simple paradigm to use to compare or contrast alternative life cycle models (e.g., waterfall, evolutionary prototyping, throwaway prototyping, software synthesis, reusable components) in terms of their degree of user needs satisfaction. 12 refs.

148. **[Davis 1989].**

Davis, A. M. "ANSI-IEEE 830—IEEE Guide to Software Requirements." In *Handbook of Industrial Automation Standards,* edited by S. Cousins. Reading, Mass.: Addison-Wesley, 1989.

Summarizes the major purposes and contents of the IEEE standard on software requirements.

149. **[Davis 1989a].**

Davis, A. M. "The Analysis and Specification of Systems and Software Requirements." In *IEEE Tutorial: Systems and Software Requirements Engineering,* R. Thayer and M. Dorfman, eds. Washington, D.C.: IEEE, 1989.

150. **[Davis 1990].**

Davis, A. M. *Software Requirements: Analysis and Specification.* Englewood Cliffs, N.J.: Prentice-Hall, 1990.

Discusses most major schools of thought on requirements. Contains an annotated bibliography of 598 entries on every known paper, book, and report about issues relating to requirements.

151. **[DavisC and Vick 1977].**

Davis, C. G., and C. R. Vick. "The Software Development System." *IEEE Transactions on Software Engineering* **3,** 1 (January 1977): 69–84.

A classic paper summarizing requirements research supported by the U.S. Army SDCATC. Describes a comprehensive software development system called SDS that supports a variety of software engineering languages and tools. SDS has been particularly designed to aid in software development of systems that are highly reliable, difficult to test in vivo, large, complex, automated, and flexible (e.g., ballistic missile defense systems). The requirements methodology was undecided at the time of the article, but three alternatives had been explored—verification graphs, Petri nets, and finite state machines. The design methodology was called Process Design Methodology (PDM). 48 refs.

152. **[DavisC and Vick 1978].**

Davis, C. G., and C. R. Vick. "The Software Development System: Status and Evolution." In *IEEE COMPSAC '78,* Washington D.C.: Computer Society Press of the Institute of Electrical and Electronics Engineers. 1978, pp. 326–31.

Although its title implies an overview of SDS, a system of tools being developed by a variety of contractors to support SDCATC's goal of producing quality, reliable software for ballistic missile defense systems, the paper actually discusses the variety of testing strategies that the Army plans to use to validate the system's performance. The paper does provide a good statement of why the missile defense problem is unique. 15 refs.

153. **[DavisC 1980].**
Davis, C. G. "Software Requirements Engineering—a Tool Developer's View." Panel session at *NCC '80,* Montvale, New Jersey: AFIPS Press of the American Federation of Information Processing Societies, 1980.

This panel session enabled the audience to compare or contrast a wide variety of currently developed tools useful for requirements analysis. Panelists included Mack Alford, Michael Bethancourt, Alan Davis, Charles Everhart, Steven Lipka, and Hassan Sayani. Commentators included Leon Stucki and Raymond Yeh.

154. **[DavisG 1982].**
Davis, G. "Strategies for Information Requirements Determination." *IBM Systems Journal* **21** (1982): 4–30.

155. **[DavisM and Addleman 1986].**
Davis, M., and D. Addleman. "Practical Approach to Specification Technology Selection." *Journal of Systems and Software* **6** (1986): 285–94.

156. **[Dearnley and Mayhew 1983].**
Dearnley, P., and P. Mayhew. "In Favour of System Prototypes and Their Integration into the Systems Development Cycle." *Computer Journal* **26,** 1 (January 1983): 36–42.

157. **[DeMarco 1979].**
DeMarco, T. *Structured Analysis and System Specification.* Englewood Cliffs, N.J.: Prentice-Hall, 1979.

Describes the use of data flow diagrams, data dictionaries, structured English, decision tables, and decision trees to create a *structured specification.*

158. **[Demetrovics et al. 1982].**
Demetrovics, J., et al. "Specification Meta Systems." *IEEE Computer* **15,** 5 (May 1982): 29–35.

Consists of three completely independent and unrelated papers arranged sequentially. The first discusses the System Description and Logical Analyzer (SDLA), which has two components: (1) a meta system that enables users to define their own specification languages and (2) an interpreter that processes specification documents written in that language. The underlying system model is based on concepts and attributes. The second paper discusses the System Encyclopedia Management System (SEMS), which is described as almost identical to SDLA except that its underlying system model is the entity–relationship–attribute model. The third paper discusses using knowledge-based systems to process specifications in particular limited application domains. 14 refs.

159. **[Department of Defense 1988].**
Department of Defense. *Military Standard: Defense System Software Development.* DOD-STD-2167A. Washington, D.C., February 1988.

The official DoD standard for all defense system software development.

160. **[Derbenwick 1979].**
Derbenwick, L. F. "Tools for Requirements and Specifications." Unpublished review from the University of Connecticut. Storrs, Conn., 1979.

Contrasts a large variety of requirements and design languages, methodologies, and tools. 62 refs.

161. **[Desclaux 1988].**
   Desclaux, C. "ECCAO: Computer-Aided Requirement Capturing." *International Workshop on Software Engineering and Its Applications,* Toulouse, France, December 1988. Nanterre, France: EC2.

162. **[Deutsch 1988].**
   Deutsch, M. "Focusing Real-Time Systems Analysis on User Operations." *IEEE Software* **5,** 5 (September 1988): 39–50.

   Describes a three-step approach to constructing real-time systems: (1) Create an operations concept model, (2) create a requirements model, and (3) create an implementation model. The second and third steps are each followed by a validation step in which models are checked for consistency with the result from the first step. The operations concept model captures the behavior of each feature of the system as a stimulus-response sequence, described in a *system-verification diagram.* Requirements and implementation models use data flow diagrams extended with Ward's SA/RT. Ward's bottle-filling example is shown using Deutsch's three-step approach. 9 refs.

163. **[Devorkin and Oberndorf 1979].**
   Devorkin, D. B., and R. T. Oberndorf. *A Survey of State-of-the-Field of Requirements Methodology.* DTIC Technical Report AD-A075227, U.S. Army Institute for Research in Management Information and Computer Science. Atlanta, May 1979.

164. **[DeWolfe 1977].**
   DeWolfe, J. "Requirements Specification and Preliminary Design for Real-Time Systems." In *IEEE COMPSAC '77,* Washington D.C.: Computer Society Press of the Institute of Electrical and Electronics Engineers. 1977, pp. 17–23.

   For some real-time systems, the problem being solved is quite vague in the requirements analysis phase. Thus this paper suggests performing a very preliminary requirements phase followed by a straw dog design, called functional design. This functional design consists of sets of cooperating abstract processes. A technique is given to document these. A set of data flow diagrams with well-defined primitives are given. Once these have been defined, one returns to a more complete requirements analysis followed by a real design. One could consider the functional design as a virtual design, done to learn more about how the system should behave. 16 refs.

165. **[DeWolfe and Principato 1977].**
   DeWolfe, J., and R. Principato. *A Methodology for Requirements Specification and Preliminary Design of Real-Time Systems.* Draper Lab Report C-4923. Lexington, Mass., July 1977.

166. **[Diaz-Gonzalez 1987].**
   Diaz-Gonzalez, J. "The Requirements Engineering of Real-Time Systems: A Temporal Logic Approach." Ph.D. diss., University of Southwestern Louisiana, 1987.

167. **[Diaz-Gonzalez and Urban 1989].**
   Diaz-Gonzalez, J., and J. Urban. "A Requirements Engineering Environment for Real-Time Systems." In *IEEE Hawaii International Conference on System Sciences—22,* Washington D.C.: Computer Society Press of the Institute of Electrical and Electronics Engineers, 1989.

Presents an approach to requirements specification that includes the hierarchical definition of objects in the real world, description of each object in a real-life visual representation, and simulation of the system by animating those objects and their visual representations. 40 refs.

168. [Dickinson 1989].
Dickinson, B. *Developing Quality Systems.* New York: McGraw-Hill, 1989.

One of the most fascinating books I have read on DeMarco's style of structured analysis. The entire methodology is described in detail in this 350-page book using the methodology itself. Other than the appendices and a few pages of text preceding each of the three chapters, this book is entirely composed of data flow diagrams, data dictionaries, and process specifications. 17 refs.

169. [Dobbins 1987].
Dobbins, J. "ASA: An Automated Structured Requirements Analyzer with Rapid Prototyping." In *Conference on Methodologies and Tools for Real-Time Systems: IV,* Washington, D.C.: National Institute for Software Quality and Productivity, 1987.

170. [Dooley et al. 1980]
Dooley, B. L., et al. "Experience with Software Tools for Nuclear Process System Applications." In *IEEE COMPSAC '80,* Washington D.C.: Computer Society Press of the Institute of Electrical and Electronics Engineers, 1980, pp. 646–54.

Describes the application of SADT, RSL, flowcharts, and hierarchy charts to the development of nonproduction nuclear reactor control software. Two projects were undertaken; one using SADT, hierarchy charts, and flowcharts; the other SADT and RSL. The paper discusses each project and the tools and techniques applied in each case. Both projects were deemed successful by the authors. 16 refs.

171. [Dorfman and Flynn 1981].
Dorfman, M., and R. F. Flynn. "ARTS–An Automated Requirements Traceability System." In *AIAA Third Computers in Aerospace Conference,* Also appears in *Journal of Systems and Software* **4,** 1 (April 1984): 63–74. Washington D.C.: American Institute of Aeronautics and Astronautics. 1981, pp. 418–28.

Describes a tool that provides for the storage and retrieval of large quantities of requirements that have been constructed in a tree. The system also maintains pointers between requirements and those requirements from which they were derived. 18 refs.

172. [Dorfman and Thayer 1989].
Dorfman, M., and R. Thayer. "System and Software Requirements Engineering." *Tutorial: System and Software Requirements Engineering,* edited by M. Dorfman and R. Thayer, Washington, D.C.: IEEE Computer Society, 1989.

173. [Dumas 1988].
Dumas, J. *Designing User Interfaces for Software.* Englewood Cliffs, N.J.: Prentice Hall, 1988.

This book does not specifically address how to specify a user interface in an SRS, but it is one of the best collections of wisdom ever compiled about how to design a user interface. The ideas in this book should be learned by anyone involved in specifying requirements for or designing a user interface. 56 refs.

174. **[Dutton 1984].**
Dutton, C. "Requirements Tools: Phase I in a Software Development Methodology." *ACM Software Engineering Notes* **9,** 1 (January 1984): 19–23.

A brief look at PSL/PSA, SREM, SADT, and HOS to report their degree of flexibility, automated completeness checking, interactive editing, and support by their vendors. 5 refs.

175. **[Dyer et al. 1977].**
Dyer, M. E. et al. *REVS Users Manual.* SREP Final Report, Vol. 2, TRW Report 27332-6921-026. Huntsville, Ala., August 1977. See Alford and Benoit for Vols. 1 and 3.

The definitive work that motivates and precisely defines TRW's REVS system and RSL language. RSL allows requirements analysts to define all elements, attributes, relationships, and structures in the requirements. Once written, such requirements can be processed by REVS. REVS stores all requirements in a relational data base for subsequent refinement, analysis, and extraction. RADX performs completeness and consistency checking as well as documentation generation. The 2-inch thick document serves as an excellent reference document with detailed descriptions and examples of RSL and its job control language. 6 refs.

176. **[Early 1986].**
Early, M. "Relating Software Requirements to Software Design." *ACM Software Engineering Notes* **11,** 3 (July 1986): 37–39.

You cannot code directly from requirements without designing. 7 refs.

177. **[Edwards 1987].**
Edwards, W. "Excelerator and CASE 2000 Design Aid: Management Considerations and Systems Analysis Support Tools." *Conference on Methodologies and Tools for Real-Time Systems,* Washington, D.C., National Institute for Software Quality and Productivity, 1987, pp. N-1–N-20.

Brief comparison of two structured analysis tools as applied to complex real-time systems. Conclusion: CASE 2000 was not as user friendly or as bug free as Excelerator. No refs.

178. **[Epple et al. 1983].**
Epple, W. K., et al. "The Use of Graphic Aids for Requirements Specification of Process Control Systems." In *IEEE COMPSAC '83,* Washington D.C.: Computer Society Press of the Institute of Electrical and Electronics Engineers, 1983, pp. 521–31.

179. **[Everhart 1978].**
Everhart, C. R. "User Experience with a Formally Defined Requirements Language IORL." *Second U.S. Army Software Symposium,* U.S. Computer System Command, October 25–27, 1978, pp. 211–19.

180. **[Everhart 1980].**
Everhart, C. R. "A Unified Approach to Software (System) Engineering." In *IEEE COMPSAC '80,* Chicago, 1980. pp. 49–55. Washington D.C.: Computer Society Press of the Institute of Electrical and Electronics Engineers.

Advocates using common languages for all phases of the system development life cycle. The author describes existing requirements languages as inadequate for a variety of reasons. He gives fourteen characteristics of ideal system definition and design languages. No attempt is made to ensure that requirements writers remain in the domain of requirements. 19 refs.

181. **[Everhart et al. 1980].**
Everhart, C. R. et al. *SAMS IORL*[2] *Demonstration Final Report.* Teledyne Brown Engineering Report SD80-AIRMICS-2428. September 1980.

182. **[EWICS 1981].**
EWICS. *Application-Oriented Specifications Glossary of Terms,* Jo Kramer, ed. Unpublished. London: Imperial College, 1981.

Collection of definitions for terms and phrases related to requirements specifications. The glossary was prepared by the European Workshop on Industrial Computer Systems (EWICS), a subcommittee of the International Purdue Workshop, an affiliate of IFIPS. No refs.

183. **[Exel and Popovic 1981].**
Exel, M., and B. Popovic. "SL1 Specification Language—a Tool for Switching Systems Software Development." In *IEEE International Conference on Communications,* Washington D.C.: Computer Society Press of the Institute of Electrical and Electronics Engineers, 1981.

184. **[Farny et al. 1981].**
Farny, A., et al. "An Application of Computer-Aided Requirements Analysis to a Real-Time Deep-Space System." In *AIAA Third Computers in Aerospace Conference,* Washington D.C.: American Institute of Aeronautics and Astronautics, 1981, pp. 531–36.

Describes the use of PSL/PSA as a tool for the requirements analysis of the sequence of commands given to a spacecraft. This work was performed at the Jet Propulsion Laboratory. 1 ref.

185. **[Federal Information Processing Standards 1979].**
Federal Information Processing Standards. *Guidelines for Documentation of Computer Programs and Automated Data Systems for the Initiation Phase.* National Bureau of Standards Publication NBS-FIPS-PUB-64. Washington, D.C., August 1979.

Provides guidelines for the content and organization of a project request document, a feasibility study document, and a cost/benefit analysis document. Officially these three documents are produced prior to the functional requirements phase. However by this guide's definition, the purpose of the three documents is to determine the software product's objectives and general requirements.

186. **[Feldman 1979].**
Feldman, C. "SADT." Panelist report in W. Bail, "User Experiences with Specification Tools." *ACM Software Engineering Notes* **4,** 3 (July 1979): 12–13.

A brief SofTech retort to Ed Jack's summary of experience using SDAT.

187. **[Feldman 1980].**
Feldman, C. G. "IDEFO: A Method for Analzying Complex Computerized Systems." Presented at *VIM 32 Conference,* San Francisco, May 1980. Reprints available from SofTech, Waltham, Mass.

---

[2]IORL is a registered trademark of Teledyne Brown Engineering.

Defines concepts behind the IDEFO method, a subset of SADT used for the functional modeling of complex systems. No refs.

188. [Fickas et al. 1987].

Fickas, S., et al. *Problem Acquisition in Software Analysis: A Preliminary Study.* University of Oregon Computer Science Department Technical Report 87-04. Eugene, November 1987.

189. [Fife et al. 1987].

Fife, D., et al. *Evaluation of Computer-Aided System Design Tools for SDI Battle Management/C^3 Architecture Development.* IDA paper P-2062, Institute for Defense Analyses. Alexandria, Va., October 1987.

A carefully thought out and thorough comparison of five systems engineering tool sets—TAGS, AUTO-G, DCDS, Teamwork, and Software through Pictures. These were evaluated from a point of view of overall systems engineering and design, not necessarily from a software requirements point of view. Nonetheless many of the evaluation criteria used here are equally applicable to software requirements. The critiera include

1. Provide effective graphics.
2. Represent timing requirements.
3. Represent process behavior formally.
4. Represent hardware allocations explicitly.
5. General SDI architecture data flow modeling technique representation.
6. Provide simulation for validation.
7. Provide requirements traceability.
8. Provide version identification.
9. Support configuration management.
10. Support user-tailorable icons and semantics.

All of the preceding are applicable to software requirements except criteria 4 and 5. It was determined that TAGS satisfied six of the eight criteria, AUTO-G satisfied five, DCDS satisfied four, Teamwork satisfied two, and Software through Pictures satisfied one. However, be cautioned that in the context of the book you are now reading, points earned might be very different when using criteria specifically developed for software requirements (see Sections 4.2.1 and 4.2.8). This report is well worth reading and represents one of the most thorough comparisons of tools anywhere in the literature. 12 refs.

190. [Finger 1981].

Finger, A. "Modeling the Man-Machine Interface." *Yourdon Report* **6**, 1 (January–February 1981): 6–7.

Describes how state transition diagrams can be used to model user interactions with interactive software. 1 ref.

191. [Finkelstein and Potts 1986].

Finkelstein, A., and C. Potts. "Structured Common Sense: The Elicitation and Formalization of System Requirements." In *Software Engineering '86,* P. Brown and D. Barnes, eds. Stevenage, U.K.: Peter Peregrinus, 1986.

192. **[Fischer and Walter 1979].**
Fischer, K. F., and M. G. Walter. "Improved Software Reliability through Requirements Verification." *IEEE Transactions on Reliability* **28,** 3 (August 1979): 233–40.

Describes a technique called System Verification Diagrams (SVD) that can be used to locate inconsistent, unclear, or incomplete requirements specifications. The technique is to manually extract the fundamental processes defined in an English language requirements specification. Once these processes (called decomposition elements—DEs) are extracted, they are recorded in a directed graph network showing their interrelationships. Each node includes stimulus, function, response, and cross-reference fields. The resulting network can then be analyzed using directed graph analysis techniques. These techniques help estimate the cost of testing the software and the number of potential problems during maintenance. 12 refs.

193. **[Floyd 1984].**
Floyd, C. "A Systematic Look at Prototyping." In *Approaches to Prototyping.* R. Budde, et al., eds. Berlin: Springer-Verlag, 1984. pp. 1–18.

One of the best papers ever published with the goal of introducing the concept of prototyping as it applies to software. Explains why prototyping software is unique; explains all types of prototyping as applied to software. Well worth reading. 11 refs.

194. **[Freeman 1980].**
Freeman, P. "Requirements Analysis and Specification: A First Step." Presented at *ASME International Computer Technology Conference,* August 1980.

195. **[Frimer and Folkes 1982].**
Frimer, M., and M. Folkes. *Standards Document: Software Requirements Specification.* Advanced Technology Laboratories, draft 2, Bellevue, Wash., March 18, 1982.

Provides a uniform set of rules for preparing a software requirements specification for use at the Advanced Technology Laboratories, Inc. The standard defines the key people involved in writing requirements, describes configuration control protocols for the SRS, and provides a detailed outline for a typical SRS. The document also includes a set of standard forms on which to record some aspects of the requirements in a uniform fashion. 6 refs.

196. **[Furia 1979].**
Furia, M. J. "A Comparative Evaluation of RSL/REVS and PSL/PSA Applied to a Digital Flight Control System." In *AIAA Second Computers in Aerospace Conference,* Washington D.C.: American Institute of Aeronautics and Astronautics, 1979, pp. 330–37.

Compares capabilities of REVS and PSL/PSA for the detailed specification of the Digital Flight Control System (DFCS). REVS is commended for its simulation and graphics capabilities and PSL/PSA for its extensive documentation capabilities. Considering the fact that REVS was designed for requirements specification, PSL/PSA for problem decomposition, and that the author is attempting to use both tools for algorithmic design (e.g., counters, loops, interaction, conditionals), a surprisingly fair comparison of the two systems is performed. Many helpful diagrams showing the relative organizations of DFCS information in the two systems are given. 5 refs.

197. **[Furtek et al. 1981].**

Furtek, F. C., et al. "DARTS: A Tool for Specification and Simulation of Real-Time Systems." In *AIAA Third Computers in Aerospace Conference,* Washington D.C.: American Institute of Aeronautics and Astronautics, 1981, pp. 390–98.

Design Aids for Real-Time Systems (DARTS) is a tool for analyzing the design of real-time systems. It enforces a functional decomposition of the system into processes. Simulation capabilities aid the designer in determining the performance capabilities of the design. 10 refs.

198. **[Gackowski 1977].**

Gackowski, Z. *An Example of How to Use PSL / PSA.* University of Michigan ISDOS Working Paper 184. Ann Arbor, June 1977.

Describes the use of PSL/PSA in specifying a student course registration system. No refs.

199. **[Gane and Sarson 1979].**

Gane, C., and T. Sarson. *Structured Systems Analysis: Tools and Techniques.* Englewood Cliffs, N.J.: Prentice Hall, 1979.

Presents a wide variety of tools and techniques useful for specifying requirements for commercial data processing systems. These techniques include hierarchical data flow diagrams, data dictionaries, decision trees, decision tables, pseudocode, data definition, and human interface specifications. The book also briefly describes the process of deriving a design from requirements specifications. Very readable with much helpful information for the commercial data processing requirements writer. 42 refs.

200. **[Gatewood 1977].**

Gatewood, F. E., ed. *A Structured Requirements Process Using the Improved Programming Technologies.* IBM Washington Systems Center Technical Bulletin GG22-9011-00, DAPS CODE 0910/0911. September 1977.

Describes the application of some tools and techniques that have generally been considered design and implementation techniques to the requirements phase of the software life cycle. These techniques includes HIPO, walk-throughs, chief requirements definer (aka chief programmer), and top-down decomposition. This report was written for the data processing professional. A complete example using a financial analysis problem is given. 4 refs.

201. **[Gatto 1964]**

Gatto, O. "Autosate." *Communications of the ACM* **7,** 7 (July 1964): 425–32.

An early paper emphasizing the need to record data flows within an organization during problem analysis. To no surprise considering the year, data flows were recorded textually rather than graphically. No refs.

202. **[Gehani 1982].**

Gehani, N. "Specifications: Formal and Informal—a Case Study." *Software Practice and Experience* **12** (1982): 433–44.

203. **[Gehani and McGettrick 1986].**

Gehani, N., and A. McGettrick, eds. *Software Specification Techniques.* Reading, Penn.: Addison-Wesley, 1986.

Collection of previously published articles on requirements and design techniques. Most are on formal specifications and design specifications.

204. **[Gishen et al. 1979].**
Gishen, J. S., et al. *A Requirements, Specification, and Design Methodology for Software Engineering.* Technical Report, IBM Federal Systems Division. 1979.

205. **[Gladden 1982].**
Gladden, G. R. "Stop the Life-Cycle, I Want To Get Off." *ACM Software Engineering Notes* **7,** 2 (April 1982): 35–39.

Claims that reasons for most software failures are (1) poorly understood requirements, (2) a software life cycle, and (3) changing requirements. In reponse Gladden suggests: (1) defining general objectives rather than requirements and (2) building a prototype instead of an SRS. 2 refs.

206. **[Glaseman and Davis 1980].**
Glaseman, S., and M. Davis. *Software Requirements for Embedded Computers: A Preliminary Report.* U.S. Air Force Document R-2567-AF, 1980.

In spite of the title, this report discusses the full software acquisition process undertaken by the Air Force. The authors explain in introductory chapters why their original goal of examining the requirements phase only was expanded to the entire development process—because the single greatest problem with requirements is the appearance of inevitable late-appearing changes to the requirements. The authors contend that the most effective means of handling this lies in the rest of the process, not just in requirements (and rightly so). In any case, this report provides an excellent description of the Air Force's embedded software acquisition process. 23 refs.

207. **[Goedicke 1986].**
Goedicke, M. "The Use of Formal Requirements Specifications in EDE in a Software Development Environment." In *IEEE COMPSAC '86,* Washington D.C.: Computer Society Press of the Institute of Electrical and Electronics Engineers, 1986, pp. 190–96.

Describes the EDE formal specification language for defining functions, processors, and signals for embedded systems. EDE is based on VDM. 7 refs.

208. **[Goldsack and Kramer 1980].**
Goldsack, S., and J. Kramer. "The Use of Invariants in the Application-Oriented Specification of Real-Time Systems." In *IFIP/IFAC Workshop on Real-Time Programming,* Oxford, England: Pergamon Press, 1981, pp. 63–72.

Uses the concepts of invariants and guarded commands to describe a method of precisely defining the requirements of a process control system. The control system and the process under control are jointly considered the system under specification. Guarded commands are used to define how a system returns to a *quiescent* state in response to a set of states of processes within the system that indicate a condition requiring action on the part of the controller. A worthwhile paper to read. 13 refs.

209. **[Gomaa and Scott 1981].**
Gomaa, H., and D. Scott. "Prototyping as a Tool in the Specification of User Requirements." In *Fifth International Conference on Software Engineering,* Wash-

ington D.C.: Computer Society Press of the Institute of Electrical and Electronics Engineers, 1981, pp. 333-42.

This excellent paper describes the implementation and use of a prototype system after an initial requirements specification is written but before requirements are finalized and approved. The rewards of this approach, as demonstrated by an actual case history, are described and well justified. The "quick and dirty" prototype was coded in APL, expended only 6% of the total development effort, and uncovered a remarkable number of flaws in the requirements that would have resulted in either gross customer dissatisfaction or very expensive changes after full system implementation. 12 refs.

210. **[Gomaa 1983].**

Gomaa, H. "The Impact of Rapid Prototyping on Specifying User Requirements." *ACM Software Engineering Notes* **8,** 2 (April 1983): 17–28.

With the assumption that requirements documents, whether textual or graphical, are difficult for a customer to understand really well, this paper proposes that system developers produce a rapid prototype of the system during the requirements phase that the customer can exercise and actually use. Feedback from the customer becomes an essential input in the requirements specification process. The author recommends that the prototype emphasize the human interface, expend no more than 10% of system development costs, and be written in an easy-to-debug, but not necessarily fast-to-execute, language. The paper supplies a wealth of similarly useful advice to rapid prototypers. A full example is given of a rapid prototyping project for a semiconductor process controller called PROMIS. A highly worthwhile paper. 12 refs.

211. **[Gomaa 1986].**

Gomaa, H. "Prototypes—Keep Them or Throw Them Away?" In *Infotech State of the Art Report on Prototyping.* M. Lipp, ed., Oxford, England: Pergamon Infotech Ltd. 1986.

Describes differences between throwaway and evolutionary prototypes. 14 refs.

212. **[Gottschalk 1979].**

Gottschalk, W. *SSP—eine Methode zum Strukturierten Systementwulf von Steuerungen fur Diskrete Technische Prozesse.* Kernforschungszentrum Karlsruhe Report 176. May 1979.

213. **[Greenspan 1982].**

Greenspan, S. "Requirements Modeling and the Design of Information Systems." In *International Symposium of Current Issues of Requirements Engineering Environments,* Y. Ohno, ed. Amsterdam: North Holland Publ., 1982, pp. 107–13.

Opening sections of this paper do an excellent job of defining precisely the problems inherent in writing requirements specifications. The author also justifies adequately the use of models and assertions for requirements. Later sections however introduce so much new and unnecessary terminology that the reader (and perhaps the author) finds it difficult to extract relevant underlying concepts. 31 refs.

214. **[Greenspan et al. 1982].**

Greenspan, S., et al. "Capturing More World Knowledge in the Requirements Specifications." In *Sixth International Conference on Software Engineering,* Washington D.C.: Computer Society Press of the Institute of Electrical and Electronics Engineers, 1982, pp. 225–34.

Most requirements specification languages and methods concentrate on modeling the behavior of a system. However as any systems analyst knows, there is a large domain of knowledge about the application environment that must be learned before an actual requirements specification can be written. This paper discusses a model sufficient for describing attributes of the application environment itself. Using the classical entity-relationship scheme, the paper offers two major contributions to the requirements discipline: (1) three types of entities are allowed (objects, activities, and assertions) and (2) the requirements specification is organized according to three types of abstraction—aggregation, classification, and generalization. The paper has basically applied technology from other disciplines to the unique problem of requirements specification. 29 refs.

215. **[Greenspan and Mylopoulos 1983].**
Greenspan, S., and J. Mylopoulos. "A Knowledge Representation Approach to Software Engineering: The Taxis Project." *Conference of the Canadian Information Processing Society,* Ottawa: Canadian Information Processing Society, May 1983, pp. 163–74.

216. **[Greenspan 1984].**
Greenspan, S. *Requirements Modeling: A Knowledge Representation Approach to Software Requirements Definition.* University of Toronto Technical Report CSRG-135. March 1984.

217. **[Grindley 1966.].**
Grindley, C. B. "Systematics—a Nonprogramming Language for Designing and Specifying Commercial Systems for Computers." *Computer Journal* (1966): 124–28.

Describes the use of simple charts and check lists to define data processing requirements in a commercial application. No refs.

218. **[Groner et al. 1979].**
Groner, C., et al. "Requirements Analysis in Clinical Research Information Processing—A Case Study." *IEEE Computer* **12,** 9 (September 1979): 100–108.

Describes a methodology used by Rand Corporation to derive a requirements specification for a clinical research information-processing problem. Key to the technique was developing a prototype that all interested parties were able to experiment with in order to understand better their own information-processing needs and the capabilities of the computer system. 17 refs.

219. **[Haase and Koch 1982].**
Haase, V. H., and G. R. Koch. "Application-Oriented Specifications: Guest Editors' Introduction." *IEEE Computer* **15,** 5 (May 1982): 10–11.

Brief introduction to a series of papers on application-oriented specifications. The editors emphasize the need always to use a qualifier with the term *specifications.* 4 refs.

220. **[Hagemann 1987].**
Hagemann, M. "Formal Requirements Specification of Process Control Systems." *ACM Software Engineering Notes* **12,** 4 (October 1987): 36–42.

221. [Hagermann 1988].
Hagermann, M. "Requirements Analysis for Real-Time Automation Projects." In *Tenth IEEE International Conference on Software Engineering,* Washington D.C.: Computer Society Press of the Institute of Electrical and Electronics Engineers, 1988.

222. [Halling et al. n. d.].
Halling, H., et al. "A Step Towards Application-Oriented Specifications." In *Real-Time Data Handling and Control,* H. Meyer. ed. Amsterdam: North Holland Publ. pp. 525–33.

223. [Hallmann 1988].
Hallmann, M. "An Operational Requirement Description Model for Open Systems." In *Tenth IEEE International Conference on Software Engineering,* Washington D.C.: Computer Society Press of the Institute of Electrical and Electronics Engineers, 1988.

224. [Hallmann 1988a].
Hallmann, M. "Installing Transactions in a Requirements Engineering Method." In *IEEE COMPSAC '88,* Washington D.C.: Computer Society Press of the Institute of Electrical and Electronics Engineers, 1988, pp. 121–26.

225. [Hamilton and Zeldin 1973].
Hamilton, M., and S. Zeldin. *Higher Order Software Requirements.* Charles Stark Draper Laboratory Report 2793. August 1973.

226. [Hamilton and Zeldin 1976].
Hamilton, M., and S. Zeldin. "Higher Order Software—A Methodology for Defining Software." *IEEE Transactions on Software Engineering* **2,** 1 (March 1976): 9–32.

Describes a formal methodology for specifying and analyzing interfaces in a hierarchy of system components. Although the authors state that HOS has been used during requirements as well as during the design stage of systems, no specific advice is given about the methodology's application to requirements. The term *higher order software* is used because all systems developed using the methodology are treated in the early stages as if they were completely software. 40 refs.

227. [Hamilton and Zeldin 1976a].
Hamilton, M., and S. Zeldin. *Integrated Software Development System / Higher Order Software Conceptual Description.* U.S. Army Electronics Command, Technical Report ECOM-76-0329-F. Fort Monmouth, N.J., November 1976.

Early report that surveys existing requirements approaches and defines the HOS methodology and associated tools. 45 refs.

228. [Hamilton and Zeldin 1977].
Hamilton, M., and S. Zeldin. *Verification of an Axiomatic Requirments Specification.* Higher Order Software, Inc., Publication 77-1466. Cambridge, Mass., 1977.

229. [Hamilton and Zeldin 1979].
Hamilton, M., and S. Zeldin. *Requirements Definition within Acquisition and Its Relationship to Post-Deployment Software Support.* Higher Order Software, Inc., TR-22, Vol. 1. November 1979. Available from DTIC. The title and most of this report's contents are consistent; however the preface and introduction steer the reader away from the actual topic of discussion. Specifically the title and the body

describe how the requirements phase of the software acquisition process should function (i.e., the report discusses the requirements phase of the system development life cycle). On the other hand, the preface and introduction treat the acquisition process itself as the system under discussion in the report and thus offer little motivation for reading the rest of the report.

Section 4 of this report details all types of information that must be contained in a properly written requirements specification. It stresses the need to define specifically the target system and its environments. It clearly defines thirty-six factors that interrelate and affect requirements of the target system. Not only is every one defined, but each is described in terms of how it affects the final product's attributes. Section 4 also does an excellent job of describing interrelationships between requirements, specifications, and implementations of a set of cooperating processes (e.g., nodes in a distributed network). The authors give a list of properties of a requirements specification: (1) full realization of the power of a definition, (2) definition in terms of a control hierarchy, (3) integration of generation and behavior, (4) interface consistency, (5) formal input for automation tools, (6) flexibility for changing requirements, (7) traceability, (8) ability to detect and recover from errors, (9) ability to relate to multiple dialects, and twelve others. 58 refs.

230. [Hamilton and Zeldin 1983].

Hamilton, M., and S. Zeldin. "The Functional Life Cycle Model and Its Automation: USE.IT." *Journal of Systems and Software* **3**, 1 (March 1983): 25–62.

The first publicly published description of Higher Order Software's tool, called USE.IT, which claims to be able to "synthesize" provably correct programs from "requirements" specifications written in AXES. Also includes data supporting major productivity increases on actual projects. 58 refs.

231. [Hammer and Kunin 1982].

Hammer, M., and J. S. Kunin. *OSL: An Office Specification Language: Language Description*. MIT Industrial Liaison Program Report 6-48-82. Cambridge, Mass., 1982.

Discusses a language for describing office procedures and functions. Note that this language is not necessarily designed to describe software requirements; however it is an excellent attempt to formulate the behavior of an office prior to automation. No refs.

232. [Hancock 1979].

Hancock, J. "Chipping Away at Productivity." *Computerworld* **13**, 42 (October 15, 1979).

233. [Harel 1987].

Harel, D. "Statecharts: A Visual Formalism for Complex Systems." *Science of Computer Programming* **8** (1987): 231–74.

The definitive work by David Harel that defines a formal-based set of extensions to finite state machines to make them much more powerful for, and suitable to, the requirements specifications of complex real-time systems. 33 refs.

234. [Harel 1987a].

Harel, D. "The STATEMATE Method for System Development Automation." In *Conference on Methodologies and Tools for Real-Time Systems: IV*, Washington, D.C.: National Institute for Software Quality and Productivity. 1987.

235. **[Harel et al. 1987].**

Harel, D. et al. "The ADCAD Methodology and STATEMATE1 Working Environment." In *Conference on Methodologies and Tools for Real-Time Systems,* Washington, D.C.: National Institute for Software Quality and Productivity, 1987. pp. I-1–I-10.

Presents the ADCAD (now called i-Logix) methodology and the STATEMATE1 (now called STATEMATE) tool that automates it. It supports requirements definition through two views (behavioral and functional) and design through an additional view (structural). STATEMATE1 allows specifiers to use any or all of the three models; the tool keeps the models integrated so that specifiers can easily move from one to the other. 2 refs.

236. **[Harel 1988].**

Harel, D. "On Visual Formalisms." *Communications of the ACM* **31,** 5 (May 1988): 514–30.

237. **[Harel et al. 1988].**

Harel, D., et al. "STATEMATE: A Working Environment for the Development of Complex Reactive Systems." In *Tenth IEEE International Conference on Software Engineering,* Washington D.C.: Computer Society Press of the Institute of Electical and Electronics Engineers, 1988.

238. **[Harris et al. 1975].**

Harris, J., et al. *Technology for the Formulation and Expression of Specifications,* Vols. 1 and 2. National Bureau of Standards Report GCR 76-55. December 1975. Available from NTIS. See Wright for Vol. 3.

Describes a method that aids in producing complete, clear, and correct specification documents. The method uses decision tables, an information precedence network, and a specification outline. Volume 1 defines the method; volume 2 is a user's manual. 22 refs.

239. **[Harrison 1985].**

Harrison, T. "Techniques and Issues in Rapid Prototyping." *Journal of Systems Management* (June 1985).

240. **[Harwood 1987].**

Harwood, K. "On Prototyping and the Role of the Software Engineer." *ACM Software Engineering Notes* **12,** 4 (October 1987): 34.

An easy-to-read position paper that takes an unpopular, but difficult-to-argue-with position that the purpose of a prototype is to educate the software engineers, not the potential customers. The idea is that customers already know their business except that they have a particular problem. The product they want must solve that problem and not introduce new problems into the part of the business that is working well. The primary purpose of the prototype is to help educate the software engineer about both the business and the problem so that the software product can do its job. 1 ref.

241. **[Hashimoto 1987].**

Hashimoto, K. "Systems Analysis by Extended Data Flow Diagrams with Events and Timing." In *IEEE COMPSAC '87,* Washington D.C.: Computer Society Press of the Institute of Electrical and Electronics Engineers, 1987, pp. 117–23.

Summarizes the works of Ward and Hatley. 12 refs.

242. **[Hasui et al. 1983].**
Hasui, K., et al. "Rapid Prototyping of Switching Software." In *IEEE COMPSAC '83,* Washington D.C.: Computer Society Press of the Institute of Electrical and Electronics Engineers, 1983, pp. 25–32.

243. **[Hatley 1984].**
Hatley, D. "The Use of Structured Methods in the Development of Large Software-Based Avionics Systems." In *AIAA/IEEE Sixth Digital Avionics Systems Conference,* Washington D.C.: American Institute of Aeronautics and Astronautics, 1984, pp. 6–15.

Describes Lear Siegler extensions to DeMarco-style structured analysis to make it more suitable for real-time applications. The extensions include control paths (in addition to data paths) and FSM descriptions of process behavior. 7 refs.

244. **[Hatley and Pirbhai 1987].**
Hatley, D., and I. Pirbhai. *Strategies for Real-Time System Specification.* New York: Dorset House, 1987.

Definitive work of Hatley and Pirbhai presents their extensions to conventional structured analysis that make it more applicable to real-time systems. In particular they recommend adding control flow diagrams and finite state machine specification. They also define an overall iterative methodology. At every step i of the methodology, ith-level requirements are defined and an architecture established for the $(i$th $+ 1)$ level. The result of applying the methodology is full system design. There is no distinct requirements stage; every design iteration defines requirements for the next. 21 refs.

245. **[Havey 1986].**
Havey, P. "Shortening the Software Development Cycle." *Hardcopy* **6,** 3 (March 1986).

Brief summary of ProMod, one of the many tools that implement structured analysis. No refs.

246. **[Haylock 1981].**
Haylock, R. H. "A Specification Methodology for Real-Time Systems." *Fourth International Conference on Software Engineering for Telecommunication Switching Systems,* London: Institution of Electrical Engineers, July 1981.

247. **[Heacox 1979].**
Heacox, H. C. "RDL: A Language for Software Development." *ACM SIGPLAN Notices* **14,** 12 (December 1979): 71–79.

Describes a non-procedural language called the Requirements and Development Language (RDL). Using the ISDOS data base and language definition capabilities, RDL uses objects, properties, and relations to define all stages of the software development process from requirements through maintenance. The author claims that his system is unique because it supports all phases of the development process. Unfortunately he only claims it; he provides no insight into how RDL can be used by anything other than design and code. One very useful but unoriginal concept emphasized by the paper is using a data base as the central repository of all software project data. 9 refs.

248. **[Hecht 1983].**
Hecht, H. "Software Requirements for the Maintenance Phase." In *IEEE Software Maintenance Workshop Record,* Washington D.C.: Computer Society Press of the Institute of Electrical and Electronics Engineers, 1983.

249. **[Hecht et al. 1986].**
Hecht, A., et al. "Automating Structured Analysis." In *IEEE COMPSAC '86,* Washington D.C.: Computer Society Press of the Institute of Electrical and Electronics Engineers, 1986, pp. 100–104.

A report on one tool (Teamwork/SA) by Cadre that implements structured analysis. 10 refs.

250. **[Heitmeyer et al. 1982].**
Heitmeyer, C., et al. "The Use of Quick Prototypes in the Secure Military Message Systems Project." *ACM Software Engineering Notes* **7,** 5 (December 1982): 85–87.

Describes the case study of a throwaway prototype. 6 refs.

251. **[Heitmeyer 1985].**
Heitmeyer, C. L. "Requirements Specifications in the Military Message System Project." In *Third International IEEE Workshop on Software Specification and Design,* Washington D.C.: Computer Society Press of the Institute of Electrical and Electronics Engineers, 1985, pp. 98–100.

Describes how the Navy Research Laboratory wrote requirements for the Military Message System (MMS) by partitioning requirements, defining the user command language using ICL, and developing a prototype of the user interface. 6 refs.

252. **[Heitmeyer and McLean 1983].**
Heitmeyer, C. L., and J. D. McLean. "Abstract Requirements Specification." *IEEE Transactions on Software Engineering* **9,** 5 (September 1983): 580–89.

Explains how any type of functional decomposition of requirements may unduly prejudice the designer into believing that the "design" in the SRS is the only possible real design. Presents a new technique that defines each system output as a composition of transformations on some original data in the real world. 23 refs.

253. **[Hekmatpour 1987].**
Hekmatpour, S. "Experience with Evolutionary Prototyping in a Large Software Project." *ACM Software Engineering Notes* **12,** 1 (January 1987): 38–41.

Brief summary of using VDM and C to evolve a prototype of a system whose purpose was to support prototyping. 29 refs.

254. **[Hekmatpour and Ince 1987].**
Hekmatpour, S., and D. Ince. *Rapid Software Prototyping.* Open University Mathematics Faculty Report, Walton Hall, Milton Keynes, U.K., February 1986.

Differentiates clearly between throw-it-away, evolutionary, and incremental prototyping. An excellent study of all the techniques, tools, and approaches available. 186 refs.

255. **[Hemdal and Reilly 1987].**
Hemdal, G., and M. Reilly. "Requirements Analysis and Design Using the Auto-G Tool System." In *Conference on Methodologies and Tools for Real-Time Systems: IV,* Washington, D.C.: National Institute for Software Quality and Productivity, 1987.

256. **[Heninger et al. 1978].**
Heninger, K. L., et al. *Software Requirements for the A-7E Aircraft.* Naval Research Laboratory Memorandum Report 3876, Washington, D.C., November 1978.

The actual SRS produced by the NRL A-7E team. The methodology used for its creation has been referenced extensively in the literature and is described in Heninger's 1979 paper. This SRS has been updated (see Alspaugh).

257. **[Heninger 1979].**
Heninger, K. L. "Specifying Software Requirements for Complex Systems: New Techniques and Their Application." In *IEEE Conference on Specifications of Reliable Software,* Washington D.C.: Computer Society Press of the Institute of Electrical and Electronics Engineers, 1979, pp. 1–14. Also in *IEEE Transactions on Software Engineering* **6,** 1 (January 1980): 2–12.

Describes the use of naming and formatting conventions for the detailed requirements specification of the U.S. Navy A-7E's operational flight program software. 22 refs.

258. **[Heninger 1979a].**
Heninger, K. L. "Limits to Specifications: Why Not More Progress?" *ACM Software Engineering Notes* **4,** 3 (July 1979): 15–16.

Panel report from the *Specifications of Reliable Software Conference* summarizes the position of five panelists, Jay McCauley, Ray Pollock, Ted Linden, Doug Ross, and Dave Parnas, on the subject of why it is so difficult to use available specification techniques.

259. **[Herndon and McCall 1983].**
Herndon, M. A., and J. McCall. "The Requirements Management Methodology." In *IEEE COMPSAC '83,* Washington D.C.: Computer Society Press of the Institute of Electrical and Electronics Engineers, 1983, pp. 640–41.

A rare content-free, albeit short, paper. 2 refs.

260. **[Hershey 1979].**
Hershey, E. A. "CADSAT." Panelist report in W. Basil, "User Experiences with Specification Tools." *ACM Software Engineering Notes* **4,** 3 (July 1979): 14.

A three-paragraph summary of ISDOS's position on using CADSAT by Logicon.

261. **[Hindin and Rauch-Hindin 1983].**
Hindin, H. J., and W. B. Rauch-Hindin. "Special Series on System Integration: Real-Time Systems." *Electronic Design* (January 6, 1983): 289–93.

A review of papers presented at the *IEEE Real-Time Systems Symposium* in 1980. In particular a paper on requirements for real-time systems is reviewed. No refs.

262. **[Hira and Mori 1982].**
Hira, H., and K. Mori. "Customer-Needs Analysis Procedures: C-NAP." In *International Symposium on Current Issues of Requirements Engineering Environments,* edited by Y. Ohno. Amsterdam: North Holland Publ., 1982, pp. 115–21.

Uses the term *needs analysis* to describe all development life cycle phases prior to design. Given the assumption that the total set of user requirements typically is not understood completely until later stages of development, C-NAP forces system customers and developers to do a total analysis of the problem before design. The method consists of two phases. The first includes problem analysis, objective setting, and defining means and methods. During each of these, information is collected, represented hierarchically, evaluated, and selected. The second phase, called *definition of detailed needs*, is not described. A full example is given of applying C-NAP methods to a beverage manufacturer's production control system. The C-NAP methods had been applied to seventy companies as of December 1982. 5 refs.

263. **[Ho and Nunamaker 1974].**

Ho, T., and J. Nunamaker, Jr. "Requirements Statement Language Principles for Automatic Programing." In *ACM '74 Conference.* New York: ACM Press of the Association for Computing Machinery, 1974, pp. 279–88.

264. **[Hoffman 1980].**

Hoffman, R. H. "Software Requirements Engineering Methodology (SREM) and the Requirements Engineering and Validation System (REVS).," *NBS/IEEE/ACM Software Tool Fair,* National Bureau of Standards Special Publication 500-80. Washington, D.C., 1980. pp. 111–16.

Brief overview and some examples of SREM and REVS. 6 refs.

265. **[Hollinde and Wagner 1984].**

Hollinde, I., and K. Wagner. "Experience of Prototyping in Command and Control Information Systems." In *Approaches to Prototyping,* R. Budde et al., eds. Berlin: Springer-Verlag, 1984. pp. 80–91.

Describes the experience of applying an operational prototype of the EMFIS system in a real environment, receiving feedback, and creating the full system. This paper represents one of the few documented cases of applying software prototyping to a real problem in the early 1970s. 4 refs.

266. **[Hooper and Hsia 1982].**

Hooper, J. W., and P. Hsia. "Scenario-Based Prototyping for Requirements Identification." *ACM Software Engineering Notes* **7,** 5 (December 1982): 88–93.

Proposes a methodology and tool that aids in the original identification of customer requirements, as opposed to most traditional requirements methodologies and tools, which assume that we already know the requirements and need only to check consistency. Once customers describe their dream system in terms of sample, representative dialogue scenarios, this tool executes the scenarios, giving the potential user a feel for how the system will behave. Once witnessed the scenarios can be modified or refined to approximate the user's needs more closely. 44 refs.

267. **[Howes 1987].**

Howes, N. "On Using the User's Manual as the Requirements Specification." In *Tutorial: Software Engineering Project Management,* R. Thayer and M. Dorfman, eds., Washington, D.C.: IEEE Computer Society, 1987.

268. **[Hruschka 1987].**

Hruschka, P. "ProMod at the Age of 5." Presented at *First European Software Engineering Conference,* Strasbourg, France, AFCET, September 1987.

269. **[Hsia 1980]**

Hsia, P. "Software Requirements Engineering—An Interdisciplinary View." In panel session at *NCC '80,* Montvale, New Jersey: AFIPS Press of the American Federation of Information Processing Societies, 1980.

Panel discussion; no written record. Panelists included Bob Balzer, Peter Dejong, and Raymond Yeh.

270. **[Hsia and Yaung 1988].**
Hsia, P., and A. Yaung. "Another Approach to System Decomposition: Requirements Clustering." In *IEEE COMPSAC '88,* Washington D.C.: Computer Society Press of the Institute of Electrical and Electronics Engineers, 1988, pp. 75–82.

Presents a unique design methodology in which the hierarchy of components is created based on satisfying related requirements. Thus the decision to decompose any subsystem X into particular subcomponents X_1, X_2, and X_3 is based on dividing requirements being satisfied by X into three subsets where all elements of a subset are strongly related. An algorithm is presented to aid a designer in identifying these so-called requirements clusters. 15 refs.

271. **[Huebner 1979].**
Huebner, D. L. "Systems Validation through Automated Requirement Verification." In *IEEE COMPSAC '79,* Washington D.C.: Computer Society Press of the Institute of Electrical and Electronics Engineers., 1979, pp. 222–27.

Describes the System Test Complex (STC), which can be attached to a telephone switching system in order to test thoroughly, accurately, and efficiently whether the system meets its requirements. 7 refs.

272. **[Huff and Madnick 1978].**
Huff, S. L., and S. E. Madnick. *An Approach to Constructing Functional Requirement Statements for System Architectural Design.* Center for Information Systems Research, MIT Sloan School of Management, Technical Report 6. Cambridge, Mass., June 1978.

Investigates using standard sentence templates for requirements specifications. Authors feel that most other requirements languages (e.g., PSL) are suitable only after a system has been designed. Templates described are to be used prior to system design. These are part of the Systematic Design Methodology (SDM). 32 refs.

273. **[IBM 1973].**
IBM. *HIPO: Design Aid and Documentation Tool.* IBM Technical Note SR20-9413-0. 1973.

274. **[IEEE 1984].**
Institute of Electrical and Electronics Engineers. *IEEE Guide to Software Requirements Specifications.* IEEE/ANSI Standard 830-1984. New York, 1984.

Discusses advantages, attributes, and recommended format of a properly written software requirements specification. 10 refs.

275. **[IEEE 1985].**
Institute of Electrical and Electronics Engineers. "Douglas Ross Talks about Structured Analysis." *IEEE Computer* **18,** 7 (July 1985): 80–88.

Candid interview with the inventor of SADT. No refs.

276. **[Ikadai et al. 1985].**
Ikadai, M., et al. "Requirements Specification with M-Box." In *Third International IEEE Workshop on Specification and Design,* Washington D.C.: Computer Society Press of the Institute of Electrical and Electronics Engineers, 1985, pp. 109–13.

Briefly describes a tool called M-Box that enables requirements writers to write requirements from five different perspectives using five different models: user objectives, conceptual data, conceptual process, data flow, and control flow. Provides little beyond the work of DeMarco, Ward, and Hatley. 6 refs.

277. [Ince and Hekmatpour 1987].

Ince, D., and S. Hekmatpour. "Software Prototyping—Progress and Prospects." *Information and Software Technology* **29,** 1 (January/February 1987): 8–14.

278. [Irvine and Wasserman 1979].

Irvine, C. A., and A. I. Wasserman. *Tutorial 2: Software Requirements Analysis and Definition. In Specifications of Reliable Software Conference,* Washington D.C.: Computer Society Press of the Institute of Electrical and Electronics Engineers, 1979.

Collection of slides that define requirements, the Structured Analysis and Design (SADT), and the Structured Systems Analysis (SSA) techniques.

279. [Jacks 1979].

Jacks, E. "SADT." Panelist report in W. Bail, "User Experiences with Specification Tools." *ACM Software Engineering Notes* **4,** 3 (July 1979): 11–12.

Brief summary of GM's experience using SADT as an aid in performing detailed design, not problem analysis.

280. [Jackson and Vermeersch 1983].

Jackson, D., and B. Vermeersch. "A Requirements Analysis and Documentation Methodology." In *Second IEEE Phoenix Conference on Computers and Communications,* Washington D.C.: Computer Society Press of the Institute of Electrical and Electronics Engineers, 1983, pp. 363–67.

Describes the Feature Analysis Description (FAD) methdology for defining system requirements for a large family of telephone switching systems. Requirements are organized into clusters of services (called features) provided to the switch user. The requirements document is stored in computer-readable form to facilitate updating and cross-referencing. No refs.

281. [JacksonM 1982].

Jackson, M. *Systems Development.* Englewood Cliffs, N.J.: Prentice Hall, 1982.

282. [Jahanian and Mok 1986].

Jahanian, F., and A. Mok. "Safety Analysis of Timing Properties in Real-Time Systems." *IEEE Transactions on Software Engineering* **6,** 1 (January 1986): 2–13.

283. [Jahanian and Mok 1989].

Jahanian, F., and A. Mok. "Modechart: A Specification Language for Real-Time Systems." unpublished manuscript. May appear in *IEEE Transactions on Software Engineering.* 1989-1990.

Similar to the work of Harel, these authors have formally defined serial and parallel decompositions of finite state machines, and extended modes even further to make them yet more useful in specifying real-time systems. 11 refs.

284. [Jakob 1983].

Jakob, R. J. "Using Formal Specifications in the Design of a Human-Computer Interface." *CACM* **26,** 4 (April 1983): 259–64.

Describes a transition-diagram-based language for specifying command language types of user–machine interactions. 19 refs.

285. [Janson and Smith 1985].

Janson, M., and L. Smith. "Prototyping for Systems Development: A Critical Appraisal." *MIS Quarterly* **9,** 4 (December 1985): 305–16.

286. [Jefferson and Taylor 1979].

Jefferson, D. K.,and D. W. Taylor. "Analysis of Requirements for Large-Scale Information Systems." In *IEEE COMPSAC '79,* Washington D.C.: Computer Society Press of the Institute of Electrical and Electronics Engineers, 1979, p. 282.

Describes the application of PSL/PSA and the Interactive Database Design Methodology (IDDM) to defining requirements of the U.S. Navy Inventory Control Program. Abstract and summary only. No refs.

287. [Jensen and Tonies 1979].

Jensen, R. W., and C. C. Tonies. *Software Engineering.* Englewood Cliffs, N.J.: Prentice Hall, 1979.

288. [Johnson 1983].

Johnson, D. "Selecting a Methodology for Requirements Analysis." In *Second Annual Phoenix Conference on Computers and Communications,* Washington D.C.: Computer Society Press of the Institute of Electrical and Electronics Engineers, 1983, pp. 357–62.

Compares and contrasts DeMarco's Structured Analysis, SADT, HIPO, Petri nets, PSL/PSA, SREM, RLP, and USE.IT. It describes the applicability of each to a range of problems. 20 refs.

289. [JohnsonL 1979].

Johnson, L. "CADSAT." Panelist report in W. Bail, "User Experiences with Specification Tools." *ACM Software Engineering Notes* **4,** 3 (July 1979): 13–14.

Brief summary of Logicon's use of PSL/PSA on two projects.

290. [JohnsonL 1983].

Johnson, L. "PSL/PSA to the Rescue." In *IEEE Symposium on Application and Assessment of Automated Tools for Software Development,* Washington D.C.: Computer Society Press of the Institute of Electrical and Electronics Engineers, 1983.

291. [JohnsonW 1988].

Johnson, W. "Deriving Specifications from Requirements." In *Tenth IEEE International Conference on Software Engineering,* Washington D.C.: Computer Society Press of the Institute of Electrical and Electronics Engineers, 1988.

292. [Jones 1976].

Jones, M. N. "HIPO for Developing Specifications." *Datamation* **22,** 3 (March 1976): 112–25.

As a solution to the difficulty of specifying requirements at project initiation time, this author proposes simultaneously developing requirements and design. This once classic paper claims that development teams would save money doing so. Since 1976 the software community has recognized that the majority of a project's costs are expended by the end of design. Thus simultaneously defining a customer's needs and developing the software design can be financially devastating. No refs.

293. [Jorgensen 1985].

Jorgensen, P. *The Use of MM-Paths in Constructive Software Development.* Ph.D. diss., Arizona State University, Department of Computer Science, 1985.

Presents a technique equivalent to Petri nets for defining process descriptions for real-time systems. MM-paths are particularly helpful in transitioning requirements to design. 66 refs.

294. [Jorgensen 1985a.]

Jorgensen, P. *Requirements Specification Overview.* Carnegie Mellon University Software Engineering Institute Curriculum Module SEI-CM-1-1.2 (preliminary). Pittsburgh, July 1987.

Provides an expanded outline for an undergraduate course in requirements specifications. Main topics are introduction (including material covering purposes, standards, attributes of an SRS, and the DoD acquisition process); information needs of the user community (including customer, project management, product developers, IV&V, and maintainers); a taxonomy of the application domains; underlying models for requirements specification (including FSMs, marked graphs, computation graphs, P/V systems, message systems, UCLA graphs and vector systems); and representations of requirements (including text and graphical). 51 refs.

295. [Kamin et al. 1983].

Kamin, S. N., et al. "The Role of Executable Specifications: The FASE System." In *IEEE Symposium on Application and Assessment of Automated Tools for Software Development,* Washington D.C.: Computer Society Press of the Institute of Electrical and Electronics Engineers, 1983.

296. [Kampen 1982].

Kampen, G. "SWIFT: A Requirements Specification System for Software." In *International Symposium on Current Issues of Requirements Engineering Environments,* edited by Y. Ohno. Amsterdam: North Holland Publ, 1982. pp. 77–84.

Describes an implementation of a requirements and design specification system with three primary advantages over existing systems: (1) It uses a relational data base; (2) it supports one common semantic framework that five different languages (i.e., command, query, design, syntactic meta, and specification) share, and (3) it enables users to tailor the data base and the language to fit their own terminology. 19 refs.

297. [Kang 1980].

Kang, K. *A Methodology for Analyzing System Descriptions for Completeness.* Ph.D. diss., University of Michigan, 1980.

298. [Kawashima et al. 1971].

Kawashima, H., et al. "Functional Specification of Call Processing by State Transition Diagram." *IEEE Transactions on Communications* **19,** 5 (October 1971): 581–87.

One of the earliest papers on the usefulness of specifying behavioral characteristics of a real-time system using finite state machines. The language used for this specification is graphical and contains two primary nodes—state nodes representing the state of a particular active process and a translation node enabling the specifier to describe how the next state is a function of states of other internal system resources. The method results in an unambiguous, implementation-independent, and flexible specification. 5 refs.

299. [Keller 1989].

Keller, S. "Specifying Software Quality Metrics." In *Tutorial: System and Software Requirements Engineering,* R. Thayer and M. Dorfman, eds. Washington, D.C.: IEEE Computer Society, 1989.

300. [Kerola and Freeman 1981].

Kerola, P., and P. Freeman. "A Comparison of Life Cycle Models." In *Fifth IEEE International Conference on Software Engineering,* Washington D.C.: Computer Society Press of the Institute of Electrical and Electronics Engineers, 1981, pp. 90–99.

Provides a four-step methodology for software development: pragmatic phase (same as problem analysis), the input/output perspective phase (same as writing the SRS), the constructive phase (same as design), and the operative phase (same as coding and testing). 25 refs.

301. [Keus 1982].

Keus, H. "Prototyping: A More Reasonable Approach to System Development." *ACM Software Engineering Notes* **7,** 5 (December 1982): 94–95.

Describes differences between types of prototypes. No refs.

302. [Kim and Kwon 1987].

Kim, M., and Y. Kwon. "An Executable System Model Based on Stream Processing for Structured Analysis." In *IEEE TENCON '87,* Washington D.C.: Computer Society Press of the Institute of Electrical and Electronics Engineers, 1987, pp. 1202–06.

303. [Kim and Kwon n.d.].

Kim, M., and Y. Kwon. "Notes on Dynamic Analysis of Structured System Specification." Unpulished manuscript.

Presents the new idea of using data dictionaries as stream generators rather than as passive data definitions.

304. [Kimura n.d.].

Kimura, I. "On Teaching the Art of Compromising in the Development of External Specifications." *Journal of Information Processing* **1,** 1.

Discusses using particular programming examples in an early programming course to demonstrate the effect of requirements specifications. A text-formatting problem specification and list of ambiguity-removing questions are given. The impact of choices made in ambiguity removal on the complexity of the resulting program (which is shown in FORTRAN) is demonstrated. 12 refs.

305. [King 1984].

King, D. *Current Practices in Software Development.* Englewood Cliffs, N.J.: Yourdon Press, 1984.

Chapters 6–8 describe problem analysis and writing an SRS for data processing applications using hierarchy charts, data flow diagrams, data dictionaries, and structure charts.

306. [Kitagawa et al. 1982].

Kitagawa, H., et al. "Toward Second-Generation Requirements Engineering." In *International Symposium on Current Issues of Requirements Engineering Environments,* edited by Y. Ohno. Amsterdam: North Holland Publ., 1982. pp. 93–99.

Criticizes PSL/PSA and SADT for failing to provide reports suitable for non–system-designers. An excellent example shows diversity of the views of an inventory control system from the perspectives of the sales office, system designers, and management. According to this paper, Japanese industry has standardized a set of customer-oriented forms for requirements specification. Given these standards, called STEPS/E-SA, the authors describe a six-step methodology: (1) formulating the problem, (2) gathering information necessary to collect alternative solutions, (3) describing alternative solutions in detail, (4) modeling solutions, (5) selecting the solution, and (6) formulating the requirements definition of the selected solution. 14 refs.

307. [Kitani et al. 1981].

Kitani, Y., et al. "Automatic Generation of Call-Handling Programs." *Fourth International Conference on Software Engineering for Telecommunication Switching Systems,* London: Institution of Electrical Engineers, July 1981, pp. 72–76.

Describes the syntax and semantics of CASTLE, a detailed function and algorithm specification language from which table-driven software can be automatically generated. 15 refs.

308. [Klausner and Konchan 1982].

Klausner, A., and T. Konchan. "Rapid Prototyping and Requirements Specification Using PDS." *ACM Software Engineering Notes* **7,** 5 (December 1982): 96–105.

Describes an extension to a design and specification language called PDS to make it applicable to requirements. The paper also proposes a model of the software development life cycle in which a prototype is built early in the coding phase—after requirements and design are complete. The only connection between rapid prototyping and requirements (as stated in the paper's title) is that both are written in the same language (i.e., PDS). 17 refs.

309. [Koch and Rembold 1980].

Koch, G., and U. Rembold. "The Necessity of Requirements Engineering in Process Automation." In *IEEE COMPSAC '80,* Washington D.C.: Computer Society Press of the Institute of Electrical and Electronics Engineers, 1980, pp. 835–41.

Classifies ten different requirements and specification tools in terms of automated/manual, direct/indirect, and suitability for real-time systems. Describes in detail two tools—the Structured System Design for Process Automation (SSP) and Entwurfunterstutzendes, PEARL-Orientiertes Spezifikations System (EPOS). SSP uses Petri nets and decision tables to define process control. EPOS is a software development methodology controlling all phases of software development. 14 refs.

310. [Komoda et al. 1981].

Komoda, N., et al. "An Innovative Approach to System Requirements Analysis by Using Structural Modelling Method." In *Fifth International Conference on Software Engineering,* Washington D.C.: Computer Society Press of the Institute of Electrical and Electronics Engineers, 1981, pp. 305–13.

Describes a part-manual and part-automated technique for recording the objectives of a system, not its functions. Using blackboard, metal boards, cards, and magnets, a technique is given for defining carefully an organization and its functions. A program, called PPDS (Planning Procedure to Develop Systems), is then used to lay out and plot an objectives tree. A short example shows how the technique can be applied to an actual computer application. This paper offers little beyond that of Nakao. 7 refs.

311. [Kono 1983].

Kono, T. "A Method of Requirements Analysis and Application to Mail Processing System." In *IEEE COMPCON '83,* Washington D.C.: Computer Society Press of the Institute of Electrical and Electronics Engineers, 1983.

312. [Konsynski 1976].

Konsynski, B. R., Jr. "A Model of Computer-Aided Definition and Analysis of Information System Requirements." Ph.D. diss., Purdue University, 1976.

Describes a model of information systems that can be used for the PSL/PSA-like specification of such systems. Once a specification is written using the model, it can be checked for consistency (a set of propositions are true) and completeness (all mandatory relations are resolved). Two languages, one based on PSL and one a structured English design language, are developed and implemented. The class of applicable systems, collectively called information systems, are defined as those solving or assisting in the solution of operational or planning problems of society or organizations. 83 refs.

313. [Kramer et al. 1988].

Kramer, J., et al. *TARA: Tool-Assisted Requirements Analysis.* Rome Air Development Center Report RADC-TR-88-71. Griffiss Air Force Base, N.Y., May 1988.

Summarizes the results of a two-year project at Imperial College of Science and Technology for RADC. The purposes were to (1) supply guidance in selecting a requirements method appropriate to a particular problem, (2) provide simulation of requirements, and (3) provide reusability of specification fragments. This work is implemented in PROLOG on Apple Macintosh computers and expands on earlier work of CORE and EMMA. See other entries for Mullery. 31 refs.

314. [Krasner 1985].

Krasner, H. "Modeling Software Systems as Unified Views." In *Third International IEEE Workshop on Specification and Design,* Washington D.C.: Computer Society Press of the Institute of Electrical and Electronics Engineers, 1985, pp. 122-24.

Advocates building models during requirements and involving users in writing the SRS. 15 refs.

315. **[Krause and Diamant 1978].**

Krause, K. W., and L. W. Diamant. "A Management Methodology for Testing Software Requirements." In *IEEE COMPSAC '78,*. Washington D.C.: Computer Society Press of the Institute of Electrical and Electronics Engineers, 1978, pp. 749–54.

Describes a methodology for requirements testing. The heart of the methodology is the test evaluation matrix, which keeps track of changing requirements, changing software, and the implications and status of each test performed. 8 refs.

316. **[Kraushaar and Shirland 1985].**

Kraushaar, J., and L. Shirland. "A Prototyping Method for Applications Development by End Users and Information System Specialists." *MIS Quarterly* **9,** 3 (September 1985): 189–97.

317. **[Kung 1989].**

Kung, C. "Conceptual Modeling in Software Development." *IEEE Transactions on Software Engineering* 15, 10 (Octover 1989).

Provides formal definitions for a hierarchy of DFDs and for checking consistency between levels well beyond DeMarco's original concept of leveling. Kung does for DFDs what Harel did for finite state machines. Well worth reading. 35 refs.

318. **[Lamb et al. 1978].**

Lamb, S. S., et al. "SAMM: A Modeling Tool for Requirements and Design Specification." In *IEEE COMPSAC '78,* Washington D.C.: Computer Society Press of the Institute for Electrical and Electronics Engineers, 1978, pp. 48–53.

By combining hierarchy charts with SADT charts, the authors have defined the Systematic Activity Modeling Method (SAMM). The computer-based support system, called SIGS, is a graphics-based system that enables one to discover incomplete requirements coverage in the design and to keep track of the multitude of inevitable changes to the requirements and design. 10 refs.

319. **[Landau 1979].**

Landau, J. V. "State Description Techniques Applied to Industrial Machine Control." *IEEE Computer* **12,** 2 (February 1979): 32–40.

Describes a finite state machine-based assembly language for specifying industrial controllers. The paper describes how the language translator (an assembler) is constructed and provides an example of using the approach in one particular application—an industrial sewing machine. 4 refs.

320. **[Lano 1989].**

Lano, R. "Operational Concept Document: The Bridge Between the User and the Developer." In *Tutorial: System and Software Requirements Engineering,* R. Thayer and M. Dorfman, eds. Washington, D.C.: IEEE Computer Society, 1989.

321. **[Larson et al. 1979].**

Larson, R. et al. "Development of a Unified Approach for Systems Requirements Engineering." In *IEEE COMPSAC '79,* Washington D.C.: Computer Society Press of the Institute of Electrical and Electronics Engineers, 1979, pp. 215–21.

Describes the Axiomatic Requirements Engineering (ARE) methodology, which is an iterative process resulting in increasingly more refined statements of requirements. The process begins with a set of system characteristics, a set of quantitative goals for those characteristics, a set of system design decisions that define the solution space, and a set of models that enable one to describe relationships between these sets. The process is iterative because new requirements are derived from previously ascertained ones. Some examples are given. 2 refs.

322. **[Lauber 1982].**

Lauber, R. J. "Development Support Systems." *IEEE Computer* **15,** 5 (May 1982): 36–46.

Presents a quick overview of eleven software development systems and classifies the tools into various categories. Describes in detail the Engineer and Process-Oriented Development Support System (EPOS). One part of EPOS, called EPOS-R, supports the requirements phase; it is basically informal natural language combined with a fixed outline and the keyword *requirement* used to identify requirements statements. It is interesting to note that the author's chart comparing EPOS and PDL reports that EPOS handles requirements but PDL does not. PDL is certainly not an ideal requirement language, but it does provide more support than EPOS-R! 25 refs.

323. **[Lausen 1988].**

Lausen, Georg. "Modeling and Analysis of the Behavior of Information Systems." *IEEE Transactions on Software Engineering* **14,** 11 (November 1988): 1610–20.

Combines the precision of Petri nets with the convenience and simplicity of hierarchical data flow diagrams to define a bottom-up methodology that captures the behavior of information systems. 33 refs.

324. **[Lee and Sluizer 1985].**

Lee, S., and S. Sluizer. "On Using Executable Specifications for High-Level Prototyping." In *Third IEEE International Workshop on Specification and Design,* Washington D.C.: Computer Society Press of the Institute of Electrical and Electronics Engineers, 1985, pp. 130–34.

Shows how GTE Laboratories is building prototypes from FSMs. 4 refs.

325. **[Levene and Mullery 1982].**

Levene, A., and C. Mullery. "An Investigation of Requirements Specification Language: Theory and Practice." *IEEE Computer* **15,** 5 (May 1982): 50–59.

An excellent description of what requirements specificaton is and what purposes it fulfills. The authors' thesis is that useful requirements languages must be sufficiently precise to enable automated consistency and completeness checking but natural enough to permit easy readablity. The paper discusses the Software Development System (SDS) in depth. SDS does not include any particular requirements language but provides extensive language definition capabilities for defining such languages. The characteristics of their first language, based on the entity–relationship–attribute model, is described. 13 refs.

326. **[Levitt et al. 1979].**

Levitt, K., et al. *The SRI International Hierarchical Development Handbook.* Vol. 3, *A Detailed Example in the Use of HDM.* SRI International, Naval Ocean Systems Center Document 366. June 1979. Available from DTIC.

327. [Lipka 1980].

Lipka, S. "Some Issues in Requirements Definition." In *IEEE COMPSAC '80,* Washington D.C.: Computer Society Press of the Institute of Electrical and Electronics Engineers, 1980, pp. 56–58.

Emphasizes the need for requirements methodologies that are data oriented rather than function oriented and enable analysts to address multiple viewpoints of the process. 4 refs.

328. [Liskov and Berzins 1978].

Liskov, B. H., and V. Berzins. "An Appraisal of Program Specifications." In *Research Directions in Software Technology,* edited by P. Wegner. Cambridge, Mass.: MIT Press, 1978.

A thorough survey of available formal techniques for specifying modules. Suggests using informal specifications to communicate salient features of a module in an understandable fashion along with formal specifications that contain all details and impart the meaning of the specification. The techniques surveyed and contrasted for sequential programs are procedural abstractions, input/output, operational, data abstraction, axiomatic, and abstract model. The techniques surveyed and contrasted for parallel programs are state variable and event approaches. 54 refs.

329. [Liskov and Guttag 1988].

Liskov, B., and J. Guttag. *Abstraction and Specification in Program Development.* Cambridge, Mass.: MIT Press, 1988.

Using CLU as a specification language, this book provides detailed information about procedural and data abstractions in programs (design and code). Introduces the concept of a *specificand set,* which is "the set of all [systems] that satisfy [the specification]." This concept is analogous to the *product space* defined in Chapter 2 of the current book. The remainder of the book addresses design, testing, and verification issues related to abstraction and specification.

330. [Lor and Berry 1987].

Lor, K.-W., and D. Berry. "A Requirement-Driven System Design Environment." In *IEEE Second International Conference on Computers and Applications,* Washington D.C.: Computer Society Press of the Institute of Electrical and Electronics Engineers, 1987, pp. 817–20.

Brief summary of how the authors combined stimulus-response sequences, data flow diagrams, and SARA. 8 refs.

331. [Loshbough et al. 1981].

Loshbough, R., et al. *Applicability of SREM to the Verification of Management Information System Software Requirements,* Vols. 1 and 2. TRW Report 37554-6950-001. Huntsville, Ala., April 1981.

Reports the successful results of a study by TRW to apply SREM to a non-BDMS application, in particular to an MIS function. Volume 1 is the actual report; volume 2 consists of four appendices that address (1) the operation of REVS on a VAX, (2) the regeneration of requirements, (3) the application of the requirements analysis and data extraction function, and (4) a list of 302 trouble reports generated by REVS when processing an army specification (DFSR for SAMS-MOM). No refs.

332. **[Ludewig 1980].**

Ludewig, J. *PCSL—A Process Control Software Specification Language.* Kernforschungszentrum Karlsruhe Report 2874. April 1980.

Detailed description of the PCSL language that can be used for the detailed specification of process control software. PCSL is closely related to PSL but has altered syntax and changes to semantics to limit the general scope of PSL to the process control problem. The primary motivation for the language development is software reliability, not readable requirements specification documents. 8 refs.

333. **[Ludewig 1980a].**

Ludewig, J. "Process Control Software Specification in PCSL." *IFAC/IFIP Workshop on Real-Time Programming,* Oxford, England: Pergamon Press, 1981, pp. 103–10.

Brief description of the capabilities of the PCSL language is given. The language is used to define a system's components and data flow. 8 refs.

334. **[Ludewig 1982].**

Ludewig, J. "Computer-Aided Specification of Process Control Systems." *IEEE Computer* **15,** 5 (May 1982): 12–20.

One of the best collections in the literature of wise (and original) thoughts about requirements specifications. To cite but a few: (1) Pure black box requirements are only an ideal, like GOTO-less programming; some design embedded in requirements, like some GOTOs in programs, is acceptable. (2) Occasionally describing a system in terms of a hypothetical architecture is perfect, especially if the requirements writer explicitly states that the architecture was chosen for easier definition, not to imply the actual design; an excellent example is given. (3) A mutual dependency may exist between design and requirements. For example, how do you know if you want the stairway in your new home carpeted if you do not know there is going to be a stairway until the floor plan has been designed? (4) A hierarchical model is absolutely necessary unless you are building something well understood, like a telephone switching system. (5) Using a tool without a technique "is a rope trick which will fail."

The latter half of the paper discusses a specification language (ESPRESO-S) and tool (ESPRESO-W) that embody Ludewig's ideas on requirements. A well-formulated language, a successor to PCSL, is carefully defined, and examples and justifications are given. The author hints at how a tool could be written that would automatically generate a large part of the actual software in PASCAL for ESPRESO-L. 24 refs.

335. **[Luqi and Berzins 1987].**

Luqi, and V. Berzins. *Rapid Prototyping of Real-Time Systems.* Naval Postgraduate School Computer Science Dept. Report 87-5. Monterey, Calif., 1987.

336. **[Luqi and Berzins 1988].**

Luqi, and V. Berzins. "Rapidly Prototyping Real-Time Systems." *IEEE Software* **5,** 5 (September 1988): 25–36.

Proposes a *design* methodology for developing prototypes using the Prototype-System Description Language (PSDL). It combines the concepts of asynchronous process design and dynamic calling hierarchy design with formal non-procedural real-time constraint specification. The paper also describes the PSDL environment in which one can define, construct, and modify prototypes efficiently.

337. [Luqi et al. 1988].

Luqi, et al. "A Prototyping Language for Real-Time Software." *IEEE Transactions on Software Engineering,* **14,** 10 (October 1988): 1409–23.

Describes the PSDL language for rapidly designing and implementing real-time systems. One application for PSDL involves constructing a rapid prototype during the problem analysis stage in order to verify the developer's understanding of requirements. PSDL has facilities for recording and enforcing timing constraints, for modeling control aspects of real-time systems and specifying operator and data abstractions. An example is given of PSDL applied to a simple system for treating brain tumors with hyperthermia. 32 refs.

338. [Luqi and Ketabchi 1988].

Luqi, and M. Ketabchi. "A Computer-Aided Prototyping System." *IEEE Software* **5,** 2 (March 1988): 66–72.

Describes the environment that suports development of PSDL programs. 10 refs.

339. [Lyytinen 1987].

Lyytinen, K. "Different Perspectives on Information Systems: Problems and Solutions." *ACM Computing Surveys* **19,** 1 (March 1987): 5–46.

Section 5 of this paper surveys types of models available for information systems and their environments—formalistic information, functional information system, information system architecture, information need, success factor, sociotechnical, evaluation, and information system development contingency. 262 refs.

340. [McCabe 1983].

McCabe, T. "Structured Requirements and Testing." *Software Outlook Newsletter,* May 1983. McCabe and Associates, Columbia, Maryland.

Provides a brief summary of SRT,[4] a proprietary methodology that enables one to define a system specification and generate test scenarios from those specificiations. No refs.

341. [McCracken and Jackson 1982].

McCracken, D., and M. Jackson. "Life Cycle Concept Considered Harmful." *ACM Software Engineering Notes* **7,** 2 (April 1982): 29–32.

Provides strong criticism for any traditional life cycle model because it fails to bridge the incredibly large gap that exists today between the user and the analyst. The authors urge (1) user-developed systems, (2) user involvement in all phases of development, and (3) recognition that all requirements cannot be understood until after a system has been employed by the user (i.e., prototyping). No refs.

342. [McFadyen 1982].

McFadyen, W. S. "A Cohesive Methodology for the Development of Large Real-Time Systems." *Journal of Telecommunication Networks* (1982): 265–80.

This paper claims that "widely accepted methodologies" have some specific deficiencies in the area of requirements and lists these deficiencies. Unfortunately the author does not list the methodologies by name or reference. Since none of the ones in this bibliography exhibit these deficiencies, one must conclude that the author

---

[4]Trademark of McCabe and Associates, Inc., Columbia, Md.

knows of others. Furthermore the paper says that requirements should come after architectural design and exhibit the same structure as the implemented system. The author is therefore using the term *requirements* instead of *design* for the design stage. In fact if you replace every occurrence of *requirements* with *design* in the paper, then it makes sense except that it completely denies the need of a requirements phase for large systems. 6 refs.

343. [McGowan and McHenry 1979].

McGowan, C. L., and R. C. McHenry. "Software Management (Requirements Specifications)." In *Research Directions in Software Engineering,* P. Wegner, ed. Cambridge, Mass.: MIT Press, 1979, pp. 226–31.

Brief overview of four graphical requirements notations (HIPO, Semantic Analysis, Structural System Analysis, and SADT) and two computer-based requirements analysis, storage, and retrieval systems (SADT and REVS). 18 refs.

344. [McGowan et al. 1985].

McGowan, C. L., et al. "The Metafor Approach to Executable Specifications." In *Third IEEE International Workshop on Specification And Design,* Washington D.C.: Computer Society Press of the Institute of Electrical and Electronics Engineers, 1985, pp. 163–69.

Brief overview of a state-transition-based operational specification technique called Metafor and provides an example of its use on a patient-monitoring system. 30 refs.

345. [McMenamin and Palmer 1984].

McMenamin, S., and J. Palmer. *Essential Systems Analysis.* Englewood Cliffs, N.J.: Prentice Hall, 1984.

As an expansion of DeMarco's methodology, this book makes considerable progress in explaining the difference between users' real needs (called essential requirements) and those requirements that represent the external behavior of one particular incarnation of a system satisfying those needs. Much helpful and specific advice is provided for modeling essential requirements (corresponding to part of problem analysis as defined by the book you are now reading). 54 refs.

346. [Maddison 1983].

Maddison, R. *Information System Methodologies.* New York: Wiley/Heyden, 1983.

347. [Maibaum et al. 1986].

Maibaum, T., et al. "A Modal Logic for Requirements Specification." In *Software Engineering '86,* P. Brown and D. Barnes, eds. London: Peter Peregrinus, 1986.

348. [Mantei and Teorey 1988].

Mantei, M., and T. Teorey. "Cost/Benefit Analysis for Incorporating Human Factors in the Software Life Cycle." *Communications of the ACM* **31,** 4 (April 1988): 428–39.

An excellent description of how incorporating human factors into software affects users; also describes how prototyping affects the software life cycle. 51 refs.

349. [Marca and McGowan 1988].

Marca, D., and C. McGowan. *SADT: Structured Analysis and Design Technique.* New York: McGraw-Hill, 1988.

The first book written to cover the most popular aspects of SADT. An excellent in-depth presentation with lots of helpful examples. 21 refs.

350. [Marker 1977].

Marker, L. R. "A Software Requirements Engineering Methodology Using a Requirements Statement Language and a Requirements Engineering Validation System." *Infotech State of the Art Report,* Oxford, England: Pergamon Infotech, Ltd. February 1977.

351. [Martin 1982].

Martin, J. *Application Development Without Programmers.* Englewood Cliffs, N.J.: Prentice-Hall, 1982.

Heavily oriented toward DP applications, this text provides an excellent one-man's view of the next twenty years in the programming industry. The book stresses that the only way of increasing programmer productivity substantially is by using data base query languages, report generators, graphics languages, application generators, very high-level programming languages, and parameterized application packages. Martin considers BASIC and APL to be very high-level languages because of the shortness of resulting programs. The author also advocates avoiding requirements languages. A particularly strong case against requirements is given in Chapter 4. 111 refs.

352. [MartinW and Bosyj 1976].

Martin, W. A., and M. Bosyj. "Requirements Derivation in Automatic Programming." In *Symposium on Computer Software Engineering.* New York: Polytechnic Press, 1976. pp. 123–31.

Describes a questionnaire for potential computer system users that can help determine the customer's real data processing requirements. The questionnaire addresses the customer's needs in only the area of operations management. Administering the well-thought out questionnaire is handled by an interactive program written in a LISP-based language called OWL. The authors claim that responses given by the user are sufficient to generate a program automatically that performs necessary tasks (i.e., solves the problem the user defined). However the software automation process has not been implemented and the authors provide no insight into how this can be achieved. 4 refs.

353. [Mason et al. 1982].

Mason, R., et al. "ACT/1: A Tool for Information Systems Prototyping." *ACM Software Engineering Notes* **7,** 5 (December 1982): 120–26.

354. [Mason and Carey 1983].

Mason, R., and T. Carey. "Prototyping Interactive Information Systems." *Communications of the ACM* **26,** 5 (May 1983): 347–54.

Describes ACT/1, a methodology and tool that enables specifiers to define user interfaces for interactive systems in terms of screen designs, data entries, and system responses that are together termed *scenarios*. Although ACT/1 supposedly generates prototypes automatically, the authors say that the prototype, with no changes, can be used as the product. 21 refs.

355. [Matsumoto 1977].

Matsumoto, Y. "A Method of Software Requirements Definitions in Process Control." In *IEEE COMPSAC '77,* Washington D.C.: Computer Society Press of the Institute of Electrical and Electronics Engineers, 1977, pp. 128–32.

Describes the application of decision tables to define the appropriate action for a process controller in response to particular sets of values of sensing ports. 5 refs.

356. [Matsumoto and Kawakita 1980].

Matsumoto, Y., and S. Kawakita. "A Method of Bridge Discontinuity Between Requirements Specification and Design." In *IEEE COMPSAC '80,* Washington D.C.: Computer Society Press of the Institute of Electrical and Electronics Engineers, 1980, pp. 259–66.

Describes Toshiba's Software Workbench System (SWB), which has helped bridge the gap between requirements and design for two thousand people working on seventy active projects. The system supports a hierarchical decomposition of function and data and uses a requirements data base, a design data base, and a data dictionary to span the two data bases. 17 refs.

357. [Matsumoto et al. 1982].

Matsumoto, Y., et al. "Specification Transformations and Requirements Specifications of Real-Time Control." In *International Symposium on Current Issues of Requirements Engineering Environments,* edited by Y. Ohno. Amsterdam: North Holland Publ., 1982. pp. 143–49.

Defines the software development life cycle as a series of model specifications where each specification is the result of a transformation on a previous specification. The paper describes three specific models in this process:(1) requirements that describe "what" entities, relationships between "what" entities, and constraints on "what" entities; (2) control and data flows specifying how to implement requirements; and (3) program structure describing software modules and their interrelationships. Concerning the requirements model, the authors strongly advocate using an applications-oriented model, language, and vocabulary. Since the authors are particularly interested in process control systems, an example is given from that domain. 12 refs.

358. [Matsumoto et al. 1984]

Matsumoto, Y., et al. "Flow Sketch Methodology: A Practical Requirements Definition Technique Based on Data Flow Concept." In *IEEE International Conference on Data Engineering,* Washington D.C.: Computer Society Press of the Institute of Electrical and Electronics Engineers, 1984.

359. [Matsumura et al. 1987]

Matsumura, K., et al. "An Application of Structural Modeling to Software Requirements and Design." *IEEE Transactions on Software Engineering* **13,** 4 (April 1987): 461–71.

Describes a methodology for creating a design from a set of fuzzy requirements using the Computer-Aided Software Design System (CASDS). 17 refs.

360. [Mayr et al. 1982].

Mayr, H. C., et al. *A Common Platform for Application System and Requirements Engineering.* Karlsruhe, W. Germany: University of Karlsruhe Fak, 1982.

361. [Mayr et al. 1984].

Mayr, H. C., et al. "Prototyping Interactive Application Systems." In *Approaches to Prototyping,* R. Budde et al., ed. Berlin: Springer-Verlag. pp. 105–21.

Describes an extension to transition diagrams, called information nets, that can be used to specify user interactions. Although the approach appears sound, there is no discussion of whether the authors have developed tools enabling the creation of prototypes from such nets automatically. This paper introduces two new terms— vertical prototyping and horizontal prototyping. Horizontal prototypes offer all (or most) functionality but in a less than perfect manner. Vertical prototypes provide complete service to only a limited number of functions. 27 refs.

362. [Meseke 1975].
Meseke, D. W. "The Data-Processing System Performance Requirements in Retrospect." *Bell System Technical Journal* (1975): S29–S37.

The Data-Processing System Performance Requirements (DPSPRs) were designed to specify performance constraints on the SAFEGUARD System. After a brief historical perspective, the paper describes what the DPSPRs contain. Although DPSPRs should have been limited solely to performance requirements, they often contained implementation details of algorithms. The author admits that this is not "pure," but explains what factors in this real case caused them to become "impure." During design the DPSPRs were used to motivate design and generate tests. In retrospect the author feels that the DPSPRs' greatest shortcoming was the lack of explicit interface specification between functions. No refs.

363. [Mical and Schwarm 1979].
Mical, R. D., and S. C. Schwarm. "SMC—A High-Level Language for Implementing State Transition Diagrams for Industrial Machine Control." Presented at *Eighth Texas Conference on Computing Systems,* Dallas, November 1979. pp. 1.5–1.13.

Describes the application of finite state machines to the requirements specification of computer-controlled machines. The Sequential Machine Controller (SMC) language enables one to specify sequences to stimuli and system responses. No refs.

364. [Miller and Taylor 1981].
Miller, T., and B. J. Taylor. "A System Requirements Methodology." In *IEEE Electro '81 Conference,* Washington D.C.: Computer Society Press of the Institute of Electrical and Electronics Engineers, 1981, pp. 18.5.1–18.5.5.

Describes a methodology for requirements specification of complex systems that often necessitate decomposing a black box into subboxes. This paper also defines the levels of automatic error checking possible with any requirements analysis tool. 9 refs.

365. [Miller and Taylor 1982].
Miller, T., and B. J. Taylor. "A Requirements Methodology for Complex Real-Time Systems." In *International Symposium on Current Issues for Requirements Engineering Environments,* edited by Y. Ohno. Amsterdam: North Holland Publ., 1982. pp. 133–41.

Defines a methodology for expressing requirements for real-time systems, given four assumptions: (1) Requirements must be easy for a customer to read, (2) different readers require different levels of detail, (3) requirements will be written by a team of analysts, and (4) requirements must be machine analyzable for the presence of ambiguity and inconsistency. The authors advocate the use of *clear-box requirements* in which the system is defined as a set of cooperating processes communicating via well-defined message over well-defined ports. The state space of the entire system is considered a subset of the cross product of the state spaces of constituent processes. An example is presented using a packet data network.

Implementation of the methodology can be achieved using a combination of PSL/PSA and RLP. 8 refs.

366. [Mills et al. 1986].

Mills, H., et al. *Information Systems Analysis and Design.* Orlando, Fla.: Academic Press, 1986.

A rigorous, professional, polished treatise on specification techniques. Three types of models are presented—black box (external view only), state machine (define external behavior using FSMs as a virtual machine), and clear box (internal view showing component interactions). Much thought has gone into this book by very well-respected authors, and the result speaks for itself. No refs.

367. [Mital and Berg 1988].

Mital, R., and R. Berg. "An Example of the Impact of CASE 2000 on Quality and Productivity." *Conference on CASE Technology,* Washington, D.C.: National Institute for Software Quality and Productivity, 1988.

368. [Mitchell 1980].

Mitchell, J. "Software Requirements Engineering from a User Viewpoint." Panel session at *NCC '80,* Montvale, New Jersey: AFIPS Press of the American Federation of Information Processing Societies, 1980.

369. [Mittermeir 1979].

Mittermeir, R. T. "Enhanced SADT for Requirements Analysis." In *IEEE COMP-SAC '79,* Washington D.C.: Computer Society Press of the Institute of Electrical and Electronics Engineers, 1979, pp. 300–305.

Extends the SADT concept to include morphological analysis. SADT is used in the usual hierarchical manner. Morphological analysis is used at each level to produce and contrast a variety of views, or dimensions, of the problem. Each of these views is then analyzed using SADT. Combination of the two techniques can result in finding a larger solution space than either technique used independently. 12 refs.

370. [Mittermeir 1980].

Mittermeir, R. T. *Semantic Nets for Modeling the Requirements of Evolvable Systems—an Example.* Inst. Digitale Anlagen Technical Report, University of Wein. Vienna, May 1980.

371. [Mittermeir et al. 1982].

Mittermeir, R. T., et al. "Alternatives to Overcome the Communications Problem of Formal Requirements Analysis." In *International Symposium on Current Issues of Requirements Engineering Environments,* edited by Y. Ohno. Amsterdam: North Holland Publ., 1982. pp. 163–69.

Compares and contrasts (1) objectives analysis, which derives the actual user, customer, and management goals; (2) prototyping, which provides a system to the user and enables analysts to quickly query its suitability for the customer; and (3) scenarios, which strike a middle ground between objectives analysis and prototyping. The three authors briefly describe their personal experiences with the three techniques and strongly advocate using them where and when appropriate. However, they specifically advocate using prototypes as the first stage only when it is believed that the prototype is likely to come close to the customer's actual needs. Otherwise objectives analysis should be performed first. 11 refs.

372. **[Mittermeir et al. 1982a].**
Mittermeir, R. T., et al. *Requirements Analysis—An Integrated Approach.* University of Maryland Technical Report TR-1155. College Park, 1982.

373. **[Miyamoto 1977].**
Miyamoto, I. "Software Requirements Engineering." Software Engineering: Current State-of-the-Arts Series, *bit,* **9,** 6 (May 1977): 86–93. Kyoritsu Publishing Company, Tokyo.

374. **[Miyamoto 1977a].**
Miyamoto, I. "Software Requirements Engineering: Methodologies and Tools." In *Record of the Symposium on Software Tools,* Tokyo: Association of Management Science, September 19–20, 1977.

375. **[Miyamoto 1978].**
Miyamoto, I. "Software Requirements and Specifications: Status and Perspective. *Bit* **10,** 10 (July 1978): 63–119.

376. **[Miyamoto 1978a].**
Miyamoto, I. "Software Requirements Engineering Methodologies for BMD Systems." *Bit* (special issue on specification) **10,** 10 (July 1978): 177–209.

377. **[Miyamoto and Yeh 1981].**
Miyamoto, I., and R. Yeh. "A Software Requirements Analysis and Definition Methodology for Business Data Processing." In *1981 National Computer Conference,* AFIPS, Vol. 50. Montvale, New Jersey: AFIPS Press of the American Federation of Information Processing Societies. pp. 571–81.

378. **[Miyamoto 1987].**
Miyamoto, I. "A Prototyping Tool for Graphical Software Engineering Tools." *ACM Software Engineering Notes* **12,** 4 (October 1987): 45–51.

Describes the Entity–Relation–Attribute (ERA) Meta-Graph System, which enables a designer to specify a system graphically using ERA diagrams. Most of the paper describes the user interface and internal design of the tool implemented on a Macintosh computer in C. 5 refs.

379. **[Montanari 1983].**
Montanari, U. "Requirements Analysis and Definition Techniques: Myth, Magic, or Reality?" In *Ninth IFIP World Computer Conference,* Amsterdam: North-Holland. 1983.

380. **[Moret 1982].**
Moret, B. "Decision Trees and Diagrams." *ACM Computing Surveys,* **14,** 4 (December 1982): 593–623.

Complete discussion of the state-of-the-art in decision trees and decision tables. 114 refs.

381. **[Morganstern 1975].**
Morganstern, M. "The Specification of Information Systems for Management." M.S. thesis, MIT, 1975.

382. **[Morrison 1988].**
Morrison, W. "Communicating with Users During Systems Development." *Information and Software Technology* **30,** 5 (June 1988): 295–98.

Advocates prototyping for systems of low complexity, conceptual modeling for complex systems with low uncertainty in requirements, and a combination of prototyping and conceptual modeling for all other systems. 22 refs.

383. [Morton and Freburger 1980].

Morton, R., and K. Freburger. "Toward Methodology for Function Specification." In *IEEE COMPSAC '80,* Washington D.C.: Computer Society Press of the Institute of Electrical and Electronics Engineers, 1980, pp. 201–6.

Explores difficulties experienced while writing a requirements specification. The paper gives a large number of very practical guidelines to follow to prevent similar difficulties. These guidelines are aimed at managers and technical staff. 9 refs.

384. [Mullery 1979].

Mullery, G. P. "CORE—a Method for Controlled Requirement Expression." In *Fourth International Conference on Software Engineering,* Washington D.C.: Computer Society Press of the Institute of Electrical and Electronics Engineers, 1979, pp. 126–35.

Describes and justifies the existence of the Controlled Requirement Expression (CORE) System. Includes an excellent summary of the aims of requirements analysis. CORE supports multiple viewpoints, numerous information types, relationships between information, and assigning attributes to the system. CORE is primarily a manual-enforced methodology supported in part by a diagram notation. Detailed rules are presented concerning construction of a variety of diagrams. Human-enforced rules are described in detail, which aid in producing a consistent and readable specification. 7 refs.

385. [Mumford et al. 1978].

Mumford, E., et al. "A Participative Approach to the Design of Computer Systems." *Impact of Science on Society* **28,** 3 (March 1978): 235–53.

386. [Murai et al. 1982].

Murai, J., et al. "A Software Development Tool under Japanese Environments." In *International Symposium on Current Issues of Requirements Engineering Environments,* edited by Y. Ohno. Amsterdam: North Holland Publ., 1982. pp. 59–67.

Describes the internal design of the tool discussed in the following bibliographic entry. 9 refs.

387. [Murai et al. 1982a].

Murai, J., et al. "Requirement Specification Description System in Japanese Language: JISDOS." In *Sixth International Conference on Software Engineering,* Washington D.C.: Computer Society Press of the Institute of Electrical and Electronics Engineers, 1982, pp. 127–36.

Describes a pre-processor and a post-processor for PSL/PSA that translate PSL to/from JPSL. JPSL is identical to PSL except that it uses Japanese characters. The input can be in Katakana or Romanji; the output can be in either Hiragana or Kanji. 9 refs.

388. [Musa et al. 1987].

Musa, J., et al. *Software Reliability.* New York: McGraw-Hill, 1987.

389. **[Myers 1976].**
     Myers, G. *Software Reliability.* New York: Wiley, 1976.
     Chapter 4 discusses specifying nonbehavioral requirements. 14 refs.

390. **[MyersM 1988].**
     Myers, M. E. "A Knowledge-Based System to Reduce Software Requirements Volatility." Presented at the *Twenty-Seventh Annual Technical Symposium of the Washington, D.C. Chapter of the ACM,* Gaithersburg, Md., June 1988.

391. **[MyersW 1978].**
     Myers, W. "The Need for Software Engineering." *IEEE Computer* **11,** 2 (February 1978): 12–26.
     An overview of 1978 state-of-the-art in software engineering principles. Mentions the requirements phase only briefly. 53 refs.

392. **[Mylopoulos and Greenspan 1983].**
     Mylopoulos, J., and S. Greenspan. "Knowledge Representation Issues for Requirements Specification." In *IFIP '83,* Amsterdam: North-Holland. 1983. pp. 135–42.

393. **[Nakao et al. 1980].**
     Nakao, K., et al. "A Structural Approach to System Requirements Analysis of Information Systems." In *IEEE COMPSAC '80,* Washington D.C.: Computer Society Press of the Institute of Electrical and Electronics Engineers, 1980, pp. 207–13.
     Emphasizes analysis and extraction of needs rather than the clarification of system functions during the requirements phase. The paper describes a methodology using matrices, objectives trees, and functional and operational activity flow diagrams to thoroughly define and relate the computerization needs of a company and the functional characteristics of the specified system. A tool, called the Planning Procedure to Develop Systems (PPDS), has been developed that supports the three-phase (needs analysis, functional requirements analysis, operational requirements analysis) requirements methodology. 7 refs.

394. **[National Aeronautics and Space Administration 1976].**
     National Aeronautics and Space Administration. *NASA Software Specification and Evaluation System Design Final Report.* NASA Report SAI-77-555-HU, NTIS N76-22945 and 6. March 1976.

395. **[National Bureau of Standards 1980].**
     National Bureau of Standards. *Guidance on Requirements Analysis for Office Automation Systems.* NBS Publication 500-72. Gaithersburg, Md., 1980.
     Describes a methodology that would aid a company in determining its individual requirements in the area of office automation. Specific attention is given to means of evaluating the increase in productivity resulting from introducing such systems. No refs.

396. **[Naumann and Jenkins 1982].**
     Naumann, J., and A. Jenkins. "Prototyping: A New Paradigm for Systems Development." *MIS Quarterly* **3** (1982): 29–44.

397. [Nelson 1989].

Nelson, E. "Solving the Requirements Allocation Mystery." In *Tutorial: System and Software Requirements Engineering,* R. Thayer and M. Dorfman, eds. Washington, D.C.: IEEE Computer Society, 1989.

398. [Nishio et al. 1982].

Nishio, T., et al. "A Requirements Definition Method Based on a Flow-Net Model." In *International Symposium on Current Issues of Requirements Engineering Environments,* edited by Y. Ohno. Amsterdam: North Holland Publ., 1982. pp. 41–49.

The authors put forth a two-level technique for decomposing system requirements. One level, the system flow diagram, shows interfaces between major system processes. The second level, the data flow diagram, shows the behavior of each process. The paper criticizes SREM, PSL/PSA, and SADT for not providing their users with criteria for decomposition. However, this paper also falls short of that target. The restriction to two levels seems to be arbitrary, and the authors provide no guidance concerning how to partition a real problem. 9 refs.

399. [Nogi 1981].

Nogi, K. "A Method for Expressing Requirements Specifications." In *Twenty-Second IPS National Conference,* Tokyo: Information Processing Society of Japan, 1981 (in Japanese).

400. [Nosek 1984].

Nosek, J. "Organization Design Choices to Facilitate Evolutionary Development of Prototype Information Systems." In *Approaches to Prototyping,* R. Budde, et al., ed. Berlin: Springer-Verlag, 1984. pp. 341–55.

401. [Nunamaker and Konsynski 1975].

Nunamaker, J., and B. Konsynski. "From Problem Statement to Automatic Code Generation." Student *Systemerring 1975,* Litteratur, Lund, Sweden, 1975.

402. [Nunamaker and Konsynski 1981].

Nunamaker, J., and B. Konsynski. "Formal and Automated Techniques of Systems Analysis and Design." In *Systems Analysis and Design—a Foundation for the 1980s,* W. W. Cotterman et al., eds. Amsterdam: North Holland Publ., 1981. pp. 291–320.

403. [Ohnishi et al. 1982].

Ohnishi, A., et al. "Improvement of Communicability of Requirements Description." In *International Symposium on Current Issues of Requirements Engineering Environments,* edited by Y. Ohno,. Amsterdam: North Holland Publ, 1982. pp. 69–74.

Begins with a very basic assumption: Formal requirements cannot be understood by customers. The authors later clarify that point: Japanese customers typically cannot read computer languages using English keywords. The goal of the project described in this paper is to provide a document, called the requirements description, that can be derived from the formal requirements specification but understood by the customer. The paper describes a system, called Translation Specification Language/Translation Specification Analyzer (TSL/TSA), designed to meet that goal. It accepts as input (1) a glossary to translate keywords and applications jargon from English into Japanese and (2) the Formatted Problem Statement (FPS) generated by PSL/PSA. It produces as output a Japanese translation of the requirements. It is not apparent how this tool achieves its goal in general. 7 refs.

404. [Ohnishi et al. 1985].
Ohnishi, A., et al. "Requirement Model and Method of Requirements Definition." In *IEEE COMPSAC '85,* Washington D.C.: Computer Society Press of the Institute of Electrical and Electronics Engineers, 1985, pp. 26–32.

Describes the Japanese Requirements Description Language (JRDL), which was created by severely restricting the natural Japanese language so that semantic analysis becomes relatively straightforward. Once an SRS is written in JRDL, it is translated into an internal form where it can be used as a basis for prototyping. Actual examples are shown in Japanese. 13 refs.

405. [Orr 1980].
Orr, K. "Structured Requirements Definition in the 80s." In *ACM '80 Conference,* New York: ACM Press of the Association for Computing Machinery, 1980, pp. 350–54.

Describes a structured requirements definition phase as part of the Langston-Kitch Structured Systems Development (SSD) Methodology. The phase is described very briefly as using Warnier–Orr and entity diagrams, both of which are demonstrated in a brief example. 11 refs.

406. [Orr 1981].
Orr, K. *Structured Requirements Definition.* Topeka, Kans.: Ken Orr and Associates, 1981.

Given that software design is accomplished by an output-driven method (as advocated in Orr's *Structured Systems Development,* Englewood Cliffs, N.J.: Yourdon, Inc., 1977), this book puts forth a specific methodology to help the analyst translate a statement of the problem being solved by the software into a definition of required system outputs. The methodology has the same name as the book, namely Structured Requirements Definition. The primary tools of the technique are entity diagrams and functional flow diagrams, both of which are profusely illustrated and described. A number of practical examples are given of the methodology in use. All the examples are of EDP problems. 26 refs.

407. [Palmer 1988].
Palmer, J. "Impact of Requirements Uncertainty on Software Productivity." Presented at *Twenty-Seventh Annual Technical Symposium of the Washington, D.C. Chapter of the ACM,* Gaithersburg, Md., June 1988.

408. [Pangalos 1986].
Pangalos, G. "Information-Oriented Approach to Structured Analysis and Design." *Information Age* **8,** 1 (January 1986).

409. [Parker 1976].
Parker, R. W. "The Development of Software Requirements Experiences from a Large Scale Program." In *IEEE COMPCON '76,* Washington D.C.: Computer Society Press of the Institute of Electrical and Electronics Engineers, 1976, pp. 45–49.

Provides a history of one particular requirements writing effort. No refs.

410. **[Parnas 1969].**
Parnas, D. L. "On the Use of Transition Diagrams in the Design of a User Interface for an Interactive Computer System." In *Twenty-Fourth ACM Conference,* New York: ACM Press of the Association for Computing Machinery, 1969, pp. 379–85.

411. **[Parnas 1972].**
Parnas, D. L. "A Technique for Software Module Specification with Examples." *Communications of the ACM* **15,** 5 (May 1972): 330–36.

Although not addressing requirements specifications per se, this classic paper contains so much of the justification for much (if not most) of subsequent research in requirements and design specifications that it must be included in this bibliography. The essence of Parnas's message is that a specification must (1) contain all information needed by a user to use the software and no more, (2) contain all the information needed by the implementer of the software to construct the software and no more, (3) be formal enough to be verified in some way, and (4) be readable enough to be understood by both user and implementer. All of these ideas seem almost trivial today, but they were not in 1972. Parnas also recognized that his approach has shortcomings, including the fact that specifications may become as complex as (or more complex than) the software itself.

412. **[Parnas 1976].**
Parnas, D. L. "On the Design and Development of Program Families." *IEEE Transactions on Software Engineering.* **2,** 1 (March 1976): 1–9.

Advocates the definition of viable subset and likely extensions in the SRS to facilitate the design process. A classic paper. 16 refs.

413. **[Parnas 1978].**
Parnas, D. L. "Desired System Behavior in Undesired Situations." *Software Engineering Principles.* U.S. Naval Research Laboratory Document UE.1. Washington, D.C., 1978.

414. **[Patton 1983].**
Patton, R. "Prototyping—A Nomenclature Problem." *ACM Software Engineering Notes* **8,** 2 (April 1983): 14–16.

A short bibliography on prototyping. 24 refs.

415. **[Perrone 1987].**
Perrone, G. "Low-Cost CASE: Tomorrow's Promise Emerging Today." *IEEE Computer* (new product review section) **20,** 11 (November 1987): 104–10.

An unbiased and thorough comparison of four structured analysis products. The four tools are Visible Systems' Visible Analyst Workbench, Cadre Technologies' Teamwork/PCSA, Advanced Logical Software's Anatool, and Iconix Software Engineering's PowerTools. No refs.

416. **[Peters 1978].**
Peters, L. "Relating Software Requirements and Design." *ACM Software Engineering Notes* **3,** 5 (November 1978): 67–71.

Proposes that requirements and design are not unique, separable, mutually exclusive phases. The author's thesis is that requirements and design phases are strongly linked and when applied iteratively result in a succession of increasingly refined models of the problem solution. 6 refs.

417. [Peterson 1987].

Peterson, V. "A Case Study in the Application of the ProMod Software Development System." In *Conference on Methodologies and Tools for Real-Time Systems*. Washington, D.C.: National Institute for Software Quality and Productivity, 1987, pp. P-1–P-8.

Presents actual results from using ProMod on a 50-month, 150-person, real-time DoD-standard system development. No refs.

418. [Petrie 1980].

Petrie, F. A., III. "The Utilization of Requirements Statement Methodologies in the United States Navy and Their Impact on Systems Acquisition." M.S. thesis, U.S. Naval Postgraduate School, 1980. Available from DTIC.

Provides extensive descriptions of REVS and PSL/PSA and describes the Navy's involvement with RSL. This report also briefly describes the variety of Navy standards relating to requirements. 28 refs.

419. [Pew and Rollins 1975].

Pew, R., and A. Rollins. *Dialog Specification Procedures*. Bolt, Beranek, and Newman Report 3129.Cambridge, Mass., 1975.

A set of guidelines to consider when specifying user interfaces using relatively old I/O devices. General principles however still hold: (1) Know the user, (2) respond consistently and clearly, (3) speak in the user's terminology, (4) adapt wordiness to expertise of user, and (5) allow user to correct errors. No refs.

420. [Pierce 1978].

Pierce, R. A. "A Requirements Tracing Tool." *ACM Software Engineering Notes* **3,** 5 (November 1978): 67–71.

Describes a tool useful for maintaining cross-references among sets of requirements and between requirements and design. 6 refs.

421. [Piperakas 1978].

Piperakas, N. "SRDM: A Software Requirements Definition Methodology." *Telecom. Report* (Germany) **1,** 3 (December 1978): 142–47.

Discusses the Software Requirements Definition Methodology (SRDM) developed by Siemens, Belgium. The six-step manual process stresses stating requirements from multiple viewpoints and organizing the specification into levels of abstraction to support the gradual exposition of detail. Although the need for consistency checking is emphasized, only manual methods of enforcement are suggested. A skeletal checklist is given to aid this manual process. 10 refs.

422. [Pirnia 1981].

Pirnia, S. "Requirements Definition Approach for an Automated Requirements Traceability Tool." In *IEEE National Aerospace and Electronics Conference,* Washington D.C.: Computer Society Press of the Institute of Electrical and Electronics Engineers, 1981, pp. 389–94.

Describes the requirements definition process used by SofTech for the functional requirements of a particular tool. That tool, an automated requirements traceability program, is described briefly. Types of analyses performed to determine the tool's data base are described. No refs.

423. [Postel 1974].

Postel, J. B. *A Graph-Model Analysis of Computer Communications Protocols.* Ph.D. diss., University of California at Los Angeles, 1974.

424. [Poston 1985].

Poston, R. "Preventing Software Requirements Specification Errors with IEEE 830." *IEEE Software* **2,** 1 (January 1985): 83–86.

Brief summary of ANSI/IEEE Standard 830. No refs.

425. [Poston and Bruen 1987].

Poston, R., and M. Bruen. "Counting Down to Zero Software Failures." *IEEE Software* **4,** 5 (September 1987): 54–61.

Short summary of nine "rules of order" for writing an SRS. 10 refs.

426. [Powell 1983].

Powell, P. B. "Software Requirements Analysis: A Disciplined Approach." In *IEEE COMPSAC '83,* Washington D.C.: Computer Society Press of the Institute of Electrical and Electronics Engineers, 1983, pp. 642–43.

Advocates writing user's manuals, generating test plans, interacting with users, and prototyping as means of uncovering problems in an SRS. Also advocates applying automated static and dynamic analyses on the SRS. 9 refs.

427. [Pressman 1982].

Pressman, R. *Software Engineering: A Practitioner's Approach.* New York: Mc-Graw-Hill, 1982.

Chapter 5 of this well-written, organized, and practical textbook on software engineering covers the requirements phase. Differentiates between problem analysis and writing an SRS. Briefly explores the applicability of DFDs, data dictionaries, Warnier diagrams, SADT, SREM, and PSL/PSA. Simple but practical examples are provided. 16 refs.

428. [Pulli 1988].

Pulli, P. "Execution of Structured Analysis Specifications with an Object-Oriented Petri-Net Approach," *IEEE International Conference on Computer Languages,* Miami Beach, October 1988.

429. [Quirk 1978].

Quirk, W. J. *The Automatic Analysis of Formal Real-Time System Specifications.* H.M.S.O. Report AERE-R 9046. London, 1978.

430. [Ramamoorthy and So 1978].

Ramamoorthy, C. V., and H. H. So. *Software Requirements and Specifications: Status and Perspectives.* Electronics Research Laboratory, University of California, Berkeley, memo UCB/ERL M78/44. June 1978.

A thorough and detailed analysis of a wide variety of requirements and design tools (including Higher Order Software, Fitzwater, SADT, F^2D^2, decision tables, information algebra, systematics, ADS, TAG, HIPO, ISDOS, SODA, BDL, structured design, LOGOS, THREADS, SREM, FSM, VG and Petri Nets). Although a very thorough analysis of each is given, it is unclear what the authors' perception is concerning differences among problem analysis, requirements specification, and design.

431. [Ratcliff 1988].

Ratcliff, B. "Early and Not-so-Early Prototyping—Rationale and Tool Support." *IEEE COMPSAC '88,* Washington D.C.: Computer Society Press of the Institute of Electrical and Electronics Engineers, 1988, pp. 127–34.

Hekmatpour defined three classes of prototypes—throw-it-away, evolutionary, and incremental. Floyd defined three classes of prototypes—exploratory, experimental, and evolutionary. Ratcaliff classifies prototypes using another dimension—the phase during which the prototype is constructed. Thus he defines three classes—early, middle, and late. Early prototyping uses VHLLs and 4GLs to explore interfaces and functions. Middle prototyping uses high-level languages to verify interfaces and functions. Late prototyping is used to perform performance evaluation. 33 refs.

432. [Rauch-Hindin 1982].

Rauch-Hindin, W. "Software Tools: New Ways to Chip Software into Shape." *Data Communications* (April 1982): 83–115.

Contains a brief introduction to the basic concepts behind PSL/PSA, REVS, and SDL. No refs.

433. [Rauscher and Ott 1987].

Rauscher, T., and L. Ott. *Software Development and Management for Microprocessor-Based Systems.* Englewood Cliffs, N.J.: Prentice Hall, 1987.

Chapters 6 and 7 provide a brief comparison of NRL's A-7E specification, RLP, HIPO, and PSL/PSA.

434. [Reifer and Trattner 1976].

Reifer, D. J., and S. Trattner. "Software Specification Techniques: A Tutorial." In *IEEE COMPCON,* Washington D.C.: Computer Society Press of the Institute of Electrical and Electronics Engineers, 1976, pp. 39–44.

Although the authors define specifications as the output of both the requirements and design stages, systems surveyed herein are almost entirely design techniques. Techniques analyzed are SADT, abstraction, top-down decomposition, Higher Order Software, LCP, information hiding, THREADS, and Structured Design. 13 refs.

435. [Reilly and Brackett 1987].

Reilly, E., and J. Brackett. "An Experimental System for Executing Real-Time Structured Analysis Models." Presented at *Twelfth Structured Methods Conference,* Chicago, August 1987. pp. 301–24.

436. [Rice 1981].

Rice, J. G. *Build Program Technique.* New York: Wiley, 1981.

Describes a language called Requirements Specification Language (RSL) developed by Olson Research that serves as input to the Automatic Software Generation System (ASGS). The ASGS generates financial data processing software directly from RSL. Includes forty pages of undocumented, poorly written, unstructured FORTRAN code that realizes the ASGS. 72 refs.

437. [Richter 1986].

Richter, C. "An Assessment of Structured Analysis and Structured Design." *ACM Software Engineering Notes* **11,** 4 (August 1986): 75–83.

A superficial review (as is this one!). 7 refs.

438. [Riddle and Edwards 1980].

Riddle, W., and B. Edwards. *Flight Software Requirements and Design Support System.* Available from NTIS Report N80-30061, University of Colorado, Boulder, August 1980.

Describes relatively unsuccessful attempts to specify flight software requirements using English prose (unstructured, hard to follow), Dream design notation (no timing facilities), and Gypsy (unsuitable for system requirements). Appendix B lists requirements tools; appendix C is a bibliography.

439. [Riddle 1984].

Riddle, W. "Advancing the State of the Art in Software System Prototyping." In *Approaches to Prototyping,* R. Budde, et al., ed. Berlin: Springer-Verlag, 1984. pp. 19–26.

Brief summary of how prototyping was applied to one particular project, the JOSEPH Software Environment. 3 refs.

440. [Riddle 1984a].

Riddle, W. "The Magic Number Eighteen Plus or Minus Three: A Study of Software Technology Maturation." *ACM Software Engineering Notes* **9,** 2 (April 1984): 21–37.

Describes technology transfer aspects of REVS, UNIX, and Smalltalk-80. The REVS description is particularly relevant to this book because it describes the eleven-year chronology of events from the idea to delivery of approximately eighty copies industrywide.

441. [Robinson 1979].

Robinson, L. *The SRI International Hierarchical Development Handbook.* Vol. 1, *The Foundations of HDM.* SRI International, Naval Ocean Systems Center Document 366, June 1979. Available from DTIC.

442. [Robson 1981].

Robson, D. "Object-Oriented Software Systems." *BYTE* (August 1981): 74–86.

443. [Rockstrom and Saracco 1982].

Rockstrom, A., and B. Saracco. "SDL—CCITT Specification and Description Language." *IEEE Transactions on Communications* **30,** 6 (June 1982): 1310–17.

444. [Roman 1982].

Roman, G.-C. "A Rigorous Approach to Building Formal System Requirements." In *IEEE COMPSAC '82,* Washington D.C.: Computer Society Press of the Institute of Electrical and Electronics Engineers, 1982, pp. 417–23.

Unlike many papers on the subject, this one provides a formal definition of requirements. Claims that finite state machines are not practical for real systems because they can not model infinite states. I know of no real systems that require modeling of infinite states. This paper is worth reading because of its excellent example of a requirements specification of a terminal-based bank teller system developed precisely in accordance with the author's definition of requirements. 11 refs.

445. [Roman 1985].

Roman, G.-C. "A Taxonomy of Current Issues in Requirements Engineering." *IEEE Computer* **18,** 4 (April 1985): 14–23.

Defines what every well-written SRS should be—appropriate, conceptually clean, constructable, precise, nonambiguous, complete, consistent, analyzable, formal, testable, traceable, expendable, tolerant of temporary incompleteness, adaptable, concise, and modifiable. Provides a useful taxonomy of requirements concerns. The author categorizes possible formal foundations for an SRS into nine models: finite state machines, data flow, stimulus response paths, communicating concurrent processes, functional decomposition, data-oriented models, and the three commonly used by compiler writers—denotational, axiomatic, and operational. He also categorizes requirements approach in terms of scope, level of formality, degree of specialization, software phase most appropriate, and development method. A paper well worth reading. 23 refs.

446. **[Rombach 1987].**
Rombach, D. *Software Specification: A Framework.* Carnegie Mellon University Software Engineering Institute Curriculum Module SEI-CM-11-1.0. Pittsburgh, October 1987.

447. **[Rosenbaum and Hackler 1980].**
Rosenbaum, J. D., and W. R. Hackler. "Requirements Specifications for Embedded Astronautic Systems." Presented at *Space-Enhancing Technological Leadership, American Astronautical Society Annual Meeting,* October 1980, pp. 1–21.

448. **[Rosenberg 1985].**
Rosenberg, D. PRISM—Productivity Improvement for Software Engineers and Managers." In *Eighth International Conference on Software Engineering,* Washington D.C.: Computer Society Press of the Institute of Electrical and Electronics Engineers, 1985, pp. 2–6.

Brief look at ICONIX's PRISM tool, which includes structured analysis capability. 6 refs.

449. **[Ross 1977].**
Ross, D. T. "Guest Editorial: Reflections on Requirements." *IEEE Transactions on Software Engineering* **3,** 1 (January 1977): 2–5.

Introduces the problems of requirements analysis and the 1977 state-of-the-art in requirements tools. No refs.

450. **[Ross 1977a].**
Ross, D. T. "Structured Analysis: A Language for Communicating Ideas." *IEEE Transactions on Software Engineering* **3,** 1 (January 1977): 16–34.

This classic paper describes the Structured Analysis and Design Technique (SADT) developed at SofTech, Inc. SADT is a graphical technique that encourages a hierarchical, top-down analysis and design of problems and their solutions from multiple perspectives. 6 refs.

451. **[Ross and Schoman 1977].**
Ross, D. T., and K. E. Schoman, Jr., "Structured Analysis for Requirements Definition." *IEEE Transactions on Software Engineering* **3,** 1 (January 1977): 6–15.

A classic paper that defines types of problems being solved during the requirments phase and presents Structured Analysis and Design Technique (SADT) as a method of recording these complex problems and their solutions. SADT is a graphical-based, hierarchically structured approach to thinking about complex problems in an orderly manner and to communicating and documenting ideas generated during analysis and design processes. 12 refs.

452. [Ross 1980].

Ross, D. T. "Removing the Limitations of Natural Language (with Principles behind the RSA Language)." In *Software Engineering,* edited by H. Freeman and P. Lewis. New York: Academic Press, 1980. pp. 149–79.

A well-written summary of Ross's philosophy of problem refinement and definition. With the premise that all communication between human beings is ultimately through natural language, Ross describes his *structured analysis* technique. Ross's Structured Analysis (RSA) embeds natural language within a well-defined framework of boxes and arrows. The content of each box serves as an abstraction for the detailed diagram representing that box at the next lower level in the hierarchy. The author carefully analyzes the ability of these diagrams to communicate ideas effectively. Pages 159–179 appear to be a compilation of vugraphs used by Ross in describing the contents of his paper at the 1979 Software Engineering Workshop in Albany, N.Y. 40 refs.

453. [Ross 1985].

Ross, D. T. "Applications and Extensions of SADT." *IEEE Computer* **18,** 4 (April 1985): 25–34.

Summarizes actual uses to which SADT has been applied. 13 refs.

454. [Roy 1983].

Roy, D.K. "A Methodology for Expressing the System Requirements of a Switching System." In *Second Annual Phoenix Conference on Computers and Communications,* Washington D.C.: Computer Society Press of the Institute of Electrical and Electronics Engineers, 1983, pp. 368–74.

States that most papers on requirements emphasize the specification document itself as opposed to methods used to arrive at a list of requirements. According to this paper, a number of problems must be addressed by a requirements methodology; these include: complexity, different levels of detail, group development of requirements, length, evolution of requirements for other related products, and slight variations between versions of the product. This author proposes dividing requirements specification into the following distinct levels—switching system, section, subsection, category, item group, and item. The author supplies no justification or motivation for the existence of or names given these levels. The paper does provide good justification for a glossary of terms, a menu of requirements elements, and definitions of system features and interfaces. A brief description is given of the physical implementation, stressing the ability to maintain proper configuration control of the very large multiproduct requirements specification. 12 refs.

455. [Royce 1975].

Royce, W. W. "Software Requirements Analysis: Sizing and Costing." In *Practical Strategies for Developing Large-Scale Software,* edited by E. Horowitz. Reading, Mass.: Addison Wesley, 1975, pp. 57–71.

Provides strong support for writing a requirements specification of high quality. There are three distinct requirements-oriented phases: (1) definition of the original set of requirements, (2) downward allocation of requirements to design components, and (3) upward modification of requirements to conform with things learned during design and implementation. There are four results of an inadequate requirements specification: (1) Top-down design is impossible, (2) testing is impossible, (3) the customer cannot steer the product to meet his needs, and (4) designers, not management, make critical decisions. Requirements definition specifies interrelationships between cost, schedule, performance, development techniques, and implementation risk. The author justifies the use of limited bottom-up design within requirements definition. A few pages of this well-written paper are devoted to the advantages of employing simulation to predict the size and cost of software development more easily. 11 refs.

456. [Russell n.d.].
Russell, L. J. "Real-Time Software Requirements." *In Infotech International Computer* State of the Art *Report,* Oxford, England: Pergamon Infotech Ltd. pp. 223–45.

457. [Rzepka 1983].
Rzepka, W. E. "RADC SREM Evaluation Program—A Status Report." *ACM Software Engineering Notes* **8,** 1 (January 1983): 20–22.

Briefly describes a Martin Marietta analysis of the applicability of SREM to command and control systems. 3 refs.

458. [Rzepka 1983a].
Rzepka, W. E. "RADC SREM Evaluation Program—Interim Results." In *IEEE COMPSAC '83,* Washington D.C.: Computer Society Press of the Institute of Electrical and Electronics Engineers, 1983, pp. 644–45.

Briefly describes the application of SREM by Martin Marietta to a command and control system. 2 refs.

459. [Rzepka 1985].
Rzepka, W. E. "A Requirements Engineering Testbed." In *Third IEEE International Workshop on Specification and Design,* Washington D.C.: Computer Society Press of the Institute of Electrical and Electronics Engineers, 1985, pp. 205–6.

Briefly describes the establishment of a testbed at Rome Air Development Center for analyzing requirements methodologies and tools. Thus far only REVS has been installed. 2 refs.

460. [Rzepka and Ohno 1985].
Rzepka, W. E., and Y. Ohno. "Guest Editors' Introduction: Requirements Engineering Environments." *IEEE Computer* **18,** 4 (April 1985): 9–12.

Provides a quick summary of the requirements domain and then introduces each of the eight papers in the special issue of *Computer* devoted to requirements engineering environments. No refs.

461. [Rzevski 1984].
Rzevski, G. "Prototypes versus Pilot Systems: Strategies for Evolutionary Information System Development." In *Approaches to Prototyping.* R. Budde, ed. Berlin: Springer-Verlag, 1984. pp. 356–67.

This paper claims that *prototypes* are ineffective because they lack robustness. Instead, *pilot systems* should be developed which do exhibit robustness. The term *prototype* is used here to be equivalent to *throwaway prototype* and *pilot system* to be equivalent to *evolutionary prototype.* 11 refs.

462. [Saito et al. 1981].
Saito, N., et al. "Japanese Translation of Requirements Specification Language, PSL." *WGSE of Information Processing Society of Japan,* February 1981 (in Japanese).

463. [Salter 1976].

Salter, K. "A Methodology for Decomposing System Requirements into Data-Processing Requirements." In *Second International Conference on Software Engineering*. Washington D.C.: Computer Society Press of the Institute of Electrical and Electronics Engineers, 1976, pp. 91–101.

Describes a requirements analysis technique based on a hierarchy of finite state machines augmented with procedural and data specification. This work was conducted by Aeronutronic Ford under contract to the U.S. Army Strategic Defense Command Advanced Technology Center. 14 refs.

464. [Samson 1988].

Samson, D. "A Knowledge-Based Requirements System." Presented at *Twenty-seventh Annual Technical Symposium of the Washington, D.C. Chapter of the ACM*, Gaithersburg, Md., June 1988.

465. [Sayani 1989].

Sayani, H. "PSL/PSA at the Age of Fifteen: Tools for Real-Time and Nonreal-Time Analysis." In *Tutorial: System and Software Requirements Engineering*, R. Thayer and M. Dorfman, eds. Washington, D.C.: IEEE Computer Society, 1989.

466. [Scharer 1981].

Scharer, L. "Pinpointing Requirements." *Datamation* **27,** 4 (April 1981): 139–51.

Emphasizes the need to define requirements before building a system. No refs.

467. [Scheffer 1979].

Scheffer, P. A. "Specification and Management of Software Requirements." In *AIAA Second Computers in Aerospace Conference,* Washington D.C.: American Institute of Aeronautics and Astronautics, 1979, pp. 409–15.

Defines the Multi-level Expression Design System (MEDL) and how it is applied to requirements using MEDL-R, design using MEDL-D, and process using MEDL-P. All three languages are translated into a relational data base so that traceability is possible between each of the levels. This paper describes the MEDL-R system in depth. The requirements document is assumed to contain large amounts of potentially ambiguous English text. The key words of the language enable requirements writers to record relationships between textual requirements, the justification for a requirement's existence, and so forth. The software system that supports MEDL-R is a specialized data base storage, edit, and retrieval system. 11 refs.

468. [Scheffer et al. 1984].

Scheffer, P. A., et al. "A Large System Evaluation of SREM." In *Seventh International Conference on Software Engineering,* Washington D.C.: Computer Society Press of the Institute of Electrical and Electronics Engineers, 1984, pp. 172–80.

469. [Scheffer et al. 1985].

Scheffer, P. A., et al. "A Case Study of SREM." *IEEE Computer* **18,** 4 (April 1985): 47–54.

Detailed account of the application of REVS to a C^3I system called ASE. The experiment showed that only 7% of errors in the requirements were found by the REVS tool itself. The remaining 93% were found through the manual application of the SREM methodology. Provides recommendations for improving the REVS tool, SREM, and the TRW training approach. 13 refs.

470. **[Searle 1978].**

Searle, L. V. *An Air Force Guide to the Computer Program Development Specification.* United States Air Force Document TM-5772/008/02. March 1978.

Intelligible digestion of early phases of the system development life cycle as defined by now-out-of-date MIL-STDs. Goes through each of the required early steps of the system acquisition process and explains each. Contains numerous references to the original standards documents.

471. **[Searle 1981].**

Searle, L. V. *An Air Force Guide to the System Specification.* United States Air Force Document TM-5772/010/00, ESD-TR-81-128. January 1981.

Provides a systems approach to the definition of computer-based (i.e., not just software) systems. The approach consists of three steps: (1) system concept, where an operational model of the requirements are defined; (2) initial systems specification, where an actual written document of the specifications is prepared; and (3) validation, where the specification is checked for validity. The author feels that it is not necessarily wrong to include design considerations in requirements; however one should not allow design considerations to divert attention from the primary purpose of identifying functional requirements. This report also states that all system requirements should be flagged to indicate their most desireable implementation—automated (i.e., implemented by software); manual (i.e., implemented by procedures); and man–machine (i.e., implemented as a software assistant to a human user). 18 refs.

472. **[Shooman 1983].**

Shooman, M. L. *Software Engineering.* New York: McGraw-Hill, 1983.

Section 6.2.2 of this book briefly discusses the contents of a requirements specification. Section 6.2.3 discusses requirements specification tools, and section 6.2.4 provides a brief example of an actual requirements specification. 3 refs.

473. **[Sievert and Mizell 1985].**

Sievert, G. E., and T. A. Mizell. "Specification-Based Software Engineering with TAGS." *IEEE Computer* **18,** 4 (April 1985): 56–65.

Using the language IORL, Teledyne Brown's TAGS has appeared numerous times in the so-called requirements literature, but all these papers, including this one, discuss designing system and software components, parameter lists between components, and the like. 2 refs.

474. **[Silver 1981].**

Silver, A. N. "Software Life Cycle Cost Estimating Using Structural Decomposition of Requirements and Design Parameters." *Fourteenth Annual IEEE Electronics and Aerospace Conference,* Washington D.C.: Computer Society Press of the Institute of Electrical and Electronics Engineers, 1981. pp. 665–73.

Defines techniques that provide measures of architectural effectiveness from a cross analysis of requirements and design. This data is then used to derive cost estimates. 17 refs.

475. **[Silverberg 1979].**

Silverberg, B. A., et al. *The SRI International Hierarchical Development Handbook.* Vol. 2, *The Languages and Tools of HDM.* SRI International Naval Ocean Systems Center Document 366. June 1979. Available from DTIC.

476. [Sklaroff and Smith 1988].

Sklaroff, J., and C. Smith. "Writing Quality Software Specifications: The Engineer's Challenge." In *AIAA/IEEE Digital Avionics Systems Conference,* Washington D.C.: American Institute of Aeronautics and Astronautics, 1988.

Briefly reviews the DoD's standards for software requirements and design with respect to documents and reviews. Justifies why all SRSs should be achievable, practical, relevant, testable, technically sufficient, well written, and not over-specified. The SRS-writing team used at IBM Owego for avionics system development consists of designers, support people, SRS document coordinators, systems engineers, data base administrators, programmers, and testers. The paper concludes with a brief description of how PSL/PSA has been interfaced with other tools and a brief set of recommendations for writing more readable specifications. 12 refs.

477. [Slegel n.d.].

Slegel, R. C. *Applying SREM to the Verification and Validation of an Existing Software Requirements Specification.* Applied Physics Laboratory, Johns Hopkins University. Laurel, Md; n.d.

478. [Slegel 1979].

Slegel, R. "SREM." Panelist report in W. Bail, chair, "User Experiences with Specification Tools." *ACM Software Engineering Notes* **4,** 3 (July 1979): 9–10. Brief summary of APL's experience using SREM.

479. [Slusky 1987].

Slusky, L. "Integrating Software Modeling and Prototyping Tools." *Information and Software Technology* **29,** 7 (September 1987): 379–87.

480. [Smith 1981].

Smith, D. *AutoidefO: A New Tool for Functional Modeling.* SofTech, Inc., Technical Report RP-125. September 1981.

Discusses the general use of AutoidefO, the interactive computer-aided graphics support tool used to define, analyze, and document the functions of complex systems. The method enforced is called IDEFO, a derivative of SADT. 10 refs.

481. [Smith 1982].

Smith, D. "Rapid Software Prototyping." Ph.D. diss., University of California at Irvine, 1982.

482. [Smith and Merrithew 1979].

Smith, D., and P. Merrithew. *Requirements Standards Study, Vols. 1–3.* Rome Air Development Center. Rome, N.Y., 1979.

Provides guidance for analyzing requirements specifications written in accordance with the DoD's MIL-STD 490 and 483. Volumes 1 and 2 describe the purpose of the study, the approach, and the history of Air Force specification techniques. They also summarize the *Requirements Engineering Guidebook* and automated tools available. Volume 3 is the guidebook itself. It defines characteristics and types of requirements and a requirements methodology. No refs.

483. [SmithG et al. 1980].

Smith, G., et al. "Incorporating Usability into Requirements Engineering Tools." In *ACM '80 Conference,* New York: ACM Press of the Association for Computing Machinery, pp. 355–68.

Provides a detailed comparison of IDEF, PSL/PSA, and REVS. Each is analyzed with respect to its language, graphics, and report generation capability, methodology, automated analysis support, simulation capability, and terminals. Conclusions are that SREM and IDEF offer more input language flexibility than PSL/PSA; IDEF provides more types of graphical presentation formats than the other two; IDEF emphasizes hierarchy, while REVS emphasizes flow; REVS and IDEF support a particular methodology, but PSL/PSA does not; REVS supports simulation, while the other two do not; and PSL/PSA offers the greatest variety of report generation facilities. The authors predict that future requirements systems will be graphics based, behavior oriented, and provide animation to help visualize tradeoffs. 21 refs.

484. [SmithS and Gerhart 1988].

Smith, S., and S. Gerhart. "STATEMATE and Cruise Control: A Case Study." In *IEEE COMPSAC '88,* Washington D.C.: Computer Society Press of the Institute of Electrical and Electronics Engineers, 1988, pp. 49–55.

Detailed analysis of MCC's experiences in applying i-Logix's STATEMATE tool to a particular problem—an automobile cruise control system. 20 refs.

485. [Smoliar and Scalf 1979].

Smoliar, S. M., and J. E. Scalf. "A Framework for Distributed Data Processing Requirements." In *IEEE COMPSAC '79,* Washington D.C.: Computer Society Press of the Institute of Electrical and Electronics Engineers, 1979, pp. 535–41.

Discusses early phases (i.e., requirements and high-level design) in developing distributed computing systems with known, fixed, and well-defined applications. Shows that it is mandatory to elaborate and repartition requirements at each level of network design. Developing distributed systems is an excellent example of how design and requirements tasks interact. 12 refs.

486. [Smoliar 1980].

Smoliar, S. M. "Operational Requirements Accommodation in Distributed System Design." In *IEEE COMPSAC '80.* Washington D.C.: Computer Society Press of the Institute of Electrical and Electronics Engineers, pp. 214–19. Also appears in *IEEE Transactions on Software Engineering* **7,** 6 (November 1981). pp. 531–37.

Distributed systems are unique because one cannot speak of the state of a system that is composed of machines each having an independent clock. This paper discusses decomposing virtual machines into hierarchies of virtual machines. One advantage of this approach is that reliability, changeability, and availability attributes can be applied to each of these machines independently. The paper describes a graphical representation, called the P-net, which provides a means of defining each processing task. These tasks can communicate with each other only via virtual queues. 14 refs.

487. [Snodgrass and Yun 1988].

Snodgrass, J., and D. Yun. "Software Requirements Specification from a Cognitive Psychology Perspective." In *IEEE International Conference on Computer Languages,* Washington D.C.: Computer Society Press of the Institute of Electrical and Electronics Engineers, 1988.

488. [SofTech 1976].

SofTech, Inc. *An Introduction to SADT—Structured Analysis and Design Technique.* SofTech Report 9022-78R. Waltham, Mass. 1976.

A basic guide to the concepts contained in SADT. Seven fundamental concepts are explained: (1) understanding via model building, (2) top-down decomposition, (3) functional modeling versus implementation modeling, (4) dual aspects of a system, (5) graphic format of a model, (6) support for disciplined teamwork, and (7) writing all decisions and comments. Help is provided to potential SADT diagram readers in understanding the meanings imparted by such diagrams. A very useful short report to assist one in learning what SADT is all about. No refs.

489. **[Solvberg 1979].**

Solvberg, A. "A Contribution to the Definition of Concepts for Expressing Users' Information Systems Requirements." In *International Conference on Entity-Relationship Approach to Systems Analysis and Design,* Washington D.C.: Computer Society Press of the Institute of Electrical and Electronics Engineers, 1979, pp. 359–80.

490. **[Sommerville 1982].**

Sommerville, I. *Software Engineering.* London: Addison-Wesley, 1982. pp. 11–37.

Describes the requirements specification phase in terms of (1) what are requirements, (2) how to express functional and nonfunctional requirements, (3) problems with specifying imprecise but inevitable requirements, (4) organizing a requirements specification, and (5) the need to validate requirements. A number of small but illustrative examples are supplied, and a few of the many tools supporting the requirements phase are briefly described. The author is a strong advocate for not using natural language in stating requirements. 22 refs.

491. **[Sroka and Rader 1986].**

Sroka, J., and M. Rader. "Prototyping Increases Change of Systems Acceptance." *Data Management* (March 1986).

492. **[Stefik et al. 1987].**

Stefik, M., et al. "Beyond the Chalkboard: Computer Support for Collaboration and Problem Solving in Meetings." *Communications of the ACM* **30,** 1 (January 1987): 32–47.

Presents a straightforward but impressive technique for interactively recording the results of brainstorming during a problem analysis session. Well worth reading. 35 refs.

493. **[Stelovsky and Sugaya 1988].**

Stelovsky, J., and H. Sugaya. "A System for Specification and Rapid Prototyping of Application Command Languages." *IEEE Transactions on Software Engineering* **14,** 7 (July 1988): 1023–32.

Describes the XS-2 system, which provides a non-procedural description language for specifying dialogs between humans and interactive programs. 23 refs.

494. **[Stephens 1978].**

Stephens, S. A. "Requirements Expression and Verification Aid." In *Third International Conference on Software Engineering,* Washington D.C.: Computer Society Press of the Institute of Electrical and Electronics Engineers, 1978, pp. 101–8.

Describes the Systematic Activity Modeling Method (SAMM) and its automation (SAMMDF). The method is based in part on, and bears a close resemblance to, SADT. A system model defined using SAMM consists of a tree where subordinate nodes represent semantic refinements (i.e., lower levels of abstraction), an SADT-like data flow activity diagram, and a condition chart, which describes behavioral requirements of the system. The paper describes types of errors that can be determined by SAMMDF—consistency and connectivity. Types of outputs generated by the tool are described. SAMM, SADT, and PSL are briefly contrasted. 8 refs.

495. [Stephens and Whitehead 1985].
Stephens, M., and K. Whitehead. "The Analyst—A Workstation for Analysis and Design." In *Eighth IEEE International Conference on Software Engineering,* Washington D.C.: Computer Society Press of the Institute of Electrical and Electronics Engineers. 1985.

496. [Svoboda 1987].
Svoboda, C. "Interfacing Excelerator/RTS with PSL/PSA to Support Development of Real-Time Systems." *Conference on Methodologies and Tools for Real-Time Systems: IV.* Washington, D.C.: National Institute for Software Quality and Productivity. 1987.

497. [Swartout and Balzer 1982].
Swartout, W., and R. Balzer. "On the Inevitable Intertwining of Specification and Implementation." *Communications of the ACM* **25,** 7 (July 1982): 438–40.

This excellent paper takes a controversial but probably altogether correct view that it is impossible to write a specification without entering the realm of implementation decisions. The first reason is that every implementation serves as the specification of the next phase. The second reason is that physical limitations specific to the choice of a particular host device (i.e., an implementation) can have major implications on what must be stated in the specifications. Third, the high level of complexity of today's problems makes it impossible to foresee all needs. An excellent example is given of a package-routing system specification, which at first glance appears ideal as a specification, but after further analysis, one notices that many assumptions were made about the physical implementation. Had other (equally acceptable) physical implementations been chosen, different requirements would have had to be written. A paper well worth reading. 23 refs.

498. [Taggart 1971].
Taggart, W. M., Jr. "A Syntactical Approach to Management Information Requirements Analysis." Ph.D. diss., University of Pennsylvania, 1971.

499. [Taggart and Tharp 1977].
Taggart, W. M., Jr., and M. O. Tharp. "A Survey of Information Requirements Analysis Techniques." *ACM Computing Surveys* **9,** 4 (December 1977): 273–90.

Describes criteria pertinent to managers when evaluating their requirements for information. A number of MIS analysis tools and techniques are described in terms of their ability to aid in each of these criteria. 69 refs.

500. [Tavolato and Vincena 1984].
Tavolato, P., and K. Vincena. "A Prototyping Methodology and Its Tool." In *Approaches to Prototyping,* R. Budde et al., eds. Berlin: Springer-Verlag, 1984. pp. 434–45.

Good introduction to prototyping for software. Uses the term *prototype* to refer to a system exhibiting the same performance characteristics as the real system, and *model* to refer to a system giving only the impression of being the real system (e.g., the software equivalent of the Hollywood stage set). Provides a brief summary of a software life cycle using both prototypes (what we call evolutionary prototypes) and models (what we call throwaway prototypes). 9 refs.

501. [Taylor 1980].
Taylor, B. J. "A Method for Expressing the Functional Requirements of Real-Time Systems." In *IFAC/IFIP Workshop on Real-Time Programming,* Oxford, England: Pergamon Press, 1981, pp. 111–20.

Describes the use of the Real-Time Requirements Language (RTRL), based on CCITT's SDL, for the requirements specification of real-time systems using a finite state machine model. 16 refs.

502. [Taylor 1980a].
Taylor, B. J. "Introducing Real-Time Constraints in Requirements and High-Level Design of Operating Systems." In *National Telecommunications Conference.* Washington D.C.: Computer Society Press of the Institute of Electrical and Electronics Engineers, 1980, pp. 18.5.1–18.5.5.

Augments the SDL language with timers. These timers can be used to define performance requirements for any arbitrary path through a state transition graph defined by the finite state machine specified using SDL. 7 refs.

503. [Taylor 1982].
Taylor, B. J. "Say What You Mean with a Language for Software Specifications." *Data Communications* **11,** 3 (March 1982): 131–43.

Excellent discussion of problems in writing a behavioral requirements specification. Puts forth excellent arguments for modeling real-time systems as sets of cooperating finite state machines. The FSMs communicate via signals over well-defined ports. SDL is used to document the resulting system. No refs.

504. [TaylorJ 1974].
Taylor, J. M. *Software Requirements for Dedicated High-Integrity Systems.* Signals Research and Development Establishment, AD-783-653. 1974. Available from NTIS. Advocates writing requirements for highly dependable software in an operational manner, that is, in terms of the behavior of a virtual machine. The Signals Research and Development Establishment of the Defense Research Information Center in England claims that such a requirements specification becomes understandable by both user and supplier. In addition the virtual system can be used as a significant part of the delivered system; that is, the requirements model is used as the design of the target system. This philosophy has been applied to a particular message switching system called HIVE. An example is given of a typical requirements specification for a dedicated high-integrity system. 9 refs.

505. [TaylorT and Standish 1982].
Taylor, T., and T. Standish. "Initial Thoughts on Rapid Prototyping Techniques." *ACM Software Engineering Notes* **7,** 5 (December 1982): 160–66.

Interesting study of the rapid prototyping research arena. Suggests that when prototyping, the developer should discard either response time or functionality that is not visible to users. Offers five alternative approaches to constructing rapid prototypes: (1) heavily parameterized models, (2) reusing software components, (3) user interface generators, (4) restricting functionality, and (5) rapid prototyping languages. Each approach is discussed briefly. No refs.

506. **[Teichroew 1972].**

Teichroew, D. "A Survey of Languages for Stating Requirements for Computer-Based Information Systems." In *1972 FJCC,* AFIPS, Montvale, New Jersey: AFIPS Press of the American Federation of Information Processing Societies, 1972, pp. 1203–24.

Classic but out-of-date survey of systems analysis and requirements specification techniques. A lengthy justification for such languages is given first. This is followed by a brief description of twenty-three systems, including ten that are either no longer being used or whose status Teichroew was unable to determine. Seven specific systems are then described in more detail and contrasted. After this analysis Teichroew describes what a requirements language should look like, then proposes PSL as that language. 70 refs.

507. **[Teichroew 1976].**

Teichroew, D. "ISDOS and Recent Extensions." In *Symposium on Computer Software Engineering.* New York: Polytechnic Press, 1976. pp. 75–81.

Brief overview of the capabilities of PSL/PSA and list of the current user population. 10 refs.

508. **[Teichroew and Winters 1976].**

Teichroew, D., and E. Winters. "Recent Developments in System Analysis and Design." *Atlanta Economic Review* (November–December 1976): 39–46.

Describes the problem of systems analysis as the accurate description of organizational information flow and decision making. The paper proposes using PSL/PSA as a tool for analyzing and documenting characteristics of an organization as a system. 8 refs.

509. **[Teichroew and Gackowski 1977].**

Teichroew, D., and Z. Gackowski. *Checking a System Description in a PSA Data Base for Consistency and Completeness.* University of Michigan ISDOS Working Paper 189. Ann Arbor. June 1977.

Describes the types of error reports generated by the PSL/PSA system. No refs.

510. **[Teichroew and Hershey 1977].**

Teichroew, D., and E. A. Hershey III. "PSL/PSA: A Computer-Aided Technique for Structured Documentation and Analysis of Information Processing Systems." *IEEE Transactions on Software Engineering* **3,** 1 (January 1977): 41–48.

This classic paper describes the primary goals and functions of the Problem Statement Language and Analyzer (PSL/PSA) developed at the University of Michigan. PSL/PSA provides a language, a data base system, an analysis system, and a report generator to aid in decomposing and analyzing system specifications and designs. 25 refs.

511. **[Teichroew et al. 1977].**

Teichroew, D., et al. *User Requirements Language (URL) User's Manual.* Hanscom Air Force Base, Electronic Systems Division Report ESD-TR-78-127. Mass. 1977.

512. **[Teichroew and Sayani 1980].**

Teichroew, D. and H. Sayani. "Computer-Aided Requirements Engineering." In *ACM '80 Conference,* New York: ACM Press of the Association for Computing Machinery, 1980, pp. 369–81.

Describes the Requirements Engineering System and how it meets the needs of systems analysts. 21 refs.

513. **[Teichroew and Chikofsky 1980].**
Teichroew, D., and Chikofsky. *An Introduction to the Problem Statement Language (PSL) and the Problem Analyzer (PSA)*. ISDOS Project, University of Michigan. Ann Arbor, August 1980.

514. **[Teledyne Brown Engineering 1980].**
Teledyne Brown Engineering. *The IORL[5] Operators Users' Language Manual*. Huntsville, Ala., 1980.

515. **[Teledyne Brown Engineering 1980a].**
Teledyne Brown Engineering. *The IORL Users' Language Manual*. Version 1-B. Huntsville, Ala., 1980.

516. **[Teledyne Brown Engineering 1987].**
Teledyne Brown Engineering. *Technology for the Automated Generation of Systems (TAGS) Overview*. Huntsville, Ala., 1987.

TAGS is a computer-aided systems engineering environment built around the Input/Output Requirements Language (IORL). TAGS enables one to define the hierarchy of system and software components comprising a system. Using both data flow and control flow, one can document a complete design of a system and have TAGS maintain the documentation and its integrity. Integrated with TAGS is a complete configuration management system and behavior simulator. This overview is well written and easy to follow. TAGS appears to make little attempt to differentiate software requirements from design. No refs.

517. **[Terrio and Vreeland 1980].**
Terrio, F. J., and J. J. Vreeland. *Task-Oriented User Requirements and Program Design, An Approach to Writing Programming Objectives and Specifications*. IBM Santa Teresa Technical Report TRO3.111. August 1980.

Describes a technique of orienting requirements specifications toward the prospective system user. The result is a specification organized into user tasks. 26 refs.

518. **[Thurber 1977].**
Thurber, K. J. "Techniques for Requirements-Oriented Design." *NCC '77*. Montvale, New Jersey: AFIPS Press. pp. 919–29. Reprinted in *Tutorial: Computer System Requirements*, K. J. Thurber, ed. IEEE Catalog EH01685, Washington D.C.: Computer Society Press of the Institute of Electrical and Electronics Engineers, 1980. pp. 4–14.

Uses the terms *requirements analysis* and *synthesis* in a marketing manner, resulting in definitions similar to those found in Webster but dissimilar to those used by requirements researchers. Requirements analysis is the process of defining how marketing needs are likely to change, creating the opportunity to produce a better product. Requirements synthesis is the process of defining how new markets will develop, creating the opportunity for a new type of product. Most of the paper is composed of examples of how the author's terminology can be applied to actual product cases. 18 refs.

[5]TAGS and IORL are registered trademarks of Teledyne Brown Engineering.

519. [Thurber 1980].

Thurber, K. J. *Tutorial: Computer System Requirements.* IEEE Catalog EH01685, Washington D.C.: Computer Society Press of the Institute of Electrical and Electronics Engineers. October 1980.

Collection of many classic requirements specification papers that have appeared in the literature. Includes seventeen reprinted articles on requirements techniques and fourteen reprinted articles of case studies.

520. [Thurber and Patton 1983].

Thurber, K. J., and P. C. Patton. *Computer-System Requirements, Techniques, and Examples.* Lexington, Mass.: D. C. Heath, 1983.

Takes a very different but very useful approach to the requirements problem. Rather than studying the requirements phase itself as an entity, this book examines how actual product development groups performed requirements analysis. IBM's and DEC's analyses of their respective marketing environments serve as the framework for the first half of the text. The second half provides more guidance to the prospective requirements writer concerned with particular applications. It describes unique requirements problems in applications, such as distributed data processing, government data bases, and microcomputer-based archeological data capture. 36 refs.

521. [Tolchin et al. 1984].

Tolchin, S. L., et al. "Computer-Assisted Requirements Specification System (CARS)." Presented at *Fourth Jerusalem Conference on Information Technology,* Jerusalem, May 1984.

522. [Topping et al. 1987].

Topping, P., et al. "Express: Rapid Prototyping and Product Development via Integrated, Knowledge-Based, Executable Specifications." In *1987 ACM/IEEE Fall Joint Computer Conference,* Washington D.C.: Computer Society Press of the Institute of Electrical and Electronics Engineers, 1987.

523. [Tozer 1987].

Tozer, J. "Prototyping as a System Development Methodology: Opportunities and Pitfalls." *Information and Science Technology* **29,** 5 (May 1987): 265–69.

524. [Treves and Caves 1979].

Treves, S. R., and K. Caves. "New Approach to Signalling System Specification and Its Implementation." Presented at *International Switching Symposium 1979,* Paris. pp. 1292–1300.

Describes the Functional Signalling and Interface Specification (FSIS) methodology for the requirements specification of signaling systems. It recognizes signal transforms that convert physical signals to logical signals, and finite state machines that describe the system's behavior in response to these logical signals. The result is a set of documents that unambiguously specify the systems behavior (not including timing constraints). 1 ref.

525. [Troy 1987].

Troy, D. A. "An Evaluation of CASE Tools." In *IEEE COMPSAC '87,* Washington D.C.: Computer Society Press of the Institute of Electrical and Electronics Engineers, 1987. pp. 124–30.

Report of a criteria-based comparison of four problem analysis tools—Excelerator, Design Aid, Information Engineering Workbench, and Structured Architect. 11 refs.

526. [TRW 1978].

TRW. *Airborne Systems Software Acquisition Engineering Guidebook for Requirements Analysis and Specification.* Aeronautical Systems Division of Wright-Patterson Air Force Base Document AST-TR-79-502, TRW Defense and Space Systems Group. Redondo Beach, Calif., 1978. Available from NTIS. A guidebook for Air Force acquisition personnel procuring software under 800-series regulations. In particular it describes the derivation, analysis, and documentation of software requirements to be included in an RFP. It precisely defines requirements and their purpose and emphasizes the need for completeness, traceability, testability, consistency, and feasibility. Requirements must include specifying interface, function, performance, human engineering, safety, failure compensation, self-test, environment, and data base. 39 refs.

527. [Tsai and Chan 1987].

Tsai, J., and O. Chan. "ISE: A User-Modeling-Based Software Development System." In *IEEE COMPSAC '87,* Washington D.C.: Computer Society Press of the Institute of Electrical and Electronics Engineers, 1987, pp. 141–47.

528. [Tsai et al. 1988].

Tsai, J., et al. "A Declarative Approach to Requirement Specification Languages." In *IEEE International Conference on Computer Languages,* Washington D.C.: Computer Society Press of the Institute of Electrical and Electronics Engineers, 1988.

529. [Tsuchiya 1980].

Tsuchiya, M. "Considerations for Requirements Engineering of Distributed Processing Systems." In *IEEE Distributed Data Acquisition, Computing and Control Symposium,* Washington D.C.: Computer Society Press of the Institute of Electrical and Electronics Engineers, 1980, pp. 61–65.

Describes extensions to the Requirements Statement Language (RSL) and the Software Requirements Engineering Methodology (SREM) that make them more suitable for distributed processing problems. 10 refs.

530. [Turner 1981].

Turner, J. A. "Achieving Consensus on System Requirements." *Systems, Objectives, Solutions* **1,** 3 (August 1981): 141–48.

Analyzes the problem of achieving consensus on a requirements document designed to meet the needs of many diverse users in a large bureaucratic organization. The paper describes how the author formed a bargaining group composed of representatives from each of the special interest (system user) groups and how problem solving, persuasion, bargaining, and politics were applied to reach agreement on system requirements. 13 refs.

531. [Uhrig 1978].

Uhrig, J. L. "System Requirements Specification for Real-Time Systems." In *IEEE COMPSAC '78,* Washington D.C.: Computer Society Press of the Institute of Electrical and Electronics Engineers, 1978, pp. 241–46.

Describes a methodology for requirements specification that recognizes ambiguity and redundancy are acceptable to some degree. The method uses flow diagrams that are similar to R-nets but can contain loops. The technique is applied in the system requirements phase and intended for use on projects where an optimal decomposition of the system into hardware, software, and humans is not known nor desired at this early stage. 15 refs.

532. [Urban et al. 1984].

Urban, S. D., et al. "Utilizing an Executable Specification Language for Information Systems." In *IEEE International Conference on Data Engineering,* Washington D.C.: Computer Society Press of the Institute of Electrical and Electronics Engineers. 1984. Also appears in *IEEE Transactions on Software Engineering* **11,** 7 (July 1985): 598 ff.

Describes the use of the Descartes specification language to define the external behavior of an information storage and retrieval system. The resulting specification is executable and used during product enhancement to compare the new behavior of the executable specification to the new behavior of the real system. 16 refs.

533. [U.S. Air Force System Command 1979].

U.S. Air Force System Command. *Requirements Specification.* Software Acquisition Engineering Guide Book Series, ASD-TR-78-45, ADA803207. Wright-Patterson Air Force Base, Ohio, January 1979.

534. [Utter 1985].

Utter, D. "Reusable Software Requirements Documents." In *IEEE COMPSAC '85,* Washington D.C.: Computer Society Press of the Institute of Electrical and Electronics Engineers. 1985, p. 204.

Brief summary of how parts of a 1978 SRS have been reused. 5 refs.

535. [Verheijen and Van Bekkum 1982].

Verheijen, G., and J. Van Bekkum. "NIAM—An Information Analysis Method." Presented at *Conference on a Comparative Review of Information System Design Methodologies,* Noordwijkerhout, the Netherlands, 1982.

536. [Vessey and Weber 1986].

Vessey, I., and R. Weber. "Structured Tools and Conditional Logic: An Empirical Investigation." *Communications of the ACM* **29,** 1 (January 1986): 48–57.

Results of an experiment comparing decision trees, decision tables, and PDL. 20 refs.

537. [Vick 1974].

Vick, C. R. "Specifications for Reliable Software." In *IEEE Electronics and Aerospace Conference,* Washington D.C.: Computer Society Press of the Institute of Electrical and Electronics Engineers, 1974.

Although this reference appears in many bibliographies in requirements-oriented publications, the subject paper does not appear in the proceedings. No refs.

538. [Vick 1977].

Vick, C. R. "First-Generation Software Engineering System." In *ACM Annual Conference,* New York: ACM Press of the Association for Computing Machinery, 1977, pp. 108–14.

Supplies a justification for the U.S. Army Strategic Systems Command (nee Ballistic Missile Defense) Advanced Technology Center (SDCATC) involvement in software engineering and requirements research. The paper begins with a summary of seven years (1969–76) of investigation into requirements and software engineering problems. The basic conclusions of those activities were that software for ballistic missile defense systems could not be tested under real conditions and some kind of verification was mandatory in a simulated environment. However, producing *perfect* code made no sense unless requirements for the software were *perfectly* understood. The SDCATC needs are listed as a methodology, a family of languages, and a set of tools. Contains an extensive bibliography of pre-1977 RSL, REVS, and SREM articles and reports. 77 refs.

539. [Vineberg 1975].
Vineberg, M. B. *Preliminary Report on System Specification and Cataloguing.* Naval Electronics Laboratory Center. San Diego, Calif., August 1975.

540. [Vitalari 1984].
Vitalari, N. "Critical Assessment of Structured Analysis Methods: A Psychological Perspective." In *Beyond Productivity: Information Systems Development for Organizational Effectiveness,* J. Bemelmans, ed. Amsterdam: North-Holland Publ., 1984. pp. 421–34.

541. [Vogel 1978].
Vogel, E. W. "Zur Formalen Berschreibung von Echtzeitsystemen." *Mitteilungen Technical Bulletin* **56,** 1 (1978): 22–30.

542. [Wallace et al. 1987].
Wallace, R., et al. *A Unified Methodology for Developing Systems.* New York: McGraw-Hill, 1987.

Presents the Systems Engineering Methodology (SEM), which combines SADT, NRL's A-7E specification techniques, and rapid prototyping in a single integrated approach. Chapters 2–5 survey a wide variety of models, including functional (SADT); behavioral (modes, events, states, activations, timing constraints all married with SADT diagrams); and other (physical, data base, and nonbehavioral "ilities"). Chapter 7 shows how to use A-7E specification techniques to write an SRS. The appendix provides a complete set of models for the home-heating problem.

543. [Wang 1986].
Wang, Y. "A Distributed Specification Model and Its Prototyping." In *IEEE COMPSAC '86,* Washington D.C.: Computer Society Press of the Institute of Electrical and Electronics Engineers, 1986, pp. 130–37. Reprinted in *IEEE Transactions on Software Engineering* **14,** 8 (August 1988): 1090–97.

Describes the State Transition Language (SXL), which specifies the behavior of real-time systems in terms of pre- and post-conditions. An example of its use in telephony is given. Brief comments are made concerning how it is executable, so that one could construct working prototypes. 10 refs.

544. [Ward and Mellor 1985].
Ward, P., and S. Mellor. *Structured Development for Real-Time Systems.* Vol. 1–3. Englewood Cliffs, N.J.: Prentice Hall, 1985.

Extensions to DeMarco-style structured analysis that facilitate specifying real-time systems. Notational extensions include control flow and finite state machines. Procedural extensions ensure that hierarchies of diagrams remain in the domain of external system behavior.

545. **[Ward 1986].**

Ward, P. "The Transformation Schema: An Extension of the Data Flow Diagram to Represent Control and Timing." *IEEE Transactions on Software Engineering* **12**, 2 (February 1986): 198–210.

546. **[Ward and Keskar 1987].**

Ward, P., and D. Keskar. "A Comparison of the Ward/Mellor and Boeing/Hatley Real-Time Methods." Presented at *Twelfth Structured Methods Conference*, Chicago, August 1987. pp. 356–66.

547. **[Wasserman 1977].**

Wasserman, A. I. "The Evolution of Specification Techniques." In *1977 ACM Conference*, New York: ACM Press of the Association for Computing Machinery, 1979.

Brief summary of why we need requirements languages. 15 refs.

548. **[Wasserman 1979].**

Wasserman, A. I. "USE: A Methodology for the Design and Development of Interactive Information Systems." In *IFIP WG8.1 Working Conference on Formal Models and Practical Tools for Information System Design*, 1979. Amsterdam: North-Holland.

549. **[Wasserman and Stinson 1979].**

Wasserman, A. I., and S. K. Stinson. "A Specification Method for Interactive Systems. In *IEEE Conference on Specifications of Reliable Software*, Washington D.C.: Computer Society Press of the Institute of Electrical and Electronics Engineers, 1979, pp. 68–79.

Assuming that requirements specifications are to be complete, comprehensible, testable, traceable, implementable, consistent, unambiguous, writable, and modifiable, this paper proposes a methodology consisting of an informal English language user view and a more formal language design and verification view. The methodology is intended for specifying interactive information systems (IIS), such as airline reservation systems. The underlying system model is one in which naïve users enter commands (via menus, command language, query language, or natural language), the system responds with results, additional prompts, or error messages. Every IIS has a data base to record data being stored and/or retrieved by its users. Transition diagrams are used to define the user language. The ANSI/SPARC framework (conceptual, external, and internal models) is used to define data base requirements. Data abstractions are used to map user requests into data base transactions. An extensive example is given. The methodology proposed here is part of User Software Engineering (USE) methodology, developed to support the entire software life cycle. 33 refs.

550. **[Wasserman and Shewmake 1982].**

Wasserman, A., and D. Shewmake. "Rapid Prototyping of Interactive Information Systems." *ACM Software Engineering Notes* **7**, 5 (December 1982): 171–80.

Early description of the USE methodology (see later Wasserman entries in this bibliography). Recognizing that well-designed user interfaces must be developed iteratively, this paper proposes generating user interface prototypes automatically from USE transition diagrams using the Transition Diagram Interpreter (TDI)

Capabilities of TDI can be expanded by using RAPID, which can provide even more realistic interactive prototypes. 32 refs.

551. [Wasserman 1985].

Wasserman, A. I. "Extending State Transition Diagrams for the Specification of Human–Computer Interaction." *IEEE Transactions on Software Engineering* **11,** 8 (August 1985): 669–713.

Detailed description of the User Software Engineering (USE) methodology and language for specifying human–computer interactions. Based on extended transition diagrams, the specification language provides facilities for defining system outputs (including cursor control, text variables that can later be referenced in order to reuse a message, tab settings, and windows); user inputs (including buffering lines versus single keystroke responsiveness, special keys, and string manipulation); and relationships between inputs and outputs (using hierarchies of USE transition diagrams). USE transition diagrams extend standard transition diagrams with the ability to decompose based on a variety of elements in the diagram, to return input values for later analysis, computation, or display and to specify stimulus-stimulus and response-stimulus timing constraints. A tool called RAPID/USE that implements the USE methodology is described. An example is provided of RAPID/USE for the specification of an interactive data dictionary tool. 23 refs.

552. [Wasserman et al. 1986].

Wasserman, A., et al. "Developing Interactive Information Systems with the User Software Engineering Methodology." *IEEE Transactions on Software Engineering* **12,** 2 (February 1986): 326–45.

Describes the User Software Engineering (USE) methodology in detail. The first step is *requirements analysis* (what we have been calling *problem analysis*), where real-world objects and required operations are identified and future users are characterized. The second step is *external design* (what we have been calling *writing the SRS*), where the user perspective is defined using extended transition diagrams. The third step involves the Transition Diagram Interpreter (TDI) to create a working prototype of the user interface. A complete example of each step is provided using a library system. 34 refs.

553. [Weinberg 1982].

Weinberg, G. *Rethinking Systems Analysis and Design.* Boston: Little, Brown, and Co., 1982.

One of the best little books on problem analysis. It is refreshing, entertaining, educational, and inspiring. Read it!

554. [WeinbergV 1980].

Weinberg, V. *Structured Analysis.* Englewood Cliffs, N.J.: Prentice Hall, 1980. Describes Yourdon-style and DeMarco-style structured analysis.

555. [White 1980].

White, S. "SRIMP—Software Requirements Integrated Modeling Program." In *NBS/IEEE/ACM Software Tool Fair,* NBS Special Publication 500-80, National Bureau of Standards. Washington, D.C. pp. 186–89.

Brief overview and examples of an interactive front end for PSL/PSA. 2 refs.

556. [White 1985].

White, S. "Requirements Modeling for Embedded Computer Systems." In *Third IEEE International Workshop on Specification and Design,* Washington D.C.: Computer Society Press of the Institute of Electrical and Electronics Engineers, 1985, pp. 238–49.

Advocates FSM-based modeling. 8 refs.

557. [White and Lavi 1985].

White, S., and J. Lavi. "Embedded Computer System Requirements Workshop." *IEEE Computer* **18,** 4 (April 1985): 67–70.

Summarizes events at the "Embedded Computer System Requirements Workshop" held in November 1984 and attended by Mack Alford, Kathryn Heninger Britton, Louis Chmura, Paul Clements, Alan Davis, Richard Edelmann, Stuart Faulk, Sandi Fryer, Evan Kessler, Bruce Labaw, H. Lubbes, David McConnell, John Mullen, Don Reifer, John Stockenberg, Dan Teichroew, Don Utter, David Weiss, and Stanley Wilson. Crucial problems recognized included the complex system design that might be necessary prior to writing requirements and ever-changing requirements. Workshop recommendations included (1) functional hierarchy with data flow is insufficient for embedded systems' requirements, (2) dynamic system views (e.g., sets of cooperating FSMs) are necessary, (3) nonbehavioral requirements are extremely important, (4) a model of an embedded computer system is required, and (5) methodologies must augment tool use. There were three areas of disagreement: (1) What model is best? (2) Should a series of steps used to transform inputs into outputs be included in the SRS, or is that the domain of design? (In my opinion there is nothing wrong with showing these steps provided it is made clear to the SRS reader that the steps have been included to help convey what the transformation is—and that the real program need not follow the same steps as long as the end result is the same.) And (3) do complex systems require system design before requirements? 15 refs.

558. [White 1986].

White, S. "Two Embedded Computer System Requirements Models Issues for Investigation." *ACM Software Engineering Notes* **11,** 4 (August 1986): 106–12.

Short synopsis of a home heating system and key questions about how various requirements techniques might model it. 7 refs.

559. [Whitis and Chiang 1981].

Whitis, V. S., and W. N. Chiang. "A State Machine Development Method for Call-Processing Software." In *Electro '81 Conference,* Washington D.C.: Computer Society Press of the Institute of Electrical and Electronics Engineers, 1981, pp. 7/2-1–7/2-6.

Describes a methodology for the functional specification of call processing in telephone switching systems. The methodology is based on the concept of layers of requirements. The layers correspond to requirements abstractions. Individual requirements defined on one layer become subautomata on the next lower level. Tools have been built to draw convenient diagrams and charts for documentation purposes. 6 refs.

560. [Whitmore 1979].

Whitmore, D. C. *Requirements Specification.* Aeronautical Systems Division of Wright-Patterson Air Force Base Document ASD-TR-78-45, Boeing Aerospace. Seattle, 1979. Available from NTIS.

A guidebook for Air Force acquisition personnel who are procuring ATE and training system software. In particular it describes the software procurement process from initial needs analysis through completion of the contract. 14 refs.

561. [Wigander et al. 1984].

Wigander, K., et al. *Structured Analysis and Design of Information Systems.* New York: McGraw-Hill, 1984.

Yet one more flavor of structured analysis; this one is called SAK. 11 refs.

562. [Williams 1988].

Williams, L. "Software Process Modeling: A Behavioral Approach." In *Tenth IEEE International Conference on Software Engineering,* Washington D.C.: Computer Society Press of the Institute of Electrical and Electronics Engineers, 1988.

563. [Wilson 1975].

Wilson, M. L. *The Information Automat Approach to Design and Implementation of Computer-Based Systems.* IBM Federal Systems Division Information Automat Technical Report. June 1975.

564. [Wilson 1979].

Wilson, M. L. "A Semantic-based Requirements and Design Method." In *IEEE COMPSAC '79,* Washington D.C.: Computer Society Press of the Institute of Electrical and Electronics Engineers, 1979, pp. 107–12.

Describes the Requirements and Design Method (RDM) developed at IBM Santa Teresa Laboratory. The thirty-step process is described in detail. The requirements specification aspects stress the detailed semantic analysis of all problem-specific terms, concepts, and relationships between terms and concepts, by human experts. The method includes three phases to define the requirements and twenty-five steps to map the requirements into a normal form system architecture. 8 refs.

565. [Wilson 1981].

Wilson, M. L. "A Requirements and Design Aid for Relational Data Bases." *Fifth International Conference on Software Engineering,* Washington D.C.: Computer Society Press of the Institute of Electrical and Electronics Engineers, 1981, pp. 283–93.

Describes a tool called the Requirements and Design Aid (RDA) that is used for requirements definition and automatic synthesis of data bases. A tool is described that analyzes a requirements specification; derives basic data base concepts from it, i.e., entities, events, relationships, attributes, and values; and builds an appropriate relational data base schema. The constructed data base is organized without biases. Optimization for particular classes of retrieval is manually performed. A five-step procedure is given for problem analysis, and the nine-step algorithm used by RDA to fabricate the data base is also given. 18 refs.

566. **[Winchester 1981].**
Winchester, J. *Requirements Definition and Its Interface to the SARA Design Methodology for Computer-Based Systems.* UCLA Technical Report UCLA-ENG-8092, UCLA-35P214-109. February 1981.

567. **[Winters 1979].**
Winters, E. W. "Experience with Problem Statement Language: A Language for System Requirements and Specification." In *IEEE COMPSAC '79,* Washington D.C.: Computer Society Press of the Institute of Electrical and Electronics Engineers, 1979, pp. 283–88.

Describes the application of PSL/PSA to a AT&T Long Lines[6] inventory system that had previously been specified in 325 pages. 8 refs.

568. **[Woodman 1988].**
Woodman, M. "Yourdon Data Flow Diagrams: A Tool for Disciplined Requirements Analysis." *Information and Software Technology* **30,** 9 (November 1988): 515–33.

Summarizes Yourdon's 1988 view of requirements analysis and data flow diagrams. After briefly introducing 1970's style structured analysis as defined by DeMarco, Woodman introduces a subset of the Ward/Mellor and Hatley/Pirhbai SA/RT extensions as Yourdon Structured Method (YSM). YSM includes three discrete steps: the feasibility study; essential modeling; and implementation modeling. The major contribution of this well-written paper is its ability to resolve ambiguities inherent in data flow diagrams. These ambiguities are related to merging two data flows into one prior to entry into a bubble, the splitting of a data flow into two data flows, the meaning of multiple arrows entering a bubble, differences between data and control flow, and legitimate combinations of data and control flows and data and control transformations. 11 refs.

569. **[Wright et al. 1975].**
Wright, R. N., et al. *Technology for the Formulation and Expression of Specifications.* Vol. 3. National Bureau of Standards Report PB-250 573. December 1975. Available from NTIS. See Harris et al. for vol. 1 and 2.

Supplies flow charts and program listings for Vol. 1 and 2. 5 refs.

570. **[Yadav 1981].**
Yadav, S. "A Methodology for Modeling an Organization to Determine and Derive Information Systems Requirements." Ph.D. diss., University of Michigan, 1981.

571. **[Yadav et al. 1988].**
Yadav, S., et al. "Comparison of Analysis Techniques for Information Requirement Determination." *Communications of the ACM* **31,** 9 (September 1988).

A thorough report that first defines criteria for evaluating a problem analysis technique and then applies those criteria to DeMarco and Ross techniques of structured analysis. 18 refs.

572. **[Yamamoto et al. 1982].**
Yamamoto, Y., et al. "The Role of Requirements Analysis in the System Life Cycle." In Montvale, New Jersey: AFIPS Press of the American Federation of Information Processing Societies, 1982, pp. 382–87.

---

[6]Registered trademark of AT&T.

573. **[Yau and Liu 1988].**
Yau, S., and C.-S. Liu. "An Approach to Software Requirements Specification." In *IEEE COMPSAC '88,* Washington D.C.: Computer Society Press of the Institute of Electrical and Electronics Engineers, 1988, pp. 83–88.

574. **[Yeh et al. 1978].**
Yeh, R. T., et al. "Software Requirements Engineering: A Perspective." In *Beyond Structured Programming, An Infotech State-of-the-Art Report,* Oxford, England: Pergamon Infotech Ltd., 1978.

575. **[Yeh et al. 1979].**
Yeh, R. T., et al. *Software Requirement Engineering—a Perspective.* University of Texas at Austin Computer Science Technical Report SDBEG-7. Austin, March 1979.

576. **[Yeh et al. 1979a].**
Yeh, R. T., et al. *Systematic Derivation of Software Requirements through Structured Analysis.* University of Texas at Austin Computer Science Technical Report SDBEG-15. Austin, 1979.

577. **[Yeh 1980].**
Yeh, R. T. *Software Requirements: A Report on the State of the Art.* University of Maryland Computer Science Department Report TR-949. College Park, October 1980.

578. **[Yeh and Zave 1980].**
Yeh, R., and P. Zave. "Specifying Software Requirements." *Proceedings of the IEEE* **68,** 9 (September 1980): 1077–85.

Recognizes that a primary cause of software problems is an improperly written requirements specification and gives the authors' view of what a properly written requirements document should and should not contain. One of the best written descriptions of differences between requirements and design. The following specification attributes are explored—understandable, formal, interpretable (i.e., simulatable), complete, and modifiable. Describes the use of conceptual models that make it easier to specify software requirements without falling into design. Although a number of models for describing data requirements are listed, only one, the relational model, is discussed. An example of process specification is given using RSL, data flow, control flow, and process. Synchronization requirements are briefly described. A sample outline for a requirements specification is given. 37 refs.

579. **[Yeh 1982].**
Yeh, R. T. "Requirements Analysis—A Management Perspective." In *IEEE COMPSAC '82,* Washington D.C.: Computer Society Press of the Institute of Electrical and Electronics Engineers, 1982, pp. 410–16.

An excellent high-level discussion of most of the issues surrounding the problem of requirements analysis and specification. Reasons for inherent difficulty in specifying requirements are listed as communication, complexity, dealing with change, and disregard for the entire life cycle when specifying requirements. General techniques for specifying requirements include modeling, decomposition, and abstraction. A properly written requirements document should include both functional and nonfunctional requirements. Modeling (data, data flow, and process) is particularly helpful for functional requirements. Nonfunctional requirements must include performance, reliability, security, operating requirements, physical constraints, and development requirements. The author also advocates involving potential users in the requirements development process. 15 refs.

580. [Yeh et al. 1984].

Yeh, R. T., et al. "Software Requirements—New Directions and Perspectives." In *Handbook of Software Engineering,* edited by C. Vick and C. Ramamoorthy. New York: Van Nostrand Reinhold, 1984. pp. 519–43.

A thorough discussion of current issues on the subject, including both problem analysis and writing an SRS. Both behavioral and nonbehavioral requirement specification techniques are discussed. 51 refs.

581. [Yeh and Welch 1987].

Yeh, R., and T. Welch. "Software Evolution: Forging a New Paradigm." In *1987 ACM/IEEE Fall Joint Computer Conference,* New York: ACM Press of the Association for Computing Machinery, 1987.

582. [Yoeli and Barzilai 1977].

Yoeli, M., and Z. Barzilai. "Behavioral Descriptions of Communication Switching Systems Using Extended Petri Nets." *Digital Processes* **3,** 4 (1977): 307–20.

Describes how Petri nets can be extended to include the ability to communicate with other Petri nets via either pulse or level signals. The authors show how this simple extension makes Petri nets a useful tool for the functional description of call-processing software. Extensive examples are given. 20 refs.

583. [Yourdon 1986].

Yourdon, E. "What Ever Happened to Structured Analysis?" *Datamation* (June 1986): 133–38.

Update on the current status of structured analysis and a prediction of the future.

584. [Yourdon 1989].

Yourdon, E. *Modern Structured Analysis.* Englewood Cliffs, N.J.: Yourdon Press, 1989.

One of the best compilations available of the collected thoughts of Ed Yourdon and the many consultants who have worked with him over the years at Yourdon, Inc., including DeMarco, Gane, Sanson, McMenamin, Palmer, Ward, and Mellor. This book presents (1) the "new" structured analysis methodology, which de-emphasizes modeling the current environment; (2) creating the essential model (as originally defined by McMenamin and Palmer and which corresponds to problem analysis in this book), including the environment model and the behavioral model; (3) the user implementation model (which corresponds closely to the concept of writing an SRS in this book); (4) Ward's real-time extensions (including control flows and processes); (5) the encouragement to use a variety of specification techniques, trying to use the one most appropriate for each situation; and (6) explicit procedures for ensuring consistency between DFDs, finite state machines, and data dictionaries. Two complete examples are given, one a traditional MIS application, and one a relatively simple real-time system. This book is well worth reading and should be mandatory for all students of structured analysis.

585. [Zave 1978].

Zave, P. "Formal Specification of Complete and Consistent Performance Requirements." Presented at *Eighth Texas Conference on Computing Systems,* Dallas, Texas, November 1978. pp. 4B-18–4B-25.

Assumes that requirements have been specified operationally and have described both the system under design and its environment as a set of asynchronously interacting digital processes. The article shows how a particular specification language can be extended to handle performance requirements. A number of examples are given. The attributes of *completeness* and *consistency* are defined when used to describe performance requirements. The author also briefly compares the relative advantages and disadvantages of black-box requirements and operationally specified requirements. 10 refs.

586. [Zave 1979].

Zave, P. "Specification of System Requirements: Functions, Time, and Money." In *IEEE COMPSAC '79,* Washington D.C.: Computer Society Press of the Institute of Electrical and Electronics Engineers, 1979, pp. 117–22.

Provides a thorough analysis of the problems of producing useful, consistent, and complete requirements specifications. The paper explores subtle differences between requirements and design and justifies and provides a preliminary definition of an operational-based, formal specification language that can be used during requirements and high-level design. The paper also emphasizes the need to address performance, cost, reliability, resource, size, and distance requirements. 12 refs.

587. [Zave 1979a].

Zave, P. "Panel Session: Approaches to Specification—Various Models, an Informal Report." *ACM Software Engineering Notes* **4,** 3 (July 1979): 17–18.

Brief report of a panel session at the *Specifications of Reliable Software Conference* attended by Bill Riddle (chair), V. Berzins, L. Robinson, D. Friedman, and D. Wise. Berzins spoke in favor of data abstractions, Robinson for parallelism, and Friedman and Wise for applicative programming.

588. [Zave 1980].

Zave, P. "Real-World Properties in the Requirements for Embedded Systems." Presented at *Annual Washington, D.C. ACM Technical Symposium,* Gaithersburg, Md., June 1980. pp. 21–26.

589. [Zave 1980a].

Zave, P. *The Operational Approach to Requirements Specification for Embedded Systems.* University of Maryland Computer Science Report TR-976. December 1980.

590. [Zave and Yeh 1981].

Zave, P., and R. T. Yeh. "Executable Requirements for Embedded Systems." In *Fifth International Conference on Software Engineering,* Washington D.C.: Computer Society Press of the Institute of Electrical and Electronics Engineers, 1981, pp. 295–304.

Emphasizes usefulness of employing formal models as early as possible in the requirements phase to define the system and its environment. Techniques described are based on the use of PAISLey (Process-oriented, Applicative, Interpretable Specification Language). Thoroughly explores the advantages and disadvantages of having interpretable requirements specifications; advantages include (1) requirements testing, (2) customer demonstrations, (3) performance simulations, (4) prototyping, and (5) serving as a test bed. 18 refs.

591. [Zave 1982].
Zave, P. "An Operational Approach to Requirements Specification for Embedded Systems." *IEEE Transactions on Software Engineering* **8,** 3 (May 1982): 250–69.

Provides a detailed definition, description, and motivation for operational specifications. Presents a description of PAISLey, including how (1) to define sets, functions, processes, and systems; (2) to specify interactions between autonomous processes; and briefly (3) to specify timing constraints. Using a simple patient-monitoring example, this article shows how PAISLey can be used. A complete grammar for PAISLey is provided in the appendix. 54 refs.

592. [Zave 1984].
Zave, P. "The Operational versus the Conventional Approach to Software Development." *Communications of the ACM* **27,** 2 (February 1984): 104–18.

Thorough comparison of conventional specification techniques and operational specification techniques. Also compares four operational approaches—JSD, PAISLey, Gist, and applicative programming. 42 refs.

593. [Zave 1985].
Zave, P. "A Distributed Alternative to Finite State Machine Specifications." *ACM Transactions on Programming Languages and Systems* **7,** 1 (January 1985): 10–36.

Recognizing that the finite state machine appears to be an extremely popular approach to writing operational specifications, this paper acknowledges the fact that single, huge, monolithic FSMs make no sense for complex systems. (REVS simplifies this by organizing the FSM into R-nets corresponding to stimuli. RLP simplifies this by organizing the FSM into stimulus-response sequences corresponding to user features from each user's perspective, and Harel simplifies this through FSM hierarchies.) This paper proposes another alternative: organizing system requirements into sets of cooperating FSMs, each separately specified. A detailed example is provided using a nontrivial telephony example (Zave deserves credit for being one of the few requirements researchers who publishes nontrivial examples!). 18 refs.

594. [Zave and Schell 1986].
Zave, P. and W. Schell "Salient Features of an Executable Specification Language and Its Environment." *IEEE Transactions on Software Engineering* **12,** 2 (February 1986): 312–25.

Describes details of the development of the tool built by AT&T to process the PAISLey language. 35 refs.

595. [Zelkowitz 1978].
Zelkowitz, M. W. "Perspectives on Software Engineering." *Computing Surveys* **10,** 2 (June 1978): 197–216.

Excellent overview of, and justification for, a rigorous software engineering methodology. The author's sections on issues relating to requirements and specifications are quite brief but raise a few interesting points. His *requirements* stage is where one analyzes such issues as the cost of the project, development computer, project schedules, configuration control needs, processing time, and so forth. Later sections briefly discuss available tools and techniques. 58 refs.

596. [Zelkowitz et al. 1979].

Zelkowitz, M. V., et al. *Principles of Software Engineering and Design.* Englewood Cliffs, N.J.: Prentice Hall, 1979.

Chapter 1 introduces the software development life cycle as requirements analysis, specification, design, and so forth. The *requirements analysis* stage describes what various prospective users of the system need (i.e., problem analysis). The *specification* stage describes what the actual product is required to do in response to those needs (i.e., writing the software requirements). Interestingly enough the book never again discusses either requirements analysis or specification except to state that Alphard, CLU, and Euclid provide abstract data types that are useful during *specification* (I would say that were suitable for *design* by Zelkowitz's definition); that PSL/PSA and SADT provide alternative design approaches (I would say they were suitable for either *requirements* or *design* by Zelkowitz's definitions); and that REVS automates the *requirements analysis* stage (I would say REVS were more appropriate for *specification* by Zelkowitz's definition). Each of these approaches is described in a half-page. The remainder of this book (which describes design, implementation, testing, and other useful concepts) is well worth reading. 47 refs.

597. [Zelkowitz 1980].

Zelkowitz, M. "A Case Study in Rapid Prototyping." *Software—Practice and Experience* **10,** 12 (December 1980): 1037–42.

598. [Zualkerman and Tsai 1988].

Zualkerman, I., and W. Tsai. "Are Knowledge Representations the Answer to Requirements Analysis?" In *IEEE International Conference on Computer Languages,* Washington D.C.: Computer Society Press of the Institute of Electrical and Electronics Engineers, 1988.

TOPIC-BIBLIOGRAPHY CROSS-REFERENCE TABLE

This table enables you easily to identify entries in the bibliography that are of interest to you. The table is organized into fifteen major topics

1. General discussion of requirements
2. System-level requirements
3. Problem analysis
4. Behavioral specification
5. User interface specification
6. Specification of timing constraints
7. Axiomatic specification techniques
8. Simulation and prototyping
9. Relationship between requirements and design

10. Software synthesis from requirements
11. Testing implications of requirements
12. Maintenance implications of requirements
13. Requirements case studies
14. General discussion of software engineering
15. Other or unknown

For each major topic, this table contains a list of all bibliographic entries related to that topic.

1. General Discussion of Requirements

Abbott and Moorhead	1981
Ardis	1979
Balzer et al.	1988
Ben-Menachem and Marliss	1980
Bianchi et al.	1980
Blum	1988
Boehm	1974
Boehm et al.	1975
Boehm	1976
Boehm	1979a
Boehm et al.	1984
Burns et al.	1979
Chmura and Weiss	1982
Conn	1977
Dasarathy	1983
Davis	1988a
Davis et al.	1988
Davis	1989
Davis	1989a
Davis	1989b
DavisC and Vick	1977
DavisC	1980
Derbenwick	1979
Dorfman and Flynn	1981
Dorfman and Thayer	1989
Everhart	1980
Freeman	1980
Gatewood	1977
Gehani	1982
Gishen et al.	1979
Gladden	1982
Greenspan	1982

Greenspan et al.	1982
Haase and Koch	1982
Hamilton and Zeldin	1979
Heninger	1979a
Hsia	1980
IEEE	1984
Irvine and Wasserman	1979
Johnson	1983
Kerola and Freeman	1981
Kimura	n.d.
Kitagawa et al.	1982
Koch and Rembold	1980
Kramer et al.	1988
Kung	1988
Lauber	1982
Levene and Mullery	1982
Lipka	1980
Ludewig	1982
Lyytinen	1987
McGowan and McHenry	1979
Mills et al.	1986
Ramamoorthy and So	1978
Reifer and Trattner	1976
Roman	1982
Roman	1985
Ross	1977
Rzepka	1985
Rzepka and Ohno	1985
Salter	1976
Scharer	1981
SmithG et al.	1980
Taggart and Tharp	1977
Teichroew	1972
Thurber	1980
Utter	1985
Vick	1977
Wasserman	1977
Weinberg	1982
White	1985
White and Lavi	1985
Yeh et al.	1978
Yeh et al.	1979a
Yeh	1980
Yeh and Zave	1980
Yeh	1982
Yeh et al.	1984
Zave	1979a

2. System-Level Requirements

Alford	1979
Alford	1985
Alford	1987
Blum	1988
Bruno et al.	1988
Cameron	1983
Cheng et al.	1982
Fife	1987
Finkelstein and Potts	1986
Hatley	1984
Jackson	1982
Larson et al.	1979
Lyytinen	1987
Miller and Taylor	1981
Miller and Taylor	1982
Rockstrom and Saracco	1982
Ross	1977a
Ross and Schoman	1977
Salter	1976
Smoliar and Scalf	1979
Smoliar	1980
Swartout and Balzer	1982
Teledyne Brown Engineering	1980
Teledyne Brown Engineering	1980a
Teledyne Brown Engineering	1987
Thurber	1980
Treves and Caves	1979
Tsuchiya	1980
Uhrig	1978
Wallace et al.	1987
Wang	1986
Ward and Mellor	1985
Ward	1986
Woodman	1988
Yourdon	1989
Zave	1978
Zave	1979
Zave	1980
Zave	1980a
Zave and Yeh	1981
Zave	1982
Zave	1984
Zave	1985
Zave and Schell	1986

3. Problem Analysis

Adler	1988
Alavi and Wetherbe	1982
Alford	1987
Averhill and Vestal	1979
Baroudi et al.	1986
Batini et al.	1986
Blum	1988
Blumofe and Hecht	1988
Bosyj	1976
Brackett and McGowan	1977
Bruyn et al.	1988
Budde and Sylla	1984
Carlson	1979
Chafin	1980
Chang et al.	1987
Chapin	1979
Coad and Yourdon	1989
Combelic	1978
Conn	1979
Cronhjort and Gallmo	1982
Davis	1989
Davis	1989b
DeMarco	1979
DeWolfe	1977
DeWolfe and Principato	1977
Diaz-Gonzalez	1987
Diaz-Gonzalez and Urban	1989
Dickinson	1989
Dorfman and Flynn	1981
Dutton	1984
Edwards	1987
Everhart	1980
Farney et al.	1981
Federal Information Processing Standards	1979
Feldman	1979
Feldman	1980
Fickas et al.	1987
Finkelstein and Potts	1986
Furia	1979
Furtek et al.	1981
Gackowski	1977
Gane and Sarson	1979
Gatto	1964
Gladden	1982

Greenspan et al.	1982
Hammer and Kunin	1982
Harel	1987
Harel	1987a
Harel et al.	1987
Harel	1988
Harel et al.	1988
Hashimoto	1987
Hatley	1984
Hatley and Pirbhai	1987
Havey	1986
Hecht et al.	1986
Hershey	1979
Hira and Mori	1982
Hruschka	1987
IBM	1973
IEEE	1985
Ikadai et al.	1985
Irvine and Wasserman	1979
Jacks	1979
Jackson	1982
Jahanian and Mok	1988
Jefferson and Taylor	1979
Johnson	1983
JohnsonL	1979
JohnsonL	1983
JohnsonW	1983
Jones	1976
Kerola and Freeman	1981
Kim and Kwon	1987
Kim and Kwon	n.d.
Kitagawa et al.	1982
Komoda et al.	1981
Konsynski	1976
Kung	1988
Lamb et al.	1978
Lano	1989
Larson et al.	1979
Ludewig	1982
Lyytinen	1987
McCracken and Jackson	1982
McMenamin and Palmer	1984
Marca and McGowan	1988
Martin	1982
Martin and Bosyj	1976
Matsumoto et al.	1982
Matsumoto	1984
Miller and Taylor	1981

Miller and Taylor	1982
Mital and Berg	1988
Mittermeir	1979
Mittermeir	1980
Mittermeir et al.	1982
Mullery	1979
Mumford et al.	1978
Murai et al.	1982a
Nakao et al.	1980
National Bureau of Standards	1980
Nishio et al.	1982
Nunamaker and Konsynski	1975
Ohnishi et al.	1982
Orr	1980
Orr	1981
Perrone	1987
Peterson	1987
Pew and Rollins	1975
Piperakas	1978
Powell	1983
Prussian and Welke	1989
Ramamoorthy and So	1978
Reilly and Brackett	1987
Richter	1986
Rosenberg	1985
Ross	1977a
Ross and Schoman	1977
Ross	1980
Royce	1975
Smith	1981
SmithG et al.	1980
SofTech	1976
Stefik et al.	1987
Stephens	1978
Svoboda	1987
Teichroew	1972
Teichroew	1976
Teichroew and Winters	1976
Teichroew and Gackowski	1977
Teichroew and Hershey	1977
Teichroew et al.	1977
Teichroew and Sayani	1980
Teichroew	1980
Teichroew and Ckikofsky	1980
Teledyne Brown Engineering	1980
Teledyne Brown Engineering	1980a
Teledyne Brown Engineering	1987
Terrio and Vreeland	1980

Thurber	1977
Thurber	1980
Troy	1987
Turner	1981
Uhrig	1978
Vitalari	1984
Wallace et al.	1987
Ward and Mellor	1985
Ward	1986
Ward and Keskar	1987
Weinberg	1982
WeinbergV	1980
White	1980
Whitmore	1979
Wigander et al.	1984
Wilson	1979
Woodman	1988
Yadav	1981
Yadav et al.	1988
Yeh et al.	1979
Yeh	1982
Yourdon	1986
Yourdon	1989
Zave	1978
Zave	1979
Zave	1980
Zave	1980a
Zave and Yeh	1981
Zave	1982
Zave	1984
Zave	1985
Zave and Schell	1986

4. Behavioral Specification

Alford and Burns	1976
Alford	1977
Alford et al.	1977
Alford et al.	1977a
Alford	1978
Alford	1980
Alford	1980a
Alford	1987
American Society For Testing Materials	1977
Balkovich and Engelberg	1976
Balzer et al.	1978
Basili and Weiss	1981
Belford et al.	1976

Belford and Taylor	1976
Belford	1978
Bell and Bixler	1976
Bell and Thayer	1976
Bell et al.	1977
Benoit et al.	1977
Berliner and Zave	1987
Berzins and Gray	1985
Bethke et al.	1981
Biewald et al.	1980
Blackhurst and Gandee	1976
Blackledge	1981
Braek	1979
Bruno and Manchetto	1986
Bruno and Morisio	1987
Bruno et al.	1988
Casey and Taylor	1981
CCITT	1977
Chang et al.	1987
Chmura and Weiss	1982
Chvalovsky	1983
Conn	1977
Conn	1979
Conn	1979a
Conn	1979b
Dasarathy	1983
Davis and Rauscher	1979
Davis and Rauscher	1979a
Davis et al.	1979
Davis	1980
Davis	1988
Davis	1989
Davis	1989a
DavisC and Vick	1977
DavisC and Vick	1978
Diaz-Gonzalez	1987
Diaz-Gonzalez and Urban	1988
Department of Defense	1988
Dutton	1984
Dyer et al.	1977
Fischer and Walter	1979
Frimer and Folkes	1982
Furia	1979
Furtek et al.	1981
Gehani	1982
Gehani and McGettrick	1986
Goldsack and Kramer	1980
Greenspan et al.	1982

Hagemann	1987
Harel	1987
Harel	1987a
Harel et al.	1987
Harel	1988
Harel et al.	1988
Harris et al.	1975
Hatley	1984
Hatley and Pirbhai	1987
Heitmeyer and McLean	1983
Heninger et al.	1978
Heninger	1979
Hoffman	1980
Howes	1987
IEEE	1984
Ikadai et al.	1985
Jackson and Vermeersch	1983
Jahanian and Mok	1988
Johnson	1983
JohnsonW	1988
Jorgensen	1985
Jorgensen	1985a
Kamin et al.	1983
Kampen	1982
Kawashima et al.	1971
Keller	1989
Kerola and Freeman	1981
Kim and Kwon	1987
Kim and Kwon	n.d.
Kitagawa et al.	1982
Kono	1983
Krasner	1985
Landau	1979
Lano	1989
Larson et al.	1979
Lauber	1982
Lausen	1988
Levene and Mullery	1982
Loshbough et al.	1981
Ludewig	1980
Ludewig	1980a
McGowan et al.	1985
Matsumoto	1977
Matsumoto and Kawakita	1980
Meseke	1975
Mical and Schwarm	1979
Miller and Taylor	1981
Miller and Taylor	1982

Ward	1986
Wasserman	1979
Wasserman and Stinson	1979
Wasserman	1985
Wasserman et al.	1986
Whitis and Chang	1981
Whitmore	1979
Wilson	1979
Wilson	1981
Woodman	1988
Yeh	1980
Yeh	1982
Yeh et al.	1984
Yoeli and Barzelai	1977
Yourdon	1989
Zave	1978
Zave	1979
Zave	1980
Zave	1980a
Zave and Yeh	1981
Zave	1982
Zave	1984
Zave	1985
Zave and Schell	1986

5. User Interface Specifications

Bass	1985
Bleser and Foley	1982
Chi	1985
Christiansen and Kreplin	1984
Dumas	1988
Finger	1981
Heitmeyer	1985
Jakob	1983
Mantei and Teorey	1988
Mason et al.	1982
Mason and Carey	1983
Mayr et al.	1984
Parnas	1969
Pew and Rollins	1975
Wasserman	1979
Wasserman and Stinson	1979
Wasserman and Shewmake	1982
Wasserman	1985
Wasserman et al.	1986

6. Specification of Timing Constraints

Boydstun et al.	1980
Cheng et al.	1982
Coolahan and Roussopoulos	1983
Dasarathy	1985
Harel	1987
Harel	1988
Jahanian and Mok	1986
Jahanian and Mok	1988
Jorgensen	1985
Taylor	1980a

7. Axiomatic Specification Techniques

Adler	1988
Agusa et al.	1979
Agusa and Ohnishi	1982
Alexander and Potter	1987
Chi	1985
Cunningham and Salih	1981
Cunningham et al.	1985
Gehani	1982
Gehani and McGettrick	1986
Goedicke	1986
Goldsack and Kramer	1980
Hamilton and Zeldin	1977
Harel	1987
Harel	1988
Heitmeyer and McLean	1983
Jahanian and Mok	1988
Liskov and Berzins	1978
Mills et al.	1986

8. Simulation and Prototyping

Alexander and Potter	1987
Babb	1982
Bally et al.	1977
Balzer et al.	1982
Basili and Turner	1975
Belkhouche	1985
Ben-Menachem et al.	1981
Blumofe and Hecht	1988
Boar	1984
Boar	1986

Boehm et al.	1984
Boehm	1986
Boydstun et al.	1980
Brandenstein et al.	1987
Bruno and Manchetto	1986
Bruno and Morisio	1987
Budde and Sylla	1984
Carrio	1987
Chen and Chou	1988
Christiansen and Kreplin	1984
Clapp	1987
Cooper and Hsia	1982
DARPA	1987
Davis	1980
Davis	1982
Davis et al.	1988
Dearnley and Mayhew	1983
Diaz-Gonzalez	1987
Diaz-Gonzalez	1989
Floyd	1984
Furtek et al.	1981
Gladden	1982
Gomaa and Scott	1981
Gomaa	1983
Gomaa	1986
Groner et al.	1979
Harel	1987a
Harel et al.	1987
Harel et al.	1988
Harrison	1985
Harwood	1987
Hasui et al.	1983
Heitmeyer et al.	1982
Heitmeyer	1985
Hekmatpour	1987
Hekmatpour and Ince	1987a
Hollinde and Wagner	1984
Hooper and Hsia	1982
Ince and Hekmatpour	1987
Janson and Smith	1985
Kamin et al.	1983
Keus	1982
Klausner and Konchan	1982
Kramer et al.	1988
Kraushaar and Shirland	1985
Lee and Sluizer	1985
Luqi and Berzins	1987
Luqi and Berzins	1988

Luqi and Ketabchi	1988
Luqi et al.	1988
McCracken and Jackson	1982
McGowan et al.	1985
Mantei and Teorey	1988
Mason et al.	1982
Mason and Carey	1983
Mayr et al.	1984
Mittermeir	1982
Miyamoto	1987
Mumford et al.	1978
Naumann and Jenkins	1982
Nosek	1984
Ohnishi et al.	1985
Patton	1983
Powell	1983
Ratcliff	1988
Reilly and Brackett	1987
Rzevski	1984
Slusky	1987
Smith	1982
Sroka and Rader	1986
Stelovsky and Sugaya	1988
Tavolato and Vincena	1984
TaylorT and Standish	1982
Topping et al.	1987
Tozer	1987
Urban et al.	1984
Wallace et al.	1987
Wang	1986
Wasserman and Shewmake	1982
Zave	1978
Zave	1979
Zave	1980
Zave	1980a
Zave and Yeh	1981
Zave	1982
Zave	1984
Zave	1985
Zave and Schell	1986
Zelkowitz	1980

9. Relationship between Requirements and Design

Adler	1988
Alford	1984
Alford	1987
Andreu and Madnick	1977

Andreu and Madnick	1977a
Balzer and Goldman	1979
Blum	1988
Chang et al.	1987
Cheng et al.	1982
Conn	1977
Dasarathy	1983
Davis	1980
Davis	1982b
DeWolfe	1977
DeWolfe and Principato	1977
Early	1986
Fischer and Walter	1979
Furia	1979
Hamilton and Zeldin	1973
Hamilton and Zeldin	1976
Hamilton and Zeldin	1976a
Hamilton and Zeldin	1979
Hamilton and Zeldin	1983
Harel	1988
Harel et al.	1988
Heitmeyer and McLean	1983
Hsia and Yaung	1988
Huff and Madnick	1978
IBM	1973
Jahanian and Mok	1988
JohnsonW	1988
Jones	1976
Jorgensen	1985
Kampen	1982
Kerola and Freeman	1981
Kim and Kwon	1987
Kim and Kwon	n.d.
Kung	1988
Lamb et al.	1978
Lor and Berry	1987
Ludewig	1980
Ludewig	1980a
Ludewig	1982
Matsumoto et al.	1982
Matsumoto et al.	1984
Matsumura et al.	1987
Meseke	1975
Miller and Taylor	1982
Mills et al.	1986
Murai et al.	1982
Murai et al.	1982a
Nelson	1989

Parnas	1972
Parnas	1976
Peters	1978
Pierce	1978
Pirnia	1981
Rockstrom and Saracco	1982
Rombach	1987
Royce	1975
Scheffer	1979
Sievert and Mizell	1985
Silver	1981
Smoliar and Scalf	1979
Smoliar	1980
Swartout and Balzer	1982
Ward and Mellor	1985
Ward	1986
Weinberg	1982
Wilson	1979
Yeh	1980
Zave	1978
Zave	1979
Zave	1980
Zave	1980a
Zave and Yeh	1981
Zave	1982
Zave	1984
Zave	1985
Zave and Schell	1986

10. Software Synthesis from Requirements

Davis	1980
Kitani et al.	1981
Martin	1982
MartinW and Bosyj	1976
Nunamaker and Konsynski	1975
Rice	1981
Wilson	1981

11. Testing Implications of Requirements

Bauer et al.	1978
Bauer and Finger	1979
Chandrasekharan et al.	1985
Chow	1977
Davis and Rataj	1978
Davis	1980
Fischer and Walter	1979

Huebner	1979
Krause and Diamant	1978
McCabe	1983
Urban et al.	1984

12. Maintenance Implications of Requirements

| Conn | 1980 |
| Hecht | 1983 |

13. Requirements Case Studies

Alexander and Potter	1987
Alford	1979a
Bail	1979
Brackett and McGowan	1977
Bruno and Morisio	1987
Celko et al.	1983
Childs et al.	1983
DavisG	1982
Dooley et al.	1980
Edwards	1987
Farny et al.	1981
Furia	1979
Gackowski	1977
Groner et al.	1979
Heitmeyer	1985
Hollinde and Wagner	1984
Hsia and Yaung	1988
Jefferson and Taylor	1979
Kono	1983
Landau	1979
Loshbough et al.	1981
Ludewig	1980
Matsumoto	1977
Meseke	1975
Mical and Schwarm	1979
Mital and Berg	1988
Parker	1976
Petrie	1980
Pirnia	1981
Riddle and Edwards	1980
Riddle	1984a
Robson	1981
Rosenbaum and Hackler	1980
Ross	1985
Rzepka	1983
Rzepka	1983a

Scheffer et al.	1984
Scheffer et al.	1985
Slegel	n.d.
SmithS and Gerhart	1988
Thurber and Patton	1983
Treves and Caves	1979
Vessey and Weber	1986
White	1986
Winters	1979
Yau and Liu	1988

14. General Discussion of Software Engineering

Abbott	1986
Birrell and Ould	1985
Blank and Krijger	1983
Charette	1986
Jensen and Tonies	1979
King	1984
Liskov and Guttag	1988
Myers	1976
MyersW	1978
Pressman	1982
Rauscher and Ott	1987
Riddle	1984a
Shooman	1983
Sommerville	1982
Zelkowitz	1978
Zelkowitz et al.	1979

15. Other or Unknown

Alford and Burns	1975
Azuma et al.	1984
Balzer	1975
Boehm	1979
Booch	1986
Borgida et al.	1985
Borgida and Greenspan	n.d.
Brathwaite	1988
Bravaco and Yadav	1985
Bryssine	1988
Cairns	1975
Canning	1977
Carrio	1987
Casey	1981
Cherry	1987
Churchman	1975

Clements	1981
Computer Sciences Corporation	1973
Cox	1973
DavisM and Addleman	1986
Demetrovics et al.	1982
Desclaux	1988
Deutsch	1988
Devorkin and Oberndorf	1979
Dobbins	1987
Epple et al.	1983
Everhart	1978
Everhart et al.	1980
EWICS	1981
Exel and Popovic	1981
Glaseman and Davis	1980
Gottschalk	1979
Greenspan	1984
Greenspan and Mylopoulos	1983
Grindley	1966
Hagermann	1988
Halling et al.	n.d.
Hallmann	1988
Hallmann	1988a
Hamilton	1973
Hamilton	1976
Hamilton	1976a
Hamilton	1976b
Hamitlon	1979
Hamilton	1983
Hancock	1979
Haylock	1981
Heacox	1979
Hemdal and Reilly	1987
Herndon and McCall	1983
Hindin and Rauch-Hindin	1983
Ho and Nunamaker	1974
Ikadi et al.	1985
Kang	1980
Kimura	n.d.
Levitt et al.	1979
McFadyen	1982
Maddison	1983
Maibaum et al.	1986
Marker	1977
Mayr et al.	1982
Mitchell	1980
Mittermeir	1982a
Miyamoto	1977

Miyamoto	1977a
Miyamoto	1978
Miyamoto	1978a
Miyamoto and Yeh	1981
Montanari	1983
Morganstern	1975
Morrison	1988
MyersM	1988
Mylopoulos and Greenspan	1983
National Aeronautics and Space Administr	1976
Nogi	1981
Nunamaker and Konsynski	1981
Palmer	1988
Pangalos	1986
Postel	1974
Poston and Bruen	1987
Pulli	1988
Quirk	1978
Rauch-Hindin	1982
Riddle	1984a
Robinson	1979
Robson	1981
Rombach	1987
Russell	n.d.
Saito et al.	1981
Samson	1988
Silverberg et al.	1979
Snodgrass and Yun	1988
Solvberg	1979
Stephens and Whitehead	1985
Taggart	1971
Teichroew et al.	1977
Tolchin et al.	1984
Tsai and Chan	1987
Tsai et al.	1988
Verheijen and Van Bekkum	1982
Vick	1974
Vineberg	1975
Williams	1988
Wilson	1975
Winchester	1981
Wright et al.	1975
Yamamoto et al.	1982
Yeh and Welch	1987
Zualkerman and Tsai	1988

INDEX